SOLVING
THE EXODUS MYSTERY

VOLUME I

DISCOVERY OF
THE TRUE KINGS AND PHARAOHS
OF
ABRAHAM, JOSEPH, MOSES
AND THE EXODUS.

By Ted T. Stewart

Published and Distributed by
BIBLEMART.COM
3710 34th Street
Lubbock, Texas 79410
1-800-221-9065

Published by Biblemart.com
Owner and author: Ted T. Stewart
3710 34th Street
Lubbock, Texas 79410

Sales@biblemart.com

1-800-221-9065

Library of Congress

I.S.B.N. 0-9718680-0-X

*Discovery of the True Pharaohs of
Joseph, Moses and the Exodus
Vol. I Solving the Exodus Mystery*

Date of 1st Printing by Lightning Source
September, 2002

SOLVING THE EXODUS MYSTERY, VOLUME I
(Discovery of the True Kings and Pharaohs of
Abraham, Joseph, Moses and the Exodus)
BY TED STEWART
TABLE OF CONTENTS

PERMISSIONS TO USE COPYRIGHTED EXCERPTS AND PHOTOS

Specific references, page numbers and dates are found in the end notes of each chapter and also in the Bibliography located in Appendix D at the end of the book.

Biblical Archaeology Review & Bible Review, Editor Harold Shank, permitted 6 sentences of quotations and 11 sentences of thought reference without cost.

Cambridge University Press granted permission to Ted Stewart to extract 31 lines without cost from the *Cambridge Ancient History*, Volumes I.1 (1970), 1.2A (1971) , & II.1 (1973): Editors: E. S. Edwards, C. J. Gadd, N. G. L. Hammond and E. Sollberger.

Doubleday (Random House, Inc.) permitted Ted Stewart to use quotations without cost.
   Editor in Chief, Noel Freeman, *Anchor Bible Dictionary* (1992): Authors: Martin Mulder, VI.99-103; Donald Redford, III.122; VI.1106; Tom Wei, V.377.
   *Archives of Eb*la by Giovanni Pettinato. *Archaeology of the Land of the Bible*, Mazar.

Eerdmans Pub. Co. granted permission without charge for Ted Stewart to extract 8 sentences from articles written in the *International Standard Bible Encyclopedia*, 1979-1980.

Facts on File, *Atlas of Ancient Egypt;* request made for quotes on March 18, 2002; no answer.

Liber AB - *Radiocarbon Variations and Absolute Chronology*, by Save Soderburgh and I. U. Olsson Permission requested; no reply received.

Metropolitan Museum of Art, William C. Hayes, *Scepter of Egypt, A Background for the Study of the Egyptian Antiquities in the Metropolitan Museum of Art, Part I From the Earliest Times to the End of the Middle Kingdom* (1990). Excerpts of 9 sentences are permitted for use in Ted Stewart's book without cost from XI, "The Middle Kingdom," pp. 171, 175-176, 183-184, and XII, and "The People of the Middle Kingdom," p. 228.

Metropolitan Museum of Art, William Hayes, *Scepter of Egypt*, 5th printing, 1990, sold 4 photos for $105.00 to Ted Stewart for use in his book: Vol. I, Figure 117 (King Senwosret I), p. 192. Figure 119   (King Sen-Wosret III as sphinx, p. 197. Figure 120 (King Sen-Wosret III, p. 198. Figure 157. (Cosmetic Box of Kemuny, the Butler of Amenemhet III), p. 245.

Oriental Institute Publications, Parker's *Calendars of Ancient Egypt*: request not answered.

Princeton University Press, Editor James B. Pritchard, *Ancient Near Eastern Texts*, copyrighted in 1950, 1955, 1969 and renewed in 1978) permitted Ted Stewart to extract 25 lines of quotations without cost.

Princeton University Press, Editor: James B. Prichard, *Ancient Near East In Pictures*, copyrighted in 1954 and 1969.   Ted Stewart was charged $160.00 for 4 photos included in his book..
   (1) Figure 383, Wooden figure of Sen-Usert I, p. 135.
   (2) Figure 384 - Sen-Usert III, an inscribed statue from Deir el-Bahri, p. 135.
   (3) Figure 385, Statue of Amen-em-het III, from Hawara, p. 135.
   (4) Figure 515 - Hammurabi before the sun-god Shamash, stela from Susa, p.175.

Random House Archive & Library in the United Kingdom permitted use of copy of David Rohl's book, *Test of Time (Pharaohs & Kings)* - Century, copy of jacket cover.

Simon & Schuster, "Reprinted with the permission of Scribner, a Division of Simon and Schuster, *Ancient Records of Egypt* by James Breasted (Russell & Russell, NY, 1962), Simon Schuster charged Ted Stewart $150 to grant permission for 142 sentences of excerpts.
   Simon & Schuster, "Reprinted with the permission of Scribner, a Division of Simon and Schuster, from   *A History of Egypt* by James Breasted (Charles Scribner's Sons, NY, 1929). Simon Schuster charged Ted Stewart $100 for 33 sentences of excerpts and figure 79 on p. 158.

University of California Press: Permission to use w/o cost 200 lines of quotations from Miriam Lichtheim's, *Ancient Egyptian Literature*, 3 volumes, copyright, 1973.

University of Chicago Press permitted without cost four sentences (direct quotes) from two articles of the *Journal of New Eastern Studies*
   (1) : Robin M. Derricourt, "Radiocarbon Chronology for Egypt and N. Africa," 42.4.271, Oct., 1983.
   (2) Ian M. E. Shaw, "Egyptian Chronology for Egypt and N. Africa, 44.4.311. Oct., 1985
      Zondervan books & *Pictorial Encyclopedia* - permission granted w/o charge

FOREWORD AND ACKNOWLEDGMENTS

Solving the Exodus Mystery, Vol. I, has the sub-title, "Discovery of the true Kings and Pharaohs of Abraham, Joseph, Moses and the Exodus." For twenty-four years I have meticulously researched the ancient documents of Babylon, Elam and Egypt and compared them with Biblical history and chronology from Abraham to the Exodus. Dr. Peter Huber, formerly of Harvard University, revised the astronomical dates of Babylon by fifty-six years, creating twenty-eight historical and chronological synchronisms between Abraham and the kings of the east in Genesis 14. In 1991 Ron Wyatt led Dot and me, plus twenty-five others to the Biblical sites of Sodom and Gomorrah on the coast of the Dead Sea. Man-made structures, destroyed by burning sulphur, with powdered sulphur balls scattered over the entire site, are among the seventeen proofs of the historicity of Genesis 19:24.

Charles Aling's *Egypt and Bible History* and Donovan Courville's *The Exodus Problem* pointed me to the twelfth dynasty as the Biblical period of Joseph and Israel in Egypt. My principal sources were James Breasted's *Ancient Records of Egypt* and *History of Egypt,* Petrie's *History of Egypt,* Miriam Lichtheim's *Ancient Egyptian Literature,* Vol. I, William C. Hayes' *The Scepter of Egypt,* Vol. 1, and John A. Wilson's translations in the *Ancient Near Eastern Texts,* edited by John Pritchard. Articles by many scholars on the twelfth dynasty in the *Cambridge Ancient History,* especially William Hayes, proved to be invaluable in my historical research. J. R. Baines and E. F. Wente gave updated historical dates and new revisions on Egyptian history in the 1991 *New Encyclopaedia Britannica.* Articles from scholarly journals kept me up to date on the most recent archaeological developments in Egypt. Large numbers of articles from the following Bible Encyclopedias have furnished excellent historical information on many topics covered in this book. I am especially indebted to the authors in *the Anchor Bible Dictionary, The International Standard Bible Encyclopedia, and the Zondervan Pictorial Encyclopedia of the Bible.* Budge's *Egyptian Hieroglyphic Dictionary* also proved to be invaluable in interpreting important words, names and locations. Dr. Richard Parker taught me in his *Calendars of Egypt* how to link lunar dates to Sothic dates in order to test the accuracy of optional astronomical chronologies. Dr. Danny Faulkner, astronomer at the University of S. Carolina at Lancaster, used the software of Dr. Brad Schaeffer, head of the Bethesda Space Center, to calculate 157 dates of Sirius' rising in different years at different latitudes to test the astronomical chronologies of Egyptologists. Dr. Faulkner used the software program of **Lunar Tables and Programs from 4000 B.C. to A.D. 8000, by Michelle Chapront-Touze and Jean Chapront** to test the lunar chronology in relation to the Sothic dates. Dr. Faulkner calculated more than 500 lunar dates. I could never have written this book without the vast historical knowledge and superior scholarship of these outstanding historians and scientists.

Dr. Dale Manor, received his doctorate in archaeology under Dr. William Dever. He wrote a number of articles in the new *Anchor Bible Dictionary* which I have used in this book. Dr. Manor read my entire book and gave me excellent suggestions for improving its contents. Dr. Truitt Adair, Director of the Sunset International Bible Institute, and Dr. Truman Scott, Dean of Sunset's eight branch schools read the entire book and improved significantly the contents. Dr. Tom Langford, Dean Emeritus of the Graduate School of Texas Tech University and a specialist in English composition and literature, critiqued the entire book, improving its clarity, accuracy and style. John Dendy, a professional Designer and owner of Dendy & Associates in Houston, Texas, expertly designed the jacket.

Ultimately, I recorded 436 synchronisms that tie the histories of Babylon, Elam and Egypt to the Biblical period from Abraham to the Exodus. A brief resume of the book is recorded on the paper jacket. **Above all, I thank God for my wife, Dot, who has been my greatest encourager, proof reader, idea source and a fellow witness of evidences that we have both seen in our travels to Israel and Egypt.**

iv

CHAPTER ONE
HISTORY'S MOST FAMOUS UNSOLVED MYSTERY

For 2,000 years scholars have searched the ancient records of Egypt to find evidence of Israel's stay in Egypt and their dramatic Exodus through the Red Sea. The search, rather than increasing faith in Biblical history, has created skepticism and unbelief. Scholars claim that Egyptian documents do not mention a single event surrounding the lives of Abraham, Jacob, Joseph and Moses.[1] This vexing enigma is called "The Exodus Problem." I call it **"History's Most Famous Unsolved Mystery."**

Even more disturbing, significant historical and archaeological evidences contradict the Biblical record of the Exodus and Conquest. In 1985 archaeologist Kathleen Kenyon claimed that the walls of Jericho fell and were burned hundreds of years before Joshua passed through the city. She also rejected the Biblical story of Israel's sojourn in Egypt, Israel's exodus from Egypt and Israel's conquest of Canaan. **Ms. Kenyon considered it a "waste of time" to study Bible history from Abraham to David.** She claimed the Biblical records are "garbled traditions," written hundreds of years after the events.[2] The Queen of England, who is the head of the church in England, knighted Ms. Kenyon as "Dame Kenyon" for her "archaeological expertise."

In 1978 I visited London and noticed that the Church of England was selling church buildings all over the city. A priest explained to me that archaeologists and Egyptologists have destroyed the faith of most Englishmen. Since they no longer believe in the Bible, they no longer go to church.

In 1991 the Biblical Archaeology Society and the Smithsonian Institute co-sponsored a symposium on the "Rise of Ancient Israel." Baruch Halpern, William G. Dever and P. Kyle McCarter, Jr., all with doctorates from Harvard University, were chosen as the principal speakers. All three agreed that Israel's Exodus from Egypt and Israel's Conquest of Canaan are **"myths" rather than true history.**

Dr. Halpern suggested that "the core truth" behind the Exodus story was two or three slaves escaping from Egypt during Ramses II's reign. He concluded that Israel always lived in Palestine, or gradually and peacefully infiltrated Canaan from the East and North, but not from Egypt.[3]

The May/June, 1995, issue of *Biblical Archaeology Review* contained lists of the top ten archaeological accomplishments in the previous twenty years. David Ussishkin, professor of archaeology at Tel Aviv University, included on his list the following **"scholarly consensus." "The archaeological data do not support the historicity" of the Biblical stories of the patriarchs, the sojourn in Egypt, the Exodus, and Joshua's conquest of Canaan in a single campaign.[4]**

In the July/August, 1996, issue of *Biblical Archaeology Review*, Hershel Shanks, the editor, interviewed William Dever. He called Dr. Dever "one of the most widely respected senior archaeologists today." Shanks asked Dever, "Many scholars have rejected the Israelite conquest of Canaan as described in the Bible." "Is that correct?" Dever answered, "I would say **all** archaeologists today."[5]

Dever's answer is certainly an overstatement. A number of competent archaeologists, such as Dr. Bryant Wood, presently defend the Biblical conquest of Canaan. However, without doubt a large majority of archaeologists have rejected the Biblical Exodus and Conquest as true history. **Some scholars consider any effort connecting excavation to Biblical events as "unscientific" and even "embarrassing." These scholars claim, "Old style biblical archaeology is dead."**[6]

In 1997, Hershel Shanks, editor of *Biblical Archaeology Review* and *Bible Review*, states that "main-stream biblical scholarship" has eroded confidence in the reliability of Old Testament history from Creation to the Conquest of Canaan.[7] In the March/April, 2000 issue of *Biblical Archaeology Review*, Thomas Thompson labeled Bible history as containing "traditions" that "do not share in reality." In the same issue the famous archaeologist, William Dever, differed with Thompson by affirming that "Ancient Israel is a fact." However, Dever admitted that "this historical Israel does not correspond in all details with the 'ideal theological Israel' portrayed in the Bible."[8]

I. CHALLENGE TO THE FAITH OF THREE WORLD RELIGIONS

The growing scholarly rejection of Biblical history from Abraham to the Exodus challenges the faith of three world religions: Judaism, Christianity and Islam. All three of these religions record in their holy Scriptures the stories of Abraham, Jacob, Joseph, Moses, Joshua, and the events of the Exodus and Conquest.

A. The Challenge to Jewish Faith

The Old Testament was written by about forty authors over a period of approximately 1,000 years. It refers to Moses as a man of God 743 times and refers to Israel in Egypt more than 500 times.[9]

Josephus, a Jewish historian of the first century, believed Moses was the author of the first five books. Josephus claimed these books contained "divine doctrines" without contamination from human ideas. He asserted that Jews had refrained from "adding to, taking from, or changing in any way," their sacred Scriptures. He also affirmed that all Jews believe in the Scriptures so firmly that, "if occasion be, they willingly die for them."[10] Indeed, Bible history from Abraham to Moses forms the core of Israel's existence, significance, purpose, life and hope.

However, most archaeologists have rejected the historicity of Abraham and Moses. They have also convinced a majority of Jews to abandon their belief in the Biblical history of ancient Israel. In June, 1991, my wife Dot and I toured the land of Israel. Our marvelous guide was Dr. Micha Ashkenazi.[11] Micha has a Master's degree in archaeology and a Doctor's degree in Jewish/Christian relations. He participated in the archaeological dig at Caesarea that uncovered the famous inscription of Pilate in honor of Tiberius Caesar.

Micha showed us the excavated remains of Jericho. He pointed out a stratum where Jericho's walls had fallen and the city had been burned. Micha said that Jewish archaeologists date the burned stratum to c. 1700 B.C., 300 years before the Biblical date of 1406 B.C. for Jericho's fall.

Micha explained that these archaeological contradictions to Biblical history have destroyed the faith of most Jews in Israel. **He estimated that only 10% of Israelites believe the Old Testament is historically reliable, and that only 5% rigorously obey Moses' law.**

In April, 1992, I lectured on the campus of the University of Arizona. A young Jewish university student doubted me when I said that many Jewish rabbis no longer believe in the Biblical account of the Exodus and Conquest. The student asked his own Jewish rabbi in Tucson if this were true. The rabbi told him, **"We rabbis are now in agreement with the archaeologists; the Exodus and Conquest, as recorded in the Bible, never occurred."**

In the "Religious" section of the Dallas Morning News, March 30, 2002, Rabbi David Wolpe, senior rabbi at Los Angeles Sinai Temple told his congregation the following words: **"The story of the Exodus did not happen the way the Bible depicts it, if it happened at all."**

Of course, some orthodox rabbis still cling to the historical truth of the Scriptures. Yet, men of intellectual integrity must face these apparent contradictions and search for an adequate solution.

One of the objectives of this book and its sequel is to restore the faith of Jews in the veracity of their own ancient history from Abraham to the Exodus, as recorded in their own Bible. The second volume of *Solving the Exodus Mystery*, which will appear in 2003, vindicates Bible history from Sinai to Solomon and beyond to the Babylonian Exile.

B. Challenge to Christian Faith

New Testament writers refer to Moses eighty-five times and mention the events surrounding the Exodus more than forty times. The New Testament teaches that God promised Abraham to bring his descendants out of Egypt, to give them the land of Canaan, and to preserve them until the Messiah would be born to bless all nations.[12]

Jesus believed He was the Messiah predicted by Abraham: "Your father Abraham rejoiced at the thought of seeing my day; he saw it and was glad."[13] Jesus believed that His coming was predicted by Moses: **"If you believed Moses, you would believe me, for he wrote about me."**[14] Jesus believed that many Old Testament passages spoke of His coming: "This is what I told you while I was still with you: Everything must be fulfilled that is written about me in the Law of Moses, the Prophets and the Psalms."[15]

Jesus believed the Old Testament was so historically accurate that **"Scripture cannot be broken."**[16] "Unbroken Scripture" obviously means that Jesus believed that the Old Testament Scriptures cannot be proved untrue.

Jesus celebrated the Passover meal in memory of Israel's salvation from the death of the firstborn and of Israel's Exodus from Egypt. That same night Jesus instituted His own "Supper" to commemorate a new Exodus from death to life and to initiate a new people of God composed of all nations.[17]

The Apostles of Christ taught the Messiahship of Jesus as part of God's promise to Abraham.[18] If the first part of Abraham's promise concerning the Exodus was not fulfilled in Moses' time, then the last part of the same promise about the Messiah cannot be fulfilled in Jesus' time. **If the Exodus is a myth, then the promise of the coming Messiah is also mythical. If the Exodus is fiction, then Jesus was wrong in teaching that it was true history.** If Jesus was wrong about the past, how can he be right about the present and the future? **Thus, the integrity of Christ and the validity of His Messiahship depend on the historicity of Abraham, Isaac, Jacob, Joseph, Moses, Joshua and Israel's Kings Saul, David and Solomon.**

Sadly, modern archaeologists have convinced many Christian professors in religious seminaries to reject the historicity of the Biblical Exodus and Conquest. Consequently, mainline Christian denominations are dividing over the historical accuracy and moral authority of the Scriptures, both Old and New Testaments.[19]

C. Challenge To The Muslim Faith

Islam's *Koran (Quran)* includes more than 200 verses about Abraham and Joseph.[20] It records 375 verses about Moses and the Exodus.[21] These Bible stories are thus essential elements of Muslim faith. Therefore, archaeologists' opposition to these Biblical characters and events applies equally against the *Koran* and Islam.

The faith of more than two billion people in three world religions is challenged by most of the world's top archaeologists and historians. This challenge increases the importance of the Exodus problem and intensifies the urgency of finding a solution.

II. THE BALANCE OF JUSTICE HANGS UNEQUALLY

The Exodus problem also involves an important principle of **"justice."** Wicked Pharaohs unjustly enslaved Israelites and cruelly oppressed them, even murdering their children to stem their population growth. **All people who believe in justice should not rest until the guilty Pharaohs are identified and condemned.** History identifies other persecutors of Jews, Christians and Muslims such as Antiochus Epiphanes, Nero, Domitian, the Roman Crusaders, Hitler and others. Their names have been condemned to eternal infamy. However, the true Egyptian Pharaohs who persecuted the Hebrews have escaped detection. The judgment of history hangs unequally in the balance until these evil Pharaohs are also identified. Modern scholars label Abraham, Isaac and Jacob as fictitious characters invented by Jewish authors who lived hundreds of years after the events. Moses is thus denied his rights as the penman of God who wrote about these Biblical characters and events. The prestigious *Cambridge Ancient History* attributes the first seven books of the Old Testament to five unknown authors. These five authors supposedly edited each other's writings between 1000 and 500 B.C. Scholars give these "ghost writers" the names of J1, J2, E, P, and D.[22] Thus, scholars' most highly esteemed history book (*Cambridge Ancient History*) gives credence to "phantom persons" that are not mentioned in any ancient document. Furthermore, the earlier copies, from which later revisions were supposedly made, have never been found.

These "ghost writers" were invented to explain alleged historical, archaeological and literary contradictions in the Old Testament. To ascribe this monumental piece of literature to unknown "ghost writers" shows total disrespect for Moses, one of the greatest authors of antiquity. **The scales of justice need to be balanced.**

III. SCOPE AND OBJECTIVE OF THIS BOOK

Chapter Two lists significant evidences that explain why historical and archaeological scholars logically reject the Biblical history of Abraham, Jacob, Joseph and Moses. The Exodus Problem is real and cannot be avoided by seekers of historical truth.

Chapter Three explains my twenty-four year search for a solution to this complex, historical enigma. The rest of the book presents 436 historical and archaeological synchronisms and discoveries between the histories of Babylon, Elam and Egypt , and Bible history from Abraham to the Exodus. This amazing evidence identifies the true kings and Pharaohs of Abraham, Joseph, Moses, and the Exodus. **However, the Egyptian documents that authenticate these Biblical stories are dated three centuries earlier than the Biblical dates.**

These **436 evidences are so abundant and significant that scholars must face a critical decision. Either Bible dates must be revised to fit the Egyptian dates, or Egyptian dates must be revised to fit the Biblical dates.** Chapters Twenty-Three and Twenty-Four present carbon-14 evidences and astronomical evidences that confirm the Biblical dates and that correct the Egyptian dates by three centuries. When you finish reading this book and its sequel (Volume II) , I hope that you will exclaim as I did when I finished my research: **"History's most famous unsolved mystery has been solved!"**

NOTES FOR CHAPTER ONE

1. John Bright, *A History of Israel*, 3rd Ed. (Philadelphia: Westminister Press, 1981), 121.

2. Kathleen Kenyon, *Archaeology of the Holy Lands*, 5th ed. (Nashville: Nelson, 1985), 204-209.

3. Halpern, Dever and McCarter, "Rise of Ancient Israel," Audio Cassette Set, Biblical Archaeology Review (Washington, D.C., Nov., 1991).

4. David Ussishkin, "Scholars Speak Out," *Biblical Archaeology Review*, (May/June, 1995), 32.

5. Hershel Shanks, "Bar Interviews With William Dever, Part I," *Biblical Archaeology Review*, (July/August, 1996), 37.

6. Neil Asher Silberman, "Lure of the Holy Land," *Archaeology* (Nov./Dec., 43.6, 1990), 33-34.

7. Hershel Shanks, "The Biblical Minimalists," *Bible Review*, (June, 1997), 32-33.

8. Thomas L. Thompson, "Can You Understand This?",36-37 & William G. Dever, "Save Us from Postmodern Malarkey," *Biblical Archaeology Review* (March/April, 2000), 36-37, 28-35.

9. Goodrick & Kohlenberger, *NIV Exhaustive Concordance*, "Egypt" and "Moses," Zondervan, (1990) 336-339, 764-766.

10. Flavius Josephus, "Against Apion," *The Works of Josephus*, updated ed. *(Peabody, Mass.:* Hendrickson Pub., 1987), I.8, 776.

11. Dr. Micha Ashkenazi lives in Jerusalem and is a government licensed tour guide. His address is P.O.B. 2316, Jerusalem, 91022, Israel. His telephone is 02-414697.

12. Genesis 12:1-3; 15:13-15.

13. John 8:56.

14. John 5:46.

15. Luke 24.44.

16. John 10:35.

17. Matthew 26:17-19.

18 Acts 3:13-26; Galatians 3:6-29.

19. "What Does God Really Think About Sex," *Time* (June 24, 1991), 48-50.

20. A. Yusuf Ali, "Index," *The Holy Quran* (Brentwood, Md.: Amana Corp., 1983), 1838.

21. Ali, 1845-46.

22. O. Eissfeldt, "Palestine in the Time of the Nineteenth Dynasty," *Cambridge Ancient History*, (Cambridge University Press, 1975), reprinted 1987, 3rd Ed., II.2.307-308.

CHAPTER TWO
CONFLICT BETWEEN BIBLICAL
AND SECULAR HISTORIES

A great conflict exists between Bible history and Babylonian and Egyptian histories. Most Christians are unaware of the complexity and gravity of the Exodus Problem. The reader cannot appreciate the solution of the Exodus Problem without recognizing its serious and enormous difficulties.

Three groups of scholars have proposed three different Pharaohs of the Exodus. (1) Scholars who believe the Bible accurately dates the Exodus in 1446 B.C. identify Thutmose III of the eighteenth dynasty as the Pharaoh of the Exodus. (2) Scholars who believe the Exodus is rooted in historical events, but is not correctly calculated in the Bible, date the Exodus c. 1250 B.C. during the reign of Ramses II of the nineteenth dynasty. (3) A growing majority of scholars reject both Thutmose III and Ramses II as the Pharaoh of the Exodus. These scholars classify the Exodus and Conquest as religious myths rather than historical truths.

My twenty-four year research for a solution to the Exodus problem led me to the conclusion that a majority of archaeologists and Egyptologists are correct in rejecting both Thutmose III and Ramses II as the Pharaoh of the Exodus. This chapter examines the reasons why these Pharaohs should be rejected as the Biblical Pharaoh of the Exodus and explains why Bible scholars should not force either Thutmose III or Ramses II into the mold of the Biblical Pharaoh of the Exodus.

Chapter Three reports how I searched for a solution to this enigmatic problem and how, by God's grace, I finally solved it. The rest of the book identifies the true kings of Abraham's time and the true Pharaohs of Joseph, Moses and the Exodus.

I. CONFLICT OVER THE HISTORICITY OF
ABRAHAM, ISAAC AND JACOB

The Bible dates the Exodus 480 years before the spring of King Solomon's fourth year (I Kings 6:1). Using links between the kings of Israel and the astronomically fixed dates of Assyrian kings, Thiele fixed Rehoboam's accession year to **931 B.C.**[1] Adding Solomon's 40-year reign to 931 B.C., we get 971 B.C. as Solomon's accession year and his fourth full year in the spring of **966 B.C.** Adding the 480 years of 1 Kings 6:1, we get **1446 B.C. as the date for the Exodus.**

The New International Version of Exodus 12:40 says, "The length of time the Israelite people lived in Egypt was **430 years**." In Chapter Four I differ with this translation of the NIV and demonstrate that Israel's 430-year sojourn in Egypt creates more problems than it solves. Other versions translate Exodus 12:40 differently so that the 430 years begin with God's Promise to Abraham, rather than Jacob's entrance into Egypt, reducing Israel's stay in Egypt to only 210 years.

However, the New International Version is the most popular version in America (and my favorite version as well). I will therefore follow the NIV dates in this chapter to demonstrate the historical conflict that it creates with the astronomical dates of Babylonian history.

Genesis 47:9 says Jacob was 130 years old when he entered Egypt. On the basis of the NIV chronology, Israel entered Egypt in 1876 B.C. (1446 + 430 = 1876). Jacob was thus born 130 years earlier in 2006 B.C. Isaac was sixty when Jacob was born, dating Isaac's birth in 2066 B.C. Abraham was 100 when Isaac was born; thus Abraham was born in 2166 B.C. Genesis 12:4 says Abraham was seventy-five when he entered Canaan in 2091 B.C. These dates follow the Bible chronology of the *NIV Study Bible* listed in Table 2-A

Table 2-A
INCORRECT CHRONOLOGY OF THE *NIV STUDY BIBLE*
FROM THE EXODUS BACK TO ABRAHAM

1 Kings 6:1	Exodus Occurred 480 Years Before Solomon's 4th Yr (966 B.C.) in:	1446 B.C.
Ex. 12:40	Jacob's Arrival in Egypt 430 Years Before The Exodus in:	1876 B.C.
Gen. 47:9	Jacob was 130 when he entered Egypt; thus his birth year was:	2006 B.C.
Gen. 25:25	Isaac was 60 when Jacob was born; thus Isaac was born in:	2066 B.C.
Gen. 21:5	Abraham was 100 when Isaac was born; thus Abraham was born in	2166 B.C.
Gen. 12:4	Abraham was 75 when he entered Canaan in:	2091 B.C.
Gen. 12:10	Abraham went to Egypt during a famine c.:	2086 B.C.
Gen 13:1	Abraham returned to Canaan with many riches three years later c.:	2083 B.C.
Gen. 14:1-16	Abraham defeats a coalition of eastern kings at night c.:	2082 B.C.
Gen. 16:15	Hagar bore Ishmael when Abraham was 86 in:	2080 B.C.

In Genesis 14 Abraham met Kedor-Laomer, king of Elam, and Amraphel, king of Shinar (Babylon) in Abraham's ninth year in Canaan, dated to 2082 B.C. However, the names of Kedor-Laomer and Amraphel are not found among the kings of Elam and Babylon during the twenty-first century B.C. Instead, *The Cambridge Ancient History* reports that Simashki was the king of Elam in 2082 B.C., not Kedor-Laomer, and that Babylon was conquered and ruled by Shulgi, the king of Ur, not Amraphel.[2] **These two serious conflicts are registered among the discovery errors that are listed at the end of this chapter in Table 2-C.**

If the NIV and Cambridge dates are both correct, the majority of scholars have rightly rejected Abraham's historicity. This historical conflict is serious and must be faced. **However, don't despair, dear reader, Chapter Five presents a unique solution to this apparent contradiction.**

II. CONFLICT BETWEEN EIGHTEENTH-DYNASTY HISTORY AND BIBLE HISTORY FROM MOSES' BIRTH TO THE EXODUS

The Bible dates the Exodus in the spring of 1446 B.C., 480 years before Solomon's fourth year of 966 B.C. (I Kings 6:1). Moses was born eighty years before the Exodus in 1526 B.C. (Exodus 7:7). Moses fled to Midian at age forty in 1486 B.C. (Acts 7:23,30). Thus, Moses returned to Egypt in 1446 B.C., the same year of the Exodus.

Most Egyptologists follow the dates of J. R. Baines in *The New Encyclopaedia Britannica,* 1991 Edition. This source dates Egypt's eighteenth dynasty from 1539 to 1292 B.C., covering the entirety of Moses' life from 1526 B.C. to 1406 B.C. Table 2-B compares Moses' chronology with eighteenth-dynasty chronology dated to the same years. However, this comparison creates conflict instead of harmony between Biblical and Egyptian histories.

Table 2-B
CORRECT BIBLICAL DATES FOR MOSES COMPARED TO EGYPTOLOGISTS' DATES FOR THE EIGHTEENTH DYNASTY

BIBLICAL CHRONOLOGY	18TH-DYNASTY CHRONOLOGY	

BIBLICAL CHRONOLOGY	18ᵀᴴ-DYNASTY CHRONOLOGY	
	1539 B.C.	AHMOSE
MOSES' BIRTH:		
80 years before the Exodus (7:7)	1526 B.C.	
	1514 B.C.	AMENHOTEP I
	1493 B.C.	THUTMOSE I
MOSES FLED TO MIDIAN 1486 B.C.		
for 40 Years, Acts 7:30	1482 B.C.	THUTMOSE II
	1470 B.C.	THUTMOSE III Reigned 53 yrs
THE EXODUS 480 Yrs. before 4ᵗʰ Yr.		
of Solomon (966 B.C.) 1 Kings 6:1	1446 B.C.	
40 Yrs. In Desert	1426 B.C.	AMENHOTEP II
THE CONQUEST 40 Yrs.	1406 B.C.	
At the end of the 40 years - Joshua 5:6	1390 B.C.	AMENHOTEP III

A. Was Ahmose the Pharaoh of Moses' Birth?

Ahmose, the founder of Egypt's eighteenth dynasty, is dated by most scholars from 1539 to 1514 B.C. The Biblical date of Moses' birth is 1526 B.C., right in the middle of Ahmose's reign: See Table 2-B above. However, if Ahmose was reigning when Moses was born, three serious problems are created.

Problem No. 1. When Moses was born, the reigning Pharaoh had previously enslaved the Israelites and forced them to construct the store cities of Pithom and Rameses (Ex.1:8-2:10). In contrast, Ahmose drove the foreigners out of the land of Goshen, rather than enslaving them.[3]

Problem No. 2. Excavations of the store cities of Pithom and Rameses and other cities in Goshen indicate that neither Ahmose, nor any other eighteenth-dynasty king, constructed them.[4] Therefore, the archaeological evidence does not support Ahmose as the Biblical Pharaoh of the Oppression, who enslaved Israelites and forced them to construct Pithom and Rameses.[5]

Problem No. 3. Each time the Bible mentions the Egyptian capital from the time of Joseph to the time of Moses, it is located close to the land of Goshen, where Israel lived in the eastern Delta of Egypt.[6] Egypt's palace was so close to Goshen that Pharaoh's daughter found baby Moses in a small papyrus boat among the reeds of the Nile where she bathed.[7] Kitchen locates Goshen in the southeastern delta of northern Egypt, called the Wadi Tumilat.[8]

However, Egyptologists, including Kitchen, unanimously locate the capital of

Ahmose and other eighteenth-dynasty Pharaohs in Thebes (modern Luxor) in southern Egypt.[9] The trip from Goshen in the north to Thebes in the south is c. 475 miles by the Nile River.[10] Moses' papyrus boat did **not** float miraculously upstream for 475 miles to encounter the Egyptian princess in her palace at Thebes.

Conclusion: Ahmose's expulsion of the foreigners in the Delta, the location of the eighteenth-dynasty capital in southern Egypt and the failure of eighteenth-dynasty kings to construct cities in the eastern Delta of Egypt, seriously militate against the identification of Ahmose or any other eighteenth-dynasty king as the Pharaoh of Moses' birth.

B. Was Thutmose III the Pharaoh of the Exodus?

We saw above that the Bible dates Moses' flight to Midian in 1486 B.C. when he was forty years old (Acts 7:23,30) and dates Moses' return to Egypt forty years later when Moses was eighty years old. (Exodus 7:7). Therefore, Moses returned to Egypt in 1446 B.C., the year of the Exodus.[11] Most modern Egyptologists date Thutmose III's reign during this same period from 1479 to 1426 B.C.[12] If the Biblical and Egyptian dates are both correct, Thutmose III was reigning in 1446 B.C., the date of the Exodus, and should be logically identified as the Pharaoh of the Exodus. Egyptologists consider Thutmose III to be the most powerful Pharaoh ever to reign over Egypt.[13] However, Thutmose III's life and reign create serious problems that negate the possibility of his being the Pharaoh of the Exodus.

Problem No. 1. Moses was born in northern Egypt in the land of Goshen and became the adopted child of an Egyptian princess, whose palace was also in northern Egypt, close to the land of Goshen. When Moses was forty years old he killed an Egyptian and fled to Midian, where he stayed for forty years. When Moses returned to Egypt at age eighty (Exodus 7:7) in 1446 B.C., the Israelites still lived in the land of Goshen. The capital of the Pharaoh was still located in northern Egypt close to the border of Goshen. The Bible describes Moses' continual trips between Goshen and the Egyptian capital to talk with Pharaoh, sometimes on a daily basis.[14] Moses' frequent trips between Goshen and the capital prove that Egypt's capital was located in northern Egypt, close to Goshen, for the entire eighty years from Moses' birth to his exile from Egypt.

However, Thutmose III's capital was located in Thebes in southern Egypt,[15] 475 miles south of Goshen by the Nile River. The distance makes it impossible for Moses to travel back and forth daily between Thebes and the land of Goshen. Thus, the southern capital of Thutmose III at Thebes clearly contradicts the Biblical picture of the northern capital near Goshen in the year of the Exodus (1446 B.C.).

Some scholars propose that Thutmose III had a second palace at Memphis in northern Egypt. However, Memphis is also too far from the land of Goshen for Moses to travel back and forth on a daily basis. Numbers 13:22 and Psalm 78:12 indicate that the Egyptian capital was in Zoan (Tanis) a few miles north of the border of Goshen in the delta of Egypt. No evidence exists that Thutmose III had a residence in Zoan. Chapter 16 presents proof for Zoan as the capital of Egypt during the time of both Joseph and Moses.

Problem No. 2. The Bible says that Moses killed an Egyptian, and the ruling Pharaoh tried to kill Moses in retribution. Moses fled to Midian where he stayed **forty years**.[16]

At the end of Moses' **forty-year exile in Midian**, God appeared to Moses in a burning bush. He told Moses that the Pharaoh and others who sought to kill him were dead. He told Moses to return to Egypt and bring Israel back to the land of Midian to worship Him on the same mountain where Moses saw the burning bush: Mount Horeb, also called Mount Sinai.[17]

> Ex. 2:23 -- During that long [forty-year] period [Acts 7:23, 30], **the king of Egypt died**. The Israelites groaned in their slavery and cried out, and their cry for help because of their slavery went up to God. (NIV)

God's words imply that the Pharaoh who tried to kill Moses died toward the end of Moses' **forty-year exile**. Thus, the Pharaoh of the Exodus had been reigning for a short time when Moses returned to Egypt. The Bible pictures only two Pharaohs reigning during Moses' forty-year exile from 1486 to 1446 B.C.

If the Biblical picture is complete, the Pharaoh who tried to kill Moses must have reigned at least 40 years, because he was reigning before Moses fled to Midian and continued to reign for most of Moses' **forty-year exile**. However, modern Egyptologists date **five different Pharaohs** between 1486 B.C. and 1446 B.C.: Amenhotep I, Thutmose I, Thutmose II, Hatshepsut and Thutmose III.[18] Five pharaohs contradict the two Pharaohs listed in the Bible for this same period.

Problem No. 3. Thutmose III reigned too long to be the Pharaoh of the Exodus. Psa 136:13-15 says: "To him who divided the Red Sea asunder . . . and brought Israel through the midst of it . . . **but swept Pharaoh and his army into the Red Sea.**" Exodus 14:28 further explains that **all of the Egyptians, including Pharaoh,** entered the Red Sea and were drowned..

> The water flowed back and covered the chariots and horsemen-- **the entire army of Pharaoh** that had followed the Israelites into the sea. **Not one of them survived.** NIV

Psalm 136:15 says that Pharaoh was swept into the Red Sea along with his army. Exodus 14:28 says that all Egyptians who entered the Red Sea died. Uniting the truths of these two Biblical passages, the Bible clearly pictures Pharaoh and his army as dying together in the Red Sea while pursuing the Israelites.

Therefore, the Pharaoh of the Exodus began his reign toward the end of Moses' forty-year exile in Midian, and died shortly afterwards in the Red Sea. Consequently, he must have reigned less than ten years. However, Thutmose III reigned **fifty-four years**,[19] **far too long to be the Pharaoh of the Exodus**.

Problem No. 4. Thutmose III led his army to Egypt's most successful military victories, dated by scholars from 1446 to 1436 B.C., ten years after the Exodus. In his thirty-third year, dated in 1446 B.C., Thutmose III led his army to Mitannia (in modern Syria) and achieved Egypt's greatest military victory.[20]   For eight consecutive years Thutmose III continued to conquer the principal cities of Syria and Canaan, subjecting them to Egyptian control and taxation.[21]

Thutmose III's successful battles from 1446 to 1436 B.C. totally contradict the Biblical picture of the Pharaoh of the Exodus, who was buried under the Red Sea with his "entire army" during these same B.C. years.

Problem No. 5. The Hebrews already inhabited Canaan before Thutmose III reigned. Idrimi, king of Alalakh, began his reign a few years before Thutmose III became king. Idrimi claimed that he lived with the "Hapiru people" in Canaan before he became king.[22] Thutmose III also mentioned his encounter with Hapiru in Canaan.[23] Also, his successor, Amenhotep II, invaded Canaan and brought back 3,600 Hapiru prisoners.[24] A growing number of scholars, such as Yohanan Aharoni, now identify these Canaanite Hapiru as the Biblical Hebrews.[25]

Joseph himself explained that he formerly lived in the land of the "Hebrews" (Exodus 40:15). When Joseph's brothers arrived in Egypt during the famine he told the Egyptians that they were "Hebrews" (Genesis 43:32). On numerous occasions God told Moses to speak to Pharaoh and tell him that "Yahweh, **the God of the Hebrews**," had commanded the Israelites to leave Egypt and worship Him in the wilderness (Exodus 3:18; 5:3; 7:16; 9:1,12; 10:3).

Abraham was also called a Hebrew in Genesis 14:13. The Hebrews descended from Eber (Heber), from whom the Hebrew language likely developed.[26] Thus, there were other Hebrews besides Abraham and his descendants.

However, Abraham did not meet other Hebrews when he entered Canaan. Neither are Hebrews mentioned among the inhabitants of Canaan in the books of Joshua and Judges when Israel entered and conquered the land in 1406 B.C.[27] Therefore, the presence of Hebrews in Canaan before and after the reign of Thutmose III implies that the Exodus and Conquest had occurred before the eighteenth dynasty came into existence. On this basis, neither Thutmose III, nor any other eighteenth-dynasty king, could have been the Pharaoh of the Exodus.

Problem No. 6. All modern archaeologists agree that the foreign conquest of Jericho and other Canaanite cities occurred during the Middle Bronze IIB/C Age.[28] This age is dated from 1800 to 1550 B.C. These same archaeologists date the eighteenth dynasty 300 years later in the Late Bronze Age, from 1550 to 1200 B.C.[29] **However, there is no evidence of a foreign conquest of Canaan during the Late Bronze Age.**

Therefore, the conquest of Jericho and other key Canaanite cities, as described in the Bible, did not occur archaeologically during the reign of any eighteenth-dynasty king. On the other hand, the archaeological evidence indicates that the Conquest occurred in the Middle Bronze Age IIB/C before the eighteenth dynasty came to power, explaining why Hebrews were living in Canaan before, during and after, the reign of Thutmose III. Therefore the Exodus and Conquest must have occurred in the Middle Bronze Age, excluding the eighteenth dynasty from being the time of Moses.

C. Conclusion: Moses Did Not Live During the Eighteenth Dynasty

I was deeply disturbed to see this serious historical conflict between eighteenth dynasty history dated to the same time of the Biblical dates for Moses. My research into the Egyptian documents of the eighteenth dynasty convinced me that Moses did not live in Egypt during the reign of any Pharaoh of the eighteenth dynasty and that Israel's Exodus and Conquest of Canaan did not occur during the reign of the eighteenth dynasty. Most Egyptologists and archaeologists and many Bible scholars had already arrived at this conclusion long before I did. When I finally recognized this conflict between eighteenth-dynasty history and Bible history of Moses' time, I fully realized the seriousness of the Exodus Problem and the reasons why many Egyptologists and archaeologists had rejected the historicity of the Biblical Exodus and Conquest of Canaan.

III. WAS RAMSES II THE PHARAOH OF THE EXODUS?

Many Bible scholars also recognized the conflict between Bible dates of the Exodus and eighteenth-dynasty history dated to the same time. Many of these Bible scholars shifted from the eighteenth dynasty to the nineteenth dynasty as the time of the Exodus and identified Ramses II as the Pharaoh of the Exodus.

Most Egyptologists date Ramses II's reign from 1279 to 1213 B.C. However, 1 Kings 6:1 says that 480 years separated Solomon's fourth year (966 B.C.) from the Exodus in 1446 B.C. Scholars who identify Ramses II as the Pharaoh of the Exodus consider the 480 years of I Kings 6:1 as **figurative of twelve generations of forty years each.** These scholars thus reduce the 480 years of 1 Kings 6:1 to only 284 years in order to date the Exodus c. 1250 B.C., in the middle of Ramses II's long reign of sixty-seven years.

In Cecil B. DeMille's *Ten Commandments,* Yul Brunner brilliantly portrayed Ramses II and Charlton Heston was a magnificent Moses. Later, an animated movie called *The Prince of Egypt,* also identified Ramses II as the Pharaoh of the Exodus. These movies represent the views of a majority of Bible scholars that accept Ramses II as the Biblical Pharaoh of the Exodus.

Seti I and his son Ramses II constructed Pi-Rameses, as their new capital, in the land of Goshen. Most Bible scholars identify Pi-Rameses as the store city that was constructed during the time of Moses in Exodus 1:11. Pi-Rameses, "the house of Rameses" that Ramses II built, appears to be the city of Rameses in Exodus 1:11. Therefore, many Bible scholars have identified Ramses II as the Pharaoh of the Exodus. However, my investigation of Ramses II's life and reign reveals compelling reasons for rejecting him as the Pharaoh of the Exodus.

Problem No. 1. Rameses was a store city in Moses' day, not a capital city. The Pharaoh of Moses' birth built Rameses and Pithom as **"store cities"** (Ex. 1:11). Ramses II built Pi-Rameses as his **capital city, not a store city.** A store city is not a capital city. If a store city were a capital city, then Pithom was also a capital of Egypt, because it is also called a "store city" in Exodus 1:11. "Store cities" were occupied by troops, weapons and supplies to protect a nearby capital from invading foreigners. Since Pithom and Rameses are both store cities, and since Pithom is listed before Rameses, it is clear that neither of these cities were capitals when Moses was born. Since both of these cities were under construction when Moses was born, the Pharaoh of the Oppression obviously lived in his palace in a different city not far from the store cities that were being built to protect it.

Problem No. 2. Zoan, not Pi-Rameses, is the implied capital of Egypt in Moses' day. Numbers. 13:22 and Psalm 78:12,43 imply that **Zoan (Tanis)** was the capital of Egypt when the plagues fell on Egypt. Kitchen presents strong evidences that Ramses II's capital was located at Qantir, not Zoan (Tanis).[30] Since the Pharaoh of Moses' birth lived in his capital at Zoan (Tanis), and since Ramses II lived in his capital at Pi-Rameses (Qantir) , Ramses II cannot be the Pharaoh of the Exodus. Chapter Sixteen discusses in depth the location of Zoan as the capital in the days of Joseph and Moses.

Problem No. 3. In Moses' day the store city of Rameses was built out of mud bricks mixed with straw (Exodus 1:11; 5:6-9), but Pi-Rameses, the capital of Ramses II, was constructed out of stone. Excavation at Qantir (Tel el-Daba = Pi-Rameses) reveals that Ramses II used **stone** to build his capital of Pi-Rameses over the ruins of the Hyksos capital of Avaris. Underneath both Pi-Rameses and the Hyksos strata was found the older, **mud-brick store city of Rameses, built by Pharaohs of the twelfth dynasty. The mud-brick city** is dated more than 200 years before the Hyksos built their capital and more than 500 years before Ramses II constructed his capital on top of the Hyksos construction.[31]

Therefore, the stone capital city of Pi-Rameses that Ramses II built cannot be the mud-brick store city of Rameses that was built in the time of Moses. The two cities cannot be the same even though they were constructed in the same location. Chapter Fifteen reveals the identity of the Pharaoh who first constructed Rameses as a store city. He is the **true** Pharaoh of Moses' birth.

Problem No. 4. The Hebrews and the tribe of Asher, lived in Canaan hundreds of years before Ramses II reigned. We have already seen that Hebrews inhabited Canaan before and during the eighteenth dynasty. Thus, the Hebrews were already living in Canaan some 350 years before Ramses II began his reign. Ramses II's **fifth year of reign** is dated by Egyptologists to **1275 B.C.** In that year Ramses II's scribe wrote that he contacted the **chief of Asher** while crossing the mountain pass of Aruna from Megiddo to the tribal territory of Asher.[32] Asher was one of the twelve tribes of Israel.[33] Therefore, the Hebrews were living in Canaan and were divided into their twelve tribal territories before Ramses II came to power. Consequently, Ramses II could not have been the Pharaoh of the Exodus.

Problem No. 5. Ramses II reigned too long to be the Pharaoh of the Exodus. Ramses II reigned sixty-seven years. We saw earlier that the Bible pictures the Pharaoh of the Exodus as coming to power toward the end of Moses' forty-year exile in Midian and dying in the Red Sea a few years later. Therefore, the Pharaoh of the Exodus must have reigned less than ten years. Consequently, the long, sixty-seven-year reign of Ramses II totally contradicts the Biblical picture of the short-reigning Pharaoh of the Exodus.

Problem No. 6. Merneptah, son of Ramses II, reported in his fifth year that Israel was desolate in Canaan.[34] This Egyptian inscription is the first to use the expression **"Israel."** Formerly, the Egyptians called the Israelites by the name, **Hebrews,** who derived their name from Eber (Heber), one of Abraham's ancestors (Genesis 10:21ff). Abraham and his descendants all spoke Hebrew.

The Bible says that Israel conquered Canaan forty years after the Exodus and remained triumphant and in peace for another forty years after the conquest.[35] **Therefore, Israel was not desolate in Canaan until at least eighty years after the Exodus.** If Ramses II were the Pharaoh of the Exodus, Israel should have been either wandering in the desert, or victorious in Canaan, in Merneptah's fifth year. Therefore, the desolate condition of Israel in Canaan in Merneptah's fifth year gives additional proof that Ramses II was not the Pharaoh of the Exodus.

Problem No. 7. The Conquest occurred in the archaeological age called Middle Bronze II, not the Late Bronze Age.

We saw earlier in this chapter that archaeologists date the fall of Jericho in Middle Bronze Age II, 500 years before the Late Bronze Age. Ramses II and Merneptah reigned in the Late Bronze Age.[36] Therefore, the desolation of Israel in Merneptah's reign cannot refer to the victorious Biblical conquest of Canaan. Volume II will show who, how, why and when Merneptah wrote about the desolation of Israel during a later period of Israel's history.

CONCLUSION

The problems presented in this chapter are complex, controversial and confounding to the mind. These conflicts demonstrate the serious reality of the Exodus Problem. **Table 2-C below summarizes eighteen discovery errors that are registered in this chapter and that were created by the NIV chronologists, that begin the 430 years of Exodus 12:40 with Jacob's entrance into Egypt instead of Abraham's departure from Ur.** The second source for this apparent conflict with Biblical dating is the incorrect dating of Babylonian history by the *Cambridge Ancient History,* **which Peter Huber of Harvard University revised 56 years earlier.** In Chapters Four and Five we apply Dr Huber's 56-year revision, creating abundant new synchronisms with my corrected Bible chronology of the 430 years of Exodus 12:40. As a result of all of these discoveries, I have been able to reveal the true kings of Abraham and the true pharaohs of Joseph, Moses and the Exodus.

TABLE 2-C
SUMMING UP EIGHTEEN DISCOVERIES OF ERRORS THAT HAVE IMPEDED THE SOLUTION OF THE EXODUS MYSTERY

Discovery Error 1. The chronologists of the New International Version date the 430 years with Jacob's entrance into Egypt whereas Paul says in Galatians 3:17 that the 430 years began with God's promise to Abraham when he lived in Ur in 1876 B.C.

Discovery Error 2. NIV chronology dates Abraham in 2082 B.C., when he confronted Kedor-Laomer of Elam , but the *Cambridge Ancient History* names Simashki as King of Elam in2082 B.C.

Discovery Error 3. NIV chronology dates Abraham in 2082, when he confronted Amraphel, king of Babylon, but Shulgi was king of Babylon and Ur in 2082 B.C.

Discovery Error 4. The NIV chronology correctly dates Moses' first eighty years from 1526 B.C. to 1446 B.C. (the Exodus). However, Ahmose was supposedly reigning when Moses was born and when Israel was enslaved. However, Ahmose drove the foreigners out of Goshen, whereas the Biblical Pharaoh of Moses' birth enslaved the foreign Israelites.

Discovery Error 5. Excavations of the store cities of Pithom and Rameses and other cities in Goshen indicate that neither Ahmose, nor any other eighteenth-dynasty king, constructed them.

Discovery Error 6. Each time the Bible mentions the Egyptian capital from the time of Joseph to the time of Moses, it is located close to the land of Goshen, where Israel lived. Eighteenth-dynasty Pharaohs had their capital in Thebes in southern Egypt.

Discovery Error 7. The eighteenth dynasty capital in southern Egypt contradicts Moses' traveling back and forth between Goshen and the Egyptian capital (Zoan) on a daily basis.

Discovery Error 8. Thutmose III of the eighteenth dynasty reigned fifty-four years in the *Britannica* dates of 1479 to 1426 B.C. and should therefore be the Pharaoh of the Exodus in the Biblical date of 1446 B.C. However, the Pharaoh of the Exodus came to power a few years before Moses returned to Egypt, and the same Pharaoh died with his army in the Red Sea shortly afterwards (Psalm 136:15). Exodus 14:28 says that all who entered the Red Sea did not survive. Thus a fifty-four-year reign cannot fit the chronology of the Biblical Pharaoh of the Exodus.

Discovery Error 9. Thutmose III led his army to conquer Canaanites and Syrians in the year following the Exodus and many years afterwards, proving that his army was not destroyed in the Red Sea, eliminating him as the true Pharaoh of the Exodus.

Discovery Error 10. Idrimi, who lived in Canaan among the Hebrews, is dated during the eighteenth dynasty, proving that the Hebrews had already left Egypt hundreds of years before the eighteenth dynasty existed.

Discovery Error 11. The foreign conquest of Jericho and other Canaanite cities occurred during the Middle Bronze IIB/C Age, dated 1800 to 1550 B.C. (on the basis of Egyptian dates), 300 years before the eighteenth dynasty came to power, proving that the Exodus occurred 300 years before the eighteenth dynasty came to power.

Discovery Error 12. The Pharaoh of Moses' birth built Rameses and Pithom as **"store cities"** (Ex. 1:11). Ramses II built Pi-Rameses as his **capital city, not a store city.**

Discovery Error 13. Numbers 13:22 and Psalm 78:12, 43 say that the plagues fell on Zoan, the capital of Egypt, whereas they did not fall on the Israelites at Rameses. Therefore Kitchen's identification of Ramses (Qantir) as a capital city contradicts the Bible.

Discovery Error 14. In Moses' day the store city of Rameses was built out of mud bricks mixed with straw (Exodus 1:11; 5:6 9), but Pi-Rameses, the capital of Ramses II, was constructed out of stone.

Discovery Error 15. The Hebrews and the tribe of Asher, lived in Canaan hundreds of years before Ramses II reigned. A scribe of Ramses II met the chief of the tribe of Asher while travelling in Canaan.

Discovery Error 16. Ramses II reigned sixty-seven years, the second longest-reigning Pharaoh in Egyptian history. The Pharaoh of the Exodus came to power shortly before Moses returned to Egypt and died with his army in the Red Sea shortly afterwards.

Discovery Error 17. Merneptah, son of Ramses II, reported in his fifth year that Israel was desolate in Canaan. The Bible says that Israel entered Canaan in 1406 B.C. and was triumphant for eighty years, whereas Merneptah is dated by Baines 1213 to 1304 B.C., 200 years later than the Exodus. Ramses II and Merneptah have nothing to do with the Exodus.

Discovery Error 18. Archaeologists say the Conquest occurred in the archaeological age called Middle Bronze II, not the Late Bronze Age. Ramses II and Merneptah lived in the Late Bronze Age, 500 years after the Middle Bronze II Age. We will see in Volume II that the walls of Jericho fell forty years after the fall of the twelfth-dynasty during the Middle Bronze Age.

When the Egyptian dates are revised by three centuries, as we will prove later in this book, the Middle Bronze Age will be dated three centuries later and thus include the 1406 B.C. date for the fall of Jericho's walls..

NOTES FOR CHAPTER TWO

1. Edwin Thiele, *Mysterious Numbers of the Hebrew Kings* (Grand Rapids: Zondervan, 1983), 67-8.
2. C. J. Gadd, "Babylonia: *c.* 2120-1800 B.C.," *The Cambridge Ancient History,* I.2B.604; "Chronological Tables," Cambridge University Press, I.2B.998.
3. T. G. H. James, *Cambridge Ancient History,* 3rd Ed., Cambridge University Press, II.1.299.
4. T. G. H. James, *Cambridge Ancient History,* 3rd Ed., II.1.304-5, 311-12.
5. Exodus 1:8-2:10.
6. Genesis 45:10; 46:28-29, 34; 47:11-16, 27; Exodus 8:22.
7. Exodus 2:1-10.
8. K. A. Kitchen, "Goshen," *Zondervan Pictorial Encyclopedia of the Bible* (Grand Rapids: Zondervan Corp., 1976), II.777-778.
9. William C. Hayes, *Cambridge Ancient History,* 3rd Ed., Cambridge University Press, II.1.323-324.
10. John Baines and J. Malek, *Atlas of Ancient Egypt,* Facts on File Pub., 1982, 43,90.
11. Acts 7:23-30; Exodus 7:7.
12. William C. Hayes, *Scepter of Egypt,* 1990 Ed., II, (New York: Metropolitan Museum of Art), 499.
13. William C. Hayes, *Cambridge Ancient History,* 3rd Ed., (Cambridge Univ. Press, 1973), II.1.319.
14. Exodus 8-10; see especially 9:26.
15. William Hayes, *Cambridge Ancient History,* 3rd Ed., II.1.323-324; John Baines & J. Malek, *Atlas of Ancient Egypt,* Facts on File Pub., 1982, 90.
16. Acts 7:23, 30.
17. Exodus 2:23; 4:19; Acts 7:30-34.
18. William C. Hayes, *Scepter of Egypt,* 1990 Ed., II, 499.
19. William C. Hayes, *Scepter of Egypt,* II, 499.
20. Margaret Drower, *Cambridge Ancient History,* 3rd Ed., *Op. Cit.* II.1.455,457.
21. James Breasted (trans.), "The Annals of Thutmose III," *Ancient Records of Egypt,* II.173-217.
22. Leon Oppenheim (Trans.), *Ancient Near Eastern Texts,* 3rd Ed. (Princeton Univ. Press, 1969), 557.
23. Wilson, John A. (Trans.), "The Taking of Joppa," *Ancient Near Eastern Texts,* 3rd Ed., 22.
24. Wilson, John A. (Trans.), "The Asiatic Campaigning of Amen-hotep II," *Ibid.,* 247.
25. Yohanan Aharoni, *The Macmillan Bible Atlas* (New York: Macmillan, 1968), 34.
26. B. J. Beitzel, "Hebrew People," *International Stand. Bible Encyc.,* 1982, Eerdmans, II.657.
27. Genesis 10:21, 24, 25; 11:14-17.
28. Amihai Mazar, *Archaeology of the Land of the Bible* (New York: Doubleday, 1990), 226-227.
29. Amihai Mazar, *Archaeology of the Land of the Bible, Ibid.,* 30.
30. K. A. Kitchen, "Raamses," *Zondervan Pictorial Bible Encyclopedia,* 5.14.
31. W. A. Shea, "Exodus, Date of," *International Standard Bible Encyclopedia,* Eerdmans,II.231.
32. Yohanan Aharoni and Michael Avi-Yonah, *Macmillan Bible Atlas,* 39.
33. Exodus 1:1-5; Joshua 19:24-31.
34. John A. Wilson, "Hymn of Victory of Merneptah," *Ancient Near Eastern Texts,"* Ed. Pritchard, Princeton Univ. Press, 378.
35. Book of Joshua.
36. Amihai Mazar, *Archaeology of the Land of the Bible, Op. Cit.* 226, 243.

CHAPTER THREE
SEARCHING FOR A SOLUTION

In 1978 I was assigned to teach an Apologetics course, which presents evidences for God as Creator and evidences for the Bible as God's Word. I have written a textbook for this course, which I revise each year to add new evidences. My textbook, *New Discoveries That Confirm the Bible,* presents answers to arguments that atheists and skeptics make for evolution and against God, Creation and the Bible. The textbook also presents positive evidences in favor of God, Creation and the historicity of the Bible. As I researched the negative evidences that archaeologists and Egyptologists make against Bible history from Abraham to the Conquest, my faith was challenged and disturbed. These serious problems that I listed in Chapter Two forced me to sympathize with scholars who reject the authenticity of Bible history.

However, my faith in God and His Word is so strong that I was determined to find a solution to the Exodus Problem. I also love mysteries and puzzles and was interested in solving the Exodus Mystery as a enjoyable hobby as well as an academic and spiritual challenge.

Hercule Poirot and Miss Marple were Agatha Christie's favorite people to solve all of her murder mysteries. Poirot often expressed, "Things that appear to be are not really what they are." After thorough investigation and intensive meditation, Poirot always arrived at a brilliant solution. Miss Marple just kept snooping and digging in her quiet manner until she found all the facts that pointed to only one person: the murderer. I hardly measure up to Hercule Perot, but my wife Dot certainly measures up to Miss Marple. Dot has contributed immeasurably to the contents of this book.

I. A COLUMBO SEARCHING FOR A SOLUTION
TO THE EXODUS MYSTERY.

I personally fit better the description of "Columbo," the TV detective played by Peter Falk. Columbo appears with ruffled hair, a crooked tie and an old trench coat. He drives an ancient car, talks incessantly about Mrs. Columbo, and looks like the lowest paid and most inept man on the police force. Matching wits with highly educated men, he disarms them with an image of incompetency. With subtle, skillful questions and persistent tenacity, he dogs his suspects to despair, until he discovers irrefutable proof of their innocence or, more often, their guilt.

While it remains to be seen if I will be as effective as Columbo in solving the Exodus Mystery, I certainly fit his humble description. I am a worn-out missionary/teacher who drives an old car and makes a low salary. Scholars consider me an academic nobody who teaches Bible, Missions, Evidences and Greek in a little-known seminary called the Sunset International Bible Institute, located in Lubbock, Texas. However, our Institute has eight branch seminaries with complete faculties in eight nations of the world and has 255 satellite schools that are increasing at the rate of twenty new satellite schools every year that are scattered throughout the U.S. and other countries. Five thousand, five hundred students are currently enrolled in all of the branches and satellite schools under the umbrella of the Sunset International Institute. Thousands of other students have taken individual courses by mail through Sunset's Extension School in Lubbock.

Academically I appear as shabby as detective Columbo appears. Columbo often refers to his wife, but we never see her by his side and she never contributes to the solution of his criminal cases. However, my wife, Dot, has always been by my side and has traveled with me to the ends of the earth in search for evidences that confirm Bible history from Abraham to the Exodus and beyond to the Conquest of Canaan. Dot also proof-reads my scripts and gives me excellent insights that have improved this book. Indeed, this book could not have been completed without Dot's indispensable assistance. My sons (Kevin and Brent) and my daughters (Cherie and Trina) have also participated in the writing of this book.

II. DR. LANGFORD'S CRITIQUE OF *SOLVING THE EXODUS MYSTERY*

Dr. Tom Langford, former Dean of the Graduate School of Texas Tech University and a specialist in English composition and literature, agreed to critique my book to improve its clarity, accuracy and style. Dr. Langford is a regular subscriber to *Biblical Archaeology Review,* and is fully aware of the Exodus Problem. When Dr. Langford considered critiquing my book, he asked this question: "Why is it that all of the top scholars of the world have failed to find an adequate solution to the Exodus Problem, whereas you, without their scholarly expertise, claim to have found a solution?" My answer is recorded below.

Foremost, I give credit and honor to my Heavenly Father, my Lord Jesus Christ and the Holy Spirit to whom and through whom I have prayed constantly for guidance to solve the "Exodus Mystery." I searched diligently in the Bible and in the ancient documents and histories of Elam, Mari, Babylon and Egypt. The following Bible verses encouraged me to trust in God to find a solution to the Exodus Mystery.

> Proverbs 2:1-5 -- "My son, if you accept my words and store up my commands within you, turning your ear to wisdom and applying your heart to understanding, and if you call out for insight and cry aloud for understanding, and if you look for it as for silver and search for it as for hidden treasure, then you will understand the fear of the LORD and find the knowledge of God." NIV

> Matthew 7:7-8 -- "Ask and it will be given to you; seek and you will find; knock and the door will be opened to you. For everyone who asks receives; he who seeks finds; and to him who knocks, the door will be opened." NIV

God gave wisdom to a slave/prisoner called Joseph to save his family and all Egypt from a seven-year famine. God chose Moses, an eighty-year old fugitive from justice, to free Israel from Egyptian bondage. God later chose Moses to reveal His omniscient knowledge of earth's history from Creation to Israel's Exodus from Egypt. At Mount Sinai God also revealed His laws and statutes to Moses. God used Joshua to lead the Israelites to destroy the high-walled cities of Canaan and defeat superior armed forces, including the giants.

God later empowered David, a poor shepherd boy, to defeat Goliath and form Israel into a powerful nation. God also inspired David with wisdom to write the most spiritually edifying "Psalms" of all history.

God appointed Jesus, the adopted son of a poor carpenter, to begin a new world religion. Jesus commissioned uneducated fishermen to expand His eternal kingdom over the world. His apostles accomplished the task in their lifetime and recorded their teachings in the New Testament, joining their words to the Old Testament. The Bible remains the best selling book every year.

God's past use of lowly men to accomplish His high purposes gave me confidence that He can use a commoner like me to solve the Exodus Problem. I do not have the plenary inspiration of the Holy Spirit as these holy men experienced. However, I trust in the same Spirit and God that they trusted. Whatever truths the readers find in this book should be credited to the Father and the Son, not to me. Whatever errors the reader may find in this book should be attributed to my human fallibility. This book records my long (24-year), intense search that led me initially in the wrong direction before finally heading me in the right direction and, ultimately, toward a complete solution of the Exodus Problem.

As Dr. Langford continued to critique the chapters of my book, his attitude gradually changed from "skepticism" to "intriguing." When he got to the middle of the book, he said, **"You are gradually winning me over."** See Dr. Langford's last judgment on the jacket of this book. Hopefully, dear reader, you will continue reading Volume I, and later Volume II, so that you will be **fully convinced that the Exodus Mystery has been truly and fully solved.**

III. VELIKOVSKY'S ATTEMPT TO SOLVE THE EXODUS PROBLEM

In 1978 Jim McGuiggan, a fellow teacher and an outstanding author, recommended that I read Immanuel Velikovsky's *Ages In Chaos*. Velikovsky claimed that Egyptian history was misdated by 300 to 600 years and would harmonize with Biblical history, if properly dated. Velikovsky identified Pharaoh Didymus I (Dudimose I or Timaios) of the thirteenth dynasty as the Pharaoh of the Exodus. Velikovsky also cited Ipuwer, an Egyptian priest of the Middle Kingdom, who recorded what appears to be an eyewitness account of the ten plagues and the Exodus. Dr. Robert Pfeiffer of Harvard University wrote the following on the jacket of the cover of Velikovsky's *Ages in Chaos:* **"If Dr.**

Velikovsky is right, this book will be the greatest contribution to the investigation of ancient times ever written."[1]

Velikovsky also identified Queen Hatshepsut of the eighteenth dynasty as the Queen of Sheba who visited Solomon in Jerusalem. Her successor, Thutmose III, was identified as Pharaoh Shishak, the Egyptian king who captured Jerusalem five years after Solomon's death. Velikovsky's identifications were supported by ancient documents and occasionally by carbon-14 dates. I was very impressed with Velikovsky's proposed solutions and I thought he had likely solved the Exodus problem. I recommended Velikovsky's books to my students.

After further reflection I decided to test Velikovsky's reconstruction of Egyptian history. I realized that my knowledge of Egyptian history was superficial. I began an intense study of Egyptian history books and especially English translations of the original documents of ancient Egypt. Then I made what I called "Chronological Clue Charts" of Biblical and Egyptian histories and compared them to charts of Velikovsky's reconstruction of Egyptian history. My comparisons showed serious contradictions in all of Velikovsky's identifications of Biblical Pharaohs.

My "Chronological Clue Charts" not only enabled me to disprove Velikovsky's reconstruction of Egyptian history, but also assisted me in discovering Bible history from Abraham to Jacob in Babylonian, Elamite and Egyptian documents. The Clue Charts further assisted me in finding Bible history from Joseph to the Exodus in the historical documents of the twelfth dynasty.

Velikovsky's principal contribution to the solution of the Exodus Problem was his discovery of *Ipuwer's Papyrus,* which is an obvious eye-witness account of the ten plagues. However, Velikovsky incorrectly dated *Ipuwer's Papyrus* to the reign of Dudimose I, a Pharaoh of the thirteenth dynasty. Appendix-A demonstrates that Dudimose I could **not** have been the Biblical Pharaoh of the Exodus and that Ipuwer did not live during the reign of thirteenth-dynasty Pharaohs. Chapter Eighteen of this book identifies the true Pharaoh of the Exodus and the specific time of his reign when Ipuwer described most of the ten plagues.

When I first read Velikovsky, I thought he had solved the Exodus Problem. Later, my bubble of hope burst when I was able to disprove all of his Egyptian identifications of Biblical Pharaohs. My faith was shaken! I was so discouraged that I almost decided to quit searching for a solution.

After much prayer and meditation, I said to myself, "Perhaps Velikovsky was correct about the misdating of Egyptian chronology, but he failed to find the correct Egyptian dynasty when the Exodus occurred." With renewed hope I began a new search to find Biblical history from Abraham to Joseph to Moses to the Exodus in Babylonian, Elamite and Egyptian documents.

IV.   COURVILLE'S PROPOSAL FOR THE PHARAOHS OF JOSEPH AND THE EXODUS

My former colleague/teacher, Jim McGuiggan, also recommended Donovan

Courville's *The Exodus Problem & Its Ramifications.*[2] Courville proposed that Sesostris I of the twelfth dynasty was the Pharaoh of Joseph. He explored the documents of the twelfth dynasty and found an inscription of a famine of many years and evidence of the canal of Joseph, both dated during the reign of Sesostris I, the second king of the twelfth dynasty.

Courville identified Joseph as Mentuhotep, the prime minister of Sesostris I's latter reign. He also identified Sesostris III, a later Pharaoh of the twelfth dynasty, as one of the Pharaohs who oppressed Israel and constructed the cities of Rameses and Pithom. To reduce the B.C. dates of Egyptian history, Courville placed the sixth dynasty parallel to the twelfth dynasty. Courville's placement of the sixth dynasty parallel to the twelfth dynasty is disproved by solid historical evidence that the twelfth dynasty was the sole dynasty that ruled over all of northern and southern Egypt. Courville's identification of Joseph as Mentuhotep, a latter vizier of Sesostris I, proved to be completely false. This evidence will be presented in later chapters of this book.

However, Courville's reference to the famine inscription and Joseph's Canal in Sesostris I's reign turned out to be accurate. Also the construction of the cities of Pithom and Rameses by Sesostris III proved to be true. I am deeply indebted to Courville for pointing me to the twelfth dynasty for the time of Joseph and Moses.

Courville followed some of Velikovsky's reconstruction of Egyptian history. However, Courville identified Koncharis of the thirteenth dynasty as the Pharaoh of the Exodus. Khoncharis reigned before Dudimose I, even though they both belonged to the same thirteenth dynasty (a family of successive Pharaohs). Appendix A demonstrates why no thirteenth dynasty Pharaoh, including Dudimose I and Koncharis, could be the Pharaoh of the Exodus.

V. ALING'S PROPOSAL FOR THE PHARAOHS OF JOSEPH AND THE EXODUS

Charles F. Aling's *Egypt and Bible History* dates Israel in Egypt for 430 years, placing Joseph in the early twelfth dynasty,[3] as Courville and I do. Aling found several synchronisms between Joseph's time and the time of Sesostris I, the second Pharaoh of the twelfth dynasty. These synchronisms are noted in later chapters of this book.

However, Aling dated the Exodus 430 years after Israel entered Egypt. This long 430-year chronology pushes Moses and the Exodus into the eighteenth dynasty where Egyptian history contradicts Bible history for the period of Moses, as we saw in Chapter Two and as will see in greater detail in Chapter Four.

Aling started well in synchronizing Joseph with Sesostris I of the twelfth dynasty, but he missed the synchronism between twelfth dynasty history and Bible history of Moses and the Exodus. Chapter Four demonstrates that Aling's designation of Israel's 430-year sojourn in Egypt is a misinterpretation of Exodus 12:40. In the next chapter, we will see that Israel lived in Egypt for only 210 years.

VI. ROHL'S AND KITCHEN'S IDENTIFICATIONS OF THE PHARAOHS OF JOSEPH AND THE EXODUS

In 1995 David Rohl published his book entitled *Pharaohs and Kings: A Biblical Quest.[4]* Rohl identifies Amenemhet III, a latter twelfth-dynasty Pharaoh, as the Pharaoh of Joseph. Rohl attributes the seven years of famine in the time of Joseph to the flooding of the Nile during Amenemhet III's reign. In Appendix B I disprove Rohl's identification of Amenemhet III as the Pharaoh of Joseph.

Rohl agrees with Velikovsky that Dudimose I of the thirteenth dynasty was the Pharaoh of the Exodus. However, Appendix A points out the incompatibility of Dudimose I as the Biblical Pharaoh of the Exodus.

Kenneth Kitchen believes a Hyksos Pharaoh appointed Joseph as his Prime Minister (Vizier).[5] The Hyksos were foreigners from Arabia who conquered northern Egypt and set up the fifteenth and sixteenth dynasties of Egypt. Kitchen logically reasoned that a foreign Hyksos Pharaoh would be more likely to appoint a foreign Prime Minister (Joseph) than a purely Egyptian Pharaoh. However, Appendix B also evaluates the Hyksos period as the time of Joseph and finds it contradictory to the Biblical record of the Pharaoh of Joseph.

Kitchen also believes that Ramses II is the Pharaoh of the Exodus. Appendix B proves that Ramses II's long sixty-seven-year reign and his supposed thirteenth-century date completely contradict the Biblical description and date of the true Pharaoh of the Exodus who reigned only ten years before Moses returned from Midian and died in the Red Sea shortly afterwards. Psalm 136:13-15 reports that the Pharaoh of the Exodus entered the Red Sea with his troops and Exodus 14:21-28 reports that all who entered the Red Sea were drowned.

VII. CHRONOLOGICAL CLUE CHARTS

My examination of all of these scholarly proposals revealed some strengths, but mostly weaknesses. The details of my critiques are discussed in Appendices A and B and in later chapters of this book. I was able to find their weaknesses by comparing what I call chronological clue charts that compare Biblical and Egyptian histories. Below I discuss the methodology behind these chronological clue charts.

A. Comparing Historical Footprints And Fingerprints of Men

To search for the Pharaoh of the Exodus I decided to use the method of detectives. Policemen interrogate witnesses as to place, time, motives and suspects. They also search for clues, including fingerprints and footprints.

Dot and I were missionaries in Brazil for thirteen years. On one occasion, we attended a party where Dot and eleven other missionary wives stood behind a curtain. The curtain covered their entire bodies, except for their bare feet showing underneath the curtain. Each husband was asked to observe the feet of all of the women and then to stand in front of his own wife's feet.

I was amazed at the different shapes of feet on those twelve women. I had never given special attention to Dot's feet, but I picked out the most delicate and beautiful pair and stood before them. When the curtain was lowered, I and nine others were standing in front of our respective wives. The two men who failed to discern the correct feet were properly reprimanded by their spouses. That experience taught me that the feet of each individual are distinctively different from the feet of others.

As feet and footprints differ, so people walk through history differently. We say that history repeats itself, and so it does in principle. But history does not duplicate itself in intricate detail and exact chronological sequence. To search for Biblical history in Egyptian documents I formulated the methodology of comparing historical patterns from the two histories. Each period of history has a unique pattern that differs from other periods of history.

Abraham was born in Ur of the Chaldees and left Ur at age seventy to go to Canaan, but stopped at Haran for five years because of his sick father. His father died five years later and Abraham thus entered Canaan at age seventy-five. During a famine he lived temporarily in Egypt, met the Pharaoh of Egypt and became wealthy. After his return to Canaan at age eighty-four he routed the troops of the kings of Elam and Babylon by surprising them at night, and thus saved his nephew Lot and Lot's family. When Abraham was ninety-nine years old, he witnessed the destruction of Sodom and Gomorrah.

Joseph was born in Canaan, was sold as a slave to Egypt at age seventeen, and was later imprisoned. He predicted seven years of abundance, followed by seven years of famine. He was appointed prime minister of all Egypt at age thirty. His father and brothers moved to Egypt when Joseph was thirty-nine years old. He died in Egypt at age 110.

Moses was born in Egypt, was saved from death by an Egyptian princess, and was reared and educated in the palace of Pharaoh. At age forty Moses fled to Midian where he lived an additional forty years. He returned to Egypt to free Israel from slavery at age eighty. After departing from Egypt, he led Israel through the Red Sea, wandered in the desert for forty years and died at age 120 in Moab.

These examples demonstrate how people leave uniquely different footprints in the sand of history. When the lives of two nationalities are intertwined, the diversity of their combined historical patterns becomes even more distinct. The Pharaoh of Joseph traded grain for all of Egypt's livestock and land. He also showed kindness to Joseph's family. This book will identify the Pharaoh of Joseph and the seven years of abundance followed by the seven years of famine, all registered in the Egyptian records of the twelfth dynasty.

In contrast, the Pharaoh of Moses' birth enslaved Israel, forced them to construct Pithom and Rameses, and killed Israelite infants by throwing them into the Nile River. This Pharaoh's daughter found baby Moses floating among the reeds of the Nile and reared him as her foster son in the Egyptian palace located close to the land of Goshen. Chapters Thirteen to Fifteen identify in Egyptian documents the Pharaoh of the Oppression, who enslaved the Israelites.

When Moses was forty years old, he killed an Egyptian slave driver who was mistreating a Hebrew slave. The new Pharaoh who had recently come to power gave orders to kill Moses to avenge the death of the Egyptian slave driver. Moses fled for his life to the land of Midian. This Pharaoh followed the same pattern of his father in mistreating the Israelites. Moses remained in Midian for forty years. At the end of those forty years God appeared to Moses and told him that the Pharaoh who had tried to kill him had died.

When Moses returned to Egypt, he faced the son of the Pharaoh who had tried to kill him. This new Pharaoh began his sole reign (after a brief co-reign) a few years before Moses left Midian and returned to Egypt. Moses appeared before the new Pharaoh and warned him that God would send plague after plague against him until he consented to free the Israelites from bondage. Because of his hardness of heart, the Pharaoh of the Exodus provoked God to send the ten worst plagues that Egypt had ever suffered. This Pharaoh ultimately lost his firstborn son, his crops and cattle, his Israelite slaves, his entire army and his own life.

Chapter Eighteen reveals from Egyptian documents the true identity of the Pharaoh of the Exodus. Chapter Nineteen also analyzes Egyptian documents of the twelfth dynasty that record most of the ten plagues that destroyed Egypt. These same Egyptian records tell of the destruction of this Pharaoh and his entire army "by pouring water."

B. God's Fingerprints

God's fingerprints must be added to the footprints of men. Joseph deciphered Pharaoh's dream to signify seven years of abundance followed by seven years of famine (Genesis 41:37-41). Pharaoh was so impressed with Joseph's interpretation that he made him his vizier (prime minister). The ten plagues so impressed the officials of the Pharaoh of the Exodus that they cried out, "This is the finger of **God**" (Exodus 8:19). God used an east wind to open a path through the Red Sea and an earthquake to topple Jericho's walls. Modern insurance companies still call natural disasters "acts of God." God's fingerprints, plus the Egyptian and Israelite footprints, form a distinct, historical pattern of amazing natural events that has never been duplicated and that can logically and chronologically fit only one period of Egyptian and Canaanite histories.

Archaeologists use mostly pottery and other Egyptian artifacts to identify the historical ages of levels they excavate. This method works because each age has its own distinctive design of pottery and scarabs. However, the unique patterns of human lives form historical designs more complex and distinct than that of pottery or scarabs. Thus, I reasoned that the best way to discover Biblical history in Babylonian and Egyptian documents was to formulate and compare the unique patterns of the two histories until I found multiple matches. **This book reveals 430 points of amazing historical and scientific synchronism that confirm the Biblical record from Abraham to the Exodus.**

Additional chronological and historical points of synchronism continue to appear in abundance in Volume II of *Solving the Exodus Mystery*. I was unwilling to publish my discoveries until I could reconcile Egyptian and Biblical histories from the Exodus to Solomon and from Solomon to the Babylonian Exile of the

Jewish Kingdom from 609 to 539 B.C. The details of this historical research for the period from the Exodus to the Exile will be found in the second volume of this work. When I was finally able to reconcile the Egyptian histories of Dynasties 12 to 26 with Biblical history from Joseph to Jeremiah, **I knew that I had finally solved the "Exodus Mystery."**

VIII. EXPAND BIBLICAL DATES, OR REDUCE EGYPTIAN DATES?

The new Bible dates for Joseph to the Exodus are dated *c.* 300 years later than the latest Sothic dates of Egypt's twelfth dynasty. In contrast, the new astronomical dates of Babylon fit the new Bible dates for Abraham. This evidence suggests that Babylonian and Biblical dates are **correct** and Egypt's astronomical dates are **incorrect by *c.* three centuries.** Therefore, Egypt's dates should be reduced by *c.* 300 years to fit the Biblical dates, instead of vice-versa.

Chapters Twenty-One and Twenty-Two disprove the Sothic dates and the Sothic Calendar that Egyptologists use to calculate their astronomical dates for Egyptian history. Chapters Twenty-Three and Twenty-Four prove by carbon-14 dating and superior astronomical dating that dynasties twelve to nineteen should be redated three centuries later than their presently assigned dates. This three-century revision of Egyptian history creates additional points of synchronism that add up to **436 historical and scientific links with Bible history from Abraham to the Exodus.** All 436 evidences are listed in Chapter Twenty-Five, summing up the discoveries in Volume I. Chapter Twenty-Five also presents a preview of Volume II, which will demonstrate that several Egyptian dynasties reigned simultaneously from different Egyptian capitals, thus reducing Egypt's chronology by about three centuries. These rival dynasties eliminate the 300 years lost when dynasties twelve to twenty are dated 300 years later than their presently assigned dates.

CONCLUSION

My search for the solution of the Exodus Mystery took me down many blind alleys, from which I had to retreat. My faith was put to a severe test during these years of trial and error. My comparative chronological charts of Biblical, Babylonian and Egyptian histories enabled me to discover how I could piece together the historical puzzle from Abraham to the Exodus. This book lists **436** points of historical, archaeological and scientific evidences. These links are too abundant and significant to be coincidental. **True synchronism is the only reasonable conclusion.**

Now, dear reader, attach your seat belt and prepare for an exciting boat ride across the Euphrates River, where Abraham crossed to go to the land of Canaan. You will also walk through the dry and desolate desert where the remains of Sodom and Gomorrah still lie. Then, you will take another boat ride down the Nile River to the Delta of Egypt, where Joseph became prime minister of all of Egypt and where Jacob and his family lived for 210 years.

You will learn the identities of the true Pharaohs of Joseph and Moses. Finally you will learn the identity of the Pharaoh of the Exodus, who provoked God to send the ten plagues upon Egypt. You will see with your own eyes the words of a twelfth-dynasty document that describes eight of the ten plagues of the Bible and the drowning of Pharaoh and his army "by pouring water."

The clues only trickle in during the early chapters. However, the evidences will gush and fall in torrents before we end our historical journey in search of Abraham, Joseph, Moses and the Pharaoh of the Exodus. We will ultimately travel through 430 years of Babylonian, Elamite, Egyptian and Biblical histories. We will include an unprecedented space trip to sun, moon and stars, especially, Sirius, the Nile Star, all of which are used to calculate astronomically correct dates of both Babylon and Egypt.

On this historical and heavenly journey we will visualize a total of **436** discoveries that link the four histories, plus additional astronomical and other scientific evidences. Hopefully, you will find what I believe I have discovered: **a historical pot of gold at the end of the astronomical rainbow**. When the reader looks back at this long journey in Volume One , hopefully, he will exclaim, **"Truly, Bible history from Abraham to Joseph to Moses to the Exodus is vindicated and the God of Israel has been glorified!"**

NOTES OF CHAPTER THREE

1. Immanuel Velikovsky, *Ages in Chaos* (New York: Doubleday, 1952), 1-142.
2. Donovan A. Courville, *The Exodus Problem & Its Ramifications*, 2 volumes (Loma Linda, California: Challenge Books), 1971.
3. Charles Aling, *Egypt and Bible History* (Grand Rapids: Baker), 1981.
4. David Rohl, David. *Pharaohs and Kings*, New York: Crown Pub., 1995.
5. K. A. Kitchen, "Joseph," *International Standard Bible Encyclopedia*, Rev. Ed., 1982, Eerdmans Pub., (1986), II.1130.

CHAPTER FOUR
DISCOVERY OF FOUR HUNDRED THIRTY YEARS FROM ABRAHAM TO THE EXODUS

Chronology bores the average reader, but true history cannot be established without accurate dates. The chronology for Jacob, Joseph, and Israel's stay in Egypt cannot be determined without **an accurate date** for God's promise to Abraham when he left Ur and headed toward Canaan land. If the date for Abraham's departure from Ur is **incorrect, we cannot know** when Joseph, Jacob and his sons were born, nor when they entered Egypt. If we do not have an accurate date for Jacob's entrance into Egypt, then we will not be able to discover the Pharaohs of Joseph, Moses and the Exodus.

Unfortunately, the NIV version of Exodus 12:40 has been incorrectly translated from the Hebrew when it says that Israel lived in Egypt for 430 years. When Exodus 12:40 is correctly translated from the Hebrew, **the 430 years will begin with Abraham's departure from Ur,** rather than Jacob's entrance into Egypt. By starting the 430 years with Abraham's departure from Ur, we will see **that Israel sojourned in Egypt for only 210 years.**

Sixteen chronological discoveries are noted in Table 4-G that confirm the 430-year period from God's Promise to Abraham to Israel's Exodus from Egypt. This 430-year chronology produces in Chapter Five **twenty-eight additional discoveries of historical synchronism between Abraham's Biblical history and scholars' recently revised astronomical dates of the kings of Babylon and Elam.**

Chapters Four and Five are more difficult to understand than the other chapters of this book. However, most of the remaining chapters of this book will be easy to understand, illuminating the mind and inspiring the soul.

I. ESTABLISHING THE DATE OF THE EXODUS

To establish the chronology for Abraham we must first establish the date of the Exodus. I Kings 6:1 enables us to establish this date.

> In the **four hundred and eightieth year after the Israelites had come out of Egypt, in the fourth year of Solomon's reign** over Israel, in the month of Ziv, the second month, he began to build the temple . . . .

The reader can see that I Kings 6:1 counts 480 years **between the Exodus and Solomon's fourth year**. The spring of **966 B.C.** is established as Solomon's fourth year. This date of 966 B.C. is determined by ten astronomically calculated dates that connect the reigns of Biblical kings to eight different Assyrian and Babylonian kings. These ten links were found by Edwin Thiele in the ancient records of

Assyria and Babylon.[1] These astronomical dates are calculated by links to nine eclipses of the sun that are recorded in Assyrian, Babylonian and Persian histories.[2]

The *Cambridge Ancient History* has accepted Edwin Thiele's chronology of Israel as "absolute" from **853 B.C. (the year King Ahab died) to 597 B.C.**, when Jerusalem fell to Nebuchadnezzar, the king of Babylon.[3] Thiele dated backward from Ahab's death to fix the accession year of Solomon to the fall of 971 B.C. and his first full year to 970 B.C. I Kings 6:1 dates the Exodus 480 years before Solomon's fourth full year in the spring of **966 B.C.** Adding the 480 years to 966 B.C., the Exodus should have occurred in the **spring of 1446 B.C.**

Tables 4-A and 4-B, below and on the next page, list the details and references of proof for the dates of these eclipses of the sun that give Biblical kings absolute dates.

TABLE 4-A
NINE ECLIPSES OF THE SUN THAT ENABLED SCHOLARS TO FIX ASTRONOMICALLY FIXED YEARS IN THE REIGNS OF ASSYRIAN, BABYLONIAN AND PERSIAN KINGS
Source: Edwin R. Thiele, *The Mysterious Numbers of the Hebrew Kings,*
Zondervan Pub., 1983, p. 229

B.C. DATE		YEAR OF KING	YEAR OF NABONASSAR ERA (Babylonian King)
June 14,	763	10th yr. of Ashurdan III (Assyria)	
March 19,	721	1st yr. of Mardokempados (Babylon)	27
March 8,	720	2nd yr. of Mardokempados (Babylon)	28
Sep't. 1,	720	2nd yr. of Mardokempados (Babylon)	28
April 22,	621	5th yr. of Nabopolassar (Babylon)	127
July 4,	568	37th yr. of Nebuchadnezzar (Babylon)	180
July 16,	523	7th yr. of Cambyses (Persia)	225
Nov. 19,	502	20th yr. of Darius (Persia)	246
April 25	491	31st yr. of Darius (Persia)	257

TABLE 4-B
LINKS BETWEEN ASSYRIAN AND BABYLONIAN KINGS AND THE BIBLICAL KINGS OF JUDAH AND ISRAEL
Source: T. C. Mitchell, "Israel and Judah Until the Revolt of Jehu,"
Cambridge Ancient History, 2nd Ed., III.1.445

KINGS OF JUDAH JUDAH AND N. ISRAEL	ASTRONOMICALLY FIXED B.C. YEAR	ENCOUNTERED AND RECORDED KINGS OF ASSYRIA & BABYLON
Ahab of N. Israel	853	Shalmaneser III of Assyria
Jehu of N. Israel	841	Shalmaneser III of Assyria
Joash of Judah	802	Adad-Nirari III of Assyria
Menahem of N. Israel	743	Tiglath-pileser III of Assyria
Ahaz of Judah	732	Tiglath-pileser III of Assyria
Hoshea: Fall of Samaria	722	Sargon of Assyria
Hezekiah of Judah	701	Sennacherib of Assyria
Manasseh of Judah	c. 670	Sennacherib of Assyria
Manasseh of Judah	c. 666	Ashurbanipal of Assyria
Fall of Jerusalem	597	Nebuchadnezzar of Babylon

II. TWO DIFFERENT INTERPRETATIONS
OF EXODUS 12:40

A. The NIV Interpretation Of The 430
Years of Exodus 12:40

The NIV translation of Exodus 12:40 claims that Israel lived in Egypt for 430 years: **"Now the length of time the Israelite people lived in Egypt was 430 years."** If this translation were true, Jacob would have entered Egypt 430 years before the 1446 B.C. date for the Exodus, or **1876 B.C.** (1446 + 430 = 1876). The chronology of the *NIV Study Bible* thus dates Abraham's entrance into Canaan in **2091 B.C.** Chapter Two names the kings of Elam and Babylon that Abraham defeated in Genesis 14, but they contradict the names of the kings of Elam and Babylon who ruled from 2091 B.C. to 2000 B.C. (*Cambridge* dates) We will prove below that the NIV dates and the Cambridge dates are **both incorrect.**

B. Paul's Interpretation of the 430
Years of Exodus 12:40

In Galatians 3:16-17 the apostle Paul gives a different interpretation of the 430 years of Exodus 12:40.

> The promises were spoken to **Abraham** and to his seed. . . . The law, **introduced 430 years later**, does not set aside the covenant previously established by God and thus do away with the promise. NIV

Paul began the 430 years of Exodus 12:40 **with God's promise to Abraham, not Jacob's entrance into Egypt.** Therefore, the NIV translation of the 430 years in Galatians 3:16-17 contradicts the NIV translation of Exodus 12:40.

C. Josephus' Interpretation of the 430 Years of Exodus 12:40

Paul is not the only one to begin the 430 years of Exodus 12:40 with God's promise to Abraham. Josephus, the Jewish historian of the first century A.D., first reported that Israel lived in Egypt 400 years.[4] Later in his book, Josephus changed his mind and shortened Israel's stay in Egypt to **215 years** and **extended the 430 years of Exodus 12:40 back to Abraham's entrance into Canaan.**

> **They left Egypt in the month Xanthicus, on the fifteenth day of the lunar month; four hundred and thirty years after our forefather Abraham came into Canaan, but two hundred and fifteen years only after Jacob removed into Egypt.**[5]

D. The Septuagint's Interpretation of the 430 Years
of Exodus 12:40 Also Agrees with the
chronology of Paul and Josephus.

Even more significant is the translation of Exodus 12:40 in the Septuagint.

The word, "Septuagint," means "seventy," referring to seventy Jewish scholars that translated the Hebrew Bible into Greek under the orders of Ptolemy II, king of Egypt from 285 to 246 B.C.[6] The Septuagint translation of Exodus 12:40 also extends the 430 years back from the Exodus to God's promise to Abraham: "The sojourning of the sons of Israel, . . . in the land of Egypt **and in the land of Canaan**, was **four hundred and thirty years."[7]**

Therefore, the apostle Paul, Josephus and the seventy Jewish scholars who translated the Septuagint from Hebrew to Greek all agree that the 430 years did not begin when Israel entered Egypt, but began with God's promise and command to Abraham to leave Ur and go to Canaan.

III. THE NIV MISTRANSLATION
OF EXODUS 12:40

Exodus 12:40 (NIV) dates the beginning of the 430 years to Jacob's entrance into Egypt, whereas the NIV translation of Galatians 3:16-17 dates the beginning of the 430 years with God's promise to Abraham in Ur. Thus, the NIV translation of Exodus 12:40 contradicts the NIV translation of Galatians 3:16-17. One of these translations must be incorrect. The Greek in Galatians 3:16-17 is accurately translated. However, the Hebrew in Exodus 12:40 is **not** accurately translated.

The Hebrew word for "length of time" in the NIV translation of Exodus 12:40 is *moshab*. *Moshab* means "dwelling," and is linked linguistically to *toshab*, "a sojourner." *Moshab* can mean "length of time," but is more frequently used to indicate the length of time that foreigners sojourned in a strange land.[8] The next page records six different versions of Exodus 12:40. Three of these versions use the idea of "sojourning" when translating *moshab*. The NIV fails to include in its translation the idea of "sojourning" in a foreign land.

The NIV rendition of Exodus 12:40 also fails to translate the Hebrew *asher*, which means "who" or "which."[9] Four of six translations on page 31 translate *asher* as "who," or "which." A fifth version, the NAS, translates *asher* as "who" in a footnote. The KJV and NKJV properly translate both *moshab* and *asher:* "The **sojourning** of the children of Israel, **who** dwelt in **Egypt,** was **four hundred and thirty years."**

"Who" links Israel's past habitation to Egypt, but does not limit Israel's total sojourning to Egypt. The Bible (Genesis 17:8; 21:23; 23:4; 28:4; 47:9; Heb. 11:9). also calls Abraham, Isaac and Jacob "foreigners and sojourners" while living in Canaan. Thus, Paul's interpretation of the Hebrew text of Exodus 12:40 can mean the following: "Israel, who lived in Egypt, sojourned as aliens for 430 years" (from the time Abraham left Ur until Israel left Egypt).

Thus, the KJV, the NKJV, the footnote in the NASV, the Septuagint, Josephus, and Paul interpret the 430 years of Exodus 12:40 **to begin with Abraham's departure from Ur in 1876 B.C. and end with the Exodus in 1446 B.C.** (1446 + 430 = 1876). Below are six different translations of Exodus 12:40.

TABLE 4-C
SIX DIFFERING TRANSLATIONS OF EXODUS 12:40

1. **King James Version**: "Now the sojourning of the children of Israel, who dwelt in Egypt, was four hundred and thirty years."
2. **Septuagint (Greek Translation)**: "And the sojourning of the sons of Israel, while they sojourned in the land of Egypt and in the land of Canaan, was four hundred and thirty years." Sir Lancelot Brenton, *The Septuagint Version: Greek and English*, Zondervan, p. 86.
3. **New King James Version:** "Now the sojourn of the children of Israel who lived in Egypt was four hundred and thirty years."
4. **New American Standard Version**: "Now the time that the sons of Israel lived in Egypt was four hundred and thirty years." Footnote in NASV reads: "Or, 'of the sons of Israel who dwelt in Egypt.'"
5. **New International Version:** "Now the length of time the Israelite people lived in Egypt was 430 years."
6. **New American Bible (St. Joseph's Ed.)** "The time the Israelites had stayed in Egypt was 430 years."

IV. A NEW INTERPRETATION OF THE
400 YEARS OF GENESIS 15:13

Many Bible scholars believe that Genesis 15:13 predicted that Israel would live in Egypt 400 years, which they interpret to be the rounded off number of the 430 years of Exodus 12:40.[10] Paul interpreted Exodus 12:40 to begin the 430 years with **God's promise to Abraham (Galatians 3:16-17).** The 400 years of Genesis 15:13 began with Abraham's **first descendant of the Promise, Isaac.**

Know for certain that your **descendants** will be strangers in a country not their own, and they will be enslaved and mistreated **four hundred years.** (NIV)

Genesis 12:4 says Abraham was seventy-five when he entered Canaan. Genesis 21:5 says he was 100 when Isaac was born, a difference of twenty-five years. Five more years are needed to fill the thirty-year gap between 430 years and 400 years. **Can we find these five extra years?**

Genesis 15:7 says God's original promise was made to Abraham when he lived in Ur. Genesis 11:31 says Abraham left Ur with his father Terah to go to Canaan, but stopped in Haran on the way and **"settled there." "Settling" indicates years, not days.**

In Acts 7:2-4 Stephen says that Abraham remained in Haran and did not enter Canaan **until his father Terah died.** Thus, Abraham was **seventy** when he left Ur with Terah in **1876 B.C.** Terah was likely too sick to travel, forcing Abraham to stop in Haran **for five years** until Terah died. Abraham was **seventy when he left Ur in 1876 B.C. and was obviously seventy-five when he left Haran (Genesis 12:4), entering Canaan in 1871 B.C. Abraham was 100 when Isaac was born in 1846 B.C.[11] The 400 years of Genesis 15:13** began in Canaan with **Abraham's** first descendant of the promise, Isaac, born in 1846 B.C. The 400 years ended in 1446 B.C. when Israel left Egypt. See **Table 4-D**.

TABLE 4-D
430 YEARS OF EXODUS 12:40 AND THE 400 YEARS OF GENESIS 15:13

ABRAHAM'S BIRTH .... 1946 B.C.
        70 Years Before the Promise   - 70 yrs.
GOD'S PROMISE TO ABRAHAM IN UR .... 1876 B.C.
    Beginning of 430 Years when Abraham was 70 years old
    Ex. 12:40, 430 Years Before the Exodus (Galatians 3:17)
Abraham's father, Terah became sick and they stopped in Haran
    for five years until he died (Acts 7:2-7).   - 5 yrs.
ABRAHAM ENTERED CANAAN   1871 B.C.
    Abraham was 75 when he entered Canaan (Genesis 12:4).
    Abraham was 100 when Isaac was born (Genesis 21:5).   - 25 yrs.
ISAAC'S BIRTH .... 1846 B.C.
    Beginning of 400 Years: 1846 -400 = 1446 B.C. Exodus
    Thirty years after the Promise in Genesis 15:13 - 430 -30 = 400
    Isaac was 60 years old when Jacob was born (Genesis 25:26).   -60 yrs.
JACOB'S BIRTH .... 1786 B.C.
    Jacob was 130 years old when he entered Egypt (Genesis 47:9) -130 yrs.
JACOB AND ISRAELITES ENTERED EGYPT .... 1656 B.C.
    Israelites remain 210 Years in Egypt after Jacob entered Egypt.-210 yrs.
DATE OF THE EXODUS .... 1446 B.C.
    Moses was eighty years old at the Exodus (Exodus 7:7).......... +80 yrs.
MOSES' BIRTH .... 1526 B.C.
    Moses was born 80 years before the Exodus   -80 yrs.
THE EXODUS .... 1446 B.C.
    480 Yrs before Solomon's 4th Yr. 1 Kings 6:1   -480 yrs.
SOLOMON'S 4TH YR. .... 966 B.C.

V. TWO HUNDRED TEN YEARS OF ISRAEL'S SOJOURN IN EGYPT INSTEAD OF 430 YEARS

This chronology of 430 years begins with Abraham's Promise in 1876 B.C. and ends with Israel's Exodus from Egypt in 1446 B.C., reducing Israel's presence in Egypt **to only 210 years.** Isaac was born in **1846 B.C.**; he gave birth to Jacob, when he was sixty years old: Genesis 25:26 (1846 B.C. - 60 years = **1786 B.C.**). Jacob was 130 when he entered Egypt: Genesis 47:9 (1786 -130 = **1656 B.C.**). Israel departed from Egypt 480 years before Solomon's fourth year: 1 Kings 6:1 (966 + 480 = **1446 B.C.**). See this entire chronology in Table 4-D above.

Therefore, this new Bible chronology, based on Paul's interpretation in Galatians 3:16-17 and Stephen's interpretation in Acts 7:2-7, has Israel in Egypt from **1656 to 1446 B.C.**, a period of **only 210 years, not the 430 years of the NIV translation of Exodus 12:40**.

VI. JOSEPH'S ARRIVAL IN EGYPT IN 1678 B.C.
TWENTY-TWO YEARS BEFORE JACOB
ENTERED EGYPT IN 1656 B.C.

Joseph entered Egypt at age seventeen as a slave in 1678 B.C. Twenty-two years later Jacob and his family entered Egypt in 1656 B.C. as guests of Joseph and Pharaoh Sesostris I.   Jacob and his family stayed in Egypt for **210 years, leaving Egypt in 1446 B.C.** Thus, Joseph's **twenty-two years** in Egypt must be added to the **210 years** that Jacob and his family lived in Egypt for a total of **232 years** that Joseph and his brothers and their ancestors lived in Egypt.

Genesis 45:6 reports that Jacob entered Egypt with his **family at the end of the second year of famine.** Therefore, the seven years of abundance, plus the second year of famine give us nine years that preceded Israel's entrance into Egypt in 1656 B.C. Adding these nine years to Israel's arrival in Egypt in 1656 B.C. gives us **1665 B.C.** as Joseph's first year as Vizier of Egypt: 1656 + 9 = 1665.

Genesis 41:46 says that Joseph **was thirty years old** when he became Vizier and that he immediately began to collect grain during the first year of abundance (1665 B.C.). Genesis 37:2,36 says that Joseph was only **seventeen years old** when his brothers sold him as a slave to Midianites, who carried Joseph to Egypt and sold him to Potiphar, the captain of Pharaoh's body guard. Thus Joseph lived in Egypt thirteen years (30 -17 = 13) before his appointment as Vizier of the ruling Pharaoh. Therefore, we must add these thirteen additional years to 1665 B.C. when Joseph became Vizier: **1665 plus 13 years gives us 1678 B.C.** as the date Joseph first entered Egypt. Therefore, Joseph and Israel together lived in Egypt for a total of **232 years** (1678 - 1446 = 232). See this chronology in Table 4-E below.

TABLE 4-E
THE CHRONOLOGIES OF JOSEPH AND JACOB
TOTAL OF 232 YEARS IN EGYPT.

JACOB (ISRAEL) ENTERED EGYPT	1656 B.C.
Jacob entered Egypt at the end of the second year of famine (Gen. 45:6)	
Thus, the first year of abundance began 9 years earlier when Joseph	
was appointed vizier of Egypt at age 30 (Gen. 41:46)	+9 yrs.
JOSEPH WAS APPOINTED PRIME MINISTER OF EGYPT AT AGE 30	1665 B.C.
Joseph was 17 when enslaved and carried to Egypt, Gen. 37:2	+13 yrs.
JOSEPH ENTERED EGYPT AS A SLAVE AT AGE 17	1678 B.C.
TOTAL YEARS OF JOSEPH IN EGYPT BEFORE JACOB ENTERED EGYPT:	22 YEARS
TOTAL YEARS THAT ISRAEL LIVED IN EGYPT	210 YEARS
TOTAL YEARS THAT JOSEPH & ISRAEL LIVED IN EGYPT	232 YEARS
1678 (Joseph) to 1446 B.C. (Exodus) = 232 YEARS (1678- 1446 = 232)	

VII. 600,000 ISRAELITES IN ONLY 210 YEARS?

Exodus 12:37 says that "about **600,000 [Israelite] men on foot, besides women and children." left Egypt.** These 600,000 Israelites were all twenty years of age or older according to Numbers 1:3ff.

Almost all scholars voice objections against this 600,000 number. Keil & Delitzsch argued that 600,000 male Israelites above 20 years of age could be produced in 430 years, but **not in "215 years."**[12] P. Kyle McCarter, Jr. denies that Israel could have grown to 600,000 men in only 430 years, much less 210 years.[13]

The Bible lists sixty-eight sons and grandsons of Jacob that were alive when Israel entered Egypt.[14] Since the 600,000 Israelites were twenty years or older at the Exodus, we must subtract these twenty years from the date of the Exodus, to calculate their rate of birth. Based on **210 years** (not 215 years) in Egypt, these sixty-eight Israelite males had to grow to 600,000 in **only 190 years (210 - 20 = 190) for all of them had to be at least twenty-years old at the Exodus.**

Moses reported Israel's remarkable population explosion before their enslavement: "But **the sons of Israel were fruitful and multiplied greatly and became exceedingly numerous, so that the land was filled with them."**[15] The Bible also reports that Israel continued to multiply after they were enslaved and even after their infants were thrown into the Nile: "So God was kind to the midwives and **the people increased and became even more numerous.**"[16] Israel experienced extraordinary growth because they were blessed by an extraordinary God. Is it impossible for Israel to have grown from sixty-eight males to 600,000 males in only 190 years?

Jody Jones, of Toluca, Mexico, my former student, calculated the growth rate on his computer at **4.9%** from sixty-eight to 600,000 in 190 years. My son-in-law, Jeff Muehring, has earned his doctorate in computer science. He wrote for me a software program that calculates growth rates. Jeff's software shows that sixty-eight males growing to 600,000 males in **190 years is a growth rate of 4.897%,** rounded off to Jody's 4.9%. While Israel's growth rate of 4.9% is higher than most countries, it is exceeded by the growth of two modern countries: **Namibia (5.3%) and Malawi (6.0%).**[17] Since these modern countries grow faster than the Israelites were growing, how can modern scholars claim that 4.9% growth is impossible for the Israelites? The truth is, Bible scholars have assumed that the growth rate is impossible and have not taken the time to calculate the growth rate and compare it with other nations. Notice the growth rates of others nations compared to Israel's growth in Table 4-F below. These rates are based on a 1990 census.

TABLE 4-F
COMPARISON OF ISRAEL'S GROWTH FROM
68 MALES TO 600,000 MALES IN 190 Years
Source: PC Globe 1990,
Calculated by Jody Jones

ANCIENT ISRAEL	=	4.9%
UNITED STATES	=	0.9%
SAUDI ARABIA	=	4.0%
KENYA	=	4.2%
NAMIBIA	=	5.3%
MALAWI	=	6.0%

CONCLUSION

The NIV Bible chronology that dates Israel in Egypt for 430 years is one of the principal reasons that scholars have been unable to find Abraham, Jacob, Joseph and Moses in the historical records of Babylon, Elam, Mari and Egypt. Paul's chronology in Galatians 3:16-17 dates the 430 years from God's Promise to Abraham in 1876 B.C. until Israel's Exodus in 1446 B.C.

Joseph arrived as a slave in Egypt at age seventeen in 1678 B.C., twenty-two years before Jacob and his family arrived in Egypt in 1656 B.C. Joseph became Vizier of Egypt at age thirty in 1665 B.C., nine years before Jacob arrived in Egypt in 1656 B.C. Moses led Israel out of Egypt 210 years later in 1446 B.C. Thus Israel lived in Egypt for 210 years (1656 B.C. to 1446 B.C.). Since Joseph went to Egypt in 1678 B.C. and Israel left Egypt in 1446 B.C., Joseph and Israel together remained in Egypt for a total of 232 years.

Israel grew from sixty-eight to 600,000 males twenty years or older in only 210 years. **Table 4-F proves that the growth rate was 4.9%, less than the growth rate of Namibia and Malawi eight or ten years ago.** Based on **210 years** (not 215 years) in Egypt, these sixty-eight Israelite males had to grow to 600,000 in **only 190 years (210 - 20 = 190) for all of them had to be at least twenty-years old at the Exodus.** This Biblical chronology from Abraham to the Exodus permitted me to find **436 synchronisms** between Bible history and the histories of Elam, Babylon, Mari and Egypt. **Without this chronology I could never have solved the Exodus Mystery.**

Chapter Four contains fifteen chronological discoveries that confirm 430 years from Abraham to the Exodus. See these discoveries in Table 4-G below.

TABLE 4-G
SIXTEEN CHRONOLOGICAL DISCOVERIES
THAT CONFIRM THE BIBLICAL DATES
FROM ABRAHAM TO THE EXODUS

Discovery 1. *The Cambridge Ancient History* accepts the chronology of Edwin Thiele that dates Solomon's fourth year at **966 B.C.**

Discovery 2. 1 Kings 6:1 dates the Exodus 480 years before Solomon's fourth year: 480 + 966 = **1446 B.C.**

Discovery 3. Exodus 12:40 says that the Israelites sojourned for 430 years. Since the Israelites sojourned in Canaan as well as Egypt, then the 430 years should logically begin before Israel went to Egypt.

Discovery 4. Paul in Galatians 3:16-17 and Josephus in his *Antiquities of the Jews,* II.XV.2 begin the **430 years of Exodus 12:40** with God's promise to Abraham when He commanded him to leave Ur.

Discovery 5. Adding the 430 years to 1446 B.C., the established date of the Exodus, we see that Abraham left Ur in **1876 B.C.** when he was **seventy-years old.** Genesis 11:31-12:5 reports that Abraham stopped and settled in Haran for **five**

years because of his sick father, Terah. (See Stephen's sermon in Acts 7:2-4)

Discovery 6. When Terah died, Abraham entered Canaan in **1871 B.C.** at **age seventy-five (Gen. 12:4).**

Discovery 7. Genesis 15:13 records that Abraham's descendants would wander as strangers for 400 years. **Isaac was Abraham's first descendant of the promise.** Abraham was 100 years old when Isaac was born (Gen. 21:5). Thus, Isaac was born thirty years after Abraham left Ur at age seventy when he left Ur in 1876 B.C. Subtracting thirty years from 1876 B.C., we **get 1846 B.C. as the birth year of Isaac, Abraham's first descendant,** which began the 400 years of Genesis 15:13, the years of sojourning for all of Abraham's promised descendants.

Discovery 8. Starting with Isaac's birth in 1846 B.C., we see that Jacob was born when Isaac was sixty years old (Gen. 25:26) in **1786 B.C.** (1846 -60 = 1786).

Discovery 9. Jacob was 130 years old when he entered Egypt at the end of the second year of famine in **1656 B.C.** (1786 B.C. - 130 = 1656 B.C.).

Discovery 10. Since 1 Kings 6:1 dates the Exodus in **1446 B.C.**, we subtract 1446 B.C. from Israel's arrival in **1656 B.C.**, and get **210 years that the Israelites sojourned in Egypt.**

Discovery 11. Subtracting the 210 years of Israel's stay in Egypt from the 430 years of Exodus 1:40, we see that Abraham and his descendants sojourned **220 years** from the time he left Ur in 1876 B.C. until Jacob (Israel) entered Egypt **in 1656 B.C.**

Discovery 12. Joseph was **thirty years old** when he was appointed Vizier of Sesostris I (Genesis 41:46).

Discovery 13. Joseph was **thirty-nine years old** when Jacob arrived in Egypt in **1656 B.C.** after seven years of abundance and two years of famine, a total of nine years (Genesis 45:2).

Discovery 14. Therefore, Joseph was appointed Vizier of Egypt when he was **thirty years old, nine years before Jacob arrived in 1656 B.C.**, dating Joseph's appointment as Vizier in **1665 B.C.** (1656 + 9 = 1665).

Discovery 15. Joseph was seventeen years old when he arrived in Egypt as a slave (Genesis 37:2), thirteen years he became Vizier of Egypt. Adding these thirteen years to Joseph's appointment as Vizier of Egypt in 1665 B.C., we get **1678 B.C. as the year Joseph entered Egypt as a slave.**

Discovery 16. Based on Israel's **210 years** in Egypt, sixty-eight Israelite males had to grow to 600,000 in **only 190 years (210 - 20 = 190) for all of them had to be at least twenty-years old at the Exodus. The growth percent for ancient Israel was only 4.9% whereas modern Nambia (5.3%) and Malawi (6%) exceed the growth rate for Israel.**

TABLE 4-H
RUNNING TOTAL OF DISCOVERIES

Chapter	Chapter Total	Running Total
2 Conflict Between Biblical and Secular Histories	18	18
4 Discovery of 430 Years from Abraham to the Exodus	16	34

NOTES FOR CHAPTER FOUR

1. Edwin Thiele, *Mysterious Numbers of the Hebrew Kings*, Zondervan, 1983, 67-103.
2. Thiele, *Mysterious Numbers of the Hebrew Kings* 229.
3. T. C. Mitchell, "Israel and Judah until the Revolt of Jehu (931-841 B.C.),"
   Cambridge Ancient History, (Cambridge Univ. Press, 1982), III, Part I.445-6.
4. Flavius Josephus, "Antiquities of the Jews," II.IX.1, *The Complete Works of Josephus*,
   (Grand Rapids: Kregel Pub. 1981), 55.
5. Josephus, II.XV.2, 62.
6. "Septuagint," *New Encyclopaedia Britannica*, 1991 Ed., 10.643.
7. Sir Lancelot Brenton, *The Septuagint Version: Greek and English*, Zondervan, 86.
8. Francis Brown, *The New Brown, Driver, Briggs, Gesenius Hebrew and English Lexicon*
   (Lafayette, Ind.: Associate Pub., 1980), 444.
9. Francis Brown, *The New Brown, Driver, Briggs Hebrew-English Lexicon*, Lafayette, Ind.,
   Associated Pub., (1980), 81-82.
10. Walter C. Kaiser, "Exodus," *The Expositor's Bible Commentary*, Zondervan, 1990, II.380.
11. Genesis 12:4; 21:5.
12. Keil, Delitzsch, *Commentaries on the Old Testament*, Eerdmans, II.28-3.
13. P. Kyle McCarter, Jr., "Exodus," *Harper's Bible Commentary*, Ed. James Luther Mays, 143.
14. Genesis 46:8-27.
15. Exodus 1:6.
16. Exodus 1:20.
17. *PC Globe*, (1990) computer soft ware.

CHAPTER FIVE
CONFIRMATION OF ABRAHAM'S HISTORICITY

In Chapter Four we established the Biblical chronology for Abraham's birth in **1946 B.C.,** his departure from Ur in **1876 B.C. at age seventy, his stay in Haran for five years until his father died, and his arrival in Canaan five years later at age seventy-five in 1871 B.C.**

Most archaeologists, historians and many religious scholars deny the historicity of Abraham and reject the Biblical dates that I have assigned to Abraham. The cover of the March, 2002 issue of *Harper Magazine* proclaimed that the Old Testament is **"A False Testament"** and affirmed in the subheading, **"Archaeology Refutes the Bible's Claim to History."** The author, Daniel Lazare, claims that Abraham, the Exodus, the Conquest of Canaan and even David and Solomon **are all "fictional" characters.**

This complex chapter is crucial to confirm the Biblical dates and historicity of Abraham and the kings he confronted in Genesis 14. This chapter also lays the chronological and historical foundation for the **discovery of the true Pharaohs of Joseph, Israel, Moses and the Exodus.**

I. ABRAHAM'S ENCOUNTER WITH THE KINGS OF THE EAST AND THE KINGS OF SOUTHERN CANAAN

While Abraham was living in Hebron in southern Canaan, his nephew, Lot, decided to separate from Abraham and move his family and flocks to a new location in the southern plain of the Jordan near the cities of Sodom and Gomorrah.

Genesis 13:10 describes the plain of the Jordan around Sodom and Gomorrah **"as the garden of the Lord."** This beautiful garden existed before the cities were destroyed by burning sulphur and before the plain became the Dead Sea.

Genesis 14 reports that the wealth of the land enticed **Kedor-Laomer, king of Elam,** to conquer these cities and place them under tribute **for twelve years**. In **the thirteenth year**, the cities rebelled. **In the fourteenth year** Kedor-Laomer led a coalition of three other kings that defeated the armies and kings of five cities in southern Canaan, including Sodom and Gomorrah. The four kings of the East carried off much booty and captives, including Abraham's nephew, Lot. Abraham gathered 318 troops from his own servants, plus troops from three Amorite allies. Leading the attack, Abraham surprised the four kings of the East and their troops at night. After routing them, Abraham recovered their captives and plunder, including Lot and his family.

About one year after Abraham's defeat of these kings Genesis 16:3 reports that Abraham had lived in Canaan **for ten years (from 1871 to 1861B.C.)** Therefore, Abraham encountered these kings one year earlier in **1862 B.C.** Genesis 14 thus dates Kedor-Laomer's **initial** conquest of Sodom and Gomorrah **fourteen**

years earlier in the Biblical date of 1876 B.C.

Genesis 14 names **Kedor-Laomer, king of Elam, as the leader of three subordinate kings** when they attacked Sodom and Gomorrah and the other cities of southern Canaan in **1862 B.C.** These three subordinate kings are listed by name in Genesis 14: **(1) Amraphel, king of Shinar, (2) Arioch, king of Ellasar and (3) Tidal, king of Goiim.**

Can extra-biblical sources verify these four kings of the East in the Bible date **of 1862 B.C.?** This chapter presents **twenty-eight synchronisms that link Abraham to these four named kings from Elam, Babylon, Mari and Ellasar in the astronomically fixed year of 1862 B.C.**

II. THE REVISION OF BABYLON'S ASTRONOMICAL DATES

The **1972 Edition** of the *Cambridge Ancient History* lists the names of the kings of Babylon and Elam, who were reigning **in the Biblical date of 1862 B.C.** when Elam and Babylon attacked Sodom and Gomorrah. **However, none of the names of these four Bible kings in Genesis 14 are listed in the 1972 Edition of the *Cambridge Ancient History* in 1862 B.C.**[1] I was deeply disappointed that I had failed to confirm the historicity of Abraham. However, several years later I found the solution to this problem. See this solution below.

In **1982 A.D. Peter Huber of Harvard University** and his colleagues restudied the **Ammisaduqa Venus Tablets of Babylon** and compared the astronomical data with **33,000 lunar dates and various solar eclipses recorded in Babylonian history.** Huber concluded that the odds **were fifteen to one that King Hammurabi of Babylon, should be redated fifty-six years earlier than the previous astronomical dates of the 1972 Edition of the *Cambridge Ancient History*.**[2] Adding the fifty-six years to Hammurabi's previous accession year of 1792 B.C., **Dr Huber revised Hammurabi's accession year to 1848 B.C.**[3]

The 1991 Edition of the *Cambridge Ancient History* confirmed the new astronomical dates of Dr. Peter Huber, redating the accession year of Hammurabi, **from the previous date of 1792 B.C. to the corrected date of 1848 B.C.** Huber's new dates for Babylon automatically modified also the ancient histories of Elam and Mari **by fifty-six years earlier.**

Huber's new astronomical dates for Hammurabi's reign are **1848 to 1806 B.C.** Therefore, Hammurabi was a contemporary of Abraham in the new Bible dates for Abraham's life in Canaan from **1871 to 1771 B.C.** (from Abraham's 75th year to his 175th year, Gen. 12:4; 25:7). See Chapter Four, Table 4-C for the detailed Biblical dates.

.   **Dr. Huber's fifty-six-year revision of Babylonian history creates twenty-eight historical synchronisms with my new Bible chronology for Abraham.** Three of the four kings of the East mentioned in Genesis 14 are found in the historical records of (1) Elam, (2) Babylon and (3) Mari/Ellasar. **These three kings are dated astronomically to the same B.C. year of 1862, the year**

Abraham confronted these kings. The fourth king, also fits remarkably well in the historical culture of Abraham's time. **These twenty-eight synchronisms confirm the historicity of Genesis 14 and are discussed in this chapter.**

III. THE THREE RULERS OF ELAM FROM 1875 TO 1862 B.C. WHEN KEDOR-LAOMER INVADED CANAAN

Walther Hinz wrote the *Cambridge Ancient History* of Elam before Peter Huber revised the astronomical dates of the reign of Hammurabi, king of Babylon. Consequently, **Hinz's Cambridge dates are fifty-six years later than Dr. Huber's dates.** Huber's new astronomical dates are fifty-six years earlier than Hinz's date, fitting perfectly with the Biblical dates for Abraham.

Huber's new astronomically fixed dates of Hammurabi are the standard by which the kings of Babylon, Elam and Mari are all to be redated. Therefore, I use the **correct historical facts of Dr. Hinz in the *Cambridge Ancient History* and I apply Huber's new fifty-six year revision of the new astronomical dates for the reign of Hammurabi.**

Hinz identified Shilkhakha as the Grand Regent of Elam in Huber's revised dates of **1886 to 1856 B.C.** Thus, Shilkhakha's reign included the **Biblical years of 1875 to 1862 B.C.** when Kedor-Laomer, king of Elam, invaded Sodom and Gomorrah and kept them under subjection for thirteen years (Genesis 14). Abraham entered Canaan in **1871 B.C.** and was thus present during most of the period that Kedor-Laomer held southern Canaan (Sodom and Gomorrah) under bondage.

Obviously, Shilkhakha's name does **not** fit the Biblical name of Kedor-Laomer. **However, Hinz explained that Elam was governed by a triumvirate (three kings)**, rather than a single king: (1) Shilkhakha, the Grand Regent was supreme over the capital and the entire country of Elam. (2) The Viceroy was the brother next in age to the Grand Regent, and heir to his throne. (3) The Regent of the provinces (outside the capital) was the responsibility of the eldest son of the Grand Regent. [4] **Thus Elam had three rulers, not one ruler.**

Hinz did not identify the name of the Regent of the Provinces, who should have been the eldest son of Shilkhakha.[5] Below we will show proof that Kudur-Mabuk was the eldest son and the Regent of the Provinces and that he is to be identified as Kedor-Laomer of Genesis 14, the third highest ruler of Elam.

IV. WAS KEDOR-LAOMER (KUDUR-MABUK) THE ELDEST SON AND REGENT OF SHILKHAKHA?

C. J. Gadd wrote the *Cambridge Ancient History* of Babylon. He reports that Kudur-Mabuk conquered Larsa, a principal city of Sumeria, and appointed two of his sons in succession as kings of Larsa, in Peter Huber's new dates of **1890 to 1819 B.C.**[6] Huber's dates for Kudur-Mabuk include the Biblical year of **1875 B.C.** when Kedor-Laomer **first** conquered Sodom and Gomorrah. Later, in **1862 B.C.** Kedor-

Laomer, king of Elam, invaded Sodom and Gomorrah again to bring them back under his control. In Genesis 14 Abraham confronted Kedor-Laomer, a king of Elam, in the Biblical date of **1862 B.C.** See Table 5-A on the next page. **Could Kudur-Mabuk be the missing son of Shilkhakha, and thus the Regent and third ruler of Elam?** Since the third ruler was in control of the provinces outside Elam, Kudur-Mabuk and Kedor-Laomer performed the same function of the ruler of the provinces that were not within Elam, but were conquered territories outside the boundaries of Elam.

Gadd identified Kudur-Mabuk's name as **"Elamite"** and admitted that **Kudur's father's name was also Elamite**: **Simti-Shilkhak.** Gadd also noted that **Shilkhak, the second name of Kudur's father, was remarkably close to the name of Shilkhakha, the Grand Regent of Elam.**[7] Only the last two letters, "ha," are missing from Shilkhak. Kudur could have shortened his father's legal name to be the affectionate name he called his father from childhood. **Abraham's name can be shortened to "Abram" or "Abe."** My legal name is Teddy, but my friends call me Ted. Shilkhakha can certainly be Shilkhak! Kudur-Mabuk's father is obviously Shilkhakha , the Grand Regent of Elam. If so, **Kudur-Mabuk was the Regent of the Provinces of Elam under his father Shilkhakha, who was the Grand Regent of Elam.** No other person, besides Kudur-Mabuk, has been identified as the Regent of the Provinces.

Gadd admitted that Kudur-Mabuk appeared to be an Elamite ruler, but he was confused that Kudur-Mabuk also called himself **"Father of Amurru and Emutbal."** This title led Gadd to identify Kudur-Mabuk as a powerful chief of the Amorite tribe of Emutbal, who moved into the boundaries of Elam and received permission from the Grand Regent of Elam to rule this Amorite tribe in Elam.[8] If Gadd is correct, **Kudur-Mabuk was also a sub-ruler of a region of Elam and was still qualified to be one of the kings of Elam.**

However, both Kudur-Mabuk and his father, Shilkhak, had Elamite names, not Amorite names. It is more reasonable that Kudur-Mabuk was the **Regent of the Provinces and the eldest son of Shilkhakha** who forced these Amorite tribes to submit to his paternal control, thus becoming the **figurative** "father and ruler of Amurru and Emutbal."

In Huber's new date of **1864 B.C.**, Kudur-Mabuk assisted his second son, Rim-Sin I, king of Larsa, **in defeating the armies of seven major cities, including Uruk, Isin and Babylon.**[9] **Elamite cities were not on the list. Why? Rim-Sin I was an Elamite and his father, Kudur-Mabuk, was the Regent of the Provinces of Elam.** If Kudur were ruler of an Amorite tribe in Elam, he would be a sub-king of a part of Elam, but could not have led an army powerful enough to conquer the armed forces of seven major cities, including Babylon. Hinz' failure to name Shikhakha's Regent of the Provinces leaves the door open for Kudur-Mabuk **to fill the vacant office of Regent of the Provinces as Shilkhakha's eldest son. What person, other than Kudur-Mabuk, could fill the powerful role of the Regent and third ruler of Elam, and conquer the mighty city of Babylon at the very time that Hammurabi and his father were reigning?**

43

V. KUDUR-MABUK IS KEDOR-LAOMER

Both Kudur-Mabuk, Regent of the Provinces of Elam, and the Biblical Kedor-Laomer, a ruler of Elam, are dated astronomically and Biblically to the same B.C. years: **1875 to 1862 B.C.** The consonants in **Kudur's and Kedor's names are identical: K-d-r.** Before 1000 B.C. only consonants were used in the Hebrew language with no vowels. The vowel sounds were memorized and handed down by tradition.[10] Vowel sounds were easily modified over the centuries before they were gradually written into the Hebrew alphabet between 1000 and 600 B.C. Since no written vowels existed in the time of Moses, **the names of Kudur and Kedor are practically identical. Kdr = Kdr.**

The two second names, "Mabuk" (Elamite source) and "Laomer" (Biblical source), may represent different gods that Kudur/Kedor worshiped.[11] However, if the vowel, "E," is placed before Laomer, we have Kedor-Elaomer, which could possibly mean, **Kedor, the Elamite.**[12] Elamite rulers could have used two different last names, since Egyptian kings used three different names (as most Americans do).

TABLE 5-A
NEW CHRONOLOGY OF BIBLICAL, BABYLONIAN
AND ELAMITE HISTORIES
(Table 5-A uses my new Bible chronology and Peter Huber's new astronomical chronology for Babylon and other nations linked to Babylon)

BIBLICAL CHRONOLOGY   BABYLONIAN/ELAMITE HISTORY
B.C.   Huber's Astronomical Dates

ABRAHAM	YEAR	BABYLON	ELAM	LARSA	MARI	ALEPPO
Birth	1946			Sons of		
Abraham in Ur	1890		Shilkhakha	Kudur-Mabuk		Iakhdunlim
			Kudur-Mabuk	Warad-Sin		
			Regent	Son		
Departure from Ur	1876	April-Sin			Rim-Sin I	Zimrilim
				Iarimlim		
Entrance into Canaan	1871	Sin-Muballit				Iasmakh-Adad
	1869				(Assyria conquers Mari)	
					Zimrilim & Arioch in exile at Allepo	
	1864	Babylon Defeated by Kudur-Mabuk & Rim-Sin I				
Encounters Kedor &	1862	Hammurabi (crown prince) is allied with Kudur-Mabuk				
Amraphel = Hammurabi						
	1848	Hammurabi (King)				Hammurabi
ISAAC'S BIRTH	1846					
	1836				Zimrilim Returns to Mari	

400 years from Isaac's Birth   Gen. 15:13
430 years from Abraham's Departure from Ur   Gal. 3:16-17; Exodus 12:40
EXODUS   1446   Moses receives God's Law at Mount Sinai.
     1876 - 1446 = 430 years

Thus, Kedor-Laomer and Kudur-Mabuk are the same person, sharing **five synchronisms**. (1) Both have the same first name. (2) Both were Elamite rulers. (3) Both had a father with Shilkhak in his name. (4) Both conquered major cities outside of Elam, including Babylon. (5) Both are dated by different historical and astronomical methods to the same B.C. years: 1875 to 1862. **Logically, Kedor-Laomer of the Bible should be Kudur-Mabuk of the Elamite records**.

VI. COULD AMRAPHEL BE HAMMURABI?

Genesis 14:4 says Kedor-Laomer, king of Elam, was the leader of three other kings, including **Amraphel, king of Shinar.** Genesis 10:10 says that the country of Shinar included the cities of Babel (Babylon), Accad (Agade), Erech (Uruk) and Calneh. **Thus, Amraphel, as king of Shinar, was also king of a province of Babylon in the new Bible date of 1862 B.C.,** nine years after Abraham entered Canaan in 1871 B.C. See Table 5-A above.

According to Huber's new astronomical dates, Sin-Muballit, was king of Babylon in 1862 B.C., not Amraphel. **However, Sin-Muballit's son, Hammurabi, was crown prince in 1862 B.C. and became king fourteen years later in 1848 B.C.**[13] If Amraphel is Hammurabi, then Amraphel was the crown prince of Sin-Muballit in 1862 B.C. and commander of a Babylonian army that assisted Kedor-Laomer (Kudur-Mabuk) when they attacked Sodom and Gomorrah.

Why did Genesis 14 call Amraphel "king," if he were only a "crown prince?" Princes are often called kings before their fathers die. Nebuchadnezzar was a crown prince and Babylonian commander, while his father, Nabopollasar, was king.[14] **However, II Kings 24:1 called Nebuchadnezzar, "king of Babylon," in 609 B.C., three and half years before he became king in 605 B.C.** In the same manner, Moses, the author of Genesis 14, knowing that Amraphel (Hammurabi) would later become king of Babylon, **called him a king, even though he was still a crown prince.**[15]

Scholars continue to debate the similarities and differences of the names of Amraphel and Hammurabi. However, the two names are practically identical. Hayden explains the names as follows.

> The . . . writing of the name from Ugarit (*mrpi*) would argue for a "p" instead of a "b," and "h" does not correctly represent the first consonant. Perhaps 'Ammurapi would be the best spelling. . . . *Ammu or Hammu* is most likely a god and . . . should be translated "Ammu Is Great."[16]

Now let us analyze the name of Amraphel. The "A" in the Hebrew of Amraphel can be aspirated in Aramaic as "Ha," as the "Apiru" in Egyptian texts is equivalent to "Hapiru" in the Mari texts. Also, the "B" is often interchanged with "P" when translating one language into another as "Hapiru" is also translated by the word "Habiru."[17] The **"el" stem** at the end of Amraphel means **"god."** Thus, Amraphel or Hamraphel in Hebrew means, "Amu [Hamu] is a Great God," whereas

Ammurapi or Hammurapi (Hammurabi) in Akkadian means, "Ammu [Hammu] is Great." Thus, Moses, the author of Genesis, interpreted the Akkadian (Babylonian) name of Hammurabi as Amraphel (Hamraphel) so that his Hebrew readers would know that it was the name of a god by the el ending. Babylonians already knew that Hammu (Ammu) was the name of one of their gods.

Some scholars argue that Hammurabi, as king of Babylon, was never in submission to Elam. They thus conclude that Hammurabi could not be Amraphel, king of Shinar, who was subject to Kedor-Laomer, king of Elam.[18] However, we previously noted that Kudur-Mabuk and his son, Rim Sin I, king of Larsa, defeated Babylon **in Rim Sin I's fourteenth year.[19] Huber's date for Rim-Sin I's fourteenth year is 1864 B.C.**

Therefore, **Babylon had been conquered by Elam two years before 1862 B.C., when Kedor-Laomer (Kudur-Mabuk) led Amraphel (Hammurabi) and other kings to reconquer Canaan in Genesis 14. The timing was thus perfect for a Babylonian king to be subject to an Elamite king.**

Thus, **four points of likely synchronism** link Amraphel to Hammurabi, the crown prince of Shinar (Babylon). **(1) Their names have the same meaning. (2) They were both rulers in Shinar (Babylon). (3) They are both dated astronomically to the same year of 1862 B.C. (4) They both were subject to a ruler of Elam called Kedor or Kudur, who had conquered them in 1864 B.C. Amraphel and Hammurabi are obviously the same person.** See Hammurabi as he worships his god Shamash in Figure 5-A below.

515. Hammurabi before the sun god Shamash, stela from Susa.

FIGURE 5-A
TOP OF MONUMENT: HAMMURABI
WORSHIPS SHAMASH
Underneath Their Figures Are Laws of Babylon
Source: James B. Pritchard, *The Ancient Near East in Pictures,* Princeton Univ. Press, 1974
Louvre. Susa. V. Scheil, Memoirs, Delegation en Perse, vol. 4, Paris, 1901 pl.3. AOB, 318.
Photograph Giraudon, Paris. Permission granted by Princeton University Press no. 4403.02

VII. WHO WAS ARIOCH, KING OF ELLASAR?

Genesis 14 also reports that Arioch, king of Ellasar, accompanied Kedor-Laomer in 1862 B.C. to conquer Sodom and Gomorrah when Abraham surprised them at night on their return home. **Zimrilim, the famous king of Mari, had a son by the name of Arioch (Arriwuuk).**[20] **Was Arioch, the son of Zimrilim, alive in 1862 B.C.?**

In Huber's astronomically revised date of 1869 B.C., Shamshi-Adad I, king of Assyria, conquered Mari and killed its king, Iakhdunlim, the father of Zimrilim. **Zimrilim took his family, including his son Arioch, and fled to his father-in-law, Iarimlim, king of Aleppo.** Zimrilim and **Arioch** remained in exile for thirty-two years before returning to reconquer Mari in Huber's new date of 1837 B.C.[21] **Thus, Zimrilim and his son, Arioch, lived in the vicinity of Aleppo from 1869 to 1838 B.C., which includes the B.C. year of 1862, when Arioch, king of Ellasar, accompanied Kedor-Laomer in Genesis 14. Can Arioch, son of Zimrilim, be Arioch, the king of Ellasar?**

Iarimlim, the father-in-law of Zimrilim, and the grandfather of Arioch, was the powerful king of the country of Iamkhad with its capital at Aleppo between the northern border of Syria and the southern border of Turkey. Iarimlim's kingdom was comprised of an alliance **of twenty sub-kings in cities located in southern Turkey and northern Syria.**[22] The capital of Aleppo was a chief market place and caravan route for those traveling south to Canaan, north to Hatti (Turkey), or east along the Euphrates to Mari, a trip of more than 200 miles.[23]

Ancient Jewish Targums on Genesis 14 locate Ellasar in Pontus or Cappadocia in modern Turkey, land of the Hittites.[24] "Alisar," almost identical to "Ellasar," is the name of several archaeological sites in Turkey.[25] One of these sites is dated continuously back to the third millennium B.C.[26] Thus, the city of Ellasar in Genesis 14 is likely Alisar in southern Turkey, north of Aleppo and Carchemish. If so, Ellasar was one of the twenty cities that made up Iarimlim's kingdom of Iamkhad. Iarimlim could have appointed his grandson, Arioch, as king of Ellasar, after his arrival in Aleppo in 1869 B.C. Therefore, Arioch was definitely alive and likely the king of Ellasar in 1862 B.C., when Kedorlaomer led Arioch, Amraphel and Tidal in an invasion of southern Canaan in the time of Abraham.

VIII. THE UNIQUE ALLIANCE OF KINGS FROM ELAM, BABYLON, AND TURKEY

Babylon and Elam were separated from Aleppo in Turkey by 200 miles. Why were these three kingdoms allied with each other? Kupper notes in the *Cambridge Ancient History* that **Iarimlim, king of Aleppo**, communicated with Babylon and sent an army to assist Sin-Muballit, who was king of Babylon and the father of Hammurabi. Sin-Muballit of Babylon likely married a daughter of Iarimlim, who gave birth to Hammurabi, just as Zimrilim of Mari married another daughter of Iarimlim (king of Aleppo) who gave birth to Arioch. **If so,**

Hammurabi of Babylon and Arioch of Mari were both grandsons of Iarimlim and therefore, cousins. Interestingly, Iarimlim also named his son "Hammurabi," who was the crown prince who inherited the throne of Aleppo when his father died. **Thus, Iarimlim of Aleppo and Sin-Muballit of Babylon both named their crown princes by the name of "Hammurabi." Both Hammurabis became full-fledged kings in the same year of Huber's astronomically-fixed date of 1848 B.C.** The two Hammurabis immediately exchanged ambassadors with each other when they became kings. Hammurabi of Aleppo later sent an army to assist Hammurabi of Babylon militarily.[27] **Thus, the two fathers and two sons constantly communicated with each other from 1869 to 1838 B.C., including 1862 B.C. when Arioch joined Amraphel (Hammurabi) to invade S. Canaan.**

In 1862 B.C. Hammurabi of Babylon, with approval of Kedor-Laomer (Kudur-Mabuk), likely invited his cousin, Arioch, king of Ellasar, to join their military alliance. Arioch likely agreed to meet Kedor and Hammurabi at a mid-way point, where they united forces and attacked cities on both sides of the Dead Sea, including the cities of Sodom and Gomorrah, where Lot lived. (Gen. 12:5-12).

This historical scenario above contains eight points of likely synchronism with the facts of Genesis 14. The similarities in names, relationships and B.C. years are too numerous, significant and remarkable to be chance coincidence. Only true historical synchronism adequately fits the evidence.

IX. WHAT ABOUT TIDAL, KING OF GOIIM?

Tidal, king of Goiim, a fourth king in Genesis 14, joined Kedor-Laomer in 1862 B.C. **Scholars agree that Tidal is uniquely a royal Hittite name in Huber's date of 1776 B.C.[28]** The city of Goiim has not yet been found in ancient sources outside the Bible. However, since Tidal is a Hittite name, **Goiim could have been a Hittite city in Turkey, not far from Ellasar where Arioch was king.** Tidal of Goiim could have been one of the twenty kings under the rule of Iarimlim of Aleppo. Iarimlim may have agreed for Tidal and Arioch to be part of a military alliance with his grandson Hammurabi, and Kedor-Laomer (Kudur-Mabuk), king of Elam.

A second possible identification of Tidal, King of Goiim, is found in Joshua 12:23. This Bible verse lists Goiim as the name of a **Canaanite city located in Gilgal, north of Jericho. The Bible reports that Hittites lived in Canaan with Abraham in the nineteenth century B.C.[29]** Thus, Tidal could be a Hittite ruler of the Canaanite city of Goiim. Since Kedor-Laomer first invaded southern Canaan in 1875 B.C., he may have conquered Tidal, the Hittite king of Goiim, in upper Canaan the same year. If Tidal remained submissive to Kedor-Laomer (Kudur-Mabuk), instead of rebelling, then Kedor-Laomer could have invited Tidal to be a part of the alliance that punished the rebellious cities of southern Canaan in Genesis 14. **These two identifications of Tidal, king of Goiim, are not absolutely synchronistic. However, they are clearly compatible with the historical picture of Canaan, Elam, Turkey and the Hittites in 1862 B.C.**

X. ABRAHAM'S CULTURE FITS ELAMITE
AND BABYLONIAN CULTURE

Abraham lived in Ur of the Chaldees for seventy years from 1946 to 1876 B.C. Thus, Abraham was steeped in Babylonian and Elamite culture when he moved to Canaan in 1871 B.C. Hinz records that Elamite kings commonly married their sisters.[30] Abraham also married his sister, Sarah, the daughter of Abraham's father, but not the daughter of his mother.[31]

Hammurabi's Code lists several customs fitting Abraham's time. Genesis 16:1-4 reports Sarah's failure to bear Abraham a son.   Sarah knew that Hammurabi's Code permitted Abraham to marry a second wife that could bear him a son. In such a case the second wife's son would become Abraham's heir and Sarah's importance as chief wife would be diminished. Sarah resolved this dilemma by giving her slave, Hagar, to Abraham as a surrogate wife. Thus, Sarah remained Abraham's number one wife, while Hagar and her son remained slaves. More important, when Hagar bore Ishmael, **Hammurabi's Law no. 144 forbad Abraham from later marrying a second free wife, preserving Sarah's position as chief wife.**

> If a man take a wife and this woman give her husband a maid-servant, and she bear him children, but this man wishes to take another wife, this shall not be permitted to him; he shall not take a second wife."[32]

Sarah used Babylonian Law masterfully to protect her rights. Sarah gave her maid to Abraham in **1861 B.C. after living in Canaan ten years (Genesis 16:3). According to Peter Huber's new date of 1861 B.C. Hammurabi was the crown prince of Babylon and a contemporary of Sarah in this same year.**

XI. OTHER CULTURAL SYNCHRONISMS
IN THE TIME OF ABRAHAM

G. Posener says Amorites entered Canaan during Egypt's tenth to the twelfth dynasties, before and after Abraham's lifetime.[33] Moses, the author of Genesis, also records the movement of Amorites into Canaan during this same period.[34] C. J. Gadd equates the Hurrians with the Biblical Horites and notes their movement in N. Syria and Canaan during Abraham's time.[35] **Notice that Genesis 14:6 says that the Horites were present in Canaan and Edom in the time of Abraham when Kedorlaomer attacked Sodom and Gomorrah in 1862 B.C.**

> Gen. 14:5-7 -- 5 In the fourteenth year, Kedorlaomer and the kings allied with him went out and defeated the Rephaites in Ashteroth 6 and **the Horites in the hill country of Seir,** as far as El Paran near the desert. 7 . . . and they conquered the whole territory of the Amalekites, as well **as the Amorites** . . . living in Hazazon Tamar.

Thus, Kedor-Laomer's defeat of the Horites in Mount Seir (Edom) in 1862 B.C. (Gen.14:5-7) is compatible with historical records of the Horites.

Egyptologist Kenneth Kitchen observed that slaves were sold for **10 to 15 shekels** from 2370 to 2000 B.C. (Akkad Empire & Third Dynasty of Ur), **20 shekels** from 1900 to 1700 B.C. (Code of Hammurabi & Inscriptions of Mari), and **30 shekels** from 1600 to 1300 B.C. (Inscriptions of Nuzi & Ugarit).[36] Kitchen noted that Joseph was sold as a slave for **20 shekels of silver** in Genesis 37:28, but the price was **30 shekels** in Moses' time (Exodus 21:32). Kitchen thus concluded that the increasing prices for slaves from Abraham to Moses matched the changing prices of eastern countries dated to the same B.C. centuries.[37]

In an attempt to refute Kitchen's argument, Ronald Hendel cited Leviticus 27:5, which lists the redemption price of 50 shekels for adults over twenty years of age and 20 shekels for males under twenty years of age.[38] However, Leviticus 27 does not give the price of slaves, but the cost that **free** Israelites gave to dedicate themselves to God. Slaves are not mentioned in Leviticus 27. Thus, Kitchen's observation of the changing prices for slaves remains valid.

For other cultural synchronisms with the Biblical patriarchs see the March/April, 1995, issue of *Biblical Archaeology Review*. Hendel's attempted refutation of Kitchen's arguments appears in the May/June, 1995, issue of *Biblical Archaeology Review*.

CONCLUSION

Incorrect Bible chronologies for Abraham and incorrect astronomical dates for Elam and Babylon have prevented the discovery of archaeological data that supports the historicity of Abraham. However, the new Bible chronology for Abraham and Huber's new astronomical dates for Babylon, Elam and Mari, position all of the pieces of a complex historical puzzle into a coherent picture. **Twenty-eight synchronistic discoveries discussed in this chapter are here summarized.**

TABLE 5-B
TWENTY-EIGHT DISCOVERIES THAT CONFIRM
ABRAHAM'S HISTORICITY

Discovery 1. Incorrect Bible chronologies for Abraham and incorrect astronomical dates for Elam and Babylon previously prevented the discovery of Abraham and his encounter with the four kings of the East in Genesis 14.

Discovery 2. Stewart's chronological discovery of **1862 B.C.** for Abraham's encounter with four kings of the East provides the chronological background to verify the historicity of the four kings that Abraham encountered in Genesis 14.

Discovery 3. Dr. Peter Huber recalculated Babylon's astronomical dates by **fifty-six years earlier** for Amraphel (Hamurapi), co-ruler of Babylon, and his father Sin-Muballit, placing Hamurapi as a contemporary of Abraham **in the Biblical and astronomically fixed year of 1862 B.C.**

Discovery 4. Genesis 14 reports that Kedor-Laomer (Kedor the Elamite), one of three kings of Elam, led the coalition of three other kings, including Amraphel of Babylon in the Biblical and Babylonian year of **1862 B.C.**

Discovery 5. Prior to 1862 B.C. Kudur-Mabuk conquered Babylon, bringing Amraphel (Hammurabi) and his father under control of Elam, confirming Genesis 14 that Amraphel of Babylon was subject to Kedor-laomer, a king of Elam.

Discovery 6. Amraphel (Hamurapi) of Gen. 14 fits Hamurabi, co-ruler with his father Sin-Muballit in **1862 B.C.**

Discovery 7. Arioch, the king of Ellasar, the third king mentioned in Genesis 14, fits perfectly as the son and co-ruler of Zimrilim, king of Mari.

Discovery 8. Arioch fled with his father Zimrilim to Iarimlim, the father-in-law of Zimrilim and the king of Aleppo, who controlled N. Syria and S. Turkey.

Discovery 9. Ellasar, where Arioch ruled, is a city in Turkey under the rule of Iarimlim.

Discovery 10. Iarimlim's heir was also named Hammurabi, the same as the name of Hammurapi (Amraphel), the king of Babylon. The two Hammurabi's were likely cousins and certainly friends that corresponded and visited each other frequently.

Discovery 11. Tidal, king of Goiim, and the fourth king mentioned in Genesis 14, fits perfectly with Hittite culture and nomenclature.

Discovery 12. Goiim is named as a Canaanite city in northern Israel. Since Hittites inhabited Canaan in Abraham's time, Tidal, a Hittite, may have been ruler of Goiim in Canaan and was a vassal of Kedor-Laomer (Kudur Mabuk).

Discovery 13. Goiim could also possibly be one of the cities of the kingdom of Iarimlim in Southern Turkey, the land of the Hittites.

Discoveries 14 to 18. The combined names and relationships of these four rulers remarkably fit historically and culturally in both the Bible and the ancient records of Babylon, Elam, Mari and Aleppo all in the same B.C. years.

Discoveries 19 to 22. All of these four rulers can be dated to the Biblical and **astronomically-fixed year of 1862 B.C.**, when Abraham confronted these kings.

Discovery 23. Abraham's marriage to his sister fits perfectly the culture of the Code of Hammurabi, dated in this very period of time.

Discovery 24. Sarah's gift of Hagar as a surrogate wife for Abraham, is approved in the Code of Hammurabi.

Discovery 25. Hammurabi's Law no. 144. forbad Abraham from later marrying a second free wife, preserving Sarah's position as his chief wife.

Discovery 26. The changing prices for slaves from the time of Abraham to Joseph in the Bible fit perfectly the changing prices for slaves from the Code of Hammurabi to latter historical documents dated to the time of Joseph.

Discovery 27. Horites in Mount Seir (Edom) in Genesis 14:5 is confirmed in the *Cambridge Ancient History* in the revised astronomical year of 1862 B.C.

Discovery 28. The presence of **Amorites in Canaan in Gen. 14:7** is confirmed in the *Cambridge Ancient History* in the period that includes Huber's date of 1862 B.C.

Twenty-eight historical matches between Biblical and Eastern histories of the time of Abraham demand historical synchronism rather than chance similarity. Table 5-C shows that the mounting total for Chapters Two, Four and Five contain a total of 62 Discoveries.

TABLE 5-C
RUNNING TOTALS OF DISCOVERIES

Chapter		Chapter Total	Running Total
2	Conflict Between Biblical and Secular Histories	18	18
4	Discovery of 430 Years from Abraham to the Exodus	16	34
5	Confirmation of Abraham's Historicity	28	62

NOTES ON NEXT PAGE

NOTES FOR CHAPTER FIVE

1. "Chronological Tables," *Cambridge Ancient History*, Vol. I.Part2B, 1000.
2. Peter Huber, *et. al.*, "Astronomical Dating of Babylon I and Ur III," *Monographic Journals of the Near East*, (June, 1982), 1-38.
3. Asger Aaboe, "Babylonian Mathematics, Astrology," *Cambridge Ancient History*, III.2.280.
4. Walther Hinz, "Persia," *c.*1800-1550 B.C.," *Camb. Ancient Hist.*, II.1.256-261, 265.
5. Walther Hinz, II.1.261.
6. C. J. Gadd, "Babylonia, *c.* 2120-1800 B.C.," *Camb. Ancient History*, I.2B.640-43 & "Chronological Tables," I.2B.1000.
7. C. J. Gadd, I.2B.640.
8. C.J. Gadd, , I.2B.640-41.
9. C. J. Gadd, , I.2B.642.
10. L. McFall, "Hebrew Language," *Intern. Stand. Bible Ency.*, Eerdmans, (1982), Rev., II.660.
11. R. K. Harrison, Chedorlaomer," *I.S. B.E.*, (1982), II.638-39
12. E. A. Wallace Budge, *An Egyptian Hieroglyphic Dictionary*, Dover Pub., II.921-23.
13. "Chronological Tables," *Cambridge Ancient History*, I.2B.1000, plus Huber's additional 56 years.
14. 2 Kings 24:1; Daniel 1:1; Jeremiah 25:11.
15. 2 Kings 24:1 - King Nebuchadnezzar made Jehoiakim his vassal in 609 B.C., 3 ½ years before Nebuchadnezzar became king in Babylon in 605 B.C. Jer. 25:1,11 and Daniel 1:1.
16. R. E. Hayden, ""Hammurabi," *International Standard Bible Encyclopedia*, Eerdmans, II.604.
17. B. J. Beitzel, "Habiru," *Ibid.*, II.586-588.
18. T. G. H. Pinches, "Amraphel," *Ibid.*, I.118-119.
19. C. J. Gadd, "Babylonia *C.* 2120-1800 B.C.," *Cambridge Ancient History*, I.2B.642.
20. Michael C. Astour, "Arioch," *Anchor Bible Dictionary*, 1992 Ed., Doubleday, I.378.
21. M. B. Rowton, "Ancient Western Asia," *Cambridge Ancient History*, I.1.210.
22. J. R. Kupper, "Northern Mesopotamia and Syria," *Ibid.*, II.1.7-10.
23. "Aleppo," *New Encyclopaedia Britannica*, 1991 Rev., I.237.
24. Michael C. Astour, "Ellasar," *Anchor Bible Dictionary*, 1992 Ed., II.476-77, Doubleday.
25. *Ibid.* 26. J. Mellaart, "Anatolia *c.* 4000-2300 B.C.," *Cambridge Ancient History*, I.2A.368, 386.
27. J. R. Kupper, "N. Mesopotamia and Syria," *Ibid.*, I.18; "Chronological Tables." *Ibid.*, II.1.820.
28. Michael C. Astour, "Tidal," *Anchor Bible Dictionary*, VI.551, Doubleday. 29. Gen. 15:20; 23:3-20.
30. Walther Hinz, "Persia *c.* 1800-1550 B.C.," *Cambridge Ancient History*, II.1.259.
31. Gen. 20:11-12.
32. L. W. King (Translator), "Code of Hammurabi," Law no. 144, *Encyclopaedia Britannica*, 1910 Ed., copied from the internet.
33. G. Poesner, "Syria and Palestine, 2160-1780 B.C.," *Cambridge Ancient History*, I.2A.535, 556-58.
34. Genesis 14:7,13; 15:6, 21.
35. C. J. Gadd, "Babylonia *c.* 2120-1800 B.C.," *Cambridge Ancient History*, I.2B.624-25.
36. K. A. Kitchen, "The Patriarchal Age: Myth or History?" *Biblical Archaeology Review*, March/April, 1995, 56.
37. K. A. Kitchen, *Ibid.*
38. Ronald Hendel, "Finding Historical Memories in the Patriarchal Narratives," *Biblical Archaeology Review*, (July/August, 1995), 56.

CHAPTER SIX
DISCOVERY OF THE REMAINS OF
SODOM AND GOMORRAH

One of the most notable events during the lifetime of Abraham was the destruction of Sodom and Gomorrah, which Abraham witnessed with his own eyes. If archaeological and scientific evidences confirm that Sodom and Gomorrah were destroyed by burning sulfur, then we have added evidence that Abraham was a **true man of history** and that the destruction of Sodom and Gomorrah was a true **event of history.** This chapter presents my eye witness testimony, plus geographical, archaeological and scientific evidences that Sodom, Gomorrah and two other cities of the Plain (Admah and Zeboim) were destroyed by burning sulfur that fell from the sky.

I. THE WEALTH AND BEAUTY OF
SODOM AND GOMORRAH

Abraham and his nephew Lot were blessed by God with great abundance of livestock and wealth in the land of Canaan. However, their herds grew so rapidly that the area where they were located could not support all of the livestock. Abraham offered Lot the option of staying on location or of moving to new territory. Lot decided to move to richer and more spacious land.

> Genesis 13:10-11-- Lot looked up and saw that the whole plain of the Jordan **was well watered, like the garden of the LORD**, like the land of Egypt, toward Zoar. (This was before the LORD destroyed Sodom and Gomorrah.). So Lot chose for himself the whole plain of the Jordan and set out toward the east. NIV

In the days of Lot the Dead Sea was a gorgeous valley. The Jordan River flowed through the valley and down into the crevices below the ground. In the summer of 1991 Dot and I photographed the sign on the Dead Sea that shows the **Dead Sea has a depth of 1,312 feet below sea level, the lowest place on earth.** It is also the hottest spot on earth we have ever experienced. Eventually, the crevices tightened and the valley became a huge lake, as it is today. **The Jordan River continually flows into the Dead Sea without a noticeable outlet.** Yet, the shore around the Dead Sea mysteriously remains the same size. One solution to this mystery is the continuous and rapid evaporation from the surface of the hottest Sea on earth. Another possibility is that water continually seeps into crevices on the sea bottom that open to underground streams that run into sub-surface lakes.

In the previous chapter we saw that Genesis 14 describes how the four kings of the east attacked Sodom and Gomorrah in the Biblical and Babylonian year of 1862 B.C. They fought against the five kings of the plain in the valley of Sidim through which the Jordan flowed and before the Dead Sea had filled the valley. The kings of Sodom, Gomorrah, Admah, Zeboim and Zoar left their cities in the plain and descended into the valley of the Jordan with their armies to meet the forces of the kings of the east (Genesis 14).

Genesis 14:10 mentions that the Siddim Valley was filled with tar pits and that some of the soldiers of the defeated Canaanites fell into the tar pits, while others escaped to the hills above the valley and above the plain where the cities of Sodom and Gomorrah were located. Bitumen is still excavated at the southern end of the Dead Sea. **Every day the Jordan River pours seven million tons of water into the Dead Sea.** The Sea has a high concentration of sodium and magnesium chloride. Seepage from the bottom of the Sea exudes salt, potash, magnesium, calcium, sulfur, petroleum and bitumen, which produces tar. The Dead Sea stores hundreds of millions of tons of each of these elements. The tar pits alone were a source of great income for the cities of Sodom and Gomorrah in the time of Abraham as they are to modern Israelites.[1] Thus, the narrative of Genesis 14:10 that tar pits existed in the time of Abraham has been confirmed by excavation.

When Dot and I visited the Dead Sea in 1991, we saw a ship in the water at its southern end. Men were cutting out blocks of solid salt from the Dead Sea and were stacking them on their ship. The blocks of salt looked like blocks of ice. Thus, the Biblical description of tar and salt in the valley is still true today as it was in the days of Abraham and Moses.

II. THE DESTRUCTION OF SODOM AND GOMORRAH

A. Abraham's Plea to Save Sodom and Gomorrah

In Genesis 18:1-3 three men appeared to Abraham. One of them is called "LORD" (*Yahweh* in the Hebrew). The other two are obviously angels. The man called "the LORD" told Abraham that his wife Sarah, who was barren, would bear a child (Isaac) the following year (Genesis 18:10). Our new Bible chronology dates Isaac's birth in 1846 B.C. when Abraham was 100 years old (Genesis 21:5). Thus, in 1847 B.C., one year before Isaac's birth, the three men appeared to Abraham. They told Abraham that Sodom and Gomorrah would be destroyed that same year along with two other cities of the plain: Admah and Zeboiim.

B. Why and How Were Sodom and Gomorrah Destroyed?

The LORD also reported to Abraham that the reason Sodom and Gomorrah and the other cities were going to be destroyed was due to their serious and wide-spread sins. Abraham asked the LORD to spare Sodom (where Lot lived), if fifty righteous souls could be found. When the LORD agreed to this request, Abraham continued to bargain for the cities by reducing the number of the righteous to forty-five, forty, thirty, or twenty. Ultimately, the LORD agreed to spare Sodom if ten righteous men could be found (Genesis 18:24-32).

While Abraham talked with the LORD, the other two men (angels) traveled to Sodom and were invited into Lot's home. In the evening "all the men from every part of the city of Sodom, both young and old, surrounded Lot's house." They demanded that Lot bring the two strangers out so they could sexually rape them. The two angels blinded the Sodomites and led Lot, his wife and his two daughters safely out of the house and out of the city (Genesis 19:1-16).

The angels instructed Lot and his family to flee to the mountains for safety and not to look back at the destruction of the cities, or they also would be destroyed. Lot asked permission to go to the city of Zoar instead of the mountains. The angels granted his request. Lot's wife looked back and turned to a pillar of salt. The rest of Lot's family reached Zoar before the dawn of day just before the destruction of the cities occurred (Gen. 19:17-29).

C. Two Yahwehs Destroyed the Cities of the Plain

In the meantime, the third man, **who was called the LORD (Yahweh)**, and who was talking to Abraham, perceived that not even ten righteous men could be found in the city of Sodom. As soon as Lot and his daughters arrived in Zoar, the LORD destroyed Sodom, Gomorrah and the other cities of the plain (except Zoar) in the following words expressed in Genesis 19:24.

> Then **the LORD [YAHWEH] rained down burning sulfur** on Sodom and Gomorrah-- **from the LORD [YAHWEH] out of the heavens**. Thus he overthrew those cities and the entire plain, including all those living in the cities-- and also the vegetation in the land. NIV

Interestingly, there are two "LORDS" (YAHWEHS) mentioned in Genesis 19:24: One LORD was on earth talking to Abraham while the second LORD was in heaven. Genesis 1:26 also shows the plurality of the Biblical Godhead: "Then God (Elohim = plural of El) said, "Let **us** make man in **our** image, in **our** likeness." David also mentioned two Lords in Psalm 110:1, **"The LORD [Yahweh] says to my Lord [Elohim]**: "Sit at my right hand until I make your enemies a footstool for your feet." (NIV). Thus, the Bible views the Godhead as a unified plurality, a divine family of actually three persons, not just two: Father, Son and Holy Spirit (Matthew 28:18-20), similar to a human family of father, mother and son, united in the same flesh with the same last name, with the Father being the chief authority.

D. What Was the Source of the Falling Sulfur?

Only volcanoes are known to spew sulfur into the sky, but no evidences of volcanoes are found in the area of the Dead Sea. Martin Mulder quotes Cornelius, who theorizes that a volcanic eruption may have destroyed Ugarit and Alalakh in Syria c.1600 B.C. and that the wind could have blown the ashes south toward Sodom and Gomorrah.[2] However, Ugarit is 300 miles north of Sodom and Gomorrah and would have destroyed cities in Syria and northern Canaan before arriving at Sodom and Gomorrah. Also, the excavations of Ugarit and Alalakh have not shown evidence of sulfur among the ancient ruins. A tectonic earthquake likely did the damage and there is no evidence that the damage spread south to Canaan and certainly not to the Dead Sea.

No scientific evidence indicates that sulfur has ever fallen to the ground from a celestial source. Most scholars have concluded that the destruction of Sodom and Gomorrah is fiction, rather than true history. Many scholars argue that this Biblical story is simply a theological allegory to teach a moral lesson against the sinful conduct of the Sodomites rather than having any relation to historical reality. Mulder claims that "Genesis 14 -19 is a construction of various genres dating from the post-exile period,"[3] that is, after 539 B.C. Later in this Chapter we will see clear evidence that Sodom and Gomorrah were destroyed by burning sulfur confirming the historicity of Moses' report of the destruction of these cities.

III. CONFIRMED ANTIQUITY AND LOCATIONS OF THE CITIES OF SODOM, GOMORRAH, ADMAH AND ZEBOIIM

Giovanni Pettinato translated the *Ebla Tablets* and found the names of Sodom and Zeboim among the many cities with which Ebla traded.[4] Pettinato dates these tablets between 2400 and 2000 B.C., confirming the ancient existence and commercial importance of Sodom and Zeboiim before Abraham's time. However, some scholars challenge Pettinato's reading of Sodom and Zeboim.[5]

Archaeologists and Bible scholars differ on the general location of the cities of the plain. (1) Some say these cities are buried beneath the southern end of the Dead Sea.[6] (2) Some say the cities are situated on the southeastern end of the Dead Sea in modern Jordan.[7] (3) Since the Jordan River flows into the Dead Sea, some locate the cities north of the Dead Sea.[8] (4) Strabo, the ancient geographer, located Sodom and Gomorrah near Massada on the western coast of the Dead Sea.[9] As we shall soon see, Strabo's location is absolutely correct.

Martin Mulder's article on "Sodom and Gomorrah" in *The Anchor Bible Dictionary* includes a thorough survey of archaeological excavations in search of Sodom and Gomorrah. (1) In the 1880's Clermont-Ganneau searched for Sodom on Mount Usdum, a mountain located southwest of the Dead Sea. (2) In the 1930's Mallon, Koppel and Neuville excavated a site north of the Dead Sea and near the mouth of the Jordan. (3) Later, W. F. Albright excavated Bab edh-Dra, southeast of the Dead Sea. (4) P. W. Lapp in 1965 and 1967 continued the excavations of Albright. (5) W. E. Rast and R. T. Schaub since 1973 excavated in the southern ghor [end of the Dead Sea]. However, they only found habitations dated to the early Iron Age, not in the Early or Middle Bronze Ages.[10]

None of these excavations have uncovered the cities of Sodom and Gomorrah. Some archaeologists believe the cities are buried beneath the waters of the Dead Sea and will never be found. Other archaeologists are now convinced that they are "mythical cities" based on a "widespread saga motif."[11]

However, Genesis 19:22 says that God destroyed "the cities of the **Plain**." The battle with the kings of the East in Genesis 14 took place in **"the Valley of Siddim,"** where the Jordan flowed and later became the Dead Sea.

Genesis 14:8 says that the kings of Sodom and Gomorrah **"marched out"** of the cities on the Plain (Gen. 13:12) and **descended into** the Jordan valley to fight the kings of the East. **Therefore, the cities were not located in the valley, but in the Plain above the "Valley of Sidim" on the western coast of the Dead Sea.**

IV. BIBLE LOCATIONS OF THE FIVE CITIES OF THE PLAIN

Genesis 10:19 -- The borders of Canaan reached from Sidon toward Gerar as far as Gaza, and then toward Sodom, Gomorrah, Admah and Zeboiim, as far as Lasha [Laish or Dan].

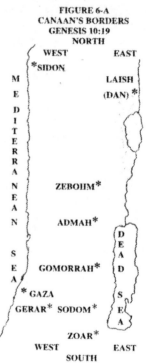

FIGURE 6-A
CANAAN'S BORDERS
GENESIS 10:19

The Bible gives us precise clues for the locations of the four cities of the plain that were destroyed . The fifth city, Zoar, is the only city of the the plain that was not destroyed by burning sulfur. These five cities are often called the Pentapolis, or Pentapoli. Notice above how Genesis 10:19 identifies the general locations of these cities.

All Bible maps agree that the **western border** of Canaan extended along the Mediterranean coast from Sidon in the north to Gerar and Gaza in the south.

Canaan's **southern border** ran from Gaza on the Mediterranean coast directly east to Gerar and on to Sodom, on the western coast of the Dead Sea. **Sodom was thus located on the south-eastern corner of Canaan's border**.

Therefore, Sodom, Gomorrah, and other cities of the plain formed the **eastern border of Canaan** along the western coast of the Dead Sea all of the way to Lasha (Laish or Dan), which is the **northeastern corner of Canaan.** The **northern border ran** from Lasha (Laish or Dan), west to Sidon. Sidon is located on the **north-western corner of Canaan on the coast of the Mediterranean Sea.** Genesis 10:19 lists five cities of the Plain as Canaan's eastern border. This arrangement **precludes** the idea of scholars that four of these cities were located closely together at the southern end of the Dead Sea. These borders also prove that Sodom and Gomorrah could not be located on the coast of Moab and Edom on the eastern coast of the Dead Sea.

V. DESCRIPTION OF THE BURNED REMAINS
OF THE CITIES OF THE PLAIN

Moses predicted how God would later devastate the entire land of Israel (Canaan) if its inhabitants sinned against God. Notice below that Moses compared Israel's future desolation to that of Sodom, Gomorrah, Admah and Zeboim.

Deuteronomy 29:23 - The whole land will be a burning waste of salt and sulfur-- nothing planted, nothing sprouting, no vegetation growing on it. It will be like **the destruction of Sodom and Gomorrah, Admah and Zeboiim, which the LORD overthrew in fierce anger**. NIV

The entire area of the Plain along the western coast of the Dead Sea fits perfectly this Biblical description. When we visited the Dead Sea in 1991, salt and sulfur were in abundance everywhere. Not a single plant grows in this entire area. It is the lowest land on earth and among the hottest places on earth. What a contrast to the beauty of the valley before God destroyed it with burning sulfur! Josephus, General of Galilee's army when the Romans captured him in 70 A.D., testified that remains of the five cities of the Plain could be seen in his own day.

Lake Asphaltitis [the Dead Sea] . . . is extended as far as Zoar, in Arabia. . . The country of Sodom borders upon it. . . The traces of the five cities are still to be seen, as well as the ashes growing in their fruits, which fruits have a colour as if they were fit to be eaten; but if you pluck them with your hands, they dissolve into smoke and ashes.[12]

Josephus also claimed that he had seen the pillar of salt into which Lot's wife was transformed because of her disobedience to God by looking back at the burning cities[13] The pillar of salt that covers Lot's wife must be located south of Sodom (Mt. Sidim) on the way to Zoar. However, we saw hundreds of pillars of salt on the western coast of the Dead Sea. It would be practically impossible to determine which pillar of salt belonged to Lot's wife.

VI. RON WYATT: THE MODERN DISCOVERER OF THE
REMAINS OF SODOM AND GOMORRAH

In the summer of 1990 I met Mr. Ron Wyatt at the Christian Booksellers Convention in Denver, Colorado. He was promoting his book on various discoveries he claimed to have made.[14] He told me that he had recently discovered Sodom and Gomorrah and that this discovery was not included in his book.

Ron Wyatt was an anesthetist who assisted surgeons in the operating rooms of hospitals in Madison, Tennessee. He was an amateur archaeologist who searched in his spare time for famous Biblical sites. I questioned him at length about all of his discoveries. His answers were impressive. However, his claims seemed too numerous and too good to be true. I wondered if he might be a fraud. He invited me to come to his house in Madison, Tennessee, and see video evidence and artifacts in his home that confirm his discoveries.

I made an appointment to see Mr. Wyatt in October of 1990. One of my students, John White, accompanied me on this trip. Wyatt showed us live videos of the sites of his discoveries and showed us artifacts that he found at the various sites. The evidences were impressive and convincing. His answers to our questions were forthright and reasonable. After seeing these amazing video evidences, plus artifacts he brought from the sites, I was convinced that Mr. Wyatt was not a fraud.

Wyatt advised me not to lecture and show his videos to anyone until I went with him to see the sites he had discovered. "Then," Wyatt concluded, "you will be an eye-witness of many of the things you will report, and not a mere reporter of what I have seen." His advice was very wise and I followed it.

In June, 1991, Dot and I, together with Virgil Yocham and Jody Jones, my colleagues in the Sunset International Bible Institute, joined Mr. Wyatt, his wife Mary Nell, plus twenty others to see the site of Sodom and Gomorrah and other sites that we will discuss in Volume II of *Solving the Exodus Mystery*.

We also traveled with Ron to Egypt, where Dot and I and my colleagues remained an extra week after Mr. Wyatt and the others returned to the U.S.A. In Egypt we discovered additional evidences that identify the true Pharaohs of Joseph, Moses and the Exodus. This journey in search of evidences proved to be the most exciting and informative trip of our lives. This chapter zeroes in on Wyatt's discovery of Sodom and Gomorrah and our eye-witness testimony of what we saw.

Most scholars scoff at Wyatt's claim to have discovered the burned remains of Sodom and Gomorrah. They call him a fraud because archaeologists have never found these remains. **However, the truth is that archaeologists have never investigated the sites that Wyatt found.**

A Palestinian peasant boy found the Dead Sea Scrolls on the northwestern coast of the Dead Sea. He reported his finding to scholars who investigated and found them to **be the greatest archaeological discovery of the twentieth century.** If a peasant boy could find the Dead Sea Scrolls, why should scholars think that an intelligent anesthetist and amateur archaeologist from Tennessee could not search and find the cities of Sodom and Gomorrah? I am not in agreement with all of Wyatt's alleged discoveries and interpretations. On the other hand, my policy is to follow the Biblical principle of I Thessalonians 5:21: **"Prove all things; hold fast to that which is good."** A sincere truth searcher should examine the eye witness evidences recorded in this chapter and purchase Wyatt's video to see the evidence for himself or herself to arrive at their own conclusion. Better still, the reader can go to these sites and examine them closely and find the same evidences that we saw with our own eyes.

Unfortunately, Ron Wyatt died in 1999. I will be eternally grateful to him for what he taught and showed me. While I am not in agreement with all of his alleged discoveries and interpretations, I am quite certain of the validity of his discoveries that I have visited and examined first hand. With written permission from Mr.

Wyatt many years before he died I condensed four of his discoveries into one video, which includes the discovery of Sodom and Gomorrah, plus other discoveries that we will discuss in Volume II of this book. The reader may order this video and a manual that I have written that includes eye-witness testimony of these sites by myself, my wife and two colleagues, Virgil Yocham and Jody Jones. The reader can obtain the video and its accompanying manual by ordering from **biblemart.com** on the internet, or by E-mailing us at sales@biblemart.com, or by calling Biblemart.com's toll-free telephone number: **1-800-221-9065.**

VII. RON WYATT'S DISCOVERY OF THE CITIES OF THE PLAIN

From 1989 to 1995 Wyatt gradually discovered the locations of all five cities of the plain mentioned in Genesis 10:19: Sodom, Gomorrah, Admah and Zeboiim, plus Zoar. Ron found evidences that confirmed that four of these five cities were destroyed by burning sulfur. Only Zoar was spared destruction. The locations of these cities are noted on the Map in Figure 6-A above.

A. The Locations of Admah and Zeboiim

After discovering the remains of Sodom and Gomorrah, Mr. Wyatt searched for the locations of Admah and Zeboiim, the other cities of the plain that the Bible says were also destroyed by burning sulfur. About two years later he found Admah to the west of, and across from, Qumran on the north-western end of the Dead Sea. Ron found sulfur balls at this location enabling him to identify the site. Later, Ron also discovered the site of Zeboiim by following the directions in 1 Samuel 13:16-18, which placed Zeboiim not far from Jericho and the Jordan River. He also found balls of powdered sulfur at this site which had caused Zeboiim's destruction. See the location in Figure 6-A above, or in Wyatt's video. We did not have time to visit the sites of Admah and Zeboiim.

B. Gomorrah

In 1989 Ron Wyatt found Gomorrah about a mile north of Mount Massada, close to the western coast of the Dead Sea. Ron had frequently driven on the road from Jericho to the Gulf of Aqaba. About a mile or so before he reached Mount Massada, Ron noticed what appeared to be the walls of an ancient city. He pulled off the road and investigated the site. He noticed that some of the walls had squared gaps spaced evenly across the top of the walls where soldiers could shoot arrows and throw missiles down upon the enemy. He saw support ramparts that were built up perpendicular to the walls to support them from the inside. He found an ancient river-bed that formerly flowed through the city from the south to the north and then curved and flowed east into the Dead Sea. Inside the walls of the city he found construction that looked like houses, some with entrances and window openings. Dot, Virgil Yocham and Jody Jones and I, plus twenty others saw with our own eyes what Mr. Wyatt had told us and showed us in his video.

Interestingly, a whole community of Jews lived in the caves of Qumran from about 150 B.C. to 100 A.D. Yet, the caves they lived in showed less architectural design than the construction sites we saw at Gomorrah. I stood in front of Qumran with a cave behind me that has a teepee-like entrance, rather than the rectangular entrances and windows I saw at Gomorrah.

Structures in the general form of a circular building, a ziggurat and a sphinx are scattered throughout the area and can be seen, especially from the top of Mount Massada, located about a mile to the south of Gomorrah. The reader can see many of these structures by ordering the video. See below my photo from the top of Massada in Figure 6-B.

**Figure 6-B - Ted Stewart's Photo from Massada,
Looking to the northwest at Gomorrah**

**Figure 6-C - Ted Stewart's Photo of Jody Jones, standing
in front of the remains of man-made structures in Gomorrah**

Wyatt's most astounding discovery was evidence that this ancient city had been destroyed by burning sulfur. Ron discovered a large slab which was peppered with burning sulfur that fell from the sky like hail. See this slab in the video. Blackened holes are evident over the entire slab. **Many of the burnt holes still have the remains of sulfur that burned partially and were smothered out by the ashes.** Mr. Wyatt carried back to the U.S. **many samples of the sulfur balls that had not been burned.** His video shows the laboratory technician testing the sulfur at **95.7% pure. Better evidence could not exist to demonstrate that all of the construction in this ancient city had been destroyed by burning sulfur.**

In 1991, our entire group of twenty-seven people scoured the area of Gomorrah, taking photos and searching for sulfur balls. Each of us picked up several sack-fulls of powdered sulfur balls and brought them back with us to the U.S. We found sulfur balls everywhere we looked. Figure 6-D shows me hunting and finding sulfur balls on the tops of hills located at Gomorah. Dot and I brought these sulfur balls back to the U.S. We have demonstrated these balls to several

**Figure 6-D
Ted searching for sulfur balls**

thousand people during the last eleven years. Figure 6-E shows a picture of some of our powdered sulfur balls which we found at Gomorrah and demonstrated to our audiences.

Figure 6-E - Ted and Dot Stewart showing some of
the sulfur balls that they found at Gomorrah

Dr. Micah Ashkenazi, our Israeli guide in Palestine, and an expert archaeologist, accompanied us on our trip from Jerusalem to Gomorrah and on to Elat (Elath). He has a master's degree in archaeology and a doctor's degree in Jewish/Christian Relations from the University of Jerusalem. Arriving at Gomorrah, the Americans spread over the site, picking up powdered sulfur balls. Micah stayed at the bus and did not venture out with the rest of us. When Dot and I returned to the bus, we found him waiting for us. I asked him why he did not survey the site with us. Micah answered, "My teachers say these sites are not the remains of ancient cities and that it would be a waste of my time to look for them." None of his teachers considered the western coast of the Dead Sea as the location of the cities of the Plain. Thus, archaeologists have not found these cities because they have not looked closely at the areas above the western coast of the Dead Sea, which are wide open for all tourists to explore and see for themselves.

Dot asked Micah, "How can you explain these balls of powdered sulfur that we found?" **Micah replied, "Those are not balls of powdered sulfur."** Dot took out one of her sulfur balls and raised it up to Micah's nose and asked him what it smelled like. Micah would not answer. Dot lowered the same ball of powdered sulfur to his lips and asked him to touch it with his tongue, but he refused.

Finally, Dot took Micah's hand, opened it and placed a ball of powdered sulfur in his palm. She told Micah, "Take this sulfur ball to a laboratory in Jerusalem and have it tested for its contents. We will do the same in America." We don't know what Micah did with the ball of powdered sulfur we gave him. The powdered sulfur balls we were finding contradicted what Micah had been taught by his teachers. He appeared to be shaken by what we claimed to have found. We hope that Micah presented his sulfur ball to be tested in a competent laboratory.

C. Sodom

Mr. Wyatt found Sodom located at the foot of Mount Siddim, which is situated on modern maps of Israel toward the southwest corner of the Dead Sea. Genesis 10:19 also locates Sodom at the southwest corner of the Dead Sea, which is also the southeastern corner of Canaan. See Sodom's location on the map in Figure 6-A above. At the bottom of Mount Sidim Wyatt found the remains of an ancient city that had been formerly destroyed by burning sulfur. The remains of burnt and unburnt sulfur are proof positive that this site is one of the cities of the Plain that God destroyed. Our time schedule did not permit us to investigate Sodom because we had already spent most of the day investigating Gomorrah, which is better preserved than Sodom. Our bus drove slowly down the highway so that we could see the remains of Sodom from a distance at the foot of Mount Sidim.

VIII. TESTING OUR SULFUR
BALLS IN THE U.S.A.

When I returned to the U.S.A., Mr. Dutton, a scientist of the Southwestern Public Service Co., heard my lecture in Amarillo, Texas. Afterwards, people lined up to see a few of the sulfur balls that I had brought back from the site of Gomorrah. Mr. Dutton asked permission to analyze one of my sulfur balls in the lab of the Southwestern Public Service Co. Figure 6-F shows a copy of the report he received from their lab in Amarillo: **96.14% pure sulfur.** See this report on the next page.

Mr. Dutton informed me that he works frequently with sulfur, but had never seen a ball of powdered sulfur lying out on the ground. He said that sulfur is found underneath the earth in crystalized form. They drill down to the sulfur strata, liquefy it and pump it out of the ground and let it dry. He said that during his lifetime he has never heard of powdered balls of sulfur lying on the ground anywhere in the world. He concluded that the sulfur balls could only have arrived on the ground by falling from the sky. He reasoned that the evidences of these powdered sulfur balls in the very area where Sodom and Gomorrah are Biblically located, give irrefutable proof that the words of Genesis 19:24 were literally fulfilled: "Then the LORD rained down **burning sulfur** on Sodom and Gomorrah-- from the LORD out of the heavens." (NIV)

SOUTHWESTERN PUBLIC SERVICE COMPANY
P. O. BOX 1261 • AMARILLO, TEXAS 79170 • 806/378-2121

SYSTEM LAB

LABORATORY ANALYSIS REPORT

TO: Ted Stewart   PR#00000

ACCOUNT: Sunset School of Preaching   DATE RECEIVED: 2/15/93
          Lubbock, Texas
                                             DATE REPORTED: 4/23/93

JOB: Material from site west of Dead Sea, Israel

ANALYSIS: Sulfur

METHOD: LECO Sulfur Analyzer
         ASTM D 4239 Method C

Sample 1: Powdery Spheres   Sample 2: Powder

% SULFUR	96.14	2.42
% CALCIUM	1.4	28.8
% SILICON	0.8	13.0
% ALUMINUM	0.2	2.8
% IRON	0.3	1.3
% MAGNESIUM	0.3	2.9

Analyst _Kathy Snodon_   Date _4-26-93_
Lab Supervisor _____

Report relates only to the item tested.

Figure 6-F - Photo copy of the Report from Southwestern Public Service Company that analyzed one of the powdered sulfur balls submitted by Ted and Dot Stewart. The result was 96.14% pure sulfur.

In the years since we visited Gomorrah I have told others where the site is located so that they too can find some sulfur balls. So far, only four of my colleagues, Hollis Maynard, Bob Anderson, and their wives have gone to the site to see the evidence for themselves. They also found balls of powdered sulfur and brought them back to the U.S. Bob Anderson took one of his sulfur balls and burned it to verify that its flame and smell indicated that it was really sulfur. However, the lab reports of Ron Wyatt and myself are more conclusive than the mere smell of burning sulfur.

CONCLUSION

The ancient remains of Sodom, Gomorrah, Admah and Zeboim, including Zoar, are still open for anyone to visit them and verify that these locations, except for Zoar, were destroyed by burning sulfur. The archaeological and scientific evidences confirm that these ancient cities that once flourished in a paradise atmosphere were totally destroyed by burning sulfur that fell from the sky. We do not know how God accomplished this task. God may have sent a comet or some other heavenly object that was stuffed with powdered sulfur and guided it so that it would pass over these cities and drop burning sulfur and unburnt sulfur on top of them. A volcano can spew out liquid sulfur, but cannot spew out dry powdered sulfur balls. The hot liquid sulfur from a volcano would cool into a crystallized form and not dry in powdered form. Regardless, no volcanoes exist in the area of the Dead Sea. Thus, a comet is the more logical choice for the source of these balls of both burning and unburnt powdered sulfur. However, the greater miracle was the prediction of the event and the warning of the angels so that Lot and his family could escape the destruction by fleeing from his home in the middle of the night.

More important, the discovery that these cities were destroyed by burning sulfur confirms the historicity of the Biblical record of this destruction. Previously we saw sixteen discoveries of the chronology of Chapter Four and twenty-eight discoveries in Chapter Five for the historical confirmation of Abraham and the kings of the East in Genesis 14. This Chapter has presented **seventeen archaeological and scientific evidences that confirm the destruction of Sodom and Gomorrah, as described in Genesis 18 and 19,** These seventeen additional synchronisms are listed in **Table 6-A below.**

Adding the synchronisms of Chapters Two, Four, Five and Six, we have a total of seventy-nine historical and archaeological discoveries that confirm the Biblical dates and historical events of the time of Abraham. We are now ready to find the same kind of historical evidences for the Biblical period from Joseph to the Exodus.

TABLE 6-A
SEVENTEEN DISCOVERIES THAT CONFIRM THE DESTRUCTION OF SODOM AND GOMORRAH BY BURNING SULPHUR

The following discoveries are pictured in Ron Wyatt's video and were witnessed by myself, my wife, Dot, and my colleagues, Virgil Yocham and Jody Jones and seventeen others.

Discovery 1. Gomorrah is located about a mile north of Mount Massada.

Discovery 2. City walls are seen with squared gaps spaced evenly across the top for soldiers to shoot arrows against the enemy and be protected.

Discovery 3. Ramparts are constructed perpendicular to the inside walls to support them.

Discovery 4. An ancient river-bed formerly flowed through the city from the south to the north and then curved and flowed east into the Dead Sea.

Discovery 5. Houses with rectangular entrances and square window openings are visibly seen on the ground and from the top of Massada..

Discoveries 6, 7 and 8: Dot and I saw (6) a circular building, (7) a sphinx, and (8) a ziggurat at Gomorrah.

Discovery 9. Our entire group of twenty that accompanied Mr. Wyatt found abundant amounts of powdered sulfur balls over the entire site. We all carried bags of sulfur balls back to the U.S., which we jealously guard.

Discovery 10. Wyatt's laboratory in Tennessee reported the powdered balls to be 95.7% pure sulfur.

Discovery 11. Mr. Dutton, of the Southwestern Public Service in Amarillo, Texas, tested one of my powdered sulfur balls as 96.14% pure sulfur.

Discovery 12. Wyatt's video shows a large slab that was peppered with burning sulfur that fell from the sky like hail. Blackened holes cover the slab, many of them with portions of unburned powdered sulfur in their centers.

Discovery 13. Mr. Dutton informed me that he drills into the earth to find crystalized sulfur, which they melt and pump out of the ground. But he had never seen a ball of powdered sulfur that had obviously fallen from the sky as described in Genesis 19:24.

Discovery 14. Mr. Wyatt found Sodom at the foot of Mount Sidim, near the southern end of the Dead Sea. He also found sulfur balls at Sodom.

Discovery 15. Mr. Wyatt found sulfur balls at the site of Admah (Gen.10:19 and Deut. 29:23), directly west of Qumran on the N.W. end of the Dead Sea.

Discovery 16. Mr. Wyatt discovered Zeboiim by following the directions in 1 Samuel 13:16-18, which placed Zeboiim not far from Jericho and the Jordan River. He also found balls of powdered sulfur at this location.

Discovery 17. I later directed my colleagues, Hollis Maynard and Bob Anderson, to the location of Gomorrah. They also picked up powdered balls of sulfur and tested them at home by burning them and smelling the sulfur.

TABLE 6-B
RUNNING TOTAL OF DISCOVERIES

Chapter		Chapter Total	Running Total
2	Conflict Between Biblical and Secular Histories	18	18
4	Discovery of 430 years From Abraham to Solomon	16	34
5	Confirmation of Abraham's Historicity	28	62
6	Discovery of the Remains of Sodom and Gomorrah	17	79

NOTES FOR CHAPTER SIX

1. G. R. Lewthwaite, "The Dead Sea," *Zondervan Pictorial Encyclopedia of the Bible*, II.50-52.

2. Martin J. Mulder, "Sodom and Gomorrah," *Anchor Bible Dictionary*, Doubleday, VI. 101-102.

3. Martin Mulder, "Sodom and Gomorrah," *Anchor Bible Dictionary*, VI.99-103

4. Giovanni Pettinato, *The Archives of Ebla*, Doubleday, 1981, 287.

5. Martin. Mulder, "Sodom and Gomorrah," *Anchor Bible Dictionary*, VI.102.

6. R. L. Alden, "Sodom," *Zondervan Pictorial Bible Dictionary*, 1976, Vol. 5, 466-68.

7. D. M. Howard, Jr., "Sodom," *International Standard Bible Encyclopedia*, 1988 Rev., Eerdmans, IV.560.

8. Martin Mulder, "Sodom and Gomorrah," *Anchor Bible Dictionary*, VI.101.

9. Martin Mulder, "Sodom and Gomorrah," *Anchor Bible Dictionary*, VI. 101.

10. Martin Mulder, "Sodom and Gomorrah," *Anchor Bible Dictionary*, VI.102.

11. Martin Mulder, "Sodom and Gomorrah," *Anchor Bible Dictionary* VI.102.

12. Josephus, *Wars of the Jews*, Book IV, Chapter 8, paragraph 4, *The Complete Works of Josephus*, Wm. Whiston (Trans.), Kregel Pub. Co., 540.

13. Josephus, *Antiquities of the Jews*, Book I, Chapter XI.4.,35.

14. Ron Wyatt, *Discovered: Noah's Ark* [which includes the discovery of Noah's Ark, Sodom and Gomorrah, the Red Sea Crossing & Mount Sinai], World Bible Society, 1989.

CHAPTER SEVEN
JOSEPH AS A SLAVE AND PRISONER IN THE REIGN OF AMENEMHET I

Jacob loved Joseph more than his other sons and gave him a richly ornamented robe. Joseph related two mysterious dreams to his brothers. In one dream Joseph and his brothers were gathering sheaves. Suddenly, Joseph's sheaf rose and stood in the middle of his brothers' sheaves. His brothers' sheaves bowed before Joseph's sheaf. In a second dream the sun, moon and eleven stars bowed down before Joseph. His brothers recognized that both dreams implied that Joseph would rule not only his other brothers, but also his father and mother.[1]

Infuriated with jealousy, his brothers bound Joseph, threw him into a pit and later sold him to Midianites traveling to Egypt. The Midianites (Ishmaelites who lived in Midian) carried Joseph to Egypt and sold him as a household slave to Potiphar, the captain of Pharaoh's body guard. Joseph was only seventeen years old at the time.[2] God blessed Joseph with great ability and success so that Potiphar soon promoted Joseph to be chief administrator over his entire house. God also blessed Potiphar and his household because of his kindness to Joseph.[3]

I. FROM SLAVERY TO PRISON

Joseph was well-built and handsome. Potiphar's wife fell in love with Joseph and often tempted him to commit adultery with her. Because of his moral and religious convictions, Joseph continually resisted her amorous advances, asking her, "How could I do such a wicked thing and sin against God?" Angry with Joseph for rejecting her, Potiphar's wife falsely accused Joseph of attempted rape. Believing his wife's accusations, Potiphar threw Joseph into prison.[4]

The prison warden soon recognized Joseph's fine qualities and placed him in charge of the other prisoners.[5] Later, Pharaoh became angry with his butler and baker and confined them in the same prison where Joseph was staying. The butler and baker each had dreams. Joseph interpreted the butler's dream to mean that he would be restored to the king's service within three days. Joseph told the butler how he had been imprisoned on false charges. He asked the butler to intercede on his behalf before Pharaoh when the butler was restored to his office.

Joseph interpreted the dream of the baker as meaning that he would be hanged, also within three days. Three days later Joseph's predictions were precisely fulfilled. The baker was hanged and the butler was restored to his former position. However, the butler forgot to speak to Pharaoh on Joseph's behalf.[6]

II. FROM PRISONER TO PRIME MINISTER
"**Two full years later**" (Genesis 41:1) Pharaoh had two dreams. The butler remembered Joseph and told Pharaoh about Joseph's ability to interpret dreams. Pharaoh released Joseph from prison and asked him to interpret his dreams. Joseph interpreted both of Pharaoh's dreams to mean that seven years of great abundance

would be followed by seven years of devastating famine. Joseph said that the seven years of abundance would begin soon.[7]

Joseph advised Pharaoh to store up grain during the years of abundance to prepare for the famine. Pharaoh was so impressed with Joseph's interpretation and advice that he appointed him Vizier (Prime Minister) of Egypt. Joseph was thirty years old when he was appointed to this office.[8] Thus, God turned Joseph's slavery and imprisonment into freedom and preeminence as the highest political official under the Pharaoh of Egypt.

Does this rags-to-riches story of Joseph fit a specific dynasty and Pharaoh in Egyptian history? An Egyptian dynasty is a single family of successive kings who rule over all of Egypt, or even a part of Egypt. When a new family of kings succeeds in ousting a former family of kings, a new dynasty is formed. Modern Egyptologists count twenty six different dynasties from the first dynasty c. 2925 B.C. to the twenty-sixth dynasty in 525 B.C., when Cambyses, king of Persia conquered all of Egypt and ended the dynasties of Egypt.[9]

III. CLUES FROM COURVILLE AND ALING THAT LINK
JOSEPH TO EGYPT'S TWELFTH DYNASTY

In Chapter Three I mentioned that Donovan Courville in his book, *The Exodus Problem & Its Ramifications*, noted twelfth-dynasty inscriptions that spoke of "years of famine" and of a canal dug at this same period that was later called the "*Bahr Yusef*, ("The Joseph Canal.). Courville's book inspired me to read every twelfth-dynasty inscription I could find in searching for more evidence for Joseph.

Charles Aling's book, *Egypt and Bible History*, also dated Israel's entrance into Egypt during the twelfth dynasty. Aling noted a papyrus of the twelfth dynasty that gives a long list of slaves in Egypt, including Canaanites purchased by private Egyptians.[10] Some of these slaves held domestic posts of responsibility just as Joseph did in Potiphar's house.[11] While these Egyptian documents do not prove that Joseph was enslaved during the twelfth dynasty, they do show that Joseph's slavery as a domestic servant fits harmoniously with twelfth-dynasty culture.

The same papyrus that mentions twelfth-dynasty slaves from Canaan also describes twelfth-dynasty prisons and the punishment of convicted criminals, including confinement, forced labor, and in serious cases, death.[12] Therefore, Joseph's imprisonment, the butler's and baker's confinement, as well as the baker's subsequent execution by hanging,[13] all fit harmoniously into the historical context of the twelfth dynasty.

A nineteenth-dynasty document, entitled *The Tale of Two Brothers*, recounts a story similar to that of Joseph and Potiphar's wife. The wife of an older brother attempted to seduce her husband's younger brother. When he refused to commit adultery with her, she falsely reported to her husband that his younger brother attempted to rape her and beat her when she resisted him. Her husband tried to kill his younger brother, but the younger brother was saved by praying to his god, Per-

Harakhti. When the older brother learned the truth, he killed his wife instead.[14]

Scholars have theorized that the Egyptian story, dated to the thirteenth century B.C., was the source for the Biblical story of Joseph. This book proposes that the Biblical story occurred in the twelfth dynasty, more than 300 years before the similar Egyptian story was written by a nineteenth-dynasty scribe.

IV. CLUES IN AMENEMHET I'S REIGN, FOUNDER OF THE TWELFTH DYNASTY

Figure 7-A
Amenemhet I
Ted Stewart's photo in the Cairo Museum

Amenemhet I (Ammenemes I) was the founder of the twelfth dynasty. See a photo of his bust in Figure 7-A. He formerly served as the Vizier (prime minister) of Nebtowy Mentuhotep IV (also Mentuhotpe IV), the last Pharaoh of the eleventh dynasty. After leading the Egyptian army in a successful effort to drive out foreigners that had entered the Delta of northern Egypt, Amenemhet I, the Vizier of Mentuhotep IV, apparently usurped the throne of his king. He then moved the government of Egypt from Thebes in southern Egypt to northern Egypt, where he built a new capital city called **"Itjtowy," which means "Seizer of the Two Lands."**[15]

The "Two Lands" refer to both Upper Egypt (higher elevation ascending to the mountains in the south) and Lower Egypt (lower elevation, ending in the Mediterranean Sea in the north).

Scholars formerly located the capital of Itjtowy at El-Lisht, about eighteen miles south of Memphis. Egyptologists chose this location as the capital because most of the pyramids of the twelfth dynasty are located across the Nile to the west of El-Lisht.[16] However, Breasted says that Itjtowy was a strong fortress with "battlemented walls."[17] No remnants of the city walls or of the palace have ever been found at El-Lisht. John Baines notes, "Nothing has yet been found of the town itself [Itjtowy], and its exact location is still unknown."[18]

Chapter Sixteen proposes a new site for Itjtowy in the Delta of Egypt that fits the description of its location in two different twelfth-dynasty documents. This new location also matches the Biblical description of Egypt's capital in the time of Joseph and Moses.

A. First Clue: The Assassination Attempt Against Amenemhet I

The first Egyptian document that I read was a letter from Amenemhet I to his son, Sesostris I. Amenemhet I's letter explained how his palace servants and officials treacherously attempted to kill him when his son, Sesostris, was away from the palace on a military expedition with the army. Amenemhet's letter warned

Sesostris not to trust his closest friends or servants.

> **Breasted (Translator)** -- Beware of **subjects** who are nobodies, of whose plotting one is not aware. **Trust not a brother, know not a friend, make no intimates,** it is worthless . . . I gave to the beggar, I raised the orphan, I gave success to the poor as well as to the wealthy; but **he who ate my food** raised opposition, **He whom I gave my trust** used it to plot. **Wearers of my fine linen** looked at me as if they were needy. . . . It was after supper, night had come. . . . As my heart began to follow sleep, **weapons for my protection were turned against me,** while I was like a snake of the desert. I awoke at the fighting, alert, and found it was a combat of the guard. . . . Thus bloodshed occurred while I was without you; **before the courtiers had heard I would hand over to you [the kingdom]; before I had sat with you as to advise you.** For I had not prepared for it, had not expected it, had not foreseen **the failing of the servants."** [19]

After reading Amenemhet's words above, my mind immediately connected **"the failing of the servants"** to the Biblical story of the baker and butler who had "offended" Pharaoh and were subsequently cast into prison. [20] Could this **"offense"** of the baker and butler be related to Amenemhet's description of the **"servants"** who ate his **"food,"** were dressed with his **"fine linen"** and either participated in the plot to kill him or failed to warn him? The fact that the baker was hanged implies that he had committed a capital offense. Could the baker's execution mean that he was found guilty of directly participating in the assassination attempt? Amenemhet's expression, "the failing of the servants," might imply that the butler had merely been negligent in defending or warning the king as the plot began to unfold, and thus deserved imprisonment, but not death.

When I first discovered this possible historical link, I thought it was only chance coincidence with small probability of being a true synchronism. However, a detective often constructs an imaginary scenario for a crime based on a few vague clues. As more clues are found, these are compared with previous clues to see if they also harmonize with the original hypothesis. If continued harmony is found with the emergence of new clues, the detective grows more confident in his original hypothesis. If later clues contradict the original hypothesis, the detective must either revise the original hypothesis, or substitute it with a new one that better explains the facts.

Little did I know when I began my research that this possible historical connection would enable me to find **436 remarkable evidences in 430 years of matching Babylonian, Egyptian and Biblical histories from Abraham, to Joseph, to Moses, to the Exodus. Many other evidences will appear in Volume II of this series.**

73

B. Second Clue: Potiphar's Likely Participation in the Coup

If the baker and butler were imprisoned with Joseph because of the assassination attempt against Amenemhet I, another possibility comes to mind. Joseph was imprisoned by his master, Potiphar, who is described as the "captain" of Pharaoh's body guard and an important "official" of Pharaoh.[21] The "captain of the body guard" was a regular position in the palace of twelfth-dynasty kings.[22] Amenemhet I specifically stated above that "**weapons for my protection were turned against me** . . . . I awoke at the fighting, alert, and found it was **a combat of the guard**."[23] Amenemhet's words imply that his body guard, who had weapons to protect the king, turned those same weapons against the king to kill him.

If Potiphar were the captain of Amenemhet I's body guard, he also would likely be one of the ring leaders of the coup. If so, he was either killed in the attempt or was executed immediately for his treachery when Amenemhet I's son, Sesostris I, arrived back at the palace with the army. Since Potiphar unjustly imprisoned Joseph earlier, God may have later justly punished Potiphar for his rebellion against the king and for Potiphar's mistreatment of Joseph. This idea would make an interesting episode in a movie about the life of Joseph.

C. Third Clue: Vacant Viziership When Joseph Was Appointed

The Bible reports that Joseph appeared before Pharaoh **"two full years"** after the butler was released from prison.[24] After interpreting the dreams of Pharaoh, Joseph was appointed Vizier (prime minister) of all of Egypt.

> Gen 41:39-44 - "Then Pharaoh said to Joseph, 'Since God has made all this known to you, there is no one so discerning and wise as you. You shall be in charge of my palace, and all my people are to submit to your orders. Only with respect to the throne will I be greater than you.' . . . Thus he put him in charge of the whole land of Egypt. Then Pharaoh said to Joseph, 'I am Pharaoh, but without your word no one will lift hand or foot in all Egypt.'" NIV

The Viziership (office of the prime minister) was a permanent position in the government of Egyptian dynasties before, during and after the twelfth dynasty.[25] Amenemhet I himself was a Vizier before he became Pharaoh of Egypt and usurped the throne of the last Pharaoh of the eleventh dynasty.[26] The fact that the Pharaoh of the Bible appointed Joseph to be his Vizier is proof within itself that the office of Vizier was vacant when Pharaoh appointed him. Obviously, the former Vizier had died, retired or had been forcibly removed from office.

Amenemhet I's letter to his son Sesostris implies that the Vizier participated in the coup and was likely executed for his crime, as was the baker in Genesis 40:18-22. In the following passage Amenemhet I appears to warn his son against appointing another Vizier and against trusting in the servants of his own household.

**Lichtheim's Translation: Trust not a brother, know not a friend,
make no intimates,** it is worthless . I gave to the beggar, I raised the
orphan, I gave success to the poor [and] to the wealthy; but **he who ate
my food** raised opposition, **He whom I gave my trust used it to plot.**[27]

Viziers of twelfth-dynasty kings called themselves **"favorite of the king"
and "his beloved among the companions."**[28] Yet, Amenemhet I's counsel to his
son Sesostris was not to trust in **"intimate friends" or even "a brother."** The
Vizier was the closest friend and adviser to the Pharaoh and was thus likely the
leader of the coup attempt to murder Amenemhet I. Amenemhet I's advice not to
trust "a brother" may indicate that his own brother also participated in the coup. He
may well have been Amenemhet I's Vizier.

The Vizier was the highest authority in Egypt next to Pharaoh. Remember that
Amenemhet I was the Vizier of the last Pharaoh of the Eleventh Dynasty and
Amenemhet I, himself, killed the Pharaoh he was serving and took over his
kingdom. What **goes** around often **comes** around to punish the original offender.

D. Fourth Clue: Evidence That Amenemhet I's Vizier
Led the Murder Coup Attempt

While the usurpers were successful in wounding Amenemhet I, they were
unsuccessful in killing him. He wrote his son Sesostris, "Thus bloodshed occurred
while I was without you." Sesostris was likely away from the palace, perhaps with
all or part of the army, when the attempted coup occurred. The usurpers may have
thought that they killed Amenemhet I. However, as we will see later, they only
wounded him and he survived. When Sesostris I and the army returned to the
palace, they likely fought with the Vizier and his cohorts and either killed them
immediately or captured them and executed them later.

Evidence also indicates that Amenemhet I's Vizier was executed for his
participation in the coup. Amenemhet I's pyramid is located a few hundred yards
west of the village of El Lisht. El Lisht guarded and maintained the royal cemetery
of the kings of the twelfth dynasty. Chapels were also built within the enclosures
of each king's pyramid to conduct religious ceremonies in memory and in worship
of the departed kings, who were also regarded as gods.

Amenemhet I's pyramid was surrounded by two walls, an inner enclosure-wall
of limestone and an outer wall of mud brick. In the area between the walls were
buried members of the royal family and six of the court officials, two of them
unnamed.[29] A stela preserved in Paris names **Khenty-bau** as the Vizier of
Amenemhet I.[30] However, Khenty-bau's name is not found among the many tombs
of Amenemhet I's other officials. The Vizier of the Pharaoh usually occupies the
largest tomb within the pyramid complex, but Rehu-er-djer-sen, the Chancellor
occupied this tomb,[31] even though his office was not as important as the Vizier's.
The absence of Khenty-bau's tomb and name in the pyramid complex implies that
he died in dishonor. Khenty-bau was likely the leader of the coup attempt against

Amenemhet I. If so, he was immediately killed by Sesostris I when he returned to the palace.

The fact that Khenty-bau, the Vizier of Amenemhet I, was not buried within the pyramid enclosure of Amenemhet I suggests that Khenty-bau died in dishonor. This fact leads to the logical conclusion that Khenty-bau was likely the perpetrator of the assassination attempt. The removal of the Vizier also explains why two years after the coup attempt, Sesostris I was still following his father's advice to refrain from trusting anyone, even a brother, to occupy the office of Vizier. **Thus, the missing tomb of the Vizier Khenty-bau fits perfectly my proposed theory that the assassination attempt of Amenemhet I occurred shortly before Joseph met the baker and butler in prison.** Two years later Joseph was appointed Vizier of Egypt by Sesostris I, the son of Amenemhet I. The Viziership had remained vacant during these two years because Sesostris I feared to trust another Vizier.

Some Egyptologists identify the Vizier of Amenemhet I as Inyotef-Okre because he was called the "Vizier and Governor of the Pyramid City."[32] These scholars conclude that the twelfth-dynasty capital was located at El Lisht, since the Vizier lived there. However, the word "Vizier" [tha-at in hieroglyphics] was also used to refer to governors of nomes (states) and mayors of cities, as well as Vizier of the entire nation of Egypt, depending on the context.[33] The small city of El Lisht was located south of Memphis (Cairo) and was very close to Amenemhet I's pyramid. Its governor was given the responsibility to oversee the pyramid. However, Amenemhet I and the Vizier he appointed over the entire nation resided in his new capital in the delta of Egypt. We will show proof in Chapter Sixteen from two twelfth-dynasty documents that the twelfth-dynasty capital of Itjtowy was located in the northeastern delta of Egypt close to the border of the land of Goshen.

I repeat that this connection between the Pharaoh of Joseph and Amenemhet I and his son Sesostris I was only hypothetical when I began this research. However, after seeing that subsequent Biblical events in the life of Joseph continued to synchronize with the events in matching years of Amenemhet I and Sesostris I, then I knew that I was on track to discover the entire history of Israel in Egypt during the twelfth dynasty alone.

To compare the two histories I established the precise years when these Biblical events are hypothetically linked to the reigns of Amenemhet I and Sesostris I. If the baker and butler are connected to this coup, they were likely suspected as participants in the plot and were thus placed in prison until their cases could be judged. The baker was found to be an active participant. Thus, his dream of birds eating the bread on his head was fulfilled by his hanging and his flesh being eaten by the birds as reported in Genesis 40:18-22.

The butler was found to be negligent, but not a participant in the coup attempt. Joseph's interpretation of the butler's dream in Genesis 40:9-23 was fulfilled by the butler's release from prison and returning to serve Pharaoh, who was now Sesostris I, co-reigning with his injured father, Amenemhet I.

Joseph had previously requested the butler to speak on Joseph's behalf to the Pharaoh. However, the butler forgot to tell Pharaoh about Joseph for two full years.

At the end of these two years Pharaoh had a dream and could not interpret it. Then the butler remembered Joseph and told Pharaoh about Joseph's ability to interpret dreams (Genesis 40:23-41:1).

This proposed scenario likely explains why Amenemhet I advised his son, Sesostris I, against confiding in a Vizier. If this is the time of Joseph, Amenemhet I's advice to Sesostris I was not to confide in a Vizier because it was the Vizier who planned the attack against Amenemhet I. The treachery of the former Vizier also explains why Sesostris I was reluctant to appoint a Vizier **in the two years after the coup attempt against his father.** On this basis we have several possible synchronisms between the assassination attempt on Amenemhet I's life and the Biblical story of the baker and butler in prison and Joseph's appointment as Vizier two years later.

Amenemhet I was seriously wounded and could not continue to serve actively on the throne. He thus appointed his son, Sesostris I, to serve in his place as co-ruler of Egypt. Sesostris I was very young when he took the throne. A wooden statue of Sesostris I in his first years as king shows him to be a young man in his early twenties. This statue is shown at the end of Chapter 8.

V. SESOSTRIS I'S TEN-YEAR CO-REIGN WITH HIS FATHER, AMENEMHET I

A. The Assassination Attempt on Amenemhet I's Life

Breasted and Petrie both concluded from the documentary evidence that the failed assassination attempt occurred in the twentieth year of Amenemhet I. They also believed that Amenemhet I was not killed, but lived for ten more years in a co-reign with his son Sesostris I. These scholars proposed that the attempted coup was "undoubtedly" the chief motivation for appointing Sesostris I as co-ruler.[34] A. H. Gardiner also argued that Amenemhet I's written explanation of the assassination attempt was given at the beginning of the co-reign.[35]

However, some modern Egyptologists believe the assassination attempt was successful and occurred in Amenemhet I's thirtieth and last year, at the end of the co-regency, rather than the beginning of co-regency.[36] This theory views the instructions of Amenemhet to his son as a fabrication by Sesostris I to justify his assumption of his father's throne.[37] Amenemhet I's instructions to Sesostris are pictured by these scholars as coming from the abode of the dead through a writer appointed by Sesostris I.[38]

B. Did the Assassination Attempt Occur in Amenemhet I's Thirtieth Year?

The theory that Amenemhet I was assassinated in his thirtieth year is based on a misinterpretation of an Egyptian document entitled, *The Story of Sinuhe*. Sinuhe was an official of the royal harem under the reign of Amenemhet I and Sesostris I. He was serving temporarily in the army in a war against Libya under the command of Sesostris I. As they were returning to Egypt, messengers brought word that Amenemhet I died "in Year 30, third month of the first season, Day 7."[39]

Upon hearing the news Sesostris I returned immediately to the palace. Sinuhe decided to flee Egypt and go to Palestine. Sinuhe wrote many years later of his motivation to flee Egypt: **"I believed there would be turmoil,"** he explained, **"and did not expect to survive it."**[40] Some scholars say that Sinuhe knew of the assassination plot, feared that his job and life might be in jeopardy. Some have even suggested that Sinuhe had participated in the plot and feared the outcome. These scholars have concluded that the death of Amenemhet I mentioned in Sinuhe's document resulted from the "coup" recorded in Amenemhet I's letter to Sesostris I. Thus, the coup is interpreted to have occurred at the death of Amenemhet I in his thirtieth year rather than in his twentieth year of reign as former Egyptologists have all concurred.

C. Stronger Evidence that the Coup Occurred in Amenemhet I's Tenth Year

However, another explanation of Sinuhe's flight is just as reasonable and fits better all of the facts of twelfth-dynasty history. Sinuhe said that "he **believed**" there would be turmoil. Thus, in fear for his own survival he fled Egypt. However, as we shall see below, Sinuhe's **"fear"** was unwarranted. After overhearing the whispered conversation between the messengers and Sesostris I about the death of Amenemhet I, Sinuhe may have imagined that a **second** attempt (after the attempt ten years earlier) had been made on the life of Amenemhet I in his thirtieth year and that the assassination this time was successful. Sinuhe thus feared that the traitors would also fight against Sesostris I and his companions when they arrived at the capital. He feared for his life and thus fled Egypt rather than return to the palace.

But Sinuhe's fears were unwarranted. Amenemhet I had merely died from old age, hastened by the wounds he suffered from the attempt on his life ten years earlier. When Sesostris I arrived at the capital, the body guards of his father had every thing under control and no attempt had been made to take over the throne. Sesostris I had already been co-reigning with his father for ten years and had the throne firmly under his grip. Years later, Sinuhe requested permission to return to Egypt. Sesostris I sent back the following response to Sinuhe which confirms the explanation I have just proposed.

> **Lichtheim (Translator):** This decree of the King is brought to you [Sinuhe] to let you know that you circled the foreign countries . . . **[and it] was the counsel of your own heart.** What had you done that one should act against you? You had not cursed, so that your speech would be reproved. You had not spoken against the counsel of the nobles, that your words should have been rejected. . . . It was not in my heart against you. This your heaven in the palace lives and prospers to this day. . . . Come back to Egypt.[41]

Sesostris specifically says that Sinuhe had **imagined "in his own heart"** a danger that did not in reality exist. Sinuhe's fear that he might have been killed if he had returned to the capital was unwarranted. When Sinuhe received the reply from Sesostris, he agreed that he was thinking illogically when he fled Egypt and called himself "a servant whom his heart led astray to alien lands." He attributed his foolish flight to **"a dream."**

Lichtheim (Translator) -- Lo, this flight which the servant made---I did not plan it. It was not in my heart; I did not devise it. I do not know what removed me from my place. **It was like a dream.**[42]

Yet, what Sinuhe considered "a dream" and what Sesostris called "imagination" some modern Egyptologists have assumed to be fact. These scholars believe that the assassination attempt against Amenemhet I occurred in his thirtieth year and that turmoil occurred at the palace both before and after Sesostris I arrived, as Sinuhe had "dreamed." Scholars who believe the assassination was successful in Amenemhet I's thirtieth year contradict Sinuhe and Sesostris I, who both agreed that Sinuhe's flight was based on imagined fears rather than factual reality.

The document concludes by narrating how Sinuhe returned to Egypt, where Sesostris I gave him a position among the nobles of the court, a large house and many riches.[43] If an assassination had really taken place when Amenemhet I died, then all servants who fled, including Sinuhe, would have been chief suspects. Sesostris I's unreserved acceptance and reward of Sinuhe are indicative that Sinuhe had nothing to do with an assassination plot on the basis that Amenemhet I was not assassinated in his thirtieth year, but died of natural causes.

Therefore, the assassination attempt occurred ten years earlier in Amenemhet I's twentieth year. However the attack succeeded only in seriously wounding Sesostris I's father rather than killing him. Amenemhet I died ten years after the assassination attempt, likely from old age, but perhaps also hastened by the severe wounds he received from the attack in his twentieth year of reign. This interpretation of the chronology of the assassination attempt and the co-reign of Sesostris with his father, fits perfectly with the Biblical description of the Pharaoh who made Joseph his Vizier.

Hayes tell us that "Year 5" of Sen-Wosret (Sesostris I) corresponded with "Year 25" of his father and that the two kings co-reigned for ten years.[44] When I visited the Cairo Museum in 1991, I found on a wall that houses twelfth-dynasty statues a framed plaque called "Stela Cairo 205." The English translation of the Stela read, **"Year 10 of Sesostris I = Year 30 of Amenemhet I."** Sinuhe affirmed in his biography that Amenemhet I died in his thirtieth year.[45] **Combining these facts, Sesostris I co-reigned with his father for ten years before his father died in his thirtieth year.** All former Egyptologists that I have read logically accept this **ten-year co-reign as a fact of twelfth-dynasty history.**

D. The Illogical Idea That Sesostris I
Fabricated His Father's Letter

As already mentioned, some modern Egyptologists claim that Sesostris I fabricated the letter from Amenemhet I after his death in the thirtieth year to justify his succession to his father's throne. However, Sesostris I's motive to justify sitting on his father's throne after his death is contradicted by the very letter Sesostris I supposedly fabricated.

Amenemhet I's letter, in two different translations, clearly claims that the attack on his life occurred before Sesostris I began co-reigning with his father.

> Breasted -- Behold the abomination occurred, while I was without thee, while the court had not yet heard that I had delivered to thee (the kingdom), **while I had not yet sat with thee.**[46]

> John A. Wilson -- Behold, bloodshed occurred while I was without thee, before the couriers had heard that I was handing over to thee, **before I had sat together with thee**.[47]

Therefore, Amenemhet I's letter specifically affirms that Sesostris I had not co-reigned with him before the assassination attempt occurred. Since all scholars admit that Sesostris I co-ruled with his father for ten years before Amenemhet I died, Amenemhet I's letter (whether written by Amenemhet I or his son Sesostris I) clearly states that the assassination attempt occurred before the co-rule began, not at the end of the co-reign.

It is illogical that Sesostris I fabricated this letter after his father's death, because he would never have put into his father's mouth that the assassination occurred before the court knew that Amenemhet I had chosen Sesostris I to be king in his place. When Amenemhet I died, the court had known full well that Sesostris I had co-reigned with his father for ten years, making Sesostris I the obvious choice of his father to succeed him when he died.

In fact, we will see in the coming chapters that Sesostris I did act as sole ruler in the place of his wounded father and thus had full control of Egypt during his ten-year co-reign. Sesostris I did not need to fabricate a letter using illogical arguments to support his rightful succession to the throne.

The "forgery theory" of modern scholars makes no logical sense in view of Sesostris I's ten-year co-rule, in which he ruled and gave commands to his officials while his father was seriously wounded and incapacitated for ten years before he died. Sesostris I ascended to the throne immediately when he found his father had been seriously wounded during the coup attempt.

In Amenemhet I's twentieth year, the Egyptians did not know for certain which son the king had chosen to succeed him. In his thirtieth year, everyone knew that Amenemhet I had chosen Sesostris I to be his successor because he had permitted Sesostris I to be his co-ruler for ten years. Therefore, we conclude that the only logical interpretation of Amenemhet I's letter, whether written by himself or by his son, is that the assassination attempt occurred in Amenemhet I's twentieth year, immediately before Sesostris I began the co-reign.

VI. AMENEMHET I'S APPOINTMENT
OF SESOSTRIS I AS CO-RULER

Although Amenemhet I did not die during the attack, he must have been seriously wounded. Ms. Lichtheim's translation indicates that Amenemhet I's own blood was shed.

> Had I quickly seized weapons in my hand, I would have made the cowards retreat in haste. But no one is strong at night; no one can fight alone; no success is achieved without a helper. Thus **bloodshed** occurred while I was without you.[48]

Amenemhet I's wounds obviously disabled him from resuming his kingly duties. If he were conscious, then he immediately appointed his son Sesostris I to act in his place as co-ruler and later wrote the document verifying what he had told Sesostris verbally, that Sesostris was to act in Amenemhet's place as the official heir and co ruler of Egypt.

If Amenemhet I was either unconscious or too disoriented to think coherently, then Sesostris I may have taken the throne on his own initiative. Amenemhet I may have earlier told Sesostris that he was the royal heir, even though he had not yet told his court. Whether Amenemhet I was conscious, or unconscious, after the attack, his writing to Sesostris I clearly says that Sesostris I became co-ruler before Amenemhet I had informed his officials that Sesostris was his choice to succeed him. Thus, when Amenemhet regained his consciousness and ability to dictate a letter, he gave Sesostris a permanent document, explaining the treacherous coup, and officially appointing Sesostris as his crown prince to co-reign with him.

If Sesostris I fabricated this letter, he did so while his father was wounded and unable to think clearly or to write. Even so, when Amenemhet I later recovered from his wounds, he could either confirm or deny the letter, for Sesostris I co-reigned with him for ten years before he died. Obviously, Amenemhet I agreed with the letter's contents whether he personally wrote it or not. Therefore, we should accept the contents of Amenemhet I's letter as true and factual.

Since Amenemhet I survived the attack and lived on for ten years, we should assume that he expressed his complete approval that Sesostris I co-rule with him. Amenemhet I certainly did not want anyone to think that his son was ruling on the throne without his approval. While still recovering from his serious wounds, he did not know whether he would live or die. Thus, he gave Sesostris I full authority to act as king in his place. Notice below Amenemhet's own words to Sesostris I.

Lichtheim's Translation -- As my feet depart, you are in my heart, My eyes behold you, child of a happy hour, before the people as they hail you. I have made the past and arranged the future. I gave you the contents of my heart. You wear the white crown of a god's son. The seal is in its place, assigned you by me. Jubilation is in the bark of Re. Kingship is again what it was in the past! [lacuna] Raise your monuments, establish your strongholds, fight [lacuna].[49]

The above words possibly imply that Amenemhet expected to die soon, because he urged Sesostris I to carry on the duties of the kingship and to erect monuments in his own honor, as if Amenemhet would no longer be around to do these things himself. As it turned out, Amenemhet lived for ten more years, longer than he, Sesostris I, or others had anticipated.

However, Amenemhet must have either retired or remained seriously disabled for most, if not all, of Sesostris' ten-year co-reign. An inscription dated in Sesostris I's third year of co-reign supports the conclusion that Sesostris I took total control of the throne while his wounded father was still alive.

Breasted's Translation -- Year 3, third month of the first season, day [?], under the majesty of the King of Upper and Lower Egypt, Kheperkere, Son of Re, Sesostris I, triumphant, living forever and ever. . . . He [the god Harakhte] appointed me shepherd of this land. . . . I am a king of his character. . . . He appointed me lord of mankind in the presence of the people.[50]

Notice in Breasted's citation above that Sesostris I is proclaimed to be King of all of Egypt in his third year even though his father was still alive in Sesostris I's tenth year. This document does not even mention the name of Amenemhet I, likely because he was too disabled to attend this ceremony.

In this same inscription Sesostris I ordered the Vizier of Egypt by the majestic authority of his own name (not Amenemhet's name) to build a temple and a monument in honor of himself.

Breasted -- **The king himself said,** "To the wearer of the royal seal, the sole companion, the overseer of the double White House, ... It is thy counsel, which shall cause the work to be done. Of which **my majesty desires,** that it should be. . . . I have commanded those who work, to do according as thou shalt exact.[51]

When the temple was later inaugurated, Sesostris I appeared at the ceremony "crowned with the diadem" and "all the people following him" as if he were the only king of Egypt.[52] These declarations of Sesostris I in his third year of co-reign prove that he was directly ruling Egypt as if the only king, even though his father continued to live until his tenth year of co-reign. In exerting this authority of sole king, Sesostris I was doing precisely what his father commanded him to do in the letter he wrote: "You wear the white crown of a god's son. . . . Kingship is again what it was in the past. Raise your monuments."[53] We conclude, therefore, that the assassination attempt was the event that thrust Sesostris I into the co-regency and that the co-rule began simultaneously in the week and year when the assassination attempt occurred.

VII. LINKING JOSEPH'S VIZIERSHIP TO THE SECOND YEAR OF SESOSTRIS I'S CO-REIGN

My hypothetical proposal identifies Sesostris I as the Pharaoh who appointed Joseph to be his prime minister. This hypothesis requires us to specify the year of Sesostris I's reign when Joseph became Vizier and when the seven years of abundance and seven years of famine occurred during Sesostris I's reign. This same chronology should determine when Jacob and his family arrived in Egypt during Sesostris I's reign. This hypothetical synchronism between Biblical and twelfth-dynasty histories can then be tested for compatibility.

Hayes' detailed study of twelfth-dynasty chronology led him to the conclusion that twelfth-dynasty kings used the accession year method of calculating the duration of their reigns. The system of accession year dating considered the year of the father's death and the son's accession to the throne as Year 0. Year 1 of the successor began on the first New Year's Day after the father's death.[54] On this basis Sesostris I's accession year (Year 0) began in Amenemhet I's twentieth year, when the assassination attempt occurred. Year 1 of Sesostris I began in Amenemhet I's twenty-first year, and thus Sesostris' Year 10 occurred in Amenemhet I's thirtieth year. See Table 7-A at the end of the chapter to visualize this co-reign as we compare it to Biblical chronology.

Amenemhet I was too disabled to function as king after the assassination attempt. Thus, his son Sesostris I actively ruled Egypt by himself in his accession year even though his father was still alive. Thus, our hypothetical connection of Biblical history to Egyptian history proposes that Sesostris I is the Pharaoh who freed the butler and executed the baker in the year of his accession to the throne, which was the twentieth year of Amenemhet I's reign, when he was seriously wounded and unable to function as king. Since Genesis 41:1 says that Joseph was appointed Vizier **two years** after the baker was executed and the butler was restored, this pinpoints Sesostris I's second full year and Amenemhet I's twenty-second year as the year of Joseph's appointment as Sesostris I's Vizier. In Chapter Eight we will test this hypothesis to see if the Vizier of Sesostris I fits the Biblical description of Joseph's Viziership.

The Bible says that the seven years of abundance began the same year that Joseph was appointed Vizier of Egypt.[55] On the same basis, the seven years of abundance began also in Sesostris I's second year of his co-reign and continued through his eighth year, followed by the seven years of famine in years nine through fifteen of his reign. The Bible also tells us that Jacob came to Egypt at the beginning of the third year of famine (after two full years of famine had already occurred),[56] which I have assigned to Sesostris I's eleventh year of reign.

These hypothetical connections enable us to test this proposed synchronism later to see if grain was stored during years two to eight of Sesostris I during the seven years of abundance . We can then observe if the stored grain was sold for all of the money, livestock and land of Egypt (except the priests' land) in years nine to fifteen of Sesostris I during the seven years of famine. We will test this hypothesis in Chapters Ten and Eleven and we will find that Sesostris I passes the test.

VIII. LINKING BIBLICAL YEARS TO SESOSTRIS I'S REIGN

Our new Bible chronology dates Joseph's appointment as Vizier of Egypt at the age of thirty in 1665 B.C. See this chronology in Table 7-A at the end of the chapter. On this basis the assassination attempt and imprisonment of the baker and butler occurred two years earlier in 1667 B.C., as specified in Genesis 41:1. I thus hypothetically connected the Biblical year of 1667 B.C. to the twentieth year of Amenemhet I, which is also the accession year of Sesostris I, when the assassination attempt took place. Since Joseph was appointed Vizier two years later in 1665 B.C., this appointment would occur in Amenemhet I's twenty-second year and Sesostris I's second year: see Table 7-A. I also note in Table 7-A the dates of the 1971 edition of the *Cambridge Ancient History* and the differing dates of the 1991 edition of the *New Encyclopaedia Britannica.* If Egyptologists agree that the synchronism is valid (after reading the entire book), but insist the Egyptian dates are correct, they have the option of expanding Biblical history to agree with one of their **differing** "astronomical chronologies." For those who believe the Biblical dates are correct, Egyptian history should be reduced to fit the Biblical dates. Chapters Twenty-Three to Twenty-Four present scientific evidences that confirm the Biblical dates, not the Egyptian dates.   I note below some of the examples of carbon-14 dating.

IX. CARBON-14 CONFIRMATION OF 1667 B.C.
AS SESOSTRIS I'S ACCESSION YEAR

The "astronomical date" of the *Cambridge Ancient History* for Sesostris I's accession year is 1972 B.C. and the "astronomical date" of the *New Encyclopaedia Britannica* for his accession is 1918 B.C., a difference of 64 years, proving that the astronomical dates are certainly not "fixed" or "absolute." Uncalibrated carbon-14 dates generally have a + or - range of forty years on each side of the middle date.

Interestingly, the uncalibrated carbon-14 dating of wood from the tomb of Nebhepetre Mentuhotep II, a Pharaoh of the eleventh dynasty, averages 1700 B.C.[57] Mentuhotep II died about forty years before Sesostris I reigned.[58]   Therefore, Sesostris I's accession year has a carbon-14-related date of 1660 B.C. (1700 -40 = 1660). 1660 B.C. is only seven years later than my 1667 B.C. Biblical date, but

312 years later than Hayes' *Cambridge* date and 258 years later than Baines' date in the *New Encyclopaedia Britannica*.

Burned wood from the Buhen fortress, constructed by Sesostris I on the southern border of Egypt, has been carbon-14 dated (uncalibrated) at 1680 B.C.,[59] only thirteen years before my date for Sesostris I's **accession year, but 238 to 291 years later than the scholars' dates.** Cedar wood from Wadi Gawasi linked to Sesostris I's reign has an uncalibrated carbon-14 date of 1605 B.C. (3555 B.P. - A. D. 1950 = 1605 B.C.).[60] B.P. means "**B**efore **P**resent," which means **before A.D. 1950,** when Libby discovered carbon-14 dating. **My Biblical date for Sesostris I's death is 1621 B.C., only sixteen years earlier than the carbon-14 date. Hayes' date for Sesostris I's death is 1928 B.C., 323 years earlier than the carbon-14 date, and Baines' date is 1875 B.C., 270 years earlier than the carbon-14 date.** See Table 7-A. Therefore, the uncalibrated carbon-14 dates strongly sustain our Biblically-designated date of 1667 B.C. for the year when Sesostris I began his co-reign, the same year that the Biblical butler was released from prison.

However, knowing that the uncalibrated carbon-14 dates of Egyptian dynasties contradict the "astronomical Sothic dates" by about three centuries, scientists now calibrate the carbon-14 dates by tree rings in an attempt to approximate their "astronomical Sothic dates". Chapters Twenty-One to Twenty-Four disprove the Sothic dates, support the uncalibrated carbon-14 dates, and confirm the Biblical dates by a recently discovered eclipse of the sun. These new scientific discoveries revise the Egyptian dynasties by three centuries and confirm the Biblical dates from Joseph to the Exodus, creating remarkable synchronism between Egyptian and Biblical histories. Volume II continues this amazing historical and scientific synchronism from the Exodus and beyond to Kings Saul, David and Solomon.

CONCLUSION

Joseph's slavery in Potiphar's household and his unjust imprisonment both fit the culture of the twelfth dynasty. Joseph's encounter with the baker and butler in prison and the subsequent hanging of the baker as capital punishment coincide with the attempt of Amenemhet I's servants to assassinate him. The vacancy of the office of Vizier when Joseph was appointed two years after the butler's release fits the hypothesis that the Vizier of Amenemhet I participated in the attempted coup and was executed for his crime. The missing tomb of Khenty-bau, the Vizier of Amenemhet I, suggests that he died in dishonor, and was likely the man who led the plot to kill the king. Amenemhet's instructions to his son Sesostris that he not trust in friends or confidants, such as a Vizier, explains why no Vizier was appointed during the two years following the release of the butler. **Table 7-B at the end of the chapter summarizes twenty-one historical links between Joseph and the twelfth-dynasty history of Pharaohs Amenemhet I and Sesostris I.**

I hypothetically linked Amenemhet I's twentieth year (when the coup occurred) to Joseph's prison encounter with the baker and butler in 1667 B.C. Thus, Joseph's appointment as Vizier of Egypt fits the second year of Sesostris I's co-reign in 1665 B.C. Uncalibrated carbon-14 dates of Sesostris I's reign agree with the Biblical dates instead of Egyptologists' dates, which are three centuries earlier. These historical and scientific links may appear as insignificant coincidence and stretched imagination. However, in the remaining chapters we will put to the test this hypothetical synchronism and find **a total of 436 points of remarkable discoveries** that link Babylonian, Elamite and twelfth-dynasty histories to Biblical history in precise chronological order from Abraham to Joseph to Moses to the Exodus. These synchronisms increase in abundance and significance with each succeeding chapter. See these growing discoveries in Table 7-B. Table 7-C pictures the growing number of synchronisms that continue to increase chapter by chapter.

TABLE 7-A
BIBLICAL CHRONOLOGY OF JOSEPH'S EARLY LIFE
IN THE TWELFTH DYNASTY

Years are approximate with a four-year margin of error on each side of these dates.

		Cambr. Date	Britan. Date	Biblical Date	Biblical Event
AMENEMHET I					
Accession		1991	1938	1688	
10		1980	1928	1678	Joseph sold into slavery at 17
18					
SESOSTRIS I		1972	1920	1670?	Joseph in Prison
20	00	1970	1918	1667	Vizier, baker killed; butler released
21	02	1968	1916	1665	Joseph released from Prison

Differing Egyptologists calculate the total reign of the Twelfth Dynasty from **182 to 235 years** from 1994 B.C. to 1759 B.C.[61] See Appendix C which discusses in depth the length of Twelfth-Dynasty chronology.

TABLE 7-B
TWENTY-ONE DISCOVERIES RELATED TO JOSEPH'S
MEETING AMENEMHET I'S BAKER AND
BUTLER IN PRISON

Discovery 1. Joseph as a slave from Canaan, purchased by an Egyptian official was a normal practice in twelfth-dynasty culture.

Discovery 2. Joseph, as a slave and supervisor of Potiphar's household, existed in the twelfth dynasty.

Discovery 3. Potiphar's position as captain of the body guard was an important position of leadership among twelfth-dynasty officials.

Discovery 4. Joseph's temptation to commit adultery with Potiphar's wife is imitated in a later nineteenth-dynasty Egyptian story.

Discovery 5. Twelfth-dynasty prisons were organized precisely in the manner of Joseph's prison.

Discovery 6. The punishment of confinement, hard labor and death also characterized twelfth-dynasty prisons and justice systems.

Discovery 7. The assassination attempt against Amenemhet I by palace servants provides the occasion for Joseph's meeting the baker and butler in prison.

Discoveries 8 and 9. Amenemhet I's report that the assassination attempt occurred because of the **"failing of the servants,"** resulting in the baker's hanging, implying his guilt in the conspiracy to kill Amenemhet I. The butler proved to be innocent and was later released.

Discovery 10. The body guard turned against Amenemhet I instead of protecting him, implying that Potiphar, the former slave master of Joseph, may have engaged in the military coup against Amenemhet I's life.

Discovery 11. The assassination attempt seriously wounded Amenemhet I, requiring that his young, inexperienced son, Sesostris I, reign in his place.

Discovery 12. The assassination attempt occurred in Amenemhet I's twentieth year, thus connecting this event to the Biblical date of 1667 B.C. when the baker was hanged.

Discovery 13. The same date of 1667 B.C. marks the accession year of Sesostris I.

Discovery 14. Amenemhet's wounded condition and letter to Sesostris I gave him full authority to reign as if the only king.

Discovery 15. Sesostris I killed the perpetrators of the coup and imprisoned participants that likely included the baker and butler ("the failing of the servants").

Discovery 16. If the Vizier led in the coup, he was immediately killed, leaving this office vacant for Joseph to fill two years later under Sesostris I.

Discovery 17. The office of Vizier was the most important office in the twelfth dynasty next only to the Pharaoh himself.

Discovery 18. Khenty-bau was the Vizier of Amenemhet I, but his tomb is missing among other lesser officials of Amenemhet I who are buried in the pyramid complex of the Pharaoh, indicating that the Vizier died in disgrace, likely as a participant in the coup, opening the office to Joseph.

Discovery 19. The Vizier was called the "favorite companion and friend of the king," but Amenemhet I instructed Sesostris I not to confide in friends or officials, explaining why Sesostris I waited two years before appointing a Vizier.

Discovery 20. Sesostris I's youth and inexperience explained his need to have a wise Vizier like Joseph.

Discovery 21. Uncalibrated carbon-14 dates of the eleventh-dynasty king Mentuhotep II and the carbon-14 dates of Sesostris I's own reign vary only 8 to 17 years from the Biblical dates I assigned to their reigns, but they differ by 238 to 323 years from scholars' dates.

TABLE 7-C
RUNNING TOTAL OF DISCOVERIES

Chapter		Chapter Total	Running Total
2	Conflict Between Biblical and Secular Histories...............	18	18
4	Discovery of 430 Years from Abraham To the Exodus	16	34
5	Confirmation of Abraham's Historicity.....................	28	62
6	Discovery of the Remains of Sodom and Gomorrah..............	17	79
7	Joseph As a Slave and Prisoner in the Reign of Amenemhet I.....	21	100

NOTES TO CHAPTER SEVEN

1. Genesis 37:3-11.
2. Genesis 37:12-36; 39:1.
3. Genesis 39:1-6.
4. Genesis 39:6-20.
5. Genesis 39:21-23.
6. Genesis 40:1-23.

7. Genesis 41:1-32.
8. Genesis 41:33-46.

9. J. R. Baines and E. F. Wente, "Egypt," *New Encyclopaedia Britannica*. 1991 Ed., 18.109-121.

10. William C. Hayes, *The Scepter of Egypt*, II, Metropolitan Museum of Art, N.Y., 498.

11. Charles F. Aling, *Egypt and Bible History*, Baker Book House, pp.30-31, citing the *Brooklyn Papyrus* 35:1446; William C. Hayes, *Papyrus*, 87, 92 ff; 133-134.

12. Aling, pp. 34-35, citing Helck, *Beziehungen*, 77, n.2, 78 and Hayes, *Papyrus*, 103.

13. Aling, . p. 37, citing Hayes, *Papyrus*, 37-42.
14. Genesis 39:20-40:22.

15. Miriam Lichtheim, *Ancient Egyptian Literature*, II.203-206, Univ. Calif. Press.

16. William C. Hayes, "Middle Kingdom in Egypt," *Cambridge Ancient History*, I.2A.493-496.
17. Hayes, I.2A.493-496.
18. Breasted, *History of Egypt*, Scribners 1937.157.
19. Baines & Malek, *Atlas of Ancient Egypt* , Facts on File, N.Y., 133.
20. M. Lichtheim, *Ancient Egyptian Literature*, Univ. of Calif. Press, I.136-137.
21. Genesis 40:1.
22. Genesis 39:1.
23. Breasted, Trans., *Ancient Records of Egypt*, I.306 (687).
24. Genesis 41:1.
25. W. S. Smith, "Old Kingdom in Egypt," *Camb. A.. Hist.,*I.2A.159-160,166,187.
26. William C. Hayes, "The Middle Kingdom In Egypt," *Cambridge Ancient History*, I.2A.493.
27. M. Lichtheim, *Ancient Egyptian Literature*, Univ. Calif. Press. I.136.
28. Breasted (Trans.), "Inscriptions of Mentuhotep," *Ancient Records of Egypt*, I.256 (no.531).
29. Wm. Hayes, *Scepter of Egypt*, I.176-177.
30. Hayes, *Scepter of Egypt*, I.176-177.
31. Hayes, *Scepter of Egypt*, I.176-177.
32. Hayes, *Scepter of Egypt*, I.176-177.
33. E. A. Wallis Budge, *An Egyptian Hieroplyphic Dictionary*, Dover Pub., N. Y., II.848.
34. Breasted, *Ancient Records of Egypt*, I.229; Petrie, *A History of Egypt*, I.138.
35. A. H. Gardner, quoted by J. Pritchard, Introduction to "The Instruction of Amen-em-het," translated by John A. Wilson, *Ancient Near Eastern Texts*, 418.

CHAPTER SEVEN – JOSEPH AS A SLAVE AND PRISONER
IN THE REIGN OF AMENEMHET I

36. William C. Hayes, *Scepter of Egypt*, Metropolitan Museum, I.179.
37. William C. Hayes, "The Middle Kingdom in Egypt," *Cambridge Ancient History*, I.2A. 498.
38. John A. Wilson (Trans.), "The Instruction of Amen-emhet," *Ancient Near Eastern Texts*, p. 418.
39. John A. Wilson (Trans.), "The Story of Sinuhe," *Ancient Near Eastern Texts*, p.18
    and James Breasted, "Year 30, second month of first season," *Ancient Records of Egypt*, I.I.235.
40. M. Lichtheim (Translator), "Story of Sinuhe," *Ancient Egyptian Literature*, I.224.
41. Lichtheim, *Ancient Egyptian Literature*, I.229.
42. Lichtheim, *Ancient Egyptian Literature*, I.230-231.
43. Lichtheim, *Ancient Egyptian Literature*, I.232-233.
44. W. C. Hayes, *Scepter of Egypt*, 5th Ed. I.172.
45. Lichtheim (Trans.), *Ancient Egyptian Literature*, "Story of Sinuhe,"
46. James Breasted (Trans.), *Ancient Records of Egypt*, I.231-232.
47. John A. Wilson (Trans.), *Ancient Near Eastern Texts*, 419.
48. Lichtheim (Trans.), *Ancient Egyptian Literature*, I.137.
49. Lichtheim (Trans.), *Ancient Egyptian Literature*, I.138.
50. Breasted (Trans.), *Ancient Records of Egypt*, I.242-243.
51. Breasted, (Trans.), *Ancient Records of Egypt*, I.245 (no. 505).
52. Breasted, (Trans.), *Ancient Records of Egypt*, I.245 (nos. 504, 506).
53. Breasted, (Trans.), *Ancient Records of Egypt*, I.245 (no. 504,506)..
54. William C. Hayes, "Chronology of Egypt to the Twentieth Dynasty," *Cambridge Ancient History*, I.1.182-183.
55. Genesis 41:32.
56. Genesis 45:6.
57. T. Save-Soderbergh and I. U. Olsson, "C14 Dating and Egyptian Chronology," *Radiocarbon Variations and Absolute Chronology*, (New York: John Wiley & Sons, 1970), pp. 43-45.
58. "Chronological Tables of the Middle Kingdom," *Cambridge Ancient History*, I.2B.996.
59. Prof. Emery, excavator, cited by T. Save-Soderberg and I. U. Olsson, "C-14 and Egyptian Chronology," *Radiocarbon Variations and Absolute Chronology*, p. 44.
60. Ian Shaw, "Egyptian Chronology & the Irish Oak Calibration," *Journal of Near Eastern Studies*, Oct., 2985, 44.4.311.

CHAPTER EIGHT
JOSEPH BECOMES THE VIZIER
OF SESOSTRIS I

Officials and palace servants attacked Amenemhet I in an effort to take over his throne. His son, Sesostris, was out of town with the army when the attack occurred. After receiving the news from a palace messenger, Sesostris returned with the army, executed the rebels and sat on the throne in the place of his wounded father. We saw in the previous chapter that the rebels included household servants. These servants likely included Amenemhet I's baker and butler.

The Bible says that Joseph became Vizier of Egypt **"two years"** after the baker was hanged and the butler was released from prison.[1] If we are correct in the proposed historical links of the previous chapter, Sesostris I is the Pharaoh who appointed Joseph as Vizier (prime minister) during his second year of co-reign. In this chapter we will show that the Biblical description of Joseph's Viziership uniquely matches the Viziership under Sesostris I. See a photo of a statue of young Pharaoh Sesostris I Figure 8-A.

I. SESOSTRIS I'S INSTRUCTIONS TO HIS FIRST VIZIER

Hayes tell us that Sesostris I had several Viziers during his forty-five-year reign.[2] In Sesostris I's **third year of reign** a scribe recorded the king's orders to his **first, unnamed** Vizier, who oversaw the treasuries and income from both Upper and Lower Egypt (the two diadems).

Lichtheim's Translation -- "The king spoke to the royal seal-bearer, sole companion, overseer of the two gold-houses and the two silver-houses and privy-councillor of the two diadems."[3]

Figure 8-A
Young Sesostris I
Permission Granted to Ted Stewart
By Metropolitan Museum of Art.
Rogers Fund supplemented by the
Contribution of Edward S. Harkness.

When we visited Cairo in 1991 we found the monument upon which this inscription was recorded. **The monument was located in a park not far from the Cairo Museum.** I recognized the monument by photos I had seen in different books. **Notice below that the words Sesostris I used to address his Vizier and describe his responsibilities, reflecting uniquely the Biblical record of Pharaoh's instructions to Joseph as his new Vizier.**

A. "The Royal Seal Bearer"

In the inscription cited above Sesostris I called his Vizier **"the royal seal-bearer."** The Pharaoh who appointed Joseph to be his Vizier gave him a "signet ring" to identify Joseph as his personal representative: "Then Pharaoh took his **signet ring** from his finger and put it on Joseph's finger" (Genesis 41:42). **Thus, Joseph bore a ring with Pharaoh's cartouche inscribed on it, identifying him as the "royal seal-bearer"** just like the ring Sesostris I's Vizier wore.

B. "Sole Companion and Privy Councillor"

Sesostris I also called his Vizier **"Sole Companion"** and **"Privy Councillor."** Many officials who were not Viziers during Sesostris I's reign, also called themselves "sole companions" and "councillors." These officials served as special advisers concerning limited aspects of Sesostris I's kingdom.[4] However, the principal Vizier of Sesostris I was his "sole companion" and "Privy-Councillor" in the closest and most complete sense, for he consulted the king on a daily basis concerning the affairs of the whole kingdom.[5] Did Joseph's responsibilities make him the "Sole Companion" and "Privy Councillor" of the King? Notice what the Bible says.

> Genesis 41:40-43 -- (40) You shall be in charge of my palace, and all my people are to submit to your orders. Only with respect to the throne will I be greater than you." (41) . . . I hereby put you in charge of the whole land of Egypt." (42) Then Pharaoh took his signet ring from his finger and put it on Joseph's finger. He dressed him in robes of fine linen and put a gold chain around his neck. (43) He had him ride in a chariot as his second-in-command, and men shouted before him, "Make way !" **Thus he put him in charge of the whole land of Egypt.** NIV

Therefore, Joseph was obviously the closest companion and adviser to the king, supervising the very palace of Pharaoh. He was, therefore, the most important official with the greatest responsibility and closest relationship to the king, in the same manner as the Vizier of Sesostris I.

C. "Overseer of the Two Gold-houses and the Two Silver-houses"

Sesostris I specifically stated that his Vizier supervised the **"Two Gold Houses and the Two Silver Houses."** Breasted explains the meaning of these houses.

> The central office of the treasury was still the "White House," which through its sub-departments of the granary, the herds, the "double gold-house," the "double silver-house," and other produce of the country, were collected into the central magazines and stock-yards the annual revenues due the Pharaoh.[6]

Since Sesostris I's Vizier was "overseer" of these houses, he was in charge of the total treasury of Sesostris I. Was Joseph in charge of the treasury and property of Pharaoh when he was Vizier of Egypt? Notice what the Bible says below.

> Genesis 47:14 -- Joseph collected **all the money** that was to be found in Egypt and Canaan in payment for the grain they were buying, and **he brought it to Pharaoh's palace.** NIV

Joseph collected "all the money" of both Egypt and Canaan; therefore, he was in charge of the collection of **all the revenue of Pharaoh**. Notice that he brought the money he collected "to Pharaoh's palace." However, the Bible tells us that Pharaoh had also put Joseph in charge of his palace.

> Genesis 41:40 - "You shall be **in charge of my palace**, and all my people are to submit to your orders. Only with respect to the throne will I be greater than you." NIV

Since Joseph was in charge of collecting the money and also in charge of the "palace," then he was also in charge of the treasury when he took the money to the palace. Therefore, Joseph supervised the "Double Gold House" and "the Double Silver House" in the same manner that the Vizier of Sesostris I did.

D. Counselor of the Two Diadems

Sesostris I also called his Vizier the "privy-councillor of the two diadems." Notice below that "Privy-Counselor of the **Two Diadems**" means to give counsel regarding the Diadem (Crown or Rule) of Lower Egypt in the North and the Diadem of Upper Egypt in the South.

> The king spoke to the royal seal-bearer, sole companion, overseer of the two gold-houses and the two silver-houses, and **privy-councillor of the two diadems**: It is your counsel that carries out all the works that my majesty desires to bring about. You are the one who is in charge of them, who will act according to my wish. Order the workmen to do according to your design.[7]

Egypt was divided into two geographical areas (Upper and Lower Egypt). At different times in Egypt's history two or more Pharaohs ruled over these areas simultaneously. At the end of the eleventh dynasty foreigners had entered northern Egypt and controlled the Delta of Lower Egypt. During this time Amenemhet I was the Vizier of Mentuhotep III, the last Pharaoh of the eleventh dynasty, who reigned in his capital in Thebes in Upper (Southern) Egypt. Amenemhet I led Egypt's army to victory over the foreigners in Lower Egypt (Northern Egypt) and declared himself to be Pharaoh of all of Egypt, usurping the authority of Pharaoh Mentuhotep II. Thus, Amenemhet I began a new family of kings, which became Egypt's twelfth dynasty.

Amenemhet I built his new capital in northern Egypt and called it Itjtowy, which means, "Seizer of the Two Lands."[8] A prophecy attributed to the sage Nefer-rehu of the time of King Snefru of the fourth dynasty supposedly predicted Amenemhet I's conquest of the foreigners from the east and west, **thus reuniting both lower and upper Egypt into one kingdom.**

> **Hayes' Translation** -- A king shall come from the south, called Amuny, the son of a woman of Nubia, and born in Upper Egypt. , , , The Asiatics shall fall before his carnage, and the Libyans shall fall before his flame. . . . There shall be built the "Wall of the Prince," and the Asiatics shall not (again) be suffered to go down to Egypt.[9]

Thus, when Sesostris I sat on the throne in the place of his wounded father, he too was **Pharaoh of the entirety of both Lower and Upper Egypt.**

Some of Sesostris I's counselors advised only in regard to a particular nome (state or principality); some advised only in regard to Upper Egypt (South) ; others only in regard to Lower Egypt (North). But Sesostris I's statement to his Vizier that he was to be his private counselor for "the two diadems," means that Sesostris I's Vizier advised the king on matters concerning all of Egypt, both north and south.

The Bible also says that Joseph supervised and advised Pharaoh concerning matters in the entirety of all Egypt, not a part of Egypt.

> Genesis 41:40, 43 -- (40) You shall be in charge of my palace, and all my people are to submit to your orders. **Only with respect to the throne will I be greater than you.** . . . (43) He had him ride in a chariot as his second-in-command, and men shouted before him, "Make way!" **Thus he put him in charge of the whole land of Egypt.** NIV

We can thus conclude that the responsibility that Pharaoh gave Joseph to be in charge of all of Egypt is the same responsibility that Sesostris I gave his unnamed Vizier.

E. "Order the Workmen According to Your Design"

Sesostris I specifically delegated authority to his Vizier to execute all of Sesostris I's works and plans and to direct all of Sesostris I's workmen according to the Vizier's own will and desire.

> **Lichtheim's Translation** -- The king spoke **to the royal seal-bearer, sole companion, overseer of the two gold-houses and the two silver-houses, and privy-councillor (*sic*) of the two diadems**: It is your counsel that carries out all the works that my majesty desires to bring about. You are the one who is in charge of them, who will act according to my wish. **Order the workmen to do according to your design.**[10]

The Pharaoh of the Bible gave Joseph this same authority over the works and workmen of Egypt that Sesostris I gave to his unnamed Vizier.

> Genesis 41 -- (40) You shall be in charge of my palace, and **all my people are to submit to your orders**. Only with respect to the throne will I be greater than you. . . ." (41) So Pharaoh said to Joseph," **I hereby put you in charge of the whole land of Egypt."** . . . (43) He had him ride in a chariot as his second-in-command, and men shouted before him, "Make way !" **Thus he put him in charge of the whole land of Egypt.** (44) Then Pharaoh said to Joseph, **"I am Pharaoh, but without your word no one will lift hand or foot in all Egypt."** . . . (55) When **all Egypt** began to feel the famine, the people cried to Pharaoh for food. Then Pharaoh told all the Egyptians, **"Go to Joseph and do what he tells you."**

Thus, the Bible says Joseph ordered all officials and workmen in Egypt in the same manner as Sesostris I authorized his first Vizier to do. Table 8-A at the end of this chapter sums up the five characteristics that unite Joseph to the Viziership of Sesostris I.

II. COMPARING THE VIZIERSHIP OF JOSEPH WITH THE VIZIERSHIP OF MENTUHOTEP

Hayes tells us that "several Viziers" held office under Sesostris I, but only two are known by name: Amuny and Montu-hotpe (Mentuhotep).[11] However, Amuny was Vizier of the Pyramid City, which Hayes assumed was Itjtowy, the capital of Egypt. In Chapter Sixteen we will see proof that Itjtowy was located in the northeastern delta, **not** at El Lisht in the Faiyum, south of Memphis.

El Lisht only supervised and protected the cemetery and pyramids of the twelfth dynasty. Thus, Amuny did not qualify to be the Vizier of all of Egypt, but only of the small region surrounding El Lisht, which had a different name from the capital city of Itjtowy, where the king had his palace and where his principal officials lived.

The term "Vizier" could be used in a limited sense in regard to a particular place (as a mayor), or a general area (such as a governor) or in an unlimited sense when it referred to the Vizier of all of Egypt who lived in the Palace or nearby in the same city (Itjtowy) with the King.

Mentuhotep indeed became the Vizier of all of Egypt in the latter reign of Sesostris I. **Before becoming Vizier, Mentuhotep was the Commander of the Egyptian army in Sesostris I's eighteenth year.**[12] Therefore, Mentuhotep could not have been the Vizier of Sesostris I in years three to eighteen, when Joseph was appointed Vizier. I identify Joseph as the first Vizier of Sesostris I.

Thus, Mentuhotep likely was appointed to office after Joseph retired in the latter half of Sesostris I's long forty-six-year reign. Mentuhotep inscribed in his tomb a description of his authority and responsibilities as Vizier.[13] If Mentuhotep succeeded Joseph to the same office of Vizier, then the description of Mentuhotep's Viziership should match the Biblical description of Joseph's Viziership. In fact, the description of Mentuhotep's Viziership is so remarkably identical to that of Joseph that Donovan Courville mistakenly concluded that Mentuhotep was Joseph.[14] However, Mentuhotep had a number of characteristics that nullify the possibility of his being Joseph.

A. Differences Between Joseph and Mentuhotep

(1) First of all, there is the difference in their names. The name Mentuhotep has no relation to the name Joseph or to his Egyptian name, Zaphenath-Paneah. The meaning of Mentuhotep in the Egyptian language also has no relation to the Hebrew meaning of Zaphenath-Paneah or of Joseph. "Mentu" is the hieroglyphic "Menthu," the name of "an ancient war-god of Hermonthis near Thebes in southern Egypt,"[15] "Hotep" from the Hieroglyphic "hetep" means "peace" and "joy."[16] Thus, Mentuhotep means, "the war god who made peace." We will discuss Joseph's Egyptian name in the next chapter and see how different it is from that of Mentuhotep.

(2) Mentuhotep was a "hereditary prince."[17] The title "prince" was reserved for a "nomarch" (governor) of Egypt who ruled a particular "nome" or "state" or "province" of Egypt. To be a "hereditary prince" it was necessary to inherit this office from one's father, who was also the former governor of that province.[18] Thus, before Mentuhotep had been appointed Vizier, he was a governor of some province of Egypt, having inherited this position through his father. Joseph was not a governor of Egypt before being appointed Vizier. Neither could he have inherited this office from his father since Jacob was a shepherd from Canaan, not a noble Egyptian. Thus, Joseph was not a "hereditary prince," and, therefore, could not have been Mentuhotep.

(3) Mentuhotep was a confessed "prophet of Mat [goddess of Truth]" and "prophet of Horus," two different Egyptian gods.[19] Joseph was a prophet of the one true God, the God of Abraham, Isaac, and Jacob. It is inconceivable that Joseph would have called himself the prophet of two different Egyptian gods.

(4) Mentuhotep arrogantly bragged about himself. Breasted notes that the account which Mentuhotep gave of himself on his tomb-stone "read like the declaration of a king's powers."[20] In Mentuhotep's later life he was discredited by Sesostris I or his successor, who defaced some of his monuments.[21] Breasted believes Mentuhotep's self-exaltation may be the cause of his ultimate disgrace.

> Mentuhotep, Sesostris I's commander . . . made himself so prominent upon the triumphal monuments of the king that his figure had to be erased, and in all likelihood the noble himself was dismissed in disgrace. Discreet conduct toward the Pharaoh was the condition of a career, and the wise praise of him who knows how to be silent in the king's service.[22]

In the Biblical account Joseph rarely spoke of himself. When he did speak, he gave God the credit rather than glorifying himself.[23] However, Pharaoh praised Joseph in the same terms that Mentuhotep praised himself.[24] The difference in attitude is striking. Solomon said, "Let another praise you and not your own mouth; someone else, and not your own lips."[25] Joseph's humble attitude stands in sharp contrast to the arrogance of Mentuhotep.

B. Conclusion of the Differences Between
Joseph and Mentuhotep I

Because of these **four significant differences** between Joseph and Mentuhotep, I conclude they were not the same person. Rather, I propose that Joseph was Sesostris I's first Vizier for about twenty to thirty years. When Joseph retired, Mentuhotep, the former general of Egypt, followed him as Vizier. Perhaps Mentuhotep was chosen to replace Joseph because of his expertise as a military commander and because of Egypt's need for military protection. Regardless, Mentuhotep proved to be too arrogant, and thus fell from grace and was replaced by another Vizier. Several Viziers may have served Sesostris I during his long reign of forty-six years. Possibly, Sesostris I called Joseph out of retirement to resume his duties as Vizier in place of the proud Mentuhotep.

III. MENTUHOTEP'S POWERS WERE
LIKE THAT OF THE KING

If Mentuhotep served as Vizier of Sesostris I in the same office that Joseph occupied, then the responsibilities and authority of Mentuhotep's Viziership should be the same as Joseph's. Breasted mentions Mentuhotep and the extraordinary power that was given to him by Sesostris I.

> **The office of the Vizier** was thus the central archives of the government as before, and all records of the land-administration with census and tax registration were filed in his bureaus. Thus he calls himself one "confirming the boundary records, separating a land-owner from his

neighbor." [Breasted here cites the writing of Mentuhotep in the *Ancient Records of Egypt*, Paragraph 531, Vol. I, p. 255] . . . He was also head of the judicial administration, presiding over the six "Great Houses" and the "House of Thirty"; and when he also held the office of chief treasurer, as did **the powerful Vizier Mentuhotep under Sesostris I, the account which he could give of himself on his tomb-stone read like the declaration of a king's powers.** [Breasted cites Paragraphs 530-534 of his *Ancient Records of Egypt*, Vol. I, pp. 255-257.][26]

Were Joseph's powers like that of a king? Pharaoh actually gave Joseph his own kingly power in the same manner that Sesostris I later gave Mentuhotep his own authority. Read what Pharaoh told Joseph in Genesis 41:40-44.

Genesis 41:40-44 -- (40) "You shall be in charge of my palace, and all my people are to submit to your orders. **Only with respect to the throne will I be greater than you."** (41) So Pharaoh said to Joseph, "I **hereby put you in charge of the whole land of Egypt. . . . ."** (43) He had him ride in a chariot as his second-in-command, and men shouted before him, "Make way !" **Thus he put him in charge of the whole land of Egypt.** (44) Then Pharaoh said to Joseph, "I am Pharaoh, but **without your word no one will lift hand or foot in all Egypt."**

How could a king give more power to a man without giving him the throne itself? Breasted's statement about the immense royal power of Mentuhotep as Vizier is no less true than the power Pharaoh gave Joseph. The difference in the two men is that Mentuhotep boasted of his own greatness in his writings, whereas Joseph was satisfied with what the king said about him.

IV. FOURTEEN SIMILARITIES BETWEEN MENTUHOTEP AND JOSEPH

Below we list fourteen characteristics of the Viziership of Mentuhotep in Sesostris I's latter reign that are uniquely found in the Biblical description of Joseph's Viziership.

(1) Mentuhotep was "pilot of the people."[27] Joseph was "governor of the people" and "all of Pharaoh's people" were "to submit to" his orders.[28]

(2) Mentuhotep judged "the Two Lands," both Upper and Lower Egypt.[29] Joseph was made "ruler" of "all Egypt;"[30] therefore, Joseph also judged both Upper and Lower Egypt.

(3) Mentuhotep was a "giver of laws."[31] Joseph established laws: "So Joseph established it as a law concerning land in Egypt, still in force to this day."[32]

(4) Mentuhotep was "wearer of the royal seal."[33] "Pharaoh took his signet ring and put it on Joseph."[34] Thus, Joseph wore Pharaoh's royal seal engraved on a ring.

(5) Mentuhotep was "chief of all works to the King."[35] Pharaoh put Joseph "in

charge of the whole land of Egypt."[36] Pharaoh told Joseph, "I am Pharaoh, but without your word no one will lift hand or foot in all Egypt."[37] Therefore, Joseph was also chief over all works of the king.

(6) Mentuhotep claimed that Sesostris I listened to him as if he were "a god" and "a favorite companion."[38] Joseph told his brothers that God had made him "father to Pharaoh, lord of his entire household".[39] Pharaoh also considered Joseph to have the spirit of God dwelling in him so that no one in Egypt was wiser than he to advise the king.[40] Joseph's name, "Zaphenath-Paneah," is interpreted by some Egyptologists to mean, "God speaks and He lives."[41] Thus, Pharaoh called Joseph by a name that included "God" in the same manner that Sesostris I considered Mentuhotep as a god.

(7) Mentuhotep claimed that he "had an advanced seat to approach the throne of the king."[42] Pharaoh said to Joseph, "Only with respect to the throne will I be greater."[43]

(8) Mentuhotep said he was "the prince over the royal palace."[44] Pharaoh told Joseph, "You shall be in charge of my palace."[45] Joseph also claimed to be "lord" of Pharaoh's "entire household."[46]

(9) Mentuhotep claimed that Sesostris I exalted him above millions "as an excellent man."[47] Pharaoh exalted Joseph before all of the Egyptians, just as Mentuhotep claimed to be exalted by Sesostris I.

> Genesis 41:42-43 - Then Pharaoh took his signet ring from his finger and put it on Joseph's finger. He dressed him in robes of fine linen and put a gold chain around his neck. He had him ride in a chariot as his second-in-command, and men shouted before him, "Make way!" Thus he put him in charge of the whole land of Egypt.

(10) Mentuhotep claimed to be "pilot of the people, giver of food."[48] Joseph fed all of Egypt during the days of famine.[49]

(11) Mentuhotep claimed to be a "prophet of Anubis," "prophet of Mat," and "prophet of Horus, master of secret things of the house of sacred writings."[50] Joseph spoke as a prophet when he predicted the seven years of abundance, followed by seven years of famine. Thus, Pharaoh considered Joseph to be "one in whom is the spirit of God" and thus one who is more "discerning and wise" than all other Egyptians.[51]

(12) Mentuhotep said he was "overseer of the double granary."[52] Joseph was overseer of all the granaries of Egypt: "Joseph stored up huge quantities of grain . . . and stored it in the cities."[53]

(13) Mentuhotep oversaw the treasury of Sesostris I, calling himself "overseer of the double silver-house" and "overseer of the double gold-house."[54] Joseph also oversaw Pharaoh's treasury, for "he collected all the money to be found in Egypt and brought it to Pharaoh's palace."[55]

(14) Mentuhotep, as the sole Vizier of Sesostris I, had to travel all over Egypt to oversee Sesostris I's work in the same manner that Joseph traveled all over Egypt

to oversee the Pharaoh's work.

Obviously, Joseph and Mentuhotep filled the identical office of Vizier. Perhaps the reader is thinking that these fourteen matching characteristics are insignificant because all Viziers of Egypt had these same responsibilities. But this is not true! See the next point.

V. JOSEPH'S VIZIERSHIP ONLY FITS THE FIRST VIZIER OF SESOSTRIS I

Below we compare the unique differences of the Viziership under Sesostris I with the Viziership of other twelfth-dynasty Pharaohs and of other dynasties.

A. The Eleventh Dynasty at Thebes
The Eleventh Dynasty lived in southern Egypt at Thebes, [56] whereas the twelfth dynasty had its capital in Itjtowy, located in northern Egypt, close to the land of Goshen.[57] Joseph was Vizier of a Pharaoh whose capital was in **northern** Egypt, close to the land of Goshen in the delta.[58] Thus, Joseph could not have been the Vizier of a Pharaoh of the eleventh dynasty.

B. The Vizier of Sesostris I Differed From the Vizier of Sesostris III.
The Viziership in the twelfth dynasty changed when Sesostris III became Pharaoh. Sesostris III lived about 100 years after Sesostris I's death. Sesostris III removed power from the local nomarchs who were governors of the provinces. He also centralized control in his capital, administering the nation under three departments: (1) Northern Egypt (2) Middle Egypt and (3) Southern Egypt. These three departments were administered by three heads who answered to the Vizier.[59]

The Vizier of Sesostris I worked directly through the various nomarchs (governors) in the many capital cities of the nomes (states). The Vizier of Sesostris III supervised only three officials who traveled only to the designated cities of each official.[60] Thus, Sesostris III's Vizier did not need to travel to all of the cities of Egypt, as the Vizier of Sesostris I did. Notice below that the Bible says that Joseph, like the Vizier of Sesostris I, traveled to all of the principal cities of Egypt to fulfill his duty as Vizier.

> Genesis 41:46-49 -- And Joseph went out from the presence of Pharaoh and **traveled throughout Egypt** . . . Joseph collected all the food produced in those seven years of abundance in Egypt and **stored it in the cities**. In each city he put the food grown in the fields surrounding it. NIV

Therefore, Joseph executed the king's work through the nomarchs in the principal cities of Egypt and traveled throughout Egypt as the Vizier of Sesostris I did, but not as the Vizier of Sesostris III did. We thus conclude that the Viziership of Joseph uniquely fits the time of Sesostris I, whereas it does not fit the Viziership that existed from Sesostris III's reign to the end of the twelfth dynasty.

C. The Vizier of Sesostris I Also Differed from the Vizier of Amenemhet III.

David Rohl proposed that Joseph was the Vizier of Amenemhet III. He attributed the seven years of famine to successive floods of the Nile that occurred in Amenemhet III's reign.[61] However, the new change in the work of the Vizier over three supervisors began with Sesostris III and continued into the reign of his son, Amenemhet III. Since Joseph oversaw all the nomarchs of Egypt, he could not be the Vizier of Amenemhet III.

However, Breasted reports that Amenemhet III "raised the productive capacity of the land to an unprecedented level" through a system of irrigation.[62] Indeed, Amenemhet III improved and deepened the canal of Joseph to siphon off the water of high Niles that were occurring in Upper Egypt, thus preventing the flooding of Middle and Lower Egypt. We will see later that it was the Vizier of Sesostris I that oversaw the original digging of the "Joseph Canal."

One of the dreams of Pharaoh predicted the seven years of famine by picturing seven heads of grain "thin and scorched by the east wind."[63] Rohl proposes that the famine resulted from excessive water during the reign of Amenemhet III. However, Pharaoh's dream clearly indicates drought instead of flooding.

In Sesostris I's reign, Breasted reports that "years of famine" were produced by low Niles and ended by years of abundance when high Niles returned,[64] **not** the reverse process suggested by Rohl.

The Bible says that the seven-year famine **affected the entire world surrounding Egypt, including Canaan.**[65] The flooding of the Jordan would not affect the area where Joseph's father, Jacob, and his eleven brothers lived. Large rains in the dry, desert regions where the Israelites lived would cause the land to flourish rather than dry up.

Also, the flooding of the Nile, which came from rain in the upper regions of South Africa, did not affect the land of Canaan and the rest of the ancient world. Most famines are caused by lack of water, not an over-abundance of it. We will discuss this famine in depth in Chapter Eleven.

> Genesis 41:46-49 -- And Joseph went out from the presence of Pharaoh and **traveled throughout Egypt.** . . . Joseph collected all the food produced in those seven years of abundance in Egypt and **stored it in the cities**. In each city he put the food grown in the fields surrounding it. NIV

Therefore, Joseph executed the king's work through the nomarchs in the principal cities of Egypt and traveled throughout Egypt as the Vizier of Sesostris I did, but not as the Vizier of Sesostris III did. We thus conclude that the Viziership of Joseph uniquely fits the time of Sesostris I, whereas it does not fit the Viziership that existed from Sesostris III's reign to the end of the twelfth dynasty.

D. The Viziership of the Thirteenth and Fourteenth Dynasties Was Different Than the Viziership of Joseph.

Joseph could not fit as Vizier of a thirteenth- or fourteenth-dynasty king because these two dynasties came into existence simultaneously at the fall of the twelfth dynasty.[66] Thus, two Pharaohs with two different Viziers reigned over a divided Egypt after the fall of the twelfth dynasty. Since Joseph served as Vizier over "all Egypt,"[67] he could not have been Vizier of a thirteenth- or fourteenth-dynasty king who ruled only part of Egypt.

However, Sesostris I of the twelfth dynasty reigned over all of Egypt without rivals, as was characteristic of all of the other kings of the twelfth dynasty.[68] Joseph thus fits the Vizier of Sesostris I, but does not fit the Vizier of any Pharaoh of the thirteenth or fourteenth dynasties.

E. The Viziership of the Fifteen to Seventeenth Dynasties Differed from the Viziership of Joseph.

Since Joseph was **"ruler of all Egypt,"** he could **not** have been the Vizier of a Hyksos Pharaoh or of any other Pharaoh of the fifteenth through the seventeenth dynasties. All of these dynasties reigned parallel to each other with three to four different Pharaohs reigning simultaneously from different capitals, each with his own Vizier.[69] However, in the time of the twelfth dynasty there was only one Pharaoh and one Vizier over all of Egypt. Thus, Joseph fits as Sesostris I's Vizier, but does not fit the Vizier of any Pharaoh of the Hyksos dynasties.

Many scholars, especially Kitchen, believe Joseph was the Vizier of one of the Hyksos Pharaohs.[70] For the interested reader, Appendix B presents a thorough case as to why Joseph could not have been the Vizier of a Hyksos Pharaoh.

F. The Viziership of the Eighteenth Dynasty Differed From the Viziership of Joseph.

During the eighteenth dynasty the kingdom was united under one Pharaoh. However, Each Pharaoh of the eighteenth dynasty appointed two Viziers, one over southern Egypt and the other over northern Egypt.[71] Thus, during the eighteenth dynasty there was not a single Vizier over all of Egypt. Since Joseph was Vizier of "all of Egypt," his Viziership was distinctly different from that of the eighteenth dynasty. But Joseph fits perfectly as Vizier in the twelfth dynasty when Sesostris I had only one Vizier over all of Egypt.

G. The Viziership of Joseph Fits Uniquely the Viziership of Sesostris I.

We have seen that Joseph's Viziership does not match the Viziership of dynasties prior to the twelfth, nor of dynasties that followed the twelfth. Even within the twelfth dynasty, Joseph's Viziership fits only that of Sesostris I, and possibly that of Amenemhet II and Sesostris II, but definitely not the Viziership under Sesostris III, Amenemhet III and his son Amenemhet IV. In these comparisons of different styles of Viziership, we have determined a unique characteristic that ties the Viziership under Sesostris I to the Viziership of Joseph: **single oversight with administration through governors of the principal cities of all Egypt.**

VI. POSSIBLE STATUES AND TOMBS OF JOSEPH

We saw above that Mentuhotep, the latter Vizier of Sesostris I, died in disgrace. He was not buried in the pyramidal complex of Sesostris I. Several Viziers served Sesostris I during his long forty-six-year reign, but the names of none of them are found in any of the tombs inside Sesostris I's pyramidal complex. However, a broken statue of one of his unnamed Viziers was found at the southeast corner of the pyramid enclosure.[72] If Joseph was Sesostris I's first Vizier, this statue could represent Joseph. I have not been able to locate a photo of this statue.

A huge tomb north of the pyramid enclosure was built by a high-ranking, unnamed official **who served under four kings,** starting with Amenemhet I. Hayes suggests that this official might be Inyotefokre, Vizier of the Pyramid City.[73] But Inyotefokre was not Vizier of all of Egypt, only a mayor of a single city. However, Joseph's long life certainly qualifies to be this "high-ranking" but unnamed official who built this tomb. Genesis 41:46 says, "Joseph was thirty years old when he entered the service of Pharaoh king of Egypt." Genesis 50:26 tells us that "Joseph died at the age of a hundred and ten. And after they embalmed him, he was placed in a coffin in Egypt." Thus, Joseph lived in Egypt for eighty years after he was appointed Vizier.

Therefore, Joseph lived long enough to qualify as the high ranking official who built the huge tomb north of Sesostris I's pyramid and served under four kings: Amenemhet I, Sesostris I, Amenemhet II and Sesostris II. Table 8-B, located at the end of this chapter, demonstrates how Joseph's long life parallels the reigns of these four kings. Joseph's body may have also been formerly buried in the large tomb. Another possibility for Joseph's tomb is "a vaulted tomb of unusual type on the west side of the pyramid," which "yielded no name."[74]

We cannot expect to find Joseph's body buried in any of these tombs. Before Joseph died he made his sons swear that they would remove his body and carry it back to Canaan when they left Egypt.[75] Exodus 13:19 reports that "Moses took the bones of Joseph with him" when the Exodus occurred. Joshua 24:32 explains that Joseph's bones "were buried at Shechem" in the tract of land that Jacob bought "from the sons of Hamor, the father of Shechem."

David Rohl identified a statue unearthed at a tomb at Tel el Daba (Avaris) as that of Joseph. Tel el Daba is located in the land of Goshen where the Israelites lived. The cover jacket of Rohl's book pictures this statue as having red hair with characteristics different from Egyptians and covered with a coat of many colors.[76] Figure 8-C is a copy of the cover of Rohl's book, which features a possible statue of Joseph . See it below.

Bietak, an Austrian archaeologist, excavated the tomb and statue that Rohl pictures on the cover of his book. He dated it to the Middle Kingdom, which includes the twelfth dynasty.[77] Rohl dated the statue to the reign of Amenemhet III, the Pharaoh he linked to the famine and Joseph. If this statue is indeed Joseph's, I would date its construction to the reigns of either Sesostris I, Amenemhet II or Sesostris II, the Pharaohs I have assigned to Joseph's lifetime. Perhaps in the future a more specific date within the Middle Kingdom can be ascribed to this statue. The statue certainly looks like a foreigner who was raised to a high position in Egypt in the land where Israel lived. Rohl's interpretation that this statue is that of Joseph is very likely. Rohl says the statue appears to have red hair and a coat of many colors.

Figure 8-C
Possible Statue of Joseph

CONCLUSION

Our circumstantial case for establishing Joseph as the Vizier of Sesostris I is gradually growing. Chapter Eight contains a total of **thirty-four points of unique parallelism** between the Viziership under Sesostris I and the Viziership under the Pharaoh of Joseph. The Viziership of Joseph is in unique contrast to later viziers of the twelfth dynasty . See these unique characteristics of Sesostris I's Vizier in Tables 8-A to 8-C.

We saw that the office of Vizier was significantly modified in the latter half of the twelfth dynasty and also in subsequent dynasties. Therefore, the Biblical description of Joseph as prime minister of Egypt uniquely matches the Viziership during the reign of Sesostris I. **The growing number of similarities between twelfth-dynasty and Biblical histories are gradually forming a matching pattern that soon will become as significant as the unique design of one's fingerprints.**

TABLE 8-A
FIVE SYNCHRONISMS BETWEEN THE EARLY
VIZIER OF SESOSTRIS I AND JOSEPH

"Building Inscription of Sesostris I," (Papyrus Berlin 3029), *Ancient Egyptian Literature*, Trans., Miriam Lichtheim, *op. cit.*, I.115-118.

EARLY VIZIER OF SESOSTRIS I	JOSEPH AS VIZIER
1. Royal Seal Bearer	1. Royal ring of Pharaoh Gen. 41:42
2. Sole-Companion	2. Closest to the King Gen. 41:40-43
3. Privy-Counselor of 2 Diadems (All Egypt)	3. Vizier over all Egypt Gen. 41:40, 43
4. Treasurer of Sesostris I's gold and silver	4. Collected & oversaw all of Pharaoh's money Gen. 47:14
5. Overseer of the Works of Sesostris I	5. Oversaw all of Pharaoh's works in all of Egypt Gen. 41:40-44, 55

TABLE 8-B
JOSEPH SERVED UNDER FIVE PHARAOHS:
5 SYNCHRONISMS

AMENEMHET I	0		1688 B.C.	ACCESSION YEAR
			1678 B.C.	JOSEPH ENTERED EGYPT AS A SLAVE
	19	S-I	1688 B.C.	JOSEPH IN PRISON
SESOSTRIS I	20	0	1667 B.C.	BAKER & BUTLER IN PRISON
Co-Reign	21	01	1666 B.C.	
	22	02	1665 B.C.	JOSEPH'S 1st Year as Vizier 1st Year of Abundance
	23	03	1664 B.C.	2ND Year of Abundance
	28	08	1659 B.C.	7TH Year of Abundance
	29	09	1658 B.C.	1st Year of Famine
	30	10	1657 B.C.	2nd Year of Famine
SESOSTRIS I: Sole Reign		11	1656 B.C.	JACOB ENTERS EGYPT
		12	1655 B.C.	4th Year of Famine
		15	1652 B.C.	7th Year of Famine
		28	1639 B.C.	JACOB'S DEATH
AMENEMHET II	0	42	1625 B.C.	
	04	46	1621 B.C.	ISRAELITE PROSPERITY
		S-II		
SESOSTRIS II	35	0	1590 B.C.	
	38	3	1587 B.C.	
		5	1585 B.C.	JOSEPH'S DEATH

TABLE 8-C
THIRTEEN ADDITIONAL SYNCHRONISMS
IN CHAPTER EIGHT

1. Sesostris I appointed Mentuhotep "Hereditary prince, Vizier and pilot of the people." Joseph was made governor and ruler of all Egyptians. Gen. 41:41; 45:9

2. Mentuhotep judged the two lands (upper and lower Egypt) and Joseph also ruled all of Egypt. Gen. 41:41; 45:9

3. Mentuhotep was a "Giver of laws" and "an Advancer of offices." Joseph also established laws for Egypt and appointed commissioners in every city. Gen. 41:34-35.

4. Mentuhotep was "wearer of the royal seal." Joseph wore the King's personal signet ring. Gen. 41:42

5. Mentuhotep was "Chief of all works of the King." Joseph was in charge of all of the works of the King. Gen. 41:40

6. Mentuhotep "counseled the king like a god." Joseph counseled Pharaoh like a "father and lord." Gen. 41:38-41; 45:8-9

7. Mentuhotep was the "favorite of the king." Joseph was greater than any Egyptian except Pharaoh. Gen. 41:44.

8. Mentuhotep was made "Prince over the royal castle." Joseph was in charge of Pharaoh's palace. Gen. 41:40.

9. Mentuhotep was exalted by Sesostris I above millions. Pharaoh dressed Joseph in robes of linen, put a gold chain on his neck and had him ride in a chariot as his second in command. Gen. 41:43.

10. Mentuhotep called himself "Giver of Food." Joseph gave away four-fifths of Pharaoh's grain to the Egyptians who were working the land. Gen. 47:24.

11. Mentuhotep called himself "Prophet of Horus." Pharaoh called Joseph a "Seer" who revealed the future. Gen. 41:37.

12. Mentuhotep was "Overseer of the double granary." Joseph oversaw all of the granaries of Egypt. Gen. 41:46ff.

13. Mentuhotep was the "chief treasurer" of Egypt. Joseph was also the chief treasurer of Egypt. Gen. 47:14ff.

These thirteen privileges and powers demonstrate that Joseph and Mentuhotep occupied the same office of Vizier that fits particularly the twelfth dynasty in the time of Sesostris I. These privileges and powers did not exist in the same manner later in the twelfth dynasty, nor in other dynasties.

TABLE 8-D
TOTAL SYNCHRONISMS IN CHAPTER EIGHT

TABLE 8-A - 5 synchronisms
TABLE 8-B - 5 synchronisms
TABLE 8-C - 13 synchronisms
TOTAL   - 23 SYNCHRONISMS

TABLE 8-E
RUNNING TOTAL OF DISCOVERIES

Chapter	Chapter Total	Running Total
2 Conflict Between Biblical and Secular Histories	18	18
4 Discovery of 430 Years from Abraham to the Exodus	16	34
5 Confirmation of Abraham's Historicity	28	62
6 Discovery of the Remains of Sodom and Gomorrah	17	79
7 Joseph As a Slave and Prisoner in Amenemhet I's Reign	21	100
8 Joseph Becomes the Vizier of Sesostris I	23	123

NOTES FOR CHAPTER EIGHT

1. Genesis 40:20-23; 41:1-12.
2. William C. Hayes, *Scepter of Egypt, Metropolitan Museum of N.Y.*, I.183-184
3. Lichtheim (Trans.), *Ancient Egyptian Literature*, I.117.
4. *Breasted (Trans.), Ancient Records of Egypt*, I. 235 (no. 490) & 248 (no. 512), Univ. of Calif. Pr.
5. William C. Hayes, "Middle Kingdom in Egypt," *Cambridge Ancient History*, I.2A.505.
6. James Breasted, *History of Egypt*, Scribners, 164.
7. Lichtheim (Trans.), *Ancient Egyptian Literature*, I.117.
8. Hayes, "Middle Kingdom of Egypt," *Cambridge Ancient History*, I.2A.496.
9. William C. Hayes, *Scepter of Egypt*, I.171.
10. M. Lichtheim (Trans.), *Ancient Egyptian Literature*, I.117.
11. William Hayes, *Scepter of Egypt*, 183-4.
12. J. Breasted (Trans.), *Ancient Records of Egypt*, I.247-249 (510-512).
13. J. Breasted (Trans.), *Ancient Records of Egypt*, I.255 (no. 530).
14. Donovan Courville, *The Exodus Problem And Its Ramifications*, I.141-142.
15. E. A. Wallace Budge, *An Egyptian Hieroglyphic Dictionary* (New York: Dover Pub., 1978), I. 306 and II.922.
16. E. A. Wallace Budge, *An Egyptian Hieroglyphic Dictionary.*, I.517; II.922.
17. Breasted (Trans.), *Ancient Records of Egypt*, I.255-256 (Nos. 531 & 532.)
18. Breasted, *History of Egypt*, pp. 126-127, 131.
19. Breasted, *Ancient Records of Egypt*, I.255-257 (531 & 533)
20. Breasted, *A History of Egypt*, 166.
21. Breasted, *History of Egypt*, 181.
22. Breasted, *History of Egypt*, 166-7.
23. Genesis 41:25, 32; 45:4-9; 48:9; 50:18-21, 25.
24. Genesis 41:39-44, 55.
25. Proverbs 27:2
26. Breasted, *History of Egypt*, 166.
27. Breasted (Trans.), *Ancient Records of Egypt*, I.255 (no. 531).
28. Genesis 41:40; 42:6
29. Breasted (Trans.), *Ancient Records of Egypt*, I.255 (no. 531).
30. Genesis 45:8
31. Breasted (Trans.), *Ancient Records of Egypt*, I.255 (no. 531).
32. Genesis 47:26
33. Breasted (Trans.), *Ancient Records of Egypt*, I.256 (no. 531).
34. Genesis 41:42
35. Breasted (Trans.), *Ancient Records of Egypt*, I.256 (no. 531).
36. Genesis 41:41
37. Genesis 41:44
38. Breasted (Trans.), I.256 (no. 531).
39. Genesis 45:8

40. Genesis 41:38-39
41. Nola J. Opperwall-Galluch, "Zaphenath-Paneah," *The International Standard Bible Encyclopedia*, Revised Ed.,IV.1173.
42. Breasted (Trans.), *Ancient Records of Egypt*, I.256 (no. 531).
43. Genesis 41:40
44. Breasted (Trans.), *Ancient Records of Egypt*, I.256 (no. 532).
45. Genesis 41:40
46. Genesis 45:8
47. Breasted (Trans.), *Ancient Records of Egypt*, I.256 (no. 532).
48. Breasted (Trans.), *Ancient Records of Egypt*, I.256 (no. 532). .
49. Genesis 47:24-25
50. Breasted (Trans.), *Ancient Records of Egypt*, I.256-7.
51. Genesis 41:25-39
52. Breasted (Trans.), *Ancient Records of Egypt*, I.257 (no. 533).
53. Genesis 41:48-49
54. Breasted (Trans.), *Ancient Records of Egypt*, I.257 (no. 533).
55. Genesis 47:14
56. William C. Hayes, *Cambridge Ancient History*, I.2A.476-496.
57. John Baines and F. Wente, "Egypt," *New Encyclopaedia Britannica*, 18.113.
58. Genesis 45:10
59. William C. Hayes, *Cambridge Ancient History*, I.2A.506.
60. William C. Hayes, *Cambridge Ancient History*, I.2A.506
61. David Rohl, *Pharaohs and Kings*, 1995, 335-343.
62. Breasted, *History of Egypt*, 191.
63. Genesis 41:6.
64. Breasted (Trans.), "Inscription of Amenemhet (Ameni)," *Ancient Records of Egypt*, I.252-253 (Nos. 522-523).
65. Genesis 41:53-57
66. William C. Hayes, *Cambridge Ancient History*, II.1.44-73, 818-819.
67. Genesis 41:41-46.
68. William C. Hayes, *Cambridge Ancient History*, I.2A.495-512.
69. Wlliam C. Hayes, *Cambridge Ancient History*, II.1.44-73, 818-819.
70. K. A. Kitchen, "Joseph," *International Standard Bible Encyclopedia*, Revised Ed. 1982, Eerdmans, II.1130.
71. William C. Hayes, " *Cambridge Ancient History*, II.1.353-354.
72. William Hayes, *Scepter of Egypt*, I.183-4.
73. William Hayes, *Scepter of Egypt.*, I.183.
74. William Hayes, *Scepter of Egypt*, I.183-184.
75. Genesis 41:57; 42:5; 43:1.
76. David Rohl, *Pharaohs & Kings*, 360-367.
77. David Rohl, *Pharaohs & Kings*, 360-367.

CHAPTER NINE
SESOSTRIS I GIVES JOSEPH
A NEW NAME AND A WIFE

"Pharaoh gave Joseph the name Zaphenath-Paneah and gave him Asenath daughter of Potiphera, priest of On, to be his wife" (Gen 41:45). This chapter investigates both Biblical and Egyptian sources to see if "Zaphenath-Paneah" and "Asenath" fit the historical, geographical and cultural context of the twelfth dynasty.

I. MEANING OF JOSEPH'S NEW NAME

The new name that Pharaoh gave Joseph appears to be associated with Joseph's skill in interpreting dreams. Several facts convinced Pharaoh that Joseph was a true prophet of God. (1) Joseph had interpreted correctly the dreams of Pharaoh's butler and baker. (2) Only Joseph could interpret Pharaoh's dream. (3) Joseph's wise counsel to store up grain during the years of abundance proved he was thinking unselfishly of Egypt's welfare, rather than his own glory. (3) Pharaoh knew he could not lose by storing up grain during the years of abundance, whether the famine came or not.

Before giving Joseph his new name, Pharaoh asked his officials, "Can we find anyone like this man, one in whom is the spirit of God?"[1] Pharaoh's idea that Joseph was a true spokesman of God seems to be at the heart of the meaning of the new name that he gave Joseph.

The names, Zaphenath and Paneah are not listed in Egyptian literature, nor have I been able to find them in a hieroglyphic dictionary. However, the syllables of these names are found quite frequently in documents of the twelfth dynasty and afterwards. G. Steindorff suggests that Zaphenath-Paneah means "the god speaks and he [Joseph] lives."[2] However, Steindorff adds several consonants to the Egyptian name to arrive at this meaning.

K. A. Kitchen changes Zaphenath-Paneah to Zathenaph-pa'anekh, which he interprets, "[Joseph] who is called Ip-'anekh."[3] Kitchen claims that Zaphenath-pa'aneah "is not anachronistic, as often alleged, but . . . fully compatible with a date for Joseph in the first half of the second millennium B.C."[4] Egyptian hieroglyphics are sometimes pronounced in reverse order and thus Kitchen may be justified in changing Zaphenath to Zathenaph.

Josephus, a Jewish scholar of the first century A.D., interpreted Joseph's Egyptian name to mean "Revealer of Secrets."[5] Josephus' interpretation fits well with my research on the meaning of the syllables of Zaphenath-Paneiah.

I researched a hieroglyphic dictionary for the meaning of the syllables found in Zaphenath-Paneah. Table 9-A (next page) lists the various meanings of the syllables found in this name. "Zaphenath" seems to be more closely represented by the words *Zeph, An*, and *Ath*. If we choose the meaning of "See" for *Zaph*, the meaning of secret or mystery for *Anh* and the definition of "Dignity or Rank" for *Aat*, then we would have "The Dignified Seer of Mysteries." Prophets were called "seers" twenty-eight times in the NIV translation of the Old Testament.

TABLE 9-A
POSSIBLE EGYPTIAN WORDS THAT MEAN
"REVEALER OF THE SECRETS OF GOD"
(*Egyptian Hieroglyphic Dictionary* by E. W. Wallis Budge (New York: Dover Pub., 1978).

IDEA OF REVEAL	IDEA OF SECRET	IDEA OF GOD
Gerp = reveal mystery	Amen = hidden thing	Aa = God or great
Shti = to penetrate	Anh = word with secret meaning	Akhem-sek = mysteries Everlasting God
Sentit = Seer		Khem = Unknown God
Sun = make an opening	Sheta = to hide or reveal	Neter = God (force or power)
Maaa = Seer	Seshetat = secret, mystery	Neter ua = Great God = One God
Petra = explain, show, reveal	Shtat = mystery, difficult	Netcherf = Limitless God
Unra = prophet or priest who reveals God's word		Akhem-sek = Everlasting God
Suh = prophesy with with emotion		Pau = Primeval God
Khenu = prophet, singer		Tepi-a = God of prophecy
Seri = prophecy or precept		

The word *Paneah* fits well with a combination of *Pan* and *Aaa* (*Pan-Aaa*). *Pan* means "Chief of the gods," and *Aaa* means "foreigner or interpreter." Thus, Zaphenath-Paneah could mean the "Interpreter of the Chief of the gods." Many other meanings are also possible. The reader is invited to look in Table 9-A to see meanings of other Egyptian syllables that are similar to *Zaphenath-Paneah*. Table 9-B (next page) lists all of the names that I could formulate from the syllables in Table 9-A. All of these names, except Kitchen's proposal, fit perfectly what the Pharaoh of Joseph thought about Joseph's ability to interpret dreams and predict the future.

II. DOES ZAPHENATH-PANEAH FIT INTO A TWELFTH-DYNASTY SETTING?

Does Joseph's Egyptian name and his ability as a prophet of God and seer of the future fit into the history and culture of Sesostris I's reign? While I was unable to find the name Zaphenath-Paneah in any twelfth-dynasty documents, I did find one name that was quite similar: **Hepzefi,** the nomarch (governor) of Asyut (Siut) in Middle Egypt. The last part of his name, *Zef* fits the first part of Jo**seph**'s name (**Zaphe**nath): (*Zaphe = Zefi*).

In reading the hieroglyphic cartouches of the Egyptian Pharaohs in Petrie's *History of Egypt*, I have observed that many hieroglyphic names are translated into

English in reverse order of the form in which they appear in their cartouches. The Hebrew language always reads from right to left, whereas we read English from left to right. If Joseph's Egyptian names were reversed, it would read as Zefihep or even Zefipah. Zefipha or Zephe-Pah are the first consonants in both names of Joseph's Egyptian name: **Zephe**nath **Pa**neah. Thus, Hepzefi's name in reverse would be Zephi-Pah and could be a shortened version of **Zaphe**nath **Pa**neah.

TABLE 9-B
POSSIBLE COMBINATIONS OF MEANINGS OF SYLLABLES
IN ZAPHENATH-PANEAH
(Meanings by E. A. W. Budge, *An Egyptian Hieroglyphic Dictionary*, op. cit.)

Z [DZ OR TCH] Vol. II, pp. 893-907	N Vol. I, pp. 341-409	P Vol. I, pp. 229,234
Za - serpent that came out from Ra	Na - this	Pa - this
	Na - wind, air	Paa - my
Za - to be sound, healthy	Na - great, pretty	Pan - Chief of the gods
Za - to stretch, extend out	Naat - prison, house	
	Naat - ordinance maker	A,E,Ah]
Za - to correct	Nat - law, rule, ordinance	Vol. I, pp. 1-141
Za - to make a journey	Nati - a god	Aa - to beget
Zaa - to possess knowledge	Nai - my, his (suffix)	Aa - to see
Za - storm god	Nah - injury, evil	Aa - glory, praise
	Naheh - eternal	Aaa - foreigner, interpreter
Zah - prison	Naa - have pity	Aaa - well, fountain
Zephen - to see	Naat - graciousness	Aat - rank, dignity
Zephen - to beget	Nait - goddess	Aat - moment, see
Zephen - child	Nati - belonging to the god of On	Aat - great canal
Zet - to speak	Nut - mass of water & the Sky goddess	Anh - word with secret meaning
PH [F] Vol. I, pp. 258-260	Neha - suffer loss	At - strong, sound
	Neht - protection	At - defeat, depression
Pha (Fa) - carry	Neti - to overcome	At - prisoner
Phen - weak, helpless	Neta - to come, to	At - to bring forth
Phenti - he of the nose (Judge)	Nether - God	Ath - to nurse, to nourish
Phennu - to create	Neth - of horsemen	Ath - prison
	Neth - nest, seat, throne	

I also found other connections between Hepzefi and Joseph. Hepzefi called himself a "Superior Prophet" and wrote out contracts with the priests that included offerings given out of the estate of Sesostris I.[6]   Joseph also was a "Superior Prophet" who interpreted Pharaoh's dreams and predicted the future (Genesis 47:20-26). Legal contracts in Hepzefi's tombs granted contributions from the king's estate to the priests. These contracts are consistent with what the Pharaoh of Joseph did in paying out allotments for the priests.[7]

James Breasted also says that Hepzefi represented a new family that Sesostris I had elevated to a position of honor by appointing him as nomarch (governor). The nomarch ordinarily inherited his office from his father with approval by the ruling Pharaoh.[8] Thus, Sesostris I's elevation of new families who had not inherited their honored positions is consistent with Pharaoh's elevation of Joseph to the position of Vizier, even though he was formerly a foreigner, a slave and a prisoner.

The many similarities between Joseph and Hepzefi tempted me to identify the two as the same person, but further research ruled out this idea. Hepzefi claimed to have inherited his personal property from his father, who was an Egyptian priest.[9] Joseph's father was not a priest of Egypt, and Joseph inherited nothing from Jacob while he was in Egypt. Rather, Pharaoh permitted Joseph to give land to his father and brothers in the eastern delta of northern Egypt. Hepzefi's property was located in Asyut (Siut) in Middle Egypt. Joseph and his family lived in northern Egypt in the delta. Therefore, Joseph did not fit the genealogy, location, or circumstances of Hepzefi and his father.

I also learned that Hepzefi's title of "Superior Prophet" was the name used for the chief of the other priests and prophets in the temple of Asyut and that he was "Superior Prophet" only of the temple where he officiated. Officials of other temples, who were contemporaneous with Hepzefi, also held the title "Superior Prophet."[10]

While Joseph could not have been Hepzefi, Joseph's situation was similar to that of Hepzefi and fits perfectly into the cultural context of the twelfth dynasty and specifically during the reign of Sesostris I. Hepzefi and Joseph were both "Superior Prophets." Their Egyptian names are very similar. They both were elevated to high positions of authority rather than inheriting these places of honor from their fathers. Thus, Hepzefi's promotion from obscurity to fame was similar to the situation of Joseph, whom Sesostris I elevated in the same manner. Therefore, Joseph's rise from slavery and imprisonment to a high office in Egypt fits well into the historical and cultural context of the twelfth dynasty and specifically in Sesostris I's reign.

III. HOW JOSEPH MET ASENATH THE DAUGHTER
OF THE PRIEST OF HELIOPOLIS

In a previous chapter we designated the second year of Sesostris I as 1665 B.C., the Biblical year Joseph was appointed Vizier. During that year Joseph visited all of the major cities of Egypt, constructing granaries and organizing the collection and registering the quantity of grain stored.[11] In the next chapter we will see proof that the first Vizier of Sesostris I accomplished this same mission.

Since Joseph organized all of the collection of grain in his first year, he likely took on a new project the second year (year three of Sesostris I). This new project brought him in contact with Asenath, the daughter of the priest of Heliopolis. The Bible implies that Pharaoh gave Asenath to Joseph as a wife soon after he become Vizier.[12] By Joseph's third year (Sesostris I's fourth year) he must have married

Asenath, because the Bible says that she bore Joseph two children (Manasseh and Ephraim) before the seven years of abundance ended.[13]

A famous Egyptian monument reveals the circumstances by which Joseph likely met, courted, and later married, Asenath. I found this monument by chance in a park close to the Cairo Museum. I recognized it from pictures I had seen in books. I photographed the monument in the park and show it in slide form to audiences. This monument is pictured in Figure 8-C of Chapter 8. **In Sesostris I's third year he inscribed on this monument orders for his Vizier to construct a new temple, a lake and this very monument in the city of On (Heliopolis), all in honor to Sesostris I and his god, Ra, whom Sesostris I calls his father.[14]** The construction of a lake to preserve water during the years of abundance was very appropriate in view of the coming famine which would arrive six years later. Notice the words of Sesostris I to his Vizier, whom I identify as Joseph.

> **Lichtheim's Translation** -- Year 3, third month 3, day 8, . . . The king spoke to the royal seal-bearer, sole companion, overseer of the two gold-houses and the two silver-houses, and privy-councillor of the two diadems: It is your counsel that carries out all the works that my majesty desires to bring about. You are the one who is in charge of them, who will act according to my wish. . . . Order the workmen to do according to your design.[15]

Notice that Sesostris I's order to his Vizier occurred in the king's third year. However, Sesostris I did not include the name of his Vizier in this inscription. If we have correctly connected Joseph's appointment as Vizier in Sesostris I's second year, these orders in the Pharaoh's third year were directly addressed to Joseph in his second year as Vizier.

After Sesostris I decreed that his Vizier supervise the construction in Heliopolis, the Pharaoh traveled with his Vizier to Heliopolis to inaugurate the laying of the foundation of the temple.

> **Lichtheim's Translation** -- The king appeared in the plumed crown, with all the people following him. The chief lector-priest and scribe of the divine books stretched the cord. The rope was released, laid in the ground made to be this temple. His majesty ordered to proceed; the king turned round before the people. Joined together were Upper and Lower Egypt . . . [the document is marred at this point and breaks off][16]

I have not found the name of the chief priest of Heliopolis during the early reign of Sesostris I. If we are in the right time period, the unnamed "chief lector-priest" of Heliopolis was likely the Biblical Potiphera, chief priest of the sun god, Ra. However, it is also possible that Potiphera was only one of several priests who served in the temple. Genesis 41:45 says, "Pharaoh gave Joseph the name Zaphenath-Paneah and gave him Asenath daughter of Potiphera, priest of On, to be his wife." Notice that the Bible does not say that Potiphera was the high priest.

Regardless, "all the people following" the king on that day included both the high priest and the common priests. Asenath was likely among the crowd that observed the inauguration of the new temple. Following the inauguration, Potiphera probably introduced his daughter, Asenath, to the King and to Joseph, the Vizier, who would oversee the construction of the new temple.

Heliopolis was on the edge of the delta, northeast of Memphis, and thus in close traveling distance from Itjtowy, the capital where Joseph lived. Itjtowy's precise location will be discussed in Chapter 16.

A better scenario could not be invented to explain how Joseph met, courted and married Asenath, the daughter of the priest of On. It may have been love at first sight, or it may have been a love that gradually blossomed during Joseph's frequent trips to Heliopolis (On) to supervise the construction of the temple, the lake and the monument. However, Joseph, a foreigner, could never marry an Egyptian of high society, without permission from Pharaoh. Later in this chapter we will see the close relationship that Sesostris I had with the priests of On (Heliopolis).

IV. ASENATH, THE WIFE OF JOSEPH

Egyptologists tell us that Asenath was a popular name for women during the Middle Kingdom (eleventh through the thirteenth dynasties).[17] "Asenath" may mean "she belongs to Neith," an Egyptian goddess. "Neith" was also a popular Egyptian goddess during the twelfth dynasty and was worshiped especially in northern Egypt where a temple was constructed for her in the city of Sais in the delta, not far from Heliopolis.[18]

According to the hieroglyphic dictionary, "Asenath" is the Greek equivalent of the Egyptian "Nesn-t."[19] Thus, "Asenath's" name also fits perfectly within the religious, cultural, linguistic, geographical, and historical scenario of the reign of Sesostris I, and especially in the location of the delta of northern Egypt.

V. POTIPHERA, THE PRIEST OF "ON"

Asenath's father was Potiphera, the priest of "On."[20] "On" is translated in the Greek Septuagint, "Heliopolis," literally "Sun City."[21] "On" was the religious capital of the worshipers of Ra, the sun-god of Egypt.[22] "On" (Heliopolis) is a suburb of northern Cairo right on the edge of the delta of Egypt.[23] Egyptologist Donald Redford defines "On" as coming from the Egyptian *Iwnw*, meaning, "a Pillar Town."[24] Interestingly, Sesostris I commanded his Vizier (Joseph) to construct a tall pillar at Heliopolis. Perhaps the city got its name from the very pillar that Sesostris I commanded Joseph to construct by the lake in front of the temple dedicated to Egypt's Ra-god.

The last syllable of the name Potiphe**ra** is "Ra." "Ra" is the name of the sun god of Egypt. The entire name of Poti-phe-**ra** likely means, "he whom Ra has given."[25] All twelfth-dynasty kings used "Ra" in their throne names. Amenemhet

I's name is more commonly found in Egyptian documents as "Se-Hetep-Ab-**Ra**."[26] The last syllable, Ra, is Egypt's sun-god. Amenemhet I gave his son, Sesostris I the throne name of "Kheper-Ka-**Ra**."[27] In fact, Sesostris I called himself the "Son of Ra" in giving his orders to his Vizier to construct the temple of Ra.[28] The last syllable **"Ra,"** the sun-god's name, is actually listed first in the hieroglyphic cartouche, but transposed as the last syllable in the English translation.[29]

We sometimes find "Ra" listed first and translated first as in the case of Ramses I.[30] Thus, the names of Amenemhet I and Sesostris I could have been translated respectively, "Ra-She-Hetep-Ab" and "Ra-Kheper-Ka" Notice in Table 9-C how the order of the syllables in these names are actually written in ancient hieroglyphics. Table 9-C also shows how scholars inconsistently transliterate or pronounce these names, sometimes from left to right, sometimes right to left, and sometimes in half-reverse order.

TABLE 9-C
COMPARISON OF HIEROGLYPHIC CARTOUCHES
OF DIFFERENT PHARAOHS
Petrie, *History of Egypt,* I.152, 161.

CARTOUCHE OF RAMSES I, 19TH DYNASTY

	RA	MES	SES	U
Petrie's: translation:	RA	MES	SU	

CARTOUCHE OF AMENEMHET I, 12TH DYNASTY

	RA	SHE	HETEP	AB	
Petrie's translation:		SE	HETEP	AB	RA

CARTOUCHE OF SESOSTRIS I, 12TH DYNASTY

	RA	KHEPER	KA	
Petrie's translation:		KHEPER	KA	RA

Therefore, Joseph's marriage to a daughter of the priest of Ra fits perfectly the marriage between the Vizier of Sesostris I and a daughter of the priest of "Ra." Sesostris I honored Ra in his throne name, called himself "the son of Ra," and showed his devotion to Ra by sending his Vizier to build the temple of Ra and a lake for the priests of Ra. The Bible story of Joseph's marriage to the daughter of Potiphera, the priest of On, thus fits perfectly the historical and religious context of the reign of Sesostris I.

Hayes affirms that I-em-hotep, the high priest of Heliopolis, was one of Sesostris I's most favored officials. He had the privilege of being buried in a large tomb within the cemetery of the king.[31] The name, I-em-hotep, certainly does not relate to the name of Potiphera. However this difference in name does not necessarily exclude Potiphera from being a high priest in Sesostris I's early reign. Sesostris I reigned for forty-six years. I-em-hotep may have been high priest in the last twenty-six years of Sesostris I's reign and Potiphera could have been high priest in the first twenty years of his reign. Also, the Bible does not say Potiphera was a "high" priest, leaving the possibility that he was just a common priest. Regardless, the close relationship between Sesostris I and the Heliopolis priests makes a marriage between his Vizier and the daughter of a priest of Heliopolis most appropriate.

Many scholars believe that Joseph's Pharaoh was a Hyksos king. The Hyksos were a foreign people from Arabia who conquered northern Egypt and set up dynasties fifteen and sixteen. However, the Hyksos did not honor "Ra" as their chief god and thus did not use Ra in their names or have a special relationship with the priests of Heliopolis. Joseph's marriage to Asenath fits perfectly the religious culture of the twelfth dynasty, not the culture of the fifteenth or sixteenth dynasties.

VI. THE FIRST TWO SONS OF JOSEPH AND ASENATH

Genesis 41:50 reports, "Before the years of famine came, two sons were born to Joseph by Asenath daughter of Potiphera, priest of On." Since Joseph hypothetically began construction of the temple of Heliopolis in Sesostris I's third year, this allowed Joseph to meet and court Asenath during his second year as Vizier. This chronology allows five years before the seven years of abundance came to an end, sufficient time for their first two sons to be born before the seven years of famine began. Notice in Table 9-D (next page) how Joseph's first seven years as Vizier of Egypt parallels Years 2 through 8 of Sesostris I's reign. This chronology demonstrates how Joseph's marriage to Asenath in his third or fourth year of service allowed time for two children to be born in year five and year seven when the seven years of plenty ended and the seven years of famine began.

CONCLUSION

Joseph's new name, his wife's name, and his father-in-law's position as priest of Heliopolis fit perfectly into the religious, political, cultural, historical and geographical background of the Vizier of Sesostris I. In Table 9-E (end of chapter) we see eleven points of similarity between twelfth-dynasty culture and Joseph's new name, wife, and father-in-law.

Chronologically, Joseph's first seven years in service to Pharaoh fit perfectly within years two to eight of Sesostris I's reign. We have already seen the remarkable resemblance of Joseph's Viziership to the Viziership in Sesostris I's reign. The capital of Sesostris I is in the right location to be the capital in which Joseph lived. The clues are mounting and a pattern is forming that is consistent with our identification of Joseph as the first Vizier appointed by Sesostris I. However, the most significant evidence is yet to come.

TABLE 9-D
COMPARATIVE CHRONOLOGICAL CHART ON
JOSEPH'S MARRIAGE TO ASENATH

BIBLE DATES	MOSES' HISTORY	EGYPTIAN HISTORY		BRITANNICA DATES - 1
	JOSEPH	SESOSTRIS I	AMENEMHET I	
1667 BC Butler & Baker in Prison		Accession Year	Year 20	1979 BC
1666 BC 2nd full year after release		Year 1	Year 21	1978 BC
1665 BC Joseph becomes Vizier		Year 2	Year 22	1977 BC
1664 BC Joseph goes to Heliopolis		Year 3	Year 23	1976 BC
1663 BC Joseph marries Asenath		Year 4	Year 24	1975 BC
1662 BC 4th year of Abundance		Year 5	Year 25	1974 BC
1661 BC Manasseh born		Year 6	Year 26	1973 BC
1661 BC 6th year of Abundance		Year 7	Year 27	1972 BC
1660 BC Ephraim born		Year 8	Year 28	1971 BC
1659 BC 1st Year of Famine		Year 9	Year 29	1970 BC
1658 BC 2nd Year of Famine		Year 10	Year 30	1969 BC

1   J. R. Baines, "Egypt," *New Encyclopaedia Britannica*, 1991 Ed. 18.113.

TABLE 9-E
ELEVEN LIKELY DISCOVERIES IN RELATION TO
JOSEPH'S NEW NAME AND WIFE

Discovery 1. Zaphenath-Paneah, Joseph's Egyptian name, fits perfectly the Biblical context of Joseph's name: "The Dignified Seer of Mysteries," or "The Interpreter of the Chief of the Gods," or Josephus' "Revealer of Secrets."

Discovery 2. Joseph's Egyptian names fit parts of several twelfth-dynasty names, especially Hep-Zephi (Zephi-Hephi).

Discovery 3. Joseph as a special prophet fits perfectly with twelfth-dynasty religion that instituted a "Superior Prophet" over each of the religious cults of Egypt.

Discovery 4. Sesostris I introduced new families and new prophets into the priesthood and governorship, such as Hepzefi, Superior Prophet of Asyut, as the Pharaoh of Joseph did.

Discovery 5. Sesostris I sent his Vizier in his third year to build a temple and monument at Heliopolis in honor of Ra, which was included in Sesostris I's own name ("Kheper-Ka-Ra."). This gave Joseph the opportunity to meet Asenath, the daughter of the priest of Heliopolis.

Discovery 6. Sesostris I's Vizier was likely introduced to the priests of Heliopolis during the inauguration of the construction of this temple.

Discovery 7. Potiphera's Biblical name fits perfectly the Egyptian name for a high priest of Ra-worship, "He whom Ra has given."

Discovery 8. Sesostris I had a close relationship with the high priest of On. The Pharaoh of Joseph gave the daughter of the priest of On to Joseph as a wife.

Discovery 9. Amenemhet I, Sesostris I and their heirs to the throne all had "Ra" in their throne names, showing their close relationship to the worship of Ra.

Discovery 10. Asenath was a popular twelfth-dynasty name.

Discovery 11. Joseph's meeting Asenath in the third year of Sesostris I and the second year of abundance gave sufficient time for Joseph to court Asenath, marry her and have two children by the time the seven years of abundance ended.

TABLE 9-F
RUNNING TOTAL OF DISCOVERIES

Chapter	Chapter Total	Running Total
2 Conflict Between Biblical and Secular Histories	18	18
4 Discovery of 430 Years from Abraham to the Exodus	16	34
5 Confirmation of Abraham's Historicity	28	62
6 Discovery of the Remains of Sodom and Gomorrah	17	79
7 Joseph As a Slave and Prisoner in Amenemhet I's Reign	21	100
8 Joseph Becomes the Vizier of Sesostris I	23	123
9 Sesostris I Gives Joseph a New Name and a Wife	11	134

NOTES FOR CHAPTER NINE

1. Genesis 41:38

2. G. Steindorff, cited by C. E. De Vrie,, "Zaphenath-Paneah," *Zondervan Pictorial Encyclopedia of the Bible, V.1033-34* and also B. J. Beitzel, *International Standard Bible Encyclopedia.* Revised., Eerdmans, IV.1173.

3. K. A. Kitchen, "Joseph," *International Standard Bible Encyclopedia.* Eerdmans, II.1129.

4. *Ibid.*

5. Josephus, "The Antiquities of the Jews," Book 2, 6:1, *The Works of Josephus,* Trans. William Whiston (Peabody, Mass.: Hendrickson Pub., 1987), 58.

6. James Breasted (Trans.), "Contracts of Hepzefi," *Ancient Records of Egypt,* I.I.260-262. (nos. 539-546).

7. Breasted (Trans.), *Ancient Records of Egypt,* I.258.

8. Breasted (Trans.), *Ancient Records of Egypt,* I.258.

9. Breasted (Trans.), *Ancient Records of Egypt,* I.263 (no. 549).

10. Breasted, (Trans.), *Ancient Records of Egypt,* I.263 (no. 552).

11. Breasted (Trans.), *Ancient Records of Egypt,* I.263 (No. 549-551).

12. Genesis 41:34-36, 45-49.

13. Genesis 41:45.

14. Genesis 41:45, 50.

15. M. Lichtheim (Trans.), " *Ancient Egyptian Literature,* I.115-118, Univ. of Calif. Press.

16. Lichtheim,, *Ancient Egyptian Literature,* I.116-117.

17. Lichtheim, *Ancient Egyptian Literature,* I.118.

18. R. K. Harrison, "Asenath," *International Standard Encyclopedia.* Rev. Ed., Eerdmans, I.314.

19. Baines and Malek, *Atlas of Ancient Egypt,* Facts on File, 81,152,170,238.

20. E. A. Budge, *An Egyptian Hieroglyphic Dictionary,* Dover Pub., I.389.

21. Genesis 41:50

22. Genesis 41:45, Sir Lancelot Brenton (Trans.), *The Septuagint Version, Greek & English.* Zondervan, 56.

23. E. M. Cook, "On," *The International Standard Encyclopedia.* Rev. Ed., Eerdmans, III.604.

24. J. Baines & J. Malek, *Atlas of Ancient Egypt,* 31.

25. Donald B. Redford, "Heliopolis," *Anchor Bible Dictionary,* Doubleday, 3.122.

26. G. Pratico, "Potiphera," *The International Standard Bible Encyclopedia,* Rev Ed., Eerdmans, III.913.

27. W. Flinders Petrie, *A History of Egypt,* I.152,161.

28. Petrie, I.160.

29. Lichtheim (Trans.), *Ancient Egyptian Literature,* 118.

30. E. A. Budge,, *Egyptian Hieroglyphic Dictionary,* II.923, no. 122.

31. E. A. Budge,, *Egyptian Hieroglyphic Dictionary,* II.934, no. 310.

32. William Hayes, *The Scepter of Egypt,* Metropolitan Museum, N. Y., I.193.

CHAPTER TEN
THE SEVEN YEARS OF ABUNDANCE
IN SESOSTRIS I'S REIGN

The seven years of abundance began immediately after Joseph interpreted the king's dream and was appointed Vizier.[1] If we have correctly linked Joseph's appointment as Vizier in Sesostris I's second year, then the seven years of abundance occurred in Sesostris I's regnal years two through eight. In his first year Joseph traveled to cities all over Egypt to organize the collection of the grain.[2] This chapter will give evidence that the Vizier of Sesostris I executed a brilliant plan to conserve not only grain, but also water, in anticipation of a coming famine.

I. THE APPOINTMENT OF ROYAL COMMISSIONERS

The Bible says that Joseph advised Pharaoh to "appoint **commissioners** over the land to take a fifth of the harvest of Egypt during the seven years of abundance" in preparation for the seven years of famine.[3] These "**commissioners**" were to collect all the grain of the seven years of plenty and store it **"in the cities"** to provide food during the famine.[4] Joseph traveled to Egyptian cities to set up the collection centers.

> **Genesis 41:46-48** -- Joseph . . . traveled throughout Egypt [and] collected all the food produced in those seven years of abundance in Egypt and **stored it in the cities. In each city he put the food grown in the fields surrounding it.** NIV

If Sesostris I was the Pharaoh of Joseph, then he should have appointed **"royal commissioners"** to collect grain in preparation for the famine. Did he? Breasted says that during the reign of Sesostris I "**a royal commissioner,** whose duty it was to look to the interests of the Pharaoh," existed in each nome (state capital).[5] Breasted's expression, **"royal commissioner"** is the same phrase that Joseph used when describing the king's officials that should be appointed over the collection of the grain. Thus, in the reign of Sesostris I commissioners were appointed to oversee the revenue that the nomarchs (state governors) were collecting for the crown.

In earlier dynasties collections of grain during harvest were common. However, no evidence of royal commissioners working side by side with officials of the nomarch (governor) is seen in **earlier** dynasties. Thus, a new system of checks and balances was introduced in the reign of Sesostris I for both national and nomarch officials to collect and account for grain and revenue. How widespread was this new system of collecting grain?

II. NATIONAL COLLECTION OF GRAIN
IN SESOSTRIS I'S REIGN

A model of a combined granary, bakery and weaving shop was found beside the tomb of Thoty within the pyramid complex of Sesostris I at el Lisht. Thoty was first a nomarch and later a high national official of Sesostris I, giving him the privilege of being buried in the king's pyramid complex. William Hayes describes the granary model in Thoty's tomb with his overseer and bookkeeper sitting side by side on a raised platform overlooking the granary. Before them is an open papyrus roll on which is recorded the number of baskets of grain that are filled and then dumped into four bins along the left side of the model.[6]

Thoty's **overseer** must be one of the **"royal commissioners"** mentioned by Breasted who checked the books of the nomarchs as to the amount of grain collected. Thoty's bookkeeper was his own state (nome) official who also kept records of the amount of grain being stored. Thus, we have a clear demonstration of the checks and balances that Breasted indicated was present in the reign of Sesostris I and that also existed in the reign of the Pharaoh of Joseph during the seven years of abundance.

Hayes tells us that other models of collecting grain during the twelfth dynasty have been found at Asyut (in Middle Egypt) and Mir (likely Mirgissa) at the southern border of Egypt,[7] demonstrating that a national program of collecting grain was instituted all over Egypt with a royal overseer present to count the grain, precisely as described in the Bible during the days of Joseph's Viziership.

The twelfth-dynasty scenes of a royal scribe overseeing a state scribe must have occurred during the first five or six years of the seven years of famine, for the Bible tells us that Joseph ceased to count the amount of grain before the seven years had expired.

> **Genesis 41:49** - Joseph stored up huge quantities of grain, like the sand of the sea; it was so much that he stopped keeping records because it was beyond measure. NIV

III. THE COLLECTION OF GRAIN BY KHNUMHOTEP

Khnumhotep, governor of the Oryx-nome, resided in the capital called Beni Hasan,[8] located on the Nile River in Middle Egypt.[9] Breasted includes in his book a scene inscribed on the walls of Khnumhotep's tomb that depicts both national and nome (state) officials collecting taxes and **storing grain in a granary.**[10] See Figure 10-A on the next page.

Above the heads of the officials in Figure10-A, hieratic inscriptions explain the titles and functions of all of the men in the picture. Hieratic handwriting is a cursive form of hieroglyphics that often was used in writing twelfth-dynasty documents. Breasted translated only two of the eight inscriptions above their heads. Notice Breasted's photo, translation and interpretation on the next page.

On the left is the chief treasurer before whom gold and silver are being weighed; in the middle is the steward of the estate, **who records the amount of grain brought in and deposited in the granary** on the right.[11]

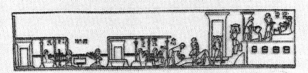

COLLECTION OF GRAIN
DURING THE REIGN OF SESOSTRIS I

AS RECORDED BY JAMES BREASTED IN *HISTORY OF EGYPT*, P. 158.

On the Right Is an Official of Sesostris I, the King, Recording Every Sack of Grain Poured into the Granary. The Sack Count Poured into the Granary Should Match the Count of Sacks Filled, as Recorded by the Nomarch (State) Official In the Middle

FIG. 79. OFFICES OF THE NOMARCH KHNUMHOTEP AT BENIHASAN.
On the left is the chief treasurer before whom gold and silver are being weighed; in the middle is the steward of the estate, who records the amount of grain brought in and deposited in the granary on the right.

FIGURE 10-A
SCENE IN THE TOMB OF KHNUMHOTEP

Notice in the center of Figure 10-A above that men are pouring grain into sacks. A scribe, whom Breasted called the steward of the estate, counts each sack filled. Going toward the right, state (nome) employees ascend the stairs, carrying the sacks of grain to the top of the granary. On the roof of the granary at the far right is another scribe of the "royal commissioner," whom Breasted mentions elsewhere in his book.[12] This royal scribe, who represents the national crown rather than the state nome, counts every sack of grain poured into the granary. Thus, both state and royal scribes record the sacks of grain, demonstrating the well organized system of checks and balances that the Vizier of King Sesostris I had instituted for the collection of the grain.

The Bible says that Joseph required the royal commissioners to keep meticulous records of the stored grain until it became so abundant that the task was meaningless: "Joseph stored up huge quantities of grain, like the sand of the sea; it was so much that he stopped **keeping records** because it was beyond measure."[13]

This painted picture was made when they were still keeping records.

Only one granary appears on the wall of Khnumhotep's tomb. However, in the tomb next to Khnumhotep's tomb, where his grandson was buried, some twenty granaries appear, proving that numerous granaries had been constructed during this period. The one granary in the tomb of Khnumhotep likely represented the many granaries pictured in the tomb next to it. Dot and I, plus Jody Jones, my student (a missionary in Toluca, Mexico for ten years), photographed these granaries inscribed on the walls of these tombs when we went to Egypt in 1991.

IV. WAS GRAIN BEING COLLECTED FOR A COMING FAMINE DURING THE EARLY REIGN OF SESOSTRIS I?

Storing grain in Egypt during harvest time was a common event in Egypt. Why did Khnumhotep and these other nomarchs think the collection of grain was such an important event to be recorded in their tombs for all posterity to remember them after their death? Collection of grain is not a common scene recorded in tombs of other dynastic periods. However, if these nomarchs under Sesostris I were collecting grain to save Egypt from the seven-year famine of Joseph's time, then these tomb scenes represent the most important service that these nomarchs accomplished during their life time. The fact that a royal commissioner was present at each of these collection scenes to verify the amount of sacks of grain deposited shows the importance that Sesostris I gave to this project.

Was the grain collected by Khnumhotep and the other twelfth-dynasty nomarchs later used to feed the hungry during a severe famine? William Hayes specifically says that the nomarchs of Sesostris I's reign improved irrigation systems to preserve water and stored up food for a future famine.

> Middle Kingdom Nomarchs in Middle Egypt . . . ruled with benevolence . . . improving the irrigation systems, restocking herds and **storing up food for use in times of famine.**[14]

I was unaware that William Hayes was alluding to Khnumhotep's collection of grain for a famine until Dot and I entered Khnumhotep's tomb in 1991. Dot made the discovery that proves this same grain stored by Khnumhotep was traded for livestock and land during "years of famine." Chapter Eleven will demonstrate that this collection of grain in Khnumhotep's storage facility was purchased by Egyptians and foreigners by trading money, livestock, land and even slaves "during the years of famine." You must read the next chapter to learn "the rest of the story."

V. WHEN DID KHNUMHOTEP COLLECT THIS GRAIN?

Did Khnumhotep collect the grain between the second and eighth years of the reign of Sesostris I? These are the years I have proposed for the seven Biblical years of abundance. Khnumhotep was appointed governor by Amenemhet I, the father of Sesostris I.[15] Therefore Khnumhotep was appointed governor before Sesostris I began his co-reign. Khnumhotep's son, Ameni, who succeeded his father as governor, tells us in his tomb that he had been governor for twenty-five years in the forty-third year of Sesostris I.[16] Subtracting twenty-five from forty-three, we see that Ameni became governor in the place of his father in the eighteenth year of Sesostris I. Therefore, Khnumhotep was ruling as nomarch before and after years 2 to 8 of Sesostris, and thus collected this grain during the years that we have hypothetically designated for the seven years of abundance described in the Bible. See Table 10-A below which graphically demonstrates this proposed chronological synchronism.

VI. WATER CONSERVATION

If Joseph was the Vizier of Sesostris I and knew a famine was coming, he would have been wise to conserve water as well as grain. Twelfth-dynasty kings dug Lake Moeris in the Faiyum of Egypt and constructed vast retention walls that eventually reached a length of twenty-seven miles. These walls gave the lake a greater depth and volume of water and, at the same time, permitted the cultivation and irrigation of the land around the lake. Twelfth-dynasty pyramids were built around, or close to, Lake Moeris.

Twelfth-dynasty kings also dug a canal that came off the Nile and ran parallel to the Nile until it finally flowed into Lake Moeris. Thus, much of the water that filled Lake Moeris actually came from the Nile River. This lake is called Birket Qarun in modern Egypt and only has a fraction of the immense size it had during the time of the twelfth dynasty.[17]

Breasted explains how twelfth-dynasty kings used Lake Moeris and its canal to **conserve water and irrigate during low Niles.**

> The kings of the Twelfth dynasty conceived the plan of controlling the inflow and outflow for the benefit of the irrigation system then in force. . . . Strabo, the most careful ancient observer of the lake . . . states that during the time of high Nile, the waters replenished the lake through the canal which still flows through the gap; but that when the river fell again, they were allowed to escape through the same canal, and be employed in irrigation.[18]

VII. THE BAHR YUSEF = THE JOSEPH CANAL

Lake Moeris was, and is still, fed by the waters of the Nile River through the **"Bahr Yusef,"**[19] a canal that branches off from the Nile at the city of Asyut.[20] This canal runs parallel to the Nile for 200 miles until it diverges from the river and circles about twenty miles to the west, flowing finally into Lake Moeris.[21]

Translated into English, the "Bahr Yusuf" means **"The Joseph Canal."**

Modern Egyptian maps still call this canal by the name of Yusef (Joseph).[22] Could the Joseph of the Bible be the brainchild of this canal which today still bears his name? When was the canal constructed or enlarged so as to reach Lake Moeris?

Breasted did not know which twelfth-dynasty king originally dug the canal and its lake, although he admits that several twelfth-dynasty kings worked on the project, especially Amenemhet III.[23] I believe that I have discovered the original Pharaoh and the exact date that the lake and its canal were initially completed.

Meri, the assistant treasurer of Sesostris I, tells us below when the lake, canal and pyramid of Amenemhet I were first constructed by his son, Sesostris I.

> **Breasted (Translator) -- Year 9** . . . under the majesty of Sesostris I, living like Re forever . . . the revered assistant treasurer, **Meri**, says: . . . My lord sent me with a commission . . . to execute for him an eternal dwelling . . . . Its columns pierced heaven; **the lake which was dug reached the river**."[24]

Notice that in "Year 9," Meri says he completed Sesostris I's commission to construct a pyramid beside a newly dug lake. Hayes tells us that transport inscriptions of the foundation stones of Sesostris I's own pyramid are not dated until Year 10, and that other stones are dated to Years 11 through 14 of Sesostris I.[25] Therefore, Meri's announcement of the completion of the lake and the pyramid in Year 9 could not be referring to Sesostris I's pyramid but to the pyramid of Amenemhet I, the wounded father of Sesostris I.

The royal cemetery of Amenemhet I was located on a desert hill several hundred yards due west of the village of El Lisht, not far from the shore of Lake Moeris.[26] Sesostris I's name and figure appear in the pyramid temple, showing the son as king, rendering gifts to his father Amenemhet I. Hayes has concluded from these scenes that Sesostris I rebuilt his father's pyramid and temple after his father's death.[27] However, we have already seen that Sesostris I was acting as sole king during their ten-year co-reign. In view of the fact that Meri said that he completed a pyramid and a lake for Sesostris I in his ninth year, whereas Sesostris I's own pyramid was not completed until his fourteenth year, it is reasonable to believe that Meri referred to Amenemhet I's pyramid and lake and not to Sesostris I's pyramid.

Since Meri completed the pyramid and lake in Year 9 and since Amenemhet I died in Year 10 of Sesostris I, the timing was perfect for the completion of his father's pyramid. Also, since Meri was the assistant treasurer, he worked directly under the supervision of the Vizier, who was the chief treasurer of Sesostris I. If that Vizier was Joseph, it was Yusef of the Bible that was the brain child of the *Bahr Yusef*, Lake Moeris, and the pyramids of Amenemhet I and Sesostris I.

The construction of the lake and pyramid likely began soon after Amenemhet I had been attacked in the assassination attempt. Therefore, the construction of the canal, the lake and the pyramid occurred during years two through eight, the years we have designated as the seven years of abundance, when Joseph was preparing for the famine. We have designated year nine as the first year of the famine. If the canal and lake were completed two or three years before the pyramid, then it could have been filled with water before the famine arrived in Year 9 of Sesostris I. See this chronological synchronism in Table10-A below.

TABLE 10-A
COMPARATIVE CHRONOLOGY OF JOSEPH,
SESOSTRIS I & KHNUMHOTEP

* The *Encyclopaedia Britiannica* revised Sesostris I's reign from 1918 to 1875 B.C.

BIBLICAL B.C. DATE	JOSEPH	SESOSTRIS I	KHNUMHOTEP (Governor)	CAMBRIDGE* B.C. DATE
1667	Baker & Butler	Year 0	Khnumhotep	1971
1666	Joseph remains in Prison	Year 1	Khnumhotep	1970
1665	Year 1 Becomes Vizier	Year 2	Khnumhotep	1969
1664	Year 2 of Abundance	Year 3	collects	1968
1663	Year 3 of Abundance	Year 4	grain	1967
1662	Year 4 of Abundance	Year 5	Meri constructs	1966
1661	Year 5 of Abundance	Year 6	canal & lake	1965
1660	Year 6 of Abundance	Year 7	Meri constructs	1964
1659	Year 7 of Abundance	Year 8	pyramid by lake	1963
1658	Year 8 = Year 1 Famine	Year 9	Meri finishes	1962
1657	Year 9 = Year 2 Famine	Year 10	Khnumhotep/Ameni	1961
1656	Year 10 = Year 3 Famine	Year 11	Khnumhotep/Ameni	1960
1655	Year 11 = Year 4 Famine	Year 12	Khnumhotep/Ameni	1959
1654	Year 12 = Year 5 Famine	Year 13	Khnumhotep/Ameni	1958
1653	Year 13 = Year 6 Famine	Year 14	Khnumhotep/Ameni	1957
1652	Year 14 = Year 7 Famine	Year 15	Khnumhotep/Ameni	1956

In Meri's quotation cited above, he mentioned that the "lake which was dug **reached the river."** How did Lake Moeris reach the Nile River when It was located about twenty miles west of the Nile? Breasted thought Meri was using "figurative language" and meant that Lake Moeris "reached" the River in the sense that it "equaled" the Nile in greatness.[28] However, Lake Moeris actually reached the Nile" through the Joseph Canal that was **"dug"** from the Nile and flowed parallel to it until it finally changed directions and flowed into Lake Moeris, thus connecting the lake to the Nile River.

The *Bahr Yusef* (Joseph Canal) had a dual purpose: (1) to fill and beautify lake Moeris and (2) to irrigate land that surrounded both the lake and the canal during low Niles and thus during periods of famine. The canal that connects Lake Moeris to the Nile River is the *Bahr Yusuf* (the Joseph Canal). Thus, the Canal of Joseph and Lake Moeris, which were improved by later Pharaohs of the twelfth dynasty,[29] were first constructed during years 2 to 8 of Sesostris I's reign. These are precisely the years that I had previously designated for the seven years of abundance when **grain and water** were being preserved during Joseph's ministry as the Vizier of Egypt.

What a brilliant idea! Joseph not only preserved grain for the famine; he also conserved water. Another coincidence, or real historical synchronism? The fact that the canal still bears the name of Joseph (Yusuf) remarkably connects Joseph to

Sesostris I's Vizier, who first designed and supervised the construction of this canal.

Interestingly, T. G. H. James, former Keeper of Egyptian Antiquities at the British Museum, writes that either Ammenemes I (Amenemhet I) or Ammenemes III (Amenemhet III) constructed the Joseph Canal and Lake Moeris. James marveled at the engineering prowess involved in their construction. He suggested that the *Bahr Yusuf* (Joseph's River) was puzzling. James suggested that Yusuf (Joseph) may have been the hydraulic engineer who masterminded the Twelfth dynasty works. He proposed that the canal may have been originally man-made, but doubted this conclusion because the canal often curved and zig-zagged at many locations along the stream.[30] However, James could have meant that it was not solely "man-made." Dot and I, along with our friends Virgil Yocham and Jody Jones, observed the canal and Lake Moeris very closely when we went to Egypt in the summer of 1991. In long sections the canal is straight as an arrow and thus looks very "man-made." In other stretches the canal curves along more natural paths. Thus, it appears that parts of the canal are man-made and part are natural river beds. The man-made sections of this 200-mile canal prevented it from running back into the Nile River. The Joseph Canal is still used for irrigation purposes in modern Egypt. However, Lake Moeris now has developed a "salty" condition and thus no longer has sweet water to irrigate Egypt's dry fields, as it once did. See the map and photos of the Joseph Canal on the next page in Figures 10-B and 10-C.

The Joseph canal and Lake Moeris stand as permanent memorials to the Vizier of Sesostris I who first constructed it during the early years of Sesostris I's reign in preparation for the years of famine. One hundred years later Amenemhet III improved the water system of the canal and the lake. However, it was Joseph who prepared for the seven years of famine by digging out the Joseph Canal and funneling the water into Lake Moeris, where it was stored for irrigation. It was also Sesostris I that authorized his Vizier (Joseph) to dig the Joseph Canal (Bahr Yusef), and to expand Lake Moeris, all in preparation for the coming famine. The finishing of the canal during the seven years of abundance just before the years of famine began is another amazing "coincidence" that confirms my identification of Sesostris I as the Pharaoh of Joseph as a true historical synchronism.

Interestingly, S. C. Burchell, author of *Building the Suez Canal*, reported that the original builder of the Suez Canal was Sesostris I of the twelfth dynasty and that it was very narrow and lasted about 1000 years before desert winds filled the canal with sand.[31] Joseph, the Vizier of Sesostris I, was likely the brain child and overseer of the original Suez Canal in Sesostris I's reign.

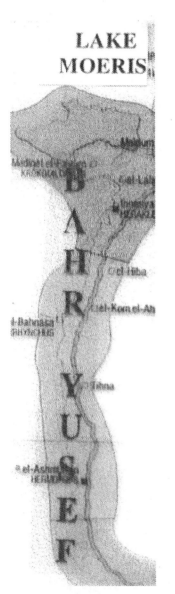

LAKE
MOERIS

B
A
H
R

Y
U
S
E
F

FIGURE 10-C
Photo by Dot Stewart
Ted Stewart and Jody Jones
Standing on Bridge over
the Bahr Yusef (Canal of Joseph)

FIGURE 10-B
MAP OF THE BAHR YUSEF
(JOSEPH CANAL)
Flows into Lake Moeris
Pyramids of 12th Dynasty
Pharaohs are constructed
around the Lake.

FIGURE 10-D
Photo by Dot Stewart
Long, Man-Made Stretch of
of the Bahr Yusef (Canal of Joseph)

CONCLUSION

We now add nine more unique "coincidences" that identify Joseph as the Vizier of Sesostris I during the years of abundance from Years 2 to 8. Table10-B below lists these eight points of synchronism. In Chapter Eleven we want to see if the grain stored by Khnumhotep was sold and traded during a famine. We also want to see if the seven years of famine during Joseph's time will fit Years 9 through 15 of Sesostris I, the years we have designated for the Biblical famine. In Chapter Twelve we will examine evidence that the Israelites entered Egypt at the end of the second year of famine. If the answers to these inquiries prove positive in Chapters Eleven and Twelve, all of these mounting "coincidences" will turn into true synchronisms that definitely identify Joseph as the first Vizier of Sesostris I.

TABLE 10-B
TEN DISCOVERIES BETWEEN JOSEPH AND SESOSTRIS I
DURING THE SEVEN YEARS OF ABUNDANCE

Discovery 1. Joseph appointed royal commissioners to represent the crown in collecting the grain as the Vizier of Sesostris I also did for the same purpose.

Discovery 2. Joseph set up the collection centers in principal Egyptian cities all over Egypt. Twelfth-dynasty nomarchs also collected grain overseen by Sesostris I in capital cities located in northern, southern and middle Egypt.

Discovery 3. Joseph required that every sack of grain stored should be recorded during the first years of abundance. Both royal and state scribes are pictured counting the grain in at least two tomb inscriptions.

Discovery 4. Khnumhotep, nomarch of Beni Hasan during Sesostris I's years two to eight stored grain at Beni Hasan during the seven years of abundance in the time of Joseph.

Discovery 5. The tomb of Khnumhotep's grandson has twenty granaries inscribed on the wall at Beni Hasan, showing the numerous grain depositories constructed in Joseph's time.

Discovery 6. Lake Moeris was dug during years two to eight of Sesostris I to conserve water and irrigate the land in time of famine.

Discovery 7. The Joseph Canal (Bahr Yusef) was dug during years two to eight of Sesostris I to increase the flow of water into Lake Moeris and also to irrigate in times of low Niles (famine).

Discovery 8. The Bahr Yusef (Canal of Joseph) still bears the name of Joseph (Yusef) to this day.

Discovery 9. Jody Jones, Virgil Yocham plus Dot and myself saw with our own eyes the sign of Bahr Yusef (Joseph Canal) on bridges and on modern maps in Egypt.

Discovery 10. As Joseph built the Bahr Yusef, he was also likely the builder of the original Suez Canal during the reign of Sesostris I.

TABLE 10-C
RUNNING TOTAL OF DISCOVERIES

Chapter		Chapter Total	Running Total
2	Conflict Between Biblical and Secular Histories	18	18
4	Discovery of 430 Years from Abraham to the Exodus	16	34
5	Confirmation of Abraham's Historicity	28	62
6	Discovery of the Remains of Sodom and Gomorrah	17	79
7	Joseph As a Slave and Prisoner in Amenemhet I's Reign	21	100
8	Joseph Becomes the Vizier of Sesostris I	23	123
9	Sesostris I Gives Joseph a New Name and a Wife	11	134
10	The Seven Years of Abundance in Sesostris I's Reign	10	144

NOTES FOR CHAPTER TEN

1. Genesis 41:32
2. Genesis 41:46-49
3. Genesis 41:34
4. Genesis 41:34-37
5. James Breasted, *History of Egypt*, pp. 162-163; also, "Twelfth dynasty: Sesostris I," *Ancient Records of Egypt*, I.252 (No. 522 and footnote a).
6. William C. Hayes, *The Scepter of Egypt*, I.264. Metropolitan Museum, N.Y.
7. Hayes, I.265.
8. Breasted, *History of Egypt*, 161-162.
9. Baines and Malek, *Atlas of Ancient Egypt*, 14.
10. Breasted, *History of Egypt*, 158-162.
11. Breasted, *History of Egypt*, note under Figure 79, 158.
12. Breasted, *History of Egypt*, 162. See end note no. 13.
13. Genesis 41:49
14. William C. Hayes, "The Middle Kingdom in Egypt," *Cambridge Ancient History*, I.2A.468.
15. Breasted, *Ancient Records of Egypt*, I.280,283. Nos.620 & 624.
16. Breasted, *Ancient Records of Egypt*, I.250, no.518.
17. James Breasted, *History of Egypt*, 191-3.
18. Breasted,, *History of Egypt*, 193.
19. Breasted, *History of Egypt*, 5.
20. Baines, *Atlas of Ancient Egypt*, 18.
21. Breasted, *History of Egypt*, 5.
22. Baines, *Atlas of Ancient Egypt*, 18.
23. Breasted, *History of Egypt*, 190-193.
24. Breasted (Trans.), "Inscription of Meri," *Ancient Records of Egypt*, I.246.
25. William C. Hayes, *Scepter of Egypt*, I.182.
26. Hayes, *Scepter of Egypt*, I.172.
27. Hayes, *Scepter of Egypt*, I.174.
28. Breasted, *Ancient Records of Egypt*, I.246, footnote h.
29. Breasted, *History of Egypt*, 193-194.
30. T. G. H. James, *Ancient Egypt, The Land & Its Legacy* (London: British Museum Pub., 1988), 73-74.
31. S. C. Burchell, *Building the Suez Canal* (New York: Harper & Row, 1966., 32.

CHAPTER ELEVEN
THE SEVEN YEARS OF FAMINE IN SESOSTRIS I'S REIGN

Famines rarely occur in Egypt because of the consistent flow of the Nile River. When a famine did occur, the event was usually noted in Egyptian inscriptions. King Unas at the end of the fifth dynasty depicted conditions of famine in his day.[1] Hundreds of years later, famines were also recorded in inscriptions from the tenth and eleventh dynasties.[2]

When Joseph was Vizier of Egypt, a seven-year famine devastated the entire land and surrounding countries. Joseph sold and traded the grain he had collected for all of the money, livestock and land of Egypt, except for the property of the priests. Afterwards, Joseph leased the land back to the Egyptians on an 80%/20% share crop basis (Genesis 47:13-27).

Other than the Bible, the only record that specifies a "seven-year famine" is found in a Greek text dated to the second century B.C. This document describes a seven-year famine during the reign of King Djoser (Zoser) of the third dynasty. The text claims that Djoser's Vizier, Imhotep, predicted the famine far enough ahead to allow Djoser to prepare for it.[3] However, our Biblical chronology dates Joseph's famine as beginning in 1658 B.C., whereas Egyptologists date Djoser's reign between 2667 B.C.[4] and 2600 B.C.[5]

Dr. Gerald Aardsma believes that Djoser's famine is the Egyptian confirmation of the Biblical story of the famine of Joseph and that Joseph needs to be redated 1,000 years earlier than the Bible dates to fit the conventional Egyptian dates of Djoser.[6] However, the Egyptian document recording the Djoser famine is very suspect. First, the text is written in Greek, not in the hieratic or hieroglyphic language of the ancient Egyptians. Second, this document did not appear until the second century B.C. Third, this famine is not mentioned in contemporary records of Djoser's time, nor is it mentioned in any other ancient Egyptian document. Fourth, the Vizier's name Imhotep means "River of Peace or Joy"[7] and thus is not similar in form or meaning to Joseph's Egyptian name, Zaphenath-Paneah.

Some scholars believe Egyptians fabricated the Djoser famine in the third or second century B.C. to justify the granting of land to the priests mentioned in the text. I agree that second-century B.C. Egyptian priests likely forged this document to prove that an Egyptian Vizier (Imhotep), predicted the famine, not Joseph, and that the Biblical narrative of Joseph imitated the earlier Egyptian story. This chapter will demonstrate that Joseph's famine was the original source for the Egyptian fabrication of the Djoser famine in the second century B.C. and that the famine actually occurred during the reign of Sesostris I of the twelfth dynasty.

I. THE YEARS OF FAMINE IN AMENI'S TIME

In the twelfth dynasty a governor by the name of Ameni reported that he distributed grain to feed the hungry during **"years of famine."**

Breasted's Translation -- When years of famine came I plowed all the fields of the Oryx nome, as far as its southern and northern boundary, **preserving its people alive and furnishing its food so that there was none hungry therein. . . . Then came great Niles, possessors of grain and all things**, but I did not collect the arrears of the field.[8]

Egyptologist Brugsch admitted that the plural years of famine in Ameni's inscription indeed sounded like the time of the Biblical Joseph:

> The concluding words of this inscription, in which Ameni sings his own praises, have given rise to the idea that they contain an allusion to the sojourn of the patriarch Joseph in Egypt and to the seven years of famine under his administration.[9]

However, Brugsch quickly dismissed the idea of linking Ameni's famine with Joseph's famine, on the basis that Joseph lived during the Hyksos dynasties (fifteenth and sixteenth) , whereas Ameni lived during the early part of the twelfth dynasty. This chapter will present historical evidences that Ameni and Joseph were contemporaries. Chapters Twenty-Three and Twenty-Four present carbon-14 dates and astronomical dates that prove the twelfth dynasty should be dated 300 years later to fit the Biblical dates for Joseph.

II. WHEN DID THE YEARS OF FAMINE OCCUR IN AMENI'S TIME?

Ameni's inscription says that his twenty-fifth year as Nomarch (governor) was Sesostris I's forty-third year.[10] Therefore, Ameni became Nomarch in Sesostris I's eighteenth year of reign, three years after the famine had ended. See Table 11-A on the next page. How could Ameni distribute grain in the seven years of famine when he did not begin to rule as governor until three years after the famine is supposed to have occurred (according to my Biblical chronology)?

When I first contemplated this chronological problem, I theorized that Ameni probably distributed to the hungry during the years of famine while assisting his father, Khnumhotep, before he was appointed Nomarch (governor). Later, I found proof for this hypothesis in Ameni's own words, recorded in *The Ancient Records of Egypt,* translated by James Breasted.

> I sailed southward as the son of a count [Nomarch], wearer of the royal seal, and commander in chief of the troops of the Oryx nome, **as a man represents his old father,** according to [his] favor in the palace and his love in the court.[11]

Khnumhotep died in Sesostris I's eighteenth year. Ameni's cited statement proves that he performed his father's functions as governor for some years before

Khnumhotep died. Ameni was likely selling the grain in the place of his aged father for all, or at least part, of the seven years of famine (years nine to fifteen of Sesostris I). Under the next point we will prove that Ameni was definitely trading grain for money, livestock and goods **during the famine.**

TABLE 11-A
COMPARATIVE CHRONOLOGICAL CHART OF JOSEPH, SESOSTRIS I, KHNUMHOTEP AND AMENI

BIBLE DATES	MOSES' HISTORY	EGYPTIAN HISTORY		
		AMENEMHET I		
1688		Year 0		
				KHNUMHOTEP
1678		Year 9		
1668		SESOSTRIS I 19		
1667 BC BUTLER HANGED		Year 0	20	?
1666		Year 1	21	?
1665 BC JOSEPH BECOMES Vizier		Year 2	22	?
1664 BC 2nd Year of Abundance		Year 3	23	?
1663 BC JOSEPH MARRIES ASENATH		Year 4	24	?
1662 BC 4th Year of Abundance		Year 5	25	?
1661 BC 5th Year of Abundance		Year 6	26	?
1660 BC 6th Year of Abundance		Year 7	27	?
1659 BC 7th Year of Abundance		Year 8	28	?
1658 BC 1st Year of Famine		Year 9	29	?
1657 BC AMENEMHET I DIES		Year 10	30	?
1656 BC JACOB ENTERS EGYPT		Year 11	31	?
1655 BC 4th Year of Famine		Year 12	32	AMENI
1654 BC 5th Year of Famine		Year 13	33	ASSISTS
1653 BC 6th Year of Famine		Year 14	34	FATHER
1652 BC 7th Year of Famine		Year 15	35	
1651 BC NILE RIVER IS FULL		Year 16	36	
1650 BC GOOD CROPS		Year 17	37	
1649 BC KHNUMHOTEP DIES		Year 18		AMENI 0
1648 BC		Year 19		
1624 BC		Year 43		25
1627 BC SESOSTRIS I DIES		Year 46		

III. DISCOVERY OF THE YEARS OF ABUNDANCE AND THE YEARS OF FAMINE IN THE SAME TOMB

Breasted reported that the collection of the grain recorded in the tomb of Ameni was located at Beni-Hasan. My wife, Dot, and I visited Egypt along with our colleagues, Virgil Yocham and Jody Jones in the summer of 1991. I was determined to see for myself the inscribed scene of Khnumhotep's collection of grain and the famine inscription of his son, Ameni. I expected to find these inscriptions in separate tombs for Khnumhotep and his son, Ameni. However, much to my surprise we found a single tomb for both father and son. To help us find these tombs we hired Badhr Sodre to be our Egyptian guide. Badhr's partner was curious when we told them what we were hoping to find. He asked permission to accompany us without charging us for his services. Both of these Egyptian guides had master's degrees in Egyptology from the University of Cairo.[12] Badhr's partner majored in hieroglyphics and helped us immensely by translating the tomb inscriptions that we later found. I fail to remember the name of Badhr's partner.

The tombs we wanted to see were located on the eastern side of the Nile River across from the town of Beni-Hasan. We crossed the Nile by boat and walked up to the tombs. We entered into many of the tombs at Beni-Hasan without finding the inscriptions we were seeking. Finally, I found an old paper sack and drew the granary scene from my memory of Breasted's book and showed it to the Egyptian guard. He immediately recognized the picture and took us back to the first tomb we had entered.

There are three reasons I did not see the granary when I entered the first tomb. (1) The guard explained that several years earlier two guards got drunk, entered the tomb and threw beer bottles at each other. The beer bottles that missed their mark seriously damaged the scene which pictured the pouring of the grain into an immense granary. (2) The tomb inscriptions and painted scenes had greatly deteriorated from exposure to the atmosphere since Breasted had photographed the scenes about eighty years earlier. (3) The stairs leading up to the top of the granary were on the opposite side of the granary when compared with Breasted's printed photo of the granary in his book (*History of Egypt*, p. 158). Breasted had copied the wrong side of the photo negative, resulting in a reverse appearance of the scenes inscribed on the southern wall of the tomb. All of these facts prevented me from recognizing the granary scene when we first entered the tomb.

When we returned to the first tomb, the guard showed me on the wall where the granary was inscribed. The stairs leading to the top of the granary with Egyptians carrying sacks of grain were barely visible. Gradually I began to see the scribes on the ground floor who counted the sacks of grain and the treasurer who collected money, but in reverse order from what I had seen in Breasted's history book.

However, the granary scene with the collection of taxes was only one of numerous pictures in this tomb. We forgot to bring our measuring tape to the tomb. We estimate that the tomb was about eighteen feet wide and thirty to thirty-five feet long. Paintings and hieroglyphic inscriptions are found on all four walls of the tomb. The granary and tax collection scenes were located on the eastern end of the southern wall of the tomb. See this scene in Figure 11-A two pages below.

While I was examining closely the granary inscription on the eastern end of the south wall, Dot backed all of the way to the north wall so that she could get an over-view of the entirety of the south wall. She saw things the rest of us had not yet seen. She excitedly yelled at me, "Look at this giant official on the western end of the south wall." "He is holding his hands out to receive rows of Egyptians and foreigners who are walking toward him, bringing to him all kinds of livestock, birds, fruit, wine, merchandise and even slaves." "Who is that man?" Dot asked me. "Are these people coming to trade for grain during the famine?" This scene occupied two thirds of the entire southern wall of the tomb. See this scene in Figure 11-B on the next page.

The guide answered Dot, "A figure that immense must be the Pharaoh of Egypt, and these people are likely bringing gifts to him." "But this is not a tomb of a Pharaoh," I told the guide, "but of Khnumhotep, a governor of Beni-hasan." "That giant figure at the west end of the wall must be Khnumhotep," I mistakenly asserted.

Our guide, who knew hieroglyphics, began to translate the inscriptions on both ends of the south wall. He confirmed that Khnumhotep was indeed the governor of Beni-Hasan and is the one who collected the grain and taxes on the eastern end of the south wall. However, the guide said that I was wrong about the identity of the giant figure on the western end of the south wall. He found that this figure was Ameni, the son of Khnumhotep who later succeeded his father as governor of the nome at Beni-Hasan.

Our guide kept reading until he finally found the hieroglyphic inscription for "years of famine." He turned to Dot and said, "You were correct; all of these Egyptians and foreigners are coming to Ameni to purchase grain in the 'years of famine.'" I had already read this inscription in Breasted's translation of the *Ancient Records of Egypt*. Our guide showed us on the wall the hieroglyphic sign for "famine," which shows a man sucking his forefinger with his mouth. On this same wall was inscribed the following quotation.

> **Breasted's Translation** -- When **years of famine** came I ploughed all the fields of the Oryx-nome, as far as its southern and northern boundary, preserving its people alive and furnishing its food, so that there was none hungry therein. I gave to the widow as to her who had a husband; I did not exalt the great above the small in all I gave. Then came great Niles, rich in grain and all things, but I did not collect the arrears of the field.[13]

I was amazed that Ameni's inscription of "years of famine" was inscribed in the same tomb with his father's inscription of the gathering of grain during the "years of plenty." This large tomb belonged to both father and son. The tomb next to this large tomb was smaller and belonged to the grandson of Khnumhotep. My presupposition that the giant figure on the west end of the south wall was Khnumhotep proved to be wrong. However, my theory that Ameni sold the grain during the years of famine in the place of his aged father proved to be correct. The pictures on the wall were so deteriorated from age and the light in the tomb was so dim that our color slide pictures were not clear enough for readers to see.

The wall pictures showed many foreigners and Egyptians walking toward Ameni at the far west end of the southern wall. They carried with them varied articles of value, different species of livestock, even a slave, to trade for grain during the years of famine.

I asked our guide if he could find the cartouche of Sesostris I to verify that the years of abundance and years of famine occurred in Sesostris I's reign. Our hieroglyphic expert searched all over the south wall and found nothing. Finally he looked at the east wall where we entered the tomb. **Above the door jam he found the cartouche of Sesostris I.** Therefore, this tomb and its drawings and inscriptions about the gathering of the grain for years of famine and the trading of grain for land, livestock and valuables during the famine confirm that Sesostris I was the Pharaoh of Joseph. **It further confirms that Joseph was the Vizier who prepared for the famine by gathering grain during the seven years of abundance.**

I then realized that Ameni built this tomb for both himself and for his aged father, Khnumhotep. The grain had been collected by the father and the grain was traded by his son, Ameni, for livestock and valuables during the famine when his father was too old to work. Both Khnumhotep and Ameni were buried in the same tomb, but their mummies had long been removed to another location.

FIGURE 11-A - (Left) Photos of the Tomb Where Grain Was Gathered During the Years of Plenty

FIGURE 11-B - (Right) Grain Sold and Traded for Money, Animals, and Land During the Years of Famine

IV. THE GRAIN DISTRIBUTION DURING THE YEARS
OF FAMINE IN SESOSTRIS I'S REIGN

As we continued to investigate the tomb, Dot called my attention to the rows of people all walking toward Ameni and bringing different items to trade for grain. Some held birds or plants. Others carried vessels of gold and silver and some bottles of wine. An entire row of men were leading livestock and even some wild animals. One Egyptian forced a slave to walk in front of him.

Our guide pointed out to us that most of the people were dressed as Egyptians, but that others were foreigners from S. Africa and the East. We were stunned almost breathless by what we were seeing. Painted pictures on the walls showed that Egyptians and foreigners were trading for grain during "years of famine" just as the Bible described during the seven years of famine.

> Genesis 41:56-57 -- (56) When the famine had spread over the whole country, Joseph opened the storehouses and **sold grain to the Egyptians**, for the famine was severe throughout Egypt. (57) And **all the countries came to Egypt to buy grain from Joseph**, because the famine was severe in all the world. (NIV)

I thanked God for enabling us to find even more than we were seeking. We found not only the inscriptions that told about these events, but also the original pictures of both the collection of the grain during the years of abundance and the selling and trading of the grain during the famine, all on one wall. This one tomb in middle Egypt described what was happening all over Egypt during the years of famine, for the Bible says that Joseph set up collection centers for grain in all of the major cities of Egypt (Genesis 41:47-49). Beni-Hasan was the capital of the Orynx Nome, a principal state or division of Egypt.

The tomb was so dark and the wall had so deteriorated that our photo, copied in Figure 11-B (above), could not capture what we could see with our naked eyes. However, on the next page the reader can see in Figure 11-C (next page) how the tomb next door had a clearer and similar scene of Egyptians and foreigners coming to trade for grain following the years of famine. The color and clarity of this photo, which I found in a magazine, enables the reader to get a clearer picture of Egyptians and foreigners who came to Beni Hasan to trade for grain when a different governor sold and traded for grain during the period following the seven years of famine.

FIGURE 11-C -This Clearer Picture of Trading & Selling of Grain is in the tomb next door to the previous tomb and pictures the normal trading for grain after the years of famine.

V. SESOSTRIS I'S WEALTH AFTER THE FAMINE

During the seven years of famine the Bible says that the Egyptians spent all of their money, traded all of their livestock and property and finally sold themselves as slaves to Pharaoh in order to purchase grain and live, rather than die.

Genesis 47:13-14 -- (13) There was no food, however, in the whole region because the famine was severe; both Egypt and Canaan wasted away because of the famine. (14) Joseph collected all the money that was to be found in Egypt and Canaan in payment for the grain they were buying, and he brought it to Pharaoh's palace. (NIV)

Ordinarily, consecutive "years of famine," such as Ameni described in his tomb, would diminish the riches of the king as well as the people. But because of the great abundance of grain that had been collected through the wisdom of Joseph, the Pharaoh of Joseph filled his treasury with all of the money of Egypt and from foreign countries as well (Genesis 47:13-14).

Does evidence exist that Sesostris I grew in wealth during this famine? The pictures engraved on the wall of Ameni's tomb show officials weighing silver and gold, no doubt given in payment for the grain purchased. Whereas Egypt should have been devastated by the "years of famine," records show that Sesostris I's treasury was so full of money that he initiated the largest expansion of Egypt in its history to that time. Hayes' describes this expansion as follows.

Secure upon his throne, he [Sesostris I] was able to devote his great energy, ability and breadth of vision to a programme [sic.] **for the enrichment and expansion of Egypt more grandiose than any heretofore undertaken.**[15]

The money Sesostris I received from selling grain in the famine enabled him to finance vast construction projects all over Egypt. Note Hayes' words below:

In Egypt itself at least **thirty-five sites**, from Alexandria on the Mediterranean coast to Aswan on the First Cataract, have yielded **buildings or other monuments** of King Sesostris I, and there was hardly a temple of any importance in Upper or Lower Egypt that was not enlarged or embellished by this great pharaoh.[16]

Sesostris I's wealth enabled him to employ men to extract even more gold, silver and precious metals and stones from mines. Hayes describes Sesostris I's riches and the extraordinary building expansion that this wealth supported.

The **gold and copper mines** of the Wadi el-Allaqi, in the desert east of Quban, were undoubtedly exploited by the **king's engineers**, and the ancient **diorite quarries** of Cheops to the north-west of Toshka apparently **swarmed with Egyptian working parties.** Amethysts of the land of Nubia were dragged on sledges from the mines of the Wadi el-Hudi, and **blocks of red granite** were extracted from the quarries at the First Cataract [first water fall on the Nile River]. . . . **Gold** was brought also from mines east of Koptos and **hard stone** from the nearby Wadi Hammamat, where, . . . an expedition of **more than seventeen thousand men** quarried the blocks **for sixty sphinxes and one hundred and fifty statues.**[17]

Abundant jewelry and exquisite artistry were more prevalent during the reign of Sesostris I and his successors than in any other time in Egyptian history. Hayes vividly describes the artistic expertise of the twelfth dynasty.

The art of the jeweler, practiced in Egypt since the Neolithic period, reached in the Middle Kingdom a degree of excellence never surpassed throughout the remainder of the country's dynastic history. An extraordinary sense of effective design, coupled with faultless taste and a complete mastery of the techniques involved in working and combining precious metals and semi-precious stones, was furthered by the existence of an almost unlimited supply of the valuable material required and by a wealthy and discriminating clientele, far more extensive than any found in our modern world.[18]

The statues sculptured by the artisans of Sesostris I are considered to be of the finest quality in the history of Egypt and even of the world.

The head . . . of Amun-em-het I . . . [father of Sesostris I] was a facial type which inspired the sculptors of the Twelfth dynasty to the creation of a series of royal portraits executed with a power and realism rarely equaled in the history of the world's art.[19]

I photographed in the Cairo Museum a magnificent ivory monument with six different ivory statues of Sesostris I facing in six different directions. Unfortunately, I misplaced the slide and have been unable to obtain a duplicate. Sesostris I appears on the monument to be in his mid-thirty's, likely in the period immediately following the "years of famine" reported by Ameni.

The wealth and expertise of Sesostris I and his monument of six ivory statues in the period following the famine stand in stark contrast to the simplicity and poverty of a wooden statue of Sesostris I when he first became king in his early twenties. Sesostris I was forced to become king when he was very young because his father was disabled by the assassination attempt. Notice Figure 11-D that pictures Sesostris I when he first was appointed Pharaoh in the place of his injured father, Amenemhet I. This simple, wooden statue shows him in scanty clothes with a shepherd's staff in his hand.

Sesostris I's early simplicity, wooden statue and lack of ostentatious wealth significantly contrast with his enormous wealth and exquisite stone and ivory sculptured statues just fifteen years later. This change demonstrates that Sesostris' wealth had multiplied by leaps and bounds during the interval. Selling grain during the seven years of famine for all of the land and money in Egypt, and much of the wealth of surrounding countries, increased Sesostris I's wealth immeasurably. See a picture of Sesostris I's statue when he was older and wealthier in Figure 11-E.

SESOSTRIS I

SESOSTRIS I

Figure 11-D	**Figure 11-E**
Photo of Wooden Statue of Young Sesostris I in Cairo Museum Photo by Ron Wyatt	Photo of a stone Statue of a more wealthy Sesostris I after the years of abundance and famine Source: Unknown

VI. SESOSTRIS I, OWNER OF MOST OF EGYPT'S LIVESTOCK

The Pharaoh of Joseph not only grew in monetary wealth during the famine, but also in ownership of livestock. When the Egyptians and foreigners spent all of their money for grain, they began to trade all of their livestock for additional grain.

> Genesis 47:15-16 -- (15) When the money of the people of Egypt and Canaan was gone, all Egypt came to Joseph and said, "Give us food. Why should we die before your eyes? Our money is used up." (16) "Then bring your livestock," said Joseph. "I will sell you food in exchange for your livestock, since your money is gone." (17) So they brought their livestock to Joseph, and he gave them food in exchange for their horses, their sheep and goats, their cattle and donkeys. And he brought them through that year with food in exchange **for all their livestock.** (NIV)

If Sesostris I is the Pharaoh of Joseph, he should have been the owner of the largest herds of livestock in the world. We saw on the wall of Ameni's tomb the livestock that Egyptians and foreigners were trading for grain. This same Ameni describes his responsibilities as Nomarch in the years following the famine.

> **The gang-overseers of the crown possessions of the shepherds of the oryx nome gave to me 3,000 bulls in their yokes.** I was praised on account of it in the palace each year of the **loan-herds.** I carried all their dues to the king's house; there were no arrears against me in any office of his.[20]

Commenting on the above citation of Ameni, Breasted noted the following:

> This means that Ameni received a herd of 3,000 cattle from the royal herds, to be maintained by him on shares. He kept them so well that he was praised each year when his payment fell due.[21]

Thus, Ameni had to pay annual **"dues"** to the king's palace to pay for these **"loan-herds"** which he leased from Sesostris I's "crown possessions." This means that Sesostris I had multiplied thousands of cattle under his own overseers, from which these 3,000 were loaned to Ameni.

Breasted also notes another governor of this time, Thuthhotep, who had "**great numbers of cattle from the king** . . . in the districts of the Hare nome."[22] Thuthhotep, like Ameni, also oversaw a very large herd of cattle that was owned by Sesostris I. Thuthhotep lived in southern Egypt; Ameni lived in middle Egypt; Sesostris I lived in northern Egypt. These loan herds, plus huge numbers of herds directly under supervision of the king's own overseers, prove that Sesostris I owned livestock all over Egypt, just as the Pharaoh of Joseph did after the famine.

The Atlas of Ancient Egypt lists twenty nomes (states or provinces) of lower Egypt and twenty-two nomes of upper Egypt for a total of forty-two nomes.[23] If each of these forty-two Nomarchs had 3,000 cows on loan from Sesostris I, that would amount to 126,000 royal cattle out on loan from Sesostris I, and this was in addition to the cattle that Sesostris I kept under the control of his own "gang overseers." Undoubtedly, Sesostris I was the richest owner of livestock in the world. Sesostris I reached the epitome of wealth in livestock, in the same manner as the Pharaoh of Joseph.

VII. SESOSTRIS I: OWNER OF ALL OF EGYPT'S LAND EXCEPT THE PRIESTS'

The Pharaoh of Joseph not only obtained all of the money and herds of Egypt, but also **all** of the land of Egypt.

> Genesis 47:18-20 -- (18) When that year was over, they came to him the following year and said, "We cannot hide from our lord the fact that since our money is gone and our livestock belongs to you, there is nothing left for our lord except our bodies and our land. (19) Why should we perish before your eyes --- we and our land as well? Buy us and our land in exchange for food, and we with our land will be in bondage to Pharaoh. Give us seed so that we may live and not die, and that the land may not become desolate." (20) So Joseph bought all the land in Egypt for Pharaoh. The Egyptians, one and all, sold their fields, because the famine was too severe for them. The land became Pharaoh's. (NIV)

Even though Egyptians no longer owned their livestock or land, Pharaoh was kind enough to lease out his newly acquired property for a 20% share cropper's lease.

> Genesis 47:23-26 -- (23) Joseph said to the people, "Now that I have bought you and your land today for Pharaoh, here is seed for you so you can plant the ground. (24) But when the crop comes in, give a fifth of it to Pharaoh. The other four-fifths you may keep as seed for the fields and as food for yourselves and your households and your children." (25) "You have saved our lives," they said. "May we find favor in the eyes of our lord; we will be in bondage to Pharaoh." (26) So Joseph established it as a law concerning land in Egypt --- still in force today --- that a fifth of the produce belongs to Pharaoh. It was only the land of the priests that did not become Pharaoh's. (NIV)

All of the land of Egypt was sold to Pharaoh with one exception. The land of the priests was not sold or traded and thus remained in their possession.

Genesis 47:22 -- However, **he [Joseph] did not buy the land of the priests,** because they **received a regular allotment from Pharaoh** and had food enough from the allotment Pharaoh gave them. That is why they did not sell their land. (NIV)

Do we find any evidence in Egyptian documents that Sesostris I owned all of the land of Egypt, except the priests' land? Did Sesostris I give the priests an allotment during the famine so that they did not need to sell their land? Do we find that Sesostris I leased the land back to the Egyptians and charged them a share-cropper's rent as did the Pharaoh of Joseph's day? Several Egyptian inscriptions written during the reign of Sesostris I give a resounding "Yes!" to all of these questions.

VIII. HEPZEFI'S CONTRACTS

Hepzefi, a Superior Prophet and priest of the temple of Upwawet was appointed by Sesostris I as Nomarch of Siut (Asyut, a capital city of Middle Egypt).[24] Hepzefi made three contracts with his fellow priests to care for his tomb and his statue in the temple and to make offerings on his behalf after his death.

(1) Contract One dealt with Hepzefi's temple income which he received as the Superior Prophet and High Priest of Upwawet.

(2) Contract Two discussed the income from King's Sesostris I's property that Hepzefi oversaw as the Nomarch or Governor of Siut. Contract Two also treated the King's property which had been rented out to the citizens of Siut.

(3) Contact Three dealt with Hepzefi's personal property that he owned as a priest and which he had received from his father, who was also a priest.

Contract One - Hepzefi's Income as
High Priest (Superior Prophet)

As Superior Prophet of Upwawet, Hepzefi was also High Priest of Upwawet and thus received a share of all of the offerings of grain and meat contributed to the Temple. In this first contract Hepzefi agreed to give all of the priests his quarter share of the bull offering that was due him as the Superior Prophet, in exchange for their making bread offerings to his statue at the end of each year.[25]

There shall be given to him (Hepzefi) a white loaf per individual priest, for his statue, . . . on the first of the five intercalary days. . . . "Behold ye [priests], I have given you this quarter [inherited portion of the bull] due to me from this temple."[26]

Contract Two, Part One: Hepzefi's Donations
From the Nomarch's Estate

In his second contract Hepzefi agreed to give the priests a bushel of grain from every field of the Nomarch's estate (owned by Sesostris I), if they would offer white bread before his statue and glorify his name every New Year's Day: "He [Hepzefi] hath given to them a heket of grain from **every field of the estate** from the first of the harvest **of the count's estate.**"[27] The count's estate is the Nomarch's estate, which was owned and controlled by Sesostris I, who appointed Hepzefi to be Nomarch and overseer of the king's property.

Hepzefi could not have contributed part of the Pharaoh's property to the priests without being instructed to do so by Sesostris I. Thus, Sesostris I had commanded that part of the proceeds of his royal property should go to the temple priests. Sesostris I's donations to the priests confirm Genesis 47:22 that says the priests of Joseph's time "received a regular allotment from Pharaoh."

Contract Two, Part 2: Proof that Sesostris I Owned All Land of Citizens

Contract Two also included donations by Sesostris I from citizens who leased property that belonged to Sesostris I. Thus, Hepzefi mentioned above that "a heket" [bushel] of grain should be given to the priests from every field of the Nomarch's estate "**as every citizen of Siut does** from the first of his harvest."[28] This statement proves that all citizens were also required by Sesostris I to give a bushel of grain from every field to the priests. Why? Because the citizens' property also belonged to Sesostris I, and thus Sesostris I had the right to require them to donate a certain amount of the produce of his land to the priests.

Remember that Genesis 47:23-26 says that Pharaoh owned all of the land of Egypt (except the priests' land) and required that the citizens to whom he rented his land should give Pharaoh 20% of the proceeds from the grain and livestock grown on the king's fields. This required donation mentioned above of one bushel of grain per year to the priests was part of the 20% proceeds that Sesostris I received from the Egyptians. Thus, Contract Two dealt only with contributions to the priests from Sesostris I's land, which he leased out either to the Nomarch or to Egyptian citizens.

Contract Three: Hepzefi's Private Land As a Priest

Contract Three deals with Hepzefi's private property which he owned as a priest. Hepzefi clearly distinguished between the donations he made to the priests from the king's property in Contract Two and the donations to the priests from Hepzefi's private property which he owned as a priest, discussed in Contract Three:

> Behold it is **my property of my paternal estate, but it is not the property of the count's estate; for I am a priest's son**, like each one of you.[29]

Breasted commented on this distinction between Hepzefi's personal property as priest and the property of the king that is leased to him because he is a governor.

> The property of the prince was held under two different titles, viz., (a) by inheritance from his father [the priest], the property being called the "paternal estate" *(nw-pr-yt)*, which he could bequeath at will; and (b) by

virtue of his appointment as "count" (*h`ty*) by the king, the property being called the "count's estate" ( *pr-h-ty`*), which he could not legally bequeath.[30]

Hepzefi's contracts prove that the property he supervised as Nomarch (count or governor) was owned by King Sesostris I. Thus, Sesostris I appointed Hepzefi as Nomarch over the king's property. On the other hand, Hepzefi justified his personal property on the basis that he inherited it as "a priest's son." Hepzefi's explanation that he had private property **because** he was a priest's son implies that **he would not have personal property, if were not a priest**, as was the case with all of the other citizens of Egypt. Hepzefi's contracts prove that the priests did not sell their property during the famine and thus retained possession of it after the famine, just as the Bible describes for the period of Joseph.

> Genesis 47:22 -- However, **he [Joseph] did not buy the land of the priests,** because they **received a regular allotment from Pharaoh** and had food enough from the allotment Pharaoh gave them. That is why they did not sell their land. (NIV)

Superior Prophets in Egypt were regarded as High Priests. Joseph was also considered as the High Priest of the God of Israel, as was Jacob, the father of Joseph. Thus, the Israelites as descendants of priests were also given an allowance from Pharaoh and were able to purchase and own land in Egypt, especially in the land of Goshen.

> Genesis 47:11-12 -- 11 So Joseph settled his father and his brothers in Egypt and gave them property in the best part of the land, the district of Rameses, as Pharaoh directed. 12   Joseph also provided his father and his brothers and all his father's household with food, according to the number of their children. (NIV)

> Genesis 47:27 -- Now the Israelites settled in Egypt in the region of Goshen. They acquired property there and were fruitful and increased greatly in number (NIV)

IX. OTHER EVIDENCE OF SESOSTRIS I'S PROPERTY ALL OVER EGYPT

Thinis, another Egyptian capital, was located about seventy-five miles south of Asyut where Hepzefi lived. In the tomb of Intefyoker at Thinis an inscription is dated to Year 33 of Sesostris I: "Supervisor of fields in the Thinite nome of the South, Imsu, southward as far as the Crocodile nome, northward as far as the Panpolite nome."[31] Thus, Sesostris I had a supervisor to check on his property in the nome of Thinis.

About 25 miles farther south was the nome (province) of Abydos. In a tomb in Abydos was found a stela (stele, monument or stone marker with an inscription) of Ikudidi, an official of Sesostris I. The stela was dated in Year 34 of Sesostris I and speaks of the "king's messenger . . . who comes inspecting the boundaries of his majesty."[32] These boundaries cannot be referring to the country of Egypt, for Abydos was 150 miles north of Egypt's southern boundary. Thus, other nomes, such as Elephantine, were farther south of Abydos. Therefore, the reference to the king's boundaries at Abydos must be referring to Sesostris I's royal property in this particular province of southern Egypt, not the boundaries of Egypt itself.

Though Sesostris I lived in northern Egypt, he owned vast tracts of land all over Egypt. These documents prove that Sesostris I, like the Pharaoh of Joseph, indeed owned land all over Egypt after a great famine, and afterwards leased it out on a share-cropper's basis. The same documents prove that the priests' land remained in their private hands, just as the Pharaoh of Joseph permitted.

X. CONTINUAL LEASING AND ALLOTMENT IN THE TWELFTH DYNASTY FROM THE TIME OF JOSEPH TO THE TIME OF MOSES

The Bible says that the land-lease laws in Egypt were originated by Joseph and continued to the days of Moses at the time of the Exodus.

Genesis 47:26 -- So Joseph established it as a law concerning land in Egypt---**still in force today [Moses' days]** ---that a fifth of the produce belongs to Pharaoh. It was only the land of the priests that did not become Pharaoh's. (NIV)

Moses wrote Genesis. Therefore, the laws by which Pharaoh leased the land back to the Egyptians originated with Joseph and continued to the time of Moses when he wrote the book of Genesis. Since these laws first appear in Sesostris I's reign, it logically follows that Joseph was the Vizier of Sesostris I.

Did these laws continue in force during the reigns of later twelfth-dynasty kings, many years after the Pharaoh of Joseph (Sesostris I) instituted them? More than 100 years after Sesostris reigned, Sehetepibre, a twelfth-dynasty nomarch in southern Egypt, wrote that he was "overseer of the royal property" and gave "contracts for the remuneration of the prophets [priests] of Abydos" during the reign of Amenemhet III.[33] His inscription proves that Egyptian kings of the late twelfth dynasty still owned property in southern Egypt, and that royal overseers still supervised that property and distributed an allotment from the king's estate to assist the prophets and priests more than 100 years after these contracts were instituted in the early reign of Sesostris I.

Therefore, these leasing laws continued in force from approximately the sixteenth year of Sesostris I's reign until the end of the twelfth dynasty. Since these leasing laws first appeared in Egyptian literature in the reign of Sesostris I, obviously these laws were originated by Sesostris I. However, the Bible says that Joseph is the Egyptian official that actually formulated and executed these lease laws for Pharaoh. Therefore, Joseph must be the first Vizier of Sesostris I.

XI. PHARAOH'S LABOR FORCE

The Bible also reports that the Egyptians sold not only their land and their livestock to Pharaoh, but also themselves.

> Genesis 47:19-21 -- Why should we perish before your eyes--we and our land as well? Buy us and our land in exchange for food, and we with our land will be in bondage to Pharaoh. Give us seed so that we may live and not die, and that the land may not become desolate. . . . The Egyptians, **one and all,** sold their fields, because the famine was too severe for them. **The Land became Pharaoh's,** and **Joseph reduced the people to servitude, from one end of Egypt to the other**. (NIV)

All Egyptians became the slaves of Pharaoh, except for the priests and their families. If Sesostris I is the Pharaoh who appointed Joseph to office, then after Year 15 of his reign, the year we have designated for the seventh year of the famine, we should expect to see enormous numbers of workers serving him in multiplied work projects all over Egypt. Hayes recorded evidence that confirms our expectations of Sesostris I's latter reign.

> The ancient diorite quarries of Cheops to the north-west of Toshka apparently **swarmed with Egyptian working parties.** . . . In Sesostris I's thirty-eighth year, an expedition of **more than seventeen thousand men** quarried the blocks **for sixty sphinxes and one hundred and fifty statues.**[34]

Hayes mentioned that Sesostris I's buildings and other monuments have been found in at least **thirty-five sites**, from Alexandria on the Mediterranean coast (northern border of Egypt) to Aswan on the First Cataract (southern border of Egypt).[35] How could Sesostris I employ 17,000 men on one work project and construct expansive building projects from one end of Egypt to the other, especially after a severe famine of many years?

The Bible clearly explains how Sesostris I acquired such wealth and manpower after seven years of famine. **Sesostris I followed the wisdom of Joseph by storing up grain during the years of abundance and then by trading the grain for all the money, livestock and land of Egypt during the famine. In the last years of famine the Egyptians even sold themselves as slaves, making themselves available for any work project Sesostris I desired.** No doubt Sesostris I paid them a just wage, but they had no choice but to work when he asked.

However, the Egyptians did not work for Sesostris I with bitterness, for Genesis 47:25 reports that the Egyptians were happy to work for him: "You have saved our lives," they said. "May we find favor in the eyes of our lord; we will be in bondage to Pharaoh." Happy are the slaves who work for a kind master who saved them from death. In his thirty-eighth year, fifteen years after the famine, Sesostris I, like the Pharaoh of Joseph, was still using enormous numbers of Egyptian laborers to execute gigantic work projects.

XII. SESOSTRIS I'S IMPACT ON HISTORY

William C. Hayes assessed the reign of Sesostris I and his impact on history in the following words.

Building upon the foundation of national unity laid down by his father, Sen-Wosret I [Sesostris I] was able through his own very great energy, ability, and breadth of vision to inaugurate and bring to fruition plans for **the enrichment and expansion of Egypt more grandiose than any heretofore conceived [emphasis mine]**.[36]

Writing in the *Cambridge Ancient History*, Hayes adds the following words.

Even in the Twelfth dynasty Sesostris I was regarded and invoked as a god. . . . The name of the king in its Greek form, **"Sesostris," is preserved in a legend of the Hellenistic Period, recounting the fabulous deeds of a pharaoh, whose heroic figures seems to have been inspired, not only by Sesostris I and II of the Twelfth dynasty, but also, in part, by Ramesses II of the Nineteenth Dynasty.**[37]

Sesostris I was immortalized by his great achievements in Egyptian history. The Pharaoh of Joseph was also immortalized in Biblical history in the same manner and for the same reasons. Because Egyptian history has been misdated by three centuries, Egyptologists have not equated Sesostris I as the Pharaoh of Joseph. **Were it not for Joseph and the blessing of Joseph's God, Yahweh, Sesostris I and Egypt would never have attained to such power, wealth and glory.**

CONCLUSION

Ameni's inscription about trading for grain during **"years of famine"** immediately after **years of collecting grain and conserving water** fits precisely the Biblical story of the seven years of plenty, followed by the seven years of famine. **The very fact that the collection of grain in years of plenty and the distribution in years of famine are found together in a single tomb dated to the reign of Sesostris I uniquely confirms the Biblical story of Joseph.**

The fourteen years of abundance and famine can be harmoniously fitted into Years 2 to 15 of Sesostris I. After the years of famine twelfth-dynasty documents demonstrate that Sesostris I became the wealthiest owner of livestock and land in the history of Egypt. The labor force and wealth of Sesostris I after the years of famine stagger the imagination and fit exactly the Biblical description of the wealth and glory of the Pharaoh of Joseph after the Biblical seven years of famine.

Sesostris I leased the land and the livestock to the Egyptians on a "share-cropper" plan exactly in the manner that Joseph did for the Pharaoh of his time. The priests who served under Sesostris I had their own private property, in addition to leased property from the king, as did the priests in Joseph's day. These priests also received allotments of food from the property of Sesostris I just as the priests did in Joseph's time. The laws of leasing royal property and giving special donations to the priests continued throughout the same span of time in the twelfth dynasty that the Bible describes from Joseph's time to the Exodus. The Bible says that these land-lease laws were originated by Joseph. These same lease laws were first enacted in Egyptian history during the reign of Sesostris I. The most logical conclusion is that Sesostris I was indeed the Pharaoh of Joseph.

A total of nineteen links of unique historical synchronism appear in this chapter alone. See them in Table 11-B. The pieces of the puzzle are beginning to come together for the time of Joseph. However, other pieces from one more chapter must be added to complete the Joseph puzzle. Chapter Twelve discusses the coming of the Israelites to Egypt and their rapid growth in the land under the benevolent rule of Sesostris I, Amenemhet II and Sesostris II.

TABLE 11-B
TWENTY DISCOVERIES DURING THE
SEVEN YEARS OF FAMINE

Discovery 1. The rarity of famines in Egypt makes the seven years of Joseph and "the years of famine" in Sesostris I's reign unique.

Discovery 2. Ameni, an Egyptian nomarch, described a famine during the reign of Sesostris I that fits precisely the famine of Joseph in the Bible.

Discovery 3. Ameni's famine occurred in years nine through fifteen of Sesostris I, the same number of years that the Bible describes for the famine of Joseph's time.

Discovery 4. Ameni's distribution of grain to the hungry appears on the same wall of the tomb where the grain was gathered by his father during the years of abundance.

Discovery 5. Egyptians are seen trading money for grain during a famine, as in Joseph's time.

Discovery 6. Egyptians were trading livestock for grain, as in Joseph's time.

Discovery 7. Foreigners are seen trading money, commodities and animals and birds for grain, as they did in Joseph's time.

Discovery 8. After seven years of famine, Sesostris I's building expansion made him wealthier than any previous Pharaoh, as the Bible describes the wealth of the Pharaoh of Joseph.

Discovery 9. Sesostris I's wooden statue as a boy/king in Figure 11-D contrasts with his exquisitely sculptured statues of marble in years sixteen forward (Figure 11-E), demonstrating how he increased in wealth as Joseph's Pharaoh did.

Discovery 10. Sesostris I's shepherd's crook as a boy/king shows the early influence that Joseph, the son of a shepherd, exerted over young Sesostris I in the beginning of his reign, even though shepherds were despised by Egyptians.

Discovery 11. Sesostris I owned vast herds of livestock all over Egypt, as the Bible describes during and after the seven years of famine.

Discovery 12. Twelfth-dynasty documents show that Sesostris I leased some of these herds to Egyptians, as the Bible says.

Discovery 13. Twelfth-dynasty documents show that Sesostris I owned all of the land of Egypt, except the priests' land, precisely as described in the Bible.

Discovery 14. Twelfth-dynasty documents show that Sesostris I leased much of the land to the Egyptians, as the Bible shows.

Discovery 15. Twelfth-dynasty documents show that only the priests retained their own land, as the Bible says.

Discovery 16. Twelfth-dynasty documents show that the priests received an annual allotment from Pharaoh, as the Bible says.

Discovery 17. Twelfth-dynasty documents show these conditions began in Sesostris I's reign and continued to the end of the dynasty.

Discovery 18. The Bible says Egyptians who were impoverished by the famine sold themselves as slaves to Pharaoh (Sesostris I), who constructed at thirty-five different sites, using 17,000 laborers on one job alone.

Discovery 19. Sesostris I supervised the greatest expansion of Egypt in its previous history.

Discovery 20. Sesostris I was one of the greatest Pharaohs of Egypt in all of its history, fitting perfectly the Biblical description of the Pharaoh of Joseph.

TABLE 11-C
RUNNING TOTAL OF DISCOVERIES

Chapter		Chapter Total	Running Total
2	Conflict Between Biblical and Secular Histories	18	18
4	Discovery of 430 Years from Abraham to the Exodus	16	34
5	Confirmation of Abraham's Historicity	28	62
6	Discovery of the Remains of Sodom and Gomorrah	17	79
7	Joseph As a Slave and Prisoner in Amenemhet I's Reign	21	100
8	Joseph Becomes the Vizier of Sesostris I	23	123
9	Sesostris I Gives Joseph a New Name and a Wife	11	134
10	The Seven Years of Abundance in Sesostris I's Reign	10	144
11	The Seven Years of Famine in Sesostris I's Reign	20	164

NOTES FOR CHAPTER ELEVEN

1. I. E. S. Edwards, "The Old Kingdom in Egypt," *Cambridge Ancient History*, I.2A.189.
2. William C. Hayes, "The Middle Kingdom In Egypt," *Cambridge Ancient History*, I.2A189, 468, 469, 475, 479.
3. John A. Wilson, "The Tradition of Seven Lean Years in Egypt," *Ancient Near Eastern Texts*, Ed. James Pritchard, 31-32.
4. "Chronological Tables," *Cambridge Ancient History*, I.2B.995.
5. J. R. Baines, "Egypt," *New Encyclopaedia Britannica*, 18.110.
6. Gerald Aardsma, *A New Approach to the Chronology of Biblical History*, (El Cajon, Calif.: Institute for Creation Research, 1992), 67-68.
7. E. A. Wallace Budge, *An Egyptian Hieroglyphic Dictionary*, I.143 & 517.
8. J. Breasted (Trans.), *Ancient Records of Egypt*, I.252-253 (Nos. 522-523).
9. Brugsch, *Egypt Under the Pharaohs*, Trans. P. Smith, 2nd Ed., 1881, cited by Donovan Courville, *The Exodus Problem & Its Ramifications*, I.134.
10. James Breasted (Trans.), *Ancient Records of Egypt*, I.250 (no. 518).
11. Breasted (Trans.), *Ancient Records of Egypt*, I.251 (no. 519).
12. Badhr Sodre; the name of the other guide has escaped us.
13. Breasted (Trans.), *Ancient Records of Egypt*, I.251 (no. 519).
14. Hayes, *Cambridge Ancient History*, I.2A.499.
15. Hayes, *Cambridge Ancient History* I.2A.501.
16. Hayes, *Cambridge Ancient History* I.2A, p. 500.
17. William C. Hayes, *Scepter of Egypt*, I.228.
18. Hayes, *Scepter of Egypt*, I.175-176.
19. Breasted (Trans.), "Inscription of Ameni," *Ancient Records of Egypt*, I.251-252.
20. J. Breasted, *Ancient Records of Egypt*, I.252, note a.
21. J. Breasted, *Ancient Records of Egypt*, I.252, note a.
22. Baines and Malek, *Atlas of Ancient Egypt*, 15.
23. Breasted (Trans.), *Ancient Records of Egypt*, I.258-260.
24. Breasted (Trans), *Ancient Records of Egypt*, I.260-261 (nos. 539-543).
25. Breasted (Trans.), *Ancient Records of Egypt*, I.260.
26. Breasted, *Ancient Records of Egypt*, I.262 (No. 546).
27. Breasted (Trans.), *Ancient Records of Egypt*, I.261-262.
28. Breasted (Trans.), *Ancient Records of Egypt*, I.261-262.
29. Breasted (Trans.), *Ancient Records of Egypt*, I.259-263 (no. 552).
30. Breasted (Trans.), *Ancient Records of Egypt*, I.254 (no. 529.)
31. Breasted (Trans.), *Ancient Records of Egypt*, I.254 no. 528.
32. Breasted (Trans.), *Ancient Records of Egypt*, I.326.
33. William C. Hayes, "Middle Kingdom of Egypt," *Cambridge Ancient History*, I.2A.500.
34. William C. Hayes, "Middle Kingdom of Egypt," *Cambridge Ancient History*, I.2A.501.
35. William C. Hayes, *Scepter of Egypt*, I.179.
36. William C. Hayes, "Middle Kingdom of Egypt," *Cambridge Ancient History*, I.2A.502.

CHAPTER TWELVE
ISRAEL ENTERS EGYPT DURING SESOSTRIS I'S REIGN

The famine that struck Egypt also devastated the land of Canaan where Joseph's father, Jacob, and his eleven brothers lived.[1]   During the first two years of famine, Jacob sent his sons to Egypt two different times to purchase grain.[2]   Each time they bowed before the Vizier without perceiving that he was their brother, Joseph.[3]   They did not realize that they were fulfilling Joseph's dreams that his brothers would bow in submission to their younger brother.[4]   Finally, Joseph revealed his true identity.   He told them that five more years of famine would devastate Egypt and Canaan.   He persuaded them to bring their father, Jacob, and all of their wives and children to Egypt.[5]   God approved Joseph's request and told Jacob, "Go to Egypt, for I will make you into a great nation there."[6]

The Pharaoh of Joseph gave Jacob's family special permission to live and own property in the land of Goshen, "the best of the land of Egypt."[7]   During the years following the famine, the Israelites "acquired property" in Goshen and "were fruitful and increased greatly in number."[8]

Previous chapters identified Sesostris I as the Pharaoh of Joseph.   If our identification is correct, then Sesostris I should be the Pharaoh who granted permission for Jacob and his family to enter Egypt and live in the land of Goshen.   Does evidence exist in twelfth-dynasty documents that shepherds from Canaan entered Egypt and lived in Goshen during Sesostris I's reign?   Did these same Canaanites grow and prosper in Egypt for about a century before being enslaved?   This chapter answers with a strong affirmative.

I. DATE OF ISRAEL'S ARRIVAL IN EGYPT

Chapter Four established the Biblical date of Israel's arrival in Egypt in 1656 B.C., 210 years before the 1446 B.C. Exodus (1446 B.C. +210 years = 1656 B.C.). Joseph said that two of the seven years of famine had expired when Jacob and his family moved to Egypt.

> Genesis 45:6-8 -- For **two years now there has been famine** in the land, and for **the next five years** there will not be plowing and reaping. But God sent me ahead of you to preserve for you a remnant on earth and to save your lives by a great deliverance.   So then, it was not you who sent me here, but God.   (NIV).

Thus, Jacob and his family arrived in Egypt at the beginning of the third year of famine, which I have assigned to Sesostris I's eleventh year.   See Table 12-A on the next page.

TABLE 12-A
COMPARATIVE CHRONOLOGICAL CHART
JOSEPH AND SESOSTRIS I

BIBLE DATES B.C.	MOSES' HISTORY	EGYPTIAN HISTORY SESOSTRIS I	AMENEMHET I	ENCY. BRIT. DATES B.C.
1665	Joseph Becomes Vizier	Year 2	Year 22	1916
1664	Joseph Marries Asenath	Year 3	Year 23	1915
1663	3rd Year of Abundance	Year 4	Year 24	1914
1662	4th Year of Abundance	Year 5	Year 25	1913
1661	5th Year of Abundance	Year 6	Year 26	1912
1660	6th Year of Abundance	Year 7	Year 27	1911
1659	7th Year of Abundance	Year 8	Year 28	1910
1658	1st Year of FAMINE	Year 9	Year 29	1909
1657	2nd Year of Famine	Year 10	Year 30	1908
1656	JACOB ENTERS EGYPT	Year 11		1907
1655	4th Year of Famine	Year 12		1906
1654	5th Year of Famine	Year 13		1905
1653	6th Year of Famine	Year 14		1904
1652	7th Year of Famine	Year 15		1903

II. ISRAEL'S NEW HABITATION IN EGYPT

Jacob and his sons were shepherds. When they came to Egypt, Pharaoh showed great favor to Joseph's family by permitting them to live and graze their flocks in the fertile land of "Goshen," called also the "district of Rameses."

Genesis 47:5-6 -- Pharaoh said to Joseph, "Your father and your brothers have come to you, and the land of Egypt is before you; settle your father and your brothers in the **best part of the land**. Let them live in **Goshen**. (NIV)

Genesis 47:11 -- So Joseph settled his father and his brothers in Egypt and **gave them property in the best part of the land, the district of Rameses**, as Pharaoh directed. (NIV)

Genesis 47:27 -- Now the Israelites settled in Egypt **in the region of Goshen**. They **acquired property there** and **were fruitful and increased greatly in number**. (NIV)

Because of Joseph's influence and Pharaoh's kindness, the Israelites were permitted to live and prosper in the most fertile land of Egypt. The Scriptures above called this section of Egypt by two different names: **"the region of Goshen" and "the district of Rameses."**

The "land of Goshen," where the Israelites lived, was later called "the Gesem of Arabia" in the Greek Septuagint Version of the Hebrew Bible.[9] Kenneth Kitchen defines the "Gesem of Arabia" as the twentieth Egyptian nome of lower Egypt, located in the Wadi Tumilat area of the eastern delta of Egypt.[10]

The eastern delta of Wadi Tumilat was conveniently located for travelers from Canaan. They could travel directly to Goshen without crossing any rivers of significant size. This unencumbered road from Canaan to Goshen facilitated the travel of Jacob's large family (sixty-six people, plus Jacob and his sons' wives).[11] Pharaoh sent many wagons, plus provisions, to transport Jacob's household and possessions to Egypt.[12]

Many years later, when Moses was born, the Israelites were enslaved and constructed the store city of Rameses in the land of Goshen, where they previously lived in complete freedom. Thus the old name of the region of Goshen may have been substituted with Rameses because the store city by this name was the regional capital at the time Moses wrote, but was not the capital of the nation of Egypt. It is also possible that both names, Rameses and Goshen, were used interchangeably from the time of Moses.

About 100 years after the twelfth dynasty fell, the store city of Rameses was conquered by the Hyksos and was rebuilt and renamed Avaris as their new capital. Centuries after the Hyksos were expelled from Egypt, Ramses II of the nineteenth dynasty built his new capital over the ruins of Avaris and called it "Per-Ramesses." An Egyptian document called *Papyrus Anastasi III* describes the beauty of the district of "Per-Ramses," where Ramses II established his new capital.[13] This Egyptian description of the district of the capital city of Pi-Rameses (Per-Ramses) fits perfectly the Biblical description of "the district of Rameses" as "the best part of the land" of Egypt (Genesis 47:5-6). Kenneth Kitchen, agrees that the district of Rameses and the region of Goshen are both located in the same general area.

> Geographically, Goshen is closely linked with the land and city of Raamses [*sic*]. . . . Goshen can readily be placed in the territory between Saft el Henneh in the South **(at the west end of Wadi Tumilat) [my emphasis]** and Qantir and El Salhieh in the North and Northeast. **It could hardly be still further extended up to Tanis [my emphasis]**.[14]

Notice above that Kitchen did not include Tanis in the land of Goshen (district of Rameses). In Chapters Fifteen and Sixteen Biblical evidence will be presented that the Egyptian capital of Tanis from the time of Joseph to the Exodus was **not** located in the region of Goshen or Rameses, but in an adjacent region called "Zoan" [the Greeks called it "Tanis"]. These two Chapters will present significant evidence from Egyptian documents that the twelfth-dynasty capital Itjtowy was located in the region of Tanis, explaining why archaeologists have never found the twelfth-dynasty capital at other locations where they searched.

III. SESOSTRIS I AND THE PHARAOH OF JOSEPH
BOTH GRAZED LIVESTOCK IN GOSHEN

Pharaoh not only permitted Jacob to live in Goshen, but he also appointed some of Jacob's sons to oversee Pharaoh's own flocks in Goshen.

Pharaoh said to Joseph, "Your father and your brothers have come to you, and the land of Egypt is before you; settle your father and your brothers in the best part of the land. Let them live in Goshen. **And if you know of any among them with special ability, put them in charge of my own livestock."**[15] NIV

If the Pharaoh of Joseph is Sesostris I, then Sesostris I should have also owned livestock in the land of Goshen. In fact, Sesostris I's father, Amenemhet I, constructed a city called "Walls of the Ruler" and located it on the eastern border of the Wadi Tumilat (the land of Goshen). Its purpose was to protect Amenemhet I's livestock in Goshen and to prevent "Asiatic" (Canaanite) nomads from bringing their livestock into this same area.[16] Obviously, Amenemhet I had large numbers of livestock to protect in the land of Goshen, or he would not have built a fortress city in Goshen to protect them. Sesostris I inherited these livestock when his father was no longer able to function as an active Pharaoh. In addition, Sesostris I wrote in his tomb about incursions of his army into Canaan to bring back livestock as booty.[17] The closest and best place to pasture cattle brought from Canaan would be in the eastern delta of Egypt, which is Goshen, where Israel lived. Thus, Sesostris I had a large number of cattle in Goshen just as the Pharaoh of Joseph had.

IV. PERMISSION FOR FOREIGN SHEPHERDS
TO LIVE IN THE LAND OF GOSHEN
DURING THE 12TH DYNASTY

The Bible specifically states that Jacob's family needed special permission from Pharaoh himself to live in the land of Goshen.

When Pharaoh calls you in and asks, "What is your occupation?" you should answer, "Your servants have tended livestock from our boyhood on, just as our fathers did." Then you will be **allowed** to settle in the region of Goshen, . . . So Joseph settled his father and his brothers in Egypt and gave them property in the best part of the land, the district of Rameses, **as Pharaoh directed.**[18] NIV

Since Amenemhet I built a city on the eastern border of the land of Goshen to

154

prevent Canaanite shepherds from entering the delta, no group could enter Goshen without special permission from Amenemhet I or his son Sesostris I. G. Posener, citing Papyrus Ermitage 1116B, verso 67-8, and Papyrus Butler 527, verso 11, tells us that during the twelfth dynasty "foreign shepherds" in Egypt were permitted access by a **special "favor"** to pasture their flocks in the Wadi Tumilat

> The founder of the Twelfth dynasty, Ammenemes I, had barely come to the throne when he expelled the bedawin and, in order to prevent further incursions, built a fortress in the eastern part of Wadi Tummilat. Access to the eastern marches was, however, not entirely forbidden to the Asiatic herdsmen, **they could be authorized to go there "as a favour in order to water their flocks".** This is the **first reference** to a practice which was continued during the New Kingdom and **brings to mind biblical memories.**[19]

Notice that Posener does not name specifically the twelfth-dynasty Pharaoh that permitted shepherds from Asia (which included Canaan) to enter the Wadi Tummilat (Goshen), but he cites this permission while discussing the reign of Amenemhet I. According to our historical synchronism between Biblical history and twelfth-dynasty history **(see 12-A below)** the famine began in Year 8 of Sesostris I's co-reign with his father Amenemhet I. Amenemhet I died in Year 10 of Sesostris I's co-reign and Israel entered Egypt at the beginning of Year 11 of Sesostris I's reign, which was the first year of his sole reign.

I have been unable to find a translation of Posener's sources that specify the name and year of reign of the Pharaoh who permitted these Canaanite shepherds to enter Goshen. If the permission was granted at the end of Sesostris I's tenth year of co-reign with Amenemhet I, or in the beginning of his eleventh year, immediately after Amenemhet I died, a remarkable synchronism occurs, confirming my hypothetical identification of Sesostris I as the Pharaoh of Joseph who graciously permitted Israel to enter the land of Goshen.

Posener admits above that this twelfth-dynasty permission for Canaanite shepherds to live in Goshen is the **"first reference"** in Egyptian literature to a practice mentioned in the Bible. Likely, Posener was thinking about Abraham's entrance into Egypt during a severe famine that affected only Canaan (Genesis 12:10-13:2). Posener likely believed that Jacob entered Egypt about 200 years after the time of Sesostris I. Little did Posener realize that he had actually uncovered the Egyptian record that confirms the Biblical story of the entrance into Egypt by Jacob and his family, not Abraham.

V. THE FAVORED STATUS OF THE ISRAELITES IN EGYPT

The Egyptians had to trade all of their land for grain during the famine. However, Pharaoh gave the Israelites property in Goshen and permitted them to purchase additional land.

> Genesis 47:11, 27 -- So Joseph settled his father and his brothers in
> Egypt and **gave them property** in the best part of the land, . . . as
> Pharaoh directed. . . . Now the Israelites settled in Egypt in the region of
> Goshen. They **acquired property** there and were fruitful and increased
> greatly in number.

The Israelites enjoyed these special privileges because they were all relatives of Joseph. Pharaoh esteemed Joseph not only for his work as Vizier, but also because he regarded Joseph as a "Superior Prophet." Pharaoh believed that "the spirit of God" resided within Joseph when he predicted the seven years of abundance and the seven years of famine. Pharaoh was himself an eyewitness of the validity of Joseph's predictions and their historical fulfillment.[20] Thus, Joseph was considered a "Superior Prophet" of the God of the Hebrews. When Joseph's family moved to Egypt, Jacob, also a prophet of the God of Hebrews, was treated with a superior status of a prophet and priest. Thus, all of Jacob's family and relatives were descendants of prophet/priests and received donations from Pharaoh as did the other priests in Egypt.[21]

Did "Superior Prophets" exist in the reign of Sesostris I? Did Sesostris I give them special privileges as the Pharaoh of Joseph gave Jacob and his family? We saw evidence in Chapter Eleven that the priests received a special allotment from the estate of Sesostris I. In these same documents, I also found that many of these priests were prophets and that a "Superior Prophet" ruled over each religious group of priests and prophets. Notice the following quotations from different twelfth-dynasty documents: bold letters are my emphasis.

1. Contract which the count, **the superior prophet, Hepzefi**, triumphant, made, with the **lay priests** of the temple of Upwawet, lord of Siut.[22]

2. Hereditary prince, Vizier and chief judge, attached to Nekhen, **prophet of Mat** (goddess of Truth). . . . **prophet of Anubis . . . Mentuhotep**, prince in the seats of Splendor.[23]

3. I [Sehetepibre] made this excellent tomb and beautified its place. I gave contracts for the remuneration of **the prophets of Abydos.**[24]

Hepzefi, the "Superior Prophet" gave some of his own private money to his under-priests in order that they might offer sacrifices on his behalf after his death. However, as a count (nomarch or governor), he also was commanded by Sesostris I to contribute to the priests a certain quantity from the estate of King Sesostris I, which Hepzefi also oversaw. These citations prove that prophets and priests were honored with special privileges and gifts by Sesostris I and by later twelfth-dynasty kings. Thus, the honors that Pharaoh bestowed upon Joseph, his father Jacob, and the family of Jacob fit perfectly with Sesostris I's practice to give the same honors and privileges to other prophets and priests of his own day.

The special favor that Pharaoh granted to Joseph's and Jacob's family enabled the Israelites to grow in number and material prosperity throughout the life time of Joseph. Joseph was about thirty-nine years old when Jacob came to Egypt in the third year of the famine.[25] Joseph was 110 years old when he died.[26] Thus, Joseph lived with his fellow Israelites in Egypt for seventy-one years, from 1656 to 1585 B.C. See this chronology paralleled to twelfth-dynasty history in Table 12-A.

The new generations of Israelites born before and after Joseph's death grew into a mighty multitude of people within the land of Egypt.

Exodus 1:6-7 -- Now Joseph and all his brothers and all that generation died, but the Israelites were fruitful and multiplied greatly and became exceedingly numerous, so that the land was filled with them. (NIV)

Genesis 46:3-4 -- "I am God, the God of your father," he said. "Do not be afraid to go down to Egypt, for I will make you into a great nation there. I will go down to Egypt with you, and I will surely bring you back again. And Joseph's own hand will close your eyes." (NIV)

Thus, God's promise was fulfilled that Jacob should go to Egypt where his descendants would become a great nation.

VI. EVIDENCE OF ISRAEL'S GROWTH IN EGYPT
IN THE REIGN OF SESOSTRIS I
AND HIS SUCCESSORS

If the Israelites entered Egypt in the eleventh year of Sesostris I and began to multiply, we should expect to find a growing presence of free foreigners in Egypt during the latter years of Sesostris I's reign and even more growth of foreigners during the reigns of his successors. Do twelfth-dynasty documents verify this growth of free foreigners?

Tomb scenes of military life dated to the reigns of Sesostris I and Amenemhet II (the son of Sesostris I) report Egyptian incursions into Canaan to plunder the livestock and possessions of the Canaanites. These scenes show that the Egyptian army included many "Oriental" or "Eastern" warriors among the Egyptians.[27] Egyptians used the expressions, "Asiatics, Orientals and Easterners" as including the inhabitants of Canaan, Syria and other people of Asia Minor. Could these "Orientals" in the Egyptian army include Israelites among their number?

The Pharaoh of Joseph specifically requested that some of Joseph's brothers take charge of Pharaoh's livestock in the Delta where the Israelites were living.[28] Since Israelites began immediately to work with the king's livestock, it is reasonable to believe they also served militarily for the king. Indeed, the Bible specifically states that Israelites who lived in Egypt participated in raids on Canaanite cities that captured livestock which they took back to Egypt.

> I Chronicles 7:21-22- - **Ezer and Elead** were killed by the native-born men of Gath, when they went down **to seize their livestock.** Their **father Ephraim** mourned for them many days, and his relatives came to comfort him.

This text says that Ezer and Elead, the grandsons of Joseph through his son Ephraim, left Egypt and went down to Gath in Canaan and were killed while attempting to rustle cattle. Ezer and Elead did not likely undertake this rustling expedition on their own. More likely, they were a part of an Egyptian military unit mentioned above that shows Canaanite faces among the native Egyptians.

When were Ezer and Elead old enough to be soldiers in the Egyptian army? Genesis 50:22-23 says, "Joseph lived a hundred and ten years and saw the third generation of Ephraim's children." Ezer and Elead were the first generation of Ephraim and were in their early twenties when Joseph was about seventy years old. According to my synchronistic chronology of Joseph's life and the twelfth dynasty, Joseph's seventieth year occurred in the eighth year of Amenemhet II. See this comparative chronology in Table 12-B below.

TABLE 12-B
CHRONOLOGY OF EPHRAIM'S SONS
WITH 12TH-DYNASTY KINGS

BIBLE MOSES' HISTORY	EGYPTIAN HISTORY	
B.C.	SESOSTRIS I	AMENEMHET I
1665 JOSEPH BECAME VIZIER	Year 2	
1663 JOSEPH MARRIES ASENATH	Year 4	Year 23
1660 EPHRAIM BORN	Year 7	Year 26
1656 JACOB ENTERS EGYPT	Year 11	Death
1652 7TH YEAR OF FAMINE	Year 15	
1648	Year 20	
1644	Year 24	
1640 EPHRAIM MARRIES	Year 28	
1638 EZER BORN	Year 30	
1636 ELEAD BORN	Year 32	
1632	Year 36	
1628	Year 40	AMENEMHET II
1623	Year 45	Year 1
1622	Year 46	Year 2
1616 EZER AND ELEAD DIED IN GATH at ages 22 and 24		Year 8

VII. GROWING NUMBERS OF CANAANITE WORKERS IN SESOSTRIS II'S REIGN

During the twelfth dynasty a gradual infiltration of free workers from Canaan (called "Asiatics") are seen side by side with Egyptians in industrial positions of service, such as mining.

William Hayes -- The mining expeditions in the peninsula, during the Twelfth dynasty, **did not include detachments of police or soldiers. Asiatics,** singly or in groups of six, ten and twenty men, came to join the mining parties. **They were not enemies who had been conquered and reduced to forced labour:** among them was the brother of a prince of the **Retenu [Canaan],** Hbdd(m), who arrived with his own escort. We may therefore only hesitate between friendly co-operation and an obligation to serve stemming from ties of vassalage.[29] [My Emphasis]

Notice that men from Canaan worked with twelfth-dynasty Egyptians in mining operations even though they "were not conquered enemies" and therefore not slaves. This picture of free Canaanites working in Egypt beside the Egyptians fits the time of Joseph before the Israelites were later enslaved by the Egyptians.

Growing numbers of men from Canaan are also found in domestic positions in Egypt, especially during the reign of Sesostris II, the grandson of Sesostris I.

Posener -- "The great majority of Asiatics [including Canaanites] who settled in Egypt **during the Middle Kingdom** were humble, peaceful people. They are to be seen in **large numbers** employed on domestic tasks in private houses, and they are also encountered in the service of temples. The earliest dated instance belongs to the reign of Sesostris II. . . . **The biblical story of Joseph** brings to mind the slave-trade; **voluntary recruitment** is, however, attested . . . ."[30] [My Emphsis]

As the Israelites began to multiply in the land of Egypt, they were likely the principal reason for this growing number of free people from Canaan who were living and serving in domestic positions in Egypt during the twelfth dynasty (the Middle Kingdom). Notice that Posener thought this growth of Canaanites in Egypt was reminiscent of **the time of Joseph,** though Posener likely believed that Joseph arrived in Egypt much later. However, Posener makes the point that Joseph was a slave when he entered Egypt, whereas he admitted that many of the Canaanite workers were **"voluntary"** laborers and thus not slaves. Again, this picture of free men from Canaan working side by side with Egyptians in the reign of Sesostris II fits the Biblical story of the growth of free Israelites permeating Egyptian society during the period after the seven years of famine and before they were enslaved.

The documents contemporary with Sesostris II are the first to show this large number of free workers from Canaan serving beside Egyptian laborers. Our reconstruction of the twelfth dynasty places the reign of Sesostris II immediately before the appearance of the Pharaoh of the Oppression (Sesostris III), who enslaved the Israelites because he feared Israel's rapid growth and strong potential to be a threat to Egyptian security.

> Exodus 1:8-10 -- (8) Then a new king, who did not know about Joseph, came to power in Egypt. (9) "Look," he said to his people, "the Israelites have become **much too numerous for us.** (10) Come, we must deal shrewdly with them or they will become even more numerous and, if war breaks out, will join our enemies, fight against us and leave the country." (NIV)

According to our comparative chronology, Joseph was still alive during the first part of the reign of Sesostris II, when free Canaanites (the Israelites) were growing so rapidly. However, the latter part of Sesostris II's reign covers the period between the death of Joseph and the birth of Moses. The Bible gives us little information about the Israelites during this period, except that they were growing and prospering. Table 12-C demonstrates that this rapid growth of people from Canaan in Sesostris II's latter reign runs perfectly parallel with the Biblical period that describes **the same rapid growth of the Israelites in Egypt** from Joseph's death to Moses' birth.

TABLE 12-C
REDATING OF TWELFTH DYNASTY TO FIT
BIBLICAL HISTORY FROM JOSEPH
TO MOSES' BIRTH

TIME B.C.	BIBLE CHRONOLOGY	12TH DYNASTY	ENCY. BRIT. B.C.
1695	Birth of Joseph		
1677		Amenemhet I	1938
1667	Baker & Butler in Prison	Assassination Attempt	
1665	Joseph Vizier of Egypt	Sesostris I	1918
1656	Jacob Enters Egypt	Shepherds Enter Goshen	
	7 Years of Famine	7 Years of Famine	
	Pharaoh Leases Property	Leases Land & Cattle	
1626		Amenemhet II	1876
	Israel Grows & Prospers	Foreigners Grow & Prosper	
1585	Joseph Dies	Sesostris II	1844
	Israel Multiplies	Foreigners Multiply	
1542	Pharaoh of Oppression Reigns	Sesostris III	1836
1526	Moses Born (Oppression)		
	Israel Enslaved	Enslaves Foreigners	
	Constructs Rameses & Pithom	Constructs Rameses & Pithom	

VIII. THE CARBON-14 DATE
OF SESOSTRIS II

According to our Biblical chronology Joseph died *c.* 1585 B.C. when he was 110 years old. We base this calculation on the fact that Joseph was **thirty years old** when he became Vizier of Egypt in 1665 B.C. (1665 B.C. - 80 = 1585). According to our parallel chronology Joseph died in about the fifth year of Sesostris II. **Sesostris II died around 1542 B.C. (my Biblically assigned date),** about forty-three years after Joseph died, according to my proposed parallel chronology. A sample from the boundary wall of Sesostris II's pyramid was carbon-14 dated at 3490 B.P. which translates into **1540 B.C.,[31] only two years after my date for his death.** Thus, we have **significant scientific as well as historical evidence** that Joseph died and Israel was a free, growing people during the reign of Sesostris II. The scientific fallacy of Egypt's Sothic Calendar and new astronomical dating and carbon-14 dating of the twelfth dynasty and other dynasties are discussed in Chapters Twenty-One to Twenty-Four. All of these carbon-14 dates and my new astronomical dates confirm my new revised dates for the twelfth dynasty. My new chronology for Sesostris II, the third Pharaoh of the twelfth dynasty, dates him from **1590 to 1542 B.C. Hayes dates Sesostris II's death in 1878 B.C. and Baines dates his death in 1837 B.C., 297 to 338 years earlier than the carbon-14 date of 1540 B.C.**

IX. THE INFLUENCE THAT JOSEPH AND ISRAEL
EXERTED OVER EGYPTIAN MORALITY
IN THE TWELFTH DYNASTY

Joseph, his brothers and their descendants no doubt influenced the Egyptians in moral, political and religious matters. Although the Egyptians considered shepherds unclean,[32] Joseph, as the son of a shepherd, no doubt influenced Sesostris I to esteem shepherds. In fact Sesostris I even adopted the figure of a shepherd as his own benevolent image in relation to his people. In Year 3 of Sesostris I, which I believe is Year 2 of Joseph as Vizier, Sesostris I inscribed on a monument that his god "appointed" him **"shepherd of this land."**[33]

A wooden statue of Sesostris I in his first years of reign picture him with a shepherd's crook in his hand. The kindness of young Sesostris I's face represents the benevolence of his reign in shepherding his people and saving them from the years of famine. Two different statues of young Sesostris I are pictured in Chapter 8, Figure 8-A, and in Chapter 11, Figure 11-D. Sesostris I is the first Egyptian king that I have noticed in Egyptian history to use a shepherd's crook in his role as king. Joseph, as a shepherd's son, may have influenced Sesostris I to adopt the image of the "Shepherd" of Egypt. Sesostris I's use of the shepherd image as king of Egypt is rather remarkable since Egyptians detested shepherds when Joseph first became Vizier.[34] Joseph no doubt influenced Sesostris I to have a new, respectful image of shepherds.

We also see a generous benevolence and a high morality in the lives of Sesostris I's officials. In an earlier chapter we saw the inscription of Ameni, who distributed to the hungry during the years of famine. Notice additional quotations from Ameni that demonstrate his high morality and benevolence toward the lowliest of Egyptians, including shepherds.

> Breasted's Translation -- There was **no citizen's daughter whom I misused; there was no widow whom I oppressed; there was no peasant whom I repulsed; there was not a shepherd whom I repelled;** there was no overseer of serf-laborers whose people I took for (unpaid) imposts; there was none wretched in my community; there was none hungry in my time. When **years of famine came** I plowed all the fields of the Oryx nome, as far as its southern and northern boundary, preserving its people alive and furnishing food so that there was none hungry therein. **I gave to the widow as to her who had a husband; I did not exalt the great above the small in all that I gave. Then came great Niles,** possessors of grain and all things, (but) I did not collect the arrears of the field.[35] (Emphasis mine)

Ameni's words, **"there was not a shepherd whom I repelled,"** implies that other Egyptians repelled and despised shepherds, as they did in Joseph's day. Ameni's specific mention that he helped "shepherds" is understandable only in a historical context where ordinarily shepherds would not receive such kind treatment. Ameni's help to widows, peasants and even shepherds reflects the kindness that Joseph, a shepherd's son, showed toward his own aged father and brothers. Sesostris I, as a shepherd king, also showed kindness to certain Canaanite shepherds who moved to Goshen. Ameni had the good examples of both King and Vizier to influence his behavior toward poor peasants and formerly despised shepherds during the years of famine. Also, Joseph's refusal to commit adultery with Potiphar's wife[36] was likely told all over Egypt after Joseph became Vizier of Egypt. Joseph's moral example no doubt influenced Ameni's stated behavior that he did not "misuse" any "citizen's daughter".

The Egyptians all knew that Joseph had revealed the interpretation of Sesostris I's dream in order to preserve the life of the people. Joseph's unselfish service on behalf of the Egyptian people and his honesty and integrity in the office of Vizier must have had an ameliorating influence on the entire Egyptian populace. These qualities of moral integrity and benevolence are expressed in many early twelfth-dynasty documents. Notice for example the tomb inscription of Intef, Son of Sent, who is dated to the reign of Sesostris I.

> Lichtheim's Translation -- I am silent with the angry, patient with the ignorant, so as to quell strife. I am cool, free of haste, knowing the outcome, expecting what comes. I am a speaker in situations of strife,

one who knows which phrase causes anger. I am friendly when I hear my name to him who would tell me his concern. I am controlled, kind, friendly, one who calms the weeper with good words. I am one bright faced to the client, beneficent to his equal. I am a straight one in his lord's house, who knows flattery when it is spoken. I am bright-faced, open-handed, an owner of food who does not cover his face. I am a friend of the poor, one well-disposed to the have-not. I am one who feeds the hungry in need, who is open-handed to the pauper. I am knowing to him who lacks knowledge, one who teaches a man what is useful to him. I am a straight one in the king's house, who knows what to say in every office. I am a listener who listens to the truth, who ponders it in the heart. I am one pleasant to his lord's house, who is remembered for his good qualities. I am kindly in the offices, one who is calm and does not roar. I am kindly, not short-tempered, one who does not attack a man for a remark. I am accurate like the scales, straight and true like Thoth.[37]

Intef expressed a high morality found frequently in the Bible and expressed personally in the life of Joseph. Joseph was likely the principal source and inspiration for this high ethical standard in the twelfth dynasty. However, in the next chapter we will see that this noble morality under the early Pharaohs of the twelfth dynasty deteriorated in the reign of Sesostris III and his successors. Unfortunately, Israel's morality also began to wane the longer they remained in Egypt. This sad corruption of morals will be discussed in Chapter Thirteen.

CONCLUSION

Amenemhet I built a city in the delta to prevent Canaanite shepherds from entering the land of Goshen. But remarkably, some twelfth-dynasty king, whom I predict will turn out to be Sesostris I, gave a special favor to one group of shepherds to enter Goshen and graze their flocks there. Our chronological clue charts show that Israel entered Egypt in Sesostris I's eleventh year of reign in the Biblical year of 1656 B.C. Sesostris I grazed his own livestock in Goshen, just as the Pharaoh of Joseph did. Inscriptions from the time of Sesostris I and his son Amenemhet II show that Canaanites (likely the Israelites) were integral members of Egyptian armies who raided Canaanite towns to plunder livestock and bring them back to Egypt. The Bible reports that two of Joseph's grandsons were killed while raiding livestock in Canaan, likely as soldiers in the Egyptian army.

Twelfth-dynasty documents record numerous evidences of a growing population of free foreigners from Canaan, who infiltrated Egyptian society, including the agricultural, military, mining and domestic areas. The growing presence of these foreigners in Egypt is especially evident in writings dated to the reign of Sesostris II. This evidence confirms the Biblical story of the significant population growth of the Israelites, turning them into an influential and powerful force in Egyptian society.

A high ethical and spiritual influence for good is seen in the first half of the twelfth dynasty whose roots can be likely traced to Joseph and his family within the early reign of Sesostris I. Table 12-D registers below fourteen historical links between the Biblical history of Israel's first hundred years in Egypt and the first-half of twelfth-dynasty history. In later chapters we will see remarkable evidence that identifies Sesostris III as the Egyptian king who enslaved and oppressed Israel.

TABLE 12-D
FOURTEEN DISCOVERIES OF ISRAEL'S ENTRANCE INTO EGYPT AND ISRAEL'S GROWTH IN THE REIGNS OF SESOSTRIS I, AMENEMHET II AND SESOSTRIS II

Discovery 1. Israel's arrival in 1656 B.C. in Sesostris I's eleventh year allows them to remain in Egypt 210 years before leaving.

Discovery 2. Goshen was "the best of the land" for cattle and easily accessible for Jacob's family coming from Canaan.

Discovery 3. Joseph's Pharaoh had livestock in Goshen. Sesostris I and his father Amenemhet I also had livestock in Goshen.

Discovery 4. Amenemhet I built a city to prevent Canaanites from grazing livestock in Goshen and to protect his own livestock.

Discovery 5. A twelfth-dynasty Pharaoh gave special permission for certain Canaanite shepherds to graze their flocks in Goshen.

Discovery 6. Joseph, as Vizier and prophet of Sesostris I, was allowed to give free property for his family in Goshen.

Discovery 7. Egyptian tombs dated to the reigns of Sesostris I and Amenemhet II show growing numbers of livestock from Canaan.

Discovery 8. Growing numbers of Canaanites are seen in the Egyptian army.

Discovery 9. Army of Sesostris I plundered Canaanite livestock. The Bible says Ephraim, Joseph's son, lost two sons in Gaza while seizing cattle.

Discovery 10. Many Canaanites are seen working among Egyptians on construction projects in the reigns of Amenemhet II and Sesostris II.

Discovery 11. Growing numbers of Canaanite miners, as voluntary workers, are seen on tomb walls dated to Sesostris II's reign.

Discovery 12. Carbon-14 date of 1540 B.C. for Sesostris II's tomb is only two years earlier than my Biblical date of 1542 B.C. for his death.

Discovery 13. Joseph's influence is seen in the change of attitude toward shepherds, both by Sesostris I and Ameni, a governor.

Discovery 14. Attributes of kindness, integrity, sexual purity and other virtues permeate the attitude of Egyptian officials from Sesostris I's reign through the reign of Sesostris II, the Pharaohs under whom Joseph lived.

TABLE 12-E
RUNNING TOTAL OF DISCOVERIES

Chapter		Chapter Total	Running Total
2	Conflict Between Biblical and Secular Histories	18	18
4	Discovery of 430 Years from Abraham to the Exodus	16	34
5	Confirmation of Abraham's Historicity...	28	62
6	Discovery of the Remains of Sodom and Gomorrah......................	17	79
7	Joseph As a Slave and Prisoner in Amenemhet I's Reign	21	100
8	Joseph Becomes the Vizier of Sesostris I	23	123
9	Sesostris I Gives Joseph a New Name and a Wife...........................	11	134
10	The Seven Years of Abundance in Sesostris I's Reign....................	10	144
11	The Seven Years of Famine In Sesostris I's Reign..........................	20	164
12	Israel Enters Egypt during Sesostris I's Reign	14	178

NOTES FOR CHAPTER TWELVE ON NEXT PAGE

NOTES FOR CHAPTER TWELVE

1. Genesis 41:56-57
2. Genesis 42-43
3. Genesis 42:6; 43:26; 44:14
4. Genesis 37:5-10.
5. Genesis 45
6. Genesis 46:2-3
7. Genesis 45:16-18; 46:34; 47:5-6, 11-12
8. Genesis 47:27
9. *The Septuagint Version: Greek and* English, 64 (Genesis 46:34), Zondervan.
10. K. A. Kitchen, "Goshen," *Zondervan Pictorial Bible Encyclopedia*, II.779; and E. D. Welch,
       "Goshen," *International Standard Bible Encyclopedia*, II.529. Eerdmans.
11. Genesis 46:26-27
12. Genesis 45:19-23
13. John Wilson (Trans.), "In Praise of the City Ramses," *Ancient Near Eastern Texts*, p. 471.
14. K. A. Kitchen, "Goshen," *Zondervan Pictorial Bible Dictionary*, II.777-78.
15. Genesis 47:5-6
16. William Hayes, "Middle Kingdom of Egypt," *Cambridge Ancient History*, I.2A.497.
17. G. Posener, "Syria and Palestine During the 12th Dynasty," *Cambridge Ancient History*,
       I.2A.538.
18. Genesis 46:33-34; 47:11
19. G. Posener, "Syria and Palestine During the Twelfth Dynasty," *Cambridge Ancient History*,
       I.2A.537.
20. Genesis 41:38
21. Genesis 47:22
22. Breasted (Trans.), "The Contracts of Hepzefi," *Ancient Records of Egypt*, I.260 (539).
23. Breasted (Trans.), "Inscriptions of Mentuhotep," *Ancient Records of Egypt*, 256-7 (533).
24. Breasted (Trans.), "Inscription of Sehetepibre," *Ancient Records of Egypt*, 326 (746).
25. Genesis 41:46; 45:6
26. Genesis 50:22
27. William Hayes, "Middle Kingdom In Egypt," *Cambridge Ancient History*, I.2A.541-2.
28. Genesis 47:6
29. William Hayes, "Middle Kingdom in Egypt," *Cambridge Ancient History*, I.2A.539.
30. G. Posener, "Syria and Palestine, c. 2160 - 1780 B.C.," *Cambridge Ancient History*,
       I.2A.541-542
31. Prof., Emery, excavator, cited by T. Save-Soderbergh and I. U. Olsson, "C14 and
       Egyptian Chronology," 44
32. Genesis 46:34
33. Lichtheim (Trans.), *Ancient Egyptian Literature*, I.116.
34. Genesis 46:34
35. Breasted (Trans.), *Ancient Records of Egypt*, I.252-253 (No. 523).
36. Genesis 39:6-23
37. Lichtheim (Trans.), *Ancient Egyptian Literature*, I.121-122.

CHAPTER THIRTEEN
SESOSTRIS III ENSLAVES THE ISRAELITES

Sesostris I and Sesostris III were the best known Pharaohs of the twelfth dynasty. Their names have been attached to legendary feats in the history of Herodotus, who wrote more than 1,000 years later.[1] Hayes estimates that Sesostris III contributed more to "the enduring glory" of the twelfth dynasty than all of its other Pharaohs.[2] I disagree! In this and the following chapters we will see that Sesostris III headed Egypt on a downward spiral to moral corruption and eventually to economic and political destruction. His apparent material gains were accomplished by inordinate pride, greed, injustice, hostility and disrespect for the humanity of others, especially foreigners. His son and grandson imitated his brutal policies, provoking God to destroy one of the most glorious dynasties of Egyptian history. In this and the next two chapters we will see that Sesostris III uniquely fits the Biblical description of the Pharaoh who hated Israelites, enslaved them, abused them, forced them to construct the store cities of Pithom and Rameses, but ironically, reared baby Moses as an Egyptian prince in his own palace.

I. SESOSTRIS III, A PHARAOH WHO KNEW NOT JOSEPH

During Joseph's life and afterwards, the Israelites grew into a "numerous people," owned property in the delta and accumulated great wealth.[3] Sesostris I appointed some of Joseph's brothers to take care of his own livestock in the delta and gave special favors to them.[4] Since Joseph was the Vizier of Egypt, some of Joseph's brothers and their descendants likely held high positions in Egyptian government, especially in the land of Goshen where most of the Israelites lived.

Exodus 1:8 reports that after Joseph's death a new Pharaoh ruled Egypt who had never known Joseph personally. This new Pharaoh feared the growing Israelites as a threat to the security of Egypt.

Table 13-A on page 169 lists my comparative chronology of Biblical and twelfth-dynasty history. Joseph died in 1585 B.C. in the fifth year of Sesostris II. This comparative chronology dates Moses' birth fifty-nine years later in 1526 B.C., in Sesostris III's sixteenth year. Since the Biblical Exodus is dated in 1446 B.C., when Moses was eighty years old (Exodus 7:7), we add 80 years to 1446 B.C. and get 1526 B.C. for Moses' birth. I thus hypothetically ascribe Sesostris III's sixteenth year to 1526 B.C. and his first year to 1542 B.C.

A statue of Sesostris III shows him to be in his mid-twenties. Sesostris III was likely born about fifteen to twenty years after Joseph died. Thus, Sesostris III obviously qualifies as "a new king, **who did not know Joseph**" (Exodus 1:8). See Sesostris III's statue in Figure 13-A on the next page.

Appendix C discusses the controversial duration of years that Sesostris III and his predecessors reigned. A newly discovered construction by Sesostris III lists his **thirty-ninth year of reign** on the corner stone.[5] **Modern Egyptologists calculate**

only an eighteen-year reign for Sesostris III. However, the recent discovery of Sesostris III's **minimum thirty-ninth year destroys the astronomical compatibility of Egyptologists' assigned B.C. years for Sesostris III.** Chapters Twenty-Two to Twenty-Four reveal scientific proof that demands that Sesostris III be redated three centuries later where the astronomical and carbon-14 evidences fit compatibly with his death in his forty-third year of reign. Figures 13-A, 13-B and 13-C show three pictures of Sesostris III as he progressed from a young Pharaoh to a middle-aged Pharaoh to an old Pharaoh, easily covering a reign of forty-three years. Sesostris III's forty-three-year reign is necessary to reach astronomical compatibility with the dates of Sirius' rising and the dates of new moons that are recorded in specific days, months and years of his reign. **See these three statues of Sesostris III.**

SESOSTRIS III AS A YOUNG MAN
Source: James B. Pritchard,
The Ancient Near East in Pictures,
Princeton University Press (New Jersey),
1969, page 135, Figure 384.
Permission granted by
Princeton Univ. Press
FIGURE 13-A

SESOSTRIS III AS A SPHINX
(MIDDLE AGE)
The Scepter of Egypt, Vol. I
by William C. Hayes
Figure 119
King Sen-Wosret III p. 197
Permission granted by
Metropolitan Museum of Art
Gift of Edward S. Harkness 1916-17.
(17.9.2)
FIGURE 13-B

SESOSTRIS III AS AN OLD MAN
The Scepter of Egypt, Vol. I
by William C. Hayes
Figure 120
King Sen-Wosret III, p.198
Permission granted by Metropolitan
Museum of Art
Carnarvon Collection,
Gift of Edward S. Harkness,
1926   (26.7.1394)
FIGURE 13-C

Table 13-A
CHRONOLOGY FROM JOSEPH TO MOSES COMPARED
WITH TWELFTH-DYNASTY CHRONOLOGY
(OVER-LAPS SHOW CO-REIGNS)

	A-I	S-I		
AMENEMHET I	0		1688	ACCESSION YEAR
	19		1668	JOSEPH IN PRISON
SESOSTRIS I	20	0	1667	BAKER & BUTLER IN PRISON
	21	01	1666	
	22	02	1665	1ST YR. OF ABUNDANCE: JOSEPH
	23	03	1664	2ND YEAR OF ABUNDANCE
	24	04	1663	3RD YEAR OF ABUNDANCE
	25	05	1662	4TH YEAR OF ABUNDANCE
	26	06	1661	5TH YEAR OF ABUNDANCE
	27	07	1660	6TH YEAR OF ABUNDANCE
	28	08	1659	7TH YEAR OF ABUNDANCE
	29	09	1658	1ST YEAR OF FAMINE
	30	10	1657	2ND YEAR OF FAMINE
		11	1656	JACOB ENTERS EGYPT
		12	1655	4TH YEAR OF FAMINE
		13	1654	5TH YEAR OF FAMINE
		14	1653	6TH YEAR OF FAMINE
		15	1652	7TH YEAR OF FAMINE
		28	1639	JACOB'S DEATH
		38	1629	
AMENEMHET II	0	42	1625	
	01	43	1624	
	02	44	1623	
	03	45	1622	
	04	46	1621	
	05	S-II	1620	ISRAELITE PROSPERITY
	35	0	1590	
SESOSTRIS II	36	01	1589	
	37	02	1588	
	38	03	1587	
		05	1585	JOSEPH'S DEATH
		30	1560	ISRAELITE GROWTH
	S-III	SII		
SESOSTRIS III		40	1550	
	0	48	1542	SLAVERY OF ISRAEL
	7		1535	CONSTRUCTION OF RAMESES
	16		1526	MOSES' BIRTH
	39		1503	
	43		1499	
AMENEMHET III		AIII		
	44	0	1498	
	45	1	1497	
	46	2	1496	
		12	1486	MOSES' EXILE TO MIDIAN
		38	1466	CONTINUED CONSTRUCTION
AMENEMHET IV				
	0	42	1456	IN GOSHEN
	6	48	1450	
	10		1446	PLAGUES AND EXODUS

II. SESOSTRIS III, SLAVE MASTER OF ISRAEL

Josephus, the Jewish historian of the first century, tells us that the Pharaoh who knew not Joseph became jealously alarmed at the prosperity, influence and growing numbers of the Israelites.[6] The Bible says that the Pharaoh of the Oppression feared that the growing Israelites might join Egypt's enemies and leave the country. He thus enslaved them and mistreated them unmercifully.

> Exodus 1:8-14 -- Then a new king, who did not know about Joseph, came to power . . . . He said, "the Israelites have become much too numerous for us. Come, we must deal shrewdly with them or they will become even more numerous and, if war breaks out, will join our enemies, fight against us and leave the country." So they put slave masters over them to oppress them with forced labor, and they built Pithom and Rameses as store cities for Pharaoh. But the more they were oppressed, the more they multiplied and spread. . . . They made their lives bitter with hard labor in brick and mortar and with all kinds of work in the fields. NIV

We saw in the previous chapter how a growing number of foreigners from Canaan were living as free citizens and prospering and participating in all sectors of Egypt's economy during the reign of Sesostris II, the father of Sesostris III. Is there any documented evidence that Sesostris III enslaved these foreigners?

Mentuemhat, the general of Sesostris III, claims on his stela that he was appreciated by the king more than his (other) officials for **"mastering the insurgents of Asia, the rebels of the northern territories."** Posener interpreted these insurgents of Asia to be those living in either Canaan or Syria.[7] However, William Simpson of Yale University says that Palestine and Syria were not considered **"northern territories"** of an Egyptian empire during the time of the twelfth dynasty.[8] Hayes agrees with Simpson by pointing out that Sesostris III recorded many military incursions into Nubia, a country of Africa,[9] but only one military campaign into Palestine that was "small in scale and unimportant.[10] In this one raid he was met by friendly people except for the inhabitants of Shechem who offered resistance and were easily conquered. This minor battle is proved by the fact that an Egyptian soldier was honored for having killed only one Canaanite.[11]

Therefore, Sesostris III did not conquer Palestine and enslave many Canaanites during his reign. In fact, we will see in a later chapter that Sesostris III feared the Palestinians and built fortress cities in the eastern delta to protect Egypt against invasions by Palestinians, Syrians, and Arabians. Since Sesostris III did not dominate Palestine, then his General Mentuemhat was not likely talking about an invasion of Palestine when he "mastered the insurgents of Asia . . . in the northern territories." Insurgents **"of"** Asia can mean "from" Canaan and the "northern territories" can refer to the northern territories of Egypt itself, which includes the land of Goshen. Therefore, General Mentuemhat was likely referring to foreigners from Canaan who were living in northern Egypt.

Mentuemhat did not say that he "conquered" these foreigners, but that he "**mastered**" them. To "master foreigners" literally means to "**enslave**" them. The order of Sesostris III to "master" or "enslave" these foreigners in northern Egypt fits precisely the words of Exodus 1:11 that the Pharaoh of the Oppression "**put slave masters**" over the Israelites of northern Egypt to "oppress them with forced labor."

Mentuemhat did not record the year of Sesostris III's reign when these foreigners were enslaved. I date Moses' birth in 1526 B.C. in Sesostris III's sixteenth year. The Bible does not tell us how many years Israel had been enslaved before Moses was born. I estimate that Sesostris III may have enslaved Israel sometime between his eighth and thirteenth years, which my synchronistic chronology dates between 1534 and 1529 B.C.: see Table 13-A above on p. 169.

III. SESOSTRIS III, MURDERER OF THE ISRAELITE INFANTS

Israel grew rapidly even while under the burden of bitter slavery.

Exodus 1:12-14 -- But the more they were oppressed, the more they multiplied and spread; so the Egyptians came to dread the Israelites and worked them ruthlessly. They made their lives bitter with hard labor in brick and mortar and with all kinds of work in the fields; in all their hard labor the Egyptians used them ruthlessly. (NIV)

The Pharaoh of the Oppression was determined to stem their population growth. He ordered the Egyptian midwives to kill all Israelite males at the moment of birth. When this order failed to get results, "Pharaoh gave this order to all his people: 'Every boy that is **born you must throw into the Nile**.'"[12]

Do any documents of Sesostris III's reign indicate that he gave instructions to **midwives and threw innocent babies into the Nile River?**

A. Egyptian Midwives

Remarkably, a treatise on duties of midwives was found dated to the time of Sesostris III and other twelfth-dynasty kings. See the proof below.

Among the papyrus documents of the Middle Kingdom, the archive from Illahun is particularly varied. It includes: **a text on midwifery**; a veterinary manual; hymns to Sesostris III on the occasion of his visit to a southern town; [etc.]. . . .[13]

This document proves that midwives constituted a special vocational class of women in the twelfth dynasty and that a twelfth-dynasty king gave them instructions concerning their profession. Since hymns to Sesostris III were found with the text of midwifery, the text about midwives was likely contemporary with the reign of

Sesostris III, lending additional evidence that is consistent with my identification of Sesostris III as the Pharaoh of the Oppression.

B. The Egyptian Meaning of Death by Water

When the midwives disobeyed Pharaoh's orders to kill newborn Israelite males, he decreed that all male Israelite infants be thrown into the Nile River.[14] The worst punishment that an Egyptian could inflict on an enemy was to cast his corpse into crocodile-infested water, where the body would be devoured and annihilated. Egyptians believed that their bodies must be embalmed and buried in a land based tomb in order to be raised to eternal life. For this reason, the Pharaohs went to great efforts to have their bodies preserved and protected in enormous pyramids that stored much of their material possessions to be utilized in the resurrection.[15]

Israelites also believed that the body should be preserved for the resurrection day.[16] Jacob and Joseph requested that their bodies be taken to Canaan land for burial.[17] The prospect of a watery grave for their children no doubt deeply disturbed the Israelites, who made every effort to bury their dead in a land-based burial ground. Imagine the emotional trauma that Israelites experienced in seeing their newborn sons cast into the Nile to be eaten by crocodiles. This inhuman atrocity must have etched on their hearts an unforgettable injury.

C. Did Sesostris III and Amenemhet III Cast
Their Enemies into the Water?

Sehetep-Ib-Re, an official who served Sesostris III and his son Amenemhet III, wrote the following about Amenemhet III.

> His eyes seek out every body. He is Re who sees with his rays. . . . Noses turn cold when he starts to rage, when he is at peace one breathes air. . . . The king's beloved will be honored, **His majesty's foe has no tomb, His corpse is cast into the water**.[18]

I have not found twelfth-dynasty Pharaohs, prior to the reign of Sesostris III, who threw their enemies into the "water." Amenemhet III likely learned this practice from his father, Sesostris III. The above citation proves that Pharaohs of the latter half of the twelfth dynasty had a practice of throwing their enemies into the water, a unique but cruel "coincidence" linking the heartless Biblical Pharaohs of the Oppression to Sesostris III and his son Amenemhet III.

IV. SESOSTRIS III'S HATRED OF FOREIGNERS

Enslaving the Israelites and murdering their infants to stem their population growth reveals a deep-seated insecurity and an intense hatred and disrespect for one's fellow man, especially foreigners. Do the writings of Sesostris III indicate that he hated foreigners? *The Execration Texts*, dated to the reigns of Sesostris III and his son Amenemhet III, further reveal the sinister hostility that these Pharaohs harbored in their hearts toward foreigners. Sesostris III commanded that curses against his enemies be inscribed upon figurines and pottery bowls and that the pottery be shattered to represent the destruction of those he hated. Broken pieces of pottery (sherds) with inscriptions have been found buried near the tombs of the dead at Thebes and Saqqara. Most texts curse the foreign enemies of Sesostris III and his son Amenemhet III. We will look at some of the significant names of these foreigners in the next chapter. These voodoo-type curses of Egypt's foreign enemies first appear in the reign of Sesostris III, marking him uniquely as the Pharaoh who showed intense hatred for the Israelite foreigners who lived in Egypt.

V. SESOSTRIS III'S ABUSE OF FOREIGNERS

Sesostris III not only cursed his foreign enemies with his lips; he also treated them cruelly. Sesostris III describes in his own words how he treated the Nubians, an African country located on Egypt's southern border.

> I am a king who speaks and acts . . . . One who attacks to conquer, who is swift to succeed . . . **Merciless to the foe who attacks him**. One who attacks him who would attack . . . Attack is valor, retreat is cowardice. . . . Since the Nubian listens to the word of mouth, to answer him is to make him retreat. **Attack him, he will turn his back**, Retreat, he will start attacking. **They are not people one respects, They are wretches, craven-hearted.** My majesty has seen it, it is not an untruth. **I have captured their women, I have carried off their dependents, Gone to their wells, killed their cattle, Cut down their grain, set fire to it.**[19] [Emphasis mine]

Egyptian kings always put their best foot forward when leaving inscriptions that will be read by future posterity. Sesostris III's stela (cited above) shows how he conquered Nubia and abused them afterwards in order to keep them under his control. He believed that the way to maintain their respect was to attack them rather than treat them kindly. Notice also the despicable terms of "wretched" and "craven-hearted" (cowardly) which Sesostris III ascribed to the Nubians. He specifically said, "**They are not people one respects**." Such oppressive tactics fit perfectly the cruel, insecure, disrespectful, oppressive Pharaoh of Moses' birth.

VI. SESOSTRIS III: OPPRESSOR
OF HIS OWN PEOPLE

The *Execration Texts* of the reigns of Sesostris III and Amenemhet III are directed mostly at foreigners. However, some of these texts show that some of Sesostris III's fellow Egyptians were also objects of his wrath. Notice below.

Egyptians, all men, all people, all folk, all males, all eunuchs, all women, and all officials, who may rebel, who may plot, who may fight, who may talk of fighting, or who may talk of rebelling, and every rebel who talks of rebelling --- in this entire land shall die. Ameni shall die . . . Sen-Usert the younger, called Ketu, shall die . . . Ameni, born to Hetep and son of Sen-Usert, shall die.[20]

Sesostris III's paranoid fear of rebellion among his own subjects reveals his insecurity, the same fear expressed by the Biblical Pharaoh of the Oppression.

Exodus 1:9-11 -- "The Israelites have become much too numerous for us. Come, we must deal shrewdly with them or they will become even more numerous and, if war breaks out, will join our enemies, fight against us and leave the country." So they put slave masters over them to oppress them with forced labor . . . .[21] NIV

In addition, Sesostris III also removed all of the Egyptian nomarchs (governors) from their positions of political power and material wealth. All of the previous Pharaohs of the twelfth dynasty appointed the nomarchs (governors of the districts of Egypt) and permitted them to grow in wealth and power, as long as they submitted to the Pharaoh's orders. However, in the latter half of Sesostris III's reign, he stripped these nomarchs of their wealth and power, placing all of the nomes (states or districts) directly under his own control. Notice Hayes' remarks below.

The situation [of wealth, power and independence of the nomarchs] evidently proved intolerable to the **autocratic nature** of the third Sesostris, and at some time during the later half of his reign he appears to have shorn the provincial nobles of their traditional rights and privileges and reduced them to the status of political nonentities. How this was achieved is not known; but in the reign of Sesostris III the series of great provincial tombs came to an end, and no more is heard of the 'Great Chiefs' of the nomes and their local courts.[22]

Sesostris III's suppression of the Egyptian nomarchs demonstrates what Hayes' called his **"autocratic nature."** His removal of the nomarchs was tantamount to robbery of their property and confiscation of the power that former twelfth-dynasty Pharaohs had granted the nomarchs. Hayes called Sesostris III's power move as a **"suppression of the landed nobility"[23]** [my emphasis]. Sesostris III achieved his "greatness" by oppressing his own Egyptian officials who had been serving his predecessors with integrity and competency. In his lust for power and wealth Sesostris III crushed not only Israel and other foreigners, but also the leaders of his own people.

Courville believed that Sesostris III enslaved Israel at the same time that he removed from power the Egyptian nomarchs.[24] However, the quotation above from

Hayes says that Sesostris III confiscated the power of the nomarchs in the "**latter part**" of his reign. Courville's dating of Israel's enslavement in Sesostris III's latter reign pushes the Exodus later into the impossible thirteenth dynasty and therefore must be rejected: see Appendix A. By dating the enslavement of Israel in the first half of Sesostris III's reign and by dating the removal of the Egyptian governors in the latter half of his reign, Sesostris III's chronology fits perfectly with the Biblical chronology of Moses' life: **see Table 13-A on p. 169.**

VII. SESOSTRIS III'S STERN APPEARANCE

Appearances can be deceiving, but they can also be revealing. Statues of Sesostris I and Sesostris III were sculptured when these Pharaohs first began their reigns as young men. They each posed for these statues and thus purposefully appeared as each wished to be seen by posterity. The statue of Sesostris I shows a gentle, loving king who holds in his hand the shepherd's crook to protect and guide his people as a shepherd cares for his sheep. In Sesostris I's third year of reign, he claimed that his Sun-god, Re, appointed him to be shepherd of the people.

> He begat me to do what should be done for him, to accomplish what he commands to do. **He appointed me shepherd of this land**, knowing him who would herd it for him. He gave to me what he protects, what the eye in him illuminates.[25]

Thus, Sesostris I's statue as a kind shepherd fits perfectly the image of the Biblical Pharaoh, who followed the counsel of Joseph, and preserved grain during the seven years of abundance so that he could provide food for his sheep (people) during the seven subsequent years of famine.

In contrast to Sesostris I's shepherd statue, Sesostris III's statue in his early years depicts a stern frown and a rigid stance of arms and hands, suggesting an angry and defiant young man. The posture of Sesostris III fits perfectly the Biblical description of the Pharaoh who enslaved the Israelites and threw their infants into the Nile River to slow their population growth. The gentle spirit of Sesostris I's statues contrasts with the cruel spirit of Sesostris III, etched in the faces and bodies of their differing statues.

When Dot and I visited the Cairo Museum in 1991 we saw a statue of Sesostris III sculptured when he was probably about forty years of age. His frown had increased rather than diminished. Sesostris III's anger and harshness are still visible in his body language. By way of contrast, we saw in the Cairo Museum a monument upon which six statues of Sesostris I were carved in ivory. It is a magnificent work of sculpture. These multiple statues of Sesostris I show him when he was older with an appearance of confidence, joy, vibrance and kindness. Unfortunately, I have lost my photo of this magnificent monument.

William Hayes, writing in the *Cambridge Ancient History*, also observed the harsh image of the statues of Sesostris III and of his son Amenemhet III.

Especially searching are the portraits of Sesostris III, whose grim, disdainful face, deeply lined with fatigue and disillusionment, is preserved to us on a score of statues from Karnak, Deir el-Bahri, El-Madamud, and elsewhere. The numerous portraits of Ammenemes III include a group of statues and sphinxes from Tanis and the Faiyum, which, from their curiously brutal style and strange accessories, were once thought to be monuments of Hyksos kings.[26]

Professor Simpson of Yale University also observed Sesostris III's statues and commented about the sphinxes of both Sesostris III and his son Amenemhet III.

The idealized, youthful and sometimes bland confidence expressed in royal statuary of the Old Kingdom changes to a brooding, concerned, and even worried strength, sometimes almost brutal, in the portraits of Sesostris III and Amunemhet [sic] III. The sphinx was revived as a medium for royal portraiture, since it so forcefully expressed the power of the kingship.[27]

Figure 13-B on page 168 displays the frown on the face of Sesostris III with the body of a lion (sphinx) ready to pounce on his prey. This is the brutal and cruel image that Sesostris III displayed to his fellow Egyptians and especially to foreigners. Sesostris III looked and acted the part of the Biblical Pharaoh of the Oppression who enslaved the Israelites, abused them and murdered their infants.

VIII. EVIL OF SESOSTRIS III CONTRASTS WITH HIGH MORALITY OF EARLIER TWELFTH-DYNASTY KINGS

Harsh brutality characterized the reigns of Sesostris III and Amenemhet III, sharply contrasting with the high morality and kind gentleness exemplified in the reign of Sesostris I, the Pharaoh of Joseph. In Chapter Eleven we saw the benevolent kindness expressed in the documents of Intef, Son of Sent[28] and Ameni, nomarch of the Oryx nome at Beni-hasan,[29] both officials of Sesostris I.

Sesostris I's emphasis on virtue and benevolence is replaced with harshness and cruelty in the reign of Sesostris III. This same change of attitude is noted in the Bible when the Pharaoh of the Oppression rose to power and abused the Israelites by forcing them to hard labor without even a day's rest each week.[30]

A heavy handed tyrant forbids criticism and eliminates the very possibility of opposition. However, I found one document of Sesostris III's reign that cried out in protest and grieved over the evil changes that had taken place: *The Complaints of Khakheperre-Sonb.* Scholars date this document to the reign of Sesostris II or shortly afterwards in the reign of Sesostris III.[31] The reason scholars think the document was written in the reign of Sesostris II is that the first part of Sonb's name, "Khakheperre," is also the throne name of Sesostris II. However, this does not necessarily mean that he wrote during the reign of Sesostris II.   Actually, Khakheperre-Sonb was only a "pen name;" his real name was Ankhu, son of Seni, priest of On (Heliopolis).[32] Ankhu obviously used the pen name of Sesostris II in honor of the king he deeply admired. Therefore, Ankhu's protests were made not against the king he honored by his own pen name, but against the king he did not respect, Sesostris III, the son and successor of Sesostris II.

Ankhu never named Sesostris III as the reigning king and could not have named him without suffering severe recrimination.   By honoring the name of Sesostris II, the father, and by attaching Sesostris II's throne name to his own pen name, Ankhu left it to the reader to deduce that he was protesting not the father's actions (Sesostris II), but the son's (Sesostris III). Notice how disturbed Ankhu became over the radical changes that Sesostris III made after his father Sesostris II died. Ankhu expresses below the radical changes for the worse that occurred when the Pharaoh of the Oppression (Sesostris III) appeared on the scene.

> I meditate on what has happened, the events that occur throughout the land. **Changes take place; it is not like last year. One year is more irksome than the other.** . . . Order is cast out. Chaos is in the council hall. The ways of the gods are violated, their provisions neglected. . . . Answer me my sayings! Unravel for me what goes on in the land, **why those who shone are overthrown.** I meditate on what has happened. While trouble entered in today, and turmoil will not cease tomorrow, **everyone is mute about it**. The whole land is in great distress. Nobody is free from crime; hearts are greedy. **He who gave orders takes orders and the hearts of both submit.** . . . A heart addressed must not be silent. Lo, **servant and master fare alike**; there is much that weighs upon you.[33] [Emphasis mine]

Ankhu spoke out against that which no one else had the courage to condemn. He was deeply disturbed because "changes take place" and **each year is worse than the other.** This change for the worse likely began when Sesostris III enslaved the foreigners in northern Egypt (the Israelites) who were formerly wealthy and politically influential. Conditions continued to worsen when Sesostris III later removed the Egyptian nomarchs from their position of power, creating disorder in the higher echelons of the Egyptian government: "Chaos is in the council hall."[34]

Many of these nomarchs were also high priests of the temples in their districts. Thus, Ankhu noted that "the way of the gods was violated" and that the "allotment" that formerly went to these nomarchs as priests was denied them, "their provisions neglected." Joseph was honored by Sesostris I as the greatest and wisest prophet in Egypt. Joseph was not only the "Superior Prophet" of the God of the Hebrews, he also married the daughter of the priest of On (Heliopolis), the priest of "Ra." Since Ankhu was himself priest of Heliopolis, and since Joseph's wife, Asenath, was the daughter of the priest of Heliopolis, Ankhu may have been related to Asenath's father and thus a relative of the descendants of Joseph and Asenath. It may have caused Ankhu painful grief to see the descendants of Asenath (Israelite descendants of Joseph) being treated so unjustly and cruelly.

Ankhu specifically laments "those who shone" formerly, but now "are overthrown." Those who shone were formerly in political and religious positions of power and influence. This expression fits perfectly the Israelites who were formerly "shining" with favor in the time of Joseph, but now have been "overthrown" through the confiscation of their property, wealth and positions of influence and by their cruel bondage. The "greedy hearts" that Ankhu observed no doubt referred to Sesostris III's selfishness in confiscating the wealth and power of the Israelites, and later, of the Egyptian nomarchs. Ankhu also complained that masters had become slaves and that both slaves and masters now had to submit to the same autocratic authority: "He who gave orders takes orders and both hearts submit. . . . Lo, servant and master fare alike." Israelites who were once wealthy, independent, in positions of authority and perhaps slave owners, were enslaved and forced to take orders. Also, the Egyptian nomarchs who once owned slaves now have none, and all must submit to Sesostris III, **the Master of Slave Masters.**

Ankhu reported that these terrible conditions brought suffering and grief to Egypt's citizens over the entire land.

The land is in turmoil; there is mourning everywhere. Towns, districts are grieving. All alike are burdened by wrongs. One turns one's back on dignity; the lords of silence are disturbed.[35]

Ankhu courageously protested Sesostris III's unjust deeds. He could not keep silent. He could only cry out in grief, for he was powerless to act against this cruel and mighty Pharaoh of Egypt. Ankhu was indeed "A Voice Crying in the Wilderness."[36]

Ankhu's document of protest shows that the outward glory, power and wealth of Sesostris III's reign was characterized by an inward corruption of greed, hostility and unending grief. Ankhu could not have better described the evil reign of the Biblical Pharaoh of the Oppression. Perhaps now the reader can understood why I disagree with Dr. William Hayes' assessment that Sesostris III contributed more to "the enduring glory" of the twelfth dynasty than all of its other Pharaohs.[37] When the truth of this book is recognized, Sesostris III's name will be named along with Antiochus Epiphanes, Nero and Hitler, **as one of history's worst tyrants, who led the twelfth dynasty down the road to ultimate destruction.**

IX. WHY DID GOD PERMIT ISRAEL'S SLAVERY?

While Sesostris III's enslavement and abuse of the Israelites is to be condemned, this is not to say that the Israelites were blameless. Unfortunately, the religious beliefs of the Egyptians gradually began to influence the Israelites who lived in Egypt. Many Israelites compromised their religious faith and abandoned the God of Abraham to worship the gods of Egypt.

Moses implied in Leviticus 17:7 that Israelites worshiped the goat-god while they lived in Egypt: "They must **no longer** offer any of their sacrifices to the goat idols to whom they prostitute themselves." Joshua 24:14 also notes the idolatry of Israel when they lived in Egypt: "Throw away the gods your forefathers worshiped beyond the River **and in Egypt**, and serve the Lord."

The prophet Ezekiel records a more detailed revelation of Israel's idolatry while they were in Egypt. Ezekiel implies that God sent prophets to Israel, warning them to put away their idols, and that God then punished Israel in Egypt when they refused to repent and turn back to the God of Abraham, Isaac, Jacob, and Joseph.

> Ezekiel 20:6-8 -- (6) On that day I swore to them that I would bring them out of Egypt into a land I had searched out for them, a land flowing with milk and honey, the most beautiful of all lands. (7) And I said to them, "Each of you, **get rid of the vile images you have set your eyes on, and do not defile yourselves with the idols of Egypt.** I am the Lord your God." (8) **But they rebelled against me and would not listen to me; they did not get rid of the vile images they had set their eyes on, nor did they forsake the idols of Egypt. So I said I would pour out my wrath on them and spend my anger against them in Egypt.** NIV

G. Posener, who reported the growth of numerous Canaanites (Asiatics) in Egyptian society during the reign of Sesostris II, also mentioned that many of them were servants in the temple worship of the Egyptians.[38] No doubt most of these Canaanites were Israelites who began to serve in the temples of the gods of Egypt, as described above in Ezekiel 20:6-8.

Thus, after many years of faithfulness to the God of Abraham, Isaac and Jacob, many Israelites apostatized and began worshiping the gods of Egypt. Ezekiel explains that God poured out His wrath on these unfaithful Israelites. **We now can see that Sesostris III was the rod of God's wrath to punish unfaithful Israel.**

Another indication of Israel's idolatry was the appearance of the Ra name of Egypt's sun-god in the names of some of Joseph's descendants. I Chronicles 7:25 lists the names of **Re**-phah and **Re**-sheph as descendants of Joseph. Genesis 41:50 says that the name of Joseph's father-in-law was Potiphera, or Poti-Phe-Ra, "priest of Heliopolis," the center of worship of Ra, the sun-god. Kitchen says that this name means, "Whom Ra, the sun-god, has given."[39] In Chapter Seventeen we will show proof that all of the twelfth dynasty Pharaohs had "Ra" in their throne names. Since Asenath was the daughter of Potiphera, the priest of Ra worship, she could also have influenced her children and grandchildren to become devoted to her father's god, Ra. Of course, it is also possible that Asenath was converted to the God of Joseph and that it was later generations that fell into the worship of Ra.

Regardless, many Israelites later became worshipers of the gods of Egypt because Ezekiel 20:6-8 reveals to us that Israel's idolatry was **the reason that God poured out his wrath on Israel while they were in Egypt.** Ezekiel's insight into the sin of ancient Israel explains why God permitted the Israelites to be enslaved and treated brutally by the cruel Pharaoh of the Oppression during the years after righteous Joseph died.

Therefore, the Israelites contributed to their own bondage and oppression by ceasing to be a leaven of righteousness in the midst of Egyptian society. **Their apostasy and slavery should be a warning for God's people in every age.** God used the evil Sesostris III to pour out his wrath upon sinful Israel. However, in spite of this religious apostasy by many Israelites, a righteous remnant remained faithful to God and produced men like Moses, Aaron, Joshua and Caleb. God used these righteous men to deliver Israel from their oppressors.

CONCLUSION

My comparative chronological charts point to Sesostris III as the infamous Pharaoh of the Oppression who did not know Joseph and who enslaved the Israelites and treated them cruelly to the point of murdering their infants by throwing them into the Nile River. Sesostris III praised his general for enslaving the Canaanite foreigners (Israelites) who lived in the northern territories (the land of Goshen). Sesostris III exhibited his great hatred of foreigners in the famous *Execration Texts* and in his cruel treatment of the Nubians who lived on Egypt's southern border. He instructed midwives to drown Israel's newborn and threw his own enemies into the water to be eaten by crocodiles.

He totally disrespected foreigners and also oppressed his own people by removing the traditional Egyptian nomarchs (governors) from office. His stern appearance and brutal sphinxes and statues demonstrate the evil reign of this Pharaoh, in contrast to earlier reigns of joy, peace and righteousness.

Ankhu, who lived under the peaceful, happy and righteous reign of Sesostris II, mourned the unjust suppression of formerly favored people (Israelites and Egyptian nomarchs) and mourned the **greedy and sinister spirit that prevailed in the reign of Sesostris III.** The prophet Ezekiel attributes the slavery of Israel to their later apostasy and idolatry. We have seen evidences of this idolatry in the Biblical record of Joseph's descendants and in the Egyptian records of the twelfth dynasty. Table 13-B on the next page lists seventeen clues that link the person and time of Sesostris III to the Pharaoh who enslaved and oppressed the Israelites. In the next two chapters we will see even more significant evidence that identifies Sesostris III as the Pharaoh who reared Moses and at the same time forced the enslaved Israelites to construct the store cities of Rameses and Pithom.

TABLE 13-B
SEVENTEEN DISCOVERIES IDENTIFY SESOSTRIS III
AS THE PHARAOH WHO ENSLAVED ISRAEL

Discovery 1. Sesostris III's chronology in relation to his predecessors' chronologies dates his reign parallel to the birth and early years of Moses.

Discovery 2. Sesostris III removed foreigners and Egyptians from their former positions of power and favor as the Pharaoh of the Oppression did in Moses' time.

Discovery 3. Sesostris III's general said he was praised most for his enslavement of the foreigners in the north (the Israelites in Goshen).

Discovery 4. "Instructions to Midwives" were found in documents dated to Sesostris III.

Discovery 5. *Execrations Texts* cursed other nations and foreigners and also rebellious Egyptians living in Egypt, showing Sesostris III's hatred for foreigners.

Discovery 6. Sesostris III's cruel treatment of Nubians (in S. Africa) shows his racial prejudice and hatred.

Discovery 7. Sesostris III's anger and harshness can be seen in the statues that he ordered his own artists to sculpture, when he was both young and older.

Discovery 8. Brutal images of sphinxes and other sculptured work reveal the sinister power that Sesostris III exercised over his subjects.

Discovery 9. Sesostris III's cruelty contrasts with the kindness of former twelfth-dynasty Pharaohs.

Discovery 10. Ankhu served under both Sesostris II and Sesostris III. He honored Sesostris II, but protested the evil changes made under Sesostris III.

Discovery 11. Ankhu protested Sesostris III's removal of important officials, who included the nomarchs (governors of Egypt), some of whom were likely Israelites.

Discovery 12. Ankhu protested the rejection and mistreatment of people formerly favored (Israelites), who were enslaved by Sesostris III.

Discovery 13. Ankhu protested the growing greed for wealth in the new regime of Sesostris III, the Pharaoh of the Oppression.

Discovery 14. Ankhu protested that former masters had become slaves, which fits perfectly the Israelites.

Discovery 15. Ankhu grieved over the growth of evil in contrast to the righteousness, peace and joy of former years.

Discovery 16. Ezekiel's revelation of Israel's idolatry as the reason for Israel's punishment by Sesostris III is also confirmed in twelfth dynasty documents showing Canaanites (Israelites) serving in the temples of the gods of Egypt.

Discovery 17. The name of Egypt's sun-god, Ra, is found in names of Joseph's descendants recorded in the Bible, indicating their apostasy from Yahweh, the God of Abraham, Isaac, Jacob, Joseph and Moses. Ra was the favorite god of twelfth-dynasty Pharaohs, all of whom used Ra's name in their throne names.

TABLE 13-C
RUNNING TOTAL OF DISCOVERIES

Chapter		Chapter Total	Running Total
2	Conflict Between Biblical and Secular Histories	18	18
4	Discovery of 430 Years from Abraham to the Exodus	16	34
5	Confirmation of Abraham's Historicity	28	62
6	Discovery of the Remains of Sodom and Gomorrah	17	79
7	Joseph As a Slave and Prisoner in Amenemhet I's Reign	21	100
8	Joseph Becomes the Vizier of Sesostris I	23	123
9	Sesostris I Gives Joseph a New Name and a Wife	11	134
10	The Seven Years of Abundance in Sesostris I's Reign	10	144
11	The Seven Years of Famine in Sesostris I's Reign	20	164
12	Israel Enters Egypt during Sesostris I's Reign	14	178
13	Sesostris III Enslaves the Israelites	17	195

Notes on Chapter 13 on next page

NOTES FOR CHAPTER THIRTEEN

1. Herodotus, *The Histories*, Trans. Aubrey de Selincourt (New York: Penguin Books, 1972), 165-169.

2. William Hayes, "The Middle Kingdom in Egypt," *Cambridge Ancient History*, I.2A,505.

3. Genesis 47:27; Exodus 1:6-7.

4. Genesis 47:5-6.

5. Josef W. Wegner, "The Nature and Chronology of the Sensosret III-Amenemhet III Regnal Succession," *Journal of Near Eastern Studies*," 55. No. 4 (1996), 249-279.

6. John Baines, "Egypt," *New Encyclopaedia Britannica*, 1991 Ed., 18.113.

7. Josephus, "The Antiquities of the Jews," II.9.1, *The Works of Josephus*, 66, Kregel.

8. G. Posener, "Syria and Palestine During Dynasty XII," *Cambridge Ancient History*, I.2A.538 (citing Janssen, *Arch. Or.* 20, 442-5).

9. William K. Simpson, *The Ancient Near East - a History* (New York: Harcourt Brace Jovanovich, Pub., 1971), 247.

10. William C. Hayes, "Middle Kingdom in Egypt," *Cambridge Ancient History*, I.2A.506-507.

11. William C. Hayes, "Middle Kingdom in Egypt," *Cambridge Ancient History*, I.2A.508.

12. William C. Hayes "Middle Kingdom in Egypt," *Cambridge Ancient History*, I.2A.508.

13. Exodus 1:6-22.

14. William K. Simpson, *The Ancient Near East - A History*," 248.

15. Exodus 1:22.

16. I. E. S. Edwards, "The Early Dynastic Period in Egypt," *The Cambridge Ancient History*, I.2A.56-57.

17. Daniel 12:1-4,13; Isa. 25:8; 26:19, Matt. 22:23-22; Acts 24:14-15; 1 Cor. 15:54-57.

18. Genesis 47:30; 49:29-32; 50:24-25; Joshua 24:32.

19. M. Lichtheim (Trans.), *Ancient Egyptian Literature*, I.128.

20. M. Lichtheim (Trans.), *Ancient Egyptian Literature*, I.119.

21. William C. Hayes, "Middle Kingdom in Egypt," *Cambridge Ancient History*, I.2A.508-9.

22. Exodus 1:9-11.

23. William Hayes, "The Middle Kingdom in Egypt," *Cambridge Ancient History*, I.2A,505-506.

24. William Hayes, "The Middle Kingdom in Egypt," *Cambridge Ancient History*, I.2A, 506.

26. M. Lichtheim (Trans.), *Ancient Egyptian Literature*, I.116.

27. William Hayes, "Middle Kingdom of Egypt," *Cambridge Ancient History*, I.2A.514.

28. William Simpson, "Dynasty 12," *Ancient Near East - a History*, 246.

29. M. Lichtheim (Trans.), "Stela of Intef Son of Sent," *Ancient Egyptian Literature*, I.121-122.

30. Breasted (Trans.), *Ancient Records of Egypt*, I.252-253 (No. 523).

31. Exodus 1:8-22

32. M. Lichtheim (Trans.), *Ancient Egyptian Literature*, I.145.

33. M. Lichtheim (Trans.), *Ancient Egyptian Literature*, I.146.

34. M. Lichtheim (Trans.), *Ancient Egyptian Literature*, I.145-148.

35. William C. Hayes, "Middle Kingdom of Egypt," *Cambridge Ancient History*, I.2A.505-506.

36. M. Lichtheim (Trans.), *Ancient Egyptian Literature*, I.145-148.

37. Isaiah 40:3

38. William Hayes, "The Middle Kingdom In Egypt," *Cambridge Ancient History*, I. Part 2A, 505.

39. G. Posener, "Syria and Palestine,"*Cambridge Ancient History*, I.2A, 542.

40. Kenneth Kitchen, "Potiphar," *Zondervan Pictorial Bible Encyclopedia*, IV.823.

CHAPTER FOURTEEN
SESOSTRIS III, FOSTER GRAND-FATHER
OF MOSES

Exodus 1:6-22 says that Israel grew rapidly even while under the burden of bitter slavery. The Pharaoh of the Oppression was determined to stem their population growth. He first ordered the Egyptian midwives to kill all Israelite males at the moment of birth. When the midwives failed to obey the king's order, Pharaoh ordered all Egyptians to throw newborn male Israelites into the Nile River.

Baby Moses was born during this terrible time in Hebrew history. Exodus 2:1-10 tells us that Moses' parents hid him for three months. When they could no longer hide the infant, Moses' mother and sister ingeniously made a basket of papyrus into a tiny boat. They placed baby Moses in the basket among the reeds of the Nile where the Egyptian princess regularly bathed. When the princess found baby Moses crying in the basket, she felt sympathy for him and decided to keep him as her own son, even though she knew he was a Hebrew. Thus, Moses providentially grew up in the Egyptian palace as the foster grandson of Sesostris III. Moses was nurtured and protected by the very Pharaoh that had ordered the death of all Hebrew infants.

According to my comparative chronology, Moses was born in the sixteenth year of Sesostris III. See this synchronistic chronology in Table 14-A on page 185. This chapter presents significant evidence that Moses was the foster grandson of Sesostris III.

I. MOSES' FOSTER MOTHER: ONE OF
SESOSTRIS III'S DAUGHTERS

Exodus 2:5-10 reports that Moses was adopted by the daughter of Pharaoh and reared and protected in the palace of the very king who was killing Israelite infants. If Sesostris III is the first Pharaoh of the Oppression, then one of his daughters was Moses' foster mother. Nefert-hent was one of two or three Queens of Sesostris III. Next to her tomb were three princesses whose names were Ment, Meryt, and Sat-hathor.[1] The Jewish historian Josephus reported a tradition that Moses' Egyptian mother was called **"Thermuthis"** and that she once saved Moses from being killed by her cruel father.[2] Two of the names of Sesostris III's daughters above have the consonants "M" and "T" (Ment, and Meryt) but the prefix, "Ther," is missing from both of them. However, "Ther" is present in the name of the third daughter, "Sat-ha-**thor**." If this third daughter's full name were "Sat-ha-**thor-muthis**," she would be indicated as Moses' foster mother, but no evidence indicates that "muthis" can be added to her name. Of course, Josephus wrote about 1600 years after Moses lived. Thus, we have no basis for knowing whether or not Josephus was accurate in naming Moses' foster mother as "Thermuthis." However, all of these names fit perfectly into the Egyptian culture of the twelfth dynasty.

Petrie listed no sons or daughters of the second Queen, Merseger, nor of Sesostris III's sister, Sentsenb, who may also have been his wife. The jewelry buried with Sentsenb is among the most valuable treasures ever found in Egypt.[3] However, silence by Petrie proves nothing as to whether Sesostris III had other daughters. With multiple wives Sesostris III certainly had many daughters, any of which could have reared Moses after finding him among the reeds of the Nile.

TABLE 14-A
CHRONOLOGY FROM JOSEPH TO MOSES COMPARED
W/ TWELFTH-DYNASTY CHRONOLOGY
(OVER-LAPS SHOW CO-REIGNS)

	A-I	S I		
AMENEMHET I	0		1688	ACCESSION YEAR
	19		1668	JOSEPH IN PRISON
SESOSTRIS I	20	0	1667	BAKER & BUTLER IN PRISON
	21	01	1666	
	22	02	1665	1ST YR. OF ABUNDANCE: JOSEPH 1ST YR. VIZIER
	23	03	1664	2ND YEAR OF ABUNDANCE
	24	04	1663	3RD YEAR OF ABUNDANCE
	25	05	1662	4TH YEAR OF ABUNDANCE
	26	06	1661	5TH YEAR OF ABUNDANCE
	27	07	1660	6TH YEAR OF ABUNDANCE
	28	08	1659	7TH YEAR OF ABUNDANCE
	29	09	1658	1ST YEAR OF FAMINE
	30	10	1657	2ND YEAR OF FAMINE
		11	1656	JACOB ENTERS EGYPT
		12	1655	4TH YEAR OF FAMINE
		13	1654	5TH YEAR OF FAMINE
		14	1653	6TH YEAR OF FAMINE
		15	1652	7TH YEAR OF FAMINE
		28	1639	JACOB'S DEATH
		30	1637	
AMENEMHET II	0	42	1625	
	01	43	1624	
	02	44	1623	
	05	S II	1620	ISRAELITE PROSPERITY
SESOSTRIS II	35	0	1590	
	38	03	1587	
	40	05	1585	JOSEPH'S DEATH
		30	1560	ISRAELITE GROWTH
SESOSTRIS III	0	48	1542	SLAVERY OF ISRAEL
	7		1535	CONSTRUCTION OF RAMESES
	16		1526	MOSES' BIRTH
	36		1506	
	43	A III	1499	
AMENEMHET III	44	0	1498	
	46	2	1496	
		12	1486	MOSES' EXILE TO MIDIAN
		32	1466	CONTINUED CONSTRUCTION
AMENEMHET IV	0	42	1456	IN GOSHEN
	6	48	1450	
Died in Red Sea	10		1446	PLAGUES AND EXODUS

II. MOSES' NAME FITS EGYPTIAN HIEROGLYPHICS

The Egyptian princess who found a Hebrew baby floating in the Nile explained why she called him Moses: "I drew him out of the water."[4] Moses comes from the same word as "Meses" in "Ra-**Meses**," which means "produced, created or born of Ra" (the Egyptian sun-god).[5] However, the Jewish historian Josephus tells us that Moses' name was originally spelled "Mouses" and comes from "mou," which the Egyptians call "water."[6] Modern lexicographers of ancient Egyptian hieroglyphics indicate that the words "ma" and "mu" do indeed mean "water."[7] If Moses' Egyptian name were "Mu-ses," then "ses" means "to raise up"[8] and thus Moses means "to raise up from the water," a prototype of Christian baptism. Josephus' interpretation fits the Bible explanation that the Egyptian princess named the baby "Moses" because she drew him out of the water.[9]

I have not yet found the name of Moses in twelfth-dynasty inscriptions. Moses' name was so hated by twelfth-dynasty kings that they likely expunged his name from all of their official records. However, Moses was highly respected by Pharaoh's officials because of his amazing predictions of the ten plagues.

> Exodus 11:3 - -The Lord made the Egyptians favorably disposed toward the people, and **Moses himself was highly regarded in Egypt by Pharaoh's officials and by the people**.

Interestingly, fifteen different Pharaohs of the eighteenth through the twentieth dynasties used Moses (Moises or Meses) as part of their names.[10] Possibly, subsequent Pharaohs used Moses' name in hopes of harnessing the same powers that Moses demonstrated through the ten plagues and the destruction of the twelfth-dynasty army in the Red Sea.

III. MOSES AS A POSSIBLE GENERAL OF SESOSTRIS III'S ARMY

If Sesostris III is the Pharaoh of the Oppression, then Moses was reared in Sesostris III's palace and was trained in the wisdom of twelfth-dynasty Egypt. Moses became a powerful and influential figure during his forty years in Egypt.

> Acts 7:20-23 -- At that time Moses was born, and he was no ordinary child. For three months he was cared for in his father's house. When he was placed outside, Pharaoh's daughter took him and brought him up as her own son. Moses was educated in all the wisdom of the Egyptians and was powerful in speech and action. When Moses was forty years old, he decided to visit his fellow Israelites. NIV

Josephus records a tradition about a military engagement between Egypt and Ethiopia (Nubia or Cush) in which Moses' ingenuity as commander brought victory to Egypt. After the battle Moses is reported by Josephus to have married "Tharbis, the daughter of the king of Ethiopia."[11] Ethiopia was called Cush or Nubia by the ancient Egyptians and also by Biblical writers. The Biblical record confirms that Moses was indeed married to a Cushite. After the Exodus and arrival at Mount Sinai, Numbers 12:1 reports that Moses' siblings, Miriam and Aaron, criticized Moses because of his **"Cushite wife."**

Josephus reports that Moses married the daughter of the king of Ethiopia before he left Egypt. Acts 7:23 tells us that Moses was forty years old when he killed an Egyptian and fled Egypt to go to the land of Midian. Moses obviously left his Ethiopian wife in Egypt when he fled to Midian.

Exodus 2:15-21 reports that while Moses was living in Midian, he met and married Zipporah, the daughter of Reuel (also called Jethro), the high priest of Midian. When Moses obeyed God's command to return to Egypt, Zipporah accompanied Moses on the journey (Exodus 4:24-26). However, Exodus 18:2 says that, after arriving in Egypt, Moses sent Zipporah and their two sons back to Midian to be with her father Jethro. Moses may have sent them away in fear that Pharaoh might harm them. However, another reason may be that Moses' Ethiopian wife was still alive when Moses returned to Egypt and Zipporah was not happy with a second wife and requested Moses to send her back to her father.

When Moses left Egypt at the time of the Exodus, he returned to the land of Midian for the second time. According to Exodus 18:5 Jethro returned Zipporah and her two sons to Moses. If Moses married the Ethiopian princess before leaving Egypt the first time, then he brought her with him when he returned to Midian. Thus, the Biblical evidence is in harmony with Josephus' claim that Moses had married an Ethiopian princess before he fled to Midian.

Moses' battle with the Ethiopians (Nubians or Cushites) harmonizes well with the reign of Sesostris III. Sesostris III himself led his army in at least four battles against "the tribesmen of Kush" (Cush) and "Nubia," the ancient names for Ethiopia.[12] The fourth battle is mentioned as "Year 19" of Sesostris III.[13] However, the records of Sesostris III's latter reign have not yet been found. The records likely lie buried in the ruins of his palace, which has also never been found.

Most modern Egyptologists have attempted to limit Sesostris III's reign to eighteen or nineteen years.[14] However, in 1996, a foundation stone of a building constructed by Sesostris III listed his **thirty-ninth year of reign**.[15] Therefore, Sesostris III could have lived on for an additional two to seven years, permitting my astronomical dating of **his sole reign at forty-three years, plus two or three years of a possible co-reign with his son Amenemhet III**. Moses likely served as General of Sesostris III's army in the latter years of Sesostris III's reign and in the early reign of Amenemhet III, the successor of Sesostris III. **A forty-three-year reign for Sesostris III creates the best compatibility with the astronomical data and with the Biblical dates of the Pharaoh of the Oppression, about 300 years later than his conventional dates.** Chapters Twenty-Two to Twenty-Four present astronomical evidence and scientific evidence of carbon-14 dating that confirms that Sesostris III should be redated to the Biblical date of the fifteenth century B.C., making him a contemporary of Moses.

IV. SESOSTRIS III AND THE SONS OF ANAK

The *Execration Texts* were written during the reigns of Sesostris III and Amenemhet III. **These texts included curses against rulers of foreign cities and countries.**[16]   Several of these names fit Biblical characters who were contemporaries of Moses.   For example, the Biblical name of "Anak" is found in these texts.

(1) The Ruler of Iy-'**anaq**, 'Erum, and all the retainers who are with him; the Ruler of Iy-'**anaq**, Abi-yamimu, and all the retainers who are with him; the Ruler of Iy-'**anaq**, 'Akirum, and all retainers who are with him.[17]

Notice in the above inscription that "Iy-'**anaq**" is the name of either a city or a territory. Three rulers of Iy-'Anaq are condemned by Sesostris III. Pritchard says that "Iy-'**Anaq**" may be related to the Biblical name of "**Anak:**" "The present name has been related to the 'Anaqim (giants) who were in the land of Canaan at the time of the Conquest.: e.g. Deut. 2:10."[18] The Bible also speaks of these Anakites (sons of Anak) in many other contexts.[19]

The Bible says that the "sons of Anak" lived in Canaan during the time that the Israelites were slaves in Egypt and were still present when the Israelites arrived in Canaan.

Numbers 13: 28, 33 -- (28) But the people who live there are powerful, and the cities are fortified and very large. We even saw descendants of Anak there. . . . (33) All the people we saw there are of great size. We saw the Nephilim there (the descendants of Anak come from the Nephilim). NIV

Egyptians are not the only ones to recognize the Anaqim or Anakites (descendants of Anak). Adad-Nirari, king of Assyria c. 1300 B.C. called the Anakites by the name of Anunaku. Notice Adad-Nirari's own words below.

Whoever blots out my name and writes his own name or breaks my memorial stele . . . may Assur, the mighty god, . . . Anu, Enlis, Ea, and Ishtar, the great gods, the Igigu of heaven, **the Anunaku of earth**, all of them, look upon him in great anger, and curse him with an evil curse.[20]

The Assyrians thus described the Anunaku as "great gods . . . of **earth**" and contrasted them with other "great gods of **heaven**." This Assyrian inscription likely equates the Anaqim with the Anunaku, revering them as earthly gods because of their enormous size and strength.

The sons of Anak were obviously present in abundant numbers when Sesostris III wrote because he cursed three of their rulers. However, the Bible is silent about the Anakites' presence in Canaan during the time of Abraham. For example, when Abraham, Isaac and Jacob lived in Canaan they lived near Hebron, a city inhabited by the Hittites, not the Anakites.[21]

However, when Moses was born, some 300 years after Abraham lived, the sons of Anak had reconstructed Hebron and renamed it Kiriath-Arba, which means the city of Arba.[22] The Bible says that Arba was the father of Anak, whose descendants became the Anakites.[23] When the Israelites later conquered Canaan, they changed the city's name back to its original name of Hebron, which continued as its only name throughout the rest of Israelite history.[24]

This change of name from Hebron to Arba after the time of Abraham, Isaac and Jacob proves that Anakites did not enter Canaan until after the Israelites moved to Egypt. Since these Anakites existed in the time of Moses and Sesostris III, but did not exist in the time of Abraham, Isaac and Jacob, **the logical conclusion is that Sesostris III must have been the contemporary of Moses, not Abraham.**

V. SESOSTRIS III AND THE MOABITES

The Execration Texts also condemned three rulers of Sheth (Shutu), identified by modern scholars as Moab.

> The ruler of **Shutu**, Ayyabu, and all the retainers who are with him; the Ruler of **Shutu**, Kushar, and the retainers who are with him; the Ruler of **Shutu**, Zabulanu, and all the retainers who are with him.[25]

Pritchard identifies the "Shutu" as "probably **Moab**; cf. the sons of Sheth."[26] Indeed, Moses called the Moabites "the sons of Sheth" in Numbers 24:17, likely because Sheth was the firstborn of Moab.

> Numbers 24:17 -- I see him, but not now; I behold him, but not near. A star will come out of Jacob; a scepter will rise out of Israel. He will crush the foreheads of **Moab**, the skulls of all the **sons of Sheth**. NIV

Thus, the rulers of Shutu (Sheth) are probably the rulers of the descendants of Moab. However, Moab was born about the same time that Isaac was born c. 1846 B.C.[27] If scholars are correct in dating Sesostris III's reign to 1846 B.C., it would be impossible for Moab to grow into a large people with many rulers in only a few years after Moab's birth. However, if Sesostris III is dated about 300 years later, as I propose in this book, then the Moabites had sufficient time to grow into a nation of people just as Israel did in Egypt. Indeed, the Bible says that the Moabites were governed by king Balak when Israel entered Canaan about 1406 B.C.[28] The co-existence of Sesostris III with the people of Moab proves that Sesostris III should be redated to be a contemporary of Moses and Moab, not Abraham.

VI. JOB: A CONTEMPORARY OF
MOSES AND SESOSTRIS III

Two of the rulers of Moab mentioned in the *Execration Texts* of Sesostris III, cited above, had Bible names: "Zabulanu" and "Ayyabum."   "Zabulanu" is cuneiform for "Zebulon."[29] Zebulon was the name of one of Jacob's twelve sons who moved to Egypt.[30] Thus, Zebulon was a common name in the land east of Egypt during the reign of twelfth dynasty kings and also in the time of Jacob, Joseph and Moses.

However, "Ayyabum," a ruler of Moab, has more significant implications. Pritchard says that "Ayyabum" is cuneiform for our English "Job."[31] Is it possible that Ayyabum, a ruler of Moab is Biblical Job? Most scholars date Job in the patriarchal period before Israel left Canaan and entered Egypt. If Biblical Job was a ruler in Moab during the reign of Sesostris III, then Job was a contemporary of Moses and Israel when they lived in Egypt.

The Bible says Job lived in "the land of Uz."[32] The land of Uz was apparently named after Uz, a son of Aram.[33]   Scholars say that the land of Uz reached all the way from Edom in the south to Syria in the north, on the east bank of the Jordan River where the modern country of Jordan is located.[34] This large area of the land of Uz included the country of Moab. Jeremiah tells us that the Land of Uz included Edom: "Rejoice and be glad, O Daughter of Edom, you who live in the land of Uz."[35] Edom was located on the southern boundary of Moab. One of Job's friends was Eliphaz who lived in Teman.[36] "Teman was a village in Edom, south of the Dead Sea,"[37] and was likely named after Teman, one of the grandsons of Esau.[38]

The mention of the "Jordan River" in Job 40:23 also implies that Job lived in an area that bordered the Jordan River. Moab's western border was the Jordan River. Thus, Job, as an inhabitant of Moab, fits well with the Jordan River and his friend Eliphaz who lived in the neighboring country of Edom.

Was Job ruler of the area where he lived? The Bible says that Job "was the greatest man among all the people of the East."[39] Job himself said that he was a ruler of the people among whom he lived: "I chose the way for them and sat as their **chief;** I dwelt as **a king** among his troops."[40] Therefore, the Job of the *Execration Texts*, who was one of the rulers of Moab in the reign of Sesostris III, amazingly harmonizes with Biblical Job, who was a ruler of part of Uz, which included Moab within its borders.

The date of Job has long been debated by the scholars. No mention is made of the Israelites in the book of Job. Therefore, Job likely lived and died before Israel arrived in Canaan. Most conservative Bible scholars place Job in the time of the patriarchs, Abraham, Isaac and Jacob. However, Eliphaz the Temanite, Job's friend,[41] was a descendant of Teman, one of the sons of Esau. Therefore, Eliphaz did not live in the time of Jacob and Esau, but in the time of the descendants of Jacob and Esau during the same period that the Israelites lived in Egypt. Job's friendship with Eliphaz places them both as likely contemporaries of Moses in his youth. We have dated Moses' birth in the sixteenth year of Sesostris III. Therefore, the Job of the *Execration Texts* of Sesostris III and the Job of the Bible fit contemporaneously with the early years of Moses' life and the first half of Sesostris III's reign. On this basis, Job likely died during Israel's forty-year wandering in the desert before they entered Canaan. Therefore, Job, Moses and Sesostris III were contemporaries in the late sixteenth century B.C.

VII. SIMILARITY OF BOOK OF JOB TO TWELFTH-DYNASTY DOCUMENTS

Modern critical Bible scholars, like Janzen, propose that Job was written between the seventh and the fourth centuries B.C.[42] However, many scholars have also recognized that Job has close affinities to the style, ideas and language of documents written during the Middle Kingdom of Egypt. Harley notes the following documents of the Middle Kingdom that are similar in style and content to Job: "The Protests of the Eloquent Peasant," "The Admonitions of Ipu-Wer," "A Dispute Over Suicide," "The Wisdom of Amenemope," "A Song of the Harper" and other Egyptian documents.[43] Many of these scholars believe that the author of Job had intimate knowledge of these writings when composing the story of Job. Even "the A-B-A style" which "sets semi-poetical speeches between a prose prologue and epilogue" is found in both Job and the Egyptian writings.[44] Job is part narrative, part dialogue and part poetry. Several twelfth-dynasty documents possess this same style.

Egyptologists consider the documents of the Middle Kingdom to represent the classical model for the literature of later Egyptian dynasties: "The Ninth to Twelfth Dynasties . . . were generally---deservedly---recognized as having sponsored the golden age of Egyptian secular literature."[45] I have read these documents and find them expressing, for the most part, a high moral standard and profound insight into human nature. These documents have a definite similarity to the contents of Job, which dealt primarily with justice, evil and human suffering.

Since the Biblical book of Job is similar in contents and style to literature of the twelfth dynasty, why have scholars not dated the book of Job to the Middle Bronze Age instead of 1,000 years later? Why do scholars believe that only Egyptian writers penned outstanding works of ancient literature in the Middle Bronze Age, and that Hebrews and their relatives (e.g. Job) were not capable of writing the same quality of literature in the same period? Why do scholars believe that the followers of the Egyptian gods of Re, Amun and Thoth wrote outstanding literature, but do not believe that the followers of the Hebrew God, Yahweh, were able to write equal or superior literature?

A certain Ayyubum (Job), ruler of Moab (Shutu), lived during the reign of Sesostris III. Biblical Job was a ruler of Moab and wrote in the same style of literature of the twelfth dynasty when Sesostris III and Ayyubum lived. All of these evidences strongly suggest that Job, Moses and Sesostris III were all contemporaries during Moses' first forty years in Egypt during the latter half of the reign of twelfth dynasty Pharaohs.

VIII. CARBON-14 DATING OF SESOSTRIS III'S REIGN CONFIRMS THAT HE WAS CONTEMPORARY WITH MOSES

T. Save-Soderbergh and I.U. Olsson from the Institute of Egyptology and Institute of Physics gathered all of the data available on carbon-14 dating of the Egyptian dynasties and shared this information in the "Proceedings of the Twelfth Nobel Symposium held at the Institute of Physics at Uppsala University."[46]

The death of Sesostris II and the accession of his son Sesostris III are both dated by the *Cambridge Ancient History* at **1878 B.C.**[47] My Biblically assigned date is **c. 1542 B.C.** A sample taken from the boundary wall of the pyramid of Sesostris II, the father of Sesostris III, was carbon-14 dated (uncalibrated) at **1545 B.C.**,[48] only three years earlier than my Biblically-assigned date, **but 333 years later than the *Cambridge* date.** Save-Soderbergh considers samples taken directly from the construction of the king's pyramid to be the best wood to test for determining the approximate year when the Pharaoh died.[49] However, Save-Soderbergh thinks more samples should be taken from the same pyramid to get an average date that is more accurate.[50] Table 14-B compares the uncalibrated carbon-14 dates of Sesostris III's reign with historians' dates and my Biblically-assigned dates.

Samples were also taken from Egyptian fortresses that archaeologists attribute to Sesostris III's constructions in the southern border between Egypt and Nubia (ancient Ethiopia). Two Egyptian inscriptions attest that Sesostris III built the fortress at Semna in either his eighth or sixteenth year. Save-Soderbergh historically dated Sesostris III's eighth year at **c. 1868 B.C.** I date his eighth year by correlation to Biblical chronology at **1534 B.C.** The uncalibrated carbon-14 dates for these fortresses remarkably average about **1550 B.C., only sixteen years earlier than my date for Sesostris III's eighth year, but 317 years later than the Cambridge date.**[51]

I did not discover these carbon-14 dates until many years after I had already predetermined the dates for twelfth-dynasty kings by connections to Biblical chronology. These carbon-14 dates for twelfth-dynasty Pharaohs agree with my Biblical dates, and prove that the historical dates assigned by scholars to the reign of Sesostris III are about three centuries too old. See Table 14-B on the next page. Egyptologists claim their historical dates are confirmed by astronomical dating and thus consider the carbon-14 dates as erroneous. In Chapters Twenty-One to Twenty-Four the reader will see that Egypt's **astronomical dates** are actually incompatible with the present dates of the twelfth dynasty and **that superior astronomical dating and carbon-14 dating confirm my three century-revision of the twelfth through the nineteenth dynasties.**

TABLE 14-B
CARBON-14 DATING OF SESOSTRIS III'S REIGN COMPARED TO BIBLICAL, CAMBRIDGE AND BRITANNICA DATES

SESOSTRIS III'S REIGN	BIBLICAL DATES	Uncalibrated CARBON-14 DATES	CAMBRIDGE DATES	BRITANNICA ENCY. DATES
ACCESSION	1542 B.C	1545 B.C.	1878 B.C.	1837 B.C.
EIGHTH YEAR	1534 B.C.	1550 B.C.	1862 B.C.	1820 B.C.

CONCLUSION

The evidences agree that Moses and Job were contemporaries in Sesostris III's reign, identifying Sesostris III as the foster grandfather of Moses. Table 14-C below lists twelve additional historical and scientific links between Sesostris III and the Biblical history of Moses' life. Admittedly, **some** of the similarities could be duplicated in other periods of Egyptian history. However, many of these historical links fit only the time of Sesostris III and Moses and cannot be found in any other period of Egyptian history. Regardless, the similarities, when added to those of previous chapters, **are too numerous and unique to be coincidental.**

Either Biblical history must be dated to fit Egyptian dates or vice-versa. The uncalibrated carbon-14 dates of Sesostris III's reign show that the historical dates of the twelfth dynasty should be reduced by 250 to 300 years to fit our Biblically assigned dates. The evidence continues to mount that twelfth-dynasty history is the time of Joseph and Moses. **An abundance of additional evidence is yet to come in the remaining chapters of this book.** The subject of the next chapter is Sesostris III, the constructor of the store cities of Pithom and Rameses.

TABLE 14-C
TWELVE DISCOVERIES OF SESOSTRIS III AS THE FOSTER GRANDFATHER OF MOSES

Discovery 1. Josephus says Thermuthis was Moses' Egyptian mother. A daughter of Sesostris III had a similar name.

Discovery 2. Moses' name means to "be raised from water," to remind his Egyptian mother and princess that she found him in a papyus boat in the Nile River. The Egyptian word, Muses (Moses) also means "raised from water.

Discovery 3. The Pharaoh of Moses reigned most of Moses' first forty years. Sesostris III's forty-year plus reign fits the length of reign of the Pharaoh who adopted Moses as his grandson.

Discovery 4. Josephus says Moses was an Egyptian general who conquered Ethiopia (Cush). Egyptian records report that Sesostris III's commander of his army conquered Ethopia (Cush).

Discovery 5. The Bible says Moses married a Cushite princess. (Numbers 12:1). The General of Sesostris III's army could certainly have captured a Cushite princess since he conquered Cush.

Discovery 6. The sons of Anak entered Canaanite cities after Israel came to Egypt. The sons of Anak were still in Canaan when Israel left Egypt and conquered Canaan. Sesostris III cursed the rulers of Anak, proving that the Anakites were contemporary with the twelfth dynasty and Moses, not the time of Abraham.

Discovery 7. Moabites grew into a nation while Israel was in Egypt. Sesostris III cursed the Moabites, proving the Moabites were contemporaries of Israel and Sesostris III.

Discovery 8. Job, a ruler of Moab, fits the time of Moses's early years. Sesostris III cursed Job (Ayabum), proving that Moses, Job and Sesostris III were contemporaries.

Discovery 9. The book of Job exhibits high ethics and profound insight into suffering. A number of twelfth-dynasty documents demonstrate the same high ethics of Job, indicating synchronism.

Discovery 10. Job is written in part narrative, part dialogue, part poetry. Some twelfth-dynasty documents show a similar literary style to that of Job.

Discovery 11. My astronomical chronology for Sesostris III's reign is dated to 1543 B.C. for his accession year, 300 years later than the scholar's dates.

Discovery 12. My astronomical chronology of 1543 B.C. for Sesostris III is **confirmed by a carbon-14 date of 1545 B.C.**

TABLE 14-D
RUNNING TOTAL OF DISCOVERIES

Chapter		Chapter Total	Running Total
2	Conflict Between Biblical and Secular Histories	18	18
4	Discovery of 430 Years from Abraham to the Exodus	16	34
5	Confirmation of Abraham's Historicity	28	62
6	Discovery of the Remains of Sodom and Gomorrah	17	79
7	Joseph As a Slave and Prisoner in Amenemhet I's Reign	21	100
8	Joseph Becomes the Vizier of Sesostris I	23	123
9	Sesostris I Gives Joseph a New Name and a Wife	11	134
10	The Seven Years of Abundance in Sesostris I's Reign	10	144
11	The Seven Years of Famine in Sesostris I's Reign	20	164
12	Israel Enters Egypt during Sesostris I's Reign	14	178
13	Sesostris III Enslaves the Israelites	17	195
14	Sesostris III, The Foster Grandfather of Moses	12	207

NOTES FOR CHAPTER FOURTEEN

1. Petrie, *A History of Egypt.* I.184-185.
2. Flavius Josephus, "The Antiquities of the Jews," II.9.5-7, *Works of Josephus.* 68.
3. Petrie, *History of Egypt.* I.184-186.
4. Exodus 2:10
5. E. A. Wallace Budge. *An Egyptian Hieroglyphic Dictionary,* I.321.
6. Josephus, "Flavius Josephus Against Apion," Book I.31, *The Works of Josephus.* 791.

7. E.A. Wallace Budge, *An Egyptian Hieroglyphic Dictionary*, I.280, 293.
8. E.A. Wallace Budge, *An Egyptian Hieroglyphic Dictionary*, II.618.
9. Genesis 2:10.
10. William C. Hayes, *Scepter of Egypt*, p. 499.
11. Josephus, "Antiquities of the Jews," II.10.1-2, *The Works of Josephus*, pp. 69-70.
12. William C. Hayes, "Reforms of Sesostris III," *The Cambridge Ancient History*, I.2A.506-507.
13. Breasted (Trans.), "Twelfth dynasty: Sesostris III - Inscription of Sisatet," *Ancient Records of Egypt*, I.301 (no. 672).
14. J. R. Baines, "Egypt," *New Encyclopaedia Britannica*, 18.113.
15. Josef W. Wegner, "The Nature and Chronology of the Senwosret III-Amenemhat III Regnal Succession: Some Considerations Based on New Evidence From the Mortuary Temple of Senwosret III at Abydos," *Journal of New Eastern Studies,* " 55, no. 4 (1996), 249-279.
16. William K. Simpson, "Dynasty 12," *Ancient Near East; A History*, 247.
17. J. Wilson (Trans.), "The Execration of Asiatic Princes," *Ancient Near Eastern Texts*, 328.
18. J. Wilson (Trans.), *Ibid.*, p. 328, footnote 2.
19. Numbers 13:22, 28, 33; Deuteronomy 1:28; 2:10,11,21; 9:2; Joshua 11:21, 22; 14:12,15; 15:13,14; 21:11; Judges 1:20
20. Luckenbill (Trans.), "Adad-Nirari I," *Ancient Records of Assyria*, (New York: Greenwood Press, 1927), I.28 (No. 76).
21. Genesis 13:18; 23:1-7; 19; 35:27-36:2; 37:14.
22. Genesis 23.2; 35:27; Joshua 14:15.;
23. Joshua 15:13-14; 21:11.   24. Joshua 14:15; 21:13; 2 Sam. 2:11; et. al
25. J, Wilson (Trans.) "The Execration of Asian Princes," *Ancient Near Eastern Texts*, 329.
26. James Pritchard, Ed., Ancient Near Eastern Texts, 329, footnotes 4 & 5.
27. Genesis 19:36-38; 21:1-7.
28. Numbers 22:4-36; 25:1; Deuteronomy 2:9-11.
29. James Pritchard (Ed.), *Ancient Near Eastern Texts*, p 329, footnote 6.
30. Exodus 1:1-3.
31. J. Pritchard, *Ancient Near Eastern Texts*, p. 329, footnote 5.
32. Job, 1:1.
33. Genesis 10.23
34. E. Smick, "Job," *Zondervan Pictorial Bible Encyclopedia*, 3.602-3.
35. Lamentations 4:21.
36. Job 2:11
37. *NIV Study Bible* comments on Job 2:11, citing also Genesis 36:11, 31, 34, 40; Jeremiah 49:7; Ezek 25:13; Amos 1:12; Obadiah 9.
38. Genesis 36:11, 34.
39. Job 1:3.
40. Job 29:25.
41. Job 2:11.
42. J. Gerald Janzen, "Job, the Book Of," *Harper's Bible Dictionary* (San Francisco: Harper & Row, 1985), 492.
43. J. E. Hartley, "Job," *International Standard Bible Encyclopedia*, II.1066-1067.
44. J. E. Hartley, "Job," *International Standard Bible Encyclopedia*, II.1066-1067.
45. William C. Hayes, "The Middle Kingdom In Egypt," *Cambridge Ancient History*, I.2A.523.
46. T. Save-Soderbergh & I.U. Olsson, *"C14 Dating and Egyptian Chronology,"* *Radiocarbon Variations and Absolute Chronology* , Ed. Ingrid U. Olsson (New York: Wiley Interscience Division, 1983), 34-55.
47. "Chronological s," *Cambridge Ancient History*, I.2B.996.
48. T. Save-Soderbergh & I.U. Olsson, *"C14 Dating and Egyptian Chronology,"* *Radiocarbon Variations and Absolute Chronology* , Ed. Ingrid U. Olsson (New York: Wiley Interscience Division, 1983), 34-55. 43 & 50.
49. T. Save-Soderbergh & I.U. Olsson, *Ibid..*, 43 & 50.
50. T. Save-Soderbergh & I.U. Olsson, *Ibid..*, 43 & 50..
51. T. Save-Soderbergh & I.U. Olsson, *Ibid..*, 43-44, 49, 50.

CHAPTER FIFTEEN
SESOSTRIS III, BUILDER OF RAMESES AND PITHOM

The Bible states that the Pharaoh of the Oppression, who enslaved Israel, forced them to construct the store cities of Pithom and Rameses.

> Exodus 1:8-11 -- Then a new king, who did not know about Joseph, came to power in Egypt. "Look," he said to his people, "the Israelites have become much too numerous for us. Come, we must deal shrewdly with them or they will become even more numerous and, if war breaks out, will join our enemies, fight against us and leave the country." So they put slave masters over them to oppress them with forced labor, and **they built Pithom and Rameses as store cities for Pharaoh.** NIV

My chronological clue charts identify Sesostris III as the Pharaoh who enslaved Israel and forced them to construct the store cities of Pithom and Rameses. His successors, Amenemhet III and Amenemhet IV, expanded and finished the construction of these cities. This chapter presents significant historical and archaeological evidence that support this proposition.

I. SESOSTRIS III, THE ORIGINAL CONSTRUCTOR OF THE STORE CITY OF RAMESES

Many scholars assume that Ramses II was the first constructor of the city of Rameses, when he made it his new capital in the eastern delta of Egypt. However, Amihai Mazar, one of the leading archaeologists in Israel, proposes that the earliest excavated remains of Tell el-Daba [Rameses] **date back to the latter kings of the twelfth dynasty.** Interestingly, Mazar says evidence exists that Canaanites (foreigners) were among the inhabitants of the city during this same period.

> MB IIA finds of **Canaanite origin** were detected at Tell el-Daba [area of Rameses] in contexts dated to **the latter part of the Twelfth Dynasty in Egypt [my emphasis].** . . as well as to the Thirteenth Dynasty.[1]

Egyptologists date the reign of Sesostris III in the MB IIA Age that includes finds of Canaanite origin at this level of Tell el-Daba. Sesostris III is the very king indicated by my comparative chronological charts as the Pharaoh who enslaved Israel and forced them to build the **store** cities of Pithom and Rameses. Baines and Malek report that a columned chapel of Amenemhet I and Sesostris III was found at Tell el-Qirqafa near Khata'na [Tell el-Daba =Rameses].[2] Sesostris III likely constructed this chapel in honor of his ancestor, Amenemhet I, who founded the twelfth dynasty. Also found near Khata'na at Tell el-Daba, was a statue of Queen Nefrusobk. This queen was both the sister and wife of Amenemhet III and the mother of Amenemhet IV, the last male Pharaoh of the twelfth dynasty.[3] These are the Pharaohs that I have identified as the oppressors of Israel during their slavery.

Thus, the twelfth-dynasty Pharaoh, Sesostris III, was the first Pharaoh to construct **Rameses as a store city 500 years before the nineteenth-dynasty Pharaoh, Ramses II,** constructed his capital city of Pi-Rameses. Actually, Ramses II constructed his capital city over the remains of four previous cities which are described below by W. H. Shea.

> Just South of Qantir is Tell el-Daba [Rameses]. **The occupation of this site under the 12th and 13th Dynasties** [emphasis mine] was brought to an end with a violent destruction. Three Hyksos strata or building phases follow this destruction and the city enlarged progressively through these three periods. The third and last Hyksos stratum was brought to an end with a violent destruction which has been connected with the conquest of Lower Egypt by the early 18th Dynasty. The 18th Dynasty appears to have left this site unoccupied (Bietak, p. 25), **but it was rebuilt under the 19th Dynasty** [emphasis mine].[4]

Note that Rameses was constructed by twelfth-dynasty kings, and was later destroyed by the Hyksos when they invaded Egypt and conquered it. Later, the Hyksos sixteenth dynasty constructed their capital, Avaris, over the ruins of the old store city of Rameses, formerly constructed by the twelfth dynasty. Three different phases of Hyksos construction occurred before Ahmose, the first Pharaoh of the eighteenth dynasty, destroyed the Hyksos capital of Avaris. However, after Ahmose destroyed the Hyksos capital, he and his successors of the eighteenth dynasty never rebuilt Avaris [ancient Rameses]. Thus, the ancient store city of Rameses remained buried under the ruins of the Hyksos capital of Avaris for about 400 years before Ramses II built his capital in the same location of the store city.

Edward F. Wente informs us that Horemheb, the last king of the eighteenth dynasty, and Seti I, the second king of the nineteenth dynasty began to construct the new capital of Piramesse (Pi-Rameses) in this very area of Qantir where the old store city of Rameses of the twelfth dynasty was first built and where the old Hyksos capital of Avaris was afterwards built. Wente also says that Ramses II, son of Seti I, expanded Rameses and reconstructed it as their new capital.[5] Thus, the store city of Rameses built by twelfth-dynasty Pharaohs lies underneath the ruins of two successive capital cities, Avaris of the Hyksos, and Pi-Ramesses completed by Ramses II. Obviously, the only time that the city of Rameses fits the Biblical description of a store city is in the reign of the latter kings of the twelfth dynasty, beginning with Sesostris III.

II. THE NAME OF RAMESES FITS THE REIGNS OF SESOSTRIS III AND AMENEMHET III

Most scholars argue that the city of Rameses fits only Ramses II, because of similar names. However, Sesostris III and Amenemhet III, both twelfth-dynasty Pharaohs, also used "Ra" in their throne names. "Rameses" is a combination of two words, "Ra," the Sun-god, and "Meses," from "mesi," which means "to bear, to give birth to, to produce, to fashion, to form, to make in the likeness of someone."[6] Thus "Rameses" may mean "Born, Created or Produced by Ra." "Ra," the sun-god, was the principal god honored by twelfth-dynasty Pharaohs.

Sesostris III, whom I identify as the first constructor of the store city of Rameses, included Ra in his throne name: "Kho-Kau-**Ra**."[7] The actual hieroglyphic inscription of his name is **Ra-Kho-Kau-Kau-Kau**, as it appears in Petrie's *History of Egypt*.[8] Thus, the "Ra" actually appears **first** in the Egyptian language, but is translated **last** in the English translation. In fact, Sesostris III specifically called himself "**the Son of Ra's body**, his beloved, the Lord of the two lands."[9] Hymns written in praise of Sesostris III actually called him by his throne name of the sun-god Ra: "How great is the lord of his city: he is **Re**, little are a thousand other men."[10] Thus, Sesostris III's throne name, "**Ra**-Kho-Kau," his designation as "**the Son of Ra**," and hymns of praise that actually call him **"Re" (Ra)**, all fit perfectly with his construction of a story city that bears the name, **Rameses,** which means "**Born of Ra**" or **"Ra Created It."**[11]

Sesostris III's son and successor, Amenemhet III, also has a throne name with **Ra** in it. From left to right Amenemhet III's throne name is **Ra-En-Maot**, or in reverse order, Maot-En-**Ra**. Thus, Amenemhet III's continued construction of Rameses harmonizes well with a store city that bears part of his own name.

III. EVIDENCE THAT SESOSTRIS III USED FOREIGN SLAVES TO BUILD RAMESES

Chapter Thirteen reported that Mentuemhat, the general of Sesostris III, enslaved foreigners in the "northern territories." We interpreted the northern territories to include the land of Goshen and interpreted the enslaved foreigners to include the Israelites. If our interpretation is correct, then Sesostris III and his successors forced these enslaved Israelites to construct the cities of Pithom and Rameses. Does evidence exist that Sesostris III used foreign slaves to construct cities in the Delta of Egypt?

Posener, writing in the *Cambridge Ancient History*, tells us that "**camps of Asiatics under the direction of Egyptian officials** . . . existed during the Middle Kingdom, **not far from the royal residence.**"[12] Egyptians used the epitaph, "Asiatics," to refer to foreigners from Canaan, Syria and points farther north. Therefore, "Asiatics" can refer to the Israelites who came to Egypt from Canaan. The fact that these Asiatics were gathered in "camps . . . under the direction of Egyptian officials" means that they were forced to live in work camps under the control of Egyptian officials. Therefore, these Asiatic Israelites were "slaves."

Furthermore, the camps of these "Asiatic" slaves were located "close" to the "royal residence." We will see in the next chapter that the twelfth-dynasty capital, Itjtowy, is located in the region of Tanis in the northeastern Delta of Egypt. The land of Goshen, where Pithom and Rameses were constructed, is located south of the border between Goshen and the district of Tanis (Zoan).

Posener's placement of these "Asiatic" work camps in the "Middle Kingdom" reports in a footnote that these Asiatic slaves first appear in the **"Twelfth dynasty."**[13] When, during the twelfth dynasty did these slave gangs appear? We saw above that Mazar dates the construction of the store city of Rameses to the "latter Twelfth dynasty." William Simpson cites twelfth-dynasty documents from the archive of Illahun and the Reisner Papyrus which describe **"deliveries and inspections . . . the expenditure of labor on building projects . . . and lists of men arranged by work gangs."**[14] Simpson also says that documents found at Illahun included hymns of praise to **Sesostris III.**[15] These documents were found at Illahun in the pyramid complex of Sesostris II, the father of Sesostris III.[16] Since this pyramid complex did not function in honor of Sesostris II until after his death, these documents mentioning deliveries, inspections, building projects and work gangs, were likely written, like the hymns, during the reign of his son, Sesostris III.

These twelfth-dynasty documents also mention "deliveries of material" for construction and "inspection" of the work of these foreign slaves. Exodus 5:3-8 confirms these Egyptian records when Moses requested Pharaoh to let the Israelites take a three-day journey into the desert to offer sacrifices to God.

> Exodus 5:5-8 -- Then Pharaoh said, "Look, the people of the land are now numerous, and you [Moses] are stopping them from working." That same day Pharaoh gave this order to the slave drivers and foremen in charge of the people: "You are no longer to supply the people with straw for making bricks; let them go and gather their own straw. But require them to make the same number of bricks as before. . . ." NIV

Therefore, Egyptian documents confirm that enslaved foreigners (from Canaan) were constructing cities in the district of Rameses under the supervision of Egyptian officials (task masters) during the reign of Sesostris III, giving us additional evidence that Sesostris III is the Biblical Pharaoh of the Oppression.

Kenneth Kitchen also confirms that twelfth-dynasty kings constructed extensively in the Wadi Tumilat area identified as the land of Goshen.

> A series of discoveries by Egyptian scholars in the Eastern Delta makes it highly probable that a royal residence existed in the 10th and 12th-13th and Hyksos dynasties (including the "Hyksos " town of Avaris) in the same region favored centuries later by Ramses II for his Delta residence Raamses sic.).[17]

IV. FORTIFIED CANAANITE CITIES IN THE REIGNS
OF SESOSTRIS III AND AMENEMHET III

Why did Sesostris III construct store cities in the eastern delta of Egypt? Amenemhet I had earlier constructed the fortified city of "Walls of the Ruler" at the eastern end of Wadi Tumilat to be a first line of defense against invading armies from Syria, Canaan and Arabia and to prevent wandering nomads from entering the land of Goshen.[18]

Sesostris III constructed the store cities of Rameses and Pithom and provided additional food and supplies for this military outpost, to protect the capital of Itjtowy against invasions from the north (Syria and Canaan) and the east (Arabia). Obviously, Canaanites were a threat to Egypt's security during Sesostris III's reign.

A. The Execration Texts and High-Walled Canaanite Cities

The *Execration Texts*, mentioned in the previous chapter, curse thirty princes from twenty countries, including Palestine, Moab, Phoenicia and Syria.[19] These texts are dated to the reigns of Sesostris III and his son Amenemhet III. These curses prove that Sesostris III considered the Canaanite rulers to be a potential danger to Egypt's sovereignty. Why was Sesostris III afraid of the Canaanites?

Archaeologists tell us that large, high-walled cities were constructed all over Canaan during the archaeological period called Middle Bronze II, which includes the twelfth dynasty. Kathleen Kenyon, the famous British archaeologist who was knighted "Dame" for her archaeological expertise in Palestine, says that the towns of Palestine in Middle Bronze II "were all enclosed by defensive walls."[20] As an example, she pointed to Middle Bronze II Jericho which "was enclosed with a brick wall about two meters thick."[21] Amihai Mazar, one of the leading archaeologists in Israel, points to the Middle Bronze IIB Age as the time that "the art of fortification reached a level of unparalleled sophistication" in Canaan.

> The idea was to surround the city with steep artificial slopes which will raise the level of the city wall high above the surrounding area and locate it as far as possible from the foot of the slope so that siege devices, such as battering rams, ladders and tunneling methods, would not be effective.[22]

Mazar admits that his chronology for the different strata of Palestine depended on the dates of the Egyptian dynasties.

> From ca. 3000 B.C. the absolute chronology of Palestine is based to a large extent on that of Egypt. . . . The dependence on Egyptian chronology is so strong that any change in the latter necessitates a parallel shift concerning Palestine.[23]

Mazar dated the Middle Bronze IIB-C Age from 1800 to 1550 B.C. This dating is based on the latest revision of the chronology of Egyptian dynasties by Krauss and Baines. Baines dates the reigns of Sesostris III and Amenemhet III from 1836 to 1770 B.C.,[24] which include the beginning of Middle Bronze IIB, precisely when these highly fortified cities first began to be constructed in Canaan. We will prove in Chapter Twenty-Three that the uncalibrated carbon-14 dates for these dynasties are about 300 years later (1536 to 1470 B.C.), fitting perfectly the time of Moses and the Pharaohs of the Oppression.

Therefore, these highly fortified cities of Canaan in Middle Bronze II began to be constructed precisely during the time that Sesostris III and Amenemhet III were involved in extensive construction in the eastern Delta as a first line of defense against the growing strength of Canaanite cities and armies. Pithom and Rameses, as store cities, were built to provide extra resources for the defense of the northern and eastern borders of Egypt.

If Sesostris III, Amenemhet III and Moses were contemporaries, we should expect to find a Biblical description of these fortified cities of Palestine in Moses' writings. Moses wrote in Deuteronomy 9:1, "You are now about to cross the Jordan to go in and dispossess nations greater and stronger than you, **with large cities that have walls up to the sky."**

The Bible does not mention high-walled cities of Canaan during the time of Abraham, Isaac and Jacob. This silence implies that these strong cities must have been constructed after Jacob and his sons left Canaan and lived in Egypt for 210 years. Therefore, the Biblical description of fortified cities in Canaan during the same period when the store cities of Rameses and Pithom were constructed in Egypt coincides perfectly with Sesostris III's construction of these store cities.

B. Most Middle Bronze II Canaanite Cities Were Destroyed Before the Middle Bronze II Age Ended

Kathleen Kenyon says that most highly fortified Canaanite cities constructed during Middle Bronze IIB/C were destroyed several times during the same age.[25] Volume Two of the series, *Solving the Exodus Mystery,* proves that the archaeological evidence of the ruins of Middle Bronze II cities in Canaan harmonizes with the Biblical account of Israel's conquest of Canaan under Joshua and the subsequent destruction of different cities during the period of the Judges.

The dates of Middle Bronze II are determined by links to the Egyptian dynasties. **When Egyptian history is redated three centuries later, the Middle Bronze II Age will also have to be redated three centuries later.** Redating Egyptian history three centuries later, the Biblical conquest of Canaan by the Israelites will coincide perfectly with the archaeological evidence of destroyed cities, including Jericho, in Middle Bronze II. **The Archaeological Ages should be dated by Biblical dates rather than the dates ascribed to Egyptian history by Egyptologists.** We will discuss in depth the destruction of Jericho and other Canaanite cities in the second volume of this series, *Solving the Exodus Mystery.*

V. DID RAMSES II CONSTRUCT THE
STORE CITY OF RAMESES?

Most scholars equate the construction of the store city of Rameses with Pi-Rameses, the capital constructed by the famous Ramses II of the nineteenth dynasty.

Kenneth Kitchen -- Raamses, Rameses . . . Residence city of the nineteenth and twentieth Egyptian dynasties in the NE Delta, where the Hebrews labored and from where they set forth on the Exodus.[26]

Edward F. Wente -- The biblical city of Rameses/Raamses should be equated with Egyptian Piramesse [Pi-Ramesse], the great delta residence of the pharaohs of the 19th and 20th Dynasties.[27]

However, the Bible says that Rameses was a **"store city," not a capital city,** when it was constructed in the days of Moses. If "store city" means "capital city," then Pithom was also a capital city because it is also called a "store city." Furthermore, Exodus 1:1 lists Pithom before Rameses ("Pithom and Rameses") in Exodus 1:11. Obviously, both Pithom and Rameses were "store cities," **proving that neither of them were capital cities during the twelfth dynasty.**

The Hebrew word, *micknah,* translated "store," is used elsewhere in the Bible to refer to "store cities" that kings of Judah built to store food and supplies for the king and his army. II Chronicles 8:5-6 reports that Solomon built his fortified cities as well as his store cities "with walls and gates and bars." These fortified cities contained soldiers, horses and chariots. Store cities contained extra food and supplies for soldiers in times of war. Thus, the store cities needed to be protected, as well as the cities housing the soldiers, chariots and horses. These store cities were strategically located "throughout all the territory" where Solomon ruled, thus protecting the country and especially the capital of Jerusalem from enemies coming from any direction.

These store cities were never equated with Jerusalem, the capital of Israel. Neither does "store city" fit the description of a Pharaoh's capital. In the next chapter I will present Biblical proof that the Egyptian capital was located outside the region of Rameses during the time of Joseph, as well as the time of Moses. On this basis Rameses was merely a store city, not a capital city in the day of Moses.

Since the Pharaoh who enslaved Israel lived in a capital other than Rameses before the city was constructed, and since he built Rameses as a store city, not a capital city, obviously the Pharaoh of Moses' birth lived in the same capital both before and after he constructed the store city of Rameses. Therefore, Rameses was not the capital of Egypt during the time that the Israelites were constructing the store city of Rameses. Consequently, Ramses II cannot be the Pharaoh of the Exodus because he constructed Pi-Rameses as a capital city, not a store city. Pi-Rameses as the capital of Ramses II of the nineteenth dynasty will be discussed in depth in Volume II of the series, *Solving the Exodus Mystery.*

VI. WHERE WAS RAMESES LOCATED WHEN
IT WAS FIRST BUILT AS A STORE CITY
AND LATER BECAME A CAPITAL?

Genesis 47:11 says that the district of Rameses where Israel lived and constructed the store city of Ramses was **"the best part"** of Egypt in the sense of being "the most fertile."

Genesis 47:11 -- So Joseph settled his father and his brothers in Egypt and gave them property **in the best part of the land, the district of Rameses,** as Pharaoh directed. (NIV)

The Egyptian document, *Papyrus Anastasi III* describes the "beauty" and "fertility" of the district of "Per-Ramses," the new capital of Ramses II.[28] Genesis 47:6 describes this district "the best part of the land" of Egypt from the time of Joseph to the Exodus. Two capital cities were built upon the ruins of the Biblical store city of Rameses: Ramses II's capital and the previous Hyksos capital. Sesostris III built the original store city of Rameses by forcing the Israelite slaves to construct it during the time of Moses. We will see in the next chapter that the twelfth-dynasty capital was **Zoan (also called Itjtowy), not Rameses**. Ramses II's capital city of Rameses cannot be the store city of Rameses during Moses' time.

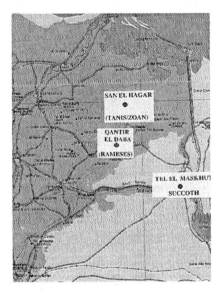

Figure 15- A
MAP OF EASTERN DELTA
Locations of Tanis/Zoan (Itjtowy),
Rameses and Succoth

VII. CONSTRUCTION OF PITHOM BY SESOSTRIS III

Israelites also constructed the store city of Pithom during the time of Moses.[29] Many Egyptologists, including T.V. Brisco, Kenneth Kitchen, Tom Wei and Redford, believe that the name Pithom is Hebrew for the Egyptian, Pi-Atum (Per-Atum or Per-Tum), which means "House of Atum."[30] Atum is part of the name of the Egyptian god, Ra. The chief temple of Ra was located in Heliopolis on the edge of the Delta and was called **Atum-Ra** or **Atum-Re,** the full name of the creator sun-god. Atum-Re was worshiped as the favorite god of most twelfth-dynasty kings.[31]

Sesostris I said that he constructed a temple in Heliopolis for "my father Atum."[32] Khnumhotep II, a governor of Egypt under Sesostris II, said that the arrival of the king was like the "shining of Atum."[33] How fitting that Sesostris III built one city honoring the name of Ra's first name, "Atum" (Pi-Atum or Pi-Tum, Pi-Thom = House of Atum or Tum) and a second city bearing his god's second name of Ra-Meses, meaning : "Born or Created by Ra".

Scholars are all agreed that Pithom is located in the land of Goshen (district of Rameses), not far from the city of Rameses. However, archaeologists differ over two possible sites: Tell el-Retabeh or Tell el-Maskhutah, both located in the eastern end of the Wadi Tumilat (land of Goshen). See the Map in Figure 15-A above.

Tom Wei reports that Naville excavated Tell el-Maskhutah and found the name "*Pr'itum*" and "*Tkw(t).*" *Pr'itum* is connected linguistically to Pi-Thom = the "House of Atum," and *Tkwt* is connected linguistically to the Hebrew "Succoth," the city where Israel traveled first after leaving Rameses.[34]

Naville argued that Pithom was the religious name of the city and that Succoth was its civil name. He found evidence of a fortress and storage building constructed with mud bricks without straw as described in Exodus 5:6-10.[35] However, the Bible distinguishes between Pithom, Rameses and Succoth.[36] Also, I have been unable to find a complete archaeological history of Tell el-Maskhutah. If this city is ancient Succoth or Pithom, its roots should go back to the twelfth-dynasty.

Gardiner located Pithom at Tell el-Retabeh on the basis of a Roman milestone found at Tell el-Maskhutah that located the house of Ero, the Greek name for the Egyptian **god, Atum (Pi- Atum = House of Atum)**, nine miles away. Tell el-Retabeh is precisely nine miles to the west from Tell el-Maskhutah.[37] Petrie excavated Tell el-Retabeh proving that the site was built in the Middle Kingdom, several hundred years before the eighteenth and nineteenth dynasties.[38] If the excavation proves to be of twelfth-dynasty origin, we have another synchronism with Sesostris III as the constructor of Biblical Pithom.

VIII. LOCATION OF BIBLICAL SUCCOTH

If the cities at Tell el-Retabeh and Tell el-Maskhutah were constructed in the twelfth dynasty, it is likely that Tell el-Retabeh is Biblical Pithom and Tell el-Maskhutah is Biblical Succoth. Kitchen points out that *Papyrus Anastas I, 19:3-8* reports that the distance between Succoth (Tjeku) and Pi-Rameses, the Egyptian capital of Ramses II, was a day's journey. Numbers 33:3-5 describes Israel's Exodus from Egypt as beginning at the city of Rameses and making its first stop at Succoth (Tjeku). This first camping stop fits Tell el-Maskhutah, but not Tell el-Retabeh, lending more evidence to the identification of Tell el-Retabeh as Pithom and Tell el-Maskhutah as Succoth.[39] Either way, we must wait for additional information to know the complete archaeological histories of these two cities. Thus far, the evidence does not contradict a twelfth-dynasty existence for Pithom or Succoth. See these locations on the map of Figure 15-A above.

IX. SESOSTRIS III AND AMENEMHET III CONSTRUCTED OUT OF MUD BRICK MIXED WITH STRAW

Moses reported in Exodus 5:7-8 that the Israelites used mud and straw bricks, rather than stone, in constructing these cities. The Pharaoh of the Exodus commanded: "You are no longer to supply the people with straw for making bricks; let them go and gather their own straw." The constructions of Sesostris III and Amenemhet III were almost entirely of mud brick mixed with straw.

William Hayes: The pyramids of the kings of the Twelfth dynasty at El-Lisht, Dahshur, El-Lahun, and Hawara followed the Old Kingdom type, but were smaller and of inferior construction. All were cased with limestone, but only the pyramid of Ammenemes I was built throughout of stone, the others being either of rubble-filled cellular construction or **of mud brick.**[40]

Different scholars identify Thutmose III of the eighteenth dynasty[41] and Ramses II of the nineteenth dynasty[42] as the Biblical Pharaoh of the Oppression. However, both Thutmose III[43] and Ramses II[44] constructed out of stone, not mud brick. **Thus, the construction of the store cities of Pithom and Rameses out of bricks composed of mud mixed with straw fits precisely the time of Sesostris III and Amenemhet III, but not the time of Thutmose III or Ramses II.**

CONCLUSION

Sesostris III used work gangs of foreign slaves to construct Rameses and Pithom with mud bricks mixed with straw in Goshen. Sesostris III's construction duplicates what the Pharaoh of the Oppression did in the Bible during Moses' lifetime. Simultaneously, Canaanites constructed high-walled, Middle Bronze II cities, fitting perfectly the Bible description of these fortified Canaanite cities that existed when Israel left Egypt. Table 15-A lists fifteen clues in this chapter that link Sesostris III to the Pharaoh who enslaved Israelites and built Pithom and Rameses. See Table 15-A below.

TABLE 15-A
FIFTEEN DISCOVERIES THAT IDENTIFY SESOSTRIS III AS THE FIRST CONSTRUCTOR OF RAMESES AND PITHOM

Discovery 1. Sesostris III and his son Amenemhet III were the first to build the store cities of Rameses and Pithom out of straw and mud brick.

Discovery 2. Sesostris III constructed other cities and temples in the district of Rameses.

Discovery 3. Most Egyptologists and archaeologists agree that Rameses was constructed in the Wadi Tumilat in the region of two villages: Qantir and El-Khatana, an area that fits the Biblical description of the store city of Rameses.

Discovery 4. Twelfth-dynasty kings were the first to build Rameses as a store city, not a capital city. The capital of the Twelfth dynasty was Zoan, not Rameses.

Discovery 5. The name of Pithom, ("House of Atum") also fits twelfth-dynasty kings who called their sun-god, Ra, by the complete name "Atum-Ra."

Discovery 6. Excavation of Tell el-Retabeh (Pithom) attributes its construction by twelfth dynasty kings **before** the eighteenth and nineteenth dynasties existed.

Discovery 7. Sesostris III and Amenemhet III constructed with mud bricks mixed with straw, as in Moses' time, whereas Ramses II constructed in stone.

Discovery 8. Egyptian records show camps of enslaved foreigners from Canaan and Syria lived close to Egypt's capital during Sesostris III's reign. The Bible confirms that Israelite slaves also lived close to Egypt's capital in Moses' day.

Discovery 9. Foreign slaves constructed in Goshen, received deliveries of materials, and were inspected by officials of Sesostris III.

Discovery 10. One hundred years after the fall of the twelfth dynasty, Hyksos kings destroyed the store city of Rameses and built their new capital of Avaris on top of the ruins of the twelfth-dynasty store city.

Discovery 11. One hundred years after Avaris was built, the eighteenth dynasty destroyed the Hyksos capital of Avaris, which was constructed over the twelfth-dynasty store city.

Discovery 12. Two hundred years later Rameses II built Pi-Rameses over the ruins of Avaris, which was built on the remains of the store city of Rameses in the twelfth dynasty.

Discovery 13. An Egyptian papyrus of Ramses II's time describes the city of Rameses as located in the most beautiful and fertile district of Egypt, in harmony with the Bible description of the district of Rameses in the time of Moses.

Discovery 14. Canaanites constructed high-walled, fortified cities in the Middle Bronze IIB/C Age. In the same age Sesostris III fortified his N.E. border to protect Egypt from the Canaanites. The Bible dates these high-walled cities in the time of Moses, proving Sesostris III was contemporary with Moses.

Discovery 15. These high-walled cities did not exist in Ramses II's reign, but did exist in Sesostris III's reign, which is carbon-14 dated to the fifteenth century B.C., the Biblical date of Moses, not Abraham.

TABLE 15-B
RUNNING TOTAL OF DISCOVERIES

Chapter		Chapter Total	Running Total
2	Conflict Between Biblical and Secular Histories	18	18
4	Discovery of 430 Years from Abraham to the Exodus	16	34
5	Confirmation of Abraham's Historicity	28	62
6	Discovery of the Remains of Sodom and Gomorrah	17	79
7	Joseph As a Slave and Prisoner in Amenemhet I's Reign	21	100
8	Joseph Becomes the Vizier of Sesostris I	23	123
9	Sesostris I Gives Joseph a New Name and a Wife	11	134
10	The Seven Years of Abundance in Sesostris I's Reign	10	144
11	The Seven Years of Famine in Sesostris I's Reign	20	164
12	Israel Enters Egypt during Sesostris I's Reign	14	178
13	Sesostris III Enslaves the Israelites	17	195
14	Sesostris III, The Foster Grandfather of Moses	12	207
15	Sesostris III, Builder of Rameses and Pithom	15	222

NOTES ON CHAPTER FIFTEEN

1. Amihai Mazar, *Archaeology of the Land of the Bible*, Doubleday, 190.

2. Baines and Malek, *Atlas of Ancient Egypt.*, Facts on File, N. Y., 175-166.
3. Baines and Malek, *Atlas of Ancient Egypt.*, 175-166.

4. W. H. Shea, "Exodus, Date of the," *International Standard Bible Encyclopedia*, II.231-232.

5. Edward F. Wente, "Rameses," *Anchor Bible Dictionary*, 5.618.

6. E.A. Wallis Budge, *An Egyptian Hieroglyphic Dictionary*, 1.321a.

7. Petrie, *A History of Egypt*, I.183.
8. Petrie, *A History of Egypt*, I.183.

9. M. Lichtheim (Trans.), *Ancient Egyptian Literature*, I.119.
10. M. Lichtheim (Trans.), *Ancient Egyptian Literature*, I.199.
11. R. W. Pierce, "Rameses," *The International Standard Bible Encyclopedia*, IV.39.
12. G. Posener, "Syria and Palestine During Dynasty XII," *Cambridge Ancient History*, I.2A.542.
13. G. Posener, "Les Asiatiques en Egypte sous les XIIe et XIIIe dynasties," *In Syria*, 34 (1957), 145-63, footnote 4. II.53,151-152 in *Cambridge Ancient History*, I.2A. 542, listed in *Cambridge Ancient History*, I.2B.954, no. 53.
14. William K. Simpson, "Dynasty 12," *The Ancient Near East, A History*, p. 248.
15. William K. Simpson, "Dynasty 12," *The Ancient Near East, A History*, p. 248..
16. Rolf Krauss, *Sothis-Und Monddadaten*, 73, translated by Richard Walker and Tom Black.
17. Kenneth A. Kitchen, "Goshen," *Zondervan Pictorial Bible Encyclopedia*, Vol. 2, 779.
18. William C. Hayes, "The Middle Kingdom in Egypt," *Cambridge Ancient History*, I.2A.497.
19. G. Posener, "Syria & Palestine, c. 2160-1780 B.C.," *Cambridge Ancient History*, I.2A.541.
20. Kathleen Kenyon, "Palestine in the Middle Bronze Age," *Cambridge Ancient History*, II.1.88
21. Kathleen Kenyon, *Archaeology in the Holy Land*, 158-159.
22. Amihai Mazar, *Archaeology of the Land of the Bible*, 198.
23. Amihai Mazar, *Archaeology of the Land of the Bible*, 28-29
24. John Baines, "Egypt," *New Encyclopaedia Britannica*, 18.113.

25. Kathleen Kenyon, *Archaeology in the Holy Land*, 158.

26. Kenneth A. Kitchen, "Raamses, Rameses," *Zondervan Pictorial Encyclopedia of the Bible*, V.14.

27. Edward F. Wente, "Rameses," *Anchor Bible Dictionary*, 5.617.

28. John Wilson (Trans.) "In Praise of the City Ramses," *Ancient Near Eastern Texts*, 471.

29. Exodus 1:11

30. T. V. Brisco, "Pithom," *International Standard Bible Encyclopedia*, III.875-6; K. Kitchen, "Pithom," *Zondervan Pictorial Bible Encyclopedia*, IV.803-4; Tom F. Wei, "Pithom," *Anchor Bible Dictionary*, 5.376.

31. W. Stevenson Smith, "The Old Kingdom in Egypt," *Cambridge Ancient History*, I.2A.202.

32. Breasted (Trans.), "Heliopolis Building Inscription,"*Ancient Records of Egypt*, I.244 (503).

33. Breasted (Trans.), "Inscription of Khnumhotep II," *Ancient Records of Egypt*, I.283 (625).

34. Tom Wei, "Pithom," *Anchor Bible Dictionary*, 5.377.

35. Tom Wei, "Pithom," *Anchor Bible Dictionary*, 5.377.

36. Exodus 1:11; 12:37.

37. T. V. Brisco, "Pithom," *International Standard Bible Encyclopedia*, 3.876.

38. T. V. Brisco, "Pithom," *International Standard Bible Encyclopedia*, 3.876.

39. Kenneth Kitchen, "Pithom," *Zondervan Pictorial Encyclopedia of the Bible*, IV.804.

40. William Hayes, "Middle Kingdom of Egypt," *Cambridge Ancient History*, I.2A.516.

41. William C. Hayes, "Egypt: Internal Affairs From Tuthmosis I to the Death of Amenophis III," *Cambridge Ancient History*, II.1.391-400.

42. James Breasted, *History of Egypt*, p. 444-445.

43. William C. Hayes, "Egypt: Internal Affairs from Tuthmosis I to the Death of Amenophis III," *Cambridge Ancient History*, II.1.391-397.

44. William C. Hayes, *Scepter of Egypt*, II.334-341.

CHAPTER SIXTEEN
ZOAN (ITJTOWY), THE CAPITAL OF THE TWELFTH DYNASTY

In order to identify criminals, detectives look for fingerprints, footprints, and other evidences left at the scene of the crime. However, a suspect cannot be convicted of a crime if he can prove he was elsewhere at the time the crime was committed.

This book identifies twelfth-dynasty Pharaohs as the rulers of Egypt during the lifetimes of Joseph and Moses. If this identification is correct, the principal capital of the twelfth dynasty should be located in the same place where the Bible situates the capital of Egypt during the time of Joseph and Moses. All Egyptologists agree that Amenemhet I, the founder of the twelfth dynasty, moved Egypt's capital from Thebes in the south to a new city called Itjtowy, located in northern Egypt. All Egyptologists agree that the twelfth-dynasty capital remained at Itjtowy during the entire duration of the dynasty.

Most Egyptologists locate the twelfth dynasty capital of Itjtowy at El Lisht south of Memphis, close to Lake Moeris, where the twelfth-dynasty pyramids are located. However, Baines admits that the remains of the twelfth-dynasty palace of Itjtowy **"paradoxically has not been found . . . and its exact location is still unknown."**[1] The reason that the twelfth-dynasty capital was not found at El Lisht, is because El Lisht was the capital of a nome (provincial capital), whose principal purpose was to guard and protect the twelfth-dynasty pyramids, not the principal capital of Egypt.

This chapter cites Egyptian documents that demonstrate that Itjtowy, the capital of the twelfth dynasty **could not have been located at El Lisht**, and that the palace and capital were actually located in **the north-eastern delta, north of, and close to, the border of Goshen.**

This chapter also presents Egyptian and Biblical evidences that the twelfth-dynasty capital of Itjtowy was previously and later called either Zoan or Tanis. When the Arabian Hyksos later invaded Egypt they called Zoan by the name of San el Hagar. **All Egyptologists agree that Zoan, Tanis and San El Hagar are the same location, but they have failed to recognize that the twelfth-dynasty capital of Ijtowy is another name for Zoan.** This chapter contains convincing evidences from twelfth-dynasty documents that prove that the twelfth-dynasty capital, Itjtowy, was located in the northeastern Delta of Egypt close to the northern border of Goshen in the same location of Zoan/Tanis.

I. ISRAEL IN THE LAND OF GOSHEN FROM JOSEPH TO THE EXODUS

Before locating the twelfth dynasty capital, let us determine Biblically where the Israelites lived in Egypt. When Israel came to Egypt, Pharaoh gave the Israelites property **in the district of Rameses, called also the land of Goshen, in the best**

part, or most fertile area, of Egypt.

> Genesis 47:6 -- Settle your father and your brothers in the best part of the land. Let them live in **Goshen.** . . . . Genesis 47:11 -- So Joseph settled his father and his brothers in Egypt and **gave them property in the best part of the land, the district of Rameses**, as Pharaoh directed. NIV

> Genesis 47:27 -- Now the Israelites settled in Egypt **in the region of Goshen.** They **acquired property there** and **were fruitful and increased greatly in number.** NIV

Genesis 47:27 says, "The Israelites settled in Egypt **in the region of Goshen,"** whereas Genesis 47:11 says Joseph gave them property "in the best part of the land, **the district of Rameses.**" Therefore, the Egyptian territory where Israel lived had **two names: (1) the land of Goshen, and (2) the district of Rameses.**

We know that the Israelites remained in the land of Goshen (district of Rameses) the entire time they were in Egypt, because the Bible says Israel was still living in Goshen at the time of the ten plagues and the Exodus from Egypt.

> Exodus 8:22 -- But on that day I will deal differently with **the land of Goshen, where my people live**; no swarms of flies will be there . . . . Exodus 9:26 -- The only place it did not hail was **the land of Goshen, where the Israelites were.** NIV

The Israelites lived in Goshen (District of Rameses) when Joseph first brought them to Egypt, and still lived in the same region at the time of the Exodus. Thus, I conclude that the Israelites continued to live in Goshen (District of Rameses) the entire 210 years they lived in Egypt.

II. LOCATION OF GOSHEN IN EGYPT

We studied in the last chapter many evidences for the location of Goshen (the District of Rameses) in the Wadi Tumilat in the eastern Delta of Egypt. Egyptologist Kenneth A. Kitchen, agrees that the district of Rameses and the land of Goshen are both located in this same area.

> Geographically, Goshen is closely linked with the land and city of Raamses. . . . Goshen can readily be placed in the territory between Saft el Henneth in the South **(at the west end of Wadi Tumilat)** [my emphasis] and Qantir and El Salhieh in the North and Northeast. **It could hardly be still further extended up to Tanis** [my emphasis].[2]

Note that Kitchen's words **exclude Tanis** from the region of Goshen (district of

Rameses). Kitchen locates Tanis in a separate district that is adjacent to Goshen's northern border. This distinction is important in locating the capital of Egypt from the time of Joseph to the Exodus.

III. THE LOCATION OF THE EGYPTIAN CAPITAL FROM JOSEPH TO MOSES

Having pinpointed the general area of Goshen where the Israelites lived and constructed cities during their 210-year stay in Egypt, let us now locate Biblically the Egyptian **capital** during this same period.

A. Egypt's Capital Was Not Located in Goshen in the Time of Joseph

Genesis 46:28-29 informs us that the Israelites knew the directions to the Egyptian capital, where Joseph lived, but did not know the directions to the land of Goshen where they were supposed to live: "Now Jacob sent Judah ahead of him to Joseph to get directions to Goshen." Israel's knowledge of the way to the capital, and their ignorance of the way to Goshen, demonstrates that the capital was not located in the district of Goshen (district of Rameses).

After Judah received directions from Joseph, and after Israel arrived in the region of Goshen, **"Joseph had his chariot made ready and went to Goshen to meet his father Israel."[3] The fact that Joseph "went to Goshen" to meet his father implies that the capital where Joseph lived was not in Goshen, which was identical to the district of Rameses.**

Furthermore, when Joseph met his family coming from Canaan, he explained in Genesis 46:33-34 why the Israelites could not live in the region of the capital.

> When Pharaoh calls you in and asks, "What is your occupation?" you should answer, "Your servants have tended livestock from our boyhood on, just as our fathers did." Then you will be allowed to settle **in the region of Goshen, for all shepherds are detestable to the Egyptians.**

Thus, Joseph explained why his family could not live in the same capital district where he lived. Shepherds were considered by Egyptians to be unclean and thus unacceptable to live in the same district of the king of Egypt. **Therefore, the capital of Egypt was not located in the region of Rameses (Goshen) where the Israelites lived.**

Exodus 8:21-23 also demonstrates that the **Pharaoh of Moses' day lived in the region of Zoan and not in the region of Rameses (Goshen) where Israel lived.**

> Ex 8:21-24 -- If you do not let my people go, **I will send swarms of flies on you and your officials, on your people and into your houses.** The houses of the Egyptians will be full of flies, and even the ground where they are. **But on that day I will deal differently with the land**

of Goshen, where my people live; no swarms of flies will be there, so that you will know that I, the LORD, am in this land. I will make a distinction between my people and your people.'" NIV

B. The Egyptian Capital Was "Close"
to Goshen in Joseph's Days

On the other hand, the Bible indicates that the capital city where Joseph lived was **"close,"** or **"near,"** to the region of Goshen.

> Genesis 45:10 -- [Joseph said:] You shall live in the region of Goshen and **be near me**-- you, your children and grandchildren, your flocks and herds, and all you have. (NIV)

As Vizier of Egypt, Joseph lived either in the king's residence or in a house close by in the same capital city, for Pharaoh told Joseph in Genesis 41:40, **"You shall be in charge of my palace,** and all my people are to submit to your orders. Only with respect to the throne will I be greater than you." Genesis 47:14 informs us that during the famine "Joseph collected all the money that was to be found in Egypt and Canaan in payment for the grain they were buying, and **he brought it to Pharaoh's palace."** The palace was obviously located in the capital of Egypt, where Pharaoh could oversee his treasury and important officials.

On the other hand, after the Israelites arrived in the land of Goshen (Rameses), they were **not far from the Egyptian capital**, because Genesis 47:1-11 informs us that Joseph introduced his father and five of his brothers to Pharaoh soon after their arrival in Egypt.

> Genesis 47:5-6-- Pharaoh said to Joseph, "Your father and your brothers have come to you, and the land of Egypt is before you; settle your father and your brothers in the best part of the land. **Let them live in Goshen.** And if you know of any among them with special ability, put them in charge of my own livestock." NIV

Since the Egyptian capital was **"near" Goshen** (district of Rameses) , **but not within Goshen (district of Rameses),** I conclude that the Egyptian capital of Joseph's day was located in another district that was adjacent to Goshen in the Delta of northern Egypt.

C. Egypt's Capital Was Still Close to Goshen
When Moses Was Born

While Pharaoh's palace was not located in Goshen at the time of Moses, it was certainly located **"near" Goshen,** as it was in the time of Joseph. Why? Because Pharaoh's daughter found baby Moses among the reeds of the Nile when she was bathing near the palace.[4] Therefore, Moses' parents must have lived on the border of Goshen, very close to the capital, where the princess lived. Remember that Joseph said that Egypt's capital in his own day was "close" to Goshen, but not within Goshen.[5] Miriam, Moses' sister, stood near by and watched the Egyptian princess take baby Moses into her arms. She then approached the princess and arranged for Jochebed, Moses' real mother, to nurse Moses before the princess began to rear him in Egypt's palace.[6] Thus, the capital must have been located very close to the border that separated the capital's district from the district of Goshen (Rameses) where Miriam and Jochebed lived.

D. The Egyptian Capital Was Still In Zoan, Not Rameses, From Moses' Fortieth Year to His Eightieth Year.

Moses was reared in the palace of the Pharaoh of the Oppression. When Moses was forty years old, he left the capital and went out to the store cities of Rameses and Pithom where his fellow Israelites were laboring.[7] Thus, forty years after Moses' birth, Rameses was still a store city, not the capital city. **Thus, the Pharaoh of Moses had not moved his capital to the land of Goshen (district of Rameses) during the past forty years.**

After killing an Egyptian who was beating an Israelite, Moses fled Egypt to live in Midian **at age forty** (Acts 7.23-29). Moses was eighty (Exodus 7:7; Acts 7:30) when he returned to Egypt at the time of the Exodus. The Bible relates specific information that locates the Egyptian capital near Goshen, but not within Goshen, during Moses first eighty years.[8] After returning to Egypt at age eighty, Egypt's capital was still located close to Goshen, but not within Goshen.[9]

When Moses went to the capital to talk to Pharaoh, he sometimes commuted back and forth between Goshen and the capital on a daily basis. God gave the following instructions to Moses in Exodus 7:15 and 8:20.

> Exodus 7:15 -- Go to Pharaoh **in the morning as he goes out to the water. Wait on the bank of the Nile to meet him**, and take in your hand the staff that was changed into a snake. NIV

> Exodus 8:20 -- **Get up early in the morning** and confront Pharaoh as he goes to the water and say to him, "This is what the LORD says: Let my people go, so that they may worship me." NIV

Thus, Moses's residence in Goshen was so close to the capital that he could get up before dawn and arrive at the palace. The palace was obviously located close to a branch of the Nile River and not far from Goshen where Israel lived.

In addition, all of the ten plagues fell upon the Egyptian capital, but the Bible specifically mentions several plagues that did not fall in Goshen (District of Rameses) where the Israelites lived. For example, Exodus 8:21-24 reports that the plague of flies filled Pharaoh's palace, but did not enter the land of Goshen where Rameses was located.

Exodus 8:21-24 -- God said: "If you do not let my people go, I will send swarms of flies on you and your officials, on your people and into your houses. The houses of the Egyptians will be full of flies, and even the ground where they are. But on that day **I will deal differently with the land of Goshen, where my people live; no swarms of flies will be there**, so that you will know that I, the LORD, am in this land . . . ." Dense swarms of flies poured into Pharaoh's palace and into the houses of his officials, and throughout Egypt the land was ruined by the flies. NIV

When hail struck the fields and livestock of Egypt, including the capital, Exodus 9:26 says, "the **only place it did not hail was the land of Goshen** where the Israelites were." Again, when the plague of darkness enveloped Egypt, Exodus 10:22-23 informs us that **Pharaoh in his palace could not see, but the Israelites in Goshen had light.**

So Moses stretched out his hand toward the sky, and **total darkness covered all Egypt** for three days. No one could see anyone else or leave his place for three days. **Yet all the Israelites had light in the places where they lived.** NIV

Since these plagues fell on the capital city of Egypt, but did not occur in Goshen, obviously the capital was not situated in the land of Goshen (also called the district of Rameses) where the Israelites lived and worked from the time of Joseph to Moses to the Exodus.

On the night that the first born of Egypt died, Pharaoh lived so close to the district of Rameses that he summoned Moses that same night to permit the Israelites to go worship their God.[10] Permission arrived in time for the Israelites to leave Rameses the following morning.[11] Therefore, from the time of Joseph to the Exodus, **Egypt's capital** was located on one of the chief tributaries of the Nile River, close to Goshen, **but not within Goshen (district of Rameses).**

IV. EGYPT'S CAPITAL IN THE TIME OF JOSEPH, MOSES AND THE TWELFTH DYNASTY

A. Zoan: The Name of Egypt's Capital in the Days of Joseph & Moses.

Zoan in Hebrew is from the Egyptian *D'nt* or *Djanet*, **which is expressed in Greek as *Tanis*.** Psalm 78:42-48 clearly names **Zoan, not Rameses,** as the region where all of the plagues fell.

They did not remember . . . the day he redeemed them from the oppressor, the day he displayed his miraculous signs in Egypt, his wonders in the region of **Zoan.** NIV

214

Zoan was not only the name of the region, it was also the name of the capital city, as Moses implies when he compared the city of Zoan with the Canaanite city of Hebron in Numbers 13:22: **"Hebron had been built seven years before Zoan in Egypt."** Genesis 13:18 and Judges 1:10 report that Hebron existed back in the time of Abraham. Therefore, Zoan existed contemporaneously with Hebron in the time of Abraham and thus existed about 200 years before Israel came to Egypt and about 300 years before Israel constructed the store city of Rameses. Other Biblical references to Zoan appear in the footnote.[12]

B. Tanis Was Not the Capital of Ramses II

Formerly, scholars thought Ramses II's capital was located at Tanis, Biblical Zoan. The excavator of Tanis, Montet, supported by the famous Egyptologist, Gardiner, advocated Tanis as the location of Pi-Rameses "mainly on the sheer quantity of monuments of Ramses II found there."[13]

However, Kenneth Kitchen, gives four excellent reasons why the weight of scholarly judgment now rejects Tanis as the capital of Ramses II.[14] (1) All monuments of Ramses II's time were found to have been moved to Tanis from other locations and reused by later kings of Egypt.[15] (2) No palaces or tombs of Ramses II and his officials were found at Tanis.[16] (3) Egyptian documents indicate that Pi-Ramesse was located on the "Waters of Ra," the old eastern arm of the Nile. However, this branch of the Nile was not navigable at Tanis during the reign of Ramses II.[17] (4) In the days of Ramses II "the fields of Tanis" are listed as a separate location from the "fields of Pi-Ramesse."[18] **Thus, Tanis and Pi-Ramesse are listed as two different cities in the Onomasticon list,[19] and cannot be the same city in the same location. Tanis is the earlier name of Itjtowy, the capital of the twelfth dynasty.** After the twelfth and thirteenth dynasties fell, Egyptians discontinued the name of Itjtowy and **reverted to the older name of Tanis.**

C. Tanis Fits Biblical Zoan

Tanis (San el-Hagar) fits perfectly the Biblical description of the Egyptian capital of Zoan in the time of Joseph and Moses. Tanis (Zoan) is located in a district that borders Goshen **on the north.** Tanis is thus located outside of Goshen and yet is near and adjacent to Goshen, where the Bible locates Zoan. In fact, a branch of the Nile directly connects Goshen to Tanis.

If Moses' mother and sister lived on this branch of the Nile in northern Goshen, they could have walked just a few miles downstream from their home in Goshen to deposit baby Moses among the reeds close to the palace at Tanis (Zoan).

Also, Tanis is not located in an area as fertile as that of the district of Rameses (Goshen), fitting Pharaoh's words that Israel was to live in the "best of the land" in Goshen. This fact implies that Pharaoh's capital was not located in the best of the land. Therefore, we conclude that the Biblical description of the location of Zoan fits perfectly with the location of Tanis (modern San el-Hagar).

Almost all scholars locate Tanis (Zoan) at modern San el-Hagar, close to the northern border of the region of Goshen (district of Rameses), precisely on

a branch of the Nile River that connects Goshen with the northern region of Tanis.[20] However, most scholars do not think that Tanis (Zoan) was the capital of the twelfth dynasty. In my opinion, the reason Egyptologists have never found Itjtowy (the capital of the twelfth dynasty) is due to a lack of more extensive excavation in the area around Tanis (San el Hagar). Notice on the map in Figure 16-A where most Egyptologists locate Tanis.

D. Zoan (Tanis) in Egyptian Literature

Egyptologists, such as Kenneth Kitchen,[21] and Donald B. Redford,[22] also distinguish between Rameses and Zoan because Egyptian documents from the time of Ramses II list the two regions as separate geographical areas. However, Redford claims that Zoan is first mentioned in Egyptian literature **as a town** "in the 23rd year of Ramesses XI of the 20th Dynasty, dated *ca.* 1183 B.C." and was later occupied as the capital of the 21st Dynasty.[23]

C. E. Devries says the name "Zoan" does not appear in Egyptian literature until the reign of Ramses II (nineteenth dynasty). Devries concluded that the city could not have existed as a capital of Egypt in earlier dynasties.[24]

However, Zoan is listed as one of the principal districts of Egypt during the **early twelfth dynasty.** William Hayes says that "a red granite altar from the pyramid temple of King Amen-em-het I" (Amenemhet I), the founder of the twelfth dynasty, contains the names of the principal districts (nomes) of upper and lower Egypt. "Tanis" (Djanet) is listed on Amenemhet I's altar among the nomes (districts) of lower Egypt,[25] where the northeastern delta of Egypt is located. Therefore, Zoan definitely existed as a district at the beginning of the twelfth dynasty. **The capital of this district was no doubt called Zoan** and thus existed before Amenemhet I established the twelfth dynasty, thus confirming Numbers 13:21 that says **Zoan was constructed seven years after Hebron was built in the land of Canaan during Abraham's days (Genesis 13:18; 23:2)**

Therefore, Tanis (Zoan) already existed as a capital of a district in the northeastern region of the delta of Egypt before the twelfth dynasty was founded. **The capital of the eleventh dynasty was located at Thebes in southern Egypt, where Nebtowyre Mentuhotep IV reigned.** Amenemhet, the Vizier of Mentuhotep IV, rebelled and took over his throne. He then moved his capital to the north eastern delta at the old city of Tanis (Zoan) and **built a a new capital, calling it Itjtowy (formerly Tanis or Zoan), and established a new dynasty (the twelfth).**

This chapter will demonstrate that the twelfth-dynasty capital of Itjtowy is located in the **northeastern delta and is to be identified with the city of Zoan, not El Lisht, south of Memphis (as Baines has incorrectly identified).**[26]

E. Royal Residence of Twelfth Dynasty
In the Eastern Delta

Kenneth Kitchen tells us that **a royal residence of the tenth through the thirteen dynasties likely existed in the eastern delta of Egypt. Notice Kitchen's** words below.

> A series of discoveries by Egyptian scholars in the Eastern Delta makes it highly probable that a royal residence existed in the 10th and 12th-13th dynasties and Hyksos dynasties (including the "Hyksos" town of Avaris) in the same region favored centuries later by Ramses II for his Delta residence of Raamses.[27]

Kitchen appears to equate Zoan with the district of Rameses, whereas Zoan and Rameses are clearly distinguished from each other. Zoan was the royal residence of the tenth, twelfth, and thirteenth dynasties that existed back in the time of Abraham and continued to the time of Joseph and Moses. Amenemhet I renamed Zoan as **"Itjtowy"** not long before Joseph and the Israelites arrived in Egypt. Many Egyptians probably continued to call the city Zoan instead of Itjtowy. Later in history, when the Hyksos reigned over north-eastern Egypt, the area of Tanis was called **San el-Hagar.**

F. Twelfth-Dynasty Statues Found At Zoan = Tanis = Itjtowy = San el-Hagar

One city with four names appears confusing, but the same city was renamed by different Pharaohs of different dynasties. Excavation of Tanis (San el-Hagar) uncovered statues from the sixth through the twenty-sixth dynasties.[28] Among these statues were a large number of twelfth-dynasty statues, including those of Amenemhet I, the founder of the twelfth dynasty, Sesostris I, Sesostris II and Sesostris III.[29] C. E. Devries tells us that a statue of Amenemhet II found in Tanis was regarded by Petrie as "in some respects the finest Egyptian statue known."[30]

G. Ancient Level of Zoan Not Yet Found

The walls and buildings thus far excavated at San el Hagar are dated to the twenty-first dynasty (1070 to 945 B.C.), leading many scholars to believe that these statues were all moved to Tanis from other locations.[31] **However, J. Yoyotte stated that further excavation at Tanis is necessary to complete the full history of this city.**[32] Other archaeologists admit that large areas around Zoan have not yet been excavated and that the older city may yet be found. **Since Zoan is named on the altar of Amenemhet I, dated 860 years before the twenty-first dynasty came to power, and since it is also named in documents of Ramses II's time, dated 200 years before the twenty-first dynasty formed, we can obviously conclude that the remains of the older city have not yet been found.** Broader and deeper excavation will likely uncover this ancient city. The older city could be buried and located not far from the ruins of the capital of the twenty-first dynasty, or may be found underneath the capital city of the twenty-first dynasty.

However, it is also possible that the ancient buildings and walls of the twelfth dynasty were so badly damaged that the kings of the twenty-first dynasty demolished them and removed the debris before constructing new walls and buildings. The statues of the sixth through the twentieth dynasties could have been transported from the old buildings at Tanis to the new buildings during the reign of the twenty-first dynasty. **Regardless, Zoan's name on the altar of Amenemhet I proves that its district and capital by the same name existed hundreds of years before the twenty-first dynasty was established.**

V. THE LOCATION OF ITJTOWY (ZOAN) IN A TWELFTH-DYNASTY DOCUMENT

We have proposed that the twelfth dynasty was reigning during the time of Joseph and Moses. If so, the capital of the twelfth dynasty should be Biblical "Zoan." William Hayes informs us that **Amenemhet I (Ammenemes I), the founder of the twelfth dynasty, "moved his residence" from Thebes in southern Egypt to northern Egypt "where . . . he built the fortified city of Itj-towy, 'Seizer-of-the-Two-Lands.'"**[33] Hayes located Itjtowy at El-Lisht, about eighteen miles south of Memphis, because most of the pyramids of the twelfth dynasty are located across the Nile to the west of El-Lisht.[34] Figure 16-A shows where Memphis is located and the reader can see where El-Lisht is 18 miles south of Memphis on the eastern side of the Nile River. See the Map in Figure 16-A, which shows Memphis, but does not have space to list El-Lisht.

However, Itjtowy was a strong fortress with "battlemented walls."[35] No remnants of the city walls or of the palace has ever been found at El-Lisht. J. R. Baines informs us, "Nothing has yet been found of the town itself [Itjtowy], and its exact location is still unknown."[36]

I believe that archaeologists have never found Itjtowy because they have been looking in the wrong place. If the twelfth dynasty capital is the capital of the Pharaohs of Joseph and Moses, then its original name was Zoan and it was located in the northeastern delta at or near San-el-Hagar, not far from Goshen. Below we show documentary evidence that confirms this conclusion.

A. Amenemhet I Located His Capital in the Delta of Egypt

After founding the twelfth dynasty, Amenemhet I, wrote this inscription, "I journeyed to Yebu [Elephantine, in southern Egypt[37]]; I returned [north] to the Delta."[38] Since he **"returned north to the Delta"** after journeying to Egypt's southern border in Elephantine, his statement implies that he started **in the Delta of northern Egypt, where his palace must have been located. Obviously, Amenemhet I's new capital was located in the Delta of northern Egypt..**

B. Sinuhe Located the Twelfth-Dynasty Capital in the N.E. Delta

"The Story of Sinuhe," a famous twelfth-dynasty document,[39] **also places the capital of "Itjtowy" in the Delta, northeast of Cairo (Memphis)** , not south of Cairo, as located by most Egyptologists. Sinuhe, an official of Amenemhet I, reported that the king had sent his son Sesostris I with the Egyptian army to fight against Libya (Tjemeh), which is located west of Egypt. Sinuhe served in the royal court and had gone with Sesostris I to assist in the battle. During the battle Amenemhet I had died in the palace at Itjtowy. Court officials sent messengers "to the **western border**" to inform Sesostris I of his father's demise. Sesostris I had already conquered the Libyans (Thekenu) and was returning to his capital in Itjtowy when he met the messengers.[40] Since the messengers were heading **west** from the capital toward Sesostris I at the Libyan border, then Sesostris I was obviously heading **east** back toward the capital of Itjtowy on the same road. Therefore, the road both groups traveled lay latitudinally in an eastern/western plane.

When Sinuhe learned of Amenemhet's death, he feared a military coup at the palace, and abandoned Sesostris I, fleeing "**southward,**" rather than continuing **eastward** with Sesostris I.[41] Sinuhe thus followed the road leading south parallel to the Nile River on its western side, heading toward the pyramids of the twelfth dynasty and the city of El Lisht. However, Sesostris I led the army east, not south, when they returned to the capital city of Itjtowy (Zoan) in the northeastern Delta. **Therefore, Sinuhe's flight toward El Lisht proves that the cemetery city was not the capital of the twelfth dynasty.**

Since Sinuhe turned south to avoid going to Itjtowy (the capital), we have additional proof that the road from the western border of Libya that led back to the capital of Itjtowy continued in an **eastern** direction toward and across the Nile River toward **Tanis, the true location of Itjtowy in the northeastern Delta.**

Sinuhe tells us that he traveled **south** for a night and a day. Then, he turned **east** and crossed the **Nile River** at "Cattle-Quay," arriving in the general region of the "Mistress of the Red Mountain."[42] Scholars have determined that the Cattle-Quay crossing is in the Giza region near modern day Cairo. Crossing the Nile River, Sinuhe continued in an eastern direction, passing beside "Red Mountain." Modern Egypt still calls Gebel Ahmar the "Red Mountain."[43] This mountain is located northeast of Cairo. See Sinuhe's journey out of Egypt toward Canaan in Figure 16-A.

Sinuhe says he then headed "north" toward Canaan and passed a fortification that Amenemhet I had erected as a barrier to the "Asiatics and sand-dwellers." From there he took the road that went along the Mediterranean coast north to Byblos in Lebanon.[44]

Since Sinuhe crossed the Nile about five miles north of Cairo after traveling south for a day and a night, this means the road that led eastward toward the twelfth dynasty capital was located north of Cairo by about forty-five miles, the distance Sinuhe likely traveled in a day and a night. This locates the road that Sesostris I was traveling toward Itjtowy on an east/west latitude of about 31 degrees.

Notice on the map in Figure 16-A that at 31 degrees the road Sesostris I was traveling from the west toward the east heads directly toward Tanis (San el Hagar). We saw above that Tanis harmoniously fits the description of the location of Biblical Zoan. Now we see that Tanis also fits Sinuhe's description of the location of Itjtowy and also fits Amenemhet I's own location of his capital in the Delta of Egypt.

VI. HOW CAN "ITJTOWY" BE "ZOAN"?

A. Name Changes

If Itjtowy and Zoan are the same city, why did it have two names? Moses tells us that **Zoan was built seven years after Hebron was built**.[45] Hebron existed before Abraham moved to Canaan.[46] Later, Hebron's name was changed to "Kiriath-Arba."[47] Joshua explains that Arba, a descendant of Anak, **rebuilt** Hebron after the time of Abraham and called it "Kiriath-Arba" (the city of Arba). After Israel conquered Canaan they changed the city's name back to Hebron.[48]

Zoan was likely the original name of the twelfth-dynasty capital. When Amenemhet I built his palace at Zoan, he changed the name of the capital from Zoan to Itjtowy, but retained Zoan as the name of the region surrounding the capital, thus explaining its name on Amenemhet I's granite altar. When the twelfth dynasty palace deteriorated in subsequent centuries, kings of later dynasties may have ceased to call it Itjtowy and may have begun to call the city by its original name of Zoan in the same manner that Israel renamed Kiriath-Arba by its older name of Hebron.

B. A Connection Between Itjtowy and Zoan

An Egyptian tomb inscription by Sebek-khu, an official of Sesostris III, a latter twelfth dynasty king, may provide us the clue that connects Itjtowy to Zoan. Sesostris III promoted Sebek-khu to be the commander of his attendants in the palace (Sesostris III's body guard). Sebek-khu decided to adopt a "nick-name" to express the importance of his new position. Sebek-khu twice calls himself, Zaa, also pronounced Tchaa or Djaa. His name is clearly related to the Hebrew Zoan,[49] and the Greek "Tanis,"[50] both coming from the hieroglyphic word "Tchaani" or "Djaani."[51] The "Z" from the Hebrew word Zoan and the "T" of the Greek word Tanis, are derived from the Egyptian hieroglyphic "Tch" or "Dj." Thus, Tch, Tj, Dj are usually translated to Hebrew and Greek as Z or T. The Egyptian Pharaoh, "Zoser,"[52] is also called "Djoser"[53] and "Tcheser or Tchoser."[54] The Libyan country, "Tehenu"[55] is also spelled, "Tjehenu"[56] and "Tchuhenu."[57]

Notice below that each time Sebek-khu mentions his new name Zaa (Djaa or Tchaa), he precedes his name with a reference to the "residence city," which was the twelfth dynasty capital and the location of the palace of Itjtowy where Sebek-khu was then residing.

> **Breasted (Translator):** The Lord of the two lands has . . . advanced . . . . the great commander of the **residence city, Zaa (Tchaa or Djaa)**. . . . . The chief attendant of the **residence city, Zaa (Tchaa or Djaa)**.[58]

Sebek-khu seems to associate his newly adopted name, Zaa (Tchaa), with the name of the capital or residence city where his duty was to protect the Pharaoh and the capital city. Notice that Sebek-khu's adopted name, "Tchaa," form the first letters of "Tchaani" (Tanis). **"Tchaa" means "to reach out the hand in protection, or with hostility."**[59] "Tchaa" thus expressed the new responsibility of

Sebek-khu to protect the king and the palace. Since Tchaa means to protect, Tchaani (Zoan) may also mean a city that protects the country of Egypt. **Thus, Sebek-khu's play on words connected the name Zoan (Tchaani) to the twelfth dynasty capital of Itjtowy.**

VII. THE TWELFTH-DYNASTY CONSTRUCTED OTHER DELTA CITIES

Before Amenemhet I became king, the Libyans from the west and Canaanites from the east had infiltrated the delta of Egypt. Amenemhet drove the Libyans and Canaanites out of the delta.[60] To protect his new capital of Itjtowy at Tanis (Zoan), he then constructed a fortress (store) city in the Delta called "Walls of the Ruler." He also built the cities of Khatana and Bubastis in the Delta to regulate the entrance of Asiatic and nomadic intruders coming by land. He fortified Memphis just south of the central Delta and also fortified cities in the western Delta to protect the capital from the Libyans in the west and from ships in the Mediterranean Sea in the north.[61] Later twelfth dynasty kings, such as Sesostris III and Amenemhet III continued to construct new store cities, including Rameses and Pithom in the eastern Delta, to protect Egypt against Canaanites and other eastern enemies. **Since these fortified cities surrounded the location of Zoan (Tanis), this intense twelfth-dynasty construction further confirms that Itjtowy, the twelfth dynasty capital, was also located in the delta and is to be identified as the famous Biblical city of Zoan (Tanis).**

VIII. PERMANENT LOCATION OF THE TWELFTH DYNASTY CAPITAL

The Biblical evidence shows that Egypt's capital of Zoan remained at the same location from the time of Joseph to the time of Moses and the Exodus. **The *Cambridge Ancient History* shows that Itjtowy remained as Egypt's capital throughout the entire duration of the twelfth dynasty and through most of the reign of thirteenth dynasty kings.**[62] Finally, we have found an Egyptian dynasty (the twelfth) whose capital remained in northern Egypt, close to the land of Goshen, but not within it, for a long enough duration to include the Biblical period from Joseph to Moses.

Remember that the eighteenth dynasty capital was located at Thebes, 400 miles south of Goshen. **Also, the nineteenth dynasty capital of Ramses II was located in the land of Goshen, not outside of Goshen.** Zoan (Tanis), however, fits perfectly the Biblical description of the Egyptian capital from the time of Joseph to Moses. Zoan's location also fits perfectly the description of twelfth dynasty documents for the location of Itjtowy, the twelfth dynasty capital. All evidence points to Itjtowy as Zoan, Egypt's capital during the days of Joseph and Moses.

Archaeologists admit that the excavation of San el-Hagar is not yet complete. Deeper and broader excavation of this area may uncover significant details of twelfth-dynasty history that will even contain the names of Joseph and Moses. **Therefore, new archaeological expeditions need be carried out in this area to uncover the secrets of ancient Zoan.**

CONCLUSION

An accused man cannot be convicted of a crime if he can prove that he was not at the scene of the crime when the crime was committed. The Bible says that the Pharaoh of the Oppression, who enslaved Israel, and the Pharaoh of the Exodus, who provoked the ruin of Egypt, reigned from their capital in Zoan, located in the north-eastern delta of Egypt close to the northern border of the land of Goshen. Egyptian documents locate Itjtowy, the capital of the twelfth dynasty, at the same latitude of the delta as Zoan. Many statutes of twelfth dynasty kings have been uncovered at Zoan (Greek city of Tanis). Another Egyptian document links the name of Zoan to the twelfth-dynasty capital of Itjtowy. **Therefore, these twelfth-dynasty Pharaohs of the Oppression were at the right location at the right time to have committed these crimes against the innocent Israelites.**

Table 16-A lists sixteen reasons for identifying Tanis (Zoan) as the location of Itjtowy, the capital of the twelfth dynasty. **Therefore, twelfth dynasty Pharaohs qualify to be the Biblical Pharaohs of Joseph, Moses and the Exodus.** Remember that neither eighteenth dynasty, nor nineteenth dynasty kings had Egyptian capitals that fit the Biblical description of Zoan. Only the twelfth-dynasty capital fits the Biblical description of Zoan and the Pharaohs of Joseph, Moses and the Exodus.

FIGURE 16-A
LOCATION OF TANIS, MEMPHIS AND THEBES

The history of twelfth dynasty Pharaohs from Amenemhet I to Sesostris III fits in duration of years and unique activities the Biblical description **of the Pharaohs who ruled Egypt from the time of Joseph to Moses.**

TABLE 16-A
SIXTEEN DISCOVERIES IDENTIFY ITJTOWY
WITH ZOAN/TANIS, AS THE TWELFTH-DYNASTY CAPITAL
FROM JOSEPH TO THE EXODUS

Discovery 1. Most Egyptologists locate the twelfth-dynasty capital at El Lisht, south of Memphis and near Lake Moeris, where the twelfth-dynasty pyramids were constructed . However, **the capital buildings and the palace have never been found at, or around El Lisht, indicating that the capital of Egypt was located in a different region of Egypt.**

Discovery 2. Genesis 47:6, 27 reports that Pharaoh permitted the Israelites to live in the land of Goshen, the best part of the land, which was also called the district of Rameses.

Discovery 3. Exodus 8:22 reports that the Israelites remained in the land of Goshen from the time of Joseph to Moses and the Exodus.

Discovery 4. Genesis 45:10 reports that Joseph, who lived in the capital, was **"near"** to the land of Goshen where Israel lived, locating the capital of Egypt north of Goshen, but close to the border of Goshen. (District of Rameses).

Discovery 5. Psalm 78:42-48 declares that most of the plagues and miraculous signs occurred in **Zoan (Tanis), the district of the capital of Egypt.**

Discovery 6. Most of the ten plagues did **not** occur in the land of Goshen, where Israel lived, proving that Egypt's capital was **not** located in the district of Rameses (Goshen) which is south of Tanis (Zoan).

Discovery 7. Scholars claim that the city of Zoan did not exist in the reign of twelfth-dynasty Pharaohs, but Hayes reports that Tanis (Djanet) is listed as one of the nomes (districts) of Egypt on a granite altar of Amenemhet I, the founder of dynasty twelve, proving that Tanis existed before the twelfth dynasty began.

Discovery 8. Genesis 47:27 clearly locates the capital of the Pharaoh of Joseph in the northeastern delta of Egypt, north of the city of Rameses distinguishing between Zoan and Rameses as two different cities and districts.

Discovery 9. A nineteenth dynasty document also lists Rameses and Tanis (Zoan) as two different locations.

Discovery 10. Amenemhet I indicated Itjtowy was in the delta after traveling to southern Egypt and **returning** to his capital in the northeastern delta.

Discovery 11. Sinuhe's travelogue locates Itjtowy in the northeastern delta at the same latitude of Tanis (Zoan) at San el-Hagar.

Discovery 12. Zaa, who served in the capital city of Itjtowy, seems to connect his nick name, Zaa, to the former name of the capital city Zaani (Zoan).

Discovery 13. Beautiful statues of most twelfth dynasty kings have been found in Tanis (San-el-Hagar).

Discovery 14. Kenneth Kitchen admits that the twelfth dynasty had a royal residence in the eastern delta of Egypt.

Discovery 15. Amenemhet I and other twelfth dynasty kings constructed store cities at strategic points in the delta to protect the capital of Itjtowy (Tanis).

Discovery 16. The twelfth dynasty occupied Itjtowy as its capital during its entire duration just as Egypt's capital remained in the same location from Joseph to the Exodus. Further excavation at Tanis (San el Hagar) may uncover the walls of Itjtowy, the ancient capital of the twelfth dynasty.

TABLE 16-B
RUNNING TOTAL OF DISCOVERIES

Chapter		Chapter Total	Running Total
2	Conflict Between Biblical and Secular Histories	18	18
4	Discovery of 430 Years from Abraham to the Exodus	16	34
5	Confirmation of Abraham's Historicity	28	62
6	Discovery of the Remains of Sodom and Gomorrah	17	79
7	Joseph As a Slave and Prisoner in Amenemhet I's Reign	21	100
8	Joseph Becomes the Vizier of Sesostris I	23	123
9	Sesostris I Gives Joseph a New Name and a Wife	11	134
10	The Seven Years of Abundance in Sesostris I's Reign	10	144
11	The Seven Years of Famine in Sesostris I's Reign	20	164
12	Israel Enters Egypt during Sesostris I's Reign	14	178
13	Sesostris III Enslaves the Israelites	17	195
14	Sesostris III, The Foster Grandfather of Moses	12	207
15	Sesostris III, Builder of Rameses and Pithom	15	222
16	Zoan (Itjtowy), the Capital of the Twelfth Dynasty	16	238

Notes on Chapter Sixteen are found on the next two pages

NOTES FOR CHAPTER SIXTEEN

1. John Baines, *Atlas of Ancient Egypt*, 133.
2. K. A. Kitchen, "Goshen," *Zondervan Pictorial Bible Encyclopedia*, II.777-78.
3. Genesis 46:29.
4. Exodus 2:1-7.
5. Genesis 45:10 .
6. Exodus 2:7-10.

7. Exodus 2:11; Acts 7:23-25.
8. Exodus 2:15; 7:7; Acts 7:23,30.
9. Exodus 4:29.
10. Exodus 12:29-32.
11. Exodus 12:42, 51; Numbers 33:3-5.
12. Psalm 78.12, 13; Isaiah 19:11, 13; 30:4; Ezek. 30:14.
13. Kenneth Kitchen, "Raamses, Rameses (City)," *Zondervan Pictorial Bible Encyclopaedia*, V.14.
14. Kenneth Kitchen, V.14.
15. Kenneth Kitchen, V.14.
16. Kenneth Kitchen, V.14.
17. Kenneth Kitchen, V.14
18. Kitchen, "Zoan," *Zondervan Pictorial Bible Encyclopedia*, V.1068.

19. Kitchen, "Raamses, Rameses (City)," *Zondervan Pictorial Bible Encyclopedia*, V.14., citing Gardiner, *Ancient Egyptian Onomastica*, II , 171 ff, 199 ff.

20. C. E. Devries, "Zoan," *International Standard Bible Encyclopedia*, IV.1201.

21. K. A. Kitchen, "Raamses," *Zondervan Pictorial Bible Encyclopedia*, "Zoan," 5.14, 1068.

22. Donald Redford, "Zoan," *Anchor Bible Dictionary*, VI.1106.

23. Donald Redford, "Zoan," *Anchor Bible Dictionary*, VI.1106.

24. C.E. Devries, "Zoan," *International Standard Bible Encyclopedia*, Rev. Ed., IV.1202.
25. William C. Hayes, *The Scepter of Egypt*, I.174-175
26. J. R. Baines, *Atlas of Ancient Egypt*, 133.

27. K. A. Kitchen, "Goshen," *Zondervan Pictorial Bible Encyclopedia*, II.779.
28. Avraham Negev, Ed., *Archaeological Encyclopedia of the Holy Land*, (Nashville: Thomas Nelson Publishers, 1986), 367.
29. Petrie, *History of Egypt*, Vol. I, 154, 155, 164, 175, 183.

30. Devries,"Zoan,"*International Standard Bible Encyclopedia*, IV.1202.

31. John Baines, *Atlas of Ancient Egypt*, 176.
32. Cited by C. E. Devries, "Zoan," *International Standard Bible Encyclopedia*, IV.1202.

33. William C. Hayes, *Cambridge Ancient History*, I.2A.496.
34. William C. Hayes, *Cambridge Ancient History*, I.2A.496.

35. Breasted, *A History of Egypt*, 157.

36. John Baines & Jaromir Malek, *Atlas of Ancient Egypt* (New York: Facts on File Pub., 1982),133
37. Breasted (Trans.), "The Teaching of Amenemhet," *Ancient Records of Egypt*, I.232.
38. Lichtheim (Trans.),"Instruction of King Amenemhet I For His Son Sesostris I," *Ancient Egyptian Literature*, I. 137.

39. Lichtheim (Trans.) "The Story of Sinuhe," *Ancient Egyptian Literature.* I.222-235.
40. Lichtheim (Trans.), I.224-235.
41. Lichtheim (Trans.), I.224-235.
42. Lichtheim (Trans.), I.224-235..
43. Lichtheim (Trans.), 224; plus footnote no. 3 on page 233.
44. Lichtheim (Trans.), 224; plus footnote no. 3 on page 233.

45. Numbers 13:22
46. Genesis 13:10-18
47. Genesis 23:1-2
48. Genesis 35:27-29; Joshua 14:15.
49. Numbers 13:22; Psalm. 78:12, 43; Isa. 19:11, 13; 30:4; Ezekiel 30:14.
50. Brenton (Trans.), *The Septuagint Version: Greek & English.* (Grand Rapids: Zondervan Pub., 1970), Psalm LXXVII.43, 745; plus other references in footnote.
51. E. Budge, *An Egyptian Hieroglyphic Dictionary,* II.1063
52. Breasted, *History of Egypt,* 597.
53. "Chronological Tables," *Cambridge Ancient History.* I 2B.995-6.
54. Budge, *An Egyptian Hieroglyphic Dictionary.* II.918. 55. Breasted, *History of Egypt.* 630.
56. "Chronological Tables," *Cambridge Ancient History.* I.2B.1054.
57. Budge, *An Egyptian Hieroglyphic Dictionary.* I.1064.
58. Breasted (Trans.), "Stela of Sebek-Khu, Called Zaa," *Ancient Records of Egypt,* I.302-306.
59. Budge, *An Egyptian Hieroglyphic Dictionary,* II.894.
60. William Hayes, *Scepter of Egypt,* I.171.
61. William C. Hayes, *Cambridge Ancient History,* I.2A.497-8;
62. William C. Hayes, II.1.45, 48.

CHAPTER SEVENTEEN
AMENEMHET III, THE PHARAOH
WHO TRIED TO KILL MOSES

Josephus reports that Moses was appointed general of the Egyptian army that defeated the Ethiopians (Nubians) and that he married Tharbis, the daughter of the king of Ethiopia. However, Moses never forgot his Israelite lineage. Genesis 2:11-15 reports that Moses later visited his fellow Hebrews and observed their hard labor. When he saw an Egyptian overseer beating a Hebrew slave, Moses killed the Egyptian and hid him in the sand. Having learned about Moses' misdeed, Pharaoh, the brother of Moses' Egyptian mother, tried to kill him. Moses fled to the land of Midian to escape his wrath. Stephen tells us in Acts 7:23-24 that Moses was **forty years old** when he fled Egypt to go to Midian. Exodus 7:7 reports that Moses was **eighty years old** when God commanded him to leave Midian and return to Egypt. **Therefore, Moses lived in Midian forty years.**

Toward the end of Moses' forty-year exile in Midian, Exodus 2:23 reports the death of the Pharaoh that tried to kill Moses. When Moses returned to Egypt, a new Pharaoh, who had not known Moses, was then sitting on the throne of Egypt. This new Pharaoh continued to mistreat the enslaved Hebrews.

In previous chapters we identified one of the daughters of Sesostris III as Moses' foster mother. On this basis Sesostris III was the foster-grandfather of Moses. If this identification is correct, Amenemhet III, the son of Sesostris III, was the brother of Moses' foster-mother, and thus Moses' foster-uncle. Does Amenemhet III fit the Biblical picture of the Pharaoh who tried to kill Moses and continued to oppress the Israelites in Goshen after Moses fled to Midian? This chapter presents significant evidence that Amenemhet III matches perfectly the Biblical description of the Pharaoh of most of Moses' forty-year Exile.

I. AMENEMHET III'S CHRONOLOGY
FITS MOSES' UNCLE

Amenemhet III's reign of forty-eight years fits perfectly the Biblical description of the Pharaoh who was reigning before and after Moses killed the Egyptian. This same Pharaoh sought to kill Moses throughout most of his forty year exile in Midian. **In Chapter Sixteen we linked Moses' birth in 1526 B.C. to the sixteenth year of Sesostris III's reign.** Appendix C shows how I determined that **Sesostris III's accession began in 1542 B.C.** and that Sirius rose on 8-16 of Egypt's calendar at Memphis on **July 15, 1535 B.C., in Sesostris III's seventh year. Appendix C also shows how I astronomically dated Amenemhet III's accession year to 1498 B.C.** Notice in Table 17-A at the end of this chapter how the Biblical history of Moses' life can be correlated to specific years of Amenemhet III's reign. Moses was twenty-eight years old when Amenemhet III began his accession year in **1498 B.C.** When Moses reached **his fortieth birthday** in **1486 B.C., Amenemhet III was in his twelfth year of reign.** Thus, Moses had been in

Midian for **thirty-six years** when Amenemhet III died in his **forty-eighth regnal year,** dated Biblically to **1450 B.C.**

Both the Bible[1] and Josephus[2] describe Moses' great accomplishments as a royal prince of Egypt during his first forty years. Amenemhet III obviously eyed the successful Moses as a threat to the throne of his own son. The achievements of Moses, an adopted Hebrew, no doubt disturbed Sesostris III and Amenemhet III, both of whom had an innate hatred and racial prejudice toward foreigners, especially Israelite inhabitants from Canaan.

When Moses killed an Egyptian slave driver in defense of his fellow Israelite, Amenemhet III had the perfect pretext to get rid of Moses forever. However, Moses' flight to the obscure and distant country of Midian prevented Amenemhet III from discovering Moses' whereabouts. Amenemhet III's long, forty-eight year reign ended thirty-six years after Moses' fled to Midian, c. 1450 B.C., thus fulfilling the Biblical condition that the Pharaoh who sought Moses' life died in the latter part of Moses' forty year exile, permitting Moses to return to Egypt as soon as all of Amenemhet III's officials who previously knew Moses had also died.[3]

Amenemhet III lived so long that one of his daughters died before he did.[4] His son, Amenemhet IV, was either a small child or had not yet been born when Moses fled Egypt forty years earlier. Thus, Amenemhet IV would not have recognized Moses when he returned to Egypt.

Moses did not return to Egypt the precise year that Amenemhet III died because many of his officials, that knew Moses, were still living and would kill him if he returned to Egypt. According to my astronomical chronology of the twelfth dynasty, Amenemhet III co-reigned with his son Amenemhet IV **for six years before Amenemhet IV began his sole reign:** see Table 17-A at the end of this chapter. Appendix C contains the details of twelfth-dynasty chronology. During the next four years all of Amenemhet III's officials that formerly knew Moses also died, because God told Moses in the beginning of 1446 B.C., **"Go back to Egypt, for all the men who wanted to kill you are dead."**[5]

Amenemhet III's long, forty-eight-year reign fits precisely the correct length of time the Bible requires for the Pharaoh who was reigning before Moses fled to Midian and who tried to kill Moses for most of the forty-years that Moses spent in Midian. Table 17-A and 17-B at the end of this chapter record this remarkable chronological harmony between the Biblical history of Moses' life and the Egyptian history of Amenemhet III's reign. I challenge Egyptologists to find another period of history when the reigns of three Pharaohs coincide so harmoniously with the eighty-year Biblical period from Moses' birth to the Exodus: **(1) the Pharaoh of Moses' birth, (2) the Pharaoh of Moses' exile to Midian and (3) the Pharaoh of the Exodus.** Table 17-B at the end of the chapter shows the over-all chronology of the twelfth dynasty in relation to Biblical history.

II. AMENEMHET III'S CONSTRUCTION
IN NORTHERN EGYPT

According to our new chronology for the twelfth dynasty, Amenemhet III had been reigning for twelve years when Moses killed the Egyptian who was mercilessly beating a fellow Hebrew. Thus, Amenemhet III continued the oppressive practice of his father, Sesostris III, in mistreating the Israelites and forcing them to continue the large building expansion in northern Egypt without adequate rest. William Hayes reports below the massive construction activities that Amenemhet III executed during his long reign.

> The growth of national prosperity under the pharaohs of the Twelfth dynasty reached its peak during the long and peaceful reign of Sesostris III's son, King Ny-ma-re Ammenemes III (1843-1797 B.C.). With Nubia completely under control, . . . the king now turned his attention whole-heartedly to the economic expansion of his country . . . carrying forward the plans of his predecessors for the development of the Faiyum.[6]

III. ISRAEL'S CONSTRUCTION OF PYRAMIDS
AND WATER CHANNELS IN THE
REIGN OF AMENEMHET III

Josephus, the Jewish historian of the first century A.D., tells us that the enslaved Israelites helped construct pyramids, water canals, and mechanical contraptions as well as walls for cities. Notice Josephus' words below.

> Having forgotten the benefits they had received from Joseph . . . they [the Egyptians] became very abusive to the Israelites, and contrived many ways of afflicting them; for they enjoined them **to cut a great number of channels for the river**, and **to build walls for their cities and ramparts, that they might restrain the river,** and hinder its waters from stagnating, upon its running over its own banks. **They set them also to build pyramids**, and by all this wore them out, and forced them to learn all sorts of mechanical arts, and to accustom themselves to hard labor.[7]

Breasted says that Amenemhet III, the son of Sesostris III, was primarily responsible for developing the irrigation system of Egypt and "undertook vast retention walls" in the process.[8] In addition, he built "a system of dikes and drainage canals" to prevent flooding of land.[9] Amenemhet III also built in northern Egypt a city, temples, colossal statues and two pyramids of uniquely designed secret passages and gigantic sliding trap-doors.[10] Thus, Josephus' ancient tradition that the Israelites built water canals, river ramparts and even mechanical contraptions (the

"Labyrinth" and its "trap-doors") matches perfectly the construction projects of Amenemhet III.

IV. AMENEMHET III USED BRICKS OF MUD AND STRAW IN HIS CONSTRUCTION PROJECTS

In the summer of 1991 my wife Dot and I visited the pyramid and "Labyrinth" that Amenemhet III constructed some 3,500 years ago. Amazingly, this construction was largely bricks composed of mud and straw, just as the Bible describes the construction by the Pharaohs who oppressed the Israelites.[11] See my photo of one of these mud/straw bricks in 17-A.

FIGURE 17-A
Ted Stewart's Photo of Mud-brick Mixed with Straw
Found Throughout Amenemhet III's Pyramid

Amenemhet III used mud/straw bricks, whereas the founder of the twelfth dynasty, Amenemhet I constructed out of stone. Also, Thutmose III of the eighteenth dynasty and Ramses II of the nineteenth dynasty constructed out of stone rather than mud bricks. William Hayes of the *Cambridge Ancient History* also observes that Amenemhet III used mud/straw bricks in his construction works.[12] However, Amenemhet III covered the mud/straw bricks of his pyramid with a beautiful stone finish.

V. DID AMENEMHET III USE SLAVES TO CONSTRUCT IN THE LAND OF GOSHEN?

Amenemhet III also constructed and repaired "store cities" in the land of

Goshen as his father Sesostris III did, and as the Biblical Pharaohs of the Oppression did. Hanks Goedicke says that a stela dated to the thirty-third year of Amenemhet III reported that **Intef, the chief of police, sent 35,300 bricks** to reinforce the defenses in the Wadi Tumilat.[13] Some scholars consider this shipment to be part of a larger order, or only for repair purposes to strengthen the frontier in Goshen.[14] **Scholars unanimously identify the "Wadi-Tumilat" as "the land of Goshen,"**[15] where the cities of Tanis, Rameses and Succoth were located. See the locations of these cities on the Map in Figure 17-B.

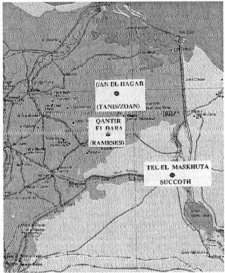

This order for bricks was given in the thirty-third year of Amenemhet III's forty-eight-year reign, underlining the continuation of Sesostris III's efforts to fortify the northeastern border of Egypt. This continued construction in Goshen fits perfectly the Biblical description of construction projects in Goshen during the entire period of Moses' first eighty years of life. For example, the Bible says that the Israelites were still making bricks for construction in Goshen when Moses returned to Egypt after his forty-year exile in Midian.[16]

The recipient of this shipment of bricks was called the "prince," possibly Amenemhet III's heir to the throne, Amenemhet IV, or perhaps the Vizier or the chief supervisor of the slaves in Goshen who would be using these bricks on construction projects.

Figure 17-B - Map of Land of Goshen where Rameses, Tanis(Zoan) and Succoth were located

Since the capital of Egypt was located in Itjtowy, just north of Goshen, the importance of a strong defense for the palace demanded a high official in charge of this construction project.

VI. POLICE CHIEFS SUPERVISED
THE MAKING OF BRICKS

Why did **Intef, the police chief cited above,** supervise brick-making? The Bible explains that the enslaved Hebrews not only constructed cities, but also formed mud and straw bricks for the construction.[17] Since the Hebrews were slaves, Pharaoh used **policemen,** armed with weapons, to force and supervise the Hebrews and other slaves, as they made bricks and as they used them in construction. Moses called these policemen "task masters" or "slave drivers."[18] Thus, chiefs of police supervised the other "slave drivers" who were actually in the field to supervise and inspect the work of the slaves. Egyptian documents describe chiefs of police and policemen supervising slave labor and delivery of bricks for construction in Goshen in the time of Amenemhet III.[19] These brick deliveries to policemen harmonize with Bible descriptions of Israel's making of bricks and using them in construction in Goshen during their years of bondage while overseen by "task masters" who are supervised by higher authorities called "policemen." Exodus 1:11-14.

VII. HIGH-WALLED BRONZE II CANAANITE CITIES BUILT IN THE REIGNS OF SESOSTRIS III AND AMENEMHET III

Middle Bronze II Canaanites, contemporary with Sesostris III and Amenemhet III, were simultaneously building high-walled cities in Canaan and training large armies. This military build-up in Canaan explains why Sesostris III and Amenemhet III strengthened the defenses of Egypt in the eastern delta. The eastern delta would be the first line of defense for Egypt if the growing Canaanite menace attacked. The continued fortification of these Canaanite cities during the reign of Amenemhet III also harmonizes with the Biblical picture of these high-walled, fortified cities that the Israelites found in Canaan after leaving Egypt and the fierce giants in Canaan, who were sons of Anak.[20]

VIII. FOREIGN WORK CAMPS NEAR THE CAPITAL OF AMENEMHET III

We mentioned in a previous chapter that work camps of "Asiatics" (a term that Egyptians used for foreigners from Canaan and Syria) worked "under the direction of Egyptian officials" on construction projects in the twelfth dynasty.[21] While our source does not say in which Pharaoh's reign these foreign work camps are found, the sending of 35,300 bricks to Goshen is sufficient evidence that these foreign work camps still existed during Amenemhet III's reign. Remember that construction by twelfth-dynasty Pharaohs reached its zenith in the time of Amenemhet III. The growing number of Israelite slaves no doubt enabled Amenemhet III to exceed the construction projects begun by his father Sesostris III.[22]

IX. LONG LIST OF FOREIGN SLAVES IN AMENEMHET III'S REIGN

The existence of foreign slaves in abundant numbers in the reign of Amenemhet III is further confirmed by a document dated to his reign that includes a list of many "**Asiatic servants**."

William Hayes: The Brooklyn Museum possesses a fragmentary papyrus with part of a prison register drawn up in the reign of King

Ammenemes III, to which were subsequently appended copies of an administrative letter and two royal decrees, and a long list of Egyptian and **Asiatic servants.**[23]

Remember that the Egyptians used the term, "Asiatics" to refer to foreigners from Canaan and Syria. Long lists of Asiatic servants harmonize perfectly with the growing numbers of Hebrew slaves in Egypt during the reign of Amenemhet III. This list of "Asiatic names" may include some of the names of the Israelites. I have been unable to find a translation of this document.

X. AMENEMHET III THREW HIS ENEMIES INTO WATER

The Bible tells us that Hebrews continued to be cruelly abused by the Egyptian Pharaoh that reigned both before and during Moses' long exile in Midian.[24] Does the historical evidence from Egyptian inscriptions support the idea that Amenemhet III oppressed others as did his father, Sesostris III? In a previous chapter we cited a passage from Sehetep-ib-re, an official who inscribed the pictures of both Sesostris III and Amenemhet III on his tomb. Sehetep-ib-re commands Egyptians to worship King Nimaatre (Amenemhet III) and warns them with these words:

> **Lichtheim's Translation:** Noses turn cold when he starts to rage. When he is at peace one breathes air. . . . Fight for his name, respect his oath! Then you stay free of betrayal. The king's beloved will be honored. **His majesty's foe has no tomb. His corpse is cast into the water.**[25]

This description of Amenemhet III proves that he threw his enemies into the water just as the Pharaohs of the Oppression did with Hebrew infants in the time of Moses.[26] Notice that noses turned cold with fear when Amenemhet III began to rage in anger. Amenemhet III, like Sesostris III, ruled by intimidation. Those who defied him were thrown in the water to be devoured by crocodiles. Like father Sesostris III, so was son Amenemhet III, both capable of throwing Hebrew infants into the Nile River to stem the population growth of Israelites and other enemies.

XI. AMENEMHET III HONORED THE CROCODILE GOD

In keeping with this evil spirit, Amenemhet III built several temples in honor of Sobek, the crocodile god. Amenemhet III also named his daughter, Sobkkare Sobknofru, in honor of this crocodile god.[27] He thus showed great appreciation to the crocodiles, who devoured the many enemies whom he threw into the water.

XII. AMENEMHET III'S ANGRY STATUES

The sphinxes of Amenemhet III also reveal his harsh attitude and abusive treatment of others: "The sphinx was revived as a medium for royal portraiture, since it **so forcefully expressed the power of the kingship**."[28] This change of architectural style and harsh tone of the sphinx that began with Sesostris III continued with his son Amenemhet III.

Hayes: "The numerous portraits of Amenemhet III include a group of statues and sphinxes from Tanis and the Faiyum, which, from their curiously **brutal style and strange accessories,** were once thought to be monuments of the Hyksos kings."[29]

Simpson: "The idealized, youthful, and sometimes bland confidence expressed in royal statuary of the Old Kingdom changes to **a brooding, concerned, and even worried strength, sometimes almost brutal**, in the portraits of Sesostris III and Amunemhet III (sic.) ".[30]

The talented Egyptian sculptors of the twelfth dynasty ably etched the sinister brutality of these Pharaohs in their very faces. Figure 17-C shows Amenemhet III with his happiest face.

It is easy to understand why Moses did not hesitate to flee Egypt when his foster-uncle learned that he had killed an Egyptian slave driver. Moses knew that there would be no mercy from a heartless man like his uncle. Amenemhet III's officials no doubt were infected with the same anger and vengeful spirit of their king. God kept Moses in Midian for forty years until Amenemhet III and all of his officials who hated Moses also died.

**Figure 17-C
Amenemhet III
Photo by Ron Wyatt**

XIII. CO-AUTHOR OF THE EXECRATION TEXTS

We saw in a previous chapter that Sesostris III gave origin to the *Execration Texts* of the twelfth dynasty, in which foreign and national enemies of Pharaoh were cursed. The hatred for enemies **increased** with alarming intensity in the reign **of** Amenemhet III. The number of foreign names and countries cursed **doubled** in comparison to Sesostris III's reign.

Posener -- For the second half of the Middle Kingdom, the Execration Texts provide long lists of Asiatic countries and their princes; the older series, which can be assigned to the reign of Sesostris III, mentions twenty countries and thirty princes; the second series, of slightly later date [Amenemhet III], gives more than sixty princes and countries.[31]

Posener's remarks above indicate that Sesostris III began the execration curses against other nations. **These curses more than doubled during the reign of Amenemhet III**, the son of Sesostris III. As Moses noted below, Amenemhet III died and **his son Amenemhet IV, the Pharaoh of the Exodus, continued and even increased the cruel oppression of the Israelite slaves.**

Exodus 2:23-24 -- During that long period, the king of Egypt died [Amenemhet III]. The Israelites groaned in their slavery and cried out, and their cry for help because of their slavery went up to God. NIV

CONCLUSION

Table 17-C at the end of this chapter contains **fifteen discoveries** that link Amenemhet III to the Biblical Pharaoh who continued to force Israelite slaves to build the cities of Rameses and Pithom and who sought to kill Moses, who fled to Midian for forty years before returning to Egypt. Table 17-D demonstrates the running total of **253 discoveries** that confirm Bible history from Abraham to Amenemhet III, the Pharaoh who tried to kill Moses. **The next chapter identifies the most sought after Pharaoh in all of Egyptian history: the illusive Pharaoh of the Exodus, who has been overlooked by Egyptologists and Bible scholars.**

Table 17-A
CHRONOLOGY OF THE REIGNS OF SESOSTRIS III,
AMENEMHET III AND AMENEMHET IV
IN RELATION TO MOSES' LIFE

B. C.	MOSES		SESOSTRIS III	AMENEMHET III
	AGE		REIGN	
1526	0	BIRTH	16th YR.	
1514	12		28th YR.	
				REIGN
1498	28		44th YR.	0-ACCESSION
1494	32		48th YR.	4th YR.
1486	40	EXILE		12th YR.
		TO MIDIAN		
			AMENEMHET IV	
1456	70		0 - ACCESSION	42ND YR.
			6th - First year of	48th Yr.
			Sole Reign	
1446	80 EXODUS		10th -Exodus/Death	

Table 17-B
BIBLICAL HISTORY FROM JOSEPH TO MOSES
COMPARED WITH TWELFTH
DYNASTY HISTORY
(Over-laps Show Co-reigns)

	A-I			
AMENEMHET I	0		1688	ACCESSION YEAR
	19	S-I	1668	JOSEPH IN PRISON
SESOSTRIS I	20	0	1667	BAKER AND BUTLER IN PRISON
	21	01	1666	
	22	02	1665	1ST YR. OF ABUNDANCE: JOSEPH 1ST YR. AS VIZIER
	23	03	1664	2ND YEAR OF ABUNDANCE
	24	04	1663	3RD YEAR OF ABUNDANCE
	25	05	1662	4TH YEAR OF ABUNDANCE
	26	06	1661	5TH YEAR OF ABUNDANCE
	27	07	1660	6TH YEAR OF ABUNDANCE
	28	08	1659	7TH YEAR OF ABUNDANCE
	29	09	1658	1ST YEAR OF FAMINE
	30	10	1657	2ND YEAR OF FAMINE
		11	1656	JACOB ENTERS EGYPT
		12	1655	4TH YEAR OF FAMINE
		13	1654	5TH YEAR OF FAMINE
		14	1653	6TH YEAR OF FAMINE
		15	1652	7TH YEAR OF FAMINE
		28	1639	JACOB'S DEATH
		30	1637	
AMENEMHET II	0	42	1625	
	01	43	1624	
	02	44	1623	
	03	45	1622	
	04	46	1621	
	05		1620	ISRAELITE PROSPERITY
SESOSTRIS II	35	0	1590	
	36	01	1589	
	37	02	1588	
	38	03	1587	
		05	1585	JOSEPH'S DEATH
		30	1560	ISRAELITE GROWTH
SESOSTRIS III	0	48	1542	SLAVERY OF ISRAEL
	7		1535	CONSTRUCTION OF RAMESES
	16		1526	MOSES' BIRTH
	36		1506	
AMENEMHET III	44	0	1498	
	45	1	1497	
	46	2	1496	
		12	1486	MOSES' EXILE TO MIDIAN
		38	1460	CONTINUED CONSTRUCTION
AMENEMHET IV	0	42	1456	IN GOSHEN
	6	48	1450	
	10		1446	PLAGUES & EXODUS

TABLE 17-C
FIFTEEN DISCOVERIES THAT IDENTIFY
AMENEMHET III AS THE PHARAOH
WHO TRIED TO KILL MOSES

Discovery No. 1. Amenemhet III's long reign of forty-eight years fits perfectly the long reign of the Pharaoh who was already reigning when Moses was forty years old and then continued to reign during the greater part of Moses' forty-year exile in Midian.

Discovery No. 2. Amenemhet III continued to expand the great construction projects begun by his father Sesostris III. Some of his construction projects were in the delta and specifically in the land of Goshen where the Israelites lived.

Discovery No. 3. Amenemhet III constructed canals, ramparts to hold water, pyramids and complicated metal contraptions with trap doors and the "Labyrinth." Josephus reported that Hebrews were involved in these same construction projects during their Egyptian bondage.

Discovery No. 4 Amenemhet III also improved the Bahr Yusef (Canal of Joseph), that had been previously constructed in the reign of Sesostris I.

Discovery No. 5. Amenemhet III constructed with bricks composed of mud mixed with straw just as the Pharaohs did who mistreated the Israelites.

Discovery No. 6. Amenemhet III sent mud bricks for construction of store cities **in the land of Goshen** to defend Egypt, as the Pharaohs of Moses' time did.

Discovery No. 7. Amenemhet III used the chief of police and policemen in providing bricks and overseeing construction by slaves just as the Pharaohs of the Oppression did when they appointed slave drivers over the Israelites.

Discovery No. 8. Camps of Canaanites, likely Hebrew slaves, worked on large construction projects in northern Egypt not far from the capital during the reign of Amenemhet III, just like the Biblical story of Moses' time.

Discovery No. 9. The building of high walled cities in Canaan during the reigns of Sesostris III and Amenemhet III paralleled the extensive construction of the high-walled store cities of Rameses and Pithom to protect Egypt from invasion. The Israelites also confronted these high-walled cities in Canaan after leaving Egypt and were fearful to enter the land. God punished the Israelites for their fear by forcing them to wander in the wilderness for forty years.

Discovery No. 10. A long list of the names of "Asiatic"(Canaanite) servants was found dated to the reign of Amenemhet III, confirming that many foreign slaves were serving the king during his reign just as they did when Moses lived.

Discovery No. 11. An Egyptian official inscribed in his tomb about the fierce anger of Amenemhet III and reported that he threw his enemies into the water, just as his father, Sesostris III, fulfilling the roles of the Biblical Pharaohs of the Oppression that threw Hebrew infants into the Nile.

Discovery No. 12. Amenemhet III built temples of worship for the crocodile god and even named his daughter with the crocodile's name (Sobek). He threw his enemies into the Nile River to be devoured by crocodiles. Amenemhet III's cruel nature, like that of his father Sesostris III, fits that of the Pharaoh who tried to kill Moses.

Discovery No. 13. Amenemhet III, following the example of his father Sesostris III, constructed a sphinx of himself as a symbol of his brutal and cruel power, which he utilized against the Hebrew slaves and his attempt to kill Moses.

Discovery No. 14. Statues of Amenemhet III and his father Sesostris III reveal angry and harsh faces which match the angry and harsh spirits of the Pharaohs of the Oppression in Moses' time.

Discovery No. 15. The *Execration Texts* begun by Sesostris III were expanded by Amenemhet III to curse all enemies of Egypt, both foreign and national. Their hateful racial bias and suspicious, jealous nature against any one who was a threat to their power and authority match the Biblical picture of the Pharaohs who considered the unarmed Israelites a threat and thus enslaved them.

TABLE 17-D
RUNNING TOTAL OF DISCOVERIES

Chapter		Chapter Total	Running Total
2	Conflict Between Biblical and Secular Histories	18	18
4	Discovery of 430 Years from Abraham to the Exodus	16	34
5	Confirmation of Abraham's Historicity	28	62
6	Discovery of the Remains of Sodom and Gomorrah	17	79
7	Joseph As a Slave and Prisoner in Amenemhet I's Reign	21	100
8	Joseph Becomes the Vizier of Sesostris I	23	123
9	Sesostris I Gives Joseph a New Name and a Wife	11	134
10	The Seven Years of Abundance in Sesostris I's Reign	10	144
11	The Seven Years of Famine in Sesostris I's Reign	20	164
12	Israel Enters Egypt during Sesostris I's Reign	14	178
13	Sesostris III Enslaves the Israelites	17	195
14	Sesostris III, The Foster Grandfather of Moses	12	207
15	Sesostris III, Builder of Rameses and Pithom	15	222
16	Zoan (Itjtowy), the Capital of the Twelfth Dynasty	16	238
17	Amenemhet III, the Pharaoh Who Tried to Kill Moses	15	253

NOTES FOR CHAPTER SEVENTEEN

1. Acts 7:22; Hebrews 11:24-25.
2. Josephus, "The Antiquities of the Jews," II.9-10, *Complete Works of Josephus*, pp. 66-70.
3. Exodus 2:23.
4. W. F. Petrie, *A History of Egypt*, I.205.
5. Exodus 4:19.
6. William C. Hayes, "Middle Kingdom of Egypt," *Cambridge Ancient History*, Vol. I.2A.509.
7. Josephus, "Antiquities of the Jews," 2.9:1, *Complete Works of Josephus*, p. 66.
8. James Breasted, *History of Egypt*, p. 193.
9. William C. Hayes, "Middle Kingdom in Egypt," *Cambridge Ancient History*, I.2A.511.
10. W. F. Petrie, *A History of Egypt*, I.194-201.
11. Exodus 5:1-16.
12. Wm. Hayes, "The Middle Kingdom in Egypt," *Cambridge Ancient History*, I.2A.511.
13. Hanks Goedicke, "Another Look At An Old Object," *Bulletin of the Egyptological Seminar* 4 (1982), 71-77
14. Hanks Goedicke, "Another Look At An Old Object," *Bulletin of the Egyptological Seminar* 4 (1982), 72.
15. E. D. Welch, "Goshen," *International Standard Bible Encyclopedia*, II.528-29.
16. Exodus 5:8-18
17. Exodus 1:9-11; 5:1-16.
18. Exodus 3:7; 5:6,10,13,14 .
19. Exodus 2:23.
20. Numbers 13:28; Deuteronomy 1:28.
21. G. Poesener, "Syria & Palestine," *Cambridge Ancient History*, I.2A,542.
22. Exodus 1:12, 20.
23. William C. Hayes, "Middle Kingdom of Egypt," *Cambridge Ancient History*, I.2A.531.
24. Exodus 2:11-15, 23-24.
25. Lichtheim (Trans.), "Stela of Sehetep-Ib-Re," *Ancient Egyptian Literature*, I.128.
26. Exodus 1:15-22.
27. Hayes, "The Middle Kingdom," *Cambridge Ancient History*, I.2A.511,520; II.1.43.
28. Hayes, *Cambridge Ancient History*, I.2A.511,520; II.1.43.
29. Hayes, *Cambridge Ancient History*, I.2A.514.
30. Simpson, *The Ancient Near East: A History*, p. 246.
31. G. Poesener, "Syria and Palestine," *Cambridge Ancient History*, I.2A.541.

CHAPTER EIGHTEEN
AMENEMHET IV, THE PHARAOH
OF THE EXODUS

Finally, we have arrived at the Egyptian king for whom we have so long searched: **The Pharaoh of the Exodus.** Amenemhet IV was the last male Pharaoh of the twelfth dynasty. He reigned only nine years, less than any other male Pharaoh of the twelfth dynasty. **He suddenly and mysteriously disappeared from the pages of history. Neither his pyramid nor his tomb have ever been found.** Neither his firstborn son, nor any other of his sons, succeeded him to the throne. Instead, his wife/sister became ruler of Egypt in his place.

When Amenemhet IV's wife died three and one half years later, **the twelfth dynasty, the most powerful and glorious Egyptian dynasty up to that time of history, mysteriously fell.** The rulership of Egypt was immediately divided into two dynasties, one of them controlled by the Libyans. Within the next 100 years, the Hyksos invaded Egypt, further dividing Egypt into two additional dynasties. At this point Egypt was then divided into four dynasties, three of which were ruled by foreigners.

In this and the next two chapters sixty historical facts will point to Amenemhet IV as the Pharaoh of the Exodus. Amenemhet IV followed his grandfather, Sesostris III, and his father, Amenemhet III, in mistreating the Israelite slaves. The mounting sins of these three Pharaohs provoked God to send on Egypt ten destructive plagues that resulted in the loss of Egypt's firstborn, slaves, Pharaoh and army. Thus, the cruelty of these three twelfth-dynasty Pharaohs led to the fall of the twelfth dynasty and its subsequent conquest and division by foreign powers.

I. THE SHORT REIGN OF THE BIBLICAL
PHARAOH OF THE EXODUS

Moses fled to Midian at age forty to escape the wrath of the Pharaoh who sought to kill him.[1] Moses stayed in Midian for forty years and was thus eighty years old when he returned to Egypt in the year of the Exodus.[2] Toward the end of this long forty-year exile, the Pharaoh who hated Moses died.[3] **At that time the Pharaoh of the Exodus came to power.** Within a few years all of the other Egyptian officials who knew Moses and sought his life also died. At that time God commanded Moses to return to Egypt.[4] **Therefore, the Pharaoh of the Exodus had been reigning only a few years when Moses returned to Egypt.** As we shall soon see, **Amenemhet IV, the last male Pharaoh of the twelfth dynasty, is the short-reigning Pharaoh of the Exodus, who died with his army in the Red Sea.**

Notice on the next page that Psalm 136:13-15 reports that God swept **Pharaoh and his army** into the Red Sea. Therefore, the Pharaoh of the Exodus did not stand on the sea shore while his army entered the Red Sea without him. Pharaoh actually led his army into the Red Sea, as was customary of Egyptian Pharaohs, such as Thutmose III and Rameses II.

Psalm 136:13-15 -- To him who divided the Red Sea asunder . . . and brought Israel through the midst of it, . . . **but swept Pharaoh and his army into the Red Sea.** NIV

Exodus 14:21-28 -- The waters were divided and the Israelites went through the sea on dry ground, with a wall of water on their right and on their left. The Egyptians pursued them, and **all Pharaoh's horses and chariots** and horsemen followed them into the sea. . . . The water flowed back and covered the chariots and horsemen---**the entire army of Pharaoh** . . . . **Not one of them survived.** NIV

Notice above that **all of Pharaoh's horses and chariots entered the sea**. **"All of Pharaoh's horses and chariots" include the horse and chariot of Pharaoh himself.** Therefore, the Bible passages, Psalm 136:13-15 and Exodus 14:21-28, clearly affirm that Pharaoh was swept into the Red Sea with his army and that **all of them drowned without a single survival.**

Since the Exodus occurred the same year that Moses returned to Egypt, then the Pharaoh of the Exodus also died in that same year. His sole reign should not have endured more than three to four years. However, as we will see later, the Pharaoh of the Exodus likely co-reigned with his father, Amenemhet III, for six or seven years.

Josephus, the Jewish historian of the first century A.D., also interpreted the Sacred Scriptures to mean that the Pharaoh of the Exodus had a very short reign.

Moses . . . came to the king, who had indeed **but lately received the government**. . . As soon, therefore, as ever the whole Egyptian army was within it, the sea flowed to its own place, . . . And thus did all these men perish, so that **there was not one man left** to be a messenger of this calamity to the rest of the Egyptians.[5]

Thus, Josephus concluded that the Pharaoh of the Exodus had reigned only a short time before the Exodus. Josephus also believed that the Scriptures indicated that the Pharaoh of the Exodus died in the Red Sea with his army.

This **short reign** of the Pharaoh of the Exodus disqualifies the principal candidates for the Pharaoh of the Exodus proposed by modern scholars. Thutmose III reigned **fifty-four years;** Amenhotep II reigned **twenty-five years** and Ramses II reigned **sixty-seven years.**[6] **None of these Pharaohs can be the short-reigning Pharaoh of the Exodus.**

II. THE SHORT-REIGN OF AMENEMHET IV

Twelfth-Dynasty history points to Amenemhet IV, the son of Amenemhet III, as the Pharaoh of the Exodus. First of all, the length of his reign is compatible with that of the short-reigning Pharaoh of the Exodus. The Turin Canon was written during the reign of Ramses II, 500 years after the fall of the twelfth dynasty. This Canon calculates Amenemhet IV's reign at precisely **nine years, three months and twenty-seven days.**[7] Notice in Table 18-A how Amenemhet IV's reign **is the shortest of all of the twelfth dynasty Pharaohs who preceded him.**

TABLE 18-A
LENGTH OF REIGNS OF TWELFTH DYNASTY PHARAOHS
(CO-REIGNS INCLUDED)

1.	AMENEMHET I	30 YEARS
2.	SESOSTRIS I	46 YEARS
3.	AMENEMHET II	38 YEARS
4.	SESOSTRIS II	48 YEARS
5.	SESOSTRIS III	44 YEARS
6.	AMENEMHET III	48 YEARS
7.	AMENEMHET IV	9 YEARS, 4 MONTHS
8.	SEBEKNEFRU (Queen)	4 YEARS

However, Amenemhet IV's sole reign is even shorter. According to my chronology of the twelfth dynasty, **Amenemhet IV co-reigned with his father Amenemhet III for six of those nine years, giving Amenemhet IV a sole reign of only three years, three months and twenty-seven days.**

TABLE 18-B
MOSES' LIFE PARALLELED TO THE REIGNS OF
SESOSTRIS III, AMENEMHET III AND AMENEMHET IV

B C		MOSES	SESOSTRIS III	
1526	0	Birth	16th	
1504	22		38th	**AMENEMHET III**
1498	28		44th	0 Accession Year
1486	40	Exile to Midian	12th	
		AMENEMHET IV		
1456	70		0	42nd
1455	71		1	43rd
1454	72		2	44th
1453	73		3	45th
1452	74		4	46th
1451	75		5	47th
1450	76		6	48th Death
1449	77		7 --- Sole Reign	
1448	78		8	
1447	79		9	
1446	80	Moses returns to Egypt and leads Israel out of Egypt	10 --- Ten Plagues	Amenemhet IV dies in the Red Sea

See the relation of Moses' chronology with that of twelfth-dynasty Pharaohs in Table 18-B above. **Table 18-B clearly shows that Amenemhet IV's less than four-year sole reign qualifies him to be the short-reigning Pharaoh of the Exodus.** More important, Amenemhet IV's reign fits perfectly the Biblical description of the Pharaoh of the Exodus, as we will see in the rest of this chapter.

III. AMENEMHET IV CONTINUED THE OPPRESSION OF HIS FATHER, AMENEMHET III

The Bible says that the Pharaoh of the Exodus continued the oppressive treatment of the Israelite slaves as did his father and grandfather.

> **Exodus 2:23-25** -- During that long period, the king of Egypt died [the Pharaoh who tried to kill Moses]. The Israelites groaned in their slavery and cried out, and their cry for help because of their slavery went up to God. God heard their groaning and he remembered his covenant with Abraham, with Isaac and with Jacob. So God looked on the Israelites and was concerned about them. NIV

When Moses returned to Egypt, Israelites were still being abused as slaves on work projects in Goshen. When Moses attempted to persuade Pharaoh to let the people take a three-day journey into the desert to worship God, the Pharaoh of the Exodus called the Israelites lazy. He also whipped the Israelite foremen and increased the work load of the other Israelite slaves by forcing them to gather their own straw to make bricks. He also demanded that the Israelite slaves continue to produce the same quota of bricks, in spite of the extra burden to gather the straw.[8]

A. Amenemhet IV's Slave Labor

In the previous chapter we saw that Amenemhet III continued Sesostris III's policy of using slave labor to construct cities in the land of Goshen. Hayes informs us that the wealth, prosperity and construction of Amenemhet III continued on through the reign of his son Amenemhet IV. Hayes specifically mentions that the monuments of Amenemhet IV are numerous and of excellent workmanship. Records also show that Amenemhet IV continued to work the turquoise mines in Sinai through his ninth year. Amenemhet IV continued Egypt's commercial trade with foreign countries. Hayes reports that a vase with Amenemhet IV's cartouche was discovered in the tomb of a prince of Byblos in Lebanon.[9] Albright also wrote that scarabs, as well as inscriptional evidence, link Tombs I & II of Byblos with both Amenemhet III and Amenemhet IV.[10] This evidence testifies to Egypt's continued influence in Palestine and Asia during the reign of Amenemhet IV. The continued prosperity and expansion of the twelfth dynasty under Amenemhet IV demonstrate that the large number of foreign slaves in his father's reign were still constructing in Goshen in the reign of this last male Pharaoh of the twelfth dynasty.

B. Amenemhet IV's Sphinx Appearance

A gold pectoral and a small sphinx of Amenemhet IV were also found in excavations at Beirut, Lebanon.[11] The sphinx expresses the figure of the king in the form of a lion, the strongest of animals capable of overpowering and devouring its foes. Amenemhet IV's Queen, Sebeknefru, also had her sculptors picture her in the form of a sphinx.[12] Sesostris III, the first Pharaoh of the oppression, was also the first twelfth-dynasty king to revive the sphinx as a symbol of his royal power and domination of others.[13] We saw previously how Amenemhet III, the father of Amenemhet IV, also used the sphinx to demonstrate his oppressive power over others. Thus, Amenemhet IV clearly displays the same abusive characteristics of his grandfather, Sesostris III, and of his father, Amenemhet III, both of whom oppressed the Hebrew slaves.

C. Amenemhet IV's Honor of the Crocodile God
And the Cobra Goddess

Amenemhet IV also gave great honor to the crocodile god, as did his father Amenemhet III. Amenemhet IV's Queen, Sebeknefru, was also his sister. Her name included that of the crocodile god, Sobek, which we pointed out in the previous chapter. As the lion of the sphinx destroyed Egypt's enemies on land, so the crocodile devoured Egypt's enemies in water.

One of Amenemhet IV's projects as king was to finish a temple that his father Amenemhet III began in honor of Renenutet.[14] Renenutet was the cobra goddess and the divine wife of Sobek (Sobk), the crocodile god.[15] The poisonous cobra also represented the sinister spirit of Amenemhet IV. On the wood and ivory cosmetic box of Kemuny, Amenemhet IV's butler, a painted picture shows Amenemhet IV seated with a crown on his head with a cobra sticking out in front.[16] See his cosmetic box in Figure 18-A below.

When the Pharaoh of the Exodus requested Moses to perform a miracle to prove that he was God's messenger, Aaron threw down his staff in front of Pharaoh and his officials and the staff became a snake, likely a cobra. When Pharaoh's magicians also turned their staffs into snakes, then Aaron's snake/staff swallowed up the snake/staffs of the magicians,[17] proving that the God of Israel was more powerful than the cobra goddess of Renenutet that appeared on the crown of Amenemhet IV. Of course, the cobra was worshiped as a god both before and after the twelfth dynasty, and thus offers no special evidence that points to Amenemhet IV as the Pharaoh of the Exodus. However, the cobra on the crown of Amenemhet IV certainly harmonizes with the Biblical picture of the Pharaoh of the Exodus as one who was very interested in snakes when Aaron's staff turned into a snake and devoured the snakes of Pharaoh's officials.

IV. THE CAPITAL OF AMENEMHET IV REMAINED
AT "ZOAN" (ITJTOWY)

Numbers 13:22 and Psalm 78:12, 43 clearly name **Zoan** as the Egyptian capital of the Pharaoh of the Exodus, not Rameses, the store city of Exodus 1:11. Chapter Sixteen presented indisputable Biblical evidence that the Pharaohs of Egypt remained in the same capital of Zoan from the time of Joseph to the time of the Exodus. Chapter Sixteen also presented solid historical evidence that the Pharaohs of the twelfth dynasty also remained in the same capital of Itjtowy during their entire reign and that Itjtowy was located in the Delta of Egypt, in the area of Zoan (Tanis). Thus, Amenemhet IV's capital of Itjtowy fits perfectly the Biblical description of Zoan from the time of Joseph to Moses and the Exodus. Zoan could have been the district in which Itjtowy was the capital, or vice versa.

FIGURE 18 A
COSMETIC BOX OF AMENEMHET IV'S BUTLER, KEMUNY, FOUND IN THEBES
Permission granted by the Metropolitan Museum of Art. (26.7.1351; 26.7.1439-1442; 27.9.1; 10.176.54; 10.130.1269a-c)

V. AMENEMHET IV WAS A "RA" PHARAOH

Amenemhet IV likely oversaw the finishing touches or improvements on the store cities of Rameses and Pithom begun by his grandfather Sesostris III, and expanded by his father Amenemhet III. Scholars have mistakenly identified Ramses II as the king who first constructed the city of Rameses because of the similarity of their names. **Actually, the original store city of Rameses was constructed by twelfth-dynasty Pharaohs. One hundred years later** the store city of Rameses was destroyed by the Hyksos, who constructed their new capital of Avaris on top of the ruins of Rameses. **Four hundred years later** Ramses II destroyed the capital city of Avaris and constructed his new capital of Pi-Ramesse on top of the ruins of Avaris and the old store city of Rameses. For details see Chapter 15.

Rameses means "born or produced by Ra, the sun-god of Egypt." The twelfth-dynasty Pharaohs, Sesostris III, Amenemhet III and Amenemhet IV were also "Ra" kings, and thus qualify as much as Ramses II to construct a city by the name of Rameses. Amenemhet IV's throne name was "Maot-Kheru-**Ra**."[18] The "Ra" at the end of his name appears first in his hieroglyphic inscription, but is usually read last by scholars. His father, Amenemhet III, also had "Ra" in his name (Maot-En-**Ra**),[19] as did his father Sesostris III (Kho-Kau-**Ra**).[20] We saw earlier that these twelfth-dynasty kings called themselves "Sons of Ra," considering themselves to be "born of Ra." Thus, the construction of a store city with the name "Rameses" fits equally well with the "Ra" Pharaohs of the twelfth dynasty as does Ramses II's capital city of Rameses, built 500 years later on the same site of the former store city.

VI. AMENEMHET IV'S MISSING TOMB

Exodus 4:19 -- Now the LORD had said to Moses in Midian, "Go back to Egypt, for **all the men who wanted to kill you are dead."**

All who tried to kill Moses died before he returned to Egypt. Therefore, the Pharaoh of the Exodus was not yet born, or was only a small child, when Moses fled Egypt. Hayes believes that Amenemhet IV's short reign indicates he died of old age.[21] However, I propose that Amenemhet IV was born about the fifteenth year of Amenemhet III's reign, shortly before Moses fled to Midian. On this basis Amenemhet IV was only a toddler when Moses left Egypt. Therefore, he never knew Moses and did not recognize Moses when he returned to Egypt.

In support of the idea that Amenemhet IV died prematurely and unexpectedly during his middle-age years, **I propose the case of his missing tomb. All of the previous twelfth-dynasty Pharaohs built magnificent pyramids for their burial.** They also built tombs within the pyramid complex for their family members and important officials. The pyramids of all of these prior twelfth-dynasty kings are located around Lake Moeris in the Faiyum. **However, the pyramid complex of Amenemhet IV and his Queen Sebeknefru has never been found.**

The remains of two small pyramids at Mazghuna, between Dahshur and El-Lisht, were once thought to have been the tombs of Ammenemes IV and his successor, Queen Sobkneferu; but their close similarity to the pyramid of King Khendjer at Saqqara makes it more probable that they are to be dated to the middle of the Thirteenth Dynasty.[22]

The absence of Amenemhet IV's tomb suggests that he died prematurely and before he was old enough to feel a need to build his own pyramid. If Amenemhet IV were already old when he became king, both he and his father would have constructed their pyramids during the same period, or at least shortly after Amenemhet III died. In fact, both father Amenemhet III and son Amenemhet IV united in constructing a temple dedicated to Renenutet, the cobra harvest goddess. The temple was located in the Faiyum not far from Amenemhet III's large pyramid complex.[23] Why did the two kings not construct Amenemhet IV's pyramid instead of the temple, if Amenemhet IV were old? This co-construction also confirms a short co-reign of both Amenemhet III and Amenemhet IV.

Indeed, if Amenemhet IV thought his death were imminent, he would have begun construction of his pyramid in the beginning of his nine-year reign and would have had sufficient time to complete it.   We have already seen above that Amenemhet IV constructed numerous monuments and had plenty of wealth to construct the pyramid of his choice. In fact Amenemhet IV inscribed his name on a door lintel of a building within the north pyramid of Amenemhet I at El Lisht.[24]

The casket of Amenemhet IV's butler, Kemuny, has been found in a tomb at Thebes with the figure and name of Amenemhet IV.   See Figure 18-A above. Kemuny's figure is seen making offerings to the deified King Amenemhet IV.[25] Strange that the tomb of Amenemhet IV's butler has been found, **but not the tomb of Amenemhet IV and his Queen, Sebeknefru.**

The unexpected and mysterious death of Amenemhet IV fits the premature death of the Pharaoh of the Exodus in the Red Sea. Christians use the **empty tomb** of Jesus Christ as a strong argument for His resurrection. The **missing tomb** of Amenemhet IV strongly suggests that he is the Pharaoh of the Exodus who died prematurely in the Red Sea. Amazing evidence will be presented in Chapters Nineteen and Twenty that Amenemhet IV died with his army by drowning in water.

VII. AMENEMHET IV'S FIRST-BORN SON DID NOT SIT ON THE THRONE

If Amenemhet IV was born a few years before Moses fled Egypt, he was about forty-five years old when Moses returned to Egypt. Amenemhet IV likely had a son between twenty and twenty-five years old. If Amenemhet IV was indeed the Pharaoh of the Exodus, the Bible says that he definitely had a firstborn son, for the tenth plague, which was the death of the firstborn of both men and livestock, included the death of **"the firstborn son of Pharaoh."**[26] In Chapter Nineteen we will see that tomb inscriptions indicate that the death of the firstborn actually occurred all over Egypt at the end of the twelfth dynasty. Is there any evidence that Amenemhet IV's eldest son died in the plague of the firstborn?

Ipuwer's papyrus, dated to the period that includes Amenemhet IV's reign, mentions the death of the king and the survival of some of his princes.[27] These princes were likely young boys who were **not the first-born and were not trained to sit on the throne of their father.** The first-born of Amenemhet IV was likely the son of Sebeknefru, the chief Queen, sister and chief wife of Amenemhet IV. Most of the twelfth dynasty kings married their sisters as their chief Queen.[28] Since Pharaohs were worshiped as gods, they believed that the divine seed would be best preserved by a union in which both the female and male were the offspring of the previous Pharaoh. **However, Amenemhet IV's firstborn son did not reign in his place because his Queen/mother, Sebeknefru, succeeded her husband to the throne.**[29] **Why?** The Bible quotation below explains why Amenemhet IV's firstborn son failed to reign after this father's death.

Exodus 11:4-7 -- So Moses said, "This is what the LORD says: 'About midnight I will go throughout Egypt. **Every firstborn son in Egypt will**

die, from the firstborn son of Pharaoh, who sits on the throne, to the firstborn son of the slave girl, who is at her hand mill, and all the firstborn of the cattle as well. **There will be loud wailing throughout Egypt--worse than there has ever been or ever will be again.'"** NIV

The tenth and last Biblical plague that killed all of the firstborn of Egypt, included **Pharaoh's firstborn son. The plague of the death of the firstborn** gives us a logical explanation as to why Amenemhet IV's firstborn did not ascend to his throne. His firstborn died shortly before Amenemhet IV himself died by drowning in the Red Sea. Thus, Queen Sebeknefru ascended the throne in view of the death of her firstborn son and the death of her brother/husband, Amenemhet IV.

In Chapter Nineteen we will show proof from Egyptian tomb inscriptions that the death of the firstborn of Egypt occurred all over Egypt at a time that is consistent with the end of Amenemhet IV's reign.

VIII. AMENEMHET IV'S BROKEN NOSE

The Cairo Museum contains an unidentified bust of a twelfth dynasty Pharaoh. The name of the Pharaoh has been scraped off and the nose has been smashed. The museum has a caption beneath the bust, attributing it to either Amenemhet IV or Sesostris II. See my photo of this bust in Figure 18-B.

FIGURE 18-B
THE SEVERED HEAD AND BROKEN NOSE OF
AMENEMHET IV'S STATUE
Photo by Ted Stewart, Cairo Museum, June, 1991

I asked my Egyptian guide, Badhr, why the Pharaoh's name was scratched off and the nose was broken? He explained that the noses of statues were sometimes accidentally broken. However, if the name was scraped off intentionally, then the broken nose was a brazen act to dishonor the Pharaoh. What Pharaoh deserved more to have his nose broken off his face than the Pharaoh of the Exodus? The statue of Amenemhet IV's broken nose is another evidence that qualifies him to be the Pharaoh, who brought upon Egypt the ten worst plagues in its entire history, plus the destruction of Egypt's army in the Red Sea.

Amenemhet IV provoked the God of Israel to send the ten worst plagues of Egyptian history, resulting in the loss of its fish industry, its crops, its livestock, its firstborn, its slaves and its army. We will show in Chapter Twenty that Amenemhet IV's actions also resulted in the fall of the glorious twelfth dynasty and the subsequent division and conquest of Egypt by foreign powers. No Pharaoh of Egypt deserved more dishonor than the Pharaoh of the Exodus. If this dishonored statue is that of Amenemhet IV, it furnishes us with another clue that he was the flint-hearted Pharaoh of the Exodus.

CONCLUSION

This chapter contains fourteen historical links between Amenemhet IV and the Biblical Pharaoh of the Exodus. These fourteen synchronisms are listed in Table 18-C and give us a review of Chapter Eighteen. In the next two chapters we will see additional evidences that support the identification of Amenemhet IV as the Pharaoh of the Exodus.

TABLE 18-C
FOURTEEN DISCOVERIES THAT IDENTIFY AMENEMHET IV
AS THE PHARAOH OF THE EXODUS

Discovery No. 1. Amenemhet IV's short reign of nine years, three months and twenty-seven days, **less 6 years of co-reign,** give the Pharaoh of the Exodus a sole reign **of only two years, three months and twenty-seven days.**

Discovery No. 2. The total years of reigns of Sesostris III, Amenemhet III and Amenemhet IV, match the Bible chronology of Moses' eighty years of age at the time of the Exodus.

Discovery No. 3. The chronological pattern of these three successive kings' reigns don't compare with reigns of three successive kings in any other dynasty.

Discovery No. 4. Carbon-14 dating of Sesostris III's reign proves that Amenemhet IV reigned in 1446 B.C., the Bible date of the Exodus.

Discovery No. 5. Amenemhet IV continued the construction in Goshen, using slave labor, as did Sesostris III and Amenemhet III, as the Bible describes.

Discovery No. 6. Amenemhet IV used the sphinx to express the lion's oppressive and devouring power that characterized his own wicked reign that fits the Biblical picture of the true Pharaoh of the Exodus.

Discovery No. 7. Amenemhet IV honored the crocodile god as his father did. His Queen bore the name of the crocodile god, who devoured the king's enemies in water, a practice imitated by the Pharaohs of the Oppression.

Discovery No. 8. Amenemhet IV honored the cobra goddess and wore a cobra on his crown, as the Pharaoh of the Exodus no doubt did when Aaron's snake (cobra) swallowed up the snakes (cobras) of Pharaoh's magicians, showing the superiority of the God of Moses.

Discovery No. 9. Amenemhet IV did not construct a new capital, but continued in the same capital of Itjtowy located in the northeastern delta of Egypt, fitting the Biblical description of the capital of the Pharaoh of the Exodus.

Discovery No. 10. Amenemhet IV was a "son of Ra" like his father and grandfather, fitting the name of "Rameses" as one of the store cities built by the Israelites and fitting the Ra god as the favorite of the twelfth dynasty.

Discovery No. 11. The missing pyramid of Amenemhet IV confirms that he died prematurely, as was the case of the Biblical Pharaoh of the Exodus.

Discovery No. 12. The tomb of Amenemhet IV's butler has been found, but the tomb and pyramid of Amenemhet IV and his Queen have never been found.

Discovery No. 13. The fact that Amenemhet IV's sister/wife took over his throne instead of his first-born son fits harmoniously with the Biblical story of the death of Pharaoh's firstborn son in the tenth and final plague that God sent upon Egypt.

Discovery No. 14. The broken nose and scraped-off name of the statue of Amenemhet IV fit the dishonor that the Pharaoh of the Exodus was given by his co-patriots after Egypt lost its slaves, its Pharaoh and its army.

TABLE 18-D
RUNNING TOTAL OF DISCOVERIES

Chapter	Chapter Total	Running Total
2 Conflict Between Biblical and Secular Histories	18	18
4 Discovery of 430 Years from Abraham to the Exodus	16	34
5 Confirmation of Abraham's Historicity	28	62
6 Discovery of the Remains of Sodom and Gomorrah	17	79
7 Joseph As a Slave and Prisoner in Amenemhet I's Reign	21	100
8 Joseph Becomes the Vizier of Sesostris I	23	123
9 Sesostris I Gives Joseph a New Name and a Wife	11	134
10 The Seven Years of Abundance in Sesostris I's Reign	10	144
11 The Seven Years of Famine in Sesostris I's Reign	20	164
12 Israel Enters Egypt during Sesostris I's Reign	14	178
13 Sesostris III Enslaves the Israelites	17	195
14 Sesostris III, The Foster Grandfather of Moses	12	207
15 Sesostris III, Builder of Rameses and Pithom	15	222
16 Zoan (Itjtowy), the Capital of the Twelfth Dynasty	16	238
17 Amenemhet III, the Pharaoh Who Tried to Kill Moses	15	253
18 Amenemhet IV, the Pharaoh of the Exodus	14	267

NOTES OF CHAPTER EIGHTEEN

1. Acts 7:23; Exodus 2:11-15.
2. Acts 7:30; Exodus 7:7.
3. Exodus 2:23.
4. Exodus 4:19.
5. Josephus, Antiquities of the Jews," 2.13.2; 2.16.3, *Works of Josephus*, 72, 76.
6. "Chronological Tables," *Cambridge Ancient History*, II.1.819 and II.2.1038.
7. Petrie, *A History of Egypt*, I.150.
8. Exodus 5:1-21.
9. William Hayes, "Egypt: From the Death of Ammenemes III to Seqenenre II," *Cambridge Ancient History*, II.1.42.
10. William Albright, *Archaeology of Palestine* (Gloucester: Peter Smith, 1971), 84.
11. Hayes, *Cambridge Ancient History*, "Egypt: From the Death of Ammenemes III to Seqenenre II," II.1.42-43.
12. Hayes, *Cambridge Ancient History*, II.1.43.
13. Hayes, *Scepter of Egypt*, I.197-199.
14. Hayes, "Middle Kingdom of Egypt," *Cambridge Ancient History*, I.2A.517
15. Hayes, *Cambridge Ancient History* I.2A.520.
16. Hayes, *Scepter of Egypt*, I.245, Figure 157.
17. Exodus 7:8-13.
18. W. F. Petrie, *A History of Egypt*, I.206.
19. Petrie, *A History of Egypt*, I.192.
20. Petrie, *A History of Egypt*, I.183.
21. Hayes, "Egypt: From the Death of Ammenemes III to Seqenenre II," *Cambridge Ancient History*, II.1.42.
22. Hayes, "Reforms of Sesostris III," I.2A.530; II.1.43. 23. *Ibid*.
24. Hayes, *Scepter of Egypt*, I.200.
25. Hayes, *Scepter of Egypt*, I.201, 246.
26. Exodus 11:5.
27. Miriam Lichtheim (Trans.), "The Admonitions of Ipuwer," *Ancient Egyptian Literature*, I.156.
28. Hayes, "Egypt: From the Death of Ammenemes III to Seqenenre II," *Cambridge Ancient History*, II.1.43.
29. Petrie, *A History of Egypt*, I.207.

CHAPTER NINETEEN
MOSES AND IPUWER REPORT
THE TEN PLAGUES

God sent ten plagues upon Egypt to convince Pharaoh to free the Israelites. The Bible (NIV) says these plagues were the worst natural calamities in all of Egyptian history.

Exodus 9:24 -- It was the **worst storm in all the land of Egypt since it had become a nation.**
Exodus 10:14 -- **Never before had there been such a plague of locusts, nor will there ever be again.**
Exodus 11:6 -- **There will be loud wailing throughout Egypt---worse than there has ever been or ever will be again.** NIV

After the eighth plague Pharaoh's officials asked the Pharaoh of the Exodus: **"Do you not yet realize that Egypt is ruined?"**[1] Egyptian writers seldom recorded the failures of Pharaohs or the calamities of Egypt. However, the historical magnitude of the ten Biblical plagues was too significant to be overlooked. **Ipuwer, the high priest of Heliopolis in the late twelfth dynasty, recorded an eyewitness account of eight calamitous plagues that devastated Egypt economically, socially and politically.** Ipuwer's description of this disastrous upheaval fits precisely the **Biblical record of eight of the ten plagues that led to the ruin of Egypt.**

The tenth and most devastating plague in the Bible was the death of the firstborn of both humans and animals. Amazingly, inscriptions about the death of the firstborn are found in tombs all over Egypt that are dated to the archaeological period that includes the twelfth dynasty. This chapter presents persuasive evidences that the ten plagues fell at the end of the twelfth dynasty during the reign of Amenemhet IV, the last male Pharaoh of the twelfth dynasty.

I. VELIKOVSKY SAW THE BIBLICAL PLAGUES IN THE IPUWER PAPYRUS

Immanuel Velikovsky, disdained by most scholars for his unorthodox ideas on Egyptian history, was the first I know to identify the *Ipuwer Papyrus* as an Egyptian record of the ten plagues and Israel's Exodus from Egypt.[2] Velikovsky dated the document to the middle of the thirteenth dynasty. He misinterpreted the document to include not only the Exodus, but also the invasion of Egypt by the Hyksos (foreigners from Palestine or Arabia).[3] Appendix A shows how Velikovsky's dating of the Exodus in the thirteenth dynasty incurs serious historical contradictions with the Biblical record. However, Velikovsky's discovery of Exodus events in the *Ipuwer Papyrus* is his greatest contribution to the solution of the Exodus problem, despite his misdating of the document.

II. THE DATE OF IPUWER'S PAPYRUS

John A. Wilson said the only extant copy of the manuscript of Ipuwer was written in the New Kingdom of either the nineteenth or twentieth dynasty. However, Wilson admitted that the orthography and language belonged to the Middle Kingdom and thus believed the manuscript was a copy of a much older document. In spite of the Middle Kingdom style of Ipuwer, Wilson dated the calamity hundreds of years earlier in the First Intermediate Period between the Old and Middle Kingdoms.[4]

A. H. Gardiner, a notable grammarian of Egyptian hieroglyphics,[5] identified the style and language of the *Ipuwer Papyrus* as the work of a **twelfth dynasty author, but** he also believed that the calamities occurred centuries earlier. He thus believed that Ipuwer wrote the narrative in the style of a "historical romance".[6]

William C. Hayes interpreted Ipuwer's work as an eye witness report of a national disaster greater than the calamities of Egypt's First Intermediate Period. He dated Ipuwer's writing to the end of the twelfth dynasty.

Hayes: When they failed [Amenemhet IV and his wife Sobeknefru, the last rulers of the Twelfth Dynasty], **the land relapsed gradually into a state as chaotic** as that of the First Intermediate period and **marked by even greater national calamities.**[7]

Thus, Hayes interpreted Ipuwer's treatise to be true history that occurred at the end of the twelfth dynasty in Ipuwer's lifetime.

Ms. Lichtheim has produced an excellent modern translation of Ipuwer's treatise. She dates the work to the "**late** Middle Kingdom," which includes the period covering the late twelfth and thirteenth dynasties. However, Ms. Lichtheim considers the document to be "non-historical" and of "purely literary inspiration."[8]

Before we discuss whether Ipuwer was writing history or fiction, let us note that most of the scholars cited above are agreed on one point: **the spelling, language and style of the document indicate a date of origin in the late twelfth dynasty or early thirteenth dynasty. Therefore, Ipuwer qualifies to be a likely contemporary of King Amenemhet IV, the last male Pharaoh of the twelfth dynasty, and the very king we have identified as the Pharaoh of the Exodus.**

III. DID IPUWER WRITE HISTORY,
OR PHILOSOPHICAL FICTION?

The reader is urged to read Ms. Lichtheim's excellent modern translation of "The Admonitions of Ipuwer."[9] All quotations in this book are taken from her translation unless otherwise stated. The document is fragmented in places. Thus, some quotations are incomplete.

Ms. Lichtheim and other modern scholars believe that Ipuwer's treatise is not based on historical fact, but is written in the style of other Egyptian literature that deals philosophically with the problem of evil and national distress. Ms. Lichtheim cites "The Complaints of Khakheperre-Sonb" as another example of philosophical literature of twelfth dynasty literature, rather than true history.[10]

However, I examined "The Complaints of Khakheprerre-Sonb" in Chapter Thirteen and it appears to me that it was a true criticism of the evil and oppressive changes that Sesostris III made when he enslaved Israel and took away the power of his Egyptian nomarchs (governors). If my interpretation is correct, this document is a historical criticism of the reign of Sesostris III, not a philosophical treatise, as Ms. Lichtheim suggests.

Ms. Lichtheim cites the work of S. Luria, a French author, to express what she believes is the strongest case against the historicity of Ipuwer's work, namely that his description of the chaos "is inherently contradictory, hence historically impossible."[11] Below we quote Lichtheim's only example of Ipuwer's "inherently contradictory" history.

> On the one hand the land is said to suffer from total want; on the other hand the poor are described as having become rich, of wearing fine clothes, and generally of disposing of all that once belonged to their masters.[12]

The Biblical Exodus rationally explains what S. Luria and Ms. Lichtheim consider historically "impossible." The land had just suffered total and sudden devastation from the ten plagues. However, the wealthy Egyptians still had their riches, food and goods stored up in their homes. When Israel left Egypt, the Bible reports that the Israelite slaves asked their Egyptian masters to share their riches with them. The Egyptians generously responded.

> Exodus 11:2-3 -- "Tell the people that men and women alike are to ask their neighbors for articles of silver and gold." The Lord made the Egyptians favorably disposed toward the people, and Moses himself was highly regarded in Egypt by Pharaoh's officials and by the people. NIV

God formerly promised in Genesis 15:14 that Israel would leave Egypt with "great substance." Thus, the Israelite slaves, included among the poor of Egypt, left with part of the stored riches of their wealthy masters, precisely as the *Ipuwer Papyrus* explains later in this chapter. Chapter Twenty will show that the departure of the Israelite slaves and the subsequent destruction of Egypt's army in the Red Sea likely enticed the non-Israelite slaves and other poor people who remained in Egypt to invade the homes of the wealthy and take away their remaining possessions by force. Therefore, what Ms. Lichtheim considered "inherently contradictory and historically impossible" is inherently consistent and historically accurate in the context of the events surrounding the Exodus. As we proceed in this chapter, we will see how Ipuwer's eyewitness testimony uniquely confirms the Biblical record of eight of the ten plagues.

IV. DID IPUWER WRITE OF PAST HISTORY,
OR CONTEMPORARY HISTORY

We saw above that the scholars, Wilson and Gardiner, believed that Ipuwer, a twelfth-dynasty author, was describing calamities that occurred hundreds of years earlier at the end of the sixth dynasty. However, notice the following excerpts from *Ipuwer's Papyrus* that clearly point to events contemporary with Ipuwer's own time. Ipuwer specifically says that he is writing of a **present fulfillment** of what was predicted in the past : Lichtheim's Translation: 2:9-10 -- Lo, the face is pale .... **What the ancestors foretold has happened.**[13] Therefore, Ipuwer **denies that he is writing of past events,** but affirms that he is writing contemporary history that fulfilled past predictions. Thus, Ipuwer himself **categorically rejects the idea that he was recording events that occurred hundreds of years earlier.**

The entire document is mostly written in the **present tense, hardly the tense to write about history that occurred hundreds of years earlier.** Ipuwer occasionally used the past tense to refer to an event that occurred immediately before the present crisis that he describes: Lichtheim's Translation: "(4:5) Lo, gone is what **yesterday** was seen. . . . . (7:1) See **now**, things are done that **never were before**."[14] "**Now**" obviously refers to the present time when Ipuwer wrote.

However, when Ipuwer writes in the present tense he constantly includes himself with the pronouns I, me, we, us and our, thus demonstrating that he and his fellow Egyptians were personally experiencing the very calamities he was describing. Notice below the we, I, my, and me pronouns of Ipuwer's personal observations of what was happening in his own lifetime.

Lichtheim's Translation,: 3:6 -- None indeed sail north to Byblos **today.** What shall **we** do for pine trees for **our** mummies? . . . 3:8 -- What good is a treasury without its revenues? . . . What shall **we** do about it? All is ruin![15] . . . 6:5 -- Had **I** raised **my** voice at that time to save **me** from the pain **I** am in! . . . 6:8 -- Woe is **me** for the grief of **this time**.[16] [Emphasis mine].

Ipuwer also constantly uses the word **"See" in the imperative** and **"Lo"** as an exclamation **to look**, each as a command or exhortation to his readers to observe for themselves the actual and present calamities he is describing. Note this below.

Lichtheim's Translation: 2:10 – **Lo**, the river **is** blood, . . . 2:11 -- **Lo**, crocodiles gorge on their catch, . . . 2:12 – **Lo**, people **are** diminished.[17] . . . 7:2 -- **See now,** the land **is** deprived of kingship . . . . 7:6 -- **See,** the land **is** tied up in gangs. . . . 7:8 -- **See,** the judges of the land **are** driven from the land.[18] (Emphasis is mine]

The expression **"Lo"** occurs **fifty-four times** in Ipuwer's first six chapters and **"See"** occurs **forty-six times** in chapters seven through nine. These exhortations for the reader to behold with his own eyes what Ipuwer was describing in the present tense is **persuasive evidence** that these events were occurring contemporaneously as Ipuwer wrote. The author of a historical romance does not exhort his readers to look for themselves at what he is describing. Rather, a historical romance simply describes the past as if in the present without urging the readers to look for themselves to verify what he describes. For these reasons and others that we could mention, Ipuwer's document should be accepted as an eyewitness report of what he and his original Egyptian readers had seen and experienced at the end of the twelfth dynasty.

V. THE LAMENTATIONS OF IPUWER

In my opinion "The Admonitions of Ipuwer" would be better named "The **Lamentations of Ipuwer.**" Ipuwer is not reminding the Egyptians of a past disaster, nor is he warning his fellow Egyptians of an impending evil. Rather, Ipuwer is expressing his profound grief over a devastation that has already brought economic, social and political chaos to Egypt and continues on as Ipuwer writes. At the end of his treatise, Ipuwer appears to criticize an Egyptian god for permitting such misery to occur in Egypt. Ipuwer admonishes little. He groans continually. He criticizes some. Yet, at the end of his treatise he hopes for better times. This chapter compares the contents and language of the *Ipuwer Papyrus* with the Biblical record of the ten plagues.

A. The Capital Was Located in Northern Egypt, Close to The Delta.

At the time of the Exodus, Moses lived with the Israelites in the land of Goshen in the southeastern delta of Egypt (Exodus 9:26; Numbers 33:3; Genesis 45:10). The Egyptian capital was close to the land of Goshen in Moses' time, as it was in the days of Joseph (Genesis 45:10), for Moses traveled between the land of Goshen and the capital sometimes on a daily basis (Exodus 8:20). In Chapter Sixteen I identified this Egyptian capital as Biblical Zoan and I equated Zoan with Tanis and Itjtowy, the capital of the twelfth dynasty. Ipuwer also implies that the capital was located in the delta in northern (lower) Egypt when he wrote.

> Lichtheim's Translation: Ch. 10 -- Lower Egypt [northern Egypt] weeps. **The king's storehouse is "I go-get-it," for everyone, and the whole palace is without its revenues.**[19] Ch. 4 -- Lo, **the whole Delta cannot be seen**, Lower Egypt puts trust in trodden roads.[20]

Ipuwer's statement in his chapter 10 implies that the king's storehouse and palace were located in the delta of Lower Egypt. Thus, the geographical location of the Egyptian capital in the *Ipuwer Papyrus* fits precisely that of **Itjtowy of the twelfth dynasty and that of the Egyptian capital of Zoan in Moses' day.** Psalm 78:12, says that God "did miracles in the sight of their fathers [Israelites] in the land of Egypt, **in the region of Zoan [Tanis].**"

B. The Plagues Covered All of Egypt

The Bible reports that many of the ten plagues affected the entire land of Egypt, not just northern Egypt.

Exodus 7: 21 -- Blood was **everywhere in Egypt.** . . . Exodus 8:17 -- All the dust **throughout the land of Egypt** became gnats. . . . Exodus 8:24 -- . . . **throughout Egypt** the land was ruined by the flies. . . . Exodus 9:9 – It will become fine dust over **the whole land of Egypt,** and festering boils will break out of men and animals **throughout the land.** . . . Exodus 9:22 - . . . hail will fall **all over Egypt** . . . Exodus 10:7 -- Do you not realize that **Egypt is ruined?** . . . Exodus 10:15 -- . . . Nothing green remained on tree or plant **in all the land of Egypt.** NIV

Ipuwer also said that the calamities of his day had occurred in **both northern (lower) and southern (upper) Egypt.**

Lichtheim: Ch. 2- - There's blood everywhere . . . Towns are ravaged, **Upper Egypt** became wasteland . . . **the land is injured.** . . . Ch. 4:5 -- Lo the **whole Delta** cannot be seen, **Lower Egypt** puts trust in trodden roads.[21] [Emphasis mine]

Therefore, Ipuwer's plagues were national in scope, often covering the entirety of Upper and Lower Egypt in the same manner as the Biblical plagues. Velikovsky quoted Gardiner as also agreeing with this "nation wide" interpretation of Ipuwer's plagues: "It is no merely local disturbance that is here described, but a great and overwhelming national disaster."[22] Hayes also believed that at the end of the twelfth dynasty Egypt suffered **"even greater national calamities"** than those that occurred at the end of the First Intermediate period (end of the sixth dynasty).[23]

C. The Plague of Water Turning to Blood

The Bible says that the first plague turned the Nile River and other bodies of water into blood.

Exodus 7:17-20 -- (17) With the staff that is in my hand I will strike the water of the Nile, and it will be changed into blood. (18) The fish in the Nile will die, and the river will stink; the Egyptians will not be able to drink its water. (19) The Lord said to Moses, Tell Aaron, "Take your staff and stretch out your hand over the waters of Egypt -- over the streams and canals, over the ponds and all the reservoirs -- and they will turn to blood. **Blood will be everywhere in Egypt, even in the wooden buckets and stone jars.**" . . . (21) **The fish in the Nile died, and the river smelled so bad that the Egyptians could not drink its water. Blood was everywhere in Egypt.** NIV

Ipuwer also reported that the Nile River had turned to blood and that blood was "everywhere" in Egypt. Ipuwer said that the Egyptians could not drink the water of the Nile, just as the Bible says in the citation above.

> Lichtheim: **Ch. 2 -- There's blood everywhere, . . . Lo, the river is blood. As one drinks of it, one shrinks from people and thirsts for water.**[24] [emphasis mine]

No other reference in ancient Egyptian literature states that "blood is everywhere," that "the river is blood," and that people who lived beside the Nile thirsted for water. Ipuwer remarkably used the same language of the Bible to describe the first plague of blood.

In Exodus 7:21 the fish in the Nile River died and began to stink horribly when the River turned to blood. **Ipuwer also implied that the fishing industry had ceased as a result of the plagues that fell upon Egypt in his day.**

> Lichtheim: Ch. 13 -- If only you would taste a little of **these miseries!** Then you would say, [lacuna] It is however good when ships sail upstream [lacuna] It is, however, good when the net is drawn in.[25]

The Bible reports that the Nile's turning to blood caused the death of all of the fish, explaining why fishermen no longer sailed on the Nile and no longer cast their nets. For this reason Ipuwer longed for the day that once again Egyptians could sail the Nile and resume their profession of fishing. The cessation of the fishing industry in Egypt thus appears in both the Bible and Ipuwer's Papyrus, another remarkable synchronism.

D.   Plagues 2, 3, & 4:   Frogs, Gnats and Flies
Upon Humans And Animals

These three plagues of frogs, gnats and flies mostly nauseated and inconvenienced both humans and animals (Exodus 8). Since these plagues did not cause permanent damage, Ipuwer may have purposefully omitted these plagues.

E.   Plagues 5, 6 & 7 - Disease, Boils and Hail Brought
Suffering and Destruction for Egypt's
Animals, Humans, and Crops.

The fifth plague spread a deadly disease among a large portion of the livestock of Egypt, while God protected the livestock of the Israelites (Exodus 9:1-7).   The sixth plague of boils on both men & animals, caused much suffering and death for many (Exodus 9:8-12) . The seventh plague of hail, the worst hail storm in the history of Egypt, killed the rest of the livestock of Egypt and also killed the Egyptian herders who remained in the open fields with the animals (Exodus 9:13-26). However, most Israelites and a few Egyptians heeded Moses' advice and sheltered their livestock from the hail. But the majority of the owners of livestock ignored Moses' advice and lost most of their livestock by these three plagues.

Notice below that *Ipuwer's Lamentations* also record the suffering of Egyptian livestock and the reduced numbers of livestock in Egypt.

> Lichtheim: Ch. 5 -- Lo, **all beasts, their hearts weep. Cattle bemoan the state of the land.** Ch. 12 -- **His herds are few**, but he spends the day herding them.[26] [emphasis mine]

Ipuwer thus confirms that the livestock of Egypt had became greatly diminished, confirming Moses' report concerning the three plagues that were directed toward the livestock of the Egyptians (Exodus 9:1-26).

F. The Seventh Plague of Hail and
the Eighth Plague of Locusts

The seventh plague of hail, plus the eighth plague of locusts combined to destroy all of the crops and the fruit trees of Egypt. However, the land of Goshen, where Israel lived, was spared from these plagues **(Exodus 9:13 -10.20)**

1. Excerpts From The Biblical Record: Exodus 9:25, 31-32 --
Throughout Egypt hail struck everything in the fields --- both men and animals; it beat down everything growing in the fields and stripped every tree. . . . (31) -- (The flax and barley were destroyed, since the barley had headed and the flax was in bloom. (32) The wheat and spelt, however, were not destroyed, because they ripen later.) NIV

Exodus 10:14-15 -- (14) . **Never before had there been such a plague of locusts, nor will there ever be again.** (15) They covered all the ground until it was black. **They devoured all that was left after the hail — everything growing in the fields and the fruit on the trees. Nothing green remained on tree or plant in all the land of Egypt.** NIV

2. *Ipuwer's Papyrus* describes below the same devastation of Egypt's crops, trees and vegetation. [emphasis mine]
Lichtheim: Ch. 3 -- **Lo, the desert claims the land,** The nomes are destroyed. . . . Noblewomen roam the land, Ladies say,'We want to eat.' . . . **Lacking are grain,** charcoal . . . brushwood.[27]
Lichtheim: Ch. 4 -- **Lo, gone is what yesterday was seen. The land is left to its weakness like a cutting of flax**.[28]
Lichtheim: Ch. 5-- **Food is lacking.** What does it taste like today? Lo the great hunger and suffer.[29]
Lichtheim: Ch. 6-- **Birds find neither fruit nor herbs.** One takes . . . from the mouth of pigs. No face is bright ----- hunger. **Lo, grain is lacking on all sides.** One is stripped of clothes, unanointed with

oil. Everyone says, 'There's nothing. The storehouse is bare"[30]

Ipuwer's comment in his chapter 4 above **("gone is what yesterday was seen")** describes the suddenness with which the abundant produce of Egypt's crops and trees disappeared. Ipuwer strangely did not mention the plagues of locusts and hail. But Ipuwer did report the results of these two plagues. Ipuwer reported the removal of Egypt's plant life **"like the cutting of flax."** The fact that **birds could find neither "fruit nor herbs"** fits precisely the Biblical expression, "Nothing remained on tree or plant in all the land of Egypt." (Exodus 10:15, NIV).

The "bare" storehouses that Ipuwer described fit exactly what would be expected after the Biblical plagues destroyed the crops of Egypt. The wheat and spelt that the Bible says were not destroyed (Exodus 9:31) enabled Egypt to survive complete loss of life, but were insufficient to fill the empty storehouses that Ipuwer reported. Ipuwer's words above precisely express the same devastation of Egypt that the Bible describes after the plagues of hail and locusts.

G. Egypt Is Ruined After the First 8 Plagues

The first eight plagues of Egypt literally destroyed Egypt. When Moses warned Pharaoh of the eighth plague, Pharaoh's officials urged the king to let the Israelites leave because Egypt had already been **"ruined."**

> Exodus 10:7 -- Pharaoh's officials said to him, "How long will this man be a snare to us? Let the people go, so that they may worship the Lord their God. **Do you not yet realize that Egypt is ruined?"**

Ipuwer also described the "ruinous" condition of the entire country of Egypt.

> Lichtheim: Ch. 2 --Towns are ravaged, Upper Egypt became wasteland. Lo, crocodiles gorge on their catch. . . . The land is injured. . . . Lo, people are diminished, . . . Ch. 3 – lo, the desert claims the land. The nomes are destroyed. . . . **All is ruin![31]**

Thus, Ipuwer used the word **"ruin"** to describe the state of Egypt in his time just as Pharaoh's officials did in the Biblical time of the ten plagues: " **Do you not yet realize that Egypt is ruined?"** (Exodus 10:7)

H. Plague 9 - The Plague Against Ra, The Sun-god

God's three-day plague of darkness was directed toward Ra, the sun-god of Egypt (Exodus 10:21-29). In previous chapters we learned that Ra was the chief god of the twelfth dynasty and that every king of this dynasty used the name of Ra in his or her name.

In a passage preceded by a long lacuna (broken space where the inscription has been damaged), Ipuwer criticizes the Egyptian god, Ra, for bringing to birth men during these evil times. Ipuwer asks Ra why he did not destroy the wicked in their first generation, so that they would not give birth to yet more evil men.

> Lichtheim: Ch. 12 -- Lo, why does he seek to fashion [men], when the timid is not distinguished from the violent? . . . Where is he today? Is he asleep? Lo, his power is not seen.[32]

Miriam Lichtheim makes the following comment on this passage:

> This section is interesting for being a criticism of the sun-god, the creator of gods and men, who is chided for passively permitting people to kill each other, instead of intervening.[33]

The ninth plague of **darkness** was directed against Egypt's **sun-god, Ra,** to show that Yahweh, the Israelite God, was superior. Ipuwer criticized Ra for not eliminating the evil men who brought these disasters upon Egypt. Ipuwer's doubt about his sun-god was provoked by the disasters that Egypt had experienced. The Bible says that the plagues fell upon Egypt, not only to punish the Egyptians for their mistreatment of the Israelites, but also in judgment of "the gods of Egypt." (Exodus 12:12). Thus, Ipuwer's criticism of Ra, the sun-god, fits perfectly with the Bible's ninth plague of darkness, which struck directly against the sun, from which the sun-god, "Ra," received his power.

I. The Tenth Plague: The Death of The Firstborn

The tenth and last plague against Egypt was the most terrifying of all: **the death of the firstborn.**

> **Exodus 11:4-7** -- So Moses said, "This is what the Lord says: 'About midnight I will go throughout Egypt. Every firstborn son in Egypt will die, from the firstborn son of Pharaoh, who sits on the throne, to the firstborn son of the slave girl, who is at her hand mill, and all the firstborn of the cattle as well. **There will be loud wailing throughout Egypt - worse than there has ever been or ever will be again.** But among the Israelites not a dog will bark at any man or animal. Then you will know that the Lord makes a distinction between Egypt and Israel.'"

> **Exodus 12:29-30** -- At midnight the Lord struck down all the firstborn in Egypt, **from the firstborn of Pharaoh**, who sat on the throne, to the firstborn of the prisoner, who was in the dungeon, and the firstborn of all the livestock as well. Pharaoh and all his officials and all the Egyptians got up during the night, and there was loud wailing in Egypt, **for there was not a house without someone dead.** NIV

Never before, and never after, has such a plague occurred in the history of any nation. Did Ipuwer testify that enormous numbers of both adults and children were killed simultaneously all over Egypt as the Bible reported concerning the death of all the firstborn of Egypt? Read and see for yourself.

> Lichtheim: Ch. 2 -- There's blood everywhere, **no shortage of dead.** The shroud calls out before one comes near it. **Lo, many dead are buried in the river. The stream is the grave,** the tomb became stream. . . . **Lo, people are diminished. He who puts his brother in the ground is everywhere.**[34]

> Lichtheim: Ch. 4-- Lo, **children of nobles** are dashed against walls; **infants** are put out on high ground. Lo, t**hose who were entombed are cast on high ground.** Embalmers' secrets are thrown away.[35]

The Bible says that a death occurred in every house in Egypt. In Chapter 2 Ipuwer says, "He who puts **his brother in the ground is everywhere,**" diminishing significantly the population of Egypt: **"Lo, people are diminished."** While Ipuwer does not mention the "firstborn," he does say **"brothers,"** not "sisters," are buried. If this were a plague or war, brothers and sisters, as well as mothers and fathers would be buried. Yet, Ipuwer and the Bible speak only of males that died. Ipuwer said above that **"children" of nobles, which include Pharaoh's child, have also died.** Exodus 12:29 says that not even Pharaoh's firstborn son was exempted. In the previous chapter we noted that Amenemhet IV's firstborn son did not succeed him to the throne, but rather his sister/wife, Sebeknefru, sat on his throne, implying that Amenemhet IV and his son had died prematurely.

In Chapter 2 Ipuwer implied that so many had died that there was a shortage of tombs. In some cases they emptied old tombs and either threw the dead bodies into the Nile, or cast them out on the ground, to make room for their newly deceased loved ones. Many could not find a tomb and were forced to bury their dead in the River. Ironically, Egyptians were casting their own dead into the Nile whereas they formerly killed Israelite infants by casting their bodies into the Nile.

The toll of death for both adults and children "everywhere" in Egypt was enormous, yet Ipuwer made no mention of a massacre by an invading army. Ipuwer's death description fits only a plague of gigantic proportions. Ipuwer was obviously describing the same plague recorded in the Bible: **"The Death of the Firstborn of Egypt."**

God promised that the death of the firstborn would destroy not only humans and animals, but also "the gods of Egypt."

> Exodus 12:12 -- On that same night I will pass through Egypt and strike down every firstborn - both men and animals - and **I will bring judgment on all the gods of Egypt.** I am the Lord. NIV

Ancient interpreters of the Bible believe that this last plague included an earthquake, which caused the death of humans, animals, and the destruction of

Egypt's gods of stone.[36] However, the firstborn of both Pharaohs and animals were also considered gods and thus the gods of Egypt were judged when God struck all of these firstborn creatures with death. While, Ipuwer does not use the word "firstborn," we will show in the point below that abundant evidence exists that great numbers of firstborn people and animals died in the time of Ipuwer.

J. Prediction of the Death of The First-born in Twelfth-dynasty Tombs

Written on the pyramid of King Unas, the last king of the fifth dynasty, is a prophecy that Unas would rise from the dead and judge with an unknown God on the day of the death of the firstborn of Egypt, including both men and gods.

> Lichtheim -- Unas has risen as Great One . . . **Unas will judge with Him-whose-name-is-hidden on the day of slaying the eldest [firstborn].** . . . Unas is he who **eats men, feeds on gods.** . . . Unas is the divine hawk, . . . Whom he finds on his way he devours whole. . . . For he has swallowed the knowledge of every god.[37]

Ziony Zevit deduced that "these texts indicate that an ancient tradition in Egypt recalled the slaying of all, or some, of the first-born **gods** on a particular night."[38] However, Zevit made no comment on the part of the quotation that says Unas killed **"men"** as well as **"gods." Notice the full quotation above.** This gruesome prophecy pictures Unas as sending messengers to kill the firstborn of **both men and gods** and to carve them up and cook them for Unas to devour so that he can assimilate their magic and knowledge into his own being.

The Bible specifically says that Yahweh, the God of Moses, judged both men and gods when the death of the firstborn occurred.

> Exodus 12:12; 13:15 -- On that same night I will pass through Egypt and strike down every firstborn - both **men** and **animals** --- and I will bring judgment on **all the gods of Egypt**. I am the Lord. . . . When Pharaoh stubbornly refused to let us go, the Lord killed every firstborn in Egypt, **both man and animal.**[39] NIV

The Pharaohs of Egypt and the animals of Egypt were worshiped as gods. Even bulls were mummified and buried with Pharaohs as gods. Thus, the death of the firstborn of animals and of the king logically led Egyptians to conclude that their gods were being killed. This ancient Egyptian prophecy also says that Unas, their ancient Pharaoh/god, will judge the firstborn **along with another God called "Him-whose-name-is-hidden."** When God appeared to Moses, He did not reveal his name until Moses asked what his name was.

> Exodus 3:13-15 -- Moses said to God, "Suppose I go to the Israelites and say to them, 'The God of your fathers has sent me to you,' and they ask

me, **'What is his name?'** Then what shall I tell them? God said to Moses, **"I AM WHO I AM."** This is what you are to say to the Israelites: **"I am has sent me to you."** God also said to Moses, "Say to the Israelites, 'The Lord, the God of your fathers --- the God of Abraham, the God of Isaac and the God of Jacob --- has sent me to you.' **This is my name forever,** the name by which I am to be remembered from generation to generation. NIV

God called himself **"I AM,"** when speaking to Moses. When Moses told others who God was, Moses said, "Yahweh sent me." Yahweh, translated above as Lord, literally means **"HE IS" or "HE EXISTS."** Yahweh is the real **"God-whose-name-is-hidden," the Ever-Existent-One,** who judged the firstborn of Egyptian men and judged the highest of the Egyptian gods, including Ra, the sun-god, by sending the ten plagues as punishment for Pharaoh's refusal to obey Yahweh.

Unas, a fifth dynasty Pharaoh, lived hundreds of years before the Middle Kingdom began. We are tempted to credit this prophecy to some twelfth dynasty priest who inscribed this prophecy on Unas' pyramid tomb to justify later the death of the firstborn on the basis that Unas predicted it and sent his messengers to accomplish the task. However the text specifically gives joint credit **to another God whose name was hidden and was thus unknown to the Egyptians**. Also, scholars claim this text has the same style, language and similar contents found in other Old Kingdom pyramid inscriptions. Scholars have concluded that this pyramid prophecy was actually inscribed in the time of Unas,[40] hundreds of years before the twelfth dynasty came into existence.

God used prophets to reveal his will in other nations not connected to the family of Abraham. Melchizedek[41] and Balaam[42] are Biblical examples of God's prophets among other nations. God also used false prophets to reveal truths and sometime half-truths in order to accomplish His will and prepare people's minds for His own purposes.[43] The Egyptian King Unas certainly did not participate in the death of the firstborn, **but the God whose name was hidden certainly did. Does any evidence exist that this prophecy of Unas was fulfilled in the time of Amenemhet IV, the last male Pharaoh to rule over Egypt?**

Unas' prophecy of the death of the firstborn is found inscribed centuries later in many Middle Kingdom tombs all over Egypt.[44] Since the Middle Kingdom includes the twelfth dynasty and the reign of Amenemhet IV, scholars need to verify precisely the date of these Middle Kingdom tombs when this prophecy is repeated. I predict that scholars will find them dated to the time of Amenemhet IV's death, toward the end of the Twelfth Dynasty.

The fact that Unas' prediction of the death of the firstborn is found in many twelfth-dynasty tombs strongly indicates that the fulfillment of Unas' prediction occurred at the very time that Ipuwer wrote of mass deaths of Egyptians both young and old, and rich and poor, all over Egypt. Remember that Ipuwer specifically wrote, **"He who puts his brother in the ground is everywhere."**[45]

Ipuwer also said that his eyewitness testimony was a fulfillment of what had been predicted by his ancestors: **"What the ancestors foretold has happened."**[46]

No other ancient inscription besides Unas' prophecy predicted the death of the firstborn of men and gods. Ipuwer likely had Unas' prophecy in mind when he described the wide spread death of Egyptians and animals (gods) all over Egypt. **Ipuwer also said that he was witnessing what his ancestors had previously prophesied.** Unas' prediction of the death of the firstborn of both men and gods (animals) in tombs all over Egypt during the Middle Kingdom (which includes the twelfth dynasty) significantly confirms the Biblical story of the death of the firstborn of both men and animals. Amenemhet IV's firstborn son did not sit on his father's throne, confirming the Biblical description of the death of the firstborn in Moses' time. The evidence strongly indicates that the ten plagues occurred in the last year of Amenemhet IV's reign.

K. Loudest Wailing in The History of Egypt

The Bible says that the death of the firstborn produced the loudest wailing in the history (past or future) of Egypt.

> Exodus 11:6 -- There will **be loud wailing throughout Egypt - worse than there has ever been or ever will be again.** NIV

> Exodus 12:30 -- Pharaoh and all his officials and all the Egyptians got up during the night, **and there was loud wailing in Egypt,** for there was not a house without someone dead. NIV

Ipuwer graphically described this same loud mourning that resounded all over Egypt because of the awesome number of deaths and agonizing destruction throughout Egypt.

> Ch. 3 -- Lo, **merriment has ceased**, is made no more. **Groaning** is throughout the land, mingled with **laments.**[47]
> Ch. 4 -- Lo, one is **numb from noise.** No voice is straight in years of shouting. **No end of shouting.** Lo, great and small says, 'I wish I were dead.' . . . What they sing to the goddess are dirges.[48]
> Ch. 5-6 -- If only this were the end of man. No more conceiving, no births! Then the land would cease to **shout. Tumult** would be no more. . . . Woe is me for the **grief** of this time.[49]
> Ch. 10 -- Lower Egypt **weeps!**[50]
> Ch. 12 -- Since giving birth is desired, **grief has come and misery is everywhere.**[51]
> Ch. 16 -- They cover their faces **in fear of tomorrow.**[52]

No other ancient Egyptian document describes such intensity of loud and grievous mourning. Therefore, the loudest mourning of Egypt is found in both Exodus 12:30

and the *Ipuwer Papyrus*, **another instance of extraordinary synchronism.**

L.   Ipuwer Blamed the Hebrews for the Plagues

The Bible clearly blames the hard-hearted Pharaoh of the Exodus for the plagues. He refused on ten different occasions to heed God's command that Israel be allowed to go into the desert to worship Him. However, Pharaoh and the Egyptians blamed the rebellious Moses and his fellow-Hebrews for the plagues.

> Exodus 10:7 -- Pharaoh's officials said to him, "How long will this man be a snare to us? Let the people go, so that they may worship the Lord their God. **Do you not yet realize that Egypt is ruined?"**   NIV

> Exodus 12:33 -- **The Egyptians urged the people to hurry and leave the country. "For otherwise," they said, "we will all die!"**   NIV

The Egyptians of Moses' time believed that the only solution to stop the plagues was to get rid of the Israelites. Ipuwer blamed some group of people "and their gods" who lived among the Egyptians for having caused the terrible plagues that Egypt was experiencing in his own day. **Ipuwer criticized Ra, his sun-god, for permitting these people to grow into large numbers, rather than destroying them in "the first generation."**

> Ch. 12 -- If only he had perceived their nature **in the first generation!** Then he would have smitten the evil, stretched out his arm against it, **would have destroyed their seed and their heirs! But since giving birth is desired, grief has come and misery is everywhere. So it is and will not pass, while these gods are in their midst.**[53]

Ipuwer does not name this group whose descendants and heirs had multiplied in the land. Since Ra was the Egyptian god that supposedly gave birth to all humans, Ra was blamed for allowing these people to multiply in number. These growing numbers of people are blamed by Ipuwer as the ones who have caused the grief and misery Egypt was suffering.

Exodus 1:6-14 says that Israel was enslaved because a previous Pharaoh feared their growing numbers would be a threat to the security of Egypt. In spite of persecutions and attempts to annihilate Israel's male infants, Israel continued to multiply: "But the more they were oppressed, the more they multiplied and spread; **so the Egyptians came to dread the Israelites**." (Exodus 1:12).

These growing Israelites fit precisely the people Ipuwer described that Ra should have killed "in their first generation." **Ipuwer could not understand why Ra, had not destroyed these people before they grew into a multitude and brought upon Egypt the worst plagues in its history. Ipuwer described the most of the plagues we find in the Bible**. Obviously, Ipuwer was blaming the same people that the Egyptians blamed in the Bible story: the Israelites. However, it was the God of Israel, not the Israelites, that sent these plagues upon Egypt because of God's justice to punish Egypt for its cruel persecution of Israelite foreigners.

CONCLUSION

Ipuwer is dated by scholars to the Middle Kingdom period that includes the reign of Amenemhet IV, the last male Pharaoh of the Twelfth Dynasty. Ipuwer's testimony of the devastation of Egypt amazingly matches Moses' description of the "ruin" of Egypt by the ten plagues. Adding the testimony of the inscriptions in Middle Kingdom tombs that record a prediction of the death of the firstborn of both men and gods, we have found **twenty-two points of synchronism** between the Biblical story of the ten plagues and the historical evidence found in *Ipuwer's Papyrus*. Ipuwer, a priest of Heliopolis, wrote this eye-witness account at the end of the twelfth dynasty, when the Exodus occurred.

These twenty-two synchronisms are listed in Table 19-A below. **They are too unique and too abundant to have occurred by chance. Ipuwer was obviously an eyewitness of the ten Biblical plagues that occurred at the end of the twelfth dynasty.** Joining these twenty-two clues of Amenemhet IV's reign in Chapter Eighteen to the fourteen historical links in this Chapter, we have thus far noted thirty-six significant clues in favor of Amenemhet IV as the Pharaoh of the Exodus. Chapter Twenty will add many more synchronisms that confirm the Biblical account of the Exodus and the destruction of Amenemhet IV and his army in the Red Sea.

TABLE 19-A
TWENTY-TWO DISCOVERIES FROM IPUWER'S
EYE-WITNESS REPORT OF MOST
OF THE TEN PLAGUES

Discovery No. 1. Scholars date Ipuwer's document to a period that includes the end of the twelfth dynasty, when Amenemhet IV died.

Discovery No. 2. Ipuwer describes Egypt's condition in historical terms, not fictional.

Discovery No. 3. Ipuwer describes slaves leaving with the riches of Egypt at a time that most of Egypt's crops and livestock were destroyed, fitting perfectly the Biblical Exodus.

Discovery No. 4. Itjtowy, the capital of the twelfth dynasty was in northern Egypt in the delta during Amenemhet IV's reign in the same location of Zoan where the Pharaoh of the Exodus lived.

Discovery No. 5. Plagues devastated all Egypt (except Goshen) as described in the Bible and in Ipuwer's Papyrus.

Discovery No. 6. The Nile and other bodies of water have turned to blood in both Ipuwer's Papyrus and Moses' testimony in the Bible.

Discovery No. 7. Ipuwer said the water was too bad to drink as in Moses' day.

Discovery No. 8. The fish had died in the Nile in Ipuwer's day and Moses' day.

Discovery No. 9. Great numbers of livestock are dead in both documents.

Discovery No. 10. The crops of Egypt are destroyed in both Ipuwer's document and the Bible.

Discovery No. 11. No fruit or leaves are on the trees for birds or man in both sources.

Discovery No. 12. Both documents say that Egypt is "**ruined.**"

Discovery No. 13. The Bible says that God used the ten plagues to "**judge the gods of Egypt.**" The plague of darkness directly attacked Ra, Egypt's sun-god. Ipuwer criticized the god of Ra because of his ineffectiveness during these plagues.

Discovery No. 14. The Biblical death of the firstborn in every house of Egypt is verified in Ipuwer's words as "**he who puts his brother in the ground is everywhere.**"

Discovery No. 15. Both adults and children were killed according to the Bible and according to Ipuwer's document.

Discovery No. 16. So many died at once that Ipuwer says all of the tombs were filled, forcing many to throw their dead into the River, duplicating what Sesostris III did by burying Israel's firstborn children in the Nile.

Discovery No. 17. Since Ipuwer does not mention an invading army, this great number of dead Egyptians must have occurred from some plague, as the Bible also reports.

Discovery No. 18. The grief and wailing of Egypt are the worst in history, according to the Bible. The wailing of Egypt is so loud that Ipuwer cannot stand the sound.

Discovery No. 19. The prophecy of the death of the firstborn appears in Middle Kingdom tombs contemporary with Amenemhet IV, confirming the tenth Biblical plague of the death of the first born that covered all of Egypt.

Discovery No. 20. The specific mention of the death of the firstborn of both men and gods in twelfth-dynasty tombs fits perfectly the Biblical plague of destroying the first born of both men and gods (animals worshiped as gods).

Discovery No. 21. The Egyptian name, "God-Whose-Name-Is-Hidden," participated in the death of the firstborn. The Bible name of "I Am" (Yahweh = "He Exists") was revealed to Moses and uniquely fits the Egyptian name of the "God-Whose-Name-Is-Hidden."

Discovery No. 22. Ipuwer blames Ra, the sun-god, for permitting a certain people (Israelites) to bring the plagues upon Egypt. Israel's God, Yahweh, sent these plagues on Egypt. Ipuwer told his Ra-god that he should have killed all of these people (Hebrews/Israelites) long ago to avoid the plagues of Egypt.

TABLE 19-B
RUNNING TOTAL OF DISCOVERIES

Chapter		Chapter Total	Running Total
2	Conflict Between Biblical and Secular Histories	18	18
4	Discovery of 430 Years from Abraham to the Exodus	16	34
5	Confirmation of Abraham's Historicity	28	62
6	Discovery of the Remains of Sodom and Gomorrah	17	79
7	Joseph As a Slave and Prisoner in Amenemhet I's Reign	21	100
8	Joseph Becomes the Vizier of Sesostris I	23	123
9	Sesostris I Gives Joseph a New Name and a Wife	11	134
10	The Seven Years of Abundance in Sesostris I's Reign	10	144
11	The Seven Years of Famine in Sesostris I's Reign	20	164
12	Israel Enters Egypt during Sesostris I's Reign	14	178
13	Sesostris III Enslaves the Israelites	17	195
14	Sesostris III, The Foster Grandfather of Moses	12	207
15	Sesostris III, Builder of Rameses and Pithom	15	222
16	Zoan (Itjtowy), the Capital of the Twelfth Dynasty	16	238
17	Amenemhet III, the Pharaoh Who Tried to Kill Moses	15	253
18	Amenemhet IV, the Pharaoh of the Exodus	14	267
19	Moses and Ipuwer Report the Ten Plagues	22	289

NOTES FOR CHAPTER NINETEEN

1. Exodus 10:7.
2. Immanuel Velikovsky, *Ages in Chaos*, pp. 22-39.
3. Velikovsky, *Ages in Chaos*, 37, 55-57.
4. John A. Wilson (Trans.), "The Admonitions of Ipuwer," *Ancient Near Eastern Texts*, p. 441.
5. Alan Gardiner, *Egyptian Grammar*, 3rd Ed., 1957.
6. Alan Gardiner, *Admonitions*, p. 111, cited by Miriam Lichtheim, *Ancient Egyptian Literature*, I.149.
7. William Hayes, *Scepter of Egypt*, I.196.
8. Miriam Lichtheim (Trans.), *Ancient Egyptian Literature*, I.149.
9. Lichtheim, *Ancient Egyptian Literature*, I.149-163.
10. Lichtheim, (Trans.), *Ancient Egyptian Literature*, I.149.
11. Lichtheim, (Trans.), *Ancient Egyptian Literature*, I.150.
12. Lichtheim, (Trans.), *Ancient Egyptian Literature*, I.150.
13. Lichtheim, (Trans.), *Ancient Egyptian Literature*, I.150.
14. Lichtheim, (Trans.), *Ancient Egyptian Literature*, I.153, 155.
15. Lichtheim, (Trans.), *Ancient Egyptian Literature*, I.152.
16. Lichtheim, (Trans.), *Ancient Egyptian Literature*, I.155.
17. Licththeim, (Trans.), *Ancient Egyptian Literature*, I.151.
18. Lichtheim, (Trans.), *Ancient Egyptian Literature*, I.156.
19. Lichtheim. (Trans.), *Ancient Egyptian Literature*, I.158-159.
20. Lichtheim, (Trans.), *Ancient Egyptian Literature*, I.153.
21. Lichtheim. (Trans.), *Ancient Egyptian Literature*, I.151,153.
22. Gardiner, *Admonitions of An Egyptian Sage*, note to 1:8, cited by Immanuel Velikovsky, *Ages In Chaos*, p. 24.
23. Hayes, *Scepter of Egypt*, I.196.
24. Lichtheim (Trans.), "The Admonitions of Ipuwer, " *Ancient Egyptian Literature*, I.151.
25. Lichtheim, (Trans.), *Ancient Egyptian Literature*, I.160.
26. Lichteim,(Trans.), *Ancient Egyptian Literature*, I.154, 159.

27. Lichtheim, (Trans.), *Ancient Egyptian Literature*, I.152.
28. Lichtheim, (Trans.), *Ancient Egyptian Literature*, I.153.
29. Lichtheim, (Trans.), *Ancient Egyptian Literature*, I.154.
30. Lichtheim, (Trans.), *Ancient Egyptian Literature*, I.154-155.
31. Lichtheim, (Trans.), *Ancient Egyptian Literature*, I. 152.
32. Lichtheim, (Trans.), *Ancient Egyptian Literature*, I.159-160.
33. Lichtheim, (Trans.), *Ancient Egyptian Literature*, I.162.
34. Lichtheim, (Trans.), *Ancient Egyptian Literature*, I.151-152.
35. Lichtheim, (Trans.), *Ancient Egyptian Literature*, I.153.
36. Eusebius, *Preparation for the Gospel*, Box IX, Ch. XXVII, cited by Velikovsky, *Ages in Chaos*, p. 31.
37. Miriam Lichtheim (Trans.), "Unas Pyramid Texts," *Ancient Egyptian Literature*, I.I.36-38.
38. Ziony Zevitt, "Three Ways to Look at the Ten Plagues," *Bible Review*, VI.13, June, 1990, 21, 42.
39. Exodus 12:12; 13:15.
40. Miriam Lichtheim (Trans.), *Ancient Egyptian Literature*, I.29-30.
41. Genesis 14:18-20.
42. Numbers 22-24.
43. I Kings 22; Ezekiel 21:18-27; John 11:49-52.
44. M. Gilula, "The Smiting of the First-Born — An Egyptian Myth?" *Tel Aviv* 4 (1977) cited by Ziony Zevit, "Three Ways to Look at the Ten Plagues," *Bible Review*, VI.13, June 1990, pp. 21,42.
45. Lichtheim (Trans.), *Ancient Egyptian Literature*, I.159-160; I.151-152.
46. Lichtheim, (Trans.), *Ancient Egyptian Literature*, I.150.
47. Lichtheim, (Trans.), *Ancient Egyptian Literature*, I.152.
48. Lichtheim, (Trans.), *Ancient Egyptian Literature*, I.153.
49. Lichtheim, (Trans.), *Ancient Egyptian Literature*, I.154, 155.
50. Lichtheim, (Trans.), *Ancient Egyptian Literature*, I.158.
51. Lichtheim, (Trans.), *Ancient Egyptian Literature*, I.159-160.
52. Lichtheim, (Trans.), *Ancient Egyptian Literature*, I. I.161.
53. Lichtheim, (Trans.), *Ancient Egyptian Literature*, I.159-160.

CHAPTER TWENTY
ISRAEL'S EXODUS AND THE DROWNING OF AMENEMHET IV AND HIS ARMY IN THE RED SEA

The ten plagues destroyed much of Egypt. However, these plagues were only the beginning of Egypt's devastation. Egypt also lost 600,000 Hebrew male slaves that were twenty years or older, plus an equal number of females, plus all of the Hebrew children that were under twenty years of age, plus non-Israelites that joined them (Exodus 12:37-38). Thus, there were about two to three million people who left Egypt, an immense loss for the labor force and economy of the country. In addition, Pharaoh and his entire army were destroyed in the Red Sea.

Ipuwer, the witness of the ten plagues, was also a witness to the loss of the Israelite slaves, the Egyptian army and the death of the Pharaoh of the Exodus. Ipuwer also described the fall of the twelfth dynasty and the social and political revolution that occurred in Egypt as a result of the Exodus. Ipuwer's continued eyewitness testimony of these dramatic events furnish additional, weighty reasons to identify Amenemhet IV as the Pharaoh of the Exodus, and to confirm the historicity of the Biblical record of the Exodus.

I. HEBREW SLAVES TOOK THE RICHES OF EGYPT

The Bible reports that the Israelites requested articles of silver, gold and clothing from their Egyptian neighbors immediately after the ten plagues and before they left Egypt. Out of respect for Moses the Egyptians responded generously.

Exodus 3:21-22 -- (21) And I will make the Egyptians favorably disposed toward this people, so that when you leave you will not go empty-handed. **Every woman is to ask her neighbor and any woman living in her house for articles of silver and gold and for clothing, which you will put on your sons and daughters. And so you will plunder the Egyptians.** NIV

Exodus 11:2-3 -- (2) Tell the people that men and women alike are to ask their neighbors for articles of silver and gold." (3) The Lord made the Egyptians favorably disposed toward the people, and Moses himself was highly regarded in Egypt by Pharaoh's officials and by the people.

Exodus 12:35-36 -- (35) The Israelites did as Moses instructed and asked the Egyptians for articles of silver and gold and for clothing. (36) The Lord had made the Egyptians favorably disposed toward the people, and they gave them what they asked for; so they plundered the Egyptians. NIV

The Biblical declaration that slaves were wearing the clothes of the wealthy and carrying away with them precious articles of gold and silver is extraordinary. Notice below how Ipuwer's document confirms this unique Biblical story.

> Lichtheim's Translation: Ch. 2 -- Lo, poor men have become men of wealth, he who could not afford sandals owns riches.
> Ch. 3 -- There are no people anywhere. Lo, gold, lapis lazuli, silver, and turquoise, carnelian, amethyst, ibht-stone . . . **are strung on the necks of female slaves.**
> Ch. 7 -- See, those who owned robes are in rags. He who did not weave for himself owns fine linen.
> Ch. 8 -- See, he who had nothing is a man of wealth. . . . See the poor of the land have become rich.[1]

Thus, Ipuwer reported precisely what the Bible said the Israelite slaves did when they left Egypt. Poor slaves suddenly became rich. Both Ipuwer and the Bible specifically refer to articles of "gold," silver" and "clothing" that the slaves were "wearing." Notice above that Ipuwer says precious stones, along with gold and silver, appear as beautiful necklaces "strung on the necks of female slaves." He also reports above that those who were in rags now wear "fine linen."

The Bible explains how these slaves obtained these riches. The Egyptians freely gave to the Israelite slaves because of their respectful fear of Moses. Moses was batting a thousand (10 for 10) in his predictions of the ten plagues that fell upon Egypt. The Egyptians preferred to lose their riches to the slaves and save their lives rather than to save their riches and lose their lives by another plague. They freely gave these rich articles and fine clothing to the Israelite slaves.

II. DISAPPEARANCE OF THE SLAVES IN THE DELTA

In Ipuwer's chapter 12 he implies that he was a chief priest.[2] His chiding of the sun-god Ra in his chapter 13 may mean that he was a priest of Ra.[3] If so, then Ipuwer lived in Heliopolis, the capital of Ra-worship, on the edge of the eastern delta, close to the area where Goshen was located and where the Israelite slaves lived. Notice below that Ipuwer's eyewitness testimony specifically mentions the delta region as the area where the Israelites formerly lived and from which they left with all of their goods and riches given them by the Egyptians. With the disappearance of the Hebrew slaves and the Egyptian army, the Delta was void of much of its population and the area was no longer defended by Egyptian soldiers.

> Lichtheim's Translation:
> Ch. 1   --   The Delta [-dwellers] carry shields.
> Ch. 4   --   Lo gone is what yesterday was seen.
> Ch. 10 -- Lower Egypt weeps. The king's storehouse is "I go-get-it.[4]

Notice above that Ipuwer located the king's store house in "Lower Egypt" (the Delta), proving that the twelfth dynasty capital was **not** located at El Lisht, south of Memphis. Egyptologists have searched for the twelfth dynasty capital at El Lisht, but without success. Ipuwer wrote much of his document in regard to what he saw occurring in the palace and the national capital (Itjtowy or Zoan) in the Delta. Since Ipuwer likely lived in on the edge of Delta at Heliopolis, then he could have been one of the Egyptians who actually saw the Israelites on the day they left Egypt. The testimony cited below implies **that he did indeed witness Israel's "Exodus."** In the same sentence in which Ipuwer noted that female slaves were seen wearing the riches of their masters, he made the statement **that people had suddenly disappeared.**

> Lichtheim (Translator): Ch. 3 -- There are no people anywhere. Lo, gold, lapis lazuli, silver, and turquoise, carnelian, amethyst, ibht-stone and ----- are strung on the necks of female slaves.[5]

The expression, "There are no people anywhere," implies that the slaves whom Ipuwer saw with their masters' riches had vanished from the delta when he wrote. The Bible depicts the Israelites leaving Egypt immediately after they obtained riches from their Egyptian neighbors.

> Numbers 33:3-4 -- The Israelites set out from Rameses on the fifteenth day of the first month, the day after the Passover. They marched out boldly in full view of all the Egyptians, who were burying all their firstborn. NIV

With the departure of about three million Israelites, no wonder that it appeared to Ipuwer that **"there are no people anywhere" in the delta of Egypt.**

III. THE REVOLT OF OTHER SLAVES AND POOR EGYPTIANS

However, many of Ipuwer's statements imply that not all of the slaves and poor people left Egypt. Other poor people and non-Israelite slaves remained in Egypt and apparently revolted shortly after the Israelite slaves left and after the Egyptian army had been destroyed in the Red Sea.

> Lichtheim (Translator): Ch. 2 -- **The servant takes what he finds.** . . .
> Lo, men's slaves, their hearts are greedy. . . . Lo, nobles lament, the poor rejoice. . . . The child of his lady became the son of his maid..[6]
> Ch. 3 -- **Noble women roam the land. Ladies say, "We want to eat!" Their bodies suffer in rags.**[7]
> Ch. 4 -- Lo, citizens are put to the grindstones, wearers of fine linen are beaten with sticks. . . . **Ladies suffer like maidservants. . . . The servant abandons his household.**[8]

Ch. 5 -- Lo, the great hunger and suffer. **Servants are served**.[9]

Thus, the example of the Israelite slaves who succeeded in achieving their freedom from the king of Egypt inspired the poor and downtrodden all over Egypt to rebel and overthrow their Egyptian masters who had also been abusing them. This rebellion of the poor could only be accomplished because the Egyptian army lay at the bottom of the Red Sea and was no longer present to protect the palace and the mansions of the rich nobles.

IV. CRIMINAL TAKE-OVER OF EGYPT

With the King and his army absent, the peasants rebelled and the social situation of Egypt deteriorated into unrestrained criminal behavior. Notice below how Ipuwer describes the chaotic situation of widespread anarchy and lawlessness as a result of the destruction of Amenemhet IV and his army in the Red Sea.

Lichtheim: Ch. 1 -- **The door [-keepers] say: "Let us go plunder."** ... **The Delta [-dwellers] carry shields**.[10] The door keepers, who were supposed to guard the royal granaries and the royal treasuries, plundered what they were supposed to protect. Murder and robbery was so rampant in the Delta that citizens had to carry shields of protection when they walked through the paths of the Delta and the streets of their cities.

> Lichtheim: Ch. 2 -- **The land is full of gangs. A man goes to plow with his shield. . . . Crime is everywhere. . . . Every town says, "let us expel our rulers." . . . Lo, the land turns like a potter's wheel. The robber owns riches. The noble is a thief**.[11]

Gangs, committing acts of violence and robbery, roamed the land. Farmers had to carry their shields and weapons with them when they went out to plow their fields. The same criminal peasants entered the administrative offices of the governors of the provinces and the mayors of cities, and expelled the officials who formerly maintained law and order. The thieves took over the land and entered the offices of the nobles. Consequently, the nobles were forced into poverty and themselves became thieves.

> Lichtheim: Ch. 6 -- **Lo, offices are opened, their records stolen**. The serf becomes an owner of serfs. Lo, [scribes] are slain, their writings stolen. Woe is me for the grief of this time! **Lo, the scribes of the land-register, their books are destroyed. The grain of Egypt is "I go-get-it."**[12]

Peasants, some of whom were slaves, entered the offices of Egypt's state and national governments. They stole the property records of both land and slaves. Afterwards they destroyed the records so that no one could again imprison them, enslave them, or repossess their newly stolen property. Some Egyptians slaves (non-Israelites) that formerly worked the land for their masters took over their masters' lands and forced free Egyptians to become their slaves. Thus, the slaves became slave masters and the slave masters became the servants of the freed slaves. The same peasants and Egyptian slaves entered state and national granaries and carried off the grain.

> Lichtheim: Ch. 7 -- **Men stir up strife unopposed.** See, the land is tied up in gangs. See now, the transformation of the people. The coward is emboldened to seize his goods. . . . He who did not build a hut is an owner of coffers. **See, the judges of the land are driven from the land. The nobles are expelled from the royal mansions. See, noble ladies are on boards . . . .** He who did not sleep on a box owns a bed. See, the man of wealth lies thirsting. He who begged dregs has overflowing bowls. See, those who owned robes are in rags. **He who did not weave for himself owns fine linen.**[13]

The success of the revolters in taking over the land of ordinary citizens encouraged the peasants to enter the state and national capitals and expel the nobles, judges and their families from the mansions owned by the King and his officials. The wives of the nobles were forced to sleep on boards outside the comfort of their mansions.

> Lichtheim: Ch. 9 -- **See, cattle stray with none to bring them back, Everyone fetches for himself and brands with his name. See, a man is slain by the side of his brother, who abandons him to save himself. . . . See the mighty of the land are not reported to. The affairs of the people have gone to ruin.**[14]

Cattle rustling was made easy. People feared to go into the pastures to care for their livestock. The peasants found straying cattle everywhere, branded them with their own name and thus became owners of livestock. Murder was common and fear filled the heart of all Egyptians. Crimes were not even reported to the authorities because these officials had been expelled from their offices by the rebelling Egyptian peasants. The law and order that had persisted during all of the previous reigns of twelfth-dynasty kings ceased to exist. As Ipuwer clearly observed, **Egypt was in chaotic ruin!**

V. THE ABSENCE OF THE EGYPTIAN ARMY

How could such anarchy and rampant crime exist? The revolt of the slaves and peasants in which masters became servants, and servants became masters, is unprecedented in Egyptian history. Scholars date Ipuwer's document in the period that includes the end of Amenemhet IV's reign, the very Pharaoh we have identified as the Pharaoh of the Exodus.

Ipuwer himself explains in chapter seven of his work why the social revolution occurred: **"Men stir up strife unopposed."** [15] The uprising of the peasants and slaves was not restrained **because the Egyptian army was not present to resist it.** There is no way that the peasant revolt could have succeeded **if the police force had been present to crush the revolt and restore law and order.**

We saw in Chapter Thirteen of this book that the Israelites were enslaved by Mentuemhat, the general of Sesostris III's army. Also, we saw in Chapter Seventeen that the Egyptian slave drivers were under the supervision of the chief of police in the reign of Amenemhet III. These same policemen were no doubt part of the Egyptian army that Amenemhet IV summoned to pursue the Israelites. If Amenemhet IV's army was destroyed in the Red Sea, then the police force of Egypt was annihilated and no longer present in Egypt to prevent the peasant revolt, restrain criminals and maintain law and order. **Ipuwer's document thus confirms the Biblical story of the disappearance of the Egyptian army.**

VI. THE KING IS DEAD BY "POURING WATER"

Ipuwer not only described an Egypt **without an army**, but **also a country without a king,** who, amazingly, had been eliminated by **"pouring water."**

> Lichtheim: Ch. 7 -- See now, the land is **deprived of kingship** by a few people who ignore custom. . . . [Stolen] is the crown of Re, who pacifies the Two Lands. . . . **If the residence [capital] is stripped, it will collapse in a moment**. See, **Egypt has fallen to pouring water, He who poured water on the ground seizes the mighty in misery.** See, **the Serpent is taken from its hole, the secrets of Egypt's kings are bared.** [16]

Notice that Ipuwer specifically says that Egypt is **"deprived of kingship,"** **proving that the King (Amenemhet IV) was dead.** Notice also that Ms. Lichtheim emended a damaged space in front of the expression, "[Stolen] is the crown of Re, who pacifies the Two Land." The words, **"[Removed]"** or **"[Destroyed]"** fits better the context than **"[Stolen]."** Notice that "He who poured water on the ground" is the one who "seizes the mighty in misery," which consisted **of taking "The Serpent . . . from its hole" and destroying it with "pouring water."**

Jehovah (Yahweh), the God of the Hebrews is the one who lured the "Serpent from its hole," by enticing Amenemhet IV away from his palace to capture the fleeing Israelite slaves who appeared to be "trapped" on the shore of the Red Sea. Then, Jehovah opened the Red Sea to allow the Israelites to escape with King

Amenemhet IV and his army following close behind. **In the middle of the night, Jehovah "seized the mighty" king Amenemhet IV and destroyed him by pouring the waters of the Red Sea upon him and his army.**

Amenemhet IV wore the crown of Re (the sun-god of Egypt). This crown had a serpent on its front. Amenemhet IV's throne name included Re (Ra): Ma-khrou-**Re**.[17] Re or Ra actually appears first in the hieroglyphic inscription of Amenemhet IV's throne name.[18] If Amenemhet IV left that crown at the palace when he led his army after the Israelites, it was likely stolen by beggars who later entered the palace, and Ms. Lichtheim would be correct in her emendation of the void space with "Stolen." However, if Amenemhet IV wore the crown of Re as he led his army into the Red Sea, then the **God of Israel, who "poured water on the ground," is the one who removed the crown of Amenemhet IV and left it at the bottom of the Red Sea.** Deep sea diving at the Red Sea Crossing Site could locate this crown and confirm that the Pharaoh of the Exodus drowned in the Red Sea (the Sea of Reeds).

VII. THE WHIRLWIND IN THE MIDST OF THE RED SEA

Exodus 14:21-22 says that God opened the waters of the Red Sea by a strong east wind. How could the Israelites walk into the face of a wind that was so strong that it could hold back millions of tons of water? Psalm 77:16-20 explains this apparent contradiction by describing this east wind as a **"whirlwind"** accompanied by a severe thunder storm.

> With your mighty arm you redeemed your people, the descendants of Jacob and Joseph. The waters saw you, O God, . . . and writhed; . . . **The clouds poured down water, the skies resounded with thunder; your arrows flashed back and forth**. Your thunder was heard in the **WHIRLWIND, ... Your path led through the sea,** your way through the mighty waters, though your footprints were not seen. **You led your people like a flock by the hand of Moses and Aaron.** NIV

Since the wind that opened the sea was a **"whirlwind,"** it could have been **either a tornado or a hurricane**. Both hurricanes and tornadoes have an **"eye"** within them where there is an **eerie calm**. If Israel were **in the eye** of this fierce storm, they could have walked across the Red Sea unhampered by the wind, while the outer edges of the storm raged against the sea and held back the waters until Israel reached the other shore. When the tornado or hurricane lifted, the walls of water would collapse upon Pharaoh and his army like **"pouring water,"** the **precise words that Ipuwer used to describe the death of Pharaoh.** Below we repeat the quote cited above for emphasis:

> Ch. 7- **Egypt has fallen to pouring water, He who poured water on the ground seizes the mighty in misery.** See, **the Serpent is taken from its hole, the secrets of Egypt's kings are bared.** [19]

"He who poured water on the ground" is likely the same God "Whose Name Is Hidden" that Unas predicted would kill the firstborn of Egypt. Remember that Ipuwer said he was writing about the fulfillment of former predictions. Yahweh, the God of the Hebrews, the Great "I AM," "poured water" on the head of the "mighty" king of Egypt and thus "seized" him in the "misery" of death by drowning. As Amenemhet IV and his predecessors threw Israelite infants to their death in the waters of the Nile River, now God punished Amenemhet IV and his army by throwing them into the water of the Red Sea.

Ipuwer's figure of the serpent being taken from his hole also amazingly fits the Biblical story of how God **lured** the Pharaoh of the Exodus to his death in the Red Sea. God purposely led the Israelites on an illogical route to the Red Sea, where it appeared that Israel was confused and trapped. God told Moses, "Pharaoh will think, 'The Israelites are wandering around the land in confusion, hemmed in by the desert.' And I will harden Pharaoh's heart, and he will pursue them."[20]

Thus, God **lured the Serpent (Amenemhet IV with a serpent on his crown)** out of his **hole (the palace)** and into the midst of the waters of the Red Sea. God then destroyed **the Serpent (the mighty Amenemhet IV)** by pouring upon him the waters of the Red Sea. As a result, the palace (where the serpent usually stayed for protection) lay unprotected by the army and open for the peasants to enter and rob the secret and hidden treasures of Amenemhet IV and his predecessors.

In this manner Ipuwer's words are fulfilled: **"the secrets of Egypt's kings were laid bare."** Ipuwer's eloquent illustration of luring the Serpent out of the hole and destroying it with **"pouring water"** uniquely fits the Biblical description of the death of the Pharaoh of the Exodus by the waters of the Red Sea.

As I pointed out in Chapter Eighteen, **all of the Pharaohs of the twelfth dynasty built enormous pyramids** where their bodies were laid to rest and where priests worshiped their mummies and their departed spirits. However, Amenemhet IV's pyramid has never been found. Why? Amenemhet IV was still young and had not started construction on his pyramid before he died in the Red Sea with his army. In the chaotic situation that ensued after the destruction of the Egyptian army, Amenemhet IV's Queen was unable to restore order or even construct a pyramid for herself. **Their missing pyramid testifies to the destruction of Amenemhet IV and his army in the Red Sea** and to the chaotic conditions of anarchy after Amenemhet IV and his army were destroyed in Ipuwer's words **"by pouring water."**

Volume II of *Solving the Exodus Mystery,* will pinpoint the precise location where the Red Sea crossing occurred. An underwater video will reveal chariot wheels and skeletons of men and horses at this amazing site.

VIII. THE ROYAL PALACE IS OVERRUN
BY PEASANTS AND CRIMINALS

With the king dead and the army destroyed, the capital and palace of Egypt were left unprotected and open to intruders. Ipuwer describes precisely what happened.

Lichtheim's Translation:
Ch. 3 -- Gold is lacking; exhausted are materials for every kind of craft. **What belongs to the palace has been stripped.**
Ch. 6 -- **The laws of the chamber are thrown out**, . . . Beggars tear them up in the alleys. **Lo the beggar comes to the place of the Nine Gods, The procedure of the House of Thirty is laid bare. Lo the great council chamber is invaded, Beggars come and go in the great mansions.**
Ch. 7 -- **See now, things are done that never were before. The king has been robbed by beggars. . . . See now, the land is deprived of kingship. . . . If the residence is stripped, it will collapse in a moment. See, Egypt has fallen to pouring water. . . . Men stir up strife unopposed. . . . See, the judges of the land are driven from the land. The nobles are expelled from the royal mansions. See, noble ladies are on boards . . . , princes in the workhouse.**
Ch. 10 -- **Lower Egypt weeps. The king's storehouse is "I go-get-it," for everyone, and the whole palace is without its revenues. . . . Destroy the foes of the noble residence, . . . The mayor of the city goes unescorted.**[21]

Notice above that beggars entered unimpeded into the Palace of Amenemhet IV and "stripped" it of its treasures. They entered the House of Thirty, the Supreme Court of Egypt, which was located within the Palace Complex in Itjtowy, and threw out the law records. Instead of paying their taxes, the people robbed the treasury and its store houses. The judges of Egypt's Supreme Court had been expelled from their offices, as well as the nobles of the royal family, including **"princes," sons of the king who were forced to live and labor "in the workhouse."** The princes were likely Amenemhet IV's young sons born by Queen Sebeknefru, or other children by minor wives of Amenemhet IV. Amenemhet IV's first-born son was killed in the plague of the death of the firstborn.

Ipuwer also said that the mayor of the capital city walked **unescorted** through the streets. Ipuwer feared that the **"residence will collapse in a moment"** if something did not happen soon. How did beggars and criminals succeed in ousting the rulers of the land and taking over the nation's capital of Itjtowy (Zoan)? Ipuwer and the Bible agree on the answer. In the words of Ipuwer, **"The land is deprived of kingship"** and **"men stir up strife unopposed:"** No king and no army!

Ipuwer specifically declared that the king is dead, the army was not present to protect the palace, and beggars and criminals were thus entering the palace without resistance. This chaotic condition existed because the Serpent was lured from his hole and was destroyed by **"pouring water."** We could not have a better historical confirmation of the Biblical description of the destruction of Pharaoh and his army

in the Red Sea, and at the precise time in twelfth-dynasty history where we find
parallels to the principal Biblical events that occurred at the Exodus.

IX. THE INVASION OF THE LIBYANS
AND NUBIANS

After Amenemhet IV's death, Egypt was destroyed not only from within, but
also from without. Foreigners began to invade Egypt from both the west and the
south. Ipuwer specifically mentions that Libyans and Nubians invaded Egypt after
the king died.

> **Lichtheim:** Ch. 1 -- **The Delta-dwellers carry shields. . . . Foreigners
> have become people everywhere.**
> Ch. 15 -- Every man fights for his sisters and protects himself. **Is it
> Nubians**? Then we will protect ourselves. There are plenty of fighters
> to repel the Bowmen. **Is it Libyans**? Then we will turn them back.[22]

The Libyans lived west of Egypt and the Nubians (Ethiopians) lived south of Egypt.
The Egyptians had periodic problems with both the Libyans and Nubians and often
warred against them. **Amenemhet I drove out Libyans and Canaanites out of
the delta and Nubians out of southern Egypt when he founded the twelfth
dynasty.**[23] Sesostris I was leading the army in a fight to drive out Libyans, who had
invaded the western delta of Egypt, when his father, Amenemhet I, died.[24]

Both Sesostris I and Sesostris III warred against the Nubians (Ethiopians) and
established the far southern boundary of Egypt with fortresses and garrisons of
soldiers stationed there on the southern border to prevent the Nubians from entering
southern Egypt. Sesostris III unmercifully abused the Nubians when he invaded
their country and brought them under his cruel submission.[25]

When king Amenemhet IV died and the army was destroyed, Ipuwer
indicated that the Libyans invaded the delta and that the Nubians invaded southern
Egypt at the same time that the peasants were revolting. Thus both civil and foreign
skirmishes were occurring spontaneously in different parts of Egypt. **Egypt was
being destroyed simultaneously from within and from without.**

X. THE FALL OF THE TWELFTH DYNASTY

The fall of the twelfth dynasty soon after the death of Amenemhet IV lends
additional evidence that we have pinpointed the Pharaoh of the Exodus. **Historians
agree that the twelfth dynasty was one of the most powerful, most prosperous
and best organized of all of the dynasties of Egypt. Hayes said that Sesostris
I, the second king of the twelfth dynasty "had a breadth of vision . . . for the
enrichment and expansion of Egypt more grandiose than any heretofore
undertaken."[26]** "The growth of national prosperity," Hayes continued, "reached

its peak during the long and peaceful reign of" Amenemhet III.[27] This wealth and progress continued on through the reign of Amenemhet IV.[28] Within ten years the line of male Pharaohs was suddenly broken with Amenemhet IV's death. Amenemhet IV's wife/sister began a reign that lasted less than four years. **After more than 200 years of continued material progress, suddenly the most glorious dynasty up to that point in Egyptian history mysteriously fell.** Hayes succinctly describes this fall below.

> With Amen-em-het IV the vigorous blood stream of the royal family was evidently beginning to run a little thin. His brief and undistinguished reign, followed by the even briefer reign of a woman, Queen Sobk-nefru, marks the end of the dynasty and the decline of the Middle Kingdom. There probably was never a period when the prosperity of the country depended so directly and so completely on the ability and tireless energy of its rulers. While these were maintained at the high standard present throughout most of the twelfth dynasty, a glorious chapter in Egyptian history was written. **When they failed, the land relapsed gradually into a state as chaotic as that of the First Intermediate period and marked by even greater national calamities.[29] (My Emphasis)**

When the twelfth dynasty fell less than four years after Amenemhet IV died, Sekhemre (Sobkhotpe I), a governor from Thebes in southern Egypt, traveled with his army north to the capital at Itjtowy (near Tanis in the Delta) and established a new family of kings, which became **"the thirteenth dynasty."**[30] When Sekhemre moved from Thebes to Itjtowy, this no doubt left the south unprotected, permitting the Nubians (Ethiopians) to enter the southern border of Egypt and take over the southern most nome of Egypt at Elephantine. John Wilson's translation of Ipuwer's document expresses clearly the consequence of this Nubian infiltration of southern Egypt.

> Ch. 3 -- Elephantine, the Thinite nome . . . of Upper Egypt do not pay taxes **because of . . . [civil] war. . . . Every foreign country [comes]!** . . . . What can we do about it? **Going to ruin!**[31]

Wilson's interposition of "**[civil]** war" is not necessary in Elephantine, which is near the southern border of Egypt. Ipuwer likely was referring to the incursion of the Nubians into southern Egypt. Ipuwer specifically named the Nubians as having entered Egypt (chapter 16). The move north by the governor and army of Thebes created a vacuum in the south, resulting in the invasion of Elephantine by the Nubians and Egypt's temporary loss of this southern nome (district). Later the thirteenth dynasty defeated the Nubians and brought Elephantine back under Egyptian authority.

With the loss of Egypt's army, the Libyans, who Ipuwer said had invaded the delta, succeeded in occupying the western delta of Egypt and establishing the fourteenth dynasty with its capital at Xois.[32] Thus, Ipuwer was not inventing a fictitious invasion by the Libyans, but a real historical event. Sekhemre, the governor of Thebes who eventually became the first king of the thirteenth dynasty, was unable to oust the Libyans of the fourteenth dynasty from the western delta. The Libyans of the fourteenth dynasty remained entrenched in the western delta for 184 years.[33] Thus, when the twelfth dynasty fell, Egypt was divided into two dynasties (the thirteenth and fourteenth). Manetho, an Egyptian priest of the third century B.C., counted **245 years of unity and independent sovereignty under twelfth dynasty kings.** Most Egyptologists do not attribute 245 years to the twelfth dynasty, as I do. See my discussion of the chronology of the twelfth dynasty in Appendix C.

The thirteenth and fourteenth dynasties were weak and unstable. The thirteenth dynasty had **sixty kings within its 153-year duration,**[34] and the fourteenth dynasty had **seventy-six kings in 184 years,**[35] **an average of only two and a half years per reign for both dynasties**. By way of contrast, the twelfth dynasty had only **eight kings that reigned 245 years for an average of thirty years per king.**

Because Immanuel Velikovsky believed that the Exodus occurred during the thirteenth dynasty, he described the invasion of foreigners as being the Hyksos who invaded Egypt from either Canaan or Arabia. However, the Hyksos did not invade Egypt until 100 years after the fall of the twelfth dynasty. Ipuwer spoke only of the Libyans and the Nubians as foreigners in Egypt. Therefore, the Hyksos had not yet invaded Egypt when Ipuwer wrote. Velikovsky thus misdated the time of Ipuwer by 100 years and consequently missed **the true identification of the Pharaoh of the Exodus: Amenemhet IV.**

However, the instability of the thirteenth and fourteenth dynasties, plus the Nubians in southern Egypt, weakened Egypt further and emboldened the Hyksos to invade northern Egypt 100 years after the twelfth dynasty had fallen. **The Hyksos later added two new dynasties (the fifteenth and sixteenth), thus dividing Egypt into four dynasties with four different Pharaohs reigning in four different capitals of Egypt.** Three of these four dynasties were ruled by foreigners. See Table 20-A on the next page. **The events surrounding the Exodus plunged Egypt into a 200-year dark age of weakness, division and foreign domination.**

XI. THE LOSS OF EGYPT'S HORSES, CHARIOTS, ARMY AND PHARAOH

Exodus 14:6-28 reports that the Pharaoh of the Exodus, whom we identify as Amenemhet IV, took all of his chariots and horses to the Red Sea to overtake the escaping Israelites. Breasted and other Egyptologists claim that Egyptian dynasties did not utilize the horse and chariot until the Hyksos brought them to Egypt from

Arabia.[36] If so, an apparent contradiction exists in my claim that Amenemhet IV was the Pharaoh of the Exodus. However, horses have been discovered in ancient Egypt. In fact, the skeleton of a horse was found **beneath** a destruction layer of the fortress at Buhen, whose builder was either Sesostris I or Sesostris III.[37] Thus horses did exist in the twelfth dynasty.

TABLE 20-A
THE FALL OF THE TWELFTH DYNASTY AND THE SUBSEQUENT DIVISION OF EGYPT

Dates: *Cambridge Ancient History,* I.2B.996; II.1.818-819

LAST TWO PHARAOHS OF THE TWELFTH DYNASTY

AMENEMHET IV - Reigned 9 years, 3 months and 27-seven days: Petrie, *Hist. Of Egypt,* p. 280
SEBEKNEFRU   - Reigned 3 years, 10 months and 24-four days. *Ibid.*

END OF THE TWELFTH DYNASTY

13TH DYN.	14TH DYN. LIBYANS		
1786 B.C.*	1786 B.C.*		
Egyptian governors	Libyans enter western		
from Thebes move	delta and build their		
north to Itjtowy	Capital at Xois		
in N.E. Delta			

13TH DYN.	14TH DYN.	15TH DYN.	16TH DYN.
1684 B.C.*	1684 B.C.*	1674 B.C.*	1684 B.C.*
Egyptian kings driven	Libyans continue	Hyksos kings	Hyksos kings
out of E. Delta by	in western delta	in E. Delta	At Memphis
Hyksos and move south	at Xois		
to Thebes (Luxor) as			
new capital			

17TH DYN.			
1650 B.C.*	Ended		
Reign in Thebes (S. Egypt)	1603 B.C.*		

Ahmosis Was the Last Pharaoh			
of the 17th Dynasty			
Who Also Began			
the 18th DYNASTY		Ended	Ended
1567 B.C.*		1567 B.C.*	1567 B.C.*

The Eighteenth Dynasty Conquers and Reunites All of Egypt

* Chapter Twenty-Four proves that the Cambridge Dates should be revised
by three centuries, thus fitting the Biblical dates.

Scholars generally recognize that horses and chariots existed in eastern countries during the time of the twelfth dynasty.[38] With the wealth of the twelfth dynasty there is no reason to doubt that they purchased horses and chariots and had them in abundance in the reign of the last male Pharaoh of the twelfth dynasty, Amenemhet IV. The reason that more horses have not been found in twelfth dynasty excavation is likely because the quantity of horses and chariots reached its highest number during the reign of Amenemhet IV and all of these horses and chariots were destroyed in the Red Sea, leaving not a trace of them in Egypt.

The material destruction of Egypt by the ten plagues, the take over of the palace and its treasuries by criminals and beggars, and the consequent decline in wealth of Egypt's citizens prevented their purchasing new chariots and horses. Thus, new horses and chariots did not reappear in Egypt until the Hyksos invaded and conquered the land.

XII. THE REIGN OF QUEEN SEBEKNEFRURE

A. Was A Woman Responsible for the Fall of the Twelfth Dynasty?

Interestingly, scholars are divided as to what brought the twelfth dynasty to an end and what subsequently caused a divided and politically unstable Egypt. Baines and Wente believe that the fall was peaceful and uneventful.

> The reigns of Amenemhet III and Amenemhet IV . . . and Sebeknefru, . . . the first certainly attested female monarch, were apparently peaceful, but the accession of a woman marked the end of the dynastic line.[39]

Baines seems to imply that a woman on the Egyptian throne explains why the twelfth dynasty fell. Yet, he inconsistently says that her reign was "apparently peaceful." How could the twelfth dynasty fall, if her reign was peaceful? The eighteenth dynasty did not fall when Hatshepsut took over the throne of Egypt. England did not fall when Queen Elizabeth ruled England, nor when Margaret Thatcher became Prime Minister of England. Did the twelfth dynasty fall merely because a woman sat on the throne?

The Bible and Ipuwer both agree as to why the twelfth dynasty fell: **Egypt was devastated by natural plagues; its king was killed; its army was not present to prevent the peasant revolt or crush the chaotic social revolution that followed**. Not even the thirteenth dynasty was able to expel the foreign Libyans who entered and remained in the western delta of Egypt for 184 years. Both the Bible and Ipuwer agree that the twelfth dynasty, one of the most powerful and glorious dynasties in Egyptian history, fell because of the ten plagues and **"pouring water,"** culminating in the death of Amenemhet IV and his army in the

Red Sea.

B. How Did Queen Sebeknefru Reign If the Exodus Occurred at Amenemhet IV's Death?

If the calamities of Egypt described in Ipuwer's document occurred at the end of Amenemhet IV's reign, how did Queen Sebeknefru, the sister/wife of Amenemhet IV, continue to reign for three years, ten months and twenty-four days before the twelfth dynasty actually fell?[40] Hayes tells us that her name is found on several monuments, one of them dated to her "Regnal Year 3." He also says that a sphinx and three statues of her person have been found at Khatana in the Delta.[41]

How could Sebeknefru continue to function as Queen under the situation of anarchy and foreign intrusion described by Ipuwer? Ipuwer said that the royal nobles and princes in the royal family had been driven away from their homes in the palace complex.

Lichtheim: Ch. 7 -- <The nobles> are expelled from the royal mansions. See, noble ladies are on boards, Princes in the workhouse. Ch. 8 See, he who slept wifeless found a noblewoman. . . . See, he who had nothing is a man of wealth, The Nobleman sings his praise.[42]

We saw above that beggars were entering the palace and carrying away the rich treasures of the Pharaoh (Amenemhet IV). Therefore, Queen Sebeknefru could not have remained inside the palace while it was being ransacked and when her own royal family had been forced into hiding and some of them into servitude. The princes mentioned by Ipuwer were forced out of the palace and lived in "work houses." These princes are likely sons of younger wives of Amenemhet IV who were not born of his sister/wife, Queen Sebeknefru, and thus were not of the royal "divine seed" and not legitimate heirs to the crown. If these princes were sons of Queen Sebeknefru, none were old or wise enough to be Pharaoh in place of their mother the Queen.

Baines apparently assumed the Queen had a peaceful and uneventful reign because she registered the height of the Nile in her third year and had a sphinx and three statues made of herself. These few inscriptions are insufficient to determine the nature of her reign. No document describes the reigns of either Amenemhet IV, or of his Queen Sebeknefru, unless it be that of Ipuwer. **No document explains why the king and his queen were not buried in a pyramid and why their tombs have never been found. Their predecessors built magnificent pyramids. The silence of their mysterious deaths and missing tombs speaks loudly that they did not die with honor and that they likely did not die naturally.**

C. A Proposed Hypothesis of Queen Sebeknefru's Reign

Below I propose a hypothetical scenario that takes into account all of the known facts of Queen Sobeknefru's reign and death in light of the historical testimony of Ipuwer and in the context of the Biblical Exodus. After the deaths of her first-born son and her husband, Amenemhet IV, Queen Sebeknefru, the wife and sister of Amenemhet IV, ascended to the throne of Egypt. When her Egyptian subjects finally learned that the entire army had been destroyed with the king in the Red Sea debacle, deep anger arose in the hearts of Egyptians against Amenemhet IV and his royal family. Amenemhet IV's hard heart had brought the ten plagues upon Egypt and destroyed their crops, their livestock, their firstborn, and now their army. The peasants and other non-Israelite slaves of Egypt realized that the absence of the Egyptian army allowed them to revolt against the Queen as well as their wealthy employers and slave masters. They seized the opportunity and turned upside down the social structure of twelfth-dynasty society, expelling the royal family and the nobles from the royal mansions of the Palace complex.

D. The Flight of Queen Sebeknefru from Itjtowy to Thebes

Queen Sebeknefru barely escaped the fury of the angry mob **by fleeing from Itjtowy to Thebes in southern Egypt, where the twelfth dynasty kings had their origin and many relatives**. Sekhemre Ammenemes Sekhemre (Sobkhotpe I) was the nomarch (governor) of Thebes and thought by some Egyptologists to be a relative of the royal family either by blood or marriage.[43] Governor Sekhemre's home in Thebes provided a safer refuge for Queen Sebeknefru than anywhere in northern Egypt, where the principal revolt was occurring.

Sekhemre's home was no doubt protected by a contingent of the Egyptian army stationed at Thebes that did not accompany Amenemhet IV's army to the Red Sea. On the other hand, if all of the southern army joined with the northern army and both armies pursued the Israelite slaves and died in the Red Sea, the Nomarch Sekhemre could easily have assembled a new army out of the youth and retired officers in southern Egypt at Thebes, the principal district of southern Egypt.

Queen Sobeknefru likely fled to Thebes under the protection of Governor Sekhemre. Interestingly, Queen Sebeknefru's name is found in an inscription at Karnak, the governor's palace at Thebes. Also, her name is inscribed in her third year on a monument on the Nile River at the Second Cataract, which is located south of Elephantine.[44] These inscriptions show that Queen Sebeknefru was active in southern Egypt and likely resided in Thebes after being forced out of her palace at Itjtowy in the Delta.

The tomb of Kemuny, the butler of Amenemhet IV, was found at Thebes.[45] The close officials and servants of previous twelfth-dynasty kings were usually buried within the same Pyramid Complex of each king in the Faiyum of northern Egypt. The fact that Kemuny was buried at Thebes in southern Egypt strongly indicates that Queen Sebeknefru indeed moved to Thebes when Amenemhet IV died and that Kemuny followed the Queen, stayed in Thebes and died there. Perhaps the Queen herself is buried in some unknown tomb of Thebes. However, her tomb has never been found to this day.

E. Governor Sekhemre Became Vizier of Queen Sebeknefru

I propose that the revolt in northern Egypt was more severe than in southern

Egypt, where Egyptian soldiers could restrain criminals and more rapidly quell the revolt. When Governor Sekhemre secured southern Egypt, he likely left the Queen protected at Thebes, and led an army to oust the Libyans in northern Egypt. Sekhemre likely fought in the Delta to quell the peasant rebellion and finally restored order to the Delta so that the Queen could return to her palace.

However, the war against the Libyans proved more difficult than Governor Sekhemre anticipated. He drove them out of the eastern delta, but failed to drive them out of the western delta. The Libyans became so firmly entrenched in the western delta that they stayed as Egypt's fourteenth dynasty for 184 years.

While Sekhemre fought against Libyans, he left a power vacuum in southern Egypt. The Nubians crossed the southern border of Egypt and began a war that prevented the province of Elephantine from sending revenue to the capital at Itjtowy. Thus, the Nubians got a momentary foothold in southern Egypt, but did not make their way as far north as Thebes, where Queen Sebeknefru had temporarily located her palace in Sekhemre's mansion.

F. The Return of Queen Sebeknefru to Itjtowy

Governor Sekhemre finally ousted the Libyans from the eastern delta, confining them in the western delta, crushing the peasant revolt, and reoccupying Itjtowy (Zoan), the capital of Egypt. About two years after the Queen fled Itjtowy, the situation was safe for her to return to Itjtowy and continue her reign in the official palace in Itjtowy. During this time a sphinx and three statues were sculptured in her image and later found at Khatana in the eastern delta, near Tanis (Zoan).[46]

G. The Mysterious Death and Dishonorable Burial of Queen Sebeknefru

Did Queen Sebeknefru die a natural death? Or did Governor Sekhemre realize that the hatred and disrespect of the populace against her and her husband, Amenemhet IV, were so intense, that she could not reign effectively and that he needed to remove her by force? With not a single document except Ipuwer's to tell us what happened during her brief reign, we cannot know for certain what occurred. **However, we do know that no pyramid was built for either Sebeknefru or her husband, Amenemhet IV. Their tombs have never been found!**

However, all of Amenemhet IV's **predecessors** were buried in honor in magnificent pyramid complexes that contain the tombs for the kings and their wives, and their entire family and important officials. Amenemhet IV, the Pharaoh of the Exodus, and his wife, Sebeknefru, **died in infamy, not honor.** A small diorite sphinx of Amenemhet IV was found in the tomb of Prince Ypshomuibi of Byblos in Lebanon.[47] We have already noted in Chapter Eighteen that the statue with the broken nose is thought to be that of Amenemhet IV. He and his wife, Sebeknefru certainly were not honored in their deaths, nor afterwards. **Amenemhet IV's tomb lies at the bottom of the Red Sea.** His wife's missing tomb and lack of honor are all consistent with what we would expect Egyptians to do **after her husband provoked the God of heaven to destroy Egypt by plagues and "pouring water."**

Sebeknefru's total reign is listed in the Turin Canon as three years, ten months and twenty-four days.[48] Her short reign implies that she was likely forced to resign as Queen at the demand of her relative, Sekhemre, former governor of Thebes.

XIII. SEKHEMRE, THE FIRST PHARAOH OF THE THIRTEENTH DYNASTY AND THE END OF THE TWELFTH DYNASTY

Governor Sekhemre became Pharaoh of Egypt in the place of Queen Sebeknefru and established a new line of thirteenth dynasty kings. Sekhemre thus started a new family of Pharaohs. Pharaoh Sekhemre made additions to the construction of the temples at Deir el-Bahri and at El-Madamud, both located in Middle Egypt. He also ordered a census of Egypt, and its lists were found at El-Lahun, in the pyramid complex of Sesostris II. During his first four years of reign, the height of the Nile was recorded on monuments at the Second Cataract (Waterfall) near Buhen, 200 miles south of Elephantine. These Nile records show that he later returned with this army and drove the Nubians out of southern Egypt. However, Sekhemre was unable to drive out the Libyans in the western delta of Egypt. His total reign lasted only five years and a fraction. The longevity of the reigns of his successors were often shorter, with sixty kings reigning in succession in only 153 years, an average of 2.55 years per reign.[49]

The glowing fire of the powerful twelfth dynasty was extinguished. Two weak and unstable dynasties stumbled in a twilight that got darker with the coming of the Hyksos 100 years later. **Amenemhet IV, the Pharaoh of the Exodus, brought upon Egypt irreparable harm that lasted for two centuries.** Hayes admits that Amenemhet III was the last great ruler of the Middle Kingdom and that "his reign was followed by a decline which opened the way to an Asiatic overlordship of Egypt and the dark days of the Hyksos Period."[50]

CONCLUSION

Ipuwer's document has provided us with twenty-six more historical links between the Biblical Pharaoh of the Exodus and Amenemhet IV, the last king of the twelfth dynasty. See these twenty-six synchronisms in Table 20-B on the next page. **Joined with the previous thirty-six links in Chapters Eighteen and Nineteen, we now have sixty-two historical facts that are consistent with, or implicate directly, Amenemhet IV as the infamous Pharaoh of the Exodus.**

TABLE 20-B
TWENTY-SIX DISCOVERIES OF ISRAEL'S EXODUS
AND THE DROWNING OF AMENEMHET IV
AND HIS ARMY

Discovery No. 1. Ipuwer reported that slaves stole the riches of Egypt. Exodus 3:21-22 says that the Egyptians freely gave the Israelites riches in fear that more plagues might fall on them.

Discovery No. 2. Ipuwer reported that female slaves were wearing gold and silver necklaces on their necks, as Exodus 11:2-3 reports.

Discovery No. 3. Ipuwer reported that the slaves suddenly vanished from the delta, as Numbers 33:3-4 reports.

Discovery No. 4. Ipuwer reported that Egypt's peasants were revolting against their Egyptian masters, because the Egyptian army was not present to exert law and order.

Discovery No. 5. Ipuwer reported that the criminal element took over Egypt because the police force (army) was not present to stop them.

Discovery No. 6. Ipuwer reported that the palace was robbed by beggars because the army was not present to restrain them.

Discovery No. 7. Ipuwer reported that the king is dead and anarchy rules.

Discovery No. 8. Ipuwer reported that the mighty Pharaoh (Amenemhet IV) had been killed by **"pouring water" (drowning in the Red Sea).**

Discovery No. 9 Ipuwer reported that Pharaoh (Amenemhet IV) was lured out of his palace like a serpent is lured from his hole and destroyed.

Discovery No. 10. Ipuwer reported that Egyptian peasants drove the judges and officials from their governmental officies and took them over because the army was not present to protect them.

Discovery 11. Ipuwer said that the Mayor of the city went unescorted (no police; army destroyed).

Discovery 12. Ipuwer reported that the capital of Egypt was about to collapse because the king and its army were not present to protect it.

Discovery 13. Libyans invaded the western Delta and began the fourteenth dynasty with no army to prevent their invasion.

Discovery 14. Nubians were threatening Egypt in the south because the army was not present to defend Egypt..

Discovery 15. Amenemhet IV's wife, Sebeknefru, reigned in her husband's place because her firstborn son died in the plague of the firstborn.

Discovery 16. Sebeknefru, the Queen, fled from her palace to Thebes for protection from the peasant revolt.

Discovery 17. The tomb of Kemuny, the butler of Amenemhet IV, was found at Thebes indicating that he followed Queen Sebeknefru when she moved to Thebes.

Discovery 18. Sekhemre , Governor of Thebes, led the southern army to recapture the eastern delta and the capital of Itjtowy.

Discovery 19. Queen Sebeknefru's short four-year reign ended abruptly and mysteriously.

Discovery 20. Queen Sebeknefru's pyramid and her tomb have not been found. She likely was removed by force, or killed by the new Pharaoh.

Discovery 21. The pyramid and tomb of Amenemhet IV are also missing. His skeleton rests on the bottom of the Red Sea.

Discovery 22. Queen Sebeknefru mysteriously disappeared and Sekhemre, Governor of Thebes, moved north to the capital city of Itjtowy and established the thirteenth dynasty with its capital at Itjtowy.

Discovery 23. The twelfth dynasty had been the most glorious and powerful of all previous dynasties, but Egyptologists simply say that this dynasty mysteriously fell at the height of its glory. Ipuwer and the Bible explain that the twelfth dynasty fell because of the ten plagues and the drowning of Amenemhet IV and his army by **"pouring water."**

Discovery 24. Libyans entered the western delta of Egypt and established the fourteenth dynasty, reigning for 184 years under seventy-six kings.

Discovery 25. The thirteenth dynasty did not have a strong enough army to expel the Libyans.

Discovery 26. One hundred years later the Hyksos arrived in Egypt, further dividing Egypt into four dynasties reigning simultaneously, in contrast to the glorious twelfth dynasty that ruled independently for more than 200 years.

TABLE 20-B
RUNNING TOTAL OF DISCOVERIES

Chapter		Chapter Total	Running Total
2	Conflict Between Biblical and Secular Histories	18	18
4	Discovery of 430 Years from Abraham to the Exodus	16	34
5	Confirmation of Abraham's Historicity	28	62
6	Discovery of the Remains of Sodom and Gomorrah	17	79
7	Joseph As a Slave and Prisoner in Amenemhet I's Reign	21	100
8	Joseph Becomes the Vizier of Sesostris I	23	123
9	Sesostris I Gives Joseph a New Name and a Wife	11	134
10	The Seven Years of Abundance in Sesostris I's Reign	10	144
11	The Seven Years of Famine in Sesostris I's Reign	20	164
12	Israel Enters Egypt during Sesostris I's Reign	14	178
13	Sesostris III Enslaves the Israelites	17	195
14	Sesostris III, The Foster Grandfather of Moses	12	207
15	Sesostris III, Builder of Rameses and Pithom	15	222
16	Zoan (Itjtowy), the Capital of the Twelfth Dynasty	16	238
17	Amenemhet III, the Pharaoh Who Tried to Kill Moses	15	253
18	Amenemhet IV, the Pharaoh of the Exodus	14	267
19	Moses and Ipuwer Report the Ten Plagues	22	289
20	Israel's Exodus and the Drowning of Amenemhet IV and His Army in the Red Sea	26	315

NOTES FOR CHAPTER TWENTY

1. Lichtheim (Trans.), "Admonitions of Ipuwer," *Ancient Egyptian Literature*, I.151-2, 156-7.
2.. Lichtheim (Trans.), I.159.
3. Lichtheim (Trans.), I.159-160.
4. Lichtheim (Trans.), I.150, 153, 158.
5. Lichtheim (Trans.), I.152.
6. Lichtheim (Trans.), I.151.
7. Lichtheim (Trans.), I.152
8. Lichtheim (Trans.), I.153.
9. Lichtheim (Trans.), I.154

10. Lichtheim (Trans.), I..150
11. Lichtheim (Trans.), I.160 151.
12. Lichtheim (Trans.), I.155.
13. Lichtheim (Trans.), I..156.
14. Lichtheim (Trans.), I.158.
15. Lichtheim (Trans.), I.156.
16. Lichtheim (Trans.), I.156
17. Hayes, *Scepter of Egypt*, I.200.
18. Petrie, *History of Egypt*, I.206.
19. Lichtheim (Trans.), I.156.
20. Exodus 14:3.
21. Lichtheim (Trans.), I.152,155,-156, 158-9.
22. Lichtheim (Trans.), I.150, 161.

23. Hayes, *Scepter of Egypt*, I.171.
24. Hayes, *Cambridge Ancient History*, "Middle Kingdom of Egypt," I.2A.498-9; 506-509.
25. Hayes, *Cambridge Ancient History*, I.2A.499, 506-507
26. Hayes, *Cambridge Ancient History Ibid.*, I.2A.499.
27. Hayes, *Cambridge Ancient History*, I.2A.509.
28. Hayes, *Scepter of Egypt*, I.196.
29. Hayes, *Cambridge Ancient History*, II.1.44-45.
30. Hayes, *Cambridge Ancient History*, II.1.45.
31. John A. Wilson (Trans.), "The Admonitions of Ipuwer," *Ancient Near Eastern Texts*, p.442.
32. Hayes, *Cambridge Ancient History*, II.1.53-54.
33. Hayes, *Cambridge Ancient History*, II.1.53-54.
34. Hayes, *Cambridge Ancient History*, II.1.44.
35. Hayes, *Cambridge Ancient History*, II.1.54
36. Breasted, *History of Egypt*, p. 222.
37. Save-Soderbergh & I. U. Olsson, *Radiocarbon Variations and Absolute Chronology*
      John Wiley & Sons, Inc. New York, p. 44
38. D. F. Morgan, "Horse," *International Bible Encyclopedia*, Rev., 1982, II.759.
39. Baines and Wente, "Egypt," *New Encyclopedia Britannica*, 18.114.
40. Petrie, *History of Egypt*, I.150.
41. Hayes, *Cambridge Ancient History*, II.1.43.
42. M. Lichtheim (Trans.,) "Admonitions of Ipuwer," *Ancient Egyptian Literature.*, I.156-7.
43. Hayes, *Cambridge Ancient History*, II.1.45.
44. Hayes, *Cambridge Ancient History*, II.1.43.
45. Hayes, *Scepter of Egypt*, I.201.
46. Hayes, *Cambridge Ancient History*, II.1.43.
47. Hayes, *Cambridge Ancient History*, II.1.42-43
48. Petrie, *History of Egypt*, I.150.

CHAPTER TWENTY-ONE
CONTINUOUS ERRORS IN EGYPT'S "ASTRONOMICALLY ABSOLUTE" DATES

Chapters Twenty-One to Twenty-Four **prove that twelfth dynasty dates should be revised about three centuries later than the Egyptologists' dates.** The reconciliation between Egyptian and Biblical chronologies depends on these four chapters.

Archaeologists depend upon the dates of the Egyptian dynasties to give astronomically absolute dates to the archaeological histories of **twenty-two nations who are linked to Egypt.**[1] Israeli archaeologist Amihai Mazar affirms that Egypt's "absolute" chronology is the model for dating most of the strata in Palestine Therefore, any revision of Egyptian chronology requires an identical revision in the dates of the archaeological ages.

> From *ca.*3000 B.C.E. the absolute chronology of Palestine is based to a large extent on that of Egypt. Egyptian objects found in Palestine . . . and founded in dated contexts provide the basis for a chronological framework. The dependency on Egyptian chronology is so strong that any change in the latter necessitates a parallel shift concerning Palestine.[2]

Mazar's admission that Egypt's dates are **being "changed"** implies that Egypt's dates are **not "absolute."** Indeed, this chapter proves that Egyptologists have **continually revised** their astronomical dates, **demonstrating** that Egypt's astronomical dates are **not "absolute."** The next three chapters prove that Egypt's earliest dynasties are dated **four to six centuries too early** and that Egypt's dynasties eleven to twenty are dated **three centuries too early.** When the dates of Egypt's dynasties twelve to twenty are **revised by three centuries later, remarkable and numerous synchronisms occur between Biblical and Egyptian histories, as already seen in the previous chapters.**

While archaeologists depend on Egypt to date strata in nations linked to Egypt, some archaeologists do not even understand the astronomical method of dating used by Egyptologists. **William Dever**, America's most famous Palestinian archaeologist, believes that the date of **1991 B.C.** for the beginning of the twelfth dynasty **"is astronomically fixed by an eclipse of the sun."**[3] However, **eclipses of the sun have nothing to do with dating the twelfth dynasty.**

Instead, Egyptologists use **dated appearances of the star Sirius, linked to lunar dates** to ascribe supposed "astronomically fixed dates" to dynasties twelve through twenty. Censorinus, a Roman scientist and Egyptologist, called the star Sirius by the name **of "Sothis."** Thus, Egyptologists call dates of Sirius' rising **"Sothic dates."**

Some archaeologists have never investigated the validity of the astronomical method by which Egyptian history is dated. Archaeologists and Egyptologists mostly confide in the astronomical conclusions **of a few Egyptologists, who are not themselves astronomers.** When Dever said that an eclipse of the sun dated the beginning of the twelfth dynasty in 1991 B.C, he was not aware that Rolf Krauss had already revised Amenemhet I's accession year of **1991 B.C. by fifty-three years** to **1938 B.C.** Baines and Wente recorded **Krauss' new date of 1938 B.C. as "absolute" in the 1991 Edition of the** *New Encyclopedia Britannica* **(18.113).**

Egyptologists **constantly revise** their Sothic dates, demonstrating that their astronomical (Sothic) method of dating is **not absolute.** This chapter is complex because of the highly technical aspects of Sothic dating. However, **we must understand Egypt's Sothic Calendar and Egyptologists' Sothic dates before we can show that the Sothic system is invalid in determining "absolute dates."**

This chapter demonstrates that continual errors, revisions and exaggerated claims of astronomical compatibility have been made by differing Egyptologists. These errors invalidate Egyptologists' claims that they have calculated astronomically absolute dates for the Egyptian dynasties. This chapter also explains the basics of "Sothic" dating and demonstrates the continual revisions and errors of incorrect Sothic dates and chronologies.

I. EGYPT'S "SOTHIC" CALENDAR

A. Egypt's 365-Day Calendar

Egypt originally used a lunar calendar, but was the first nation to devise a 365-day schematic calendar.[4] Its 365 days were divided into three seasons, each with four months. Each of the twelve months had thirty days for a total of 360 days. A five-day period was inserted between the twelfth and first months, making it a 365-day calendar. **Egypt's 365-day calendar is first seen in inscriptions** of the fifth dynasty and is repeated in later documents of the twelfth dynasty.[5] See how this calendar is organized in Table 21-A on page 294.

B. Failure to Adjust Egypt's Sothic Calendar For Leap Year

We must first learn how Sothic dates are calculated. Egyptologists claim that Egypt's 365-day calendar **was never revised, nor adjusted for Leap Year, during its entire B.C. history.** In contrast, the Julian Calendar of 365 days **added an extra day every four years for Leap Year.** Since the Egyptians **did not adust their civil calendar one day every four years for Leap Year,** Egypt's New Year's Day shifted **backward one day every four years on the Julian Calendar.** Simultaneously, Sirius' heliacal rising **theoretically** shifted forward one day every four years on the Julian Calendar.

TABLE 21-A

EGYPT'S 365-DAY CALENDAR

ACHET			
1	-	30	
2	-	30	
3	-	30	
4	-	30	120 days
PERET			
1	-	30	
2	-	30	
3	-	30	
4	-	30	120 days
SHEMU			
1	-	30	
2	-	30	
3	-	30	
4	-	30	120 days
SUB-TOTAL			**360 DAYS**
END OF YEAR FEAST			**5 DAYS**
TOTAL			**365 DAYS**

C. The Heliacal Rising of the Star Sirius

The **heliacal** rising of Sirius refers to its annual appearance **each July in the early dawn just before sunrise.** Sirius is also called **"the Nile Star,"** because it first appears over the Nile River every summer. Each succeeding day, Sirius gradually rises earlier in the darkness of night **in reverse order** from sunrise, until its final appearance occurs at sunset. Then, the star Sirius **disappears for seventy days** (at the latitude of 30°) before reappearing in the early morning darkness just before dawn one year later. Since the reappearance of Sirius announces the dawn of a new year and a new day, the Bible calls Sirius **"the morning star"** and sometimes uses it figuratively to refer to the dawning of Jesus Christ in the hearts of his disciples, or to His final coming to glorify His followers.[6]

D. Five Dates of Sirius' Rising

Rekhmire, Vizier of Thutmose III, wrote in his tomb that one of his duties was to **record** the dates of the annual rising of Sirius and the high Nile.[7] However, Egyptologists claim that only **five observed dates of Sirius' rising** are preserved in documents of ancient Egypt. See these dates in Table 21-B on page 295.

Based on the **major premise that Egypt never adjusted or revised its 365-Day Calendar,** Egyptologists use these **five dates of Sirius' rising** to calculate their **"astronomically absolute"** chronology of Egyptian history. However we will see in Chapter Twenty-Two that Egypt's calendar was significantly revised from a 365-day calendar to a 360-day calendar during Egypt's eighteenth dynasty. This 360-day calendar broke the Sothic Cycle, permitting the Egyptian dynasties to be redated three centuries later. Carbon-14 dating and an eclipse of the sun prove beyond doubt that the eighteenth dynasty must be **dated three centuries later than**

its Sothic dates. In the next chapter we will also see **a sixth observed rising of Sirius** in the reign of Ramses III of the Twentieth Dynasty, which also proves that Egypt's Sothic Cycle was broken, permitting dynasties twelve to twenty to be **redated three centuries later than their previous Sothic dates. However, we must first understand the basics of Sothic dating and its value before revealing its serious weaknesses.**

TABLE 21-B
EGYPTOLOGISTS REGISTER ONLY FIVE DATES
OF OBSERVED RISINGS OF SIRIUS

8-16 means the 8th month and the 16th day on Egypt's Calendar.
(1) 8-16 in year 7 of Sesostris III, a twelfth-dynasty king[8]
(2) 11-9 in year 9 of Amenhotep I, an eighteenth-dynasty king[9]
(3) 11-28 in an unknown year of Thutmose III, an eighteenth-dynasty king[12]
(4) 10-1 on July 19 (Julian), 238 B.C., in Ptolemy III's eighth year[13]
(5) 1-1 on July 20 (Julian), A. D. 139/140[14]

E.   Censorinus' 1460-Year Sothic Cycles
Censorinus, **a Roman astronomer of the third century A.D.,** reported the rising of Sirius at Memphis (30°) on July 20, A.D. 140, on Egypt's New Year's Day (1-1). Censorinus claimed that Sirius' rising shifted forward on Egypt's 365-day calendar at the rate of one day every four years. At this rate, Sirius' rising rotated completely around Egypt's 365-day calendar to coincide once again with Egypt's New Year's Day, **every 1,460 years** (4 years X 365 days = 1460 years). Egyptians called the star Sirius by the name of **Sopedt.** However, Censorinus called the star Sirius by the Roman name of **Sothis,** and called these **1460-year periods "Sothic Cycles."**[15] **Modern Egyptologists still use "Sothic Cycles" to date Egypt's so-called "astronomically absolute chronology."**

II.   CONTINUAL REVISIONS OF
EGYPT'S "SOTHIC" DATES

A. Petrie's Astronomical Chronology
W. F. Petrie, "father of modern archaeology" from England, calculated that **four previous Sothic Cycles of 1460 years occurred previously in A. D. 140 in 1320 B.C., 2780 B.C., 4240 B.C. and 5700 B.C.** Based on his calculations of the total reigns for each dynasty, Petrie dated the beginning of the first dynasty in **5546 B.C.,** the beginning of the twelfth dynasty in **3579 B.C.** and the beginning of the eighteenth dynasty in **1587 B.C.**[16]

B. Breasted's Astronomical Chronology and His Key to
Reducing Egyptian History by 1,460 Years
James Breasted of the University of Chicago was America's foremost Egyptologist during his lifetime. Breasted also believed that Egypt's 365-day

calendar originated with the rising of Sirius on Egypt's New Year's Day. Breasted accepted Censorinus' Sothic Cycles of 1460 years. However, Breasted **reduced** Petrie's chronology **by an entire Sothic Cycle of 1460 years** by finding that dynasties thirteen through seventeen **reigned simultaneously, and thus parallel to each other, rather than consecutively. Parallel or rival dynasties are the keys that can reduce Egyptian history by hundreds and even thousands of years.** In the next chapter I will use the same method of finding rival dynasties that enable a three-century reduction for the dates of the twelfth dynasty.

Breasted calculated that Sirius rose on **July 19** of the Julian calendar at the latitude of Memphis for many thousands of years until it finally appeared on **July 20** toward the end of the first millennium B.C.[17] Breasted calculated more specifically that **previous Sothic Cycles of 1460 years ended and began on July 20, 140 A.D., July 19, 1320 B.C., July 19, 2780 B.C., and July 19, 4240 B.C.** Breasted thus declared that Egypt began its 365-day Calendar with the rising of Sirius on "**July 19, 4241 B.C., the oldest fixed date in history.**"[18]

Breasted dated the beginning of the first dynasty to **3400 B.C.,**[19] **reducing Petrie's date of 5546 B.C. by 2,146 years**. Breasted confirmed this 3400 B.C. date by **"dead reckoning" of the total minimum reigns of Egypt's kings.**[20] He predicted, **"It is highly improbable that future discovery will shift these dates [including the 3400 B.C. date], more than a century in either direction."**[21] Little did Breasted know that modern Egyptologists would reduce his 3400 B.C. date to 2925 B.C., **a reduction of 475 years**, which we will examine later.

To calculate astronomically absolute dates for the twelfth dynasty, Breasted noted that **Sirius rose on 8-16 (Egyptian) in the seventh year of Sesostris III**. Breasted calculated that this 8-16 (Egyptian) date occurred 225 days after Egypt's New Year's Day (1-1). Since Sirius' rising shifted one day every four years, Breasted multiplied this **225-day shift by four years**, and calculated that **900 years** (225 X 4 = 900) had transpired since Sirius' rising had last coincided with Egypt's New Year's Day on **July 19, 2780 B.C.** Subtracting these 900 years from 2780 B.C., when Sirius' rising last coincided with New Year's Day, Breasted astronomically fixed **July 19, 1880 B.C.** (+ or - three years), for Sirius' rising in **Sesostris III's seventh year**.[22] Breasted considered this date for Sirius' rising in Sesostris III's seventh year as **"astronomically fixed."**[23]

The next recorded rising of Sirius occurred on 11-9 (Egyptian) in the ninth year of Amenhotep I, the second king of the eighteenth dynasty. The shift from 8-16 in Sesostris III's seventh year to 11-9 in Amenhotep I's ninth year covers eighty-three days on Egypt's 365-day, unadjusted Calendar. At the rate of one day every four years, Breasted calculated that this eighty-three-day shift occurred over **332 years** (83 X 4 = 332). **Subtracting 332 years from 1880 B.C.,** when Sirius rose on Sesostris III's seventh year, Breasted astronomically fixed **July 19, 1548 B.C.,** for Sirius' rising on 11-9 of Amenhotep I's ninth year.

Breasted confirmed this Sothic date by **"dead reckoning"** the total minimum reigns of all Egypt's kings from the Persian Conquest of Egypt in 525 B.C. backward to the ninth year of the eighteenth-dynasty Pharaoh, Amenhotep I.

Breasted thus used **Sothic dating** to fix Amenhotep I's ninth year to **1548 B.C.** and
the beginning of the eighteenth dynasty to **1580 B.C.**[24] Breasted put asterisks on
the dates of the twelfth and eighteenth dynasties that he considered to be
"astronomically absolute."

C. Richard Parker's Discovery of Egypt's
Religious Lunar Calendar

In 1950 Richard Parker wrote his famous book, *The Calendars of Ancient
Egypt.* Parker proposed that Egypt originally used **a lunar calendar of 354 to 355
days** with **twelve months of varying twenty-nine and thirty-day months.**[25]
Parker demonstrated from ancient documents that Egypt began its new lunar month
when **the old moon was no longer visible just before dawn.**[26]   Later, Egypt
developed a **365-day civil calendar that began with the first rising of Sirius,
which also occurs just before dawn.**[27] Thus, Egypt began its day and its new
lunar month **at dawn,** whereas Babylon began its day and new lunar month at
sunset. In contrast, Rome began its old lunar month and its later 365-day Julian
Calendar at **midnight.** The modern western world still follows the Roman model
of beginning the day at midnight.

Parker explained that Egypt's lunar calendar was not abandoned after
inventing its 365-day civil calendar. Egypt continued to use its lunar calendar for
celebrating **religious feasts.** Thus, the priests often noted the beginning of a lunar
month on a specific day and month of the civil calendar. In this manner **the lunar
religious calendar**, which averages **354.36 days, was superimposed** on Egypt's
365-day civil calendar.[28] This dual relationship can be compared to two roulette
wheels with 365 slots in the outer wheel and 355 slots on the inner wheel, that freely
rotate so as to connect at different points with each roll of the wheel.

Thus, **each year a different astronomical pattern of twenty-nine to thirty-
day lunar months was registered on Egypt's civil calendar of 365 days.** I will
explain later in this chapter how Egyptologists use this unique pattern of lunar dates
to test the astronomical compatibility of their Sothic dates for the twelfth dynasty.[29]

D. Parker's Twenty-Five Year Lunar Cycle

Parker also discovered that new moon months consistently changed on Egypt's
365-day Calendar and repeated the same pattern in a twenty-five year cycle. **Thus,
the first day of a new moon month coincided with Egypt's New Year's Day
every twenty-five years.** Parker used Table 21-C (p. 298) to develop his own
astronomical chronology of the twelfth dynasty. I also found Parker's twenty-five-
year table of lunar dates invaluable in searching for lunar compatibility in my own
proposed astronomical chronology of the twelfth dynasty in Chapter Twenty-Four.
I am deeply indebted to Parker for his keen insight of relating new moon dates to
Egypt's civil dates on their 365-day calendar. Parker's Twenty-Five-Year Lunar
Cycle can be seen below.

TABLE 21-C
THE 25-YEAR LUNAR CYCLE (NEW MOONS)
ON EGYPT'S 365-DAY CALENDAR

YEAR	ACHET				PERET				SHEMU				EPAG.
	I	II	III	IV	I	II	III	IV	I	II	III	IV	
1	1	1	1-30	30	29	29	29	28	27	27	27	26	
2	20	20	19	19	18	18	18	17	16	16	16	15	
3	9	9	8	8	7	7	7	6	5	5	5	4	4
4	28	28	27	27	26	26	26	25	24	24	24	23	
5	18	18	17	17	16	16	16	15	14	14	14	13	
6	7	7	6	6	5	5	5	4	3	3	3	2	2
7	26	26	25	25	24	24	24	23	22	22	22	21	
8	15	15	14	14	13	13	13	12	11	11	11	10	
9	4	4	3	3	2	2	2	1	1-30	30	30	29	
10	24	24	23	23	22	22	22	21	20	20	20	19	
11	13	13	12	12	11	11	11	10	9	9	9	8	
12	2	2	1	1	1-30	30	30	29	28	28	28	27	
13	21	21	20	20	19	19	19	18	17	17	17	16	
14	10	10	9	9	8	8	8	7	6	6	6	5	5
15	30	30	29	29	28	28	28	27	26	26	26	25	
16	19	19	18	18	17	17	17	16	15	15	15	14	
17	8	8	7	7	6	6	6	5	4	4	4	3	
18	27	27	26	26	25	25	25	24	23	23	23	22	
19	16	16	15	15	14	14	14	13	12	12	12	11	
20	6	6	5	5	4	4	4	3	2	2	2	1	1
21	25	25	24	24	23	23	23	22	21	21	21	20	
22	14	14	13	13	12	12	12	11	10	10	10	9	
23	3	3	2	2	1	1	1-30	30	29	29	29	28	
24	22	22	21	21	20	20	20	19	18	18	18	17	
25	12	12	11	11	10	10	10	9	8	8	8	7	

E. Parker's Dating of Sirius' Rising
in Sesostris III's Seventh Year

The twelfth-dynasty Pharaoh, Sesostris III, buried his father, Sesostris II, in a pyramid close to Lake Moeris (Birket Qarun) about forty miles southwest of Cairo. A temple within the pyramid complex was devoted to the worship of the departed Sesostris II. Within this temple were found numerous papyri fragments containing the civil dates of the first days of new moon months when sacrifices were offered by Sesostris III and his son Amenemhet III in behalf of their deceased father and grandfather, Sesostris II, who was regarded as a god.

One of the fragments found in the temple predicted **that the star Sirius would rise on 8-16 of the seventh year of the king.** The handwriting on this fragment was the same as that of a priest who named Sesostris III as the king he served. **Thus, Parker logically identified Sesostris III as the king in whose seventh year Sirius rose on 8-16 (Egyptian).**[30]

Parker said the traditional location of the observatory for Sirius' rising was in Memphis, which has a latitude of about 30°.[31] Parker calculated the date of Sirius' rising in the nineteenth century B.C. **He found that Breasted's date of July 19**

was incorrect by two days and that the correct date was July 17. Using the Sothic [Sothis = Sirius] method, Parker dated Sirius' rising on 8-16 Egyptian (in Sesostris III's seventh year) to the Julian date of July 17 during the quadrennium **(four year period) from 1873 to 1870 B.C.** Parker's date of July 17, 1873/70 B.C. for Sirius' rising **revised Breasted's date of July 19, 1880 B.C., by two days and seven to ten years. Each day of error for the date of Sirius' rising results in a four-year revision for the year of its rising.**

F. How Parker Decided Which Year Was
Sesostris III's Seventh Year

In order to ascertain which of these four years was Sesostris III's seventh year, Parker developed a brilliant method of comparing the calculated Julian date of Sirius' rising with a series of twelve new-moon dates observed and recorded during the thirtieth and thirty first years of Amenemhet III, the son of Sesostris III. Using the Julian date of July 17 for Sirius' rising on 8-16 (Egyptian), and utilizing his chart of the Twenty-Five-Year Cycle of New Moon Dates. Parker was able to calculate the predicted Julian dates of the twelve Egyptian new moon month dates. Then, Parker scientifically calculated the actual Julian lunar dates and compared them with his twelve predicted dates. Parker claimed that **ten of the twelve lunar dates tested correct (83%)**, when he dated Sirius' rising on 8-16 (Egyptian), **July 17 (Julian), only in the year 1872 B.C.**[32]

The observation of a series of new moon dates is never perfect because of bad weather, haze, or even white clouds. Neglect or lack of good eye sight of the observer can also cause errors. Peter Huber, formerly of Harvard University, calculated 33,000 Babylonian lunar dates. He found that the accuracy of late Babylonian administrators ranged from **66% in month lengths to 83% in crescents.**[33]

Thus, Parker's claim of 83% lunar accuracy led him to say, "The results obtained from the lunar dates . . . justify the **astronomical correctness** of the forecast of the heliacal rising of Sothis, which must have taken place on **July 17, 1872 B.C.**" **(in Sesostris III's seventh year)**.[34] Parker's pronouncement moved Sir Alan Gardiner to write, "**1872 B.C. is the earliest relatively certain fixed date in Egyptian history**."[35] William Hayes recorded in the ***The Cambridge Ancient History*** Parker's date of **1872 B.C.** for Sesostris III's seventh year as **"fixed"** in twelfth-dynasty chronology.[36]

Edgerton accepted Parker's date of July 17, 1872 B.C., as **"absolute"** for Sesostris III's seventh year. Edgerton then revised Breasted's date for **Sirius' rising in Amenhotep I's ninth year (the second Pharaoh of the eighteenth dynasty) from July 19, 1548 B.C., to July 16, 1537 B.C., a revision of only eleven years.** Hayes, writing in the *Cambridge Ancient History,* **also accepted Edgerton's date as "astronomically fixed" for the eighteenth dynasty.**[37]

G. Hayes' Revised Chronology in the
Cambridge Ancient History

William Hayes presented sound arguments for **rejecting** Breasted's date of **July 19, 4241 B.C.**, as the origin of Egypt's 365-day calendar and **"the oldest fixed date in history."**[38] Hayes **reduced** Breasted's date of **3400 B.C.** for the first dynasty **by 300 years to 3100 B.C.**[38] To harmonize this three-century reduction Hayes found **150 years of co-reigns** in dynasties 1 to 9, and **142 years of rival reigns** in dynasties 10 and 11.[39] Thus, Breasted's "astronomically absolute" chronology for Egypt suffered **an additional three-century reduction.   The reader can easily see how the discovery of parallel dynasties and co-reigns can quickly reduce Egyptian history by hundreds and even thousands of years.**

H.   Ingham's Revised Dates For Sirius' Rising

In 1969, M. Ingham, an English astronomer, recalculated the date of Sirius' rising at 30° on **July 16** from 1900 to 1700 B.C. and beyond. Ingham said that Sirius' rising gradually shifted to **July 19 in 238 B.C., and to July 20 by A.D. 139.** Ingham concluded that **Parker's date of July 17, 1872 B.C.**, for Sesostris III's seventh year, was **wrong by one day and several years.** Ingham's astronomical date of **July 16** for Sirius' rising **completely nullified all of the astronomical chronologies of Breasted, Parker and Edgerton simply because they had miscalculated the dates for Sirius' rising during the nineteenth century B.C.**[40] Thus, John Baines and E. W. Wente concluded the following in the 1991 Edition of the *New Encylopaedia Britannica.*

> The chronologies offered in most publications **up to 1985 have been disproved** [my emphasis] **for the Middle and New kingdoms** [of Egypt] **by a restudy of the evidence for the Sothic and especially the lunar dates.**[41]

Furthermore, astronomer Ingham determined that Sirius' rising did **not** produce 1,460-year Sothic Cycles, as Egyptologists had previously thought. Ingham calculated that the Sothic Cycle from 2768 B.C. to 1314 B.C. was **1454 years** and that the Sothic Cycle from 1314 B.C. to A.D. 139 was only **1,452 years.**[42] Ingham's new dates of Sirius' rising **invalidated all formerly calculated astronomical chronologies of Egypt, including those listed in the 1971 edition of the *Cambridge Ancient History.*** Thus the Sothic dates of Breasted, Parker and Edgerton were disproved by Ingham's new dates for Sirius' rising.

Thus, Egypt's "astronomically absolute" chronology suffered another blow that dented its reputation as the standard for the archaeological ages. However, these revised chronologies did not significantly change the dates of the twelfth dynasty, even though dynasties one through ten suffered a three century revision.

I. Rolf Krauss' Revised Chronology

Rolf Krauss, a German Egyptologist, calculated an entirely new and revolutionary astronomical chronology for the twelfth dynasty. **Krauss first moved the latitude of the observation of Sirius' rising from Memphis at 30° in N. Egypt to Elephantine at 24° at the southern border of Egypt**. The star Sirius rose at Elephantine **six days earlier** than it did at Memphis during the nineteenth century B.C. Krauss justified the Elephantine location by pointing out that the 11-28 (Egyptian) rising of Sirius in an unknown year of Thutmose III (eighteenth dynasty) was inscribed on a monument **at Elephantine** on the southern border of Egypt. Krauss reasoned that Elephantine was a more logical choice for the observatory because Sirius' yearly heliacal rising was **first seen in southern Egypt at Elephantine at the latitude of 24°.**

Neguebauer, an astronomer and an Egyptologist, calculated that Sirius rose **at 24° latitude (Elephantine) on July 9 (Julian) from 2000 to 1317 B.C.**[43] Using Neguebauer's date, Krauss dated Sirius' rising on 8-16 in Sesostris III's seventh year on **July 9, 1838 B.C.** Krauss compared this date with twenty lunar dates, including the twelve lunar dates that Parker used. However, Krauss **did not find sufficient astronomical compatibility for a true astronomical chronology.**[44]

In order to achieve astronomical compatibility, Krauss created the following **radical changes**. (1) He dated Sirius' rising on July 9, 1838 B.C. to the seventh year of **Sesostris II, the father of Sesostris III. However, all former Egyptologists were certain that Sesostris II was dead and his son Sesostris III was alive when the date of Sirius' rising was registered in the mortuary of Sesostris II, the dead father of Sesostris III.** (2) Krauss shortened the reign of Sesostris II **from a previous minimum reign of nineteen years to only nine years.** (3) Even more outrageous, Krauss proceeded to shorten the reign of Sesostris III from a previous minimum reign **of thirty-six years to only eighteen years.**[45] We will later see a new discovery of Sesostris III's **thirty-ninth year.**

After all of these **arbitrary** chronological changes, Krauss claimed that **fourteen of the twenty Egyptian lunar dates (70%) were correct** in relation to the July 9 date of Sirius' rising in Sesostris II's seventh year. He proceeded to **revise the six incorrect dates by one day** and claimed an adjusted astronomical accuracy of 90% (18 out of 20).[46] I personally believe one should not adjust an astronomical chronology in order to make it look better than it really is.

Krauss also calculated Sirius' rising on 11-9 of the ninth year of the **eighteenth dynasty king, Amenhotep I.** This 11-9 rising occurred eighty-three days after the 8-16 rising. Krauss multiplied the eighty-three days by four years, subtracted the 332 years from 1838 B.C., and got **July 9, 1506 B.C.,** for Sirius' rising at 24° on 11-9 in Amenhotep I's ninth year. Krauss interpreted the document that recorded this rising of Sirius to mean **a new moon month began the same day Sirius rose.** He astronomically calculated the date of this new moon month and found that it **indeed began on the same day that Sirius rose on July 9, 1506 B.C., a rare coincidence (odds are 30 to 1).** Krauss thus concluded that his dates for **July 9, 1838 B.C., for Sesostris II's seventh year and July 9, 1506 B.C., for Amenhotep I's ninth year, were "absolutely" correct.**[47] As we shall see later in this and the next chapter, Krauss' chronologies for the twelfth and eighteenth dynasties are **"absolutely incorrect."**

J. Krauss' Revised Chronology Was
Accepted by Baines and Wente

J. R. Baines and E. F. Wente **accepted both of Krauss' dates** of July 9, 1838 B.C., for Sesostris II's seventh year, and July 9, 1506 B.C., for Amenhotep I's ninth year as **"absolute."** They incorporated these dates into their revised chronology of Egyptian history and recorded them in their article on "Egypt" in the 1991 edition of the *New Encyclopaedia Britannica.*[48]

Baines and Wente also lowered the beginning of the first dynasty to **2925 B.C.,**[49] **475 years later** than Breasted's date of 3400 B.C. and **175 years later** than the *Cambridge* date of 3100 B.C. Baines and Wente accomplished this last 175-year reduction by finding **122 additional years of co-reigns and rival reigns in the first eleven dynasties.** Baines and Wente also **reduced** the Cambridge date of the beginning of the twelfth dynasty by **fifty-three years from 1991 B.C. to 1938 B.C.,** following the lead of Krauss' new astronomical chronology.[50]

K. Ulrich Luft's Revised Astronomical Chronology

In 1992, Ulrich Luft **rejected** Krauss' dating of the 8-16 rising of Sirius in **Sesostris II's** seventh year. Luft cited documentary evidence demonstrating that this 8-16 rising of Sirius was celebrated by priests **in memory of the deceased Sesostris II** in the temple of his pyramid complex at el Lahun in northern Egypt while **Sesostris III was alive and reigning after the death of his father Sesostris II.** The handwriting of the 8-16 rising is identical to that of a companion document dated specifically to **Sesostris III's reign.** Thus, Luft, like Breasted and Parker, dated this 8-16 Egyptian rising in the seventh year of **Sesostris III, in contrast to** Krauss' designation of **Sesostris II,** the father of Sesostris III.[51] Krauss' inaccurate identification of Sesostris II instead of Sesostris III invalidated his so called "astronomically absolute" chronology of the twelfth and eighteenth dynasties and annulled the fifty-three-year reduction of the twelfth dynasty chronology by Baines and Wente. I will also prove later in this chapter that Krauss exaggerated the accuracy of his lunar chronology, nullifying the accuracy of his astronomical dating of both Sesostris II and Sesostris III. See my critique of Krauss' chronology in **Table 21-J on page 315.**

Luft calculated two chronologies: one based on Sirius' rising at 30° (Memphis) and the other at 24°(Elephantine). Sirius rises six days earlier at 24° than it does at 30°. **The 30° chronology proved to be superior in astronomical compatibility with the lunar dates.** The 30° latitude at Memphis is also more logical because the document containing the date was found at el Lahun, not far from Memphis, fitting perfectly the 30° latitude of observation. **Also, it is not logical that the priests at el Lahun (30◦) celebrated the rising of Sirius six days before they saw the star, which Krauss' view required.**

Using Ingham's date for Sirius' rising at 30° on July 16, 1866 B. C., Luft

compared this date with **thirty-nine lunar dates and claimed that twenty-five
were correct: 64%.**[52] Luft's 64% accuracy is only 6% less than Krauss' claim of
70% accuracy. **Later in this chapter we will also disprove Luft's claim of 64%
accuracy.**

L. Confusion Among Egyptologists

Egyptologists are confused as to **which** of these **"astronomically absolute
dates"** they should accept. However, most Egyptologists still follow Krauss' dates
because they work better with the dates for Amenhotep I's reign in the eighteenth
dynasty and Ramses II's reign in the nineteenth dynasty. **Later in this chapter we
will test these lunar and Sothic dates of Krauss and Luft. We will see that
neither of these Egyptologists has established "absolute" dates for the twelfth
through the nineteenth dynasties.**

III. FAULKNER'S EVALUATION OF EGYPTOLOGISTS' ASTRONOMICAL DATING

In the fall of 1994 I secured the services of **Danny Faulkner.** Faulkner's
doctorate is in astronomy. He teaches astronomy and physics at the University of S.
Carolina at Lancaster and also serves as the chairman of the faculty. Faulkner
explained to me the basics of astronomy as applied to days and dates on earth. He
worked with me for two years, calculating multiple dates of Sirius' rising at four
different latitudes of Egypt. He also calculated scores of new moon dates to test the
scholars' dates and calculated hundreds of other lunar dates before I found matches
for my revised chronology of the twelfth through the twentieth dynasties. I will be
eternally grateful to God for leading me to Dr. Faulkner who provided me with
invaluable and abundant astronomical knowledge and data. I could never have
solved the Exodus Mystery without Dr. Faulkner's invaluable assistance.

A. Faulkner's Explanation of Four Different Years
1. The Tropical Year

Faulkner informed me that the Tropical Year measures the time it takes for the
earth to rotate completely around the sun. The Tropical Year averages **365.242199
days and measures the four seasons of the year.**

2. The Gregorian Year

Our modern Gregorian calendar (now in use) averages **365.2425 days per year**
(over a four year-period) and is man's best measurement of earth's rotation around
the sun. The Gregorian Calendar exceeds the actual length of the Tropical Year by
only .000301 of a day = 26 seconds.

3. The Sidereal (Stellar) Year determines the dates of Sirius' rising.

The Sidereal Year averages **longer than** the Tropical Year, the Gregorian
Calendar and the Julian Calendar (see below). The **Sidereal Year** measures the time
that the earth rotates around the sun until it reaches the same position with the **stars**

(not the sun). **Thus, when the earth reaches the same position with the sun, it must rotate a little farther to arrive at the same position with the stars outside our solar system.** Faulkner says that the Sidereal Year averages **365.256484 days over a 13,000-year cycle.** However, the relationship between earth and the stars has gradually changed so that the Sidereal Year averaged a fraction of a day slower **(365.2520796 days)** during the years **1698 B.C. to 238 B.C.** Most Egyptologists are unaware of the difference between the lengths of the Sidereal and Tropical Years when they calculate their astronomical chronologies for Egyptian history.

4. The Julian Calendar is precisely 365.25 days

The Julian Calendar is closer in length to the average Sidereal Year than the Gregorian Calendar, but **still falls short of the average Sidereal Year.** Most modern scholars use the Julian Calendar to calculate their astronomical dates rather than the superior Gregorian Calendar. **Why? Because the Julian Calendar of 365.25 days is easier to calculate than our modern Gregorian Calendar of 365.2425 days per year.**

B. Faulkner's Explanation of the Backward Shift of Sirius' Rising On Both the Gregorian and Julian Calendars

1. Egyptologists and the astronomers Neguebauer and Ingham assumed that Sirius' rising always shifted gradually forward on both the Julian and Gregorian Calendars.

This assumption has caused Egyptologists to err in some of their calculations of the dates of Sirius' rising, **which sometimes retrogress rather than progress.** Notice below the explanation of this unusual astronomical phenomenon.

2. Schaeffer's Software to Calculate Dates of Sirius' Rising

Faulkner informed me that **Brad Schaeffer, head of the Bethesda Space Center in Maryland, has done the most thorough study of the Sidereal Year, which determines the dates of Sirius' rising.** Faulkner called Schaeffer and received permission to use his computer software program which calculates precise dates of Sirius' heliacal rising throughout ancient antiquity from any longitude and latitude.

At my request, Faulkner calculated **130 pairs of Julian/Gregorian dates for Sirius' annual appearance at four different latitudes of Egypt from 2000 B.C. to A.D. 300.** These dates are listed in **Table 21-D on page 306.** Table 21-D shows that Sirius' rising at the same latitude occasionally **fluctuated back and forth** on different dates of the **Julian Calendar between centuries and within the same century.** Sirius' rising **fluctuated** less frequently on the **Gregorian Calendar than it fluctuated on the Julian Calendar.** But all Egyptologists use the Julian Calendar, not the Gregorian Calendar, to calculate their astronomical dates because its number of **365.25 days** is easier to work with than the shorter, but more accurate Gregorian Calendar of **365.2425 days.**

Table 21-D (p. 306) notes that Sirius' rising at **30° latitude fluctuated back and forth five different times** between the Julian dates of **July 14 and July 15** during the years 2000 to 1200 B.C. Sirius' rising at **24° latitude fluctuated back and forth six different times** between the Julian dates of **July 7, 8, and 9 from 2000 to 1210 B.C., before shifting forward to July 10, in 1200 B.C.**

Table 21-D (p. 306) also shows **fluctuations in the midst of a century**. At 30° latitude Sirius rose on July 14 in 1900 B.C. and 1880 B.C., but shifted to July 15 by 1838 B.C. and back again to July 14 in 1800 B.C.

Fluctuations also occurred occasionally on the Gregorian calendar. At the latitude of Canopus, **Sirius rose on June 29 in 2000 B.C., shifted forward to June 30 in 1900 B.C., but shifted backward to June 29 in 1880 B.C.** The same phenomenon occurred at the latitude of Canopus by **Sirius' rising on July 3 in 1546 B.C., shifting backward to July 2 in 1506 B.C. and forward again to July 3 in 1400 B.C.**

Egyptologists, including the astronomer Ingham, never observed these fluctuations in the dates of Sirius' rising within centuries and between centuries. Why? Because they were **unaware of the precise wobble of the earth on its axis and because they did not calculate a sufficiently large number of dates to note these fluctuations.** Also, most Egyptologists, including the astronomer Ingham, who calculated only a few of the dates of Sirius' rising, did not have sufficiently precise methods of calculating the precise wobble of the earth on its axis in comparison to the modern computer software designed by the world's best astronomers, in this case by **Brad Schaeffer, Director of Bethesda Space Center in Bethesda Maryland.**

Thus, Sirius' rising fluctuated back and forth on the Julian calendar and occasionally on the Gregorian calendar. Recognizing this fluctuation demands that one calculate the Julian and Gregorian dates of **precise B.C. years for Sirius' rising in order to calculate a correct Egyptian chronology. These precise dates have been calculated by Faulkner's utilization of Schaeffer's sophisticated software. One hundred thirty pairs of dates for Sirius' rising are listed for four latitudes in Egypt over many centuries in Table 21-D (p. 306).** Notice the fluctuations back and forth on different Gregorian dates and especially Julian dates.

TABLE 21-D
130 PAIRS OF DATES OF SIRIUS' HELIACAL RISING
CALCULATED BY DR. DANNY FAULKNER
COMPUTER SOFTWARE BY
DR. BRAD SCHAEFFER

Astronomical Dates Subtract 1 Year from the B.C. Dates and Place a minus in Front of the Date: e.g. 2001 B.C. = -2000 Astronomical

B.C. YR.	CANOPUS 31°19' Greg.	Jul.	MEMPHIS c. 30° Greg.	Jul.	THEBES 25° 42' Greg.	Jul.	ELEPHANTINE 24° 05' Greg.	Jul.	B.C. YR.
2001	6-29	7-16	6-27	7-14	6-23	7-10	6-21	7-08	2001
1901	6-30	7-16	6-28	7-14	6-23	7-09	6-22	7-08	1901
1880	6-29	7-15	6-28	7-14	6-23	7-09	6-22	7-08	1880
1838	6-30	7-16	6-29	7-15	6-24	7-10	6-23	7-09	1838
1801	6-30	7-15	6-29	7-14	6-24	7-09	6-23	7-08	1801
1701	7-01	7-15	6-30	7-14	6-25	7-09	6-23	7-07	1701
1601	7-02	7-16	6-30	7-14	6-26	7-10	6-24	7-08	1601
1546	7-03	7-17	7-01	7-15	6-27	7-11	6-25	7-09	1546
1506	7-02	7-16	7-01	7-15	6-27	7-11	6-25	7-09	1506
1501	7-02	7-15	7-01	7-14	6-27	7-10	6-25	7-08	1501
1401	7-03	7-15	7-02	7-14	6-27	7-09	6-26	7-08	1401
1317	7-04	7-16			6-28	7-10			1317
1301	7-04	7-15	7-03	7-14	6-28	7-09	6-27	7-08	1301
1211	7-05	7-16	7-03	7-14	6-29	7-10	6-28	7-09	1211
1201	7-06	7-17	7-04	7-15	6-30	7-11	6-29	7-10	1201
1101	7-07	7-17	7-05	7-15	7-01	7-11	6-29	7-09	1101
1001	7-07	7-16	7-06	7-15	7-02	7-11	6-30	7-09	1001
970	7-07	7-16	7-06	7-15	7-01	7-10	6-30	7-09	970
901	7-08	7-16	7-07	7-15	7-03	7-11	7-01	7-09	901
801	7-09	7-17	7-08	7-16	7-03	7-11	7-02	7-10	801
701	7-10	7-17	7-08	7-15	7-04	7-11	7-03	7-10	701
601	7-10	7-16	7-09	7-15	7-05	7-11	7-04	7-10	601
501	7-11	7-16	7-10	7-15	7-06	7-11	7-04	7-09	501
401	7-12	7-17	7-11	7-16	7-07	7-12	7-05	7-10	401
301	7-14	7-18	7-13	7-17	7-09	7-13	7-07	7-11	301
238	7-14	7-18	7-12	7-16	7-09	7-13	7-07	7-11	238
201	7-15	7-18	7-13	7-16	7-09	7-12	7-08	7-11	201
101	7-15	7-17	7-14	7-16	7-10	7-12	7-09	7-11	101
A.D.									A.D.

IV. SHIFT OF EGYPT'S NEW YEAR'S DAY BASED ON THE PREMISE THAT EGYPT NEVER REVISED ITS 365-DAY CALENDAR

While the dates of Sirius' rising fluctuated back and forth on the Julian Calendar, Egypt's New Year's Day consistently fell back on the Julian Calendar one day every four years. The reason for this retrogression is Egypt's failure to adjust an extra day for Leap Year every four years on their 365-day calendar.

Based on the presupposition that Egypt never adjusted or revised its 365-day calendar, **Table 21-E** (pp. 322-325) calculates the specific **quadrennium (four-year period)** when Egypt's New Year's Day coincided with a specific Julian date from 1,900 B.C. to A.D. 148.   Table 21-E is calculated on the basis of the date of the Canopus Decree, 5-17 (Egyptian) − **March 7, 238 B.C. (Julian).** This Julian date of the Canopus Decree **has been astronomically fixed by an eclipse of the sun** and is accepted as **"absolute"** by all astronomers and historians.

On the basis of **5-17 Egyptian = March 7, 238 B.C.**, Egypt's New Year's Day (1-1) must be dated 136 days earlier on **October 22, 239 B.C. (Julian).** By dating backward and forward from this Julian date I was able to determine the Julian date of Egypt's New Year's Day in every quadrennium (four-year period) throughout Egyptian history. **Table 21-E (pp. 322-325) is thus based on the presupposition that Egypt never revised its 365-Day Calendar and thus never added an extra day every four years for Leap Year.**

I used Table 21-F (p. 308) to test the astronomical chronologies of Egyptologists for accuracy **according to their own presupposition that Egypt never revised its 365-day calendar. Table 21-F** lists the Julian and Gregorian dates for **Egypt's New Year's Day** as it shifted backward on the Julian and Gregorian calendars, **based on the presupposition that Egypt never revised its 365-day Sothic Calendar.**   Table 21-F is found on the next page.

However, In the next chapter **I will prove that Egypt's 365-day Sothic calendar was revised several times, invalidating all of the B.C. dates that Egyptologists have assigned to Egypt's Dynasties One to Twenty-Two.** In this chapter we will learn how Sothic dates are determined. We will also see how Egyptologists have continued to revise Egypt's Sothic chronology on the basis of **inaccurate dates of Sirius' rising and exaggerated claims of the accuracy of the lunar dates.**

TABLE 21-F
EGYPTIAN/JULIAN DATES OF SIRIUS' RISING
IN SPECIFIC ASTRONOMICAL YEARS
Years Based on Dates in Tables 21-D & 21-E

B.C. YEAR	New Year's Day EGYPT		Day JULIAN	Sirius' Rising Day EGYPT		Day JULIAN	Sirius' Rising Day EGYPT		Day JULIAN
1885	1-1	=	12-07	8-16	-140	7-20	8-17	=	7-21
1881	1-1	=	12-06	8-16	-140	7-19	8-17	=	7-20
1877	1-1	=	12-05	8-16	-140	7-18	8-17	=	7-19
1873	1-1	=	12-04	8-16	-140	7-17	8-17	=	7-18
1869	1-1	=	12-03	8-16	-140	7-16	8-17	=	7-17
1865	1-1	=	12-02	8-16	-140	7-15	8-17	=	7-16
1861	1-1	=	12-01	8-16	140	7-14	8-17	=	7-15
1857	1-1	=	11-30	8-16	-140	7-13	8-17	=	7-14
1853	1-1	=	11-29	8-16	-140	7-12	8-17	=	7-13
1849	1-1	=	11-28	8-16	-140	7-11	8-17	=	7-12
1845	1-1	=	11-27	8-16	-140	7-10	8-17	=	7-11
1841	1-1	=	11-27	8-16	-140	7-09	8-17	=	7-10
1837	1-1	=	11-26	8-16	-140	7-08	8-17	=	7-09
1833	1-1	=	11-25	8-16	-140	7-07	8-17	=	7-08
1549	1-1	=	09-14	11-9	-57	7-19			
1545	1-1	=	09-13	11-9	-57	7-18			
1541	1-1	=	09-12	11-9	-57	7-17			
1537	1-1	=	09-11	11-9	-57	7-16			
1533	1-1	=	09-10	11-9	-57	7-15			
1529	1-1	=	09-09	11-9	-57	7-14			
1525	1-1	=	09-08	11-9	-57	7-13			
1521	1-1	=	09-08	11-9	-57	7-12			
1517	1-1	=	09-07	11-9	-57	7-11			
1513	1-1	=	09-06	11-9	-57	7-10			
1509	1-1	=	09-05	11-9	-57	7-09			
1505	1-1	=	09-04	11-9	-57	7-08			
241	1-1	=	10-22	10-01	-95	7-19			
241	1-1	=	10-22	09-30	-96	7-18			

V. METHOD OF CALCULATING LUNAR DATES

Parker, the brilliant Egyptologist from the University of Chicago, found in Egyptian documents that Egypt used a religious lunar calendar that was superimposed upon its 365-day civil calendar. **Parker calculated all of his dates manually. As we shall see later, Parker made significant errors in some of his calculations.**

To calculate accurate lunar dates Faulkner used the computer software of the book, *Lunar Tables and Programs from 4000 B.C. to A.D. 8000,* by **Michelle Chapront-Touze and Jean Chapront.** The authors claim their program is accurate to within **"a few arcseconds"** [*sic.*] back to 4000 B.C.[53] This software calculates the precise time and day of an **"astronomical new moon,"** which occurs when the center of the moon is aligned with the center of the earth in relation to the center of the sun **in the middle of its invisibility**. Thus, it is necessary to calculate **the length of time from astronomical new moon back to the dawn of day** to determine whether the old moon had already disappeared or could still be seen just before dawn. We must remember that Egyptians, in contrast to Babylonians, began the first day of their lunar month when the **moon could no longer be seen just before dawn.** The Babylonians began their new lunar month on the first evening **when the new moon first appeared in the evening.** Thus, Egypt began its day and new month at **sunrise** and Babylon began its day and new month at **sunset.**

In cases where **astronomical new moon occurs about midnight**, it is difficult to know whether or not the old moon could have been seen by an observer just before the previous dawn. Sometimes **the season of the year** determines whether or not the old moon could have been seen on the previous dawn. **Only an expert astronomer, such as Faulkner, knows best how to make this determination.** Sometimes the time of invisibility is so close to the hour of dawn that it is a tossup as to whether the Egyptian observer could see the Old Moon at dawn, or not. In such rare cases, Faulkner calls it a tie and lists both dates and we call it a match rather than a miss. We followed this policy with all of the astronomical chronologies we tested, including our own.

Faulkner calculated the lunar dates of all of the chronologies we tested. He also calculated about **350 lunar dates** in our search for a new astronomical chronology **based on a three-century revision of the twelfth through the nineteenth dynasties.** The key lunar dates for the twelfth dynasty are discussed in depth in this chapter and in Chapter Twenty-Four. Many of Faulkner's lunar dates will appear later in **Volume II** of *Solving the Exodus Mystery.*

VI. FAULKNER'S TESTING OF THE SOTHIC DATES OF BREASTED, PARKER, EDGERTON, INGHAM AND LUFT

A. Breasted's Astronomical Chronology

Breasted cited a document of the twelfth dynasty that claimed that Sirius had risen on **8-16 (Egyptian)** of Sesostris III's seventh year. Breasted dated this rising on **July 19, 1880 B.C. (+ or - 3 years) at the latitude of Memphis (30°).** However, Faulkner's dates for Sirius' rising in **Table 21-D (p. 306) show** that Sirius rose at 30° on the **Julian date of July 14** from 1901 B.C. to 1858 B.C., **five days earlier** than **Breasted's date of July 19.** Thus, Breasted's date of July 19, 1880 B.C., is **incorrect by five days and nineteen to twenty-two years.**

B. Testing of Parker's Astronomical Chronology

Table 21-D (p. 306) shows that **Parker's date of July 17, 1872 B.C.**, for Sirius' rising on 8-16 (Egyptian), is contradicted by **Faulkner's date of July 14, 1861 to 1858 B.C., an error by Parker of three days and eleven to fourteen years.** **Parker's three-day error in dating Sirius' rising reduced his claim of 83% lunar accuracy to zero.**

Parker also failed to list a single Julian equivalent date of his twelve Egyptian lunar dates and **also failed to list a single astronomically-calculated Julian date** to compare to the Julian equivalent dates. Of **thirty-six dates** that Parker should have listed, he only recorded **the twelve Egyptian lunar dates and indicated which of them were correct.**[54] **Parker freely listed in his book the astronomically calculated Julian lunar dates for other Egyptian dynasties, but not for the twelfth dynasty, a serious oversight.**[55]

I tested Parker's astronomical chronology **based on his erroneous date for Sirius' rising on July 17.. Parker claimed that ten of his twelve lunar dates were correct (83%).** Faulkner calculated these twelve lunar dates and found that only **seven out of the twelve lunar dates were correctly dated (58%).** See Faulkner's test of Parker's claim in **Table 21-H (p. 311).**

In Table 21-H (p. 311) Parker's date of Sirius' rising on July 17, 1872 B.C. **is inaccurate by three days. Faulkner's date is July 14, 1872 B.C. at the latitude of Memphis (30°), nullifying Parker's entire astronomical chronology. Parker significantly exaggerated his claim of "astronomically absolute dates."**

Parker's claim of astronomically absolute dates turns out to be totally erroneous on the basis of his three-day error in dating Sirius' rising in 1872 B.C. Yet, all historians at that time accepted Parker's date of July 17, 1872 B.C., for Sirius' rising in Sesostris III's seventh year as **"astronomically absolute."** Parker's date was canonized as **"fixed"** by William Hayes in the reputable *Cambridge Ancient History.*[56] **Little did Hayes know that he would later have to retract Parker's date.**

C. Testing of Edgerton's Astronomical Date for Amenhotep I.

Sirius rose on 11-9 (Egyptian) in Amenhotep I's ninth year. Edgerton assumed the latitude was 30° and dated this rising of Sirius on **July 16, 1537 B.C.** However, Faulkner's Table 21-E (pp. 322-325) shows that Sirius rose at 30° on **July 15, from 1546 to 1506 B.C.** Table 21-G is located in the larger Table 21-H (p. 311), which shows that this **July 15 rising coincided with 11-9 Egyptian only in the years 1533 to 1530 B.C.** Thus, Edgerton's date of July 16, 1537 B.C. is **incorrect by one day and four to seven years.**

The inscription recording this 11-9 date of Sirius' rising was found **at Thebes.** On the basis of Sirius' rising at the latitude of Thebes, Table 21-E (pp. 322-323) and Table 21-F (p. 308) together show that Sirius rose on **July 11 and coincided with 11-9 Egyptian only in the years from 1517 to 1514 B.C.** Therefore, Edgerton's date of July 16, 1537 B.C. is **incorrect by five days and twenty years.**

TABLE 21-H
FAULKNER'S TESTING OF PARKER'S
ASTRONOMICAL CHRONOLOGY

Based on Sirius' Rising at 30°on July 17, 1872 B.C. in Sesostris III's Seventh Year

King's Name	Regnal Year	Document I.D.	B.C. Year	Egypt's Lunar Date	Julian Equivalent Lunar Day TABLE 21-G	Lunar Date Accuracy	Faulkner's Dates	Month Length Accuracy
AIII	30	D-1	1813	10-26	= 09-10	0	09-10	
AIII	30	D-2	1813	11 25 +29 =	10-09	0	10-09	
								0
AIII	30	D-3	1813	12-25 +30 =	11-08	+1	11-07	+1
AIII	31	D-4	1813	01-19 +29 =	12 07	0	12-07	-1
AIII	31	D-5	1812	02-20 +31 =	01-07	+2	01-05	+2
AIII	31	D 6	1812	03-19 +29 =	02-05	+1	02-04	-1
AIII	31	D-7	1812	04-19 +30 =	03-07	+1	03-06	0
AIII	31	D-8	1812	05-18 +29 =	04-05	0	04-05	-1
AIII	31	D-9	1812	06-18 +30 =	05-05	+1	05-04	+1
AIII	31	D-10	1812	07-17 +29 =	06-03	0	06-03	-1
AIII	31	D-11	1812	08-17 +30 =	07-03	0	07-03	0
AIII	31	D 12	1812	09-16 +29 =	08-01	0	08-01	0

	FAULKNER'S LUNAR DATES	ASTRO-DATES MONTH LENGTHS
FAULKNER'S TESTING OF PARKER	7/12	5/12
	58%	42%

PARKER'S CLAIM OF ACCURACY	10/12
Seriously Exaggerated	83%

Parker's date of Sirius' rising on July 17, 1872 B.C. is inaccurate by three days (Faulkner's date is July 14, 1872 B.C. at the latitude of Memphis (30°), nullifying Parker's entire astronomical chronology. Parker significantly exaggerated his claim of "astronomically absolute dates."

D. Testing of Ingham's Sothic Dates and Cycles

Ingham, the British astronomer, calculated that **Sirius rose at 30°on July 16** during the first half of the nineteenth century B.C. **Faulkner's date of July 14 at 30° in Table 21-E (pp. 322-325) shows that Ingham's date is incorrect by two days.**

Ingham thought that Sirius' rising shifted **only forward on the Julian Calendar**. Table 21-E (pp. 322-325) demonstrates that Sirius' rising actually fluctuated back and forth between pairs of Julian dates between the centuries and often within the same century. **Ingham apparently was unaware of this fluctuation**, which is caused by the wobble of the earth on its axis. Notice this fluctuation at different latitudes in Table 21-E (pp. 322-325).

Thus, Ingham's calculations of the Sothic Cycle at **1454 years** from 2768 to 1314 B.C. and **1,452 years** from 1314 to 139 B.C. are **both incorrect.** Sirius' rising fluctuates back and forth on the Julian calendar **differently in each century and at each latitude. Thus, the length of the Sothic Cycle also varies from latitude to latitude, from century to century, and even within the century.**

On the other hand, New Year's Day of Egypt's 365-day calendar **did not fluctuate** as it shifted backward on the Julian Calendar **consistently at the rate of one day every four years,** rotating completely around the Julian Calendar in **1,460 years.** Of course this cycle is based on the **presupposition** that Egypt's 365-day calendar was **never revised or adjusted during its entire history.**

In the next chapter we will **disprove the 1460-Year Sothic Cycle of New Year's Day by proving that Egypt replaced its 365-day calendar with a 360-day calendar during the eighteenth dynasty.** We will also see that foreign calendars were later introduced into Egypt, further breaking the Sothic Cycle.

E. Testing of Luft's Astronomical Chronology

Ulrich Luft used Ingham's date of **July 16, 1866 B.C.,** for Sirius' rising at **30°** on 8-16 (Egyptian) in Sesostris III's seventh year. Faulkner's date for Sirius' rising at 30° in **Table 21-E** (pp. 322-325) is **July 14, two days earlier than Luft's date.** Table 21-G (on Table 21-H, p. 311) shows that the Egyptian date of 8-16 coincided with Sirius' rising on July 14 only in the years **1861 to 1858 B.C.** Thus, Luft's date is **incorrect by two days and five to eight years.**

Luft also claimed that twenty-five of his thirty-nine lunar dates proved to be correct, an accuracy of **64.1%.** Nevertheless, his **two-day error for Sirius' rising reduces this lunar accuracy to zero percent accuracy.** Since this error invalidated the accuracy of his lunar dates, we did not bother to test the accuracy of Luft's lunar chronology.

However, Lynn Rose, assuming that July 16 was a correct date, tested Luft's lunar chronology in the *Journal of Near Eastern Studies.*[57] Rose reported that Luft used thirty-nine lunar dates, including Krauss' twenty lunar dates, to calculate two astronomical chronologies, one based on Sirius' rising at 30° and the other based on Sirius' rising at 24°. The 30° chronology proved to be superior. **Rose invalidated six of Luft's thirty-nine dates** as inapplicable or too uncertain to be considered true new-moon dates. Rose tested the remaining thirty-three dates and found an accuracy of **eighteen out of thirty-three (55%), less than Luft's claim of 64% accuracy, and too low to constitute a true astronomical chronology.** Regardless, **Luft's two-day error on the date of Sirius' rising nullifies the entirety** of his proposed astronomical chronology for the twelfth dynasty.

VII. THE TESTING OF ROLF KRAUSS' ASTRONOMICAL CHRONOLOGY

I am deeply indebted to my friends, Richard Walker and Tom Black, former missionaries to Germany, who translated Rolf Krauss' work from German into English so that I could understand how Krauss calculated and tested his astronomical chronology. Krauss' date of **July 9, 1838 B.C.**, for Sirius' rising at the latitude of 24° **proved to be correct, though quite by chance.** He likely used Neguebauer's date of **July 9** for Sirius' rising at 24° from 2000 to 1400 B.C.[58]

Faulkner's dates in **Table 21-E (pp. 322-325)** show that Sirius rose at 24° on July 8 in 2000 B.C., shifted to July 9 in 1838 B.C. and shifted back and forth between July 7, 8 and 9 over the next 500 years. Thus, Krauss used the **wrong date of July 9** for Sirius' rising in 2000 B.C. to get a **correct date for Sirius' rising** in 1838 B.C.

Krauss claimed to have **70% lunar accuracy (14 of 20).** However, Table **21-I** (p. 312) shows that Krauss provided only **twenty-six of the sixty dates** needed to prove this accuracy. These sixty dates constitute twenty Egyptian lunar dates, twenty Julian equivalents of the Egyptian lunar dates, and twenty astronomically calculated Julian lunar dates. Krauss provided **only the twenty Egyptian lunar dates** and **only six of his astronomically calculated Julian lunar dates**.

Krauss' significant omission of twenty Julian equivalent dates and fourteen astronomically calculated dates followed the questionable practice of R. A. Parker, who failed to list a single Julian equivalent date or a single astronomically calculated Julian date in his astronomical chronology of the twelfth dynasty.

Krauss failed to calculate and record fourteen of the Julian equivalent dates for the Egyptian lunar dates. I found it necessary to calculate his dates myself. Krauss' Julian dates are calculated in **Table 21-I** (p. 312) and the results are recorded in **Table 21-J** to complete the assessment of Krauss' accuracy. **Table 21-J appears on page 315.**

Table 21-I (p. 312) compares Krauss' claim of 70% accuracy with the testing of his lunar dates by Dr. Faulkner and Dr. Rose. Faulkner's astronomically calculated lunar dates show that **Krauss' accuracy was only 55% (11 of 20)**, significantly less than **Krauss' claim of 14 of 20 (70%)**. I also calculated the accuracy of the month-lengths in Krauss' chronology, which Krauss did not consider. Krauss' dates show a month-length accuracy of **7 out of 12 (58%)**. But Faulkner's dates in Table 21-I (p. 312) shows that the month-length accuracy of Krauss' chronology is only 17% **(2 out of 12)**.

I later learned that Lynn Rose also tested Krauss' chronology in the *Journal of Near Eastern Studies*.[59] Table 21-H (p. 311) shows that Rose misinterpreted six of the equivalent Julian dates in Krauss' chronology. We corrected these six dates listed in Rose's twenty Julian dates in Table 21-I (p. 312), comparing them with Krauss' and Faulkner's dates. Rose showed that **only eight of Krauss' twenty lunar dates were correct (40%), whereas Faulkner and I found 11 of 20**

correct: 55%. Table 21-I also shows that Rose's dates give Krauss **a 42% accuracy on the month lengths (5 out of 12)**, whereas Faulkner's evaluation is only **2 out of 12 dates (17%).**

Faulkner's testing shows that Krauss' total chronology **has only 13 correct measurements out of 32: 11 lunar dates plus two month lengths, or 42**%. Rose's testing also shows **13 of 32 measurements were correct: 8 lunar dates, plus 5 month lengths, also 42%. 42% accuracy is proof of a totally unacceptable astronomical chronology. Therefore, Krauss' claim of 70% lunar accuracy is grossly exaggerated and insufficient to be a true astronomical chronology.**

Table 21-I below shows that Faulkner's twenty astronomically calculated lunar dates **differed with three of Rose's dates**, and thus **agreed with Rose on seventeen dates**. Since Faulkner is a Doctor of Astronomy and used the most modern and sophisticated software programs to calculate Sothic dates and lunar dates, Faulkner's dates are more likely superior to Rose's manually calculated dates. Remember that Faulkner is an astronomer and Rose is a historian, not a scientist. **Table 21-J** on the next page shows the testing of Krauss' chronology.

TABLE 21-I
CONVERSION OF KRAUSS' EGYPTIAN LUNAR DATES INTO
JULIAN LUNAR DATES TO TEST KRAUSS' ACCURACY

Document	Year	New Year's Day Egypt		New Year's Day Julian	Lunar Dates Egypt	After, or Before 1-1	Date Julian
E	-1827	1-1	=	11-23	07-10	-176	05-31
F	-1822	1-1	=	11-22	02-17	+ 46	01-07
G	-1818	1-1	=	11-21	10-01	- 95	08-18
A	-1814	1-1	=	11-20	11-16	- 50	10-01
H	-1808	1-1	=	11-18	10-13	- 83	08-27
B	-1788	1-1	=	11-13	09-08	-118	07-18
D1	-1787	1-1	=	11-13	10-26	- 70	09-04
D2	-1787				11-25	+ 29	10-03
D3	-1787				12-25	+ 30	11-02
D4	-1787				01-19	+ 29	12-01
D5	-1786				02-20	+ 31	01-01
D6	-1786				03-19	+ 29	01-30
D7	-1786				04-19	+ 30	03-01
D8	-1786				05-18	+ 29	03-30
D9	-1786				06-18	+ 30	04-29
D10	-1786				07-17	+ 29	05-28
D11	-1786				08-17	+ 30	06-27
D12	-1786				09-16	+ 29	07-26
C1	-1786				02-09	+148	12-21
C2	-1785				03-08	+ 29	01-19

TABLE 21-J
TESTING OF ROLF KRAUSS' LUNAR DATE ACCURACY
Sirius Rose at 24° on 8-16 Egyptian, 7-9 Julian in Sesostris II's 7th Year in 1838 B.C. (-1837)

Doc. King Year	Krauss B.C. Year	Krauss Egypt Dates p.95	Krauss Claim Correct. Egypt. Dates p.96	Krauss Astron Calc. Julian Dates p.100	Stewart Julian Equiv. Krauss Dates Table	Faulkner Astron Calc. Dates Julian Krauss	Krauss Lunar Accuracy	Accuracy Calc. Month Julian Length Julian Date w/Stewart's Jul. Equiv. Krauss Accuracy	Rose Accur. Astro.Calc. Mo. Length Julian Date w/Stewart's Jul. Equiv.	
SII 7	1838	08-16		07-09	07-09		Accuracy	Accuracy		
E S III 9	1828	07-10	0	05-30	05-31	05-31	0	NA	05-30	-1 NA
F S III 14	1823	02-17	-1	01-07	01 07	01-08	-1	NA	01-08	-1 NA
G SIII18	1819	10 01	0	?	08-18	08-18	0	NA	08-18	0 NA
A AIII 3	1815	11-16	-1	10-01	10-01	10-01	0	NA	10-01	0 NA
H AIII 9	1809	10-13	0	?	08-27	08-26	-1	NA	08-26	+1 NA
B AIII 29	1789	09-08	+1	07-16	07-18	07-17	+1	NA	07-17	+1 NA
D1 AIII 30	1788	10-26	0	?	09-04	09-03	+1	NA	09-03	+1 NA
		↓30			+29	+30		-1	+29	0
D2	1788	11-25	0	?	10-03	10-03*	0		10-02*	+1
		+30			+30	+29		+1	+30	0
D3	1788	12-25	0		11-02	11-01	+1		11-01	-1
		+29			+29	+30		-1	+30	-1
D4 AIII 31	1788	01-19	0	?	12-01	12-01	0		12-01	0
		+31			+31	+30		+1	+30	-1
D5	1787	02-20	+1	12-30	01-01	12-31	+1		12-31	-1
		+29			+29	+30		-1	+30	-1
D6	1787	03-19	0	?	01-30	01-30	0		01-30	0
		+30			+30	+29		+1	+29	+1
D7	1787	04-19	+1	02-28	03-01	02-28	+1		02-28	+1
		+29			+29	+30		-1	+30	-1
D8	1787	05-18	0	?	03-30	03-30	0		03-30	0
		+30			+30	+30		0	+30	0
D9	1787	06-18	0	?	04-29	04-29	0		04-29	0
		+29			+29	+29		0	+29	0
D10	1787	07-17	0	?	05-28	05-28	0		05-28	0
		+30			+30	+29		+1	+29	+1
D11	1787	08-17	0	?	06-27	06-26	+1		06-26	+1
		+29			+29	+30		-1	+29	0
D12	1787	09-16	0	?	07-26	07-26*	0		07-25*	+1
		+148			+148	+148		NA	+148	NA
C1 AIII 32	1787	02-09	+1	?	12-21	12-20	+1		12-20	+1
		+29			+29	+30		-1	+30	+1
C 2 AIII 32	1786	03-08	0	?	01-19	01-19	0		01-19	0

R. KRAUSS Claim W/O Evidence	FAULKNER W/Evidence	L. ROSE W/Evidence
Accuracy of Lunar Dates 14/20	Accuracy of Lunar Dates 11/20	Lunar Dates 8/20
Only 6 Julian dates listed 70%	20 Julian dates listed 55%	20 Jul. Dates 40%
Accuracy of Mo. Lengths 7/12	Accuracy of Mo. Lengths 2/12	Month Lengths 5/12
58%	17%	42%
Average Total Accuracy 21/32	Average Total Accuracy 13/32	13/32
Avg. Total Claim 66%	% Average Accuracy 41%	41%

Faulkner differs with Rose's dates by one day in documents E, D2 & D12

Krauss later dated Sirius' rising on **July 9, 1506 B.C.**, in the ninth year of Amenhotep I, the second king of the eighteenth dynasty. However, this date is **entirely dependent on the accuracy of Krauss' lunar chronology based on Sirius' rising on July 9, 1838 B.C., in Sesostris II's seventh year.** Since Faulkner and Rose have **disproved** Krauss' lunar chronology based on Sirius' rising in Sesostris II's seventh year, **Krauss' date of July 9, 1506 B.C. date** for the ninth year of the eighteenth dynasty Pharaoh Amenhotep I is **also disproved.** These two chronologies of the twelfth and eighteenth dynasties are dependent on each other. **Since Krauss' twelfth-dynasty chronology has been refuted, the July 9, 1506 B.C. for the eighteenth dynasty (ninth year of Amenhotep I) must also be rejected.** The new moon date that occurred on the same day of Sirius' rising in 1506 B.C. was merely coincidental.

Summing up, Krauss committed the following serious errors in calculating his Sothic chronology of the twelfth dynasty. After coming to the conclusion that he could not find astronomical compatibility when he dated Sirius' rising in Sesostris III's seventh year, Krauss made the following unwarranted changes that differed from the interpretation of all previous Egyptologists: (1) Krauss shortened Sesostris III's reign to only eighteen years, whereas a monument was recently found with Sesostris III's thirty-ninth year inscribed on it. (2) Krauss dated the rising of Sirius in the seventh year of Sesostris II instead of the seventh year of Sesostris III. (3) Krauss diminished the reign of Sesostris II to only nine years, in spite of the fact that Manetho ascribed forty-eight years to the reign of Sesostris II. (4) Krauss moved the latitude of Sirius' rising to 24° on the southern border of Egypt, where Sirius rises six days earlier than at Memphis (30°). Sirius' rising was registered by priests at el Lahun, just below Memphis. Therefore, Krauss was unwarranted in moving the location of Sirius' rising to 24°, because this rising of Sirius' was recorded in northern Egypt, not southern Egypt.

In addition, this rising of Sirius occurred in the seventh year of **Sesostris III, not** in the seventh year **of his father, Sesostris II.** Krauss could not find astronomical compatibility when he dated Sirius' rising in Sesostris III's seventh year. Thus, Krauss arbitrarily switched to the seventh year of **Sesostris II** against all the evidence that points to Sesostris III as the Pharaoh in whose seventh year Sirius' rising was recorded. However, switching to Sesostris II did not help, because the astronomical chronology based on Sesostris II's seventh year also failed to achieve sufficient astronomical compatibility to be a true chronology. Yet, Baines and Wente totally endorsed Krauss' astronomical chronology for the twelfth dynasty and recorded the alleged astronomical date in the *New Encyclopaedia Britannica of 1991.*

VIII. SESOSTRIS III'S THIRTY-NINTH YEAR
CANCELS PREVIOUS ASTRONOMICAL
CHRONOLOGIES

Current Egyptologists give Sesostris III **a maximum reign of only eighteen years** in order to find astronomical compatibility with three lunar dates in the reign of Sesostris III and seventeen lunar dates in the reign of Amenemhet III, the son of Sesostris III. Therefore, **the correct length of Sesostris III's reign is crucial in calculating a correct astronomical chronology of the twelfth dynasty.**

Since the dated rising of Sirius was recorded in the seventh year of either Sesostris II (Krauss) or Sesostris III , then Krauss and Luft had to have **absolutely correct lengths of reign for both Sesostris II and Sesostris III** in order to compare the date of Sirius' rising with the twenty lunar dates in the reigns of Sesostris III and his son, Amenemhet III. Parker's astronomical chronology demanded that Sesostris III have a reign of **thirty-six years.** The astronomical chronologies of Krauss and Luft required that Sesostris III reign **only eighteen years**. Krauss' chronology, unlike Parker's, required that Sesostris II reign **only eight years**. Luft, like Parker, dated Sirius' rising in Sesostris III's seventh year, which is far more logical than Krauss' dating Sirius' rising in Sesostris II's seventh year. The reason for these different and specific years of reign for Sesostris II and Sesostris III is that Krauss could not find sufficient astronomical compatibility between the date of Sirius' rising and the lunar dates when he used **their traditional years of reign. He only found compatibility (which proved insufficient) when he reduced their traditional reigns by one half.**

However, Krauss and Luft were not warranted in reducing the traditional reign of Sesostris III to only eighteen years. **Figure 13-A in Chapter Thirteen** pictures three statues of Sesostris III that indicate **his aging from his twenties to his forties to his sixties.** Krauss and Luft were apparently unaware of these statues, or they **would not have limited Sesostris III's reign to eighteen years.**

However, the statues were superceded in chronological value in 1996, when a mortuary temple of Sesostris III was excavated near Karnak. **Sesostris III's name was inscribed in rock throughout the temple. On one of its foundation stones was found the year thirty-nine, which must be the current year of Sesostris III when the temple was constructed, because only his name appears in the temple.**[60] The **excavator** admitted that **the year thirty-nine must belong to Sesostris III.** However, in order to preserve the astronomical chronology of Krauss and Luft, the author suggested the possibility that Sesostris III co-reigned with Amenemhet III for twenty years.[61] Yet, no document or inscription says that Amenemhet III co-reigned with his father, nor is Amenemhet III's name found inscribed in Sesostris III's temple. **The autocratic and egotistical attitude of Sesostris III, which I discussed in my historical chapters as the evil Pharaoh who enslaved Israel, would not permit his son to share his throne for twenty years.**

Since Sesostris III was **alive in his thirty-ninth year**, when he began construction of this building, then his reign likely continued **into the forties.** All of the astronomical chronologies proposed by twentieth-century Egyptologists **have less than thirty-nine years** for Sesostris III's reign. Therefore, **all** their astronomical chronologies **are nullified by this one fact alone.** The discovery of Sesostris III's thirty-ninth year of reign confirms what we have already proved by astronomical testing, namely that **all astronomical dates calculated by Egyptologists for the twelfth and eighteenth Dynasties are incorrect.**

IX. SIRIUS' RISING IN THE CANOPUS DECREE

In 238 B.C. Ptolemy III signed the Canopus Decree in the city of **Canopus, Egypt** on the Mediterranean coast. **Canopus** is a Greek name for a **star, thus marking this city as one that observed the stars.** The decree occurred on **5-17 (Egyptian) of Ptolemy III's eighth year,** which is dated astronomically by links to eclipses of the sun to **May 7, 238 B.C.** The decree ordered **one day to be added to Egypt's 365-day calendar every four years to compensate for Leap Year** and maintain Sirius' rising on 10-1 (Egyptian) throughout their future history.

The decree **predicted that Sirius would rise on 10-1 (Egyptian), which is March 7 (Julian), 238 B.C.** The purpose of the decree appears **to fix the rising of Sirius on 10-1 (Egyptian), July 19 (Julian),** rather than permitting Sirius' rising to shift one day later every four years on Egypt's unadjusted 365-day calendar, as had been the previous practice.[62]

This decree has led Egyptologists and M. Ingham, the English astronomer, to believe that **Sirius' rising at 30°definitely occurred on 10-1 Egyptian, July 19 (Julian) in 238 B.C.**[63] However, Faulkner's calculations, using Brad Schaeffer's precise software, demonstrate in **Table 21-E (pp. 322-325)** that **Sirius never rose on July 19 (Julian) at any latitude of Egypt during its entire B.C. history.** Table 21-E (pp. 322-325) shows that the date should be **July 18, 238 B.C., at the latitude of Canopus (31° 19'),** where the decree was made.

How could this error of one day for Sirius' rising have occurred? **Obviously, atmospheric conditions, perhaps clouds or haze) prevented the sighting of Sirius' rising at Canopus on 9-30 (Egyptian), July 18 (Julian) in 238 B.C. The priests obviously did not see the star rise on 9-30 (July 18), but saw it on the next day 10-1 (Egyptian), July 19, 238 B.C.** They assumed that the star would rise again on 10-1, the following year (237 B.C.) and thus predicted this same date for 237 B.C. and recorded such in the Canopus Decree.

However, when July 18, 237 B.C. arrived, lo and behold they saw Sirius' rising on 9-30 (July 18), one day earlier than 10-1 (July 19). The astronomers under Ptolemy III then realized that their prediction of 10-1 was incorrect because of bad atmospheric conditions the previous year. They thus realized that they must wait for two to three years before the date of Sirius' rising shifted to 10-1 on the Egyptian calendar. Thus, they could not execute the Canopus Decree and add an extra day to their calendar for two or three years. During the next two or three years they forgot about the decree and it was never obeyed. **Thus, Egypt's 365-day calendar continued unadjusted for Leap Year as previously practiced.**

Obviously, the plan to revise Egypt's 365-day calendar one day every four years failed. All Egyptologists and historians freely admit **that the Canopus Decree was never executed.**[64] Therefore, **the July 19 date** for Sirius rising at 30°in 238 B.C. is **another astronomical error** that has caused Egyptologists and astronomers to miscalculate the Sothic Cycle.

X. TESTING CENSORINUS' DATE OF SIRIUS' RISING

Censorinus, the Roman astronomer, reported that Sirius rose at Memphis (30°) on July 20 (Julian) about A.D. 140. Egyptologists and even the astronomer Ingham still believe this date is correct. However, Faulkner's dates in Table 21-E below (pp. 322-325) show that **Sirius never rose in Egypt on July 20 at any latitude in Egypt from 2000 B.C. to A.D. 300.** At the **latitude of Canopus,** Sirius rose on **July 18** during the second century **A.D. and coincided with Egypt's New Year's Day only in the years 144 to 147 A.D. Thus, Censorinus' claim that Sirius' rising on July 20 at 30°coincided with Egypt's New Year's Day in A.D. 140 is totally inaccurate.** Furthermore, (pp. 310-312) **shows that July 20 (Julian) did not coincide with 1-1 (Egyptian) in A.D. 140, but rather in the years, A.D. 136 to 139.** Tables 21-D (p. 298) and 21-E (pp. 311-313) show that Sirius rose on **July 17 at Memphis (30°) and coincided with Egypt's New Year's Day only in the years from 148 to 151 A.D. Whichever latitude is chosen, Censorinus was wrong about the date of July 20 for Sirius' rising at either of these latitudes and he was also wrong about the years when Sirius' rising coincided with Egypt's New Year's Day.**

Why did Censorinus err in this astronomical calculation? First of all, Censorinus lived in the third century A.D., 100 years after the date of Sirius' rising was observed. Secondly, Censorinus lived in the country of Italy, where the latitude causes Sirius to rise many days later than it does in Egypt. Thirdly, Censorinus could have simply made an error in his calculation of the Julian date of Sirius' rising and its coincidence with Egypt's New Year's Day in the second century B.C. Fourthly, Censorinus may have simply estimated the date and missed it by three days. **Whatever the reasons for Censorinus' mistaken date, the computer software of Brad Schaeffer is the most sophisticated and accurate method of calculating the dates of Sirius' rising and should be accepted as superior to Censorinus' unobserved guess a century after the event occurred.**

CONCLUSION

Egypt's astronomically fixed and absolute chronology **has never been fixed or absolute**. Egypt's chronology has already suffered **four major revisions** in the twentieth century. The **first dynasty** has been redated four times from 5546 B.C. (Petrie) to 3400 B.C. (Breasted) to 3100 B.C. (Hayes: Cambridge), to 2925 B.C. (Baines), **a total revision of 2,621 years.** Chapter 24 will demonstrate that the first dynasty **must still be revised centuries later than Baines' date.**

The beginning of the **twelfth dynasty** was dated "astronomically" by Petrie to 3579 B.C., by Breasted to 2000 B.C., by Parker and Hayes to 1991 B.C., and by Krauss and Baines to 1938 B.C., **a total revision of 1,641 years.**

Using the computer software of Brad Schaeffer of Bethesda Space Center,

Faulkner's dates in Table 21-E (pp. 322-325) show that Breasted, Parker, Edgerton, Luft and Ingham, all calculated **incorrect dates** for Sirius' rising at the latitude of 30°. Their errors of Sirius' rising **invalidated** their attested lunar compatibility and **thus nullified their astronomical chronologies.**

Only Krauss' date of July 9, 1838 B.C., for Sirius' rising at 24° proved to be correct. However, Krauss' claim of **70% lunar compatibility** proved to be **only 55%** for twenty lunar dates and only **17%** for twelve month lengths. Krauss' claim of an "astronomically absolute" chronology turns out to be significantly exaggerated and too low to be a true astronomical chronology. This **incorrect date** for Sesostris II's seventh year (instead of Sesostris III's seventh year) **also invalidates the 1506 B.C.** date for the ninth year of the eighteenth-dynasty king, Amenhotep I, because it is **totally dependent** on the **inaccurate date of 1838 B.C.** date for Sesostris II instead of Sesostris III.

We also saw proof that Sesostris III had a reign of **at least thirty-nine years and likely more**. All Egyptologists worked on the assumption that Sesostris III reigned **from eighteen to thirty-six years.** This record of Sesostris III's **thirty-ninth year** in and of itself **completely annuls all of the astronomical chronologies of the twelfth dynasty that have been calculated by twentieth-century Egyptologists, including Breasted, Parker, Krauss and Luft.** Krauss and Luft gave Sesostris III only eighteen years of reign.

The **"astronomically absolute Sothic dates"** for Egypt's dynasties are **constantly revised.** Egyptologists need to go back to the drawing board to formulate new astronomical chronologies for the twelfth dynasty based on correct dates of Sirius' rising in the proper quadrennium of years when the Egyptian date of 8-16 coincides with the correct Julian date for Sirius' rising. In addition, their new astronomical chronologies must be based on a reign of thirty-nine years or more for Sesostris III.

In spite of all of these astronomical errors for specific dates of Sirius' rising in the twelfth and eighteenth dynasties, the Sothic Cycle continues to tie these dynasties to their currently assigned B.C. centuries. Therefore, I cannot redate the twelfth and eighteenth dynasties three centuries later unless I can break the Sothic Cycle. This crucial problem is completely solved in Chapter 22, which I have entitled, **"The Myth of Egypt's Unbroken Sothic Cycles."**

TABLE 21-K
THIRTY DISCOVERIES OF CONTINUAL ERRORS IN EGYPT'S "ASTRONOMICALLY ABSOLUTE DATES."

Discovery Error 1. W. F. Petrie used Sothic dating to begin the first dynasty of Egypt in **5546 B.C.**

Discovery Error 2. James Breasted fixed **July 19, 4241 B.C.** as the origin of Egypt's 365-day calendar, calling it **"the oldest fixed date in history."**

Discovery Error 3. James Breasted revised Petrie's Sothic date **of 5546 B.C.** for the first dynasty **by 2,146 years to 3400 B.C.**

Discovery Error 4. William Hayes in the *Cambridge Ancient History* reduced Breasted's date of 3400 B.C. for the first dynasty **to 3100 B.C. , a three century revision.** Hayes was able to accomplish this reduction by finding that the first to the eleventh dynasties ran parallel to each other in different centuries.

Discovery Error 5. W. F. Petrie used Sothic dating to begin the twelfth dynasty in **3579 B.C.**

Discovery Error 6. James Breasted revised Petrie's Sothic date of 3579 B.C. for the twelfth dynasty to **2000 B.C., a difference of 1,379 years.**

Discovery Error 7. James Breasted astronomically dated the rising of Sirius' in Sesostris III' seventh year on **July 19, 1880 B.C.**

Discovery Error 8. Richard Parker dated Sirius' rising at 30° **on July 17 (Julian) in 1872 B.C.,** two days and eight years later than Breasted's date, nullifying Breasted's astronomical dates. Parker called his date of July 17, 1872 B.C. "the earliest relatively certain fixed date in Egyptian history."

Discovery Error 9. William Hayes recorded Parker's date as "fixed" in the chronology of the twelfth dynasty and recorded it in the *Cambridge Ancient History.*

Discovery Error 10. Parker compared his date for Sirius' rising with twelve lunar dates and determined that **ten of the twelve lunar dates tested correctly (83%).** Many years later Dr. Danny Faulkner tested Parker's chronology and found **only seven of the twelve lunar dates were correct (58%),** nullifying Parker's entire astronomical chronology.

Discovery Error 11. Edgerton accepted Parker's date of July 17, 1872 B.C. as **"absolute"** and calculated that Sirius' rising in Amenhotep I's ninth year occurred **on July 16, 1537 B.C.** Edgerton's date was also recorded in *The Cambridge Ancient History* as absolute.

Discovery Error 12. In 1969 A.D., M. Ingham, an English astronomer, determined that Sirius rose on July 16 from 1900 to 1700 B.C. As a result of Ingham's calculations, John Baines wrote in the *Encyclopaedia Britannica* that all astronomical chronologies of the Middle and New Kingdoms of Egypt since 1985 A.D. have been **disproved** by a restudy of the Sothic and lunar dates.

Discovery Errors 13 to 16. Rolf Krauss presented a new Sothic and Lunar chronology for the twelfth through the eighteenth dynasties, claiming an accuracy of 75% (15 out of 20) for the lunar dates. Dr. Danny Faulkner, astronomer from the

University of South Carolina at Lancaster, recalculated the astronomical chronology of Krauss and found that Krauss's actual accuracy was only 55% in lunar dates (11 out of 20): **four serious errors.**

Discovery Errors 17 to 26. Krauss failed to test the 12 month lengths. Faulkner tested Krauss' twelve month lengths and found only two of the twelve month lengths to be correct, **only 17%: ten serious errors.**

Discovery Error 27. Krauss' astronomical chronology rests on the premise that Sirius rose in Sesostris II's seventh year. Former Egyptologists believed that Sirius' rising occurred in the seventh year of Sesostris III.

Discovery Error 28. Krauss' astronomical chronology was based on the date of Sirius' rising at 24° whereas all other Egyptologists dated Sirius' rising at 30° where the date was recorded in northern Egypt.

Discovery Error 29. Krauss calculated his astronomical chronology on the basis that Sesostris III reigned for only eighteen years from 1836 to 1818 B.C. Recently, a new discovery of a building with Sesostris III's name on it in his thirty-ninth year, completely invalidated Krauss' astronomical chronology for the twelfth dynasty.

Discovery Error 30. Dr. Danny Faulkner tested the date of July 20 for Sirius' rising at 30° in A.D. 140 as recorded by Censorinus, a Roman astronomer. Faulkner's calculations show that Sirius' rising occurred on New Year's Day in July 17 only in the years from A.D. 148 to 151 A.D., disproving the 140 A.D. date.

TABLE 21-L
RUNNING TOTAL OF DISCOVERIES

Chapter		Chapter Total	Running Total
2	Conflict Between Biblical and Secular Histories	18	18
4	Discovery of 430 Years from Abraham to the Exodus	16	34
5	Confirmation of Abraham's Historicity	28	62
6	Discovery of the Remains of Sodom and Gomorrah	17	79
7	Joseph As a Slave and Prisoner in Amenemhet I's Reign	21	100
8	Joseph Becomes the Vizier of Sesostris I	23	123
9	Sesostris I Gives Joseph a New Name and a Wife	11	134
10	The Seven Years of Abundance in Sesostris I's Reign	10	144
11	The Seven Years of Famine in the Sesostris I's Reign	20	164
12	Israel Enters Egypt during Sesostris I's Reign	14	178
13	Sesostris III Enslaves the Israelites	17	195
14	Sesostris III, the Foster Grandfather of Moses	12	207
15	Sesostris III's Construction of Rameses and Pithom	15	222
16	Zoan (Itjtowy), the Capital of the Twelfth Dynasty	16	238
17	Amenemhet III, the Pharaoh Who Tried to Kill Moses	15	253
18	Amenemhet IV, the Pharaoh of the Exodus	14	267
19	Moses and Ipuwer Report the Ten Plagues	22	289
20	Israel's Exodus and the Drowning of Amenemhet IV and His Army in the Red Sea	26	315
21	Continuous Errors in Egypt's "Astronomically Absolute" Dates	30	345

TABLE 21-E
JULIAN/ GREGORIAN DATES OF EGYPT'S NEW YEAR'S DAY (1-1)
IF EGYPT NEVER ADJUSTED ITS 365-DAY CALENDAR
Based on Date of Canopus Decree, 5-17 (Egyptian) = March 7, Julian, 238 B.C.
Previous 1-1 (Egyptian) = October 22, 239 B.C. (Julian)

TABLE 21-E CONTINUED				TABLE 21-E CONTINUED				TABLE 21-E CONTINUED			
A.D.	EGYPT	JUL	GREG	B.C.	EGYPT	JUL.	GREG.	B.C.	EGYPT	JUL	GREG
152	1-1	07-16	07-15	117	1-1	09-21	09-18	381	1-1	11-26	11-21
148	1-1	07-17	07-16	121	1-1	09-22	09-19	385	1-1	11-27	11-22
144	1-1	07-18	07-17	125	1 1	09 23	09-20	389	1-1	11-28	11-23
140	1-1	07-19	07-18	129	1 1	09-24	09-21	393	1-1	11-29	11-24
136	1-1	07-20	07-19	133	1-1	09-25	09-22	397	1-1	11-30	11-25
132	1-1	07-21	07-20	137	1-1	09-26	09-23	401	1-1	12-01	11-26
128	1-1	07-22	07-21	141	1-1	09-27	09-24	405	1-1	12-02	11-27
124	1-1	07-23	07-22	145	1-1	09-28	09-25	409	1-1	12-03	11-28
120	1-1	07-24	07-23	149	1-1	09-29	09-26	413	1-1	12-04	11 29
116	1-1	07-25	07-24	153	1-1	09-30	09-27	417	1-1	12-05	11-30
112	1-1	07-26	07-25	157	1-1	10-01	09 28	421	1-1	12-06	12-01
108	1-1	07-27	07 26	161	1-1	10-02	09-29	425	1-1	12-07	12-02
104	1-1	07-28	07-27	165	1-1	10-03	09-30	429	1-1	12-08	12 03
100	1-1	07 29	07-28	169	1-1	10-04	10-01	433	1-1	12-09	12-04
096	1-1	07-30	07-28	173	1-1	10-05	10-02	437	1-1	12-10	12-05
092	1-1	07-31	07 29	177	1-1	10-06	10-03	441	1-1	12-11	12-06
088	1-1	08-01	07-30	181	1-1	10-07	10-04	445	1-1	12-12	12-07
084	1-1	08-02	07-31	185	1-1	10-08	10-05	449	1-1	12-13	12-08
080	1 1	08-03	08-01	189	1-1	10-09	10-06	453	1-1	12-14	12-09
076	1-1	08-04	08-02	193	1-1	10-10	10-07	457	1-1	12-15	12-10
072	1-1	08-05	08-03	197	1-1	10-11	10-08	461	1-1	12-16	12-11
068	1-1	08-06	08-04	201	1-1	10-12	10-08	465	1-1	12-17	12-12
064	1-1	08-07	08-05	205	1-1	10-13	10 09	469	1-1	12-18	12-13
060	1-1	08-08	08-06	209	1-1	10-14	10-10	473	1-1	12-19	12-14
056	1-1	08-09	08-07	213	1-1	10-15	10-11	477	1-1	12-20	12-15
052	1-1	08-10	08-08	217	1-1	10-16	10-12	481	1-1	12-21	12-16
048	1-1	08-11	08-09	221	1-1	10-17	10-13	485	1-1	12-22	12-17
044	1-1	08-12	08-10	225	1-1	10-18	10-14	489	1-1	12-23	12-18
040	1-1	08-13	08-11	229	1-1	10-19	10-15	493	1-1	12-24	12-19
036	1-1	08-14	08-12	233	1-1	10-20	10-16	497	1-1	12-25	12-20
032	1-1	08-15	08-13	237	1-1	10-21	10-17	501	1-1	12-26	12-21
028	1-1	08-16	08-14	238 *	5-17 *	03-07 *	03-14*	505	1-1	12-27	12-21
024	1 1	08 17	08 15	239	5-1	10-22	10-18	509	1-1	12-28	12-22
020	1-1	08-18	08-16	241	1-1	10-22	10-18	513	1-1	12-29	12-23
016	1-1	08-19	08-17	245	1-1	10-23	10 19	517	1-1	12-30	12 24
012	1-1	08-20	08-18	249	1 1	10-24	10-20	521	1-1	12-31	12-25
008	1-1	08-21	08-19	253	1-1	10-25	10-21	525	1-1	01-01	12-26
004	1-1	08-22	08-20	257	1-1	10-26	10-22	529	1-1	01-02	12-27
B.C.				261	1-1	10-27	10-23	533	1-1	01-03	12-28
001	1-1	08-23	08-21	265	1-1	10-28	10-24	537	1-1	01-04	12-29
005	1-1	08-24	08-22	269	1-1	10-29	10 25	541	1-1	01-05	12-30
009	1-1	08-25	08-23	273	1-1	10-30	10-26	545	1-1	01-06	12-31
013	1-1	08-26	08-24	277	1-1	10-31	10-27	549	1-1	01-07	01-01
017	1-1	08-27	08-25	281	1-1	11-01	10-28	553	1-1	01-08	01-02
021	1-1	08-28	08-26	285	1-1	11-02	10-29	557	1-1	01-09	01-03
025	1-1	08-29	08-27	289	1-1	11-03	10-30	561	1-1	01-10	01-04
029	1-1	08-30	08-28	293	1-1	11-04	10-31	565	1-1	01-11	01-05
033	1-1	08-31	08-29	297	1-1	11 05	11-01	569	1-1	01-12	01-06
037	1-1	09-01	08-30	301	1-1	11-06	11-02	573	1-1	01-13	01-07
041	1-1	09-02	08-31	305	1-1	11-07	11-02	577	1-1	01-14	01-08
045	1-1	09-03	09-01	309	1-1	11-08	11-03	581	1-1	01-15	01-09
049	1-1	09-04	09-02	313	1-1	11-09	11-04	585	1-1	01-16	01-10
053	1-1	09-05	09-03	317	1-1	11-10	11-05	589	1-1	01-17	01-11
057	1-1	09-06	09-04	321	1-1	11-11	11-06	593	1-1	01-18	01-12
061	1-1	09-07	09-05	325	1-1	11-12	11-07	597	1-1	01-19	01-13
065	1-1	09-08	09-06	329	1-1	11-13	11-08	601	1-1	01-20	01-13
069	1-1	09-09	09-07	333	1-1	11-14	11-09	605	1-1	01-21	01-14
073	1-1	09-10	09-08	337	1-1	11-15	11-10	609	1-1	01-22	01-15
077	1-1	09-11	09-09	341	1-1	11-16	11-11	613	1-1	01-23	01-16
081	1-1	09-12	09-10	345	1-1	11-17	11-12	617	1-1	01-24	01-17
085	1-1	09-13	09-11	349	1-1	11-18	11-13	621	1-1	01-25	01-18
089	1-1	09-14	09-12	353	1-1	11-19	11-14	625	1-1	01-26	01-19
093	1-1	09-15	09-13	357	1-1	11-20	11-15	629	1-1	01-27	01-20
097	1-1	09-16	09-14	361	1-1	11-21	11-16	633	1-1	01-28	01-21
101	1-1	09-17	09-14	365	1-1	11-22	11-17	637	1-1	01-29	01-22
105	1-1	09-18	09-15	369	1-1	11-23	11-18	641	1-1	01-30	01-23
109	1-1	09-19	09-16	373	1-1	11-24	11-19	645	1-1	01-31	01-24
113	1-1	09-20	09-17	377	1-1	11-25	11-20	Continued on Next Page			

TABLE 21-E CONTINUED			
B.C.	EGYPT	JUL	GREG
649	1-1	02-01	01-25
653	1-1	02-02	01-26
657	1-1	02-03	01-27
661	1-1	02-04	01-28
665	1-1	02-05	01-29
669	1-1	02-06	01-30
673	1-1	02-07	01-31
677	1-1	02-08	02-01
681	1-1	02-09	02-02
685	1-1	02-10	02-03
689	1-1	02-11	02-04
693	1-1	02-12	02-05
697	1-1	02-13	02-06
701	1-1	02-14	02-06
705	1-1	02-15	02-07
709	1-1	02-16	02-08
713	1-1	02-17	02-09
717	1-1	02-18	02-10
721	1-1	02-19	02-11
725	1-1	02-20	02-12
729	1-1	02-21	02-13
733	1-1	02-22	02-14
737	1-1	02-23	02-15
741	1-1	02-24	02-16
745	1-1	02-25	02-17
749	1-1	02-26	02-18
753	1-1	02-27	02-19
757	1-1	02-28	02-20
761	1-1	02-29*	02-21
762	1-1	03-01*	02-21
765	1-1	03-02	02-22
769	1-1	03-03	02-23
773	1-1	03-04	02-24
777	1-1	03-05	02-25
781	1-1	03-06	02-26
785	1-1	03-07	02-27
789	1-1	03-08	02-28
793	1-1	03-09	02-29*
794	1-1	03-09	03-01*
797	1-1	03-10	03-02
801	1-1	03-11	03-03
805	1-1	03-12	03-04
809	1-1	03-13	03-05
813	1-1	03-14	03-06
817	1-1	03-15	03-07
821	1-1	03-16	03-08
825	1-1	03-17	03-09
829	1-1	03-18	03-10
833	1-1	03-19	03-11
837	1-1	03-20	03-12
841	1-1	03-21	03-13
845	1-1	03-22	03-14
849	1-1	03-23	03-15
853	1-1	03-24	03-16
857	1-1	03-25	03-17
861	1-1	03-26	03-18
865	1-1	03-27	03-19
869	1-1	03-28	03-20
873	1-1	03-29	03-21
877	1-1	03-30	03-22
881	1-1	03-31	03-23
885	1-1	04-01	03-24
889	1-1	04-02	03-25
893	1-1	04-03	03-26
897	1-1	04-04	03-27
901	1-1	04-05	03-27
905	1-1	04-06	03-28
909	1-1	04-07	03-29
913	1-1	04-08	03-30
917	1-1	04-09	03-31
921	1-1	04-10	04-01
925	1-1	04-11	04-02
929	1-1	04-12	04-03
933	1-1	04-13	04-04

TABLE 21-E CONTINUED			
B.C.	EGYPT	JUL	GREG
937	1-1	04-14	04-05
941	1-1	04-15	04-06
945	1-1	04-16	04-07
949	1-1	04-17	04-08
953	1-1	04-18	04-09
957	1-1	04-19	04-10
961	1-1	04-20	04-11
965	1-1	04-21	04-12
969	1-1	04-22	04-13
973	1-1	04-23	04-14
977	1-1	04-24	04-15
981	1-1	04-25	04-16
985	1-1	04-26	04-17
989	1-1	04-27	04-18
993	1-1	04-28	04-19
997	1-1	04-29	04-20
1001	1-1	04-30	04-20
1005	1-1	05-01	04-21
1009	1-1	05-02	04-22
1013	1-1	05-03	04-23
1017	1-1	05-04	04-24
1021	1-1	05-05	04-25
1025	1-1	05-06	04-26
1029	1-1	05-07	04-27
1033	1-1	05-08	04-28
1037	1-1	05-09	04-29
1041	1-1	05-10	04-30
1045	1-1	05-11	05-01
1049	1-1	05-12	05-02
1053	1-1	05-13	05-03
1057	1-1	05-14	05-04
1061	1-1	05-15	05-05
1065	1-1	05-16	05-06
1069	1-1	05-17	05-07
1073	1-1	05-18	05-08
1077	1-1	05-19	05-09
1081	1-1	05-20	05-10
1085	1-1	05-21	05-11
1089	1-1	05-22	05-12
1093	1-1	05-23	05-13
1095	1-1	05-24	05-14
1101	1-1	05-25	05-15
1105	1-1	05-26	05-15
1109	1-1	05-27	05-16
1113	1-1	05-28	05-17
1117	1-1	05-29	05-18
1121	1-1	05-30	05-19
1125	1-1	05-31	05-20
1129	1-1	06-01	05-21
1133	1-1	06-02	05-22
1137	1-1	06-03	05-23
1141	1-1	06-04	05-24
1145	1-1	06-05	05-25
1149	1-1	06-06	05-26
1153	1-1	06-07	05-27
1130	1-1	06-08	05-28
1161	1-1	06-09	05-29
1165	1-1	06-10	05-30
1169	1-1	06-11	05-31
1173	1-1	06-12	06-01
1177	1-1	06-13	06-02
1181	1-1	06-14	06-03
1185	1-1	06-15	06-04
1189	1-1	06-16	06-05
1193	1-1	06-17	06-06
1197	1-1	06-18	06-07
1201	1-1	06-19	06-08
1205	1-1	06-20	06-09
1209	1-1	06-21	06-10
1213	1-1	06-22	06-11
1217	1-1	06-23	06-12
1221	1-1	06-24	06-13
1225	1-1	06-25	06-14
1229	1-1	06-26	06-15

TABLE 21-E CONTINUED			
B.C.	EGYPT	JUL	GREG
1233	1-1	06-27	06-16
1237	1-1	06-28	06-17
1241	1-1	06-29	06-18
1245	1-1	06-30	06-19
1249	1-1	07-01	06-20
1253	1-1	07-02	06-21
1257	1-1	07-03	06-22
1261	1-1	07-04	06-23
1265	1-1	07-05	06-24
1269	1-1	07-06	06-25
1273	1-1	07-07	06-26
1277	1-1	07-08	06-27
1281	1-1	07-09	06-28
1285	1-1	07-10	06-29
1289	1-1	07-11	06-30
1293	1-1	07-12	06-31
1297	1-1	07-13	07-02
1301	1-1	07-14	07-02
1305	1-1	07-15	07-03
1309	1-1	07-16	07-04
1313	1-1	07-17	07-05
1317	1-1	07-18	07-06
1321	1-1	07-19	07-07
1325	1-1	07-20	07-08
1329	1-1	07-21	07-09
1333	1-1	07-22	07-10
1337	1-1	07-23	07-11
1341	1-1	07-24	07-12
1345	1-1	07-25	07-13
1349	1-1	07-26	07-14
1353	1-1	07-27	07-15
1357	1-1	07-28	07-16
1361	1-1	07-29	07-17
1365	1-1	07-30	07-18
1369	1-1	07-31	07-19
1373	1-1	08-01	07-20
1377	1-1	08-02	07-21
1381	1-1	08-03	07-22
1385	1-1	08-04	07-23
1389	1-1	08-05	07-24
1393	1-1	08-06	07-25
1397	1-1	08-07	07-26
1401	1-1	08-08	07-26
1405	1-1	08-09	07-27
1409	1-1	08-10	07-28
1413	1-1	08-11	07-29
1417	1-1	08-12	07-30
1421	1-1	08-13	07-31
1425	1-1	08-14	08-01
1429	1-1	08-15	08-02
1433	1-1	08-16	08-03
1437	1-1	08-17	08-04
1441	1-1	08-18	08-05
1445	1-1	08-19	08-06
1449	1-1	08-20	08-07
1453	1-1	08-21	08-08
1457	1-1	08-22	08-09
1461	1-1	08-23	08-10
1465	1-1	08-24	08-11
1469	1-1	08-25	08-12
1473	1-1	08-26	08-13
1477	1-1	08-27	08-14
1481	1-1	08-28	08-15
1485	1-1	08-29	08-16
1489	1-1	08-30	08-17
1493	1-1	08-31	08-18
1497	1-1	09-01	08-19
1501	1-1	09-02	08-19
1505	1-1	09-03	08-20
1509	1-1	09-04	08-21
1513	1-1	09-05	08-22
1517	1-1	09-06	08-23
1521	1-1	09-07	08-24
1525	1-1	09-08	08-25

CHAPTER 21 -CONTINUOUS ERRORS IN EGYPT'S "ASTRONOMICALLY ABSOLUTE" DATES

TABLE 21-E CONTINUED B.C.	EGYPT JUL.	GREG.
1529 1-1	09-09	08-26
1533 1-1	09-10	08-27
1537 1-1	09-11	08-28
1541 1-1	09-12	08-29
1545 1-1	09-13	08-30
1549 1-1	09-14	08-31
1553 1-1	09-15	09-01
1557 1-1	09-16	09-02
1561 1-1	09-17	09-03
1565 1-1	09-18	09-04
1569 1-1	09-19	09-05
1303 1-1	09-20	09-06
1307 1-1	09-21	09-07
1581 1-1	09 22	09-08
1585 1-1	09-23	09-09
1589 1-1	09 24	09-10
1593 1-1	09-25	09-11
1597 1-1	09-26	09-12
1601 1-1	09-27	09-13
1605 1-1	09 28	09-14
1609 1-1	09-29	09-15
1613 1-1	09-30	09-16
1617 1-1	10-01	09-17
1621 1-1	10 02	09-18
1625 1-1	10-03	09-19
1629 1-1	10-04	09-20
1633 1 1	10 05	09-21
1637 1-1	10-06	09-22
1641 1-1	10-07	09-23
1645 1-1	10 08	09-24
1649 1-1	10-09	09-25
1653 1-1	10-10	09-26

B.C. EGYPT	JUL.	GREG
1657 1-1	10-11	09-27
1661 1-1	10-12	09-28
1665 1-1	10-13	09-29
1669 1-1	10-14	09-30
1673 1-1	10-15	10-01
1677 1-1	10-16	10-02
1681 1-1	10-17	10-03
1685 1-1	10-18	10-04
1689 1-1	10-19	10-05
1693 1-1	10-20	10-06
1697 1-1	10-21	10-07
1701 1-1	10-22	10-07
1705 1-1	10-23	10-08
1709 1-1	10-24	10-09
1713 1-1	10-25	10 10
1717 1-1	10-26	10-11
1721 1-1	10-27	10 12
1727 1-1	10-28	10-13
1729 1-1	10-29	10-14
1733 1-1	10-30	10-15
1737 1-1	10-31	10 16
1741 1-1	11-01	10-17
1745 1-1	11-02	10-18
1749 1-1	11-03	10-19
1753 1-1	11-04	10-20
1757 1-1	11-05	10-21
1761 1-1	11-06	10-22
1765 1-1	11 07	10-23
1769 1-1	11-08	10-24
1773 1-1	11-09	10-25
1777 1-1	11-10	10 26
1781 1-1	11-11	10-27

TABLE 21-E CONTINUED B.C.	EGYPT JUL.	GREG
1785 1-1	11-12	10-28
1789 1-1	11-13	10-29
1793 1-1	11-14	10-30
1797 1-1	11-15	10-31
1801 1-1	11-16	10-31
1805 1-1	11-17	11-01
1809 1-1	11-18	11-02
1813 1-1	11-19	11-03
1817 1-1	11-20	11-04
1821 1-1	11-21	11-05
1825 1-1	11-22	11-06
1829 1-1	11-23	11-07
1833 1-1	11-24	11-08
1837 1-1	11-25	11-09
1841 1-1	11-26	11-10
1845 1-1	11-27	11-11
1849 1-1	11-28	11-12
1853 1-1	11-29	11-13
1857 1-1	11-30	11-14
1861 1 1	12-01	11-15
1865 1-1	12-02	11-16
1869 1-1	12-03	11-17
1873 1-1	12-04	11-18
1877 1-1	12-05	11-19
1881 1-1	12-06	11-20
1885 1-1	12-07	11-21
1889 1-1	12-08	11 22
1893 1-1	12-09	11-23
1897 1-1	12-10	11-24
1901 1-1	12-11	11-25
1905 1-1	12-12	11-26
1909 1 1	12-13	11 27

NOTES FOR CHAPTER TWENTY-ONE

1. Peter James, *Centuries of Darkness*, Rutgers University Press, 1993, chart inside front cover.
2. Amihai, Mazar, *Archaeology of the Land of the Bible*, 1990, 28-29.
3. William G. Dever, "The Middle Bronze Age," *Biblical Archaeologist*, Sept.. 1987, 171.
4. Richard Parker, *Calendars of Ancient Egypt* (Univ. of Chicago Press, 1950), 30-56.
5. Anthony Spalinger, "Some Remarks on the Epagomenal Days in Ancient Egypt," *Journal of New Eastern Studies* (Univ. of Chicago, 1995), 54.1.33-34.
6. Richard Parker, *The Calendars of Ancient Egypt*, 30-56.
7. Baines & Wente, *New Encyclopaedia Britannica*, 1991 Ed., 15:435-36.
8. Isaiah 14:12; 2 Peter 1:19; Revelation 2:28; 22:16.
9. James Breasted, Trans., "Tomb of Rekhmire," *Ancient Records of Egypt*, II.280.
10. Richard Parker, *The Calendars of Ancient Egypt*, 63.
11. Parker, *The Calendars of Ancient Egypt*, 37.
12. James Breasted, *Ancient Records of Egypt*, II.177 (410), footnote a.
13. Rolf Krauss, *Sothis -Und Monddadaten* (Hildesheim: 1995), 56.
14. Krauss, *Sothis -Und Monddadaten*, 57.
15. Breasted, *Ancient Records of Egypt*, I.26-27.
16. Petrie, *History of Egypt*, 10th Ed., 1923, 7.
17. James Breasted, *Ancient Records of Egypt*, I.26 and 26.footnotes a. & b.
18. Breasted, *A History of Egypt*, 1937, p. 32 and *Ancient Records of Egypt*, 1962,I.26.note a
19. Breasted, *Ancient Records of Egypt*, I.39-40.
20. Breasted, *Ancient Records of Egypt*, I.39.
21. Breasted, *Ancient Records of Egypt*, I.39.
22. Breasted, *Ancient Records of Egypt*, I.26, footnote a; I.31, footnote a.
23. Breasted, *History of Egypt*, 597-599 "all dates with asterisk = astronomically fixed."
24. Breasted, *Ancient Records of Egypt*, I.32.
25. Parker, *Calendars of Ancient Egypt*, 24-31.
26. Parker, *Calendars of Ancient Egypt*, 9-10.
27. Parker,.*Calendars of Ancient Egypt*, 7, 63.
28. Parker, *Calendars of Ancient Egypt*, 57-62.
29. Parker, *Calendars of Ancient Egypt*, 63.
30. Parker,, *Calendars of Ancient Egypt*, 63.
31. Parker, *Calendars of Ancient Egypt*, 65-66.
32. Peter Huber, *Astronomical Dating of Babylon I and Ur III*, 26-28.
33. Richard Parker, *Ancient Calendars of Egypt*, 66.

34. Alan H. Gardiner, *Egypt of the Pharaohs* (Oxford, 1961), 66, quoted by Lynn E. Rose, "The Astronomical Evidence for Dating the End of the Middle Kingdom of Ancient Egypt," *Journal of Near Eastern Studies*, 53 no. 4 (1994), 237.
35. William Hayes, *Cambridge Ancient History*, 3rd Ed., I.1.173-174 .
36. Hayes, *Cambridge Ancient History*, I.1.183.
37. Hayes, *Cambridge Ancient History*, I.1.183.
38. Hayes, *Cambridge Ancient History*, I.1.183.
39. Hayes, *Cambridge Ancient History*, I.1.174-181; "Chronological Tables", I.2B.994-996.
40. M. F. Ingham, "The Length of the Sothic Cycle," *Journal of Egyptian Archaeology* 55 (1969), 39-40.
41. John Baines & E. F. Wente, "Egypt," *New Encyclopaedia Britannica*, 1991 Ed., 18.107.
42. M. F. Ingham, "The Length of the Sothic Cycle," *Journal of Egyptian Archaeology* 55 (1969), pp. 39-40.
43. Rolf Krauss, *Sothis -Und Monddaten*, 56..
44. Krauss, *Sothis -Und Monddaten*, 47.
45. Krauss,*Sothis -Und Monddaten*,100.
46. Krauss, *Sothis -Und Monddaten* 100-101.
47. Krauss, Krauss, *Sothis -Und Monddaten*, 96-101.
48. Krauss, *Sothis -Und Monddaten* 109.
49. J. R. Baines, E. F. Wente, "Egypt," *New Encyclopaedia Britannica*, 1991 Ed., 18.107,113-115.
50. Baines & Wente, 18.109.
51. Baines & Wente., 113.
52. Ulrich Luft, *Chronologische Fixierung*, 1991, cited by Lynn Rose, "Astronomicial Evidence for the Dating the End of the Middle Kingdom," *Journal of Near Eastern Studies*, 53.4 (1994), 258-261.
53. Luft, *Chronologische Fixierung*, 1991,cited by Lynn Rose, "Astronomicial Evidence for the Dating the End of the Middle Kingdom," *Journal of Near Eastern Studies*, 53.4 (1994), 258-261.
54. Michhelle Chapront-Touze and Jean Chapront, *Lunar Tables and Programs From 4000 B.C. to A. D. 8000* (Richmond, Va.: Willmann-Bell, Inc., 1991, Foreword. iii.
55. R. A. Parker, *The Calendars of Ancient Egypt*, 67.
56. Parker,*The Calendars of Ancient Egypt*, 48-50
57. William Hayes, "Chronology: Egypt to End of Twentieth Dynasty, *Cambridge Ancient History*, 3rd Ed., I.1.173-174.
58. Lynn Rose, "Astronomical Evidence for Dating the End of the Middle Kingdom," *Journal of Near Eastern Studies*, 53.4 (1994), 259-261.
59. Krauss, *Sothis-Und Monddaten* (Hildesheim: 1995), p. 47.
60. Lynn Rose, "Astronomical Evidence for Dating the End of the Middle Kingdom," *Journal of Near Eastern Studies*, 53.4 (1994), 259-261. 259-261.
61. Josef W. Wegner (Univ. of Pa.) "The Nature & Chronology of the Senwosret III-Amenemhat III Regnal Successions:" *Journal of Near Eastern Studies, JNES 55*, No. 4 (1966), Univ. of Chicago, 250-267.
62. Wegner, "The Nature & Chronology of the Senwosret III-Amenemhat III Regnal Successions," *Journal of Near Eastern Studies, JNES 55*, No. 4 (1966), Univ. of Chicago, 250-267.
63. Krauss, *Sothis-Und Monddaten*, 57
64. M. F. Ingham, *"The Length of the Sothic Cycle," Journal of Egyptian Archaeology* 5 (1969), 39-40.
65. Ingham, *The Length of the Sothic Cycle." Journal of Egyptian Archaeology* 5 (1969), 39-40.

CHAPTER TWENTY-TWO
THE MYTH OF EGYPT'S UNBROKEN SOTHIC CYCLES

Chapter Twenty-One recorded continuous revisions, disproving Egypt's astronomically absolute dates. The refutation of all of the Sothic chronologies of the Egyptian dynasties prove that Egypt's astronomical chronology **is defective and has never been "absolute."** In spite of the continual revisions, parallel dynasties and astronomical errors of Egyptologists, the Sothic Cycle continues to bind the twelfth-dynasty between 1938 and 1756 B.C. (Dates of Baines and Wente in the *New Encyclopaedia Britannica*, Vol. 18, p. 113.)

I call Egypt's Sothic Calendar the **"Goliath of Egyptian History"** that has **opposed Biblical history and dating**. For the last twenty years I have felt like young David praying to God for a victory over **"the Goliath of the Sothic Cycle."** By God's grace I finally found the stone that pierces Goliath's forehead and destroys him forever. **This chapter presents incontrovertible evidence that breaks the Sothic Cycle, permitting a three-century revision of dynasties twelve to twenty.**

I. ORIGIN AND DURATION OF EGYPT'S 365-DAY CALENDAR

Anthony Spallinger has noted that the fifth dynasty was the first to introduce a 365-day calendar of twelve months of thirty-days each, **plus a five-day feast at the end of the twelfth month.**[1] The 365-day calendar endured through the twelfth dynasty.[2] When the twelfth dynasty fell, the thirteenth dynasty continued to use the traditional 365-day calendar. A stela of Sobekhotep VIII, the last Pharaoh of the thirteenth dynasty, reported in his fourth year that the Nile flooded the temple at Karnak (Thebes) **during the five epagomenal days that occurred between the end of the twelfth month and New Year's Day.**[3] **This five-day feast proves Egypt's 365-day calendar was still in use at the end of the thirteenth dynasty.**

With the thirteenth dynasty located in the Eastern Delta, the Libyans entered the Western Delta, establishing the fourteenth dynasty.[4] I have found no evidence as to which calendar the foreign Libyans used.

About 100 years after the twelfth dynasty fell, **Hyksos (foreigners from Arabia) conquered the eastern Delta of Egypt and established the fifteenth and sixteenth dynasties.** The capital of the fifteenth dynasty was located at Avaris, which was built over the ruins of Rameses, the former store city built by Israelites. A new group of Hyksos later entered Egypt and established the sixteenth dynasty with its capital at Memphis.[5] The Hyksos drove the thirteenth dynasty south to occupy Thebes as its capital.[6] Sixty years later the Hyksos drove the fourteenth dynasty back into their native country of Libya.[7] The Hyksos likely brought to Egypt **a lunar calendar of 354 to 355 days,** which was used by most eastern nations. The lunar calendar was adjusted every three years by adding a thirteen lunar month.

We have demonstrated that the thirteenth dynasty used a 365-day calendar when the Hyksos forced them to leave Itjtowy (Zoan) in northern Egypt and moved to Thebes in southern Egypt.[8] After some years, the thirteenth dynasty became the seventeenth dynasty when a new family of Pharaohs began to reign over southern Egypt.[9] The seventeenth dynasty undoubtedly retained the 365-day calendar they inherited from the thirteenth dynasty. However, the two Hyksos dynasties from Arabia that settled in northern Egypt likely continued to use a lunar calendar of 354/355 days with a thirteenth intercalary lunar month every three years.

After 200 years of three to four rival dynasties in Egypt, Ahmose, the last king of the seventeenth dynasty, expelled the Hyksos and established the eighteenth dynasty as the sole rule of Egypt.[10] Ahmose likely continued the traditional 365-day calendar inherited from the twelfth, thirteenth and seventeenth dynasties. The eighteenth dynasty maintained the southern city of Thebes as the capital of Egypt,[11] as did the previous seventeenth dynasty.

II. EGYPT'S NEW 360-DAY CALENDAR
BROKE THE SOTHIC CYCLE

A. Amenhotep I's Introduction
of a 360-Day Calendar

After Ahmose established the eighteenth dynasty with Thebes as the capital, his son Amenhotep I took over the reign. **In Amenhotep I's ninth year he replaced the traditional 365-day calendar with a new 360-day calendar.** Amenhotep I called this new calendar "Eber's calendar." This 360-day Eber's calendar registered the rising on 11-9 (eleventh month, ninth day) of Amenhotep I's ninth year. **The traditional calendar of 365 days was reduced to 360 days by removing the five-day feast at the end of the old 365-day year.**

Parker was the first to observe the **"failure of the scribe to reckon the [five] epagomenal days" of the Eber's Calendar of Amenhotep I.[12] Krauss also admitted that the five-day "epagomena is not contained in the scheme of the [Eber's] calendar."[13] Yet, both Parker and Krauss illogically ignored the significance of the 360-day Eber's calendar, not realizing that this 360-day calendar broke the Sothic Cycle, making it impossible to calculate the B.C. year of Amenhotep I's ninth year.** All Egyptologists who calculate the Sothic dates of Egypt have either ignored, or were ignorant of, this 360-day calendar. **It is ironic that Parker and Krauss recognized this 360-day calendar without perceiving that it broke the Sothic Cycle, nullifying their Sothic dates.**

B. How Long Did Amenhotep I's 360-day Calendar Endure?

Senmut was the chief steward of Hatshepsut, the fifth Pharaoh of the eighteenth dynasty. Senmut died in Hatshepsut's eighteenth year.[14] Parker described Senmut's calendar on the ceiling of his tomb. It was divided into twelve circles with the same names of the twelve months found on the Eber's Calendar of

Amenhotep I. While Parker described every detail of this calendar, **he did not mention the five-day epagomenal feast**, the same omission in the Eber's Calendar of Amenhotep I.[15] Therefore, Amenhotep I's 360-day calendar still existed in Hatshepsut's eighteenth year, **about 56 years after Amenhotep I introduced his 360-day calendar in his ninth year.**

C. Repercussions of a 360-day Calendar for 56 Years

A 56-year duration of a 360-day calendar in the eighteenth dynasty **significantly broke the Sothic Cycle.** In a 365-day calendar, Egypt's New Year's Day shifts one day from Sirius' rising every four years. On a **365-day** Calendar during a **56-year span** (from the 9th year of Amenhotep to the 18th year of Hatshepsut), Egypt's New Year's Day shifted **14 days** from Sirius' rising.

However, on the actual **360-day calendar** of the early eighteenth dynasty, Egypt's New Year's Day and Sirius' rising shifted on the Julian Calendar in opposite directions by five days each year for three years (15 days), and six days every Leap Year **for a total of twenty-one days (15 + 6 = 21) every four years.**

Over a 56-year period of a 360-day calendar (from Amenhotep I to Hatshepsut) Sirius' rising and Egypt's New Year's Day would have shifted from each other on the Julian Calendar by **294 days (56 ÷ 4 = 14 X 21= 294).** In contrast, during the same 56-year period of a **365-day calendar,** the shift would be **only 21 days**. Thus, Sirius' rising on a 360-day calendar in the early eighteenth dynasty shifted **14 times faster than Sirius' rising on Egypt's previous 365-day calendar: 294 ÷ 21 = 14.** The 360-day calendar of the early eighteenth dynasty completely broke the traditional Sothic Cycle of 1460 years, **invalidating** all previous and later Sothic dates.

III. RETURN TO A 365-DAY CALENDAR IN THUTMOSE III'S REIGN

Evidence exists that Egypt's previous 365-day calendar was reintroduced by the twenty-third year of Thutmose III, after the death of Hatshepsut. Hatshepsut had previously co-reigned with Thutmose III from the beginning of her reign.[16] Krauss listed two inscribed new moon dates in successive years of Thutmose III's reign: (1) the Egyptian date of 9-21 in Thutmose III's twenty-third year and (2) the Egyptian date of 7-1 in Thutmose III's twenty-fourth year.

Table 21-C in the previous chapter contains a chart of new moon dates that repeat themselves every twenty-five years on a 365-day calendar that is not adjusted for Leap Year. I used Parker's chart to test the compatibility of the 9-21 new moon date in Thutmose III's twenty-third year with the 7-1 new moon date in his twenty-fourth year. I first thought that the chart disproved that Thutmose III was using a 365-day calendar, because these two Egyptian dates are not compatible in successive years of Parker's chart. However, I later learned that Thutmose III's coronation began on 9-4 (Egyptian).[17] I then realized that the 9-21 lunar date occurred at the beginning of his twenty-third year in one B.C. year and that the 7-1 lunar date occurred late in his twenty-fourth year, covering parts of three B.C. years. When two B.C. years separate these two dates, they are perfectly compatible on Parker's chart of lunar dates, which fit only on a 365-day, unadjusted calendar. **I was thus forced to conclude that Thutmose III rejected the new 360-day calendar in his twenty-third year, and reinstated the 365-day calendar**. A group of traditional priests apparently persuaded Thutmose III to abandon the new 360-day calendar and return to Egypt's ancient 365-day calendar.

Anthony Spalinger reports that a document of the mid-eighteenth dynasty copied a twelfth dynasty document to explain the meaning of each of the five epagomenal days that turn a 360-day calendar into a 365-day calendar.[18] The need to copy a twelfth dynasty document to explain the five epagomenal days in the mid-eighteenth dynasty (during Thutmose III's reign) further **testifies to the earlier 360-day calendar that was introduced by Amenhotep I.** If the eighteenth dynasty had always used a 365-day calendar, without the interruption of the 360-day calendar, there would have been **no reason** to copy a twelfth-dynasty explanation of these extra five days in the middle of the eighteenth dynasty.

However, the return to the 365-day calendar in the reign of Thutmose III did not repair the broken Sothic Cycle caused by the 360-day Calendar of the earlier eighteenth dynasty. This 360-day calendar was introduced in the eighth year of Amenhotep I and continued for about 56 years before Thutmose III restored the old 365-day calendar. **During these 56 years of a 360-day calendar,** Sirius' rising advanced from Egypt's retreating New Year's Day on the calendar by **294 days (56 years X 5 days = 280 days, plus 14 days for Leap years = 294 days).** In contrast, the traditional 365-day Calendar would have advanced Sirius' rising **by only 14 days** during these same 56 years. Thus, the Sothic Cycle of 365 days was severely broken by the 360-day calendar that was introduced by Amenhotep I and maintained by Hatshepsut.

IV. NEW RETURN TO A 360-DAY CALENDAR IN THE LATTER EIGHTEENTH DYNASTY

However, after Thutmose III's death **the 360-day calendar made an amazing comeback.** Anthony Spalinger writes in the *Journal of Near Eastern Studies* that a 360-day civil calendar was also in use in the **latter eighteenth dynasty**.

> Perhaps of greater significance to a **chronologist** than to a student of Egyptian religion is the **frequent occurrence** of a truncated or simplified civil year **comprising only 360 days** . . . . The **"absence"** of the five epagomenal days was part and parcel of the water clocks known in the Nile valley as early as the close of Dynasty XVIII. Other evidence, also covered by Leitz, **gives additional support to the feeling that these five days need not have been placed in all liturgical or calendrical systems.**[19]

Richard Parker included a drawing of one of these 360-day calendars of the latter eighteenth dynasty in his book, *Calendars of Ancient Egypt*. Parker called this calendar "the Karnak water clock of Amenhotep III,"[20] the ninth king of the eighteenth dynasty. **The five-day feast between the twelfth and first month is clearly missing.** The drawing is found on page 40 of Parker's *Calendars of Egypt*. The five-day feast between the twelfth and first months is missing. **However, Parker made no mention of the missing five days.** Parker's picture of this 360-day water calendar in the reign of Amenhotep III is likely the forerunner of a plurality of water clocks that Spalinger and Leitz have found dated in the latter eighteenth dynasty. **Therefore, the 360-day calendar of Amenhotep I and Hatshepsut was interrupted by Thutmose III's return to the 365-day calendar, but the 360-day calendar was restored in the latter eighteenth dynasty.**

Spalinger's reference above **to a plurality of 360-day water calendars** in the latter eighteenth dynasty implies that the 360-day calendar endured for a considerable length of years. Spalinger also noted in the quotation above that these multiple 360-day calendars should be of great interest to chronologists. **Why?** Obviously, Spalinger realized that these 360-day calendars **broke the 365-day Sothic Cycle,** upon which Egyptologists depend for their astronomical dates.

Spalinger attempted to explain away the significance of the 360-day calendars by suggesting that the eighteenth dynasty **may have used simultaneously both 360-day and 365-day civil calendars.** However, it would be **utter confusion to impose Egypt's religious lunar calendar of 354/55 days on top of both 360-day and 365-day civil calendars simultaneously. Logically, the 365 day and 360-day calendars could not have co-existed.** Therefore, the 365-day calendar and the 360-day calendar obviously were used **consecutively** rather than simultaneously. Also, both calendars obviously retained the religious lunar calendar on top of the original 365-day calendar and also on top of the subsequent 360-day calendars in both the early and latter periods of the eighteenth dynasty. **Chronological confusion obviously reigned during the switch-backs of two different calendars during the reign of eighteenth-dynasty Pharaohs.**

V. FINAL PROOF THAT THE SOTHIC
CYCLE WAS BROKEN

Amenhotep III reigned for thirty-eight years in the latter half of the eighteenth dynasty. **Amenhotep III used a 360-day water clock.** Parker described in detail this water clock. See Parker's words below.

The theory of the clock is quite simple. It was filled to the brim with water at sunset. When the water, flowing out slowly through an outlet in the bottom of the clock, had dropped in level to the first of the appropriate month-scale, the second hour of the night began. The shortest scale is that of II smw [Shemu, the third and last season} and the longest IIII Achet [fourth month of the first season]. From this one may conclude that I Achet 1 [Egypt's New Year's Day (1-1)] was near the autumn equinox, about October 5 [Julian date] in the time of Amenhotep III.[21]

Notice that Parker concluded from Amenhotep III's water calendar that Egypt's New Year's Day (I Achet I = 1-1) occurred about **October 5, near the autumn equinox.** Parker is obviously using a Julian date since the autumn equinox generally occurs on September 21 (Gregorian), which is equivalent to October 5 (Julian) in relation to the autumn equinox.

Table 21-E in the previous chapter is based on the presupposition that Egypt always had a 365-day, unadjusted and unrevised calendar. Table 21-E shows that Egypt's New Year's Day on a 365-day Calendar coincided with October 5 (Julian) only in the years 1633 to 1630 B.C., whereas Baines dates Amenhotep III's reign from 1390 to 1353 B.C., **a discrepancy of 243 to 280 years. This discrepancy confirms my proposed three-century revision of Egypt's dynasties.**

Parker did not realize that his interpretation of Amenhotep III's water clock of 360 days proves that the Sothic Cycle was previously broken by the 360-day calendars of Amenhotep I and Hatshepsut. Thus, the previous 360-day calendars and the latter 360-day calendars of the eighteenth dynasty **nullified the Sothic dates of the twelfth through the twentieth dynasties.**

As we saw in Chapter 21, modern Egyptologists have constantly revised the Sothic dates, proving that the Sothic dates were "never absolute." With the Sothic Cycle broken, the dates of dynasties twelve to twenty can be redated three centuries later on the B.C. calendar, creating amazing and abundant synchronism with Bible history.

VI. SWITCH-BACK TO A 365-DAY CALENDAR IN THE NINETEENTH DYNASTY

Evidence indicates that Egypt **abandoned the 360-day calendar for the second time and finally returned permanently to its traditional 365-day calendar during the reign of the early nineteenth dynasty**. Richard Parker describes the astronomical ceiling of the Ramesseum, in which Ramses II made offerings to twelve deities who represent the twelve months of Egypt's calendar, plus a thirteenth deity who is worshiped in the feast called *Dhwtyt*, which is positioned between the twelfth and first months.[22] Parker notes that Ramses II's calendar is similar to the calendar of Senmut, the steward of the eighteenth-dynasty queen, Hatshepsut, **with the exception of the additional thirteenth deity.**[23] The fact that Senmut's calendar does **not** have the thirteenth period of five days and Ramses II's calendar contains the thirteenth period, **clearly distinguishes Ramses II's 365-day calendar from the 360-day calendars of eighteenth dynasty Pharaohs, Amenhotep I, Hatshepsut and Amenhotep III.**

However, Parker interpreted Ramses II's calendar to be a religious **lunar** calendar, rather than a 365-day civil calendar. He also interpreted the Egyptian word *Dhwty* to be a thirteenth intercalary lunar month, instead of the traditional five-day feast.[24] If Parker is correct, Ramses II replaced the 360-day calendar of the late eighteenth dynasty with a lunar calendar of 354/55 days that is adjusted every three years with a thirteenth month. **If so, Ramses II's Lunar Calendar created an additional breaking of the Sothic Cycle.**

Replying to Parker, Rolf Krauss logically pointed out that Parker's interpretation of a thirteenth lunar month would cause the rising of Sirius to shift an extra twenty-five days before it coincided with New Year's day, which would require an additional 100 years for such a shift to occur at the rate of one day every four years.[25] Remarkably, Krauss' proposal that this extra century was needed for Sirius' rising to coincide with Egypt's New Year's Day fits perfectly with the 365-day calendar of Ramses III, which I describe under the next point.

VII. A NEW 365-DAY CALENDAR IN THE REIGN OF RAMSES III OF THE TWENTIETH DYNASTY

In 1982 I found in an Egyptian document that Sirius rose on Egypt's New Year's Day in the twelfth year of Ramses III, the second king of the twentieth dynasty. This date of Sirius' rising contradicts Sothic dates by 100 years, precisely the period of time that Krauss suggested would be needed for Sirius' rising to coincide with Egypt's New Year's Day, if a lunar calendar and extra lunar month were added every three years. The twelfth year of Ramses III's reign and Sirius' rising on Egypt's New Year's Day are dated 102 years later than Ramses II's second year of reign, precisely what Parker interpreted and what Krauss noted as an objection to Parker's interpretation.

Krauss also noted the rising of Sirius on New Year's Day in Ramses III's reign. **Krauss recognized that Ramses III's 365-day calendar was completely contradictory to the supposed "unbroken Sothic Cycle".** Using the Sothic method of dating, Krauss calculated that Sirius' rising at 24°coincided with Egypt's New Year's Day **in 1278 B.C., the second year of Ramses II's reign.**[26] However, Krauss **did not cite a single Egyptian document or inscription that testifies to Sirius' rising on New Year's Day, or any other day, during Ramses II's reign.** Krauss assumed that Sirius rose on New Year's Day in Ramses II's reign, based on the false presupposition that all of Egypt's dynasties used **only a 365-day, unadjusted and unrevised calendar.** Krauss noted the missing five-day feast in Amenhotep I's reign, but ignored its significance in breaking the Sothic Cycle. Krauss was apparently ignorant of the **360-day calendars of Hatshepsut and later of Amenenhotep III.**

Krauss' claim that Sirius' rising coincided with Egypt's New Year's Day in Ramses II's second year **is disproved** by an inscription in the Medinet Habu Temple of Ramses III that states that **Sirius rose on Egypt's New Year's Day in Ramses III's twelfth year**. Krauss and Baines date Ramses III's twelfth year to **1176 B.C.,**[27] **102 years after their 1278 B.C. date** in the second year of **Ramses II** (on the basis of **unbroken** Sothic Cycles).[28] Remember that Ramses II was the second king of the nineteenth dynasty and that Ramses III was the second king of the twentieth dynasty and was separated from Ramses II by 102 years.

James Breasted admitted that Sirius' rising on New Year's Day in Ramses III's calendar **contradicted the theory of a continuous and unbroken Sothic Cycle.** He attempted to reconcile this discrepancy by calling Ramses III's calendar **"a religious calendar" (lunar) that differed from Egypt's "civil calendar."**[29]

I read Breasted's own translation of Ramses III's calendar that states that the calendar had **365 days, and thus was not a religious lunar calendar of 354/55 days.** Breasted's translation of the calendar also states that Ramses III united **on the same calendar both religious and civil events, including Ramses III's inauguration as king and his victories in war.**[30] Thus, Breasted's interpretation that Ramses III's calendar was **solely a religious calendar contradicts Breasted's own translation of the calendar as containing civil and religious events.**

Therefore, Sirius' rising on Egypt's New Year's Day in Ramses III's twelfth year proves that the Sothic Cycle had been previously broken and that Sirius did not rise on New Year's Day in Ramses II's early reign. Rather, Sirius rose on New Year's Day in Ramses III's twelfth year, 102 years later than Ramses II's second year, **proving that the 360-day calendars of the eighteenth dynasty broke the Sothic Cycle.**

Parker also saw the problem of Sirius' rising on New Year's Day in Ramses III's twelfth year. He attempted to dissolve this apparent discrepancy by saying, "it is well known that Ramses III's calendar is a copy of Ramses II's."[31] However, this calendar of Ramses III is found inscribed in stone in the **Medinet Habu Temple, which Ramses III built for himself in his twelfth year.** This 365-day calendar also lists the coronation and military conquests **of Ramses III,** not of Ramses II. The dates of the religious feast days on Ramses III's calendar **were determined by New Moon dates,** which change every year on a 365-day Calendar. Therefore, these New Moon feast days only applied to the twelfth year of Ramses III, and certainly not to the second year of Ramses II's reign 102 years earlier. **All of the facts unite in concluding that the Medinet Habu Temple calendar of 365 days was uniquely designed for Ramses III, and certainly not for Ramses II.** Sirius' rising on New Year's Day in Ramses III's twelfth year provides additional and conclusive proof that the Sothic Cycle was broken by the 360-day calendars of the earlier eighteenth dynasty.

Krauss dated Sirius' rising on New Year's Day in Ramses II's second year, but **ignored the 360-day calendars of the eighteenth dynasty,** even though he admitted that the Eber's Calendar of Amenhotep I **was a 360-day calendar.**[32] **The 360-day calendars of the eighteenth dynasty broke the Sothic Cycle and nullified all Sothic dates calculated by Egyptologists!!! These famous Egyptologists were aware of the 360-day calendars, but ignored their significance in order to maintain their traditional unbroken Sothic Cycles.**

VIII. WHY DID EIGHTEENTH DYNASTY KINGS
FLUCTUATE BETWEEN 360-DAY AND
365-DAY CALENDARS?

Why was Egypt's calendar revised at least three times during the eighteenth dynasty? The Hyksos likely used a **354/355-day lunar calendar** during their **110-year reign over N. Egypt.** During this long period, the Hyksos probably forced the priests in N. Egypt to follow only a lunar calendar rather than their 365-day calendar. When Ahmose expelled the Hyksos and established the eighteenth dynasty, he brought with him from Thebes **to N. Egypt the 365-day calendar used in S. Egypt.** This introduction of a 365-day calendar likely **caused friction with the priests of N. Egypt,** who were probably using the 354/55-day lunar calendar of the Hyksos. After some years of controversy, Amenhotep I, the son of Ahmose, likely proposed a 360-day calendar as a compromise, halfway between the 365-day calendar of S. Egypt and the 355-day lunar calendar of N. Egypt. The 360-day calendars of Amenhotep I and of Senmut, the prime minister of Hatshepsut, all testify in favor of such a compromise.

The 360-day calendar of Amenhotep I was not new to Egyptian thought. Spalinger points out, "For Djefahapy, a temple year, which was defined in an economic-religious setting by this individual, comprised **360 days.**"[33] The only Djefahapy I have found was a nomarch (governor) of the twelfth dynasty. His remarks imply that a 360-day calendar was under consideration as far back as the twelfth dynasty and was thus likely the first influence to modify Egypt's 365-day calendar to a 360-day calendar. However, a second Djefahapy may have also lived during the eighteenth dynasty. **Either way, a 360-day calendar was definitely used during both the early and latter eighteenth dynasty.**

Let us now return to my theoretical explanation of the reasons motivating the switch between 365-day and 360-day calendars in the eighteenth dynasty. After many years of trial and dissatisfaction by both groups of priests, **the southern priests convinced Thutmose III to return to a 365-day calendar.** Earlier in this chapter we saw evidence of this 365-day calendar in Thutmose III's twenty-third and twenty-fourth years.

However, the return to the 365-day calendar did not satisfy the northern priests and the debate continued as to which calendar to use. Finally, the northern priests convinced Amenhotep III of the latter eighteenth dynasty to switch back to the 360-day calendar. In view of the multiple 360-day calendars that Spalinger found in the latter eighteenth dynasty, it is clear that these 360 calendars substituted the traditional 365-day calendar, breaking the Sothic Cycle, and annulling the Sothic chronologies that Egyptologists have so religiously followed.

A final switch back to the traditional 365-day calendar occurred when the nineteenth dynasty came to power. If the eighteenth dynasty had not introduced the 360-day calendar, Sirius' rising would have coincided with Egypt's New Year's Day in the early reign of Ramses II. **The 360-day calendars interrupted the Sothic Cycle causing Sirius' rising to occur on New Year's Day 100 years later**

in the twelfth year of Ramses III, the second king of the twentieth dynasty.

I have served as an instructor, and later as Academic Dean of Sunset International Bible Institute from 1976 to 2002. During these twenty-six years we changed the calendar five times and the curriculum eight times. We also switched back to previous calendars and curriculum. Thus, these calendrical changes in the eighteenth dynasty appear in my mind to be both reasonable and natural, especially after foreign Libyan and Hyksos lunar calendars were introduced into Egypt for an entire century. The eighteenth dynasty was the beginning of what Egyptologists call the "The New Kingdom of Egypt." The "New Kingdom" **brought new changes and experimentations with two different 360-day calendars** (in the beginning of the eighteenth dynasty and in the latter eighteenth dynasty) before finally settling for their old 365-day calendar in the nineteenth dynasty.

Regardless of the number of years attributed to these two phases of 360-day calendars, each phase of 360-day calendars **broke the Sothic Cycle**. The broken Sothic Cycle **forever nullified Egypt's Sothic method to determine even the century, much less the B.C. year of Sirius' rising during the twelfth and eighteenth dynasties.**

IX. THE SOTHIC CYCLE OF
A 360-DAY CALENDAR

Egypt's New Year's Day in an unadjusted 365-day calendar shifted completely around the Julian Calendar in **1460 years** at the rate of **one day every four years**: 4 X 365 = 1460. However, Egypt's New Year's Day in an **unadjusted 360-day calendar** shifted completely around the Julian Calendar in **69.5 years** at the rate of **5.25 days every year**: $365 \div 5.25 = 69.52$ **years**. What a contrast! Sirius' rising took **1460 years to rotate around a 365-day calendar**, but Sirius took only **seventy years (69.52) to rotate around a 360-day calendar.**

Egypt's **365-day calendar** shifted on the Julian calendar **one day every four years.** Egypt's **360-day calendar** shifted on the Julian calendar **twenty-one days every four years: 5.25 X 4 = 21.** Therefore, Sirius' rising shifted on a **360-day calendar twenty-one times faster than it shifted on a 365-day calendar.**

On a 365-day Calendar, Sirius' rising on 11-9 (Egyptian) in Amenhotep I's ninth year had to shift **fifty-seven days** to coincide with Egypt's New Year's Day in Ramses III's twelfth year. At the rate of one day every four years, it took **228 years** for this shift to occur: **57 X 4 = 228**, assuming that Sirius' rising did not shift to a different Julian day in the interim. However, Krauss and Baines date Ramses III's twelfth year **330 years** after Amenhotep I's ninth year. The fact that Sirius rose on New Year's Day in Ramses III's twelfth year provides additional proof that the 360-day calendars broke the traditional Sothic rate of one day every four years.

On a 360-day Calendar, Sirius rising on 11-9 (Egyptian) in Amenhotep I's ninth year had to **shift fifty-two days to reach New Year's Day (1-1) on the basis of Amenhotep I's calendar of only 360 days.** However, a 360-day calendar omitted the five-day feast at the end of the year, whereas the 365-day calendar of the twelfth dynasty included the five-day feast at the end of the 360 regular calendar days. Thus, at the **Sothic rate of 5.25 days every year on a 360-day calendar**, Sirius' rising shifted **fifty-two days** to coincide with New Year's day **in only ten years** (52 days ÷ 5.25 days per year = 9.9 years.). What an astounding contrast! The **365-day** calendar took **228 years** (57 X 4) for Sirius' shift from 11-9 (Egyptian) to Egypt's New Year's Day (1-1), whereas the **360-day** calendar shifted from 11-9 to New Year's Day in **only ten years (52 days ÷ 5.25 = 9.9 = 10 years).**

Egypt's New Year's Day shifted completely around Egypt's **365-day calendar in 1460 years (365 X 4 = 1460)**. Egypt's New Year's Day shifted around **a 360-day calendar in only sixty-nine years (360 ÷ 5.25 = 68.57 years).**

However, the historical evidence indicates that Egypt fluctuated back and forth between 360-day and 365-day calendars, making it difficult to know the precise number of years that the 360-day calendar was utilized and the precise number of years that the 365-day calendar was used. The correct combination of these two calendars ultimately culminated with Sirius' rising on Egypt's New Year's Day in Rameses III's twelfth year.

The history of the eighteenth through the twentieth dynasties and the lengths of reign of their Pharaohs are controversial. In Volume II of my series, *Solving the Exodus Mystery,* I will propose my new chronology for the eighteenth through the twentieth dynasties. In Volume II I will also show a different combination of shifts on the 360-day and 365-day calendars that reconcile Sirius' rising on 11-9 on a 360-day calendar in Amenhotep I's ninth year with Sirius' rising on 1-1 on a 365-day calendar in Ramses III's twelfth year.

X. RAMSES III'S 365-DAY CALENDAR DOES NOT FIT THE 365-DAY CALENDAR OF PTOLEMY III.

All Egyptologists agree that Ramses III's calendar is **not compatible** with either the Sothic Cycle, or the 365-day calendar of Ptolemy III's eighth year in 239/38 B.C. Volume II will point out four different foreign groups that entered Egypt and started four rival dynasties that reigned simultaneously from different Egyptian capitals. These foreign dynasties likely brought differing calendars with them. Any of these calendars could have been the progenitor of Ptolemy III's 365-day calendar. In Volume Two we will discuss each of these calendars in depth and point out which of these four calendars was the precursor of Ptolemy III's calendar.

CONCLUSION

The Goliath of the Sothic Cycle has held Egyptian chronology in bondage for an entire century. The introduction of 360-day calendars during the eighteenth dynasty broke the Sothic Cycle and made it impossible to use Sothic dates to determine the B.C. centuries of the twelfth and eighteenth dynasties. **Table 22-A lists thirteen discoveries that are listed in this chapter. These thirteen**

discoveries break the Sothic Cycle, making it impossible to assign astronomically absolute dates to Egypt's dynasties twelve through twenty. **With Goliath dead, Dynasties One to Twenty can now slide three centuries later on the B.C. calendar.** The result of this three-century revision is abundant and amazing synchronism with the histories of Egypt, Israel, Assyria and Babylon.

TABLE 22-A
THIRTEEN DISCOVERIES THAT DESTROY THE MYTH OF EGYPT'S UNBROKEN SOTHIC CYCLES

Discovery 1. Amenhotep I, the second Pharaoh of the eighteenth dynasty introduced a new 360-day calendar by omitting the five-day feast at the end of the 360th day. Parker and Krauss recognized this revision of Egypt's 365-day calendar, but ignored its importance without realizing that this 360-day calendar invalidated all previous and later Sothic Cycles, which require uninterrupted 365-day calendars.

Discovery 2. A 360-day calendar causes New Year's Day to rotate around the calendar **every 70 years**, whereas a 365-day calendar causes New Year's Day to rotate around the calendar every **1460 years.**

Discovery 3. Parker was the first to observe the **"failure of the scribe to reckon the [five] epagomenal days"** of the Eber's Calendar of Amenhotep I.

Discovery 4. Krauss also noted the missing five-day feast day of the Eber's calendar, but ignored its significance without perceiving that it broke the Sothic Cycle of previous and later 1460-year cycles.

Discovery 5. Amenhotep I's 360-day calendar continued for **fifty-six years** up to Hatshepsut's eighteenth year. This fifty-six period of a 360-day calendar caused New Year's Day to **shift 294 days** on Egypt's calendar. On the other hand, the 365-day calendar caused New Year's Day to shift **only 14 days.** Thus, the 360-day calendar completely destroyed the Sothic Calendar of Egypt, annulling all Sothic dates both before and afterwards.

Discovery 6. Thutmose III of the mid-eighteenth dynasty returned to a 365-day Sothic Calendar for a number of years, **but in the latter period of the eighteenth dynasty Amenhotep III reinstated the 360-day calendar**, once again destroying further the Sothic Cycle.

Discovery 7. Amenhotep III constructed a water calendar that also contained 360 days instead of the traditional 365 days, further nullifying all Sothic dates of Egypt.

Discovery 8. Amenhotep III's calendar located Egypt's New Year's Day on October 5 (Julian date). **Uninterrupted Sothic Cycles on a 365-day calendar dates October 5 only in the years 1633 B.C. to 1630 B.C.** whereas Egyptologists date Amenenhotep III from 1390 to 1353 B.C., **a discrepancy of 243 to 280 years, confirming a three-century revision of the Egyptian dynasties** that I have been proposing for many years before finding this proof.

Discovery 9. Ramses II of the nineteenth dynasty returned to the traditional 365-day unadjusted calendar, rather than following the non-traditional 360-day calendars of the eighteenth dynasty. I have not been able to find the precise year and month when Ramses II returned to the 365-day calendar.

Discovery 10. The calendar of Ramses III of the twentieth dynasty began a new 365-day calendar with New Year's day coinciding with Sirius' rising, an additional breaking of the Sothic Cycle.

Discovery 11 - The Sothic Cycle of an unadusted 360-Day Calendar causes New Year's Day to shift around the Julian Calendar in **69.52 years.** New Year's Day shifts around a 365-day calendar in **1,460 years. What a contrast!.**

Discovery 12. Ramses III's 365-day calendar does not agree with Egypt's 365-day Calendar during the reign of Ptolemy III, who reigned hundreds of years later, indicating that other revisions of Egypt's calendar occurred after the reign of Ramses III.

Discovery 13. All of the discoveries above destroy the continuity and consistency of Sothic Cycles, which Egyptologists accept, while continually revising their Sothic dates.

TABLE 22-B
RUNNING TOTAL OF DISCOVERIES

Chapter		Chapter Total	Running Total
2	Conflict Between Biblical and Secular Histories	18	18
4	Discovery of 430 Years from Abraham to the Exodus	16	34
5	Confirmation of Abraham's Historicity	28	62
6	Discovery of the Remains of Sodom and Gomorrah	17	79
7	Joseph As a Slave and Prisoner in Amenemhet I's Reign	21	100
8	Joseph Becomes the Vizier of Sesostris I	23	123
9	Sesostris I Gives Joseph a New Name and a Wife	11	134
10	The Seven Years of Abundance in Sesostris I's Reign	10	144
11	The Seven Years of Famine in Sesostris I's Reign	20	164
12	Israel Enters Egypt during Sesostris I's Reign	14	178
13	Sesostris III Enslaves the Israelites	17	195
14	Sesostris III, The Foster Grandfather of Moses	12	207
15	Sesostris III, Builder of Rameses and Pithom	15	222
16	Zoan (Itjtowy), the Capital of the Twelfth Dynasty	16	238
17	Amenemhet III, the Pharaoh Who Tried to Kill Moses	15	253
18	Amenemhet IV, the Pharaoh of the Exodus	14	267
19	Moses and Ipuwer Report the Ten Plagues	22	289
20	Israel's Exodus and the Drowning of Amenemhet IV and His Army in the Red Sea	26	315
21	Continuous Errors in Egypt's "Astronomically Absolute" Dates..	30	345
22	The Myth of Egypt's Unbroken Sothic Cycles	13	358

NOTES FOR CHAPTER TWENTY-TWO

1. Anthony Spalinger, "Some Remarks on the Epagomenal Days in Ancient Egypt," *Journal of New Eastern Studies,* (Univ. of Chicago, 1995), 54.1.33-34.
2. Richard Parker, *The Calendars of Ancient Egypt,* 30-50.
3. David Rohl, *Pharaohs & Kings,* 391-2.
4. "Chronological Tables," *Cambridge Ancient History,* II.1.818.
5. "Chronological Tables," *Cambridge Ancient History,* II.1.818.
6. William C. Hayes, "Egypt: From the Death of Ammenemes III to Seqenenre II," *Cambridge Ancient History,* 3rd Ed., II.1.52-53.
7. William C. Hayes, II.1.54;
8. William C. Hayes, II.1.52-54
9. William C. Hayes, II.1.64-73.
10. T. G. H. James, "Egypt: From The Expulsion of the Hyksos to Amenophis I," *Cambridge Ancient History,* 3rd Ed., II.1.289-312.
11. T. G. H. James, II.1.311-312.
12. Richard Parker, *The Calendars of Ancient Egypt,* 42.
13. Rolf Krauss, *Sothis -Und Monddadaten* (Hildesheim: 1995), 107.
14. William C. Hayes, "Egypt: Internal Affairs From Tuthmosis I to the Death of Amenophis III," *Cambridge Ancient History,* II.1.318.
15. Richard Parker, *The Calendars of Ancient Egypt,* 42.
16. J. R. Baines, "Egypt," *New Encyclopaedia Britannica,* 1991 Ed., 18.115.
17. James Breasted, *Ancient Records of Egypt,* II.234 (592).
18. Anthony Spalinger, "Some Remarks on the Epagomenal Days in Ancient Egypt," *Journal of New Eastern Studies,* (Univ. of Chicago, 1995), 54.1.34-36.
19. Anthony Spalinger, "Some Remarks on the Epagomenal Days in Ancient Egypt," *Journal of New Eastern Studies,* 54.1.33-34.
20. Richard Parker, *The Calendars of Ancient Egypt,* 40.
21. Richard Parker, *The Calendars of Ancient Egypt,* 40.
22. Richard Parker, *The Calendars of Ancient Egypt,* 40.
23. Richard Parker, *The Calendars of Ancient Egypt,* 42-43.
24. Richard Parker, *The Calendars of Ancient Egypt,* 42-43.
25. Rolf Krauss, *Sothis -Und Monddadaten,* 17.
26. Rolf Krauss, *Sothis -Und Monddadatenauss,,*142.
27. Rolf Krauss, *Sothis -Und Monddadaten,* p. 107.
28. Baines, "Egypt," 18.118.
29. Breasted, *Ancient Records of Egypt,* IV.83.
30. Breasted, *Ancient Records of Egypt,* IV.84.143.
31. Parker, *The Calendars of Egypt,* p. 40.
32. Krauss, *Sothis -Und Monddadaten,*107.
33. Anthony Spalinger, "Some Remarks on the Epagomenal Days in Ancient Egypt," *Journal of New Eastern Studies,* 34.

CHAPTER TWENTY-THREE
CARBON-14 DATES CONFIRM A THREE -CENTURY REVISION OF EGYPTIAN HISTORY

The previous chapter demonstrated that the Sothic Cycle has been broken, freeing Egypt's Dynasties One to Twenty to be redated five to three centuries later. This chapter presents carbon-14 dating that confirms this amazing revision.

I. THE SCIENTIFIC METHOD
OF CARBON-14 DATING

Carbon-14 dating, also called radiocarbon dating, depends upon the constant and consistent rate of decay of radiocarbon (carbon 14) in living organisms, including trees and plants. Trees, for example, absorb carbon dioxide from the atmosphere. When the tree is cut or dies, it ceases to absorb carbon dioxide and the carbon 14 within the organism's tissues begins to decay at a constant rate.

In A. D. 1950 Dr. Libby discovered that carbon 14 had a half life of 5,570 years, meaning that half of the amount of radiocarbon will disintegrate within 5,570 years.[1] By measuring the residual carbon-14 in the cut wood of a tree, scientists are able to estimate the year when the specimen died with a margin of error of forty years either way. Modern scientists have corrected Dr. Libby's half-life of carbon-14 to 5,730 years instead of 5,570 years.[2]

The starting date of all uncalibrated carbon-14 dates is **A.D. 1950**, the year Dr. Libby discovered carbon-14 dating. Thus, 1950 is subtracted from what is called the B.P. radiocarbon date to get the proper A.D. or B.C. date when the living matter died and began to decay. For example, a B.P. date of 3400 is reduced by 1950 to get 1450 B.C. as the uncalibrated carbon-14 date.

However, the uncalibrated carbon-14 dates fall hundreds of years short of the so called "astronomically absolute Sothic dates" of ancient Egyptian history. Modern scientists and Egyptologists were unhappy with these carbon-14 dates because of the discrepancy between the Sothic dates and the carbon-14 dates,

Modern scientists decided to **calibrate** the carbon-14 dates in order to move them closer to the **"astronomically absolute" dates of Egyptian history**. This calibration revises the carbon-14 dates earlier **on the basis of tree rings.** Toward the end of this chapter I will explain specifically how scientists use these tree rings to calibrate their revised dates. I will point out the false premises that support these calibrated dates.

In 1990 I decided to research the subject of carbon-14 dating in relation to the dating of Egyptian and Biblical histories. My daughter Trina and my wife Dot helped me search in the Texas Tech University library for a book on carbon-14 dating. Dot found a book entitled the *Radiocarbon Variations And Absolute Chronology* (the Twelfth Nobel Symposium held at Upsalla University, in Sweden). An entire chapter by T. Save-Soderbergh and I.U. Olsson was devoted to "Carbon-14 Dating and Egyptian Chronology."[3] This book contains a chart that compares the historical dates of Egyptian history with the **uncalibrated carbon-14 dates. I was amazed to find that the uncalibrated carbon-14 dates confirmed my newly proposed dates of Egyptian history.** Another chart in Save-Soderbergh's book showed that **the calibrated dates, based on tree rings**, were closer to Egypt's historical dates, but still more than 100 years off the Sothic dates. We will explain the calibrated dates later in this chapter and disprove their alleged accuracy.

II. CARBON-14 DATING OF EGYPT'S FIRST FIVE DYNASTIES

The chart from the article by T. Save-Soderbergh and I. U. Olsson demonstrates that **the uncalibrated radiocarbon dates of the first through the fifth Egyptian dynasties average 735 years later than Breasted's dates, 444 years later than Hayes' dates, and 364 years later than Baines' dates.**[4] See this comparison in Table 23-A.

TABLE 23-A
SIX CARBON-14 DATES FOR EGYPTIAN
DYNASTIES 1 TO 5

DYN.	Breasted B.C.	Hayes B.C.	Baines B.C.	Carbon-14 Dates B.C.	Difference in years of age
I. DEN	3280	2940	2820	2350	-930 TO -470
II. KHASEKHEMWY	3000	2703	2667	2270	-730 TO -497
III. DJOSER	2980	2667	2670	2150	-830 TO -520
IV. SNEFRU	2924	2523	2574	2150	-774 TO -424
IV. CHEOPS	2887	2590	2551	2600	-287 TO -49
V. NEFERIRKARE	2731	2473	2444	2000	-731 TO -444

T. Save-Soderbergh and I.U. Olsson, "C14 Dating and Egyptian Chronology," *Radiocarbon Variations and Absolute Chronology*, Ed. I.U. Olsson (New York: John Wiley & Sons, 1983), pp. 45,49,50.

The earliest dynasties in Mesopotamia are dated by Mallowan in the *Cambridge Ancient History* back to *c.* 3100 B.C.,[5] which is also the Cambridge date for the beginning of the first dynasty of Egypt.[6] **Yet Mallowan admits that the carbon-14 dates for these earliest dynasties are 600 to 700 years later than the historical dates.**

Unfortunately, this apparently satisfactory estimate for the length of the E.D. period does not agree with recent carbon-14 findings, particularly for material from Nippur lately tested, which may require a reduction of third millennium dates by as much as **six or seven centuries**. We have to face the possibility that if the newly emerging carbon-14 pattern for the third millennium is the right one, we must jettison the whole of the previously accepted basis of Egyptian chronology upon which the Mesopotamian in large part depends. But we should be reluctant to do this without much stronger evidence, for Egyptian calculations based on written evidence can be checked on astronomical grounds with but a comparatively small margin of error. . . . Some authorities are therefore for the present inclined to believe that at the end of the third millennium there was some physical disturbance in the solar magnetic field, which may have affected the level of the carbon-14 activity in the carbon exchange reservoir. . . . **But the problem is unreal [my emphasis].**[7]

In a footnote Mallowan noted that carbon-14 dates of third millennium levels at Saqqara, Egypt, were also **four to seven centuries lower than the historically assigned dates.**[8] Interestingly, all of these carbon-14 dates reduce Egypt's and Mesopotamia's first dynasties to about 2300 B.C. or later, a date that is about 100 to 200 years after the Biblical date of the Flood.

III. CARBON-14 DATES FOR DYNASTIES ELEVEN TO NINETEEN

The reader can see in Table 23 B that the uncalibrated carbon-14 dates for Egypt's eleventh to the nineteenth dynasties are about **three centuries younger than the historical and supposed "astronomical" dates of the twelfth dynasty.** Thus, the uncalibrated carbon-14 dates confirm my three-century revision of the eleventh through the nineteenth dynasties.   Notice the evidence below.

A. Carbon-14 Dating of Mentuhotep II and Amenemhet I

The *Cambridge Ancient History* dates **Mentuhotep II,** an eleventh-dynasty king, from **2060 to 2010 B.C.**[9] The *Britannica* revised Mentuhotep II's dates from 1957 to 1945 B.C.[10] **The average uncalibrated carbon-14 date of wood in Mentuhotep II's tomb was 1700 B.C.**[11] Thus, the uncalibrated carbon-14 dates are **245 to 310 years later than the established Sothic dates** for Mentuhotep II's death.

Amenemhet I, the former Vizier of Mentuhotep II, became the first Pharaoh of the twelfth dynasty. Baines dates Amenemhet I's reign from 1938 to 1908 B.C., **only seven years after Mentuhotep II's death.**[12] My newly proposed Biblical chronology for Amenemhet I dates his accession year in **1687 B.C.**, **only thirteen years after the 1700 B.C. carbon-14 date for Mentuhotep II.**   Therefore, the uncalibrated carbon-14 date of **1700 B.C. for Mentuhotep II confirms a three-century revision of the eleventh and twelfth dynasties, but negates by three centuries the Sothic dates of modern Egyptologists.**

B. Carbon-14 Dating of Sesostris I

The reader can see in Chapters Seven and Eight how I linked Joseph's first year as prime minister to the second year of Sesostris I, the second Pharaoh of the twelfth dynasty. Since Joseph's first year as vizier is dated Biblically to **1665 B.C., Sesostris I's second year should also be dated to 1665 B.C.** and his entire reign from **1667 to 1621 B.C. However, Breasted dated Sesostris I's coronation to 1980 B.C. Hayes dated it to 1971 B.C. and Baines dated it in 1918 B.C.** Egyptologists' dates differ from my 1667 B.C. date of his coronation **by 253 to 315 years.** Which of these dates are confirmed by carbon-14 dating? Burned wood from the Buhen fortress, constructed by Sesostris I on the S. border of Egypt, was carbon-14 dated **at 1680 B.C.**[13] Cedar wood from Wadi Gawasis from Sesostris I's reign, is dated at B.P. 3555. Subtracting 1950 A.D. from this B.P. date gives a **carbon-14 date of 1605 B.C.**[14] Averaging these two dates we get **1642 B.C., in the middle of my Biblical dates for Sesostris I's reign from 1667 to 1621 B.C., but 313 to 251 years later than Egyptologists' dates for Sesostris I.**

C. Carbon-14 Dating of Sesostris II

My new Biblical chronology for Sesostris II, the third Pharaoh of the twelfth dynasty, dates him from **1590 to 1542 B.C.** A sample from the boundary wall of Sesostris II's pyramid is carbon-14 dated at 3490 B.P. which translates into **1540 B.C.,**[15] **only two years after my date for his death.** Hayes dates Sesostris II's death in 1878 B.C. and Baines dates his death in 1837 B.C., **297 to 338 years earlier than the carbon-14 date of 1540 B.C.**

Five carbon-14 dates of objects related to Sesostris II have an average B.P. date of 3530, which is **1580 B.C., only ten years after my proposed Biblical date of 1590 B.C. for Sesostris II's first year of reign.** Consistently, the 1580 B.C. carbon-14 average date is **264 to 317 years later** than the Egyptologists' differing dates for Sesostris II's accession year.

On the other hand, a grave of a common Egyptian man by the name of **Ahanakht** lived in the reign of Amenemhet II and died during the reign of Sesostris II. Several samples from Ahanakht's grave were carbon-14 dated variously from 1650 to 1850 B.C. with an average age of **1750 B.C.**[16] This tomb date is 200 years earlier than the carbon-14 date for Sesostris II's tomb, and 100 years earlier than the carbon-14 date of Sesostris I's reign, even though Ahanakht lived and died 100 years later than Sesostris I. This apparent discrepancy is dissolved if Ahanakht's relatives buried him in an old, reused casket. Common Egyptians, and sometimes even kings, reused the caskets of their ancestors or stole or purchased old caskets in which to bury their relatives.

D. Carbon-14 Dating of Sesostris III

Sesostris III's reign is dated by Hayes **at 1878-1843 and by Baines at 1836-1818 B.C.** My new Bible chronology dates Sesostris III's reign from **1542 to 1498 B.C., a difference of 294 to 337 years.** I noted above that a sample from the boundary wall of Sesostris II's pyramid **is carbon-14 dated at 1540 B.C.**[17] Sesostris III became king the same year that Sesostris II died. **Thus the 1540 B.C.**

date is only two years later than my Biblical date of 1542 B.C. for Sesostris III's accession year, but 303 to 338 years later than the dates of Egyptologists.

Five different samples from boats buried outside the pyramid of Sesostris III were carbon-14 dated at 1570 B.C., 1590 B.C., 1660 B.C., 1665 B.C. and 1670 B.C.[18] These boats were likely built many years before Sesostris III began to reign and thus were older than Sesostris III. **Two of these carbon-14 dates fall within the forty-year range of my reconstructed date of 1542 B.C. for Sesostris III's accession to the throne, but are about three centuries later than the dates Egyptologists ascribe to Sesostris III.** Even the oldest date of 1670 B.C. falls 148 to 173 years after the dates of Egyptologists for Sesostris III's death.

A fortress at Semna on the southern border of Egypt contains a text that says the frontier was established **by Sesostris III in his sixteenth year.** Other fortresses in this area are also thought to have been constructed during the twelfth dynasty and likely by Sesostris III, or one of his predecessors.[19] **The average carbon-14 date for samples from these fortresses is about 1550 B.C., another confirmation of my 1543 to 1505 B.C. date for Sesostris III's reign, 250 to 300 years later than Egyptologists' dates for Sesostris III's reign.**

E. Carbon-14 Dates of the Eighteenth and Nineteenth Dynasties

Table 23-B also lists the carbon-14 dates of the eighteenth and nineteenth dynasties along with the carbon-14 dates of the eleventh and twelfth dynasties. The reader can see that the carbon-14 dates of eighteenth- and nineteenth-dynasty Pharaohs also show a **three-century discrepancy with the dates assigned by Egyptologists.** Volume II of *Solving the Exodus Problem* treats in detail the historical records of the eighteenth and nineteenth dynasties and shows how their new Biblical dates, confirmed by the carbon-14 dates, produce numerous synchronisms with Biblical history. Table 23-B is located on the next page.

IV. SCIENTISTS ADMIT THE INADEQUACY OF THE CALIBRATED CARBON-14 DATES

In order to reduce the three-century discrepancy between historical dates and carbon-24 dates, **Egyptologists have attempted to calibrate (change) the carbon-14 dates by tree rings (dendro-chronology) to move them closer to their Sothic dates.** Some Egyptologists imply that the calibrated carbon-14 dates confirm the astronomical dates of conventional Egyptian chronology. However, even the average of the calibrated dates are younger by about 100 years than the calculated Sothic dates. Thus, some Egyptologists argue, **"the dendro-chronological correction [for carbon-14 dates] are inappropriate to Egypt for the period 2200-1250 B.C."** These scholars claim the Irish Oak does not grow in Egypt and therefore should not be used to calibrate carbon-14 dates for Egyptian objects.[20] This problem led Egyptologist, H. McKerell to argue that **"conventional Egyptian chronology might itself be the basis for a calibration curve."**[21]

TABLE 23-B
NINE OF ELEVEN UNCALIBRATED CARBON-14 DATES CONFIRM
STEWART'S DATES FOR DYNASTIES 11 TO 19
Dates of Kings Are Accession years of these Pharaohs

DYNASTY PHARAOH	HAYES' DATES	BAINES' DATES	DIFFERENCE Hayes/Baines Vs. Carbon Dates	CARBON-14 DATES Uncalibrated	DIFFERENCE Stewart Vs. Carbon Dates	STEWART'S BIBLE DATES
DYNASTY 11						
MENTUHOTEP II	2060	1957				
Death	2009	1945	-360/270	1700	+8	1708
DYNASTY 12						
AMENEMHET I	1991	1938	-310/-257	1681	+7	1688
SESOSTRIS I	1971	1918	-291/-238	1680	-13	1667
AMENEMHET II	1928	1876	-178/-126	1750	-125	1625
SESOSTRIS II	1897	1844	-347/-294	1550	+40	1590
SESOSTRIS III	1878	1836	-336/-286	1550	-8	1542
DYNASTY 18						
THUTMOSE III	1504	1479	-353/-328	1151	-5	1146
TUTANKHAMUN	1361	1332	-336/-307	1025	+1	1035
HOREMHEB	1348	1319	-398/-359	960-926	0	979-910
DYNASTY 19						
SETI I	1318	1290	-218/-190	1100	-180	920
RAMSES II	1304	1279	-329/-304	975	-65	910

Source of Carbon-14 Dates: T. Save-Soderbergh and I. U. Olson, "C14 Dating and Egyptian Chronology," *Radiocarbon Variation and Absolute Chronology.* Ed. Ingrid U. Olsson (N.Y.: John Wiley & Sons, Inc. 1983), p. 50

In 1983 the discrepancy between carbon-14 dates and historical dates was so serious that many Egyptologists rejected the evidence of carbon-14 dating as having any relevance to the chronology of Egyptian history.

As the number of . . . dated samples increased, numerical discrepancies have been observed, with radiocarbon dates for Egyptian historic finds considerably lower than the calendar dates established from textual evidence. **This discrepancy has led many Egyptologists either to cast doubt on the C-14 method or to reject its applicability to Egypt.**[22] [my emphasis].

In addition, the calibrated carbon-14 dates are given a range + or - 100 years, giving a total possible range of 200 years.[23] A 200-year range is hardly precise enough for determining the validity of Egypt's historical dates. **Let us now examine why carbon-14 dates should not be calibrated by tree rings.**

V. CRITIQUE OF THE CALIBRATION
OF CARBON-14 DATES BY
TREE RING DATES

In 1994 I submitted my chapter on Carbon-14 dating to Dr. Gerald Aardsma, then living in El Cajon, California, as a part of the faculty of Creation Research Institute.   Dr. Aardsma has his doctorate in Physics and wrote his doctoral dissertation on carbon-14 dating.   Dr. Aardsma informed me that my carbon-14 dates for Egyptian kings were invalid for determining true historical dates because they had not been calibrated by tree rings. He explained that carbon-14 ages of tree rings dated to the periods before 1,000 B.C. gradually become younger than the tree ring ages **(on the basis of one year per ring)** as one proceeds backward in history toward 6,000 B.C. Aardsma said that scientists attribute this apparent discrepancy to some "globally active physical phenomenon which impacted the atmospheric concentration of radiocarbon from time to time."[24]

Dr. Aardsma told me that Dr. Libby, the scientist who invented carbon-14 dating and won the Nobel Prize for his achievement, argued in the beginning that tree rings do occasionally produce more than one ring per year and that on this basis **that carbon-14 dates are more accurate than the tree ring dates.**

However, Dr. Aardsma went on to say that the astronomical dating of the Egyptian dynasties demonstrates that the traditional Sothic dates of Egyptian chronology are correct and that the uncalibrated carbon-14 dates are too young by about three centuries. Since the tree-ring dates are older then the carbon-14 dates, and are closer in age to the Sothic dates of Egyptian history, scientists have concluded **that the tree ring dates are closer to the Egyptian dates and that carbon-14 dating should be calibrated by the tree ring dates.** We thus see how **Egyptologists convinced the scientists that the astronomical (Sothic) dates are correct and that the carbon-14 dates are incorrect and need to be calibrated.**

I asked Dr. Aardsma whether or not trees produced more than one ring per year under certain climatic conditions (such as a drought). Dr. Aardsma admitted that Walter E. Lammerts had experimented with bristlecone pine seedlings and found **"they could be induced to grow an extra ring by subjecting them to a two- or three-week drought late in the growing season followed by a resumption of normal watering."[25]**

Astronomers have discovered that the sun gradually increases the intensity of its output of heat over an **eleven-year cycle**. A *Time* article in its September 14, 1998, issue said that the sun is **"approaching the peak of its 11-year cycle of activity around 2001."[26]**   Interestingly, the year of 1998 produced record high temperatures and drought in many places over the world, including where I live in Texas. More droughts have occurred from 1999 to 2002, when the sun reached the peak of its eleventh year of output of heat. **Since Lammerts claims that trees produce an extra ring in times of drought, it is likely that most trees produce an extra ring at least once in every eleven-year solar cycle.** Going back **thirty-six centuries from A.D. 1950 to 1665 B.C.** (when Joseph became prime minister of Egypt), **327 extra rings were likely added to the tree ring data because of the eleven-year solar cycle.** These 327 extra rings would make it appear that these pieces of wood were **327 years older than their actual age**. Therefore, tree rings are not a safe basis of calibrating carbon-14 dates. **I thus conclude that Libby's original idea was correct when he suggested that carbon-14 dating should calibrate the tree-ring dates rather than vice-versa.**

The uncalibrated carbon-14 dates consistently confirm the proposal that Egypt's dynasties, twelve to nineteen, should be redated about three centuries later than the traditional Sothic dates. Furthermore, these uncalibrated carbon-14 dates confirm the astronomical evidence for the twelfth dynasty, which I will present in the next chapter. The reader has already seen the abundant and remarkable synchronism that occurs between twelfth-dynasty history and Biblical history from Joseph to the Exodus. Table 23-B (p. 346) lists the uncalibrated carbon-14 dates of Dynasties 1 to 12, which confirm my proposed Biblical and astronomical chronology for these Pharaohs.

CONCLUSION

In Chapter Twenty-One we saw the multiple errors and revisions of Egypt's "Astronomically-Dated Calendar." Chapter Twenty-Two reveals incontrovertible evidence that the **Sothic Cycle**, by which Egyptologists ascribe astronomical dates to the twelfth and eighteenth dynasties, **has been invalidated by 360-day calendars, permitting the** twelfth and eighteenth dynasties to be redated **three centuries later** than their conventional dates. .

Tables 23-A and 23-B indicated that **15 of 17 uncalibrated carbon-14 dates confirm a four to six century revision of the earliest Egyptian dynasties and a three century revision of the eleventh through the nineteenth dynasties.**

Thus, the astronomical evidence for the time of Abraham and the uncalibrated carbon-14 dates combine to agree with the Biblical dates from Abraham to the Exodus. **The misdating of Egyptian history has distorted ancient history and even scientific dating. Now that the Sothic method of dating Egyptian history has been broken, the twelfth through the nineteenth dynasties can be redated three centuries later, and scientists can reclaim Libby's uncalibrated radio-carbon-14 dating as accurate.** On the next page Table 23-C totals the discoveries of this chapter and Table 23-D registers the mounting discoveries from Chapters Two to Twenty-Three.

The next chapter reveals **new astronomical data** that confirm a three-century revision of the twelfth through the nineteenth dynasties. This new astronomical data also confirm the uncalibrated carbon-14 data, producing **unique and numerous Biblical synchronisms.**

TABLE 23-C
FIFTEEN DISCOVERIES OF CARBON-14 DATES
THAT REDUCE EGYPTIAN DATES BY
THREE TO FIVE CENTURIES

Discoveries 1. to 5. Five of the six uncalibrated carbon-14 dates prove that Dynasties One to Five should be redated from 424 to 530 years later than Baines' most recent dates. See Table 23-A in Chapter Twenty-Three.

Discoveries 6. to 14. Nine of eleven uncalibrated carbon-14 dates confirm a three century revision that fits Stewart's Bible dates for Pharaohs of Dynasties Eleven to Nineteen. See Table 23-B in Chapter Twenty-Three.

Discovery 15. The calibrated carbon-14 dates are "corrected" by tree rings. However, every eleven years a drought adds an extra tree ring, proving that carbon-14 dates should **NOT** be calibrated by tree rings.

TABLE 23-D
RUNNING TOTAL OF DISCOVERIES

NOTES FOR CHAPTER TWENTY-THREE

1. T. Save-Soderbergh and I.U. Olsson, "C-14 Dating and Egyptian Chronology," *Radiocarbon Variations and Absolute Chronology* (New York: John Wiley & Sons, *New York: John Wiley, 1979),* 49.

2. "Carbon-14 Dating," *New Encyclopaedia Britannica,* 2.850.

3. T. Save-Soderbergh and I.U. Olsson, "C-14 Dating and Egyptian Chronology," *Radiocarbon Variations and Absolute Chronology,* 35-49.

4. T. Save-Soderberg amd I. U. Olsson, 50.

5. Max Mallowan, "The Early Dynastic Period In Mesopotamia," *Cambridge Ancient History, 3rd Ed.,* I.2A.242.

6. "Chronological Tables," *Cambridge Ancient History, 3rd Ed.,* I.2B.994.

7. Mallowan, "The Early Dynastic Period In Mesopotamia," *Cambridge Ancient History, 3rd Ed.,* I.2A.242-43.

8. Mallowan, *Cambridge Ancient History,* I.2A.242. footnote 2.

9. "Chronological Tables," *Cambridge Ancient History,* I.2B.996.

10. Baines, "Egypt," *New Encyclopaedia Britannica,* 1991 Ed., 18.113.

11. T. Save-Soderbergh and I.U. Olsson, "C-14 Dating and Egyptian Chronology," *Radiocarbon Variations and Absolute Chronology,* 45,49,50.

12. Baines, "Egypt," " *New Encyclopaedia Britannica,* 1991 Ed., 18.113.

13. Prof. Emery, excavator, cited by T. Save-Soderbergh and I. U. Olsson, "C14 and Egyptian Chronology," 44.

14. Ian M. E. Shaw, University of Cambridge, "Egyptian Chronology & the Irish Oak Calibration," *Journal of Near Eastern Studies,* Oct., 1985, #4, Vol. 44, 311.

15. T. Save-Soderbergh and I. U. Olsson, "C-14 Dating and Egyptian Chronology," *Radiocarbon Variations and Absolute Chronology* 43, 50.

16. T. Save-Soderbergh and I. U. Olsson, "C-14 Dating and Egyptian Chronology," 44,50.

17. T. Save-Soderbergh and I. U. Olsson, "C-14 Dating and Egyptian Chronology," 50.

18. T. Save-Soderbergh and I. U. Olsson, "C-14 Dating and Egyptian Chronology," 44.

19. Ian M. E. Shaw, "Egyptian Chronology & the Irish Oak Calibration," 44.311.

20. Ian M. E. Shaw, "Egyptian Chronology & the Irish Oak Calibration," 44.296.

21. Ian M. E. Shaw, "Egyptian Chronology & the Irish Oak Calibration," 44.296.

22. Robin M. Derricourt, University of Cambridge, "Radiocarbon Chronology for Egypt and N. Africa," *Journal of Near Eastern Studies,* 42.4., Oct. 1983, 271.

23. Robin M. Derricourt, *Ibid.,* 313-315.

24. Gerald E. Aardsma, "Tree-Ring Dating and Multiple Ring Growth Per Year," *Creation Research Society Quarterly,* Vol. 29, March, 1993, 186.

25. Gerald E. Aardsma, , citing W. E. Lammerts, "Are Bristlecone Pine Trees Really So Old?" *Creation Research Society Quarterly,* Vol. 29, March 1993, 184.

26. Leon Jaroff, "Lost and Found in Orbit," *Time,* Vol. 152, No. 11, Sept. 14, 1988, 66.

CHAPTER TWENTY-FOUR
NEW ASTRONOMICAL DATING CONFIRMS
A THREE-CENTURY REVISION OF
EGYPTIAN DYNASTIES

Chapter Twenty-Two broke the Sothic Cycle, thus annulling the Sothic dates assigned by Egyptologists for the twelfth through the twentieth dynasties. Chapter Twenty-Three presented carbon-14 evidence that confirms that Egypt's eleventh through the nineteenth dynasties should be dated about three centuries later than the Sothic dates of Egyptologists. This Chapter presents **new astronomical evidences** that confirm the carbon-14 dates and that establish correct dates for Sirius' rising in the reigns of Sesostris III, Amenhotep I, Ramses III, and Ptolemy II, confirming my three century revision of the dates of Egyptian dynasties twelve to eighteen.

I. A NEW ASTRONOMICAL CHRONOLOGY
FOR THE TWELFTH DYNASTY

I have identified **Sesostris III** of the twelfth dynasty as the Pharaoh who enslaved Israel and permitted Moses to live in his palace. **1526 B.C.** is the Bible date for Moses' birth. Appendix C shows how I determined that **Sesostris III's accession year began in 1542 B.C.** and that Sirius rose on 8-16 (Egyptian) at Memphis on **July 15, 1535 B.C., in Sesostris III's seventh year.** Appendix C also shows how I astronomically dated Amenemhet III's accession year to 1498 BC.

To determine this astronomical chronology I used Faulkner's Julian date of July 15 for Sirius' rising at 30° at the latitude of Memphis/Heliopolis in the sixteenth century B.C. I also used the twenty Egyptian new moon dates that Krauss used to formulate and test his astronomical chronology. I experimented with different lengths of years of reign for Sesostris III and Amenemhet III and different Julian dates of Sirius' rising at different latitudes before finding the best astronomical matches. Dr. Faulkner calculated **over 100 new-moon Julian dates** to test optional astronomical chronologies.

My best astronomical chronology achieved **75% compatibility with the twenty new moon dates, based on Sirius' rising at 30°on July 15, 1535 B.C. The twelve lunar-month lengths of this chronology also had 75% accuracy.** In contrast, **Krauss' claim of 70% accuracy turned out to be a poor 55% accuracy on new moon dates and a terrible 17% accuracy on the twelve month lengths.** See these comparative results in Table 24-A on the next page.

Peter Huber calculated 30,000 Babylonian lunar dates. He found that the Late Babylonian astronomical texts average **94.5% accuracy** in the dates of **lunar crescents and 81% accuracy in consecutive month lengths.**[1] The Babylonian astronomers were experts on lunar observation. On the other hand Huber found that the accuracy of late **Babylonian administrators, who were not astronomers, averaged 83% accuracy in crescents and 66% accuracy in month lengths.**[2]

Thus, errors occurred about 17% to 33% of the time due to bad weather, hazy skies, or because of poor eye sight or neglect by the observer.

TABLE 24-A

STEWART'S ASTRONOMICAL CHRONOLOGY FOR SESOSTRIS III OF THE TWELFTH DYNASTY
CALCULATED BY DR. DANNY FAULKNER

Based on Sirius' Rising on July 15, 1535 B.C.(Julian) , in , 8-16 (Egyptian), Sesostris III's 7th Yr.

		Year	Pharaoh	Egyptian	B.C.	Sirius' Rising			
		7	SIII	8-16	1535	July 15			
From previous charts			30°	ACCURACY	INVIS.	ASTRO.			VIS.
	7 S III	8-16 1535	7-15						
E	9 S III	7-10 1533	6-08	0	6-8/7	6-8/7 12:30am			6-8/9
F	14 S III	2-17 1528	1-15	0	1-15	1-15			1-16
G	18 S III	10-01 1524	8-26	0	8-26	8-26			8-27
New Data #1									
	7 S III	11-16 1535 +90	10-13						
A	3 A III	11-16 1495 -10	10-03	-1	10-4	10-4			10-5
	7 S III	10-13 1535 +57	9-10						
H	9 A III	10-13 1489 -12	8-29	0	8-29	8-29			8-30
	7 S III	9-08 1535 +22	8-06						
B	29 A III	9-08 1469 -17	7-20	0	7-19/20	7-19			7-20/21

					MO.				
	7 S III	10-26 1535 +70	9-23		LENGTH				
				ACCURACY		ACCURACY			
D1	30 A III	10-26 1468 -17	9-06	0	9-6	9-6			9-7
D2		11-25 1468 +29	10-05	0	10-5	29	0	10-5 3 p.m.	10-6
D3		12-25 1468 +30	11-04	0	11-4/3	30	0	11-3/4 m.n.	11-5
D4	31 AIII	1-19 1468 +29	12-03	0	12-3	29	0	12-3	12-4
D5		2-20 1467 +31	1-03	+1	1-2	30	-1	1-2/3 m.n.	1-4
D6		3-19 1467 +29	2-01	+1	1-31	29	0	1-31 11 p.m	2-1
D7		4-19 1467 +30	3-03	+1	3-2	30	0	3-2 5 p.m.	3-3
D8		5-18 1467 +29	4-01	0	4-1	30	+1	4-1 12 noon	4-2
D9		6-18 1467 +30	5-01	0	5-1	30	0	5-1 12 m.n.	5-2
D10		7-17 1467 +29	5-30	0	5-30	29	0	5-30	5-31
D11		8-17 1467 +30	6-29	0	6-29	30	0	6-29	6-30
D12		9-16 146 7 +29	7-28	0	7-28	29	0	7-28 11 a.m.	7-29
C1	32 A III	2-09 1467 +148	12-23	+1	12-22			12-22	12-23
C2	32 A III	3-08 1466 +29	1-21	0	1-21	30	+1	1-21 7 p.m.	1-22

15/20	9/12
75%	75%
LUNAR DATES	MONTH LENGTH
STEWART/ FAULKNER	STEWART/FAULKNER

SIRIUS' RISING AT 30° ON 7-15, 1535 B.C.

15 correct out of 20	9 correct out of 12
75%	75%

Compared to:

KRAUSS	KRAUSS
11 correct out of 20	2 correct out of 12
55%	17%

Egyptian priests were not expert astronomers, as the Babylonians were. Thus, I would expect the accuracy of Egyptian priests to approach the accuracy of the Babylonian administrators rather than that of Babylonian astronomers.

My proposed twelfth-dynasty chronology of **75% accuracy for both lunar dates and month lengths** thus exceeds the Babylonian administrative average of 66% in month lengths and is only 7% below the 83% average for observing new moon dates. Faulkner's evaluation of Krauss' actual chronology was **55% for lunar dates and 17% for month lengths, far inferior to Krauss' exaggerated claim of 70% for lunar dates and 58% for month lengths.**

With the breaking of the Sothic cycle by 360-day calendars in the eighteenth dynasty, I am free to redate the twelfth through the twentieth dynasties three centuries later than their previous, inaccurate Sothic dates. **In the sixteenth century B.C. the lunar dates have a higher accuracy rating than they do three centuries earlier.** Furthermore, Chapter Twenty-Three has already demonstrated that **carbon-14 dates also confirm that Sesostris III's seventh year was in the sixteenth century B.C.** (7th year = 1535 B.C.), **not the nineteenth century B.C. as claimed by Egyptologists.**

II. NEW ASTRONOMICAL CHRONOLOGY FOR THE EIGHTEENTH DYNASTY

Chapter Twenty-Two showed evidence that the 365-day calendar of the twelfth dynasty likely continued in use from the twelfth through the seventeenth dynasties and on into the eighteenth dynasty until the ninth year of Amenhotep I, the second king of the eighteenth dynasty. Krauss noted that **Sirius rose on 11-9 of Amenhotep I's ninth year and also coincided with the first day of a new moon month on the same day Sirius first appeared.**

However, Krauss and Parker both noted that this calendar (called the Eber's Calendar) only contained **360 days and not the traditional 365 days of Egypt's previous calendars.** Since this 360-day calendar was first introduced by Amenhotep I in his ninth year and preserved in stone for posterity, his action implies that this calendar was **the first instance of Egypt's new 360-day calendar.**

However, the 365-day calendar was still in force in Amenhotep I's ninth year when Sirius' rising was observed on 11-9 of Egypt's calendar, because the 360-day calendar did not come into effect **until the end of Amenhotep I's ninth year of reign, when the 5-day epagomenal feast was eliminated, reducing Egypt's calendar to only 360 days.** Thus, Sirius' rising shifted **eighty-three days** on Egypt's 365-day calendar between 8-16 (Egyptian) in Sesostris III's seventh year and 11-9 (Egyptian) of Amenhotep I's ninth year.

This eighty-three-day shift is proof that Sirius' rising was previously shifting forward on Egypt's 365-day calendar at the rate of 1 day every four years on Egypt's unadjusted and unrevised 365-day calendar from the time of the twelfth dynasty and into the early eighteenth dynasty.

Therefore, **we multiply the eighty-three days by four years and get 332 years that separated the two risings, assuming that Sirius' rising had not shifted on the Julian calendar and assuming that Sirius' rising was observed from the same latitude of 30° in both cases.** If this assumption is true, I can subtract 332 years from 1535 B.C., and get **1203 B.C.** (+ or - 2 years) as the date for Sirius' rising in Amenhotep I's ninth year.

However, Sesostris III's capital was located in **northern Egypt** and the date of Sirius' rising in Sesostris III's seventh year was also registered in documents found in northern Egypt. On the other hand, Amenhotep I's capital was located at **Thebes in southern Egypt,** and the date of Sirius' rising in Amenhotep I's ninth year was inscribed and **preserved on a stone erected in Thebes.**

Therefore, it is more logical that the rising of Sirius was dated on **July 15** (8-16 Egyptian) **at the latitude of 30° (Memphis) in northern Egypt** during Sesostris III's reign, whereas the rising of Sirius in the ninth year of Amenhotep I was dated on **July 11 at the latitude of 25°42' (Thebes) in southern Egypt: See Table 21-D in Chapter Twenty-One to confirm this date of July 11.**

This four-day difference in the dates for Sirius' rising adds sixteen years to the 332 years already calculated as the time that intervened between Sesostris III's seventh year and Amenhotep I's ninth year. Therefore, we must multiply these extra four days by 4 years and get 16 years that we should add to the 332 years above calculated, producing a total of 348 years that separated the two risings of Sirius from two different latitudes (Memphis and Thebes).

Subtracting these 348 years from Sirius' rising on July 15, 1535 B.C., we **get July 11, 1187 B.C. (+ or - 3 years) as the new astronomical and Biblical date for the eighteenth-dynasty Pharaoh, Amenhotep I in his ninth year.**

The Biblical date of 1187 B.C. (+ or - 3 years) **occurs in the middle of the Biblical period of the Judges, 349 years after Sirius' rising at the latitude of Memphis in Sesostris III's seventh year on July 15, 1535 B.C.** The first regnal year of Amenhotep I should have occurred eight years earlier than 1187 B.C. in **1195 B.C.** (+ or - 3 years). The accession year of Ahmose, the first king of the eighteenth dynasty fell in **1220 B.C. (+ or - 3 years)**, right in the middle of the Biblical period of the Judges. See this parallel chronology in **Table 24-B.** Based on this date for the eighteenth dynasty, Volume II of *Solving the Exodus Mystery* will present numerous synchronisms between the Bible and the eighteenth through the twenty-second dynasties.

III. THE COINCIDENCE OF SIRIUS' RISING IN THE NINTH YEAR OF AMENHOTEP I ON A NEW MOON DAY

The Eber's Calendar recorded Sirius' rising on 11-9 (Egyptian) in the ninth year of Amenhotep I and was inscribed in stone at Thebes. The Calendar began each new moon month on the same day that Sirius' rose. Krauss interpreted this unusual phenomenon as indicating that a new moon month began on the same day (11-9 - Egyptian) that Sirius rose. Indeed the odds of a new moon month beginning on the same day that Sirius rose are only **1 in 30 each year.** Krauss actually found that a new moon began when Sirius rose on July 9, 1506, at the latitude of Elephantine (24°), instead of Thebes (25° 42'), where the date was inscribed in stone. The coincidence of a new moon month and Sirius' rising was remarkable. But the accuracy claims of Krauss' astronomical compatibility with twenty new moon dates were exaggerated: 55% in lunar dates and only 17% in lunar month lengths instead of Krauss' claim of 75% compatibility. **Krauss did not register his findings on month links (obviously because the accuracy was only 17%).**

To find astronomical compatibility Krauss also reduced the actual years of reign of Sesostris III to nineteen years, whereas a recent discovery gives a minimum thirty-nine-year reign of Sesostris III. This discovery of Sesostris III's thirty-ninth year completely invalidates Krauss' entire astronomical chronology for the twelfth dynasty.

In my new Biblical date of **1187 B.C.** (+ or- 3 years) **for Amenhotep I's ninth year, Sirius rose on July 11 at the latitude of Thebes from 1201 to 1101 B.C. Did a new moon month begin on July 11 during the years 1184 to 1190 B.C.?** Dr. Faulkner calculated the Julian date of Egypt's new moon month in July of the years 1184 to 1190 B.C. Faulkner was unable to find in these years a new moon month that **began on July 11. However, Dr. Faulkner did find a new moon month that began on July 12 in the year, 1186 B.C.,** within the parameter of the four-year period in which Sirius rose on the same Julian day. **The new moon month that began on July 12 occurred one day after Sirius' rising at Thebes on July 11.**

We must remember that Egypt's new moon month day began when the lunar **crescent was no longer visible just before the dawn of day.** On the other hand, Sirius' rising occurs when it first appears in the sky just before the dawn of day. If a cloud in the sky prevented the Egyptian priest from seeing the last sliver of the moon on July 11, and the sky was clear where Sirius had first appeared, then the priest would have believed **that the new moon month and Sirius' rising had coincided on the same day of July 11, one day before the moon actually disappeared on July 12.** Cloudy weather occasionally prevented priests from accurately recording the correct new moon day, or even the day of the first appearance of Sirius.

Therefore, I set **July 11, 1186 B.C.** as the ninth year of Amenhotep I when **Sirius' rising first appeared in 1186 B.C.** When a cloud hid the moon on July 11, it appeared that a new moon month had begun. **However it actually disappeared on the next day of July 12.** But the priests sincerely but inaccurately thought that the new moon month coincided with Sirius' rising on **July 11.**

This date of July 11, 1186 B.C. for Sirius' rising in Amenhotep I's ninth year and the date of July 15, 1535 B.C. for Sirius' rising in Sesostris III's seventh year can now replace Krauss' former dates of 1838 B.C. for Sesostris III's seventh year and 1506 B.C. for Amenhotep I's ninth year.

This dramatic **three-century astronomical revision** of the dates of the twelfth and eighteenth dynasties are also confirmed by the **carbon-14 dates of these same dynasties, as we saw** in Table 23-B in Chapter Twenty-Three. Thus, carbon-14 dates of the twelfth and eighteenth dynasties and this new astronomical chronology between the twelfth and eighteenth dynasties confirm each other as accurate. Notice the comparison on the next page.

IV. FINAL CONFIRMATION OF STEWART'S ASTRONOMICAL CHRONOLOGY FOR THE EIGHTEENTH DYNASTY

David Rohl's book, *Pharaohs and Kings*, refers to a letter that Abimilku, ruler of Tyre, wrote to Akhenaten soon after his father Amenhotep III had died.[3] Both of these Pharaohs lived in the latter half of the eighteenth dynasty. Abimilku reported to Akhenaten, in the *Amarna Letters* that **"Fire destroyed the palace at Ugarit; (rather), it destroyed half of it and so half of it has disappeared."**[4]

Dr. Rohl pointed out that Nikmaddu II, ruler of Ugarit, was a contemporary of Amenhotep III and Akhenaten (Amenhotep IV) when this burning occurred. Archaeologists found in one of the burnt palace rooms a clay tablet that was blackened from the fire. The tablet reported that **an eclipse of the sun occurred at sunset on the same evening that a new moon appeared.** The eclipse and new moon were dated on the first day of the month of Hiyyaru, which occurs in the Julian months of April and May.

The reverse of the tablet predicted that a disaster would soon follow this astronomical warning.[5] The fact that this tablet was found in a burned room of Nikmaddu II's palace proves **that the eclipse, the new moon and the prediction of a disaster all occurred before Ugarit was burned, likely in the late reign of Amenhotep III or the early reign of Akhenaten, the son of Amenhotep III.**

Dr. Rohl contracted Wayne Mitchell, who used the software program of Dr. Peter Huber to search for an eclipse of the sun that occurred just before sunset at the latitude and longitude of Ugarit. During the entire second millennium (2000 B.C. to 1,000 B.C.), he found only one eclipse of the sun that occurred at Ugarit just before sunset. **The time was 6:09 p.m., May 9, 1012 B.C.**[6] Thus, **no eclipse of the sun** occurred at sunset at Ugarit during the fourteenth century B.C., when most Egyptologists date Amenhotep III and his son Akhenaten. However, **this May 9, 1012 B.C., eclipse confirms the conclusion I have been teaching for the last sixteen years, and that Rohl arrived at more recently, namely that Akhenaten was a contemporary with David the King, who began his reign in 1010 B.C.**

Now let us take Rohl's and Mitchell's astronomical date of **May 9, 1012 B.C.**, as falling in the latter reign of Amenhotep III or the early reign of his son, Amenhotep IV (Akhenaten), and let us combine it with Faulkner's and my astronomical date of **July 11, 1186 B.C.**, for Sirius' rising in Amenhotep I's ninth year. July 11, 1186 B.C. minus May 9, 1012 B.C. equals **173 years and 10 months. Breasted calculated exactly 174 years between Amenhotep I's ninth year and Akhenaten's first year.**[7] Therefore, these two astronomical dates of **July 11, 1186 B.C. and May 9, 1012 B.C.,** calculated by two different astronomical methods and coming from opposite chronological directions, **fit perfectly together in my new astronomical chronology for the eighteenth dynasty. Visualize this new chronology in Table 24-B below.** See all of the discoveries in this chapter in Table 24 C on the next two pages. These new dates for the eighteenth dynasty produce abundant synchronism with Biblical history from the middle of the period of the Judges to the end of Solomon's reign and beyond to the Babylonian Exile. This synchronism will be discussed in depth **in Volume II of the series, *Solving the Exodus Mystery.***

TABLE 24-B
CARBON-14 TESTING OF KRAUSS' AND STEWART'S SOTHIC DATES FOR SESOSTRIS III'S SEVENTH YEAR

KRAUSS/BAINES' SOTHIC DATES	CARBON-14 DATE	STEWART'S SOTHIC DATES
Sesostris III's 7thYear **July 15, 1838 B.C.**	**Sesostris III's Reign** ***C.* 1550/1540 B.C.**	**Sesostris III's 7th Year** **July 15, 1535 B.C.**
Amenhotep I's 9th Year **July 11, 1506 B.C.**	**Amenhotep I's Reign** ***C.* 1190 B.C.**	**July 11, 1186 B.C.**

TABLE 24-C
TWENTY-SIX DISCOVERIES CONFIRM A THREE-CENTURY REVISION OF EGYPTIAN DYNASTIES TWELVE TO NINETEEN

Discoveries 1 to 6. The carbon-14 dates confirm Stewart's Sothic dates for Sesostris III and Amenhotep I and disprove Krauss/Baines's dates for Sesostris III and Amenhotep I. I propose **a three-century revision** of twelfth-dynasty chronology that dates Sirius' rising on **July 15, 1535 B.C.,** in Sesostris III's seventh year, three centuries later than Krauss' date for Sirius' rising. **Carbon-14 dating shown above in Table 24-B rejects Krauss' Sothic dates and confirms my Sothic dates.**

Discoveries 7 to 20. My chronology for Sesostris III has **fifteen out of twenty lunar dates** that are compatible with Sirius' rising, a **75% accuracy,** in contrast to Krauss' eleven out of twenty tested dates, a **55% accuracy** that is insufficient for a true astronomical compatibility.

Discoveries 21 to 29. My chronology for Sesostris III has **nine accurate month lengths out of twelve month lengths listed: 75% accuracy**, in contrast to Krauss' 17% accuracy in month lengths (two out of twelve tested), far insufficient to be a true astronomical chronology.

Discovery 30. In Discovery No. 1 above I dated Sesostris III's seventh year
in 8-16 Egyptian) to July 15, 1535 B.C. Using Faulkner's table of dates for Sirius'
risings, I calculated the distance and date of the 11-9 Egyptian date to **July 11,
1186 B.C. for Sirius' rising in Amenhotep I's ninth year**, three centuries later
than Krauss' date. Amenhotep I is the second king of the eighteenth dynasty.

Discoveries 31 to 32. Toward the end of the eighteenth dynasty an eclipse
of the sun occurred at sunset at Ugarit during the reign of Amenhotep IV
(Akhenaten). From 2,000 to 1,000 B.C. the eclipse of the sun occurring at sunset
at Ugarit only occurred in **1012 B.C.**, proving that Akhenaten should be redated
three centuries later than the dates of Egyptologists.[1] Therefore Akhenaten was a
contemporary of David, which will be discussed in depth in Volume II.

CONCLUSION

We have seen three astronomical dates that form the major chronological
platform for my newly proposed chronology of Egyptian history. **(1) Sirius' rising
on 8-16 (Egyptian), July 15 (Julian), 1535 B.C., in Sesostris III's seventh year
of reign. (2) Sirius' rising on 11-9 (Egyptian), July 11 (Julian), 1186 B.C., in
Amenhotep I's ninth year of reign**, and **(3) An eclipse of the sun at Ugarit just
before sunset at 6:09 p.m., May 9, 1012 B.C., in the early reign of Amenhotep
IV (Akhenaten).** This astronomical date falls in the last two years of King Saul's
reign when the Hapiri (Saul and David) were fighting the Canaanites, who were
under the control of the Egyptian kings of the latter eighteenth dynasty.

These three astronomical dates form three key chronological synchronisms
that redate the twelfth through the eighteenth dynasties three centuries later than
Egypt's Sothic dates. More important these three astronomical dates confirm my
new Biblical dates from Moses' birth in 1526 B.C. to the Exodus in 1446 B.C. to
Solomon's fourth year in 967/66 B.C. (1 Kings 6:1). **Table 24-E finalizes the total
number of discoveries that have accumulated in Chapters Two to Twenty-
Four: 405 points of discovery and synchronism. Appendices A, B and C
contain additional discoveries that are added in Chapter Twenty-Five.**

TABLE 24-D
REVISED CHRONOLOGY OF THE 12ᵀᴴ THROUGH
THE 18ᵀᴴ DYNASTIES TO FIT BIBLE HISTORY
from Moses' Birth to the Middle Period of the Judges
B.C.   * Astronomically Calculated Dates

1535* SESOSTRIS III'S 7ᵀᴴ YEAR   Rising of Sirius 8-16 (Egyptian) July 15 (Julian)

B.C.		
1526	SESOSTRIS III'S 16ᵀᴴ YR.	MOSES' BIRTH
1498	AMENEMHET III'S ACCESSION	
1486	AMENEMHET III'S 12ᵀᴴ YR.	MOSES' FLIGHT TO MIDIAN
1456	AMENEMHET IV'S ACCESSION YR.	
1450	AMENEMHET III'S 48ᵀᴴ YEAR & DEATH	
1446	AMENEMHET IV'S 10ᵀᴴ & LAST YR.	MOSES' RETURN AND EXODUS
		HEBREWS AT SINAI
1443	SOBEK-NEFERU - DEATH	HEBREWS IN WILDERNESS
1442	13ᵀᴴ & 14ᵀᴴ DYNASTIES REIGN	
1406	37ᵀᴴ YEAR OF THE 13ᵀᴴ DYNASTY	HEBREWS DESTROY JERICHO
1396	36ᵗʰ YEAR OF THE 13ᵀᴴ DYNASTY	HEBREWS CONQUER CANAAN & DIVIDE
		INTO TRIBAL AREAS
1367	65ᵀᴴ YEAR OF THE 13ᵀᴴ DYNASTY	OTHNIEL CONQUERS CUSHAN
		RISHATHAIM (SYRIA)
1330	ARRIVAL OF HYKSOS - 16ᵀᴴ DYNASTY	
1320	ARRIVAL OF HYKSOS - 15ᵀᴴ DYNASTY	AMON & AMALEK
1309		EHUD CONQUERS MOAB.
1301	17ᵀᴴ DYNASTY BEGINS AT THEBES	80 YEARS OF PEACE
1218	HYKSOS DRIVEN OUT OF EGYPT	
1219	18ᵀᴴ DYNASTY BEGINS: AHMOSE	
1209		DEBORAH DEFEATS JABIN, KING- HAZOR
1194	AMENHOTEP I	
1186*	**9ᵀᴴ YEAR *Rising of Sirius on 11-9**	
1165	THUTMOSE I	GIDEON DEFEATS MIDIANITES
1153	THUTMOSE II	AND AMALEKITES
1140	THUTMOSE III	
1106		JEPHTHAH DEFEATS THE AMMONITES
1105		SAMUEL'S BIRTH
1086	AMENHOTEP II	
1060	THUTMOSE IV	
1050	AMENHOTEP III reports that:	KING SAUL BEGINS HIS REIGN, DEFEATS
	HAPIRU (HEBREWS) FIGHT	& MAKES PEACE WITH AMORITES
	CANAANITE KINGS	1 SAM. 7:14
	HAPIRU KING IS KILLED	KING SAUL KILLED IN BATTLE
1012*	**AMENHOTEP IV (AKHENATEN)**	***ECLIPSE OF SUN AT UGARIT**
1010	HAPIRU FIGHTS CANAANITE KINGS	KING DAVID BEGINS HIS REIGN;
		DAVID FIGHTS THE PHILISTINES
1003	HAPIRU KING	KING DAVID, KING OF THE
		HEBREWS,
	CAPTURES JERUSALEM	CAPTURES JERUSALEM

*THE THREE DATES ABOVE WITH AN ASTERISK ARE
ASTRONOMICALLY CALCULATED.*

TABLE 24-E
RUNNING TOTAL OF DISCOVERIES

Chapter		Chapter Total	Running Total
2	Conflict Between Biblical and Secular Histories	18	18
4	Discovery of 430 Years from Abraham to the Exodus	16	34
5	Confirmation of Abraham's Historicity	28	62
6	Discovery of the Remains of Sodom and Gomorrah	17	79
7	Joseph As a Slave and Prisoner in Amenemhet I's Reign	21	100
8	Joseph Becomes the Vizier of Sesostris I	23	123
9	Sesostris I Gives Joseph a New Name and a Wife	11	134
10	The Seven Years of Abundance in Sesostris I's Reign	10	144
11	The Seven Years of Famine in Sesostris I's Reign	20	164
12	Israel Enters Egypt during Sesostris I's Reign	14	178
13	Sesostris III Enslaves the Israelites	17	195
14	Sesostris III, The Foster Grandfather of Moses	12	207
15	Sesostris III, Builder of Rameses and Pithom	15	222
16	Zoan (Itjtowy), the Capital of the Twelfth Dynasty	16	238
17	Amenemhet III, the Pharaoh Who Tried to Kill Moses	15	253
18	Amenemhet IV, the Pharaoh of the Exodus	14	267
19	Moses and Ipuwer Report the Ten Plagues	22	289
20	Israel's Exodus and the Drowning of Amenemhet IV and His Army in the Red Sea	26	315
21	Continuous Errors in Egypt's "Astronomically Absolute" Dates..	30	345
22	The Myth of Egypt's Unbroken Sothic Cycles	13	358
23	Carbon-14 Dates Confirm a Three-Century Revision of Egyptian History	15	373
24	New Astronomical Dating Confirms a Three-Century Revision of Egyptian Dynasties	32	405

NOTES FOR CHAPTER TWENTY-FOUR

1. Peter Huber, *Astronomical Dating of Babylon I and Ur III*, pp.*25-28*.
2. Peter Huber *Astronomical Dating of Babylon I and Ur III*, pp.*25-28*.
3. David Rohl, *Pharaohs and Kings*, 237.
4. William Moran (Editor and Translator), *The Amarna Letters*, EA 151, 238.
5. David Rohl, *Pharaohs and Kings*, 237-238.
6. David Rohl, *Pharaohs and Kings*, 239.
7. James Breasted, *History of Egypt*, 599.

CHAPTER TWENTY-FIVE
SUMMATION OF THE DISCOVERIES AND
A PREVIEW OF VOLUME II

I. CRISIS OF FAITH

Most archaeologists and Egyptologists reject the historicity of Abraham, Jacob, Joseph, Moses and Israel's Exodus from Egypt. Dr. Micha Ashkenazi, an archaeologist and tourist guide in Israel, estimated that only 10% of the Israelis believe in their Holy Scriptures and that only 5% of the believers actually observe the laws of their Sacred Scriptures. He pointed out that the walls of Jericho fell 300 years before Joshua arrived in Canaan. A rabbi in Tucson told one of my students, that most rabbis are now agreed with the archaeologists that the Exodus and Conquest, as recorded in the Bible, never occurred. I know personally former Christians who have lost their faith because of the Exodus problem. The subtitle on the recent cover of the March, 2002 issue of *Harper's Magazine* proclaimed the Old Testament Scriptures to be **"The False Testament."**

Chapter Two records eighteen points of conflict between Biblical and Egyptian histories. The more I studied the Exodus Problem the more confused I became. In 1978 I began to pray fervently to my Heavenly Father to open my mind and strengthen my heart and faith to find a solution to this perplexing problem.

II. THE CHRONOLOGICAL KEY TO SOLVING
THE EXODUS MYSTERY

In Chapter Four I determined to calculate a correct Bible chronology from Abraham to the Exodus to the reign of Solomon. I Kings 6:1-4 dates the Exodus 480 years before Solomon's fourth year, astronomically dated to **966 B.C.** Adding the 480 years to 966 B.C. we get **1446 B.C. as the date of the Exodus.**

However dating the period from Abraham to the Exodus was more difficult. Most Bible versions translate Exodus 12:40 to mean that Israel lived in Egypt for 430 years. **However, Paul the Apostle in Galatians 3:15-17 dated the 430 years as beginning with God's promise and command to Abraham to leave Ur and go to Canaan.** Accepting Paul's interpretation, I date Abraham's departure from Ur in **1876 B.C., 430 years before the Exodus date of 1446 B.C. Without this chronology I could never have solved the Exodus Mystery.** Chapter Fourteen records **sixteen discoveries** that prove the 430 years extended from Abraham to the Exodus.

III. VERIFYING THE HISTORICITY OF ABRAHAM

Chapter Five cites Genesis 14 which records Abraham's encounter with four kings of the East, including the kings of Elam, Babylon and Mari. These named kings listed in the Bible could never have been identified when following the dates of earlier volumes of the *Cambridge Ancient History*. However, Dr. Peter Huber, formerly of Harvard University, examined the astronomical data for Babylon and learned that the former astronomical conclusion was **in error by fifty-six years. Huber redated** Hamurabi, king of Babylon **fifty-six years earlier than the previous dates in the** *Cambridge Ancient History*. Huber's new dates enabled me to find the names of three of the four Biblical kings in the newly dated histories of Babylon, Elam and Mari, thus proving the historicity and Biblical chronology of Abraham. I am deeply indebted to Dr. Huber, without whom I could never have solved the Exodus Mystery. Chapter Five records **28 synchronisms for the Period of Abraham.**

Chapter Six provides **seventeen additional discoveries** for Abraham's eye-witness account of the destruction of Sodom and Gomorrah and other cities of the plain. In 1991 Dot and I accompanied Ron Wyatt along with many others to see astounding evidences that the city of Gomorrah, about a mile north of Mount Massada, was destroyed by burning sulphur that fell from the sky. We observed and photographed shapes of houses, a pyramid, the walls of the city, a sphinx and many thousands of powdered sulphur balls lying all over the site along with other evidences that confirm the historicity of the time of Abraham.

IV. DISCOVERY OF THE TRUE PHARAOHS OF JOSEPH, MOSES AND THE EXODUS.

A. Chapters Seven to Twelve

Joseph arrived in Egypt as a slave in **1678 B.C.** in the ninth year of Amenemhet I, the founder of the twelfth dynasty. Israel arrived in Egypt **twenty-two years later in 1656 B.C.** Thus Joseph and Israel together lived in Egypt for **232 years, from 1678 B.C. to 1446 B.C. However, Israel lived in Egypt for only 210 years from 1656 to 1446 B.C. Appendix C demonstrates how precisely the twelfth dynasty fits the total of 232 Biblical years.**

Joseph's slave owner was Potiphar, the captain of the body guard of Amenemhet I. Potiphar's wife falsely accused Joseph of raping her. Potiphar cast Joseph into prison where he later met the baker and butler of Amenemhet I. Twelfth-Dynasty documents report that Amenemhet I's body guard, likely headed by Potiphar, attempted to kill Amenemhet I. However, Sesostris I, the son of Amenemhet I, arrived at the palace from a military expedition. He killed the usurpers, who were likely the armed guards headed by Captain Potiphar. Sesostris I revived his father and took over the throne because his father was seriously injured and was incapable of resuming his duties.

While in prison Joseph interpreted the dreams of the baker and butler. Both dreams were fulfilled when the baker was hanged and the butler was released, implying that the baker had participated in the attempted assassination of Amenemhet I, whereas the butler was found to be innocent.

Two years later Sesostris I had a dream that could not be interpreted by anyone. The butler remembered Joseph and told Sesostris I about Joseph's talents in interpreting dreams. Joseph successfully interpreted the dream and was appointed the Vizier of Sesostris I, beginning the seven years of abundance, which would be followed by seven years of famine. Jacob and his family arrived in Egypt in **1656 B.C. at the end of the second year of famine**. Twelfth-dynasty documents gave special permission to permit Canaanite shepherds to live and graze their sheep in the land of Goshen. Twelfth-dynasty documents and pictorial scenes record the growing numbers of Canaanites (Israelites) in all areas of Egyptian society during the reigns of Sesostris I, Amenemhet II and Sesostris II.

The Pharaohs of Joseph have been discovered. These early Pharaohs of the Twelfth Dynasty should be honored for their benevolence toward Joseph and his Israelite relatives.

B. Chapters Thirteen to Sixteen

Sesostris III changed everything when he became Pharaoh. He enslaved the Israelites and forced them to construct the cities of Rameses and Pithom, as documented in Egyptian records and archaeological excavation. Sesostris III threw his enemies into the Nile River as the Pharaoh of the Oppression did to the Israelite children. Sesostris III cursed the sons of Anak, the giants who lived in Canaan when the Israelites left Egypt and entered Canaan, proving that Sesostris III reigned parallel to the time of Moses and the Israelites. Sesostris III cursed Job, proving that the two were contemporaries. The literary style of Job is duplicated by twelfth-dynasty authors.

While the Israelite infants were being thrown into the Nile River, Moses' mother carried him to a location on a Nile tributary where the daughter of Pharaoh daily washed. Sesostris III's daughter took Moses from the water and reared him as the grandson of Sesostris III. Moses grew and became a famous general in the army of Sesostris III. Moses conquered the southern region of Cush (Ethiopia) and married a Cushite princess. **Sixty synchronisms appear in Chapters Thirteen to Sixteen.**

C. Chapters Seventeen to Twenty

When Sesostris III was approaching death, he appointed Amenemhet III to take his place on the throne. Moses went out to see his Hebrew brothers and saw a slave master cruelly beating a fellow Jew. In the struggle Moses killed the slave master. When Anememhet III learned about Moses' treachery, he sought to kill him. Moses fled to the land of Midian and remained there for forty years until Amenemhet III and his officials had died. When Moses returned to Egypt, Amenemhet III's son, Amenemhet IV, was reigning.

Chapter Eighteen presents **fourteen synchronisms that identify Amenemhet IV as the infamous Pharaoh of the Exodus**. Among these synchronisms are Amenemhet IV's short sole reign, his continual construction by slave labor (the Israelites), his sudden disappearance (death in the Red Sea) and his missing pyramid and tomb. In addition, Amenemhet IV's wife ascended to the throne instead of her son, who died in the plague of the death of the first-born.

Chapter Nineteen registers twenty-two synchronisms of Ipuwer's eye-witness report of **eight of the ten plagues and the devastating consequences on the land, the rivers, the animals, the people, and Pharaoh and his officials.**

Chapter Twenty follows *Ipuwer's Paprus,* recording **twenty-six points of synchronism** that describe the Exodus of the Israelites and the destruction of Amenemhet IV and his army by **"pouring water."** With Pharaoh Amenemhet IV and his army buried under the Red Sea, the peasants and slaves in Egypt rebelled, ransacked the palace and the treasury and took over the home of the nobles. Amenemhet IV's wife fled to Thebes in southern Egypt. Anarchy ruled in northern Egypt, bringing about the fall of the twelfth dynasty, the greatest and most powerful of the dynasties that had existed up to that time.

The Pharaohs who enslaved the Israelites and cruelly oppressed them have been clearly identified. Justice has prevailed! The Pharaoh of the Exodus has been discovered! His name will go down in infamy.

V. SCIENTIFIC PROOF FOR REVISING THE DATES OF THE TWELFTH DYNASTY BY THREE CENTURIES TO FIT BIBLICAL DATES

Chapter Twenty-One records the continual errors and contradictory revisions of "astronomically absolute" dates, by successive Egyptologists, **proving that they never were absolute.** Chapter Twenty-Two **breaks the Sothic Cycle, destroying the entire system of Sothic dating, permitting all of Egypt's Dynasties One to Twenty to be redated three centuries later than their current dates**. This three-century revision creates abundant synchronisms with Israelite history from Joseph to the Exodus to the Conquest to the reign of Solomon and beyond into the Divided Kingdom of Judah and Israel.

Chapter Twenty-Three registers fifteen synchronisms of carbon-14 dating that confirm my Biblical dates for the twelfth and eighteenth dynasties. Chapter Twenty-Four registers thirty-two astronomical synchronisms that together form **forty-seven scientific synchronisms** that confirm my Biblical dates for Egyptian dynasties twelve to nineteen. **Appendix A, B and C contribute an additional thirty-one synchronisms for a grand total of 436 unique discoveries over 430 years of Bible history.**

Thus, we have traveled **430 historical years** of Bible history from Abraham's Promise in 1876 B.C. to the Exodus in 1446 B.C. We have found a remarkable **436 historical, archaeological and scientific discoveries and synchronisms that confirm this 430-year period of Biblical history.** These **436 evidences** are scattered at the end of each Chapter from Two to Twenty-Four. See these synchronisms summed together in Table 25-A below.

These 436 historical and scientific evidences are too abundant and too unique to explain away as chance coincidence. The only rational conclusion is

true historical synchronism, based on a **three-century revision of Egyptian dynasties twelve to twenty.** **God has truly answered my prayers in helping me to find all of this information that confirms the Bible from Abraham to the Exodus.** The reader may question a number of my alleged synchronisms or differ with the interpretation of certain data I have recorded. However, if only half of these 436 discoveries/synchronisms were correct, the conclusions would still be confirmed. These 436 discoveries/synchronisms appear in Table 25-A below.

TABLE 25-A
FOUR HUNDRED THIRTY-SIX DISCOVERY/SYNCHRONISMS
CANNOT BE COINCIDENTAL

Chapter		Chapter Total	Running Total
2	Conflict Between Biblical and Secular Histories	18	18
4	Discovery of 430 Years from Abraham to the Exodus	16	34
5	Confirmation of Abraham's Historicity	28	62
6	Discovery of the Remains of Sodom and Gomorrah	17	79
7	Joseph As a Slave and Prisoner in Amenemhet I's Reign	21	100
8	Joseph Becomes the Vizier of Sesostris I	23	123
9	Sesostris I Gives Joseph a New Name and a Wife	11	134
10	The Seven Years of Abundance in Sesostris I's Reign	10	144
11	The Seven Years of Famine in Sesostris I's Reign	20	164
12	Israel Enters Egypt during Sesostris I's Reign	14	178
13	Sesostris III Enslaves the Israelites	17	195
14	Sesostris III, The Foster Grandfather of Moses	12	207
15	Sesostris III, Builder of Rameses and Pithom	15	222
16	Zoan (Itjtowy), the Capital of the Twelfth Dynasty	16	238
17	Amenemhet III, the Pharaoh Who Tried to Kill Moses	15	253
18	Amenemhet IV, the Pharaoh of the Exodus	14	267
19	Moses and Ipuwer Report the Ten Plagues	22	289
20	Israel's Exodus and the Drowning of Amenemhet IV and His Army in the Red Sea	26	315
21	Continuous Errors in Egypt's "Astronomically Absolute" Dates	30	345
22	The Myth of Egypt's Unbroken Sothic Cycles	13	358
23	Carbon-14 Dates Confirm a Three-Century Revision of Egyptian History	15	373
24	New Astronomical Dating Confirms a Three-Century Revision of Egyptian Dynasties	32	405
	Appendix A - Velikovsky's and Courville's Misconstruction of Egyptian History	11	416
	Appendix B - Evaluation of Different Pharaohs of Joseph	06	422
	Appendix C - Reconciling Twelfth-Dynasty and Biblical Chronologies	14	436

VI. PREVIEW OF VOLUME II OF *SOLVING THE EXODUS MYSTERY*

Volume Two demonstrates how a three-century revision of Egyptian history continues to produce historical and archaeological synchronism with Bible history from the Exodus to the Conquest of Canaan to the Kingdoms of Saul, David and Solomon and on through the Divided Kingdom to the Assyrian Conquest of Northern Israel and eventually the Exile of Judah by the Babylonians and their release from Exile by Cyrus the Persian. Below are some of the chapter titles in Volume Two.

A. Discovery of the Site of the Red Sea Crossing

This site fits perfectly Josephus' directions to the Red Sea Crossing. An underwater video camera records the remnants of chariot wheels, skeletons of men and horses at the bottom of the Gulf of Aqaba. You can order this video from biblemart.com or call 1-800-221-9065.

B. Discovery of the True Site of Mount Sinai

This same video thoroughly covers the true site of Mount Sinai. The same video that pictures Sodom and Gomorrah and the Red Sea Crossing also visualizes in detail the actual location of Mount Sinai in Arabia that fits to a "T" the Biblical description of Mount Sinai. This video can be purchased separately, or along with Volume I or II of *Solving the Exodus Mystery.* Volume II will be published in 2003.

C. Discovery of Archaeological Sites Where Israel Camped Before Entering Canaan Permanently

Volume II will also reveal Biblical, historical, archaeological and visual evidences that identify the precise route Israel took from the true site of Mount Sinai to Kadesh Barnea where they stayed for long periods of time on two different occasions during their forty-year wilderness wanderings. Evidences in our next book will show that traditional Kadesh Barnea that appears on our maps contradicts both Biblical descriptions of its location and the archaeological evidence of its excavation. Volume II will identify a new location that fits perfectly the Biblical description of Kadesh Barnea, including the rock which Moses struck and from which water flowed. Dot and I visited this site and were amazed. Other places where the Israelites camped will be disclosed as to their true location.

D. Discovery of Jericho's Fall in the Bible Date of 1406 B.C.

Volume II traces the forty years of the wilderness wanderings and the Conquest of Jericho and Canaan. **The archaeological excavation of Jericho depends on the Egyptian dates.** When Egypt's dates are revised by three centuries, the fall of Jericho's walls fits precisely the Biblical dates and the carbon-

14 dates. **The three-century revision of the Egyptian dates automatically demands a three-century revision of the archaeological ages,** creating multiple synchronisms between Biblical and Egyptian histories during the period of the Judges and early Kings of Israel. See Table 25-B below.

E. Dating Dynasties Thirteen to Eighteen by Biblical Chronology

Volume II will show that Dynasties Thirteen to Seventeen ran parallel to each other for the first half of the period of the Judges. The Eighteenth Dynasty runs parallel with the last half of the period of Judges and the period of Kings Saul, David and the early reign of Solomon. Unique synchronisms occur between Egyptian history and Bible history when the Egyptian dynasties are redated three centuries later. **Carbon-14 dates and an eclipse of the sun confirm the Biblical dates assigned to these dynasties.**

TABLE 25-B
DATES OF THE ARCHAEOLOGICAL AGES
MAZAR'S EGYPTIAN DATES VERSUS BIBLE DATES
Amihai Mazar, *Archaeology of the Bible*, p. 30

	MAZAR'S B.C. DATES	EGYPTIAN DYNASTIES	BIBLICAL B.C. DATES
MIDDLE BRONZE II A	2000 - 1750	11 and 12	1695 - 1443
MIDDLE BRONZE II B/C	1750 - 1550	13 to 17	1443 - 1217
LATE BRONZE I	1550 - 1400	18	1217 - 1150
LATE BRONZE II A/B	1400 - 1200	18/19	1150 - 814
IRON I A	1200 - 1150	20	814 - 695
IRON I B	1150 - 1000	21	868 - 713
IRON II A	1000 - 925	22, 25	800 - 656
IRON II B	925 - 720	22, 23, 24, 26	672 - 570
IRON II C	720 - 586	26	720 - 525

F. Recouping the 300 Years Lost from Revising Dynasties 12 to 20

Volume II of *The Exodus Mystery* will prove that **parallel dynasties** will recoup the 300 years that were lost by redating dynasties twelve to twenty 300 years later than their conventional dates. This new parallel arrangement of Egypt's dynasties twenty-one to twenty-six results in unique synchronism with Biblical events. Dynasties 21 to 26 run parallel to the latter 19th & 20th dynasties and to each other to make up for the 300 years lost in moving Dynasties 12 to 20 later by three centuries.

G. New Discoveries from Sinai to the Conquest of Canaan

The three-century revision of Egyptian history reduces the dates of the archaeological ages by three centuries, **producing extraordinary archaeological synchronism with Biblical history.** The new Biblical dates for the twelfth dynasty thrust the Middle Bronze IIB/C Age into the Biblical period of Israel's Exodus from Egypt, their one-year stay at Mount Sinai, their forty-year wandering in the wilderness, and their conquest of Jericho and the rest of Canaan.

Kathleen Kenyon believed that Jericho's walls fell several hundred years before Joshua arrived. However, her decision was based on the dating of the Middle Bronze II Age by links to the erroneous Sothic dates of the Egyptian dynasties. **By revising the Egyptian Dynasties three centuries later, the Middle Bronze II Age fits perfectly with Kathleen Kenyon's description of Jericho's fall and also fits the carbon-14 dates that confirm the Biblical date of 1406 B.C. for the fall of Jericho.**

H. New Synchronisms Between Bible
History and Dynasties 13 to 18

My new chronology places Dynasties 13 to 17 parallel to the first half of the period of the Biblical Judges. Biblical and historical evidences identify the Hyksos dynasties (15 & 16) as Amalekites from Arabia, explaining the strong Amalekite (Hyksos) presence in Canaan during the first half of the Biblical period of the Judges. Ahmose, the first eighteenth-dynasty Pharaoh, expelled the Hyksos, driving them back into Canaan and Arabia. Velikovsky was the first to identify the Hyksos as the Amalekites. This identification of Velikovsky was one of the few that turned out to be correct in his books on Egyptian history and the Bible. Volume Two critiques Velikovsky's misconstruction of Egyptian history for the period leading up to Israel's Conquest of Canaan and the two periods of the Judges and Kings.

After conquering the Hyksos dynasties in N. Egypt, the Eighteenth Dynasty established itself as the sole rule of Egypt. My new chronology for Dynasty 18 begins in the middle of the period of the Judges, explaining the repeated references of eighteenth-dynasty Pharaohs to the Hapiru (Habiru) = Hebrews in Canaan.

The last half of the eighteenth dynasty parallels the latter period of the Judges and the Hebrew monarchies of Saul, David and Solomon. The famous *Amarna Letters* were written by Canaanite kings who were subject to the eighteenth-dynasty Pharaohs, Amenhotep III and Amenhotep IV (Akhenaten). I analyzed these letters fifteen years ago and immediately saw how they fit the reigns of Saul, David and Solomon. These Canaanite kings continually wrote Egypt, requesting military aid to fight against the growing menace of the Hebrews who were taking over Canaanite cities. These were the same Hebrews who lived in Canaan and are mentioned by kings of the early eighteenth dynasty about 100 years before the *Amarna Letters* were written. Carbon-14 dates confirm the three-century revision of eighteenth dynasty Pharaohs .

In Volume II I will also point out references from the *Amarna Letters* that refer to Saul's battles with the Philistines and Saul's ultimate death at their hands. These letters also chronicle David's battles with the Canaanites and his eventual victory over all of Canaan and the establishment of his new capital in Jerusalem.

I. *Pharaohs & Kings* by David Rohl

In Volume Two I glean invaluable material from David Rohl's book, *Pharaohs and Kings,* that also identifies the Amarna Letters as contemporary with Saul and David. **Rohl found an eclipse of the sun at Ugarit during the early reign of Akhenaten or in the last reign of his father, Amenhotep III, that is dated to May 9, 1012 B.C.**[1] This eclipse confirms that these eighteenth-dynasty kings should be dated parallel to the Hebrew monarchy. I have been dating Akhenaten to the reign of King David for the last fifteen years without knowledge of the eclipse of the sun at Ugarit. Now Rohl has provided the astronomical confirmation for my previous redating of the Egyptian dynasties Thirteen to Twenty by historical synchronism.

Readers of my next book will be impressed with the **unique evidence that the last king of the eighteenth dynasty gave his daughter in marriage to Solomon and was the true Pharaoh Shishak who invaded Jerusalem after Solomon died (1 Kings 14:25-26).** Almost all scholars identify Sheshonk I of the twenty-second dynasty, as Pharaoh Shishak of the Bible. Volume II reveals who was the real Pharaoh Shishak that invaded Jerusalem after Solomon's death.

David Rohl, in his excellent book, *Pharaohs and Kings,* carefully analyzed the Egyptian inscriptions of Sheshonk I's military incursion into Palestine and found invaluable information that proves Sheshonk I cannot be Pharaoh Shishak of the Bible.[2] Rohl has identified Ramses II as Pharaoh Shishak. However, I have identified a better candidate than Ramses II. His name and activities fit perfectly the Biblical description of Pharaoh Shishak. Volume II will reveal his identity and the evidence supporting it.

Solomon's reign paralleled the latter eighteenth dynasty, thrusting Solomon into the Late Bronze II Age, not in the impoverished Iron II Age, where archaeologists presently date Solomon. My next book will present abundant archaeological evidences that confirm the glory, power and wealth of Solomon when he is dated to the proper Pharaoh and the proper archaeological age.

Scholars argue that the twelfth through the eighteenth dynasties cannot be redated three centuries later without encountering serious synchronistic problems with other nations. In Volume II I will present significant evidences that dissolve these synchronistic problems, proving that Kings of the same name lived 300 years apart. Each of these problems will be treated in depth.

J. Nineteenth-Dynasty Kings in the Time of Israel's Divided Kingdom

My new chronology pushes the nineteenth-dynasty Pharaohs, Ramses I, Seti I and Ramses II, parallel to the divided kingdom of northern Israel under Jeroboam I, and of Judah under Rehoboam, and their successors. Volume II finds remarkable synchronism between Seti I and a named King of northern Israel. We will also see significant synchronism between Ramses II and other Biblical characters. We will see Ramses II's encounter with Shalmaneser III, the famous Assyrian king, who is astronomically dated from 858 to 824 B.C., revealing the true dates of Ramses II's reign. Hittite kings known to be contemporary with Ramses II will also be found contemporaneous with Shalmaneser III. When Egyptian history is redated 300 years later, so also will Hittite history be redated three centuries later. As a result, a three-century dark age in Hittite history will disappear and new synchronisms will occur between the Bible and Hittite, Assyrian and Egyptian histories.

K. Centuries of Darkness Turned into Light
Peter James and his four colleagues, all English archaeologists, wrote *Centuries of Darkness*, based on the fact that twenty-two nations linked to the Egyptian dynasties have 250-year dark periods in which no history is recorded. James has provided significant evidence of anomalies that appear in art, archaeology and history that contradict each other by 250 years in their dating. James is convinced that Egyptian chronology is at the center of this chronological problem and that Egyptian history should be redated later by about 250 years to reconcile these problems.

The evidence that James has uncovered will contribute significantly to my proposed reconstruction of Egyptian history in my next volume. However, David Rohl is closer to my chronology than Peter James. Rohl's book, *Pharaohs and Kings*, has furnished abundant evidence that generally supports both James' chronology and my own, even though our chronologies are not the same. Volume II will explain how and why I differ from the chronologies of James and Rohl.

However, I will use many ideas from both James and Rohl, plus many other evidences I have found, to support my reconstruction of Egyptian history. Their contributions to my next book are significant and I am deeply indebted to them for their independent research.

L. More Parallel Dynasties
Modern Egyptologists presently date dynasties twenty-two to twenty-six parallel to each other in different B.C. years. This period is called the Third Intermediate Period (T.I.P.) when multiple dynasties ruled over Egypt. Egyptologists date dynasty twenty-six as the sole dynasty until the conquest of Egypt by Cambyses, the Persian in 525 B.C.

By moving dynasties **twelve to twenty** about three centuries later than their conventional dates, the 300 years lost are compensated by additional parallel reigns for dynasties twenty to twenty-six that Egyptologists have not observed. With help from Peter James and David Rohl, plus my own research, I have discovered how to arrange dynasties twenty through twenty-six in a harmonious manner with the result that unique historical synchronisms occur between these Egyptian dynasties and Biblical history and other nations' histories. My arrangement differs considerably from that of James and Rohl. However, I could not have succeeded in arranging these parallel dynasties without the significant evidences that James and Rohl have presented in their books.

Manetho, the Egyptian priest of the Ptolemaic period of Egypt, thought that dynasties one to twenty-six all reigned in succession to one another and thus extended back in history for many millennia. Petrie, believing that dynasties thirteen to seventeen reigned consecutively, dated the first dynasty in 5546 B.C. and dynasty twelve in 3579 B.C. Breasted, Hayes, and Baines found progressively new evidence of parallel dynasties, first during dynasties thirteen to seventeen, and later in dynasties one to eleven. Thus, rival dynasties enabled Baines to redate the first dynasty in 2925 B.C. and the twelfth dynasty in 1938 B.C., a reduction of 2,621 years from Petrie's 5546 B.C. date for the first dynasty and a reduction of 1,641 years from Petrie's date of 3579 B.C. for the twelfth dynasty. If Egyptologists were able to reduce twelfth-dynasty dates by 1,641 years by finding previously unknown parallel dynasties, it is certainly possible for me to reduce by three centuries the dates of the twelfth through the twenty-sixth dynasties by also finding additional rival dynasties during the Third Intermediate Period (T.I.P.).

M. Synchronism Between Bible History and Assyrian, Babylonian and Persian Histories

Many are not aware of the many points of historical synchronism that occur between Biblical, Assyrian, Babylonian and Persian histories. These nations' histories are astronomically dated by eclipses of the sun and do not need to be revised a single year. These astronomically dated nations refer to numerous Biblical events and Biblical persons in specific B.C. years, transferring these astronomically-fixed years to specific years of Hebrew Kings. The details of this synchronism will be presented in Volume II.

The numerous points of historical and archaeological synchronism between Israelite and Assyrian, Babylonian and Persian histories stand in stark contrast to the lack of synchronism between Israel and Egyptian history, according to modern Egyptologists. However, when Egyptian history is revised three centuries later, it produces more abundant synchronism with Bible history than it produces with Assyrian, Babylonian and Persian histories. The reason for this abundant synchronism between Egyptian and Biblical chronology is that Israel lived in Egypt for 210 years, whereas Israel and Judah had only occasional encounters with Egypt, Assyria, Persia, plus seventy years of bondage in Babylon.

N. Vindication of Bible History as Divine Truth

Christians and Jews who abandoned their faith in the Bible because of the conflict with Egyptian history can return to the Bible with full confidence that it is not only true history, but the wisdom and will of God for the lives of all men. With a renewed trust in the Old Testament, hopefully, Jews, Muslims, wavering Christians and unbelievers will seriously look at Jesus Christ as the Messiah predicted in the Old Testament and fulfilled in the New Testament.

My search for harmony between Egyptian history and Biblical history has lasted twenty-four years. I must give credit to the God of Abraham, Isaac and Jacob and to God's Son, Jesus Christ, for guiding me, strengthening me, and helping me to make the discoveries I have shared in this book. I could not have made it this far without divine assistance. Attribute all of the errors in this book to me, for I am a fallible servant of God and Christ. Attribute whatever is correct to the Father and Son. Hopefully, you will see yet other treasures of wisdom, knowledge and equally exciting discoveries in Volume II, soon to come. May God bless you, dear reader, in your study as you seek the truth of history, which leads to the truth of spiritual and moral life today and the truth of eternal life in the unknown future.

CONCLUSION

Four hundred thirty-six Biblical, archaeological, historical and chronological evidences cry out in behalf of the historicity of the biblical record of 430 years from Abraham to Joseph to Moses to the Exodus. True historical synchronism is the only reasonable conclusion.

However, the Egyptian dates for the twelfth dynasty are three centuries earlier than the Biblical dates. Either Biblical history must be redated three centuries earlier to coincide with Egyptian history or Egyptian dates must be reduced by three centuries to coincide with Biblical dating.

Interestingly, Dr. Peter Huber redated Babylon's astronomical chronology about fifty-six years earlier,[3] synchronizing the new Biblical chronology of Abraham with Babylonian history of Hammurabi and his father, Sin-Muballit. The fact that a revision of Babylonian history fits the Biblical dates for the time of Abraham suggests that a chronological revision of the dates of Egypt's twelfth dynasty will also match the Biblical dates from Joseph to the Exodus.

Egyptologists claim that Egypt's history is astronomically fixed and cannot be revised by three centuries. In the last four chapters (Twenty-One to Twenty-Four) we saw that Egypt's "astronomically absolute" dates are **absolutely incorrect** and that new carbon-14 dates and new astronomical dates prove that Egypt's Sothic dates should be revised by three centuries later, which fit and confirm the Bible dates from 1876 B.C. to 1446 B.C. The evidence of true astronomical dating and accurate carbon-14 dating will provide numerous, interesting, exciting and significant synchronisms between Bible history and other nations' histories in Volume II of the series, *Solving the Exodus Mystery.*

Truly, Bible history from Abraham to Joseph to Moses to the Exodus is vindicated and the God of Israel has been glorified! When Volume II has been finished, we will be able to exclaim: "History's Most Famous Unsolved Mystery Has Been Solved!"

NOTES FOR CHAPTER TWENTY-FIVE

1. David Rohl, *Pharaohs And Kings,* 239.
2. David Rohl, *Pharaohs And Kings,* 120-128.
3. Asger Aaboe, quoting Peter Huber, "Babylonian Mathematics, Astrology, and Astronomy," *Cambridge Ancient History,* III. Part 2, 279-280.

APPENDIX A
VELIKOVSKY'S AND COURVILLE'S MISCONSTRUCTION OF EGYPTIAN HISTORY

INTRODUCTION

In Chapters One to Three we saw how the history and archaeology of both the eighteenth and nineteenth dynasties contradict the Biblical account of the Exodus and Conquest. These discrepancies have led many scholars to reject the historical reliability of the Biblical account. However, scholars have not considered looking for the Exodus and Conquest in historical periods that precede the eighteenth and nineteenth dynasties.

In 1952 Immanuel Velikovsky theorized that the Exodus problem was not due to erroneously recorded Biblical history, but to the misdating of Egyptian history. He proposed that Egyptian history would coincide with the Bible, if the dates of Egyptian history were revised by hundreds of years on the B.C. time scale.[1]

Velikovsky's reconstruction of Egyptian history met with strong resistance from scholars, who believe that Egyptian history is astronomically dated and therefore chronologically immovable. However, Velikovsky's *Ages in Chaos* highly impressed Dr. Robert H. Pfeiffer, chairman of the Department of Semitic Languages and History at Harvard University.

> Dr. Velikovsky discloses immense erudition and extraordinary ingenuity. He writes well and documents all his statements with the original sources. . . . His conclusions are amazing, unheard of, revolutionary, sensational . . . If Dr. Velikovsky is right, this volume is the greatest contribution to the investigation of ancient times ever written.[2]

In 1978 I began an intensive study of Velikovsky's books. For several years I thought Velikovsky had indeed solved the Exodus Mystery. In 1982 I learned about Dr. Donovan Courville's two-volume book, *The Exodus Problem and Its Ramifications*. Courville accepted most of Velikovsky's ideas, but revised and amplified parts of Velikovsky's reconstruction of Egyptian history.[3]

I soon recognized that my ignorance of Egyptian history prevented me from testing the ideas of Velikovsky and Courville. I began to research translations of the original Egyptian documents from which Egyptian history is derived. Some of the proposals of Velikovsky and Courville proved to be accurate. However, my studies of the ancient Egyptian literature enabled me to see many flaws in their reconstruction of Egyptian history.

A school of disciples followed the original ideas of Velikovsky for many years. They advertised their meetings in the *Biblical Archaeological Review*.[4] The excellent conservative Bible scholar Norman Geisler also proposed the views of

Velikovsky and Courville as a possible reconciliation of the Exodus problem.[5]

I feel deeply indebted to Velikovsky and Courville for giving me invaluable ideas that led me ultimately to what I believe to be the true solution of the Exodus Mystery. However, the weaknesses of Velikovsky and Courville were so serious that I was compelled **to reject totally** their identifications of the Pharaoh of the Exodus, as well as Velikovsky's identifications of Hatshepsut as the Queen of Sheba who visited Solomon, and Thutmose III as Pharaoh Shishak who invaded Jerusalem after Solomon died.

I. DISCOVERY OF EXODUS EVENTS
IN THE IPUWER PAPYRUS

Velikovsky was the first to call attention to the *Ipuwer Papyrus*, an ancient Egyptian document dated to the middle kingdom (eleventh through thirteenth dynasties) that pictures the nation of Egypt devastated by what appears to be the ten plagues.[6] **I predict that Velikovsky's discovery of Exodus events in *Ipuwer's Papyrus* will one day prove to be one of the most significant contributions made toward the historical confirmation of the Biblical record of the ten plagues.** Chapters Nineteen and Twenty examine the *Ipuwer Papyrus* in great depth, confirming the Biblical events of eight of the ten plagues, the departure of the Israelite slaves from Egypt and the destruction of Pharaoh and his army in the Red Sea, plus the fall of the twelfth dynasty. Velikovsky only noticed the plagues. He failed to see the destruction of Pharaoh and his army by **"pouring water."**

II. VELIKOVSKY'S IDENTIFICATION OF
DUDIMOSE I AS THE PHARAOH
OF THE EXODUS

Velikovsky wrongly interpreted the *Ipuwer Papyrus* to include the invasion of Egypt by the **Hyksos, foreigners from Arabia,** who conquered northern Egypt **during the reign of thirteenth dynasty Pharaohs.** Velikovsky believed that the events surrounding the Exodus so crippled Egypt that the Hyksos were able to conquer northern Egypt. Thus, Velikovsky wrongly dated the Exodus to the period immediately preceding the Hyksos' invasion of Egypt.[7]

To determine when the Hyksos invaded Egypt, Velikovsky followed Josephus' citation of Manetho, an Egyptian priest who recorded Egypt's history *c.* 300 B.C. Manetho reported that the Hyksos invasion occurred in the reign of "Timaus".[8] Timaus is identified by modern scholars as **"Dudimose I,"** a later Pharaoh of the **thirteenth dynasty.**[9] Since Velikovsky believed the Exodus occurred just prior to the Hyksos invasion, he identified Dudimose I as the Pharaoh of the Exodus, and dated the *Ipuwer Papyrus* to the same Pharaoh.[10] In 1995, David Rohl, an Egyptologist, wrote his book, *Pharaohs and Kings, a Biblical Quest,* endorsing Velikovsky's identification of Dudimose I as the Pharaoh of the Exodus.

III. DISCOVERY EVIDENCES AGAINST DUDIMOSE I AS
THE PHARAOH OF THE EXODUS

Velikovsky and Rohl proposed that the Exodus and the destruction of Dudimose I's army in the Red Sea opened the door for Hyksos to enter Egypt and control Egypt's eastern delta. However, my study of the history of the thirteenth through the sixteenth dynasties indicates that neither Dudimose I, nor any other thirteenth dynasty Pharaoh, could have been the Biblical Pharaoh of the Exodus.

Discovery Error No. 1. When the twelfth dynasty fell, a governor of Thebes moved north to take over Itjtowy, Egypt's capital, establishing the thirteenth dynasty. Simultaneously, the fourteenth dynasty, composed of Libyans, took over the western delta of Egypt. In contrast, the Pharaoh of the Exodus in the Bible had control over all of Egypt without rival dynasties.

Discovery Error No. 2. In contrast to the stable twelfth dynasty, the thirteenth dynasty was characterized by chaos and instability from its inception. Egyptian sources list from **fifty to sixty kings for the thirteenth dynasty during a period of only 153 years, whereas the twelfth dynasty and the Bible only pictures seven Pharaohs from the time of Joseph to the Exodus.**[11]

Discovery Error No. 3. The political instability of the thirteenth dynasty did not match the long, stable reigns of the Pharaohs contemporary with Moses. The Pharaoh who sought to kill Moses reigned at least forty years, because he was reigning for some time before Moses fled Egypt, and then he reigned for most of Moses' forty years' exile in Midian.[12] **The longest any king reigned in the thirteenth dynasty was twenty-three years.**[13] Consequently, not a single thirteenth dynasty king lived long enough to qualify as the Pharaoh who tried to kill Moses. **Table A-1, on the next page, shows this significant disharmony between thirteenth dynasty history and the Biblical history of Moses' life.**

Discovery Error No. 4. Dudimose I was one of the latter Pharaohs of the thirteenth dynasty, dated by the *Ancient Cambridge History* to *c.* 1674 B.C. If Dudimose I were the Pharaoh of the Exodus, as claimed by Velikovsky and Rohl, then Dudimose I's predecessor would have to be the Pharaoh who tried to kill Moses during his forty-year exile in Midian. But Merhetepre Ini, the predecessor of Dudimose I, reigned **only two years and two months.**[14] Obviously, **Merhetepre Ini was not the Pharaoh who tried to kill Moses during most of his forty-year exile in Midian.**

Discovery Error No. 5. In fact, four Pharaohs of the thirteenth dynasty reigned during the forty years preceding Dudimose I. Yet, the Bible says **only one king of Egypt** died in the forty years prior to the Exodus.[15] **Therefore, Dudimose I does not qualify biblically as the Pharaoh of the Exodus.**

The **duration of the reigns** in the *Cambridge Ancient History* **are more important than the B.C. dates** in this comparison **because the Cambridge dates are wrong, but the duration of reigns are correct.** Baines later revised the *Cambridge* dates for the reigns of thirteenth dynasty Pharaohs in the 1991 edition of the *New Encyclopaedia Britannica*.

Discovery Error No.6. The first contingent of Hyksos invaded Egypt about ten years before Dudimose I began his reign.[16] Neither Josephus nor Velikovsky were aware of this prior invasion of the Hyksos. Modern scholars have discovered in ancient Egyptian inscriptions that Manetho's reference to the Hyksos invasion in the time of Dudimose I referred to their conquest of the fortified city of Memphis, formerly under control of the thirteenth dynasty. When this conquest occurred, Dudimose was forced to move the capital from northern Egypt to Thebes in southern Egypt. **However, Egyptologists now know that the Hyksos had already conquered the eastern delta of Egypt and had built the capital of Avaris ten years before Memphis was conquered by another group of Hyksos.** Thus, the Hyksos had already conquered the eastern delta of Egypt where the Israelites had lived **ten years before Dudimose even began to reign.[17]** **Thus, Dudimose never had control over the land of Goshen. In contrast, the Bible clearly shows that the Pharaoh of the Exodus had control over the land of Goshen and over the rest of Egypt.[18] Therefore, Dudimose I could not have been the biblical Pharaoh of the Exodus.** Velikovsky's and Rohl's identification of Dudimose I as the Pharaoh of the Exodus is seriously flawed.

TABLE A-1
THIRTEENTH-DYNASTY CHRONOLOGY OF DUDIMOSE I COMPARED TO MOSES' CHRONOLOGY AS INTERPRETED BY VELIKOVSKY

MOSES' CHRONOLOGY B.C.	DUDIMOSE'S CHRONOLOGY B.C.*	
Pharaoh of Oppression reigns		
1527 MOSES' BIRTH (0 years old)	KHASEKHEMRE NEFERHOTEP I	1740
Moses grows up as a prince	KHANEFERRE SOBKHOTPE IV	1730
in Palace of Pharaoh	Hyksos conquer Delta	
of the Oppression	KHAANKHRE SOBKHOTPE V	
	MERSEKHEMRE NEFERHOTEP II	
Pharaoh who Hates	KHAHETEPRE SOBKHOTEP VI	
Moses Seeks his Death	SEKHEMBRE SANKHTOWY	
1487 MOSES' EXILE (40 years old)	WAHIBRE YAYEBI	1709
Pharaoh who Hates Moses	MERNEFERRE IY	1699
continues to reign		
Pharaoh who Hates Moses	MERNETEPRE INI	1676
dies & new Pharaoh reigns	DUDIMOSE I	1674
1447 THE EXODUS (80 years old)	HYKSOS CONQUERED MEMPHIS	1684

*Dates taken from "Chronological Tables," *Cambridge Ancient History, op. cit.,* II.1.818. Baines in the *Encyclopedia Britannica* revised these dates later.

IV. COURVILLE'S IDENTIFICATION OF KHONCHARIS
AS THE PHARAOH OF THE EXODUS

Recognizing the difficulties surrounding Dudimose I, Courville identified Khoncharis (Khaankhre Sobkhotpe V) as the Pharaoh of the Exodus. Khoncharis was another thirteenth dynasty Pharaoh who ruled about forty years before Dudimose I. Courville stated three reasons for choosing Khoncharis.[19]

(1) Courville dated the first Hyksos invasion during the reign of Pharaoh Khoncharis. (2) Eusebius, the church historian of the fourth century, named "Cencheres" of the eighteenth dynasty as the Pharaoh of the Exodus. Since "Cencheres" and "Khoncharis" are similar in sound, Courville reasoned that Eusebius had the right name of the Pharaoh of the Exodus, but the wrong dynasty. (3) Khoncharis' name in Egyptian hieroglyphics was spelled Kha-Ankh-Re, with the last syllable, "Re" standing for the Egyptian sun-god. Courville believed that the "Re/Ra" name of Khoncharis, plus the "Re/Ra" names of his predecessors fit the land and city of Rameses that was constructed by the Pharaohs of Moses' time.

V. DISCOVERY EVIDENCES AGAINST KHONCHARIS
AS THE PHARAOH OF THE EXODUS

Discovery Error No. 1. If Khoncharis were the Pharaoh of the Exodus, then his predecessor, Khaneferre Sobkhotep IV, would have to be the Pharaoh that tried to kill Moses and lived for most of Moses' forty-year exile in Midian. But Khaneferre only reigned **about eight years,** and thus did not reign long enough to qualify as the predecessor of the Pharaoh of the Exodus who reigned for a minimum of forty years (Exodus 2:23; Acts 7:23, 30).

Discovery Error No. 2. In fact, **eight** thirteenth-dynasty Pharaohs reigned in the forty- year period preceding the reign of Khoncharis,[20] contradicting the Biblical scenario of only one Pharaoh dying during the forty years prior to the Exodus. (Exodus 2:23; Acts 7:23, 30). See in Table A-2 on the next page how the duration of years of Khoncharis and of his predecessors does not fit the duration of years for Moses. Since Khoncharis' predecessors do not fit the Biblical chronology preceding the Pharaoh of the Exodus, **then Khoncharis himself is unqualified to be the Pharaoh of the Exodus.**

Discovery Error No. 3. The Hyksos did not invade Egypt during the reign of Khoncharis, as Courville theorized, but in the reign of his predecessor, Khaneferre Sobkhotpe IV.

Discovery Error No. 4. Ancient inscriptions reveal that Avaris was already in the hands of the Hyksos during the days of Khaneferre Sobkhotep IV.[21] Artapanus, a historian of the first century B.C., confirms the claims of modern scholars by stating that King Chenefres (Khaneferre) was ruler of the regions "above Memphis" (southern Egypt is higher than lower Egypt in the north): "for there were at that time **several kings in Egypt."[22] These "several kings" were reigning simultaneously in the time of Khaneferre Sobkhotep IV, representing**

three different dynasties: (1) Khaneferre of the thirteenth dynasty ruled all of Egypt south of Memphis. (2) Kings of the fourteenth dynasty ruled the western delta with its capital at Xois. (3) Kings of the sixteenth "Hyksos" dynasty ruled the eastern delta from its capital in Avaris. See this complex historical division of Egypt in Table A-3 on the next page.

Discovery Error No. 5. Since the Bible says that **the Pharaoh of the Exodus ruled over all of Egypt,**[23] Khoncharis cannot be the Pharaoh of the Exodus because **three Pharaohs reigned simultaneously over Egypt during Khoncharis' reign.**

TABLE A-2
CHRONOLOGY OF KHONCHARIS COMPARED WITH
MOSES' CHRONOLOGY

BIBLICAL CHRONOLOGY B.C. DATES OF MOSES' LIFE	EGYPTIAN CHRONOLOGY OF THE 13TH DYNASTY	CAMBRIDGE B. C. DATES
Pharaoh Enslaves Israel	SOBKHOTPE I Reigns & Dies	1786
1527 MOSES' BIRTH	SEKHEMKARE Reigns & Dies	
	SEHETEPIBRE Reigns & Dies	
	SANKHIBRE Reigns & Dies	
	HETEPIBRE Reigns & Dies	
	SOBKHOTPE II Reigns & Dies	
	RENSENEB Reigns & Dies	
	AWIBRE HOR Reigns & Dies	
	SEDJEFAKARE Reigns & Dies	
	KHUTOWYRE Reigns & Dies	
1487 MOSES FLEES TO MIDIAN	SENEFERIBRE Reigns & Dies	
Pharaoh Tries to Kill Moses	USERKARE Reigns & Dies	
	SEMENKHKARE Reigns & Dies	
	SEKHEMRE I Reigns & Dies	
	SEKHEMRE II Reigns & Dies	
	KHASEKHEMRE Reigns & Dies	1740
PHARAOH OF EXILE DIES	KHANEFERRE Reigns	
PHARAOH OF EXODUS REIGNS	HYKSOS CONQUER DELTA	
1447 THE EXODUS	KHAANKHRE Reigns & Dies	1700
Moses is 80 years old	DUDIMOSE I (Pharaoh of the Exodus?)	1674

SOURCE OF DATES
"Chronological Tables," *Cambridge Ancient History,* II.Part I, p. 818.

Thus, both Velikovsky and Courville erred in thinking the *Ipuwer Papyrus* told of the Hyksos invasion of Egypt. However, they were correct in interpreting the document of Ipuwer as an eye-witness testimony to the ten plagues of Egypt.

TABLE A-3
THE THIRTEENTH DYNASTY REIGNED PARALLEL
WITH THREE OTHER DYNASTIES
(From 1786 to 1633 B.C. - Dates of *Cambridge Ancient History*, II.1.818)

13TH DYNASTY	14TH DYNASTY	15TH DYNASTY	16TH DYNASTY
C. 1786 -1633 B.C.	*C.* 1786 - 1603 B.C.		
SOBKHOTPE I	76 Libyan Kings Reign		
SEKHEMKARE	in the Western		
SEHETIBRE II	Delta of Egypt		
SANKHIBRE			
HETEPIBRE			
SOBKHOTPE II			
KHUTOWRYE			
USERKARE			
SEMENHKHKARE			16TH DYNASTY
SOBKHOTPE III			*C.* 1684 B.C.
KHASEKHEMRE			HYKSOS Invade
KHANEFERRE			Eastern Delta & make
KHAANKHRE			AVARIS their Capital
SOBKHOTPE VI			ANATHER
WAHIBRE			
MERNEFERRE		*C.* 1674 - 1567 B.C.	
MERHETEPRE		15TH DYNASTY	SEMQEN
DUDIMOSE I	14TH DYNASTY	HYKSOS Conquer	
CAPITAL MOVES	Libyan Kings	MEMPHIS	
FROM N. EGYPT	Continue to Reign in		KHAUSERRE
KHAUSERRE	the Western Delta	SHEHSHI	
TO SO. EGYPT			
DUDIMOSE II		YAKUBHER	SEKET
SEWAHENRE			
MERYANKHRE		KHYAN	
DJEDANKHRE			
MENKHAURE		APOPHIS I	AHETEPRE
NEHAY			
C. 1633 B.C.			
13TH DYNASTY			
ENDS			
C. 1650 -1567 B.C.			SEKHAENRE
17TH DYNASTY	14 TH DYNASTY		
Capital in	Libyan Kings		
Thebes	Continue to Reign		
SEKHEMRE	In Western Delta	APOPHIS II	
SOBKEMSAF II	ENDS *C.*1603 B.C.		AMU
NEFERKARE II			
SEUSERENRE		ASEHRE KHAMUDY	APOPHIS III
KAMOSE			
ENDS *C.* 1567 B.C.		ENDS *C.* 1567 B.C.	ENDS *C.* 1567 B.C.

VI. VELIKOVSKY AND *THE IPUWER PAPYRUS*

Most of Velikovsky's historical identities were erroneous. However, he correctly interpreted the *Ipuwer Papyrus* as an Egyptian eye-witness-account of the ten plagues. However, Velikovsky **misidentified** Dudimose I of the thirteenth dynasty as the Pharaoh of the Exodus. **Chapters Eighteen to Twenty identify Amenemhet IV of the twelfth dynasty as the true Pharaoh of the Exodus.**

In Volume II of this series I will critique Velikovsky's other identifications that he proposed in *Ages In Chaos* and his subsequent *books.* I once thought that Velikovsky had solved the Exodus Problem. After several years of research I was able to refute all of Velikovsky's identifications and interpretations, except for the Ipuwer document that Velikovsky dated to the wrong dynasty.

CONCLUSION

Velikovsky, Rohl and Courville contributed toward the solution of the Exodus Problem, but failed to identify the proper Pharaohs and dynasties that ran parallel to the Biblical chronology from Joseph to the Exodus. Eleven principal errors are explained above and are added to the running totals of discoveries listed below.

TABLE A-4 - RUNNING TOTAL OF DISCOVERIES

Chapter		Running Total	Chapter Total
2	Conflict Between Biblical and Secular Histories	18	18
4	Discovery of 430 Years from Abraham to the Exodus	16	34
5	Confirmation of Abraham's Historicity	28	62
6	Discovery of the Remains of Sodom and Gomorrah	17	79
7	Joseph As a Slave and Prisoner in Amenemhet I's Reign	21	100
8	Joseph Becomes the Vizier of Sesostris I	23	123
9	Sesostris I Gives Joseph a New Name and a Wife	11	134
10	The Seven Years of Abundance in Sesostris I's Reign	10	144
11	The Seven Years of Famine in Sesostris I's Reign	20	164
12	Israel Enters Egypt during Sesostris I's Reign	14	178
13	Sesostris III Enslaves the Israelites	17	195
14	Sesostris III, The Foster Grandfather of Moses	12	207
15	Sesostris III, Builder of Rameses and Pithom	15	222
16	Zoan (Itjtowy), the Capital of the Twelfth Dynasty	16	238
17	Amenemhet III, the Pharaoh Who Tried to Kill Moses	15	253
18	Amenemhet IV, the Pharaoh of the Exodus	14	267
19	Moses and Ipuwer Report the Ten Plagues	22	289
20	Israel's Exodus and the Drowning of Amenemhet IV and His Army in the Red Sea	26	315
21	Continuous Errors in Egypt's "Astronomically Absolute" Dates..	30	345
22	The Myth of Egypt's Unbroken Sothic Cycles	13	358
23	Carbon-14 Dates Confirm a Three-Century Revision of Egyptian History	15	373
24	New Astronomical Dating Confirms a Three-Century Revision of Egyptian Dynasties	32	405
	Appendix A - Velikovsky's and Courville's Misconstruction of Egyptian History	11	416

NOTES FOR APPENDIX A

1. Immanuel Velikovsky, *Ages in Chaos* (Doubleday, 1952), v.- ix.
2. Robert H. Pfeiffer, in Immanuel Velikovsky's *Ages in Chaos* (Garden City, N.Y.: Doubleday, 1952), inside of fly cover.
3. Donovan Courville, *The Exodus Problem & Its Ramifications*, 2 volumes (Loma Linda, Ca.: Challenge Books, 1971).
4. Supporters of Velikovsky, "Catastrophism and Ancient History," 3431 Club rive, Los Angeles, Ca., 90064, advertizement in *Biblical Archaeological Review*, May/June, 1991, XVII.3, 9.
5. Norman Geisler and Ron Brooks, *When Skeptics Ask* (Wheaton, Il.: Victor, 1990), 191-198.
6. Velikovsky, *Ages in Chaos*, 22-39.
7. Velikovsky, pp. 5-6,37-39,55-86.
8. Josephus, "Against Apion," I.14., *Complete Works of Josephus*, 610.
9. William C. Hayes, "Egypt: From the Death of Ammenemes III to Seqenenre II, *Cambridge Ancient History*, II.1.52-53.
10. Velikovsky, *Ages in Chaos*, 45.
11. William C. Hayes, "Egypt: From the Death of Ammenemes III to Seqenenre II," *Cambridge Ancient History*, II.1.44.
12. Exodus 2:11-15, 23; 4:19; 7:7; Acts 7:23.
13. "Chronological Tables," *Cambridge Ancient History*, II.1.818.
14. *Ibid.*
15. Exodus 2:23.
16. "Chronological Tables," *Cambridge Ancient History*, II.1.818.
17. William C. Hayes, "Egypt: From the Death of Ammenemes III to Seqenenre II," *Cambridge Ancient History*, I.1.57-58, 818.
18. Exodus 2:23; 3:10,18; 6:10; 7:20-21; 8:24; 9:8,9,25-26;14:7.
19. Courville, *The Exodus Problem & Its Ramifications*, I.122-129.
20. "Chronological Tables," *Cambridge Ancient History*, II.1.818.
21. William C. Hayes, "Egypt From the Death of Ammenemes III to Seqenenre II," *Cambridge Ancient History*, II.1.50.
22. Hayes, II.1.51.
23. Exodus 2:23; 3:10,18; 6:10; 7:20-21; 8:24; 9:8,9,25-26;14:7.

APPENDIX B
EVALUATIONS OF DIFFERENT PHARAOHS
OF JOSEPH AND MOSES

INTRODUCTION

Courville, Aling, Rohl and Kitchen have all proposed different Pharaohs of Joseph and the Exodus.

Courville identified Sesostris I, the second Pharaoh of the twelfth dynasty, as the Pharaoh of Joseph. He also identified Koncharis of the thirteenth dynasty as the Pharaoh of the Exodus.

Ailing identified Sesostris II, also of the twelfth dynasty, as the Pharaoh of Joseph. Ailing made this identification on the basis of a 430-year stay of Israel in Egypt, rather than a 210-year stay in Egypt. Thus, Ailing identified an eighteenth-dynasty Pharaoh as the Pharaoh of the Exodus.

Rohl identified Amenemhet III of the twelfth dynasty as the Pharaoh of Joseph and followed Velikovsky in identifying Dudimose I of the thirteenth dynasty as the Pharaoh of the Exodus.

Kenneth Kitchen proposed a Hyksos ruler of the sixteenth dynasty as the Pharaoh of Joseph and proposed Ramses II of the nineteenth dynasty as the Pharaoh of the Exodus. The Hyksos came to power after the fall of the twelfth dynasty.

I. COURVILLE'S IDENTIFICATION OF JOSEPH
AND MOSES DURING THE REIGN OF
TWELFTH-DYNASTY PHARAOHS

Donovan Courville and Josephus used a short chronology of 215 years (not the correct 210 years) for Israel's stay in Egypt. See proof of a 210-year stay in Egypt for Israel in Chapter Four. However, Courville believed that Egyptian history was misdated by hundreds of years. Thus, Courville did not accept the traditional scholarly dates of the Egyptian dynasties. Instead, Courville searched for parallel events rather than parallel dates between Biblical and Egyptian histories, in the same manner as I have done.

Courville discovered a remarkable twelfth-dynasty inscription that spoke of distributing grain to the hungry during "years of famine." The author of this inscription was Ameny, a governor of middle Egypt, who began his term of office in Sesostris I's eighteenth year of reign, and who wrote the famine inscription close to his death in the forty-third year of Sesostris I's reign. Courville interpreted the famine inscription to be equated with the seven years of famine in the Biblical narrative, and identified Sesostris I as the Pharaoh that appointed Joseph to be his Vizier in the latter half of his forty-three-year reign.[1]

In addition, Courville found that the Canal of Joseph, still used in modern Egypt for irrigation and water conservation, was first constructed during the latter reign of Sesostris I.[2]   I researched Egyptian documents to confirm or reject

Courville's proposal and found that these remarkable synchronisms occurred in **Sesostris I's early reign** rather **than his latter reign.**

Using a 215-year chronology for Israel's stay in Egypt, Courville identified Sesostris III as the Pharaoh who did not know Joseph and enslaved Israelites. Courville also learned that Sesostris III stripped the governors of Egypt of their authority, linking this event with Israel's slavery.[3] **Courville's perception on this point turned out to be right on target with my own research. See Chapters Thirteen through Fifteen.**

Courville also noted that Sesostris III and his successor, Amenemhet III, engaged in vast building projects, including the construction of cities in the delta region where the Israelites lived. Courville cited authorities that affirmed that the cities attributed to Ramses II were actually renovations of older cities constructed by Sesostris III and Amenemhet III. He noted that Ramses II constructed of stone, whereas Sesostris III and Amenemhet III originally used mud bricks mixed with straw in constructing these delta cities. Thus, Courville found other important historical links between the twelfth dynasty and the Biblical story that the Israelites constructed the store cities of Rameses and Pithom out of mud bricks (Exodus 1:11and Exodus 5:6-14).[4] My research confirmed Courville's identification of Sesostris III as the builder of Rameses and Pithom.

However, dating Joseph as the Vizier of **Sesostris I's latter reign** resulted in Courville's misidentification of Mentuhotep as Joseph. Courville noted the unique similarity of the Egyptian descriptions of Mentuhotep's office as Vizier and the Biblical description of Joseph's office. Since Mentuhotep was the name of the Vizier of Sesostris I **in the latter half of his reign,** and since Courville believed that Ameni's famine inscription also was recorded in this same period, Courville deduced that Mentuhotep must be Joseph.[5]

I agree that Mentuhotep's description of his own Viziership remarkably matches that of Joseph's Viziership. In Chapter Eight the reader can see how similar are the descriptions of their respective offices. On the other hand Courville committed many misidentifications and errors which are listed below.

II. DISCOVERY ERRORS OF COURVILLE'S IDENTIFICATION OF MENTUHOTEP AS JOSEPH

Discovery Error No. 1. Joseph's Egyptian name was "Zaphenath-Paneah,"[6] not Mentuhotep.

Discovery Error No. 2. Mentuhotep was born of Egyptian parents, whereas Joseph's parents were Hebrews.

Discovery Error No. 3. Mentuhotep served as a priest of a false Egyptian god, whereas Joseph worshiped the God of Abraham, Isaac and Jacob.

Discovery Error No. 4. Mentuhotep demonstrated arrogance and other negative qualities totally opposed to the humble and righteous character of Joseph.

Discovery Error No. 5. Courville also placed the second, fifth, sixth and thirteenth dynasties of Egypt parallel to the twelfth dynasty during the time of Joseph.[7]

This division of multiple dynasties reigning simultaneously contradicts **Genesis 41:41 that says Joseph was the one and only Vizier over all of Egypt.** during the time of Joseph, Moses and the Exodus. **Exodus 14:5-7 also affirms clearly that the Pharaoh of the Exodus was also the sole Pharaoh over all of Egypt, because "he took his army with him to the Red Sea along "with all the other chariots of Egypt."** See other verses that apply here in the footnote.[8]

The records of the twelfth dynasty also affirm that no rival kings reigned over Egypt during its entire existence. All Egyptologists agree that the twelfth dynasty was the **sole dynasty of Egypt during its entire reign.** Amenemhet I, the founder of the twelfth dynasty, moved the capital from southern Egypt to northern Egypt. He built a fortress city in the eastern delta to prevent Canaanite shepherds from entering the area. He also invaded upper Egypt (in the south) and established his reign as far south as Elephantine, **thus establishing control over all of Egypt.[9]** Therefore, **the twelfth dynasty fits the Biblical picture of one Pharaoh over all of Egypt from Joseph to the Exodus, whereas the multiple division of Egypt's later dynasties contradict the Biblical picture of one Pharaoh over all of Egypt from Joseph to the Exodus.**

Courville also dated Moses' birth in the reign of Amenemhet III, who reigned in the latter quarter of the twelfth dynasty. By dating Moses' birth late in the twelfth dynasty, rather than earlier, as I have done, Courville dated the Exodus after the fall of the twelfth dynasty and during the reign of Khoncharis a king of the mid-thirteenth dynasty.[10] However, we have already seen in earlier chapters that the *Cambridge Ancient History* has proved that Egypt was divided into four rival dynasties when Khoncharis was reigning over only a part of Egypt. Courville, who is a firm believer in the Bible, did not realize that Exodus 14:6-9 clearly teaches that the Pharaoh of the Exodus was the sole Pharaoh of Egypt.

Amenemhet I's successors expanded the Egyptian kingdom even farther south to include the land of Cush (Ethiopia). Inscriptions on monuments and buildings by twelfth dynasty Pharaohs have been found from the extreme south of Egypt to the extreme north of Egypt, testifying to their rule over the entire country.[11] **Since the twelfth dynasty was clearly the sole dynasty over all of Egypt during its entire existence, Courville seriously erred in placing the second, fifth, sixth and thirteenth dynasties contemporary to the twelfth. Thus, Courville's placement of rival dynasties parallel to the twelfth contradicts both twelfth-dynasty history and Bible history. All Egyptologists agree that the twelfth dynasty had no rival dynasties during its entire history.**

The Bible clearly teaches that **only one Pharaoh ruled Egypt at the time of the Exodus.[12]** When God punished Pharaoh with the ten plagues for his hardness of heart, "all of Egypt" suffered, not just part of Egypt.[13] All of Egypt did not need to suffer if there were two innocent Pharaohs ruling over the rest of Egypt. Furthermore, the Bible says that Pharaoh decided to chase the Israelites to the Red Sea and took with him "six hundred select chariots and **all the other chariots of**

Egypt with officers over **all of them.**"[14] The Pharaoh of the Exodus could not have taken **"all of the chariots of Egypt"** if there were two or three other Pharaohs reigning in Egypt at the same time, all with independent armies and chariots.

Courville ended the twelfth dynasty during Moses' exile in Midian, leaving the thirteenth and sixth dynasties still reigning parallel to each other at the time of the Exodus. Courville was apparently unaware that modern Egyptologists place the fourteenth dynasty as another parallel dynasty over Egypt during the time of the thirteenth dynasty. The twelfth dynasty had no rival dynasties in its entire duration. Thus, Courville contradicted both Bible history and twelfth-dynasty history by placing multiple dynasties parallel to each other both during and after the fall of the twelfth dynasty.

III. ALING'S PROPOSAL OF SESOSTRIS II
AND SESOSTRIS III AS THE
PHARAOHS OF JOSEPH

Charles F. Aling accepted the dates of the *Cambridge Ancient History* for the Egyptian dynasties. Calculating 1446 B.C. as the date for the Exodus, Aling placed the Exodus in the reign of **Amenhotep II of the eighteenth dynasty.** We have already seen the numerous historical conflicts with the Bible when the Exodus is dated in the eighteenth dynasty. Ignoring these contradictions, Aling maintained the Biblical date of 1446 B.C. for the Exodus and accepted the *Cambridge* dates for the eighteenth dynasty as astronomically fixed.

Having interpreted Exodus 12:40 to mean that the Israelites remained in Egypt for a total of 430 years, Aling added these 430 years to the 1446 B.C. date, establishing Israel's entrance into Egypt at 1876 B.C. He then estimated that Joseph was appointed Vizier of Egypt about eight years earlier in 1884 B.C.

Since the *Cambridge Ancient History* affirms that Sesostris II was reigning in 1884 B.C., Aling identified Sesostris II as the Pharaoh who appointed Joseph to be his Vizier. However, since Aling dated Jacob's arrival in Egypt in 1876 B.C. during the second year of famine, Joseph thus became the Vizier of Sesostris III, who succeeded his father Sesostris II when he died in 1878 B.C., according to the dates of the *Cambridge Ancient History.*[15]

However, numerous verses in the Bible imply that the Pharaoh that appointed Joseph as Vizier was the same Pharaoh that was reigning nine years later when Israel came to Egypt.[16] In fact the Bible also implies that the same Pharaoh was in power when Jacob died, seventeen years after Jacob's arrival in Egypt.[17] Thus, Aling's placement of two Pharaohs (Sesostris II and Sesostris III) in Joseph's first nine years appears to contradict the Biblical story.

Since Aling wrote, Egyptologists have revised the astronomical dates of the twelfth dynasty. The 1991 Ed. of *The New Encyclopaedia Britannica* assigns 1884 B.C. to the thirty-fourth year of Sesostris I's reign, very close to where Courville dated Joseph's appointment, but still too late to find the synchronisms that I found and recorded in this book.

Aling identified Sesostris III as the Pharaoh who reigned longest during Joseph's tenure as prime minister. However, Sesostris III reorganized the Egyptian government after taking over the throne, brutally removing officials formerly in power, and placing new men in control of newly designated positions.[18] This situation implies that Sesostris III also appointed a new Vizier when he became king, as was traditional among most heirs to the throne. If Joseph were prime minister of the previous king, Sesostris II, he would have been abruptly removed from office by Sesostris III when he became king.

Sesostris III also reorganized Egypt under **two** Viziers, one over lower Egypt and one over upper Egypt. However, the Bible clearly states that Joseph traveled over **the entirety of Egypt** when setting up the collection centers and that he was also in charge of the total collection and distribution of the grain **all over Egypt.**[19] Joseph was clearly **the only Vizier of Egypt**. Since Sesostris III had two Viziers, **Joseph could not have been Sesostris III's Vizier.** Obviously Ailing, who believes the Bible account that Joseph was the only Vizier of Egypt, **did not know that Sesostris III had two viziers after the deaths of Sesostris I and Joseph**.

Aling claimed that Joseph lived in the twelfth dynasty and also claimed that Moses did not appear until the eighteenth dynasty. **However, the Bible says that after Joseph bought all of the land of Egypt during the years of famine, he leased this land back to the Egyptians on the basis of a 20% share-cropper's rent. Moses said that this law remained in force throughout Egyptian history until his own day.**[20] Since Aling dated Joseph in the **twelfth dynasty** and Moses in the **eighteenth dynasty**, then these lease laws made by Joseph in the twelfth dynasty had to remain in effect for 430 years (according to Aling's interpretation) which included all of the dynasties from the twelfth and into the middle of the eighteenth dynasty.

However, after the twelfth dynasty fell, Egypt divided into two dynasties, one of them foreign. One hundred years later the Hyksos established two other dynasties over Egypt, making four dynasties, three of them foreign. One hundred sixty years later, the eighteenth dynasty expelled three of the dynasties and became the sole dynasty over Egypt since the fall of the twelfth dynasty.

How could Joseph's land-lease laws remain in effect for 430 years when three of the four dynasties were foreign and divided up the land of Egypt, canceling all of the twelfth-dynasty laws? Therefore, multiple dynasties reigning simultaneously are totally incompatible with Moses' statement that these land-lease laws remained to the very end of Moses' life. These contradictions occur if Israel actually lived in Egypt for 430 years. But we proved in Chapter Four that the 430 years began with Abraham's departure from Ur and included Israel's sojourn in Canaan and Egypt.

The apostle Paul in Galatians 3:16-17 clearly begins the 430 years with God's promise to Abraham when he lived in Ur. Therefore, the 430 years of Exodus 12:40 must extend from Abraham's Promise in 1876 B.C. to the Exodus in 1446 B.C., minimizing Israel's stay in Egypt to only 210 years. The 210-year sojourn in Egypt fits perfectly with the land-lease laws being confined to the end of the twelfth dynasty.   See Chapter Four for the detailed proof.

While Aling came close to dating Joseph in the right time period of the early twelfth dynasty, he seriously erred in believing that 430 years separated the time of Joseph from the time of the Exodus.   Had Aling calculated the correct time at 210 years and retained his identification of Joseph as a twelfth-dynasty Vizier, then the Exodus could have occurred at the end of the twelfth dynasty, as I date it.   Aling admitted that he did not find any inscriptions contemporary with Sesostris II and Sesostris III that explain Joseph's meeting the baker and butler in prison, Joseph's appointment as Vizier, the years of abundance and famine, or Pharaoh's acquiring all of the livestock and land of Egypt by trading for grain.   Neither could he find any indication in the reign of Sesostris III that Jacob's family arrived in the delta and began to grow and prosper among the Egyptians.[21]

However, Aling did find in scattered Egyptian documents of the twelfth dynasty a number of illustrative background data that generally harmonized with the Biblical story of Joseph and Jacob in Egypt.   Aling cited the twelfth-dynasty practice of slavery and the appointment of some slaves as a steward of an Egyptian house.   Aling also noted that twelfth-dynasty Pharaohs gave a gold chain to the prime minister, as practiced also by the Pharaoh of Joseph.   The names of Potiphera, the priest of On (Heliopolis) and Asenath, his daughter, the worship of Ra (the sun god) in Heliopolis were also found in Egyptian documents.   The Biblical expression that Joseph was called "father to Pharaoh" and "chief of the entire land," was also found by Aling in twelfth-dynasty documents.[22]   The Bible mentions the embalming of Jacob and Joseph (Gen. 50:2-3, 26).   Twelfth-dynasty documents also refer to the embalming of Pharaoh's important officials.[23]   Since Aling found no specific reference in Egyptian documents to specific Biblical events, his main motivation for identifying the twelfth dynasty as the time of Joseph was simply that the dates of the twelfth dynasty and the dates of Joseph, based on the long 430 year chronology from the Exodus, happened to coincide with the general culture of the time.

However, Aling used the dates of the 1971 edition of the *Cambridge Ancient History*.   The 1991 edition of the *New Encyclopedia Britannica* declares that the *Cambridge* dates were incorrect, and that the great majority of Egyptologists now follow the *Britannica* dates instead of the *Cambridge* dates.   If the revised *Britannica* dates are correct, Aling needs to modify his former identification of Joseph's Pharaoh to the latter reign of Sesostris I (1918-1875 B.C.) with Amenemhet II's (1876-1842 B.C.) taking over as Pharaoh in the last four years of the famine, in contradiction to the Bible that pictures the same Pharaoh as reigning during the seven years of abundance and the seven years of famine. Aling's trust in Egypt's inaccurate and constantly changing Sothic dates prevented him from finding the great majority of the 436 points of historical discoveries and synchronisms that I have recorded in this book.   However, a small number of Aling's findings in the twelfth dynasty were correct and contributed to a few of the general synchronisms that occurred during the time of Joseph and the early twelfth dynasty.

III. ROHL'S IDENTIFICATION OF AMENEMHET III
AS THE PHARAOH OF JOSEPH

David Rohl accepted Velikovsky's identification of Dudimose I of the thirteenth dynasty as the Pharaoh of the Exodus in 1447 B.C. He calculated that Israel came to Egypt 215 years earlier in 1662 B.C. and that Joseph was appointed Vizier eight years earlier in 1670 B.C., which Rohl attached to the thirteenth year of Amenemhet III of the twelfth dynasty.[24]

Rohl noted fifteen records of high Niles in Amenemhet III's reign.[25] Rohl proposed that these floods destroyed the crops and caused the seven years of famine during the time of Joseph.[26] Rohl claimed that Amenemhet III and his father, Sesostris III, were noted as "caring monarchs" and that they constructed their pyramids and the famous labyrinth of mud bricks.[27] Rohl also claimed that these two Pharaohs constructed the Bahr Yusef ("waterway of Joseph).[28] Rohl noted that a complete reorganization of Egyptian government occurred during the reigns of Sesostris III and Amenemhet III, which Rohl attributed to the skill of Joseph.[29]

Finally, Rohl identified a statue unearthed at a tomb at Tel el Daba (Avaris) as that of Joseph. The cover jacket of his book pictures this statue as having red hair with characteristics different from Egyptians and covered with a coat of many colors. This statue can be seen in Figure 8-B in Chapter Eight.. Bietak, the Austrian archaeologist who excavated the tomb and statue, dated it to the Middle Kingdom, which includes the twelfth dynasty.[30]

However, Rohl's dating of the flooding of the Nile to the seven years of famine is contrary to the dream of Pharaoh that Joseph interpreted in Genesis 41:17-27. Pharaoh dreamed of seven heads of grain that were "withered, thin and scorched by the east wind." The heads of grain did not deteriorate by being soaked with water, but by being scorched by a dry wind. Thus, the famine occurred because of lack of water rather than an over-abundance of water.

Genesis 41:53-42:5 reports that the famine was so severe that it extended to all countries, including Canaan. The flooding of the Nile only affected Egypt, **not Canaan.** The flooding of the Jordan River did not affect Hebron, which was in the Negev, where Jacob and his sons were living at the time of the famine.

Furthermore, the Canal of Joseph was first constructed during the reign of Sesostris I, not the reign of Amenemhet III. Chapters Ten and Eleven clearly show that the Joseph Canal, the years of abundance and the years of famine were all recorded in documents of the reign of Sesostris I, the true Pharaoh of Joseph.

However, Egyptian documents indicate that Amenemhet III improved the Joseph Canal and used it to siphon off water during times of high Niles so as to diminish the flooding of the Nile and to prevent harm to the crops. Rohl found no inscriptions of famines during the time of Amenemhet III, only instances of high Niles. He assumed that the high Niles caused famines, but presented no proof that a seven-year famine occurred in Amenemhet III's reign. Since the Joseph Canal siphoned off the water of the high Niles into Lake Moeris, the high Niles would not have destroyed the crops during the reign of Amenemhet III.

In Chapters Ten and Eleven the reader can see that grain was stored for the seven years of famine and that the Joseph Canal was dug to store water in Lake Moeris during the early reign of **Sesostris I more than 100 years before Amenemhet III began to reign**. Chapters Ten and Eleven also show that the stored grain was traded for money, livestock and land during the years of famine, during the reign of Sesostris I

.

IV. KITCHEN'S VIEW THAT JOSEPH WAS THE VIZIER OF A HYKSOS PHARAOH

Egyptologist Kenneth Kitchen has influenced most Bible scholars to identify **Ramses II as the Pharaoh of the Exodus** *c.* **1250 B.C. and to identify Joseph as the Vizier of a Hyksos Pharaoh** *c.* **1680 B.C.** Believing that Israel remained in Egypt for **430 years (Exodus 12:40)**, Kitchen added these 430 years to Ramses II's mid-reign *c.* 1250 B.C. (Kitchen's date for the Exodus), creating the date of 1680 B.C. for Israel's entrance into Egypt during the reigns of the Hyksos kings.[31]

Kitchen proposed that the selection of Joseph as Vizier of Egypt harmonizes well with a Hyksos Pharaoh, who himself was a foreigner and likely an Arabian. Kitchen is correct in saying that a full blooded Egyptian Pharaoh would not be as likely to appoint a Semite like Joseph to the important position of Vizier. Also the Egyptians of Joseph's time would not eat at the same table with foreign shepherds and thus ate separately from Joseph and separately from his brothers.[32] Kitchen and other scholars believe that the Egyptians' eating separate from Joseph indicates that this was the period when the foreign Hyksos were ruling over Egypt.[33]

V. REFUTATION OF KITCHEN'S VIEW THAT JOSEPH WAS THE VIZIER OF A HYKSOS PHARAOH

A. Kitchen's Date of the Exodus (1250 B.C.) Contradicts 1 Kings 6:1

1 Kings 6:1-- In the **four hundred and eightieth year** after the Israelites had come out of Egypt, in the **fourth year of Solomon's reign** over Israel, . . . he began to build the temple of the Lord." NIV

In the second (1982) edition of the *Cambridge Ancient History,* Vol.III, Part I, pp. 445, 451, T. C. Mitchell approved Edwin Thiele's chronology (*Mysterious Numbers of the Hebrew Kings,*pp. 51-53*).*[34] **Mitchell confirmed Thiele's date for Solomon's death in 931 B.C. in his fortieth year.** The fourth year of Solomon's forty-year reign is therefore 967/966 B.C. which began in the fall of 967 B.C. and continued into the spring of 966 B.C. when the Passover was celebrated.

Adding the 480 years of 1 Kings 6:1 to the Spring, 966 B.C. date for Solomon's fourth year, we get 1446 B.C. for the date of the Exodus. Therefore,

Kitchen has ignored the 480 years of 1 Kings 6:1 and has ignored Thiele's date and Mitchell's *Cambridge* date for Solomon's fourth year in 966 B.C. Kitchen thus reduced the Exodus date of 1446 B.C. by 196 years later to fit his own date of *c.* 1250 B.C. in the middle of Ramses II's reign from 1279 to 1213 B.C. David Rohl records Kitchen's chronology of the nineteenth dynasty in Rohl's book, *Pharaohs and Kings,* p. 20.

Kitchen also ignored Paul's interpretation in Galatians 3:16-17 that dates the 480 years of Exodus 12:40 as beginning with God's promise to Abraham in Ur and extending to the Exodus and Mount Sinai, where Israel received God's Law.

Gal 3:16-17 -- The promises were spoken to Abraham and to his seed. The Scripture does not say "and to seeds," meaning many people, but "and to your seed," meaning one person, who is Christ. What I mean is this: The law, introduced **430 years later,** does not set aside the covenant previously established by God and thus do away with the promise. (NIV)

Instead of accepting the Biblical chronologies of I Kings 6:1 and Galatians 3:16-17, Kitchen reduced by 196 years the Biblical date of the Exodus in 1446 B.C. to 1250 B.C. (1446 B.C. - 1250 B.C.= 196). Using his own date of 1250 B.C. for the Exodus, Kitchen added the 430 years of 1 Kings 6:1 to get **1680 B.C.** as the date Israel arrived in Egypt and was received by Joseph. Kitchen identified the Hyksos (foreigners from Arabia) as Egypt's sixteenth dynasty. Kitchen reasoned that a foreign dynasty in Egypt would most likely receive Joseph as a foreign Vizier. (Kenneth Kitchen, "Joseph and Asenath," *The International Bible Encyclopedia,* 1982 Ed., II.1130.)

Kitchen explains that the Hyksos conquered the northeastern delta of Egypt and built their capital of Avaris over the same area where Rameses II later built his Capital of Pi-Rameses. The thirteenth dynasty fled south to Thebes.

The fourteenth dynasty, composed of Libyan Pharaohs, took over the northwestern delta of Egypt. **Another Hyksos dynasty arrived ten years later** and established the fifteenth dynasty with its capital at Memphis. The *Cambridge Ancient History* dated the fifteenth dynasty from 1674 to 1567 B.C. **Thus, four dynasties reigned over a divided Egypt when Joseph was supposedly the Vizier of a Hyksos Pharaoh.** However, the *Cambridge Ancient History* dates the period from 1680 to 1662 as the time of the early Hyksos.[31]

The **two capitals of the Hyksos dynasties,** Memphis and Avaris, were located in northern Egypt. **(1) Memphis** is located just below the southern boundary of the Delta where the Nile enters and branches in different directions which flow through the Delta and into the Mediterranean Sea. **(2) Avaris** was located at the eastern edge of the land of Goshen and was constructed over the destroyed remains of the earlier store city of Rameses that was built by twelfth-dynasty Pharaohs.[32] The Hyksos dynasties thus lived in the same area where Joseph and the Israelites lived in the land of Goshen.[33]

B. Evidence That Joseph Could Not Have Been
the Vizier of a Hyksos Pharaoh

While the above evidence seems to fit the time of Joseph, a closer examination of the historical data for the Hyksos period reveals serious conflicts with the Biblical data.

1. No Hyksos Pharaoh Reigned Over All of Egypt

The Bible clearly declares that the Pharaoh who appointed Joseph to office ruled all of Egypt, not part of it. The Bible (NIV) also emphasizes that Joseph was the only Vizier of all of Egypt.

> Genesis 41:41 -- "So Pharaoh said to Joseph, 'I hereby put you in charge of **the whole land of Egypt.**'"
> Genesis 41:43 -- "He had him ride in a chariot as his second-in-command, and men shouted before him, "Make way!" Thus he put him in charge of the **whole land of Egypt**.
> Gen 41:44 -- "Then Pharaoh said to Joseph, 'I am Pharaoh, but without your word no one will lift hand or foot in **all Egypt**.'"
> Genesis 41:55 -- "When **all Egypt** began to feel the famine, the people cried to Pharaoh for food. Then Pharaoh told all the Egyptians, 'Go to Joseph and do what he tells you.'"
> Gen 41:56 -- "When the famine had spread over **the whole country**, Joseph opened the storehouses and sold grain to the Egyptians, for the famine was severe throughout Egypt."
> Gen. 45:8 -- "So then, it was not you who sent me here, but God. He made me father to Pharaoh, lord of his entire household and **ruler of all Egypt.**"
> Gen. 45:26 -- "They told him, 'Joseph is still alive! In fact, he is **ruler of all Egypt**.' Jacob was stunned; he did not believe them.

According to Hayes the **twelfth dynasty ruled over the entire land of Egypt** from c. 1990 to 1786 B.C. When the twelfth dynasty mysteriously fell about 1786 B.C., two dynasties simultaneously emerged: (1) the thirteenth dynasty with its capital in Itjtowy, the former capital of the twelfth dynasty in northeastern delta of Egypt and (2) the fourteenth dynasty with its capital at Xois in the western delta of northern (lower) Egypt. Thus, two dynasties reigned over Egypt from c. 1786 to 1684 B.C. with the thirteenth dynasty maintaining control over most of Egypt.[34]

About 1684 B.C. the Hyksos invaded the northeastern delta of lower Egypt, built the city of Avaris and established what Manetho called the sixteenth Egyptian dynasty. At this time the thirteenth dynasty fled south and established their capital in Thebes. Ten years later, c. 1674 B.C., another group of Hyksos conquered Memphis and began what Manetho called the fifteenth dynasty.[35]

In 1665 B.C. our Biblical chronology tells us that Joseph was appointed prime minister of Egypt. However, Egyptian history shows **four different Pharaohs** with four different prime ministers of four different dynasties were reigning simultaneously in four different capitals of Egypt. These four parallel dynasties continued until c. 1603 B.C. when the fourteenth dynasty was conquered by the fifteenth (Hyksos) dynasty, thus reducing the Egyptian dynasties to three. From c. 1603 B.C. to 1567 B.C. three Pharaohs continued to rule simultaneously over different parts of Egypt.[36] **The Hyksos period of multiple Pharaohs and dynasties reigning simultaneously contradicts the Biblical picture of Joseph as Vizier of a Pharaoh who was the sole ruler of all of Egypt (not part of it).**

2. Joseph Could Not Have Been the Vizier of Mayebre Sheshi

As a specific example, Mayebre Sheshi, the founder of the fifteenth Hyksos dynasty, conquered Memphis as his new capital in 1674 B.C. and reigned for thirteen years until 1661 B.C. If *Cambridge Ancient History* dates are correct, then Joseph was appointed Vizier of Mayebre Sheshi in the Biblical date of 1665 B.C. However, Mayebre Sheshi appointed a Vizier with the name of Hur or Har. Hur or Har hardly fits the Hebrew name of "Joseph" or Joseph's Egyptian name of "Zaphenath-Paneah".[37] Of course, we will later prove that the *Cambridge* dates are also erroneous even after the revision of Baines and Wente in the 1991 Edition of *The Encyclopaedia Britannica*, XVIII, p. 114, giving the dates of 1630 to 1523 B.C. for the sixteenth dynasty.

Furthermore, Hur, a sixteenth dynasty official, wrote on his tomb that he was "Treasurer of the King of **Lower** Egypt."[38] Since "Lower" Egypt covered only northern Egypt, not southern Egypt, Hur's statement proves that Viziers of the Hyksos dynasties did not have power over all of Egypt. In fact, "Lower Egypt" in this case did not even include the Delta of northern Egypt, because two Pharaohs were reigning over the delta at this same time, the fourteenth Libyan dynasty over the western delta and the sixteenth Hyksos dynasty over the eastern delta.[39] A divided Egypt cannot be the time of Joseph who was Vizier of a Pharaoh who ruled all of Egypt.

3. Joseph Could Not Buy All of the Land of Egypt During the Time of the Hyksos Pharaohs

The Bible says that during the years of famine Joseph bought all of the land of Egypt for one Pharaoh.

> Genesis 47:20-21 -- "(20) So Joseph bought **all the land in Egypt** for Pharaoh. **The Egyptians, one and all**, sold their fields, because the famine was too severe for them. **The land became Pharaoh's**, (21) and Joseph reduced the people to servitude, **from one end of Egypt to the other.**" NIV

Which of the Viziers of the three or four Pharaohs ruling Egypt bought all of the land of the other Pharaohs? Obviously, Joseph cannot belong to the Hyksos period because a single Pharaoh did not own all of the land of Egypt during this period.

4. Absence of Evidence for Joseph's Presence in the Time of the Hyksos Dynasties

Argument from silence is not strong, but lends additional weight to an over-all case either for or against a particular proposition. I have searched the records of the Hyksos era, which are admittedly sparse, but have found **no** evidence of any of the characteristic clues of the time of Joseph: **no** collection of grain during years of abundance, **no** feeding of the hungry during the years of famine, **no** trading of grain for all of the herds and land of the Egyptians, **no** evidence that the Israelites entered Egypt and **no** laws enacted by the Hyksos that continued down into the eighteenth dynasty when Moses is supposed to have lived. This absence of solid evidence connecting the Hyksos era to the time of Joseph and the historical picture of a divided Egypt during the entire Hyksos rule, cannot be reconciled with the Biblical pattern of Egyptian history when Joseph was Vizier of a Pharaoh who reigned over a united Egypt without rivals.

C. JOSEPH'S VIZIERSHIP DOES NOT FIT THE TIME OF THE THIRTEENTH DYNASTY

Most scholars who have argued in favor of a Hyksos Pharaoh have used the dates of the *Cambridge Ancient History* listed above. However these dates are now considered obsolete by many modern Egyptologists. J. R. Baines wrote in the 1991 edition of the *New Encyclopaedia Britannica* the following words.

> The chronologies offered in most publications up to 1985 have been disproved for the Middle and New kingdoms by a restudy of the evidence for the Sothic and especially the lunar dates.[40]

Whereas, the *Cambridge Ancient History* dated the beginning of the fifteenth and sixteenth dynasties at 1674 B.C. and 1684 B.C., respectively, the 1991 edition of the *New Encyclopedia Britannica* has revised these dates to about 1630 B.C.[41] Thus, the dates we cited above from the *Cambridge Ancient History* have now been reduced by forty years. This now places the thirteenth & fourteenth dynasties parallel with the Biblical date for Joseph's appointment as Vizier. However, in this new scenario Joseph still could not be a Vizier of one Pharaoh over all over Egypt, since Pharaohs of the thirteenth and fourteenth dynasties reigned simultaneously over a divided Egypt after the fall of the twelfth dynasty.

Remember also that Joseph bought all of the land of Egypt for Pharaoh during the years of famine and passed a law that the land be rented back to the Egyptians on a 20% share cropper's lease. Moses said that Joseph's law was still operative at the time of the Exodus.[42] This law could not have been enacted in the thirteenth dynasty, because the two Hyksos dynasties (fifteenth and sixteenth) that invaded Egypt **thirty years later** annulled all of these laws and took over the land of northern Egypt for themselves. The thirteenth dynasty, thus was unable to collect rent in northern Egypt after the invasion of the Hyksos. Therefore, Joseph could not have passed a law affecting all of the land of Egypt that remained in force for more than two hundred years to the time of Moses.

Furthermore, we have already proved astronomically and scientifically that all of the dynasties from the twelfth to the twentieth need to be revised about three centuries later than the constantly changing Sothic dates presently assigned to these dynasties.

VI. DISCOVERY ERRORS IN IDENTIFYING THE PHARAOH OF JOSEPH

Discovery Error No. 1. We have seen that Aling's dating of Joseph in the later twelfth dynasty harmonizes generally with the Egyptian culture of this period of Egyptian history. However, his dating of Joseph in the reigns of Sesostris II and Sesostris III contradicts the Biblical picture of one Pharaoh ruling during the seven years of abundance and the seven years of famine.

Discovery Error No. 2. The Biblical description of Joseph's traveling all over Egypt to set up the grain collection contradicts the two prime ministers of Sesostris III over northern and southern Egypt.

Discovery Error No. 3. Aling dated Joseph too late in the reign of Sesostris I to discover the seven years of abundance, the seven years of famine, and the arrival of the Israelites in Egypt.

Discovery Error No. 4. Courville found many evidences for Joseph, but erroneously identified Joseph as Mentuhotep, the Vizier of Sesostris I's last years of reign.

Discovery Error No. 5. David Rohl identified Dudimose I of the thirteenth dynasty as the Pharaoh of the Exodus, as did Velikovsky. Rohl failed to see the famine inscription in the reign of Sesostris I that was caused by lack of rain. Rohl's proposal that the flooding of the Nile in the reign of Amenemhet III caused the seven years of famine does not fit the scorching of the grain by a hot east wind in the dream of Pharaoh, nor does it fit the famine in Canaan and other countries not linked to the Nile River.

Discovery Error No. 6. Kitchen identified Joseph as the Vizier of a Hyksos Pharaoh. However, the Hyksos had two capitals in northern Egypt. The Libyans had a third capital in the western delta and the thirteenth dynasty had a fourth capital in southern Egypt, all in contradiction to the twelfth-dynasty and the Bible, which pictures **only one Pharaoh and one Vizier over all of Egypt..**

CONCLUSION

The reader can understand now why some scholars doubt that Joseph ever existed and why others suggest that he was only an administrator of grain, rather than Vizier of all of Egypt. But Moses clearly said that Pharaoh made Joseph "his second-in-command," and **"put him in charge of the whole land of Egypt."** So vast were his responsibilities that Pharaoh said, "You shall be in charge of my palace, and all my people are to submit to your orders. Only with respect to the throne will I be greater than you." Also, he said, "I am Pharaoh, but without your word no one will lift hand or foot **in all Egypt**."[43] Since Joseph could not have possessed these immense powers during the multiple dynasties of the thirteenth through the seventeenth dynasties, we conclude that this Egyptian period of history cannot be the time of Joseph. Seeing the disharmony between the Biblical history of Joseph and the time of the Hyksos dynasties will enable the reader to appreciate the unique harmony that is found in the twelfth dynasty in Chapters Seven to Twelve.

TABLE B-1
RUNNING TOTAL OF DISCOVERIES

NOTES FOR APPENDIX B

1. Donovan Courville, *The Exodus Problem and Its Ramifications* (Loma Linda, Calif.: Challenge Books), I.134.
2. Courville, I.142-143.
3. Courville, I.146-147.
4. Courville, I.147-148.
5. Courville, I.142.
6. Genesis 41:45.
7. Courville, I.151 (Fig. 3); 223 (Fig. 9).
8. Courville, I.150-157, 122-129.
9. Gen. 41:33,41,43,44,46,54,56; 47:6,14,20,22.
10. William C. Hayes, "Middle Kingdom of Egypt," *Cambridge Ancient History*, I.2A.495-497.
11. Hayes, I.2A.499-505.
12. Exodus 2:23; 3:18-19; 4:21 23; 5:1; 6:11.
13. Exodus 7:14-21; 8:6,17,24; 9:6,9,22,25; 10:7,14-15,19,22; 11:5-6; 12:29-30.
14. Exodus 14:6-9.
15. Charles Ailing, *Egypt and Bible History* (Grand Rapids: Baker,1981), 21-31.
16. Gen. 41:46-55; 45:8,16-19; 47:20-26.
17. Gen. 47:9,28; 50:1-8.
18. Hayes, *op. cit.*, I.2A.505-6.
19. Gen. 41:41,46-49, 55-57; 42:6; 45:8; 47 14-21.
20. Genesis 47:20-26.
21. Ailing, *Egypt & Bible History*, 28-29.
22. Ailing, 29-52.
23. Ailing, *Ibid.*
24. David Rohl, *Pharaohs & Kings* (New York: Crown Pub.1995), 335-343.
25. Rohl, 342-343.
26. Rohl, 335-342.
27. Rohl, 343-46.
28. Rohl, 346-47.
29. Rohl, 348-50.
30. Rohl, 360-367.
31. Kenneth Kitchen, "Hyksos," *Zondervan Pictorial Encyclopedia of the Bible*, III.232-233.
32. "Chronological Tables," *Cambridge Ancient History*, II.1.818.
33. John Baines & Jaromir Malek, *Atlas of Ancient Egypt*, 167.
34. Genesis 45:10.
35. Genesis 43:32; 46:34.
36. K. A. Kitchen, "Joseph," *Intern. Stand. Bible Encyclopedia*, II.1130.
37. William C. Hayes, "Egypt: From the Death of Ammenemes III to Seqenenre II," *Cambridge Ancient History*, II.1.44,50-54. 38. Hayes,, II.1.50-55. 39. Hayes, II.1.64-73.
40. Gen. 41:45.
41. Hayes,, *Cambridge Ancient History*, II.1.60.
42. Hayes, II.1.50-51.
43. Baines, "Egypt," *New Encyclopedia Britannica*, 18.107.
44. Baines, 18.114.
45. Genesis 47:20-26.
46. Genesis 41:40-44.

APPENDIX C
RECONCILING TWELFTH-DYNASTY
AND BIBLICAL CHRONOLOGIES

Calculating correct twelfth-dynasty dates and correct Bible dates are crucial to solving the Exodus Mystery. This chapter demonstrates **how 232 years of twelfth-dynasty history coincide perfectly with 232 years of Biblical chronology from Joseph's entrance into Egypt until Israel's Exodus from Egypt.**

I. TWO HUNDRED THIRTY-TWO YEARS OF JOSEPH'S
AND ISRAEL'S RESIDENCE IN EGYPT

A. ISRAEL'S 210 YEARS IN EGYPT

Chapter Four explains in depth the Biblical chronology of 430 years from Abraham's departure from Ur in 1876 B.C. to Jacob's entrance into Egypt in 1656 B.C. to Israel's exodus from Egypt in 1446 B.C. **Thus, the Israelites lived in Egypt for 210 years: 1656 B.C. - 1446 B.C. = 210 years**. See Table C-1 below.

Table C-1
**THE 430 YEARS OF EXODUS 12:40 FROM ABRAHAM TO THE EXODUS,
THE 400 YEARS OF GENESIS 15:13 FROM ISAAC TO THE EXODUS,
AND ISRAEL'S 210-YEAR STAY IN EGYPT**

ABRAHAM'S BIRTH	1946 B.C.
70 Years Before the Promise	-70 yrs.
GOD'S PROMISE TO ABRAHAM IN UR	1876 B.C.
Beginning of 430 Years when Abraham was 70 years old	
Ex. 12:40, - 430 Years Before the Exodus, Galatians 3:17	
Abraham Stayed in Haran for 5 Years Until His Father Died Gen. 11:32	- 5 yrs.
ABRAHAM ENTERED CANAAN when he was 75 years old, Gen. 12:4	1871 B.C.
Abraham Was 100 Years Old when Isaac was Born , Gen. 21:5 (100 -75) =	-25 yrs.
ISAAC'S BIRTH: Beginning of 400 Years of Abraham's descendants (Gen. 15:13)	1846 B.C.
Jacob was born when Isaac was 60 years old, Genesis 25:26	-60
JACOB'S BIRTH	1786 B.C.
Jacob Entered Egypt at Age 130 - Gen. 47:9	-130 yrs.
JACOB (ISRAEL) ENTERED EGYPT	1656 B.C.
ISRAEL'S DEPARTURE FROM EGYPT (I KINGS 6:1)	-1446 B.C.
YEARS THAT THE ISRAELITES REMAINED IN EGYPT (1656 - 1446 = 210)	210 yrs.

B. JOSEPH'S TWENTY-TWO YEARS IN EGYPT
BEFORE ISRAEL CAME TO EGYPT

Joseph entered Egypt at age seventeen as a slave in 1678 B.C. Twenty-two years later Jacob and his family entered Egypt in **1656 B.C.** as guests of Joseph and Pharaoh Sesostris I.   Jacob and his family stayed in Egypt for 210 years, leaving Egypt in 1446 B.C. Thus, Joseph's **22 years in Egypt must be**

added to the **210 years that Jacob and his family lived in Egypt.** Israel's **210 years,** plus Joseph's **extra 22 years,** give us a total duration of **232 years** that Joseph, Jacob, and Jacob's sons and descendants lived in Egypt before leaving Egypt in **1446 B.C. xx.**

Genesis 45:6 reports that Jacob entered Egypt with his **family at the end of the second year of famine.** Therefore, the seven years of abundance, plus the second year of famine give us **nine years** that preceded Israel's entrance into Egypt in 1656 B.C. Adding these nine years to Israel's arrival in Egypt in 1656 B.C. gives us **1665 B.C.** as Joseph's first year as Vizier of Egypt: 1656 + 9 = 1665.

Genesis 41:46 reports that Joseph **was thirty years old** when he was appointed Vizier and that Joseph immediately began to collect grain during the first year of abundance (1665 B.C.). However, Genesis 37:2,36 reports that Joseph was only **seventeen years old** when his brothers sold him as a slave to Midianites, who carried Joseph to Egypt and sold him to Potiphar, the captain of Pharaoh's body guard. Thus Joseph lived in Egypt **thirteen years** (30 -17 = 13) **before his appointment as Vizier of the ruling Pharaoh.** Therefore, we must add these thirteen additional years to 1665 B.C. when Joseph became Vizier: **1665 B.C. plus 13 years gives us 1678 B.C.** as the date Joseph first entered Egypt at age seventeen. Therefore, Joseph and Israel together lived in Egypt for a total of **232 years** (1678 - 1446 = 232). See this chronology in Table C-2 below.

TABLE C-2
THE CHRONOLOGY OF JOSEPH AND THE ISRAELITES
TOTAL 232 YEARS IN EGYPT

JOSEPH ENTERED EGYPT AS A SLAVE AT AGE 17 Genesis 37:2	1678 B.C.
	-22 Yrs.
ISRAEL ENTERED EGYPT AT THE END OF THE SECOND YEAR OF FAMINE	
Gen. 45:6	1656 B.C.
Israel stayed in Egypt for 210 years s	-210 Yrs.
ISRAEL LEFT EGYPT IN THEIR EXODUS THROUGH THE RED SEA	1446 B.C.
JOSEPH AND ISRAEL LIVED IN EGYPT FROM 1678 TO 1446 B.C. =	232 Yrs.

Joseph entered Egypt in 1678 B.C. and Israel left Egypt in 1446 B.C., **a total period of 232 years (1678 - 1446 = 232). Therefore, I needed to find 232 years in twelfth-dynasty history to match these 232 Biblical years. This Chapter shows how I was able to find 232 years of twelfth-dynasty history that parallel Joseph's and Israel's stay in Egypt. My sources were contemporary inscriptions from monuments and documents of the twelfth-dynasty. I also utilized the chronology of the Turin Canon, a document dated to the reign of Ramses II, and the chronology of Manetho, an Egyptian priest of the third century B.C.**

C. DISCOVERY OF 232 YEARS OF BIBLICAL HISTORY IN THE TWELFTH DYNASTY

Having calculated 232 Biblical years for Joseph's and Israel's sojourn in

Egypt, we must now examine twelfth-dynasty chronology to see if it contains 232 corresponding years that will match the 232 biblical years.

W. M. Flinders Petrie, a famous British Egyptologist and archaeologist, stated that the twelfth dynasty "is perhaps the best known chronologically of any before the Greek times; **yet here in some reigns uncertainties beset us." Petrie attributed Manetho, a priest of the third century B.C., with a count of 245 years for the twelfth dynasty.**[1]

Manetho had access to chronological data that we do not have in our possession today. Manetho was the first person to divide all of the Egyptian Pharaohs under dynasties (families of kings). His chronology of the dynasties is still used by modern Egyptologists.

Most Egyptologists calculate the twelfth dynasty with lower duration of years than Manetho. Breasted says it endured 212 years; Hayes says it lasted 205 years and Baines gives the twelfth dynasty only 182 years. **While I am not in agreement with all of Manetho's years of reign for each of these twelfth-dynasty Pharaohs, I do agree with Manetho's total number of 245 years for the entire duration of the twelfth dynasty. This Appendix demonstrates how the 232 Biblical years began with Joseph's entrance into Egypt as a slave in 1688 B.C. in Amenemhet I's ninth year. Counting Amenemhet I's accession year, we subtract nine years from the total of 245 years of Manetho's chronology, leaving a balance of 236 years: 245 - 9 = 236.**

Amenemhet IV was the last male Pharaoh of the twelfth dynasty and died in the Red Sea with his army in the biblical date of 1446 B.C. An ancient Egyptian record called the **"Turin Canon" states that Amenemhet IV died in the twenty-seventh day of the third month of his tenth year.**[2] **Thus Amenemhet IV, the Pharaoh of the Exodus, reigned nine years, three months and twenty-seven days.** His death marked the end of the 232 years from Joseph's entrance into Egypt as a slave in 1678 B.C. to the exodus of Israel in Amenemhet IV's last year in 1446 B.C.

His wife Sebeknefru, continued to reign for four years before disappearing from the scene. Breasted provided the precise reign of **three years, ten months and twenty-four days for the reign of Sebeknefru,** the sister/wife of Amenemhet IV who succeeded her husband after he had died in the Red Sea.[3] Subtracting her four-year reign from Manetho's remaining 236 years, we get precisely **232 years that fit the Bible dates and Manetho's dates for the twelfth-dynasty. Table C-3 on page 400 and and Table C-4 on page 409 provide the chronological information that demonstrates this remarkable synchronism, confirming that the twelfth dynasty is definitely the time of Joseph, Israel, Moses and the Exodus.**

I found these **232 years** of the twelfth-dynasty by starting at the end of the twelfth dynasty and counting backwards. Chapter 18 identifies Amenemhet IV as the last male king of the twelfth dynasty and identifies him as **the Pharaoh of the Exodus. I assigned 1446 B.C., the Biblical date of the Exodus, to Amenemhet IV's death.**

TABLE C-3
232 MATCHING YEARS OF TWELFTH-DYNASTY AND BIBLICAL
HISTORIES FROM JOSEPH AS A SLAVE (1678 B.C.)
TO ISRAEL'S EXODUS (1446 B.C.)

(Over-laps show co-reigns)

A-I		B.C.		Years in Egypt
AMENEMHET I	0		1688 ACCESSION YEAR	
	09		1678 JOSEPH ENTERS EGYPT AS A SLAVE	0
	19	S-I	1668 JOSEPH IN PRISON...	10
SESOSTRIS I	20	0	1667 BAKER & BUTLER IN PRISON	
	21	01	1666	
	22	02	1665 1ST YR. - ABUNDANCE: JOSEPH VIZIER...	13
	23	03	1664 2ND YEAR OF ABUNDANCE	
	24	04	1663 3RD YEAR OF ABUNDANCE	
	25	05	1662 4TH YEAR OF ABUNDANCE	
	26	06	1661 5TH YEAR OF ABUNDANCE	
	27	07	1660 6TH YEAR OF ABUNDANCE	
	28	08	1659 7TH YEAR OF ABUNDANCE	
	29	09	1658 1ST YEAR OF FAMINE	
	30	10	1657 2ND YEAR OF FAMINE	
		11	1656 JACOB ENTERS EGYPT (Age 130)	22
		12	1655 4TH YEAR OF FAMINE	
		13	1654 5TH YEAR OF FAMINE	
		14	1653 6TH YEAR OF FAMINE	
		15	1652 7TH YEAR OF FAMINE	
		28	1639 JACOB'S DEATH (Age 147)..............................	39
		30	1637	
AMENEMHET II	0	42	1625	
	01	43	1624	
	02	44	1623	
	03	45	1622	
	04	46	1621	
	05	S II	1620 ISRAELITE PROSPERITY...............................	58
SESOSTRIS II	35	0	1590	
	36	01	1589	
	37	02	1588	
	38	03	1587	
		05	1585 JOSEPH'S DEATH (Age 117).........................	93
	S III	30	1560 ISRAELITE GROWTH	
SESOSTRIS III	0	48	1542 SLAVERY OF ISRAEL	
	7		1535 CONSTRUCTION OF RAMESES	
	16		1526 MOSES' BIRTH...152	
	36	A III	1506	
AMENEMHET III	44	0	1498	
		1	1497	
		2	1496	
		12	1486 MOSES' EXILE TO MIDIAN (Age 40) 192	
	A IV	38	1466 CONTINUED CONSTRUCTION	
AMENEMHET IV	0	42	1456 IN GOSHEN	
	6	48	1450	
	10		1446 PLAGUES & EXODUS Moses at age 80..........	232

My Biblical chronology shows that Joseph arrived in Egypt as a slave in **1678 B.C. in Amenemhet I's ninth year.** Chapter Seven shows that Joseph met the baker and butler in prison eleven years later in **1667 B.C.** during Amenemhet I's twentieth year, which **is also Sesostris I's accession year as co-ruler.** I thus needed to find **232 years between Amenemhet I's ninth year in 1678 B.C. and Amenemhet IV's death in his tenth year in 1446 B.C.**, the date of Israel's Exodus from Egypt. I **used optional lengths of king's reigns until I found a combined twelfth-dynasty chronology of exactly 232 years that fit every year of my Biblical chronology from Joseph to the Exodus.**

II. ACCESSION YEAR METHOD OF DATING KINGS' REIGNS

Hayes tells us that twelfth dynasty kings used the accession year method of counting their years of reign.[4] **The accession year is regarded as year zero.** **Year one** does not begin until New Year's Day of the following year. Thus, the entire last calendar year in which the king died is given to the dead king, making that year zero for his successor, regardless of the number of months that the successor may have reigned. My research of twelfth-dynasty chronology confirms Hayes' observation of the method of accession-year dating. This chronological principle is very important, because I cannot reconcile twelfth-dynasty history with Biblical history without using the accession-year system of counting kings' reigns. Interestingly, Hayes also discovered that the kings of the eighteenth and nineteenth dynasty **rejected the accession-year method**, using the non-accession year method, which counts their accession to the throne as Year One instead of Year Zero.

III. THE REIGNS OF AMENEMHET I AND SESOSTRIS I IN RELATION TO JOSEPH'S AND JACOB'S ARRIVALS IN EGYPT

I previously noted that Joseph at age seventeen arrived in Egypt in **1678 B.C. as a slave in Amenemhet I's ninth year. This date of 1678 B.C. marks the beginning of the 232 years from Joseph's arrival in Egypt as a slave to Israel's entrance into Egypt in 1656 B.C. and their later Exodus from Egypt in 1446 B.C.**
In 1991 I copied the words of Intef's stela in the Cairo Museum. This stela records year **30** of Amenemhet I as equal to year **10** of Sesostris I, proving that Sesostris I's co-reign began in **year 20** of Amenemhet I, the father of Sesostris I. James Breasted agrees in his *Ancient Records of Egypt* that Sesostris I's tenth year was the **Amenemhet I's thirtieth year.** [5]
"The Tale of Sinuhe" was written during **Sesostris I's tenth year of reign, telling us that Amenemhet I died in his thirtieth year.**[6] This evidence proves that Amenemhet I and Sesostris I **co-reigned for ten years.** See the length of reigns of all twelfth-dynasty kings in Table C-4 at the end of this Appendix.

Chapters 7 and 8 show how an assassination attempt against Amenemhet I occurred in his twentieth year in the Biblical date of **1667 B.C. In this same year the baker and butler were thrown into prison as likely suspects in the assassination attempt.** Thus, Sesostris I took over the throne of Egypt in place of his wounded father.

Genesis 41:1 says that Pharaoh had a dream two years after the butler had been released from prison in the year **1665 B.C.** Joseph interpreted the dream of Pharaoh, who immediately appointed Joseph as his prime minister in this same **year of 1665 B.C., which is Sesostris I's second year of co-reign.**

Connecting this coup with Joseph's encounter with the baker and butler in prison, **I dated Amenemhet I's twentieth year and Sesostris I's accession year (as co-ruler) in the Biblical year of 1665 B.C. Thus, Sesostris I's accession year pinpoints the first year of abundance when Joseph became Vizier of Egypt.**

Genesis 41:31 says the **seven years of abundance** began the same year that Joseph was appointed prime minister **in Sesostris I's second year in 1665 B.C. These seven years terminated in 1659 B.C. in Sesostris I's eighth year. The seven years of famine commenced in 1658 B.C. in Sesostris I's ninth year of reign and ended in 1652 B.C. in Sesostris I's fifteenth year.** The reader can see how these years connect in Table C-4 at the end of Appendix C. In Chapters Ten and Eleven I show proof from Egyptian documents **that the fourteen total years of abundance and famine** are registered in Egyptian records dated between Sesostris I's **second and fifteenth years.**

Jacob entered Egypt **after two full years of famine. Thus, the beginning of the third year of famine in 1656 B.C. corresponds to Sesostris I's eleventh year.** Jacob was 130 years old when he entered Egypt in 1656 B.C. (Sesostris I's eleventh year). **Jacob died at 147, seventeen years later in 1639 B.C., which corresponds to Sesostris I's twenty-eighth year.** See Chapter Four for proof of this Biblical chronology and see Chapters Seven, Eight and Twelve for the correlation between Israel's arrival in Egypt and Sesostris I's eleventh year of reign. Table C-4 at the end of this appendix also shows the synchronism of Biblical events of Joseph's and Moses' life with the chronology of all of the twelfth-dynasty kings.

Sesostris I reigned forty-five to forty-six years, according to the Turin Canon and Manetho's chronology. However, the *Stela of Upwaweto* at Leyden, a contemporary monument of Sesostris I's time, records the double date: **Year 44 of Sesostris I = Year 2 of Amenemhet II.**[7] **Thus, Sesostris I's Year 43 was Year 1 of Amenemhet II and Year 42 was Amenemhet II's accession year as co-ruler: see C-3 above.** I thus assigned Sesostris I forty-two years as his sole reign.

IV. THE REIGN OF AMENEMHET II

Scholars differ over the duration of the reign of Amenemhet II. Manetho, the Egyptian priest, attributed **thirty-eight years to his reign.** The Turin Canon was written 600 years after the twelfth dynasty, during Ramses II's reign.[8] **It did not** mention Amenemhet II's name, nor his years of reign. The priest who compiled the Turin Canon accidentally omitted Amenemhet II's name or was copying from a defective manuscript. **However, two contemporary inscriptions register Amenemhet II's thirty-fifth and thirty-sixth years of reign.**

Two contradictory options face us as to the length of Amenemhet II's duration of reign. The *Inscription of Hapu*, **translated by Breasted, dates the third year of Sesostris II to Amenemhet II's thirty-fifth year.**[9] However, Hayes cites another inscription that dates **Amenemhet II's thirty-sixth year in Sesostris II's first year.**[10] Hayes' source gives Amenemhet II **three more years of reign than Breasted's inscription.** Only Hayes' source will fit the 232 years of Biblical and Egyptian chronologies. Thus, I opted for **Amenemhet II's thirty-sixth year as Sesostris II's first year.** Ultimately, the Biblical records will be shown to be more accurate and precise than the Egyptian records.

Manetho listed Amenemhet II's total reign **at thirty-eight years** from his **accession in 1625 B.C. to 1587 B.C.** However, since he co-reigned with his father and son, **his sole reign totals only thirty years from year five in 1620 B.C. to his thirty-fifth year in 1590:** see Table C-4 at the end of the Appendix. In Chapter Twelve the reader can see inscriptions dated to Amenemhet II's time that reveal Israel's growth and infiltration into Egyptian society.

V. THE PROBLEMATIC REIGN OF SESOSTRIS II

Manetho attributes forty-eight years to the reign of Sesostris II. The Turin Papyrus is fragmented with only a nine showing. Petrie says that a papyrus from Kahun [el-Lahun] dates Sesostris II's reign from his first to his nineteenth year and then stops.[11] **Thus, Petrie, Breasted and Hayes all gave Sesostris II a reign of nineteen years.** However, Baines and Rolf Krauss reduced Sesostris II's reign **to only nine years, two of which were a co-reign with his father Amenemhet II.**[12] Their only basis for reducing his reign to the **nine years of the Turin Canon** was to fit Krauss' astronomical dating, **which has since been disproved (see Chapter Twenty-One).**

Breasted argued that the nineteen-year reign of Sesostris II was more feasible than the forty-eight-year reign of Manetho because a tomb inscription of **Sebek-khu** says he was born in the twenty-seventh year of Amenemhet II and that he served as a warrior during the reign of Sesostris II and was later promoted to be Commander of the body guard of Sesostris III. Breasted cited another document where a "Sebek-khu" measured the height of the Nile in the ninth year of Amenemhet III. **Breasted interpreted this Sebek-khu to be the same Sebek-khu of the reigns of Amenemhet II, Sesostris II and Sesostris III.** Breasted thus concluded that Amenemhet II could not have reigned more than nineteen years because Sebek-khu lived during the reigns of four different Pharaohs and the forty-eight years that Manetho attributed to his reign would make Sebek-khu 103 years old when he was measuring the Nile during Amenemhet III's ninth year.[13]

Breasted said that Sebek-khu was about twenty-four when he served as commander of Sesostris III's body guard and led sixty men in a military invasion of Nubia. This conjecture is based on a nineteen-year reign for Sesostris II. However, if Manetho's forty-eight-year reign for Sesostris II is correct, then Sebek-khu was about fifty-six years old when Sesostris III became king. A fifty-six year old man is more likely to be the Commander of Sesostris III's body guard, and lead part of the army, than a young man of twenty-four years old.

More important, Sebek-khu's tomb inscription mentions only three Pharaohs: Amenemhet II, Sesostris II and Sesostris III. Amenemhet III is not mentioned in the tomb inscription. **Therefore, the Sebek-khu listed in another document of Amenemhet III's reign is obviously not the same person that made the tomb inscription.** Twelfth-dynasty documents show that Egyptians frequently gave their sons their own names, as is evidenced by Sesostris I, Sesostris II and Sesostris III. The name of Amenemhet was used not only by kings, but also by certain governors of Egypt. Khnumhotep was another popular name.[14] The Sebek-khu that wrote the tomb inscription in Sesostris III's reign could be the father of the Sebek-khu who lived in Amenemhet III's reign, or he could be simply another Egyptian that had the same name. Two persons listed with the same name are not necessarily the same person. **Therefore, Breasted's argument about Sebek-khu does not nullify Manetho's forty-eight year reign for Amenemhet II.**

Another argument for reducing Amenemhet II's reign to only nineteen years is given by William Hayes, which reports that "the reigns of Sesostris III's predecessors amount to a total of 120 years."[15] Thus, Hayes apparently reduced Sesostris II's reign so it would fit within this 120-year period mentioned in the Turin Canon. However, the Turin Canon left out the thirty-eight-year attested reign of Amenemhet II, demonstrating that the Turin Canon, written at least 600 years later than Amenemhet II's reign, has some serious errors in it. Thus, Hayes used the interrupted chronology of the El Lahun scribe and the defective chronology of the Turin Canon to limit Sesostris II's reign to only nineteen years.[16] While such a conjecture is possible, Manetho's forty-eight years must have been based on ancient sources not now available to modern scholars.

No contemporary inscriptions tell us how long Sesostris II reigned. The Turin Canon's number of years for Sesostris II's reign is damaged. Manetho's forty-eight years thus represent the only ancient Egyptian source for Sesostris II's total reign. Most of Manetho's chronologies for other twelfth-dynasty kings have proved accurate within only a few years. **Therefore, I incorporated Manetho's long forty-eight-year reign for Sesostris II into my chronology, and the result was a perfect match with Biblical chronology, allowing me to reach the 232 years of Biblical history from Joseph's slavery in 1678 B.C. and his later meeting of the baker and butler in prison in 1667 B.C. until the Exodus in 1446 B.C. (1678 B.C. minus 232 years = 1446 B.C.)**

VI. THE CHRONOLOGY OF SESOSTRIS III

There is **only one recorded rising of Sirius during the entire duration of the twelfth dynasty. All Egyptologists base their Sothic dates for the twelfth dynasty on this single recorded rising of Sirius in the fifteenth day of the eighth month in the seventh year of Sesostris III.** This dated rising of Sirius is the key date by which all Egyptologists calculate their Sothic dates for the twelfth dynasty. However, the ancient sources differ with each other as to the duration of Sesostris III's reign. This duration of reign is extremely important because Egyptologists compare this dated rising of Sirius' in Sesostris III's seventh year to twenty lunar dates, which were recorded in the reigns of Sesostris III and his son Amenemhet III. The number of years of Sesostris III's reign is extremely important because Egyptologists cannot determine the B.C. year of Sirius' rising unless it is found compatible with twenty lunar dates in later years of the reigns of Sesostris III and Amenemhet III. Manetho, the Egyptian priest of the third century B.C. lists **only eight years for Sesostris III.** The Turin Canon for Sesostris III reads **only three years, with the second number obliterated, indicating a thirty-plus years reign.** Breasted and Petrie combined the three of the Turin Canon with the eight of Manetho and attributed **thirty-eight years to Sesostris III's reign.**

To achieve astronomical compatibility between Sirius' rising in Sesostris III's seventh year and twelve lunar dates in the reign of his son, Amenemhet III, Parker and Hayes reduced Sesostris III's reign **from thirty-eight to thirty-six,** keeping the three of the Turin Canon and ignoring the eight of Manetho. However, Chapter Twenty-One shows that Parker's astronomical chronology was **inaccurately calculated and was not compatible with the true date of Sirius' rising in relation to twelve lunar dates.**

Rolf Krauss and J. R. Baines used astronomical dating **to reduce Sesostris III's reign from Breasted's thirty-eight years and Parker's thirty-six years to only eighteen years.**[17] Petrie claimed that a monument recorded Sesostris III's **twenty-eighth year**[18] and Breasted says the highest date on the monuments is year **thirty-three. Breasted says that Sethe's reconstruction of the Turin Papyrus indicates that the year thirty-eight should be restored.**[19] If Petrie's monument has twenty-eight years and Breasted's monument has thirty-three years, **it is difficult to see how Krauss and Baines reduced Sesostris III's reign to eighteen years,** even on the basis of astronomical compatibility. Chapter 21 proves that Krauss' claim of "astronomically absolute dates" had a compatibility **of only 55% for lunar dates instead of his claim of 75% compatibility. He had only 17% compatibility with the twelve month-lengths in the same chronology. 55% accuracy for lunar dates and 17% accuracy for month lengths is certainly not a true astronomical chronology.**

Since Parker, Hayes, Krauss and Baines all used astronomical dating to arrive at differing years of reign for Sesostris III (thirty-six years and eighteen years), obviously the precise number of years of Sesostris III's reign is unknown and thus uncertain. However, three photos of Sesostris III in Figures 13-A, 13-B and 13-C in Chapter 13 **show him at three successive ages, ranging at least from his mid twenties to his forties to his early seventies. This evidence indicates a reign of forty-plus years.**

Since writing this Chapter years ago, a new discovery was made in 1996 that verifies that **Sesostris III reigned a minimum of thirty-nine years.** Excavation of Sesostris III's mortuary temple revealed Sesostris III's name in notable stones all over the temple. **One of the foundation stones was dated in the thirty-ninth year of the king.** Since Sesostris III's name is the only name that appears in the temple, the thirty-ninth year obviously belongs to Sesostris III, as interpreted by the excavator of the temple. **Thus, the excavator of the temple logically concluded that this thirty-ninth year belongs to Sesostris III.**[20]

This minimum thirty-ninth year of Sesostris III's reign completely nullifies all previous astronomical chronologies calculated by Parker, Krauss and others. The reason for their incorrect chronologies is that all of them attributed less than thirty-nine years to Sesostris III's reign. However, Sesostris III likely lived on for several more years after the temple was constructed and thus could easily have advanced to forty plus years.

VII. STEWART'S PROPOSED ASTRONOMICAL CHRONOLOGY FOR SESOSTRIS III

Since the Sothic Cycle is broken, and since carbon-14 dates reduce the traditional dates of the twelfth dynasty by three centuries, I have developed a new Sothic chronology for the twelfth dynasty. I thus redated Sesostris III's reign by three centuries, where the carbon-14 dates place him.

As previously stated, I have identified **Sesostris III** as the Pharaoh who enslaved Israel and permitted his daughter to rear Moses in the Egyptian palace. The Bible date for Moses' birth is **1526 B.C.** I determined that Sesostris III began his reign somewhere between **1544 and 1541 B.C.**, giving optional dates for Sirius' rising in Sesostris III's seventh year between **1537 and 1534 B.C.**

After experimentation with each of these four years, I found astronomical compatibility only when I dated **Sesostris III's accession year to 1542 B.C., and his seventh year to Sirius' rising on July 15 (Julian), 1535 B.C.** After further experimentation to find astronomical compatibility with the seventeen lunar dates in Amenemhet III's reign, **I astronomically dated Amenemhet III's accession year to 1498 B.C**

To calculate this astronomical chronology I used Faulkner's Julian date of July 15 for Sirius' rising at 30° in the late sixteenth century B.C., plus the twenty Egyptian new moon dates that Krauss used to formulate his astronomical chronology. I experimented with different lengths of years of reign for Sesostris III and Amenemhet III and different Julian dates of Sirius' rising at different latitudes before finding the best astronomical matches. Dr. Faulkner calculated **over 100 new-moon Julian dates** to test the optional astronomical chronologies for Sesostris III.

My best astronomical chronology achieved 75% compatibility with the twenty new moon dates based on Sirius' rising at 30°on July 15, 1535 B.C. The twelve lunar-month lengths of this chronology **also had 75% accuracy.** In contrast, **Krauss' claim of 70% accuracy turned out to be a poor 55% accuracy on new moon dates and a terrible 17% accuracy on the twelve month lengths.** See the actual dates and results in **Chapter 21, Table 21-I.**

Peter Huber calculated 30,000 Babylonian lunar dates. He found that the Late Babylonian **astronomical** texts average **94.5% accuracy** in the dates of **lunar crescents and 81% accuracy in consecutive month lengths.**[21] The Babylonian astronomers were experts on lunar observation. On the other hand Huber found that the accuracy of late **Babylonian administrators averaged 83% accuracy in crescents and 66% accuracy in month lengths.**[22] Thus, **errors occurred about 17% to 33% of the time due to bad weather, hazy skies, or because of poor eye sight or neglect by the observer.**

Egyptian priests were not expert astronomers, as the Babylonians were. Thus, I would expect the accuracy of Egyptian priests to compare with that of the Babylonian administrators rather than that of Babylonian astronomers.

My proposed twelfth-dynasty chronology of **75% accuracy for both lunar dates and month lengths** thus exceeds the Babylonian administrative average of 66% in month lengths and is only 7% below the 83% average for observing new moon dates. Faulkner's evaluation of Krauss' actual chronology showed to be **55% for lunar dates and 17% for month lengths,** far inferior to Krauss' claim of 70% for lunar dates and 58% for month lengths.

Therefore, the Sothic cycle is broken and my fifteen correct new moon dates out of twenty are astronomically compatible (75% for lunar dates and month lengths) with Sirius' rising on **July 15, 1535 B.C.** in Sesostris III's seventh year. I am now free to date the twelfth dynasty in the sixteenth century B.C. instead of the nineteenth century B. C. **In the sixteenth century B.C. the lunar dates have a higher accuracy rating than they do three centuries earlier.** Furthermore, Chapter Twenty-Three has already demonstrated that **carbon-14 dates also confirm that Sesostris III's seventh year was in the sixteenth century B.C.** (7th year = 1535 B.C.) See my new chronology for the twelfth dynasty in Table 24-A and 24-B at the end of Chapter Twenty-Four.

VIII. THE CHRONOLOGY OF AMENEMHET III

Breasted agrees with the reconstructed numbers of Manetho and the Turin Canon for the forty-eight-year reign of Amenemhet III.[23] Hayes and Petrie both list **forty-six years:** see Table C-4 at the end of Appendix C. However, Breasted says that Amenemhet III was still putting his name on monuments in Year **forty-six.** My chronology works under forty-six or forty-eight years for Amenemhet III, because I have him co-reigning with his son Amenemhet IV for four to six years, depending on whether Amenemhet III reigned forty-six or forty-eight years. Either of these lengths of years fits the Biblical Pharaoh that was reigning before Moses fled to Midian at age forty and continued to reign during most of Moses' forty-year exile in Midian.

IX. AMENEMHET IV'S REIGN

Finally we arrive at the reign of Amenemhet IV, the Pharaoh of the Exodus. The Turin Papyrus gives Amenemhet IV a reign of precisely **nine years, three months and twenty-seven days.**[24] My astronomical chronology causes Amenemhet IV's accession year to begin in Amenemhet III's forty-second year of reign, resulting in a six-year co-reign until Amenemhet III died in his forty-eighth year of reign. **See Table C-4.** Amenemhet IV's short reign fits the Biblical description of the short reigning Pharaoh of the Exodus, who came to sole power only a few years before Moses returned to Egypt and died in the Red Sea in the year of the Exodus. **His pyramid and tomb have never been found. By way of contrast, all of the other Pharaohs of the twelfth dynasty had magnificent pyramids and tombs within them for their high officials. The glorious and powerful twelfth dynasty came to an abrupt and mysterious end.**

When Amenemhet IV and his army were destroyed in the Red Sea, the peasants rebelled, expelling the royal family and officials from the palace and governor's mansions. Amenemhet IV's wife, Sebeknefru, reigned in the place of her dead husband. However, she was forced to leave Itjtowy, the capital of the twelfth dynasty, moving to Thebes in southern Egypt. **She reigned 3 years, ten months and 24 days. She disappeared without a known grave or pyramid for her body.** Sekhemre, governor of Thebes, likely disposed of Sebeknefru and moved with his army to Itjtowy in the north-eastern Delta of Egypt. He reestablished law and order, calming the peasant rebellion, and took over the throne of Egypt, establishing the thirteenth dynasty.

SUMMING UP THE DISCOVERIES

Seven Biblical Pharaohs ruled Egypt from Joseph's slavery in 1668 B.C. to Israel's Exodus in 1446 B.C., **a total period of 232 years. Seven twelfth-dynasty Pharaohs** duplicate these same 232 years from Amenemhet I's ninth year to the death of Amenemhet IV. The seven Pharaohs of the Bible match the seven Pharaohs of the twelfth-dynasty in events of history and years of reign, all within 232 years. Twelfth-Dynasty history, as calculated from ancient sources and sharpened by astronomical dating, coincide with the 232 years of Biblical history from Joseph's entrance into Egypt as a slave in 1678 B.C. to Israel's Exodus in 1446 B.C. See Table C-3 above and Table C-4 below. **The seven Pharaohs of the twelfth dynasty and the seven Pharaohs of the Bible that match each other in exactly 232 years create a total of fourteen synchronistic discoveries.** See Table C-5 at the end of this Appendix.

My new dates are as follows: **(1) 1678 B.C. for Joseph's entrance into Egypt as a slave, (2) 1667 B.C.** for Joseph's meeting the butler and baker in Sesostris I's accession year, **(3) July 15, 1535 B.C.** for Sirius' rising in Sesostris III's seventh year, **and (4) 1446 B.C. for the death of Amenemhet IV in the Red Sea when the Exodus occurred.**

Egyptologists are divided among themselves over the length of the twelfth dynasty. **However, solid evidence supports this 232-year chronology of the twelfth dynasty (beginning with Amenemhet I's ninth year when Joseph entered Egypt in 1678 B.C. until the Exodus in the ninth year of Amenemhet IV in 1446 B.C.)** The beginning of the twelfth dynasty occurred nine years earlier when Amenemhet I founded the twelfth dynasty **in the year 1688. Thus, the twelfth dynasty ended** with the death of Amenemhet IV's wife, Sebek-Nefru, in 1443 B.C., three and a half years after her husband died. **Thus my over-all chronology of the twelfth dynasty covers a total of 245 years. The Egyptian priest, Manetho, also registered 245 years for the total length of the twelfth dynasty, a perfect match.**

TABLE C-4
DURATION OF REIGN OF TWELFTH DYNASTY PHARAOHS
AS CALCULATED BY DIFFERENT SCHOLARS

	MANETHO-1	PETRIE-2	BREASTED-3	HAYES-4	BAINES-5	Monuments-6
AMENEMHET I	16	30	30	30	29	20
SESOSTRIS I	46	45	45	45	43	43
AMENEMHET II	38	36	36	35	33	35
SESOSTRIS II	48	22	22	19	19	7
SESOSTRIS III	(3)8	38	38	38	35	39 Wegner
AMENEMHET III	(4)8	46	46	48	45	48
AMENEMHET IV	8	9	9	9	8	10
SEBEKNEFRURE	4	4	4	4	3	4
TOTALS	245	230	230	228	206	185
Minus Co-Reigns	?	?	-19	-1 5	0	-15
NET TOTALS	245	213	211	213	206	170

* 39th year of Sesostris III was recently discovered engraved on a newly discovered building

Sources For Table C-4

1. Courville, *The Exodus Problem and Its Ramifications*, Vol. I, p. 214.
2. W. M. Petrie, *A History of Egypt*, Vol. I.152.
3. Breasted, *A History of Egypt*, pp. 598-599.
4. Wm C. Hayes, "Chronology of Egypt to the Twentieth Dynasty," *Cambridge Ancient History*, Vol. I, Part I, p. 182.
5 Baines and Wente, "Egypt," *New Encyclopaedia Britannica*, 18.113-114.
6. Josef Wegner, "The Nature & Chronology of the Senwosoret III-Amenemhet III Regnal Succession," *Journal of New Eastern Studies*, 55. No. 4. (1996). 249-279.

TABLE C-5
FOUR HUNDRED THIRTY-SIX DISCOVERY/SYNCHRONISMS
CANNOT BE COINCIDENTAL

NOTES FOR APPENDIX C

1. W. M. Flinders Petrie. *A History of Egypt*, I.152.
2. James Breasted, *Ancient Records of Egypt*, I.221.
3. *Petrie*, I.150
4. William C. Hayes, "Chronology: Egypt to the End of the Twentieth Dynasty," *Cambridge Ancient History*, I.1.183.
5. James Breasted, *Ancient Records of Egypt*, I.221, note b (No. 460).
6. James Breasted (Trans.) "Tale of Sinuhe," *Ancient Records of Egypt*, I.235 (491).
7. James Breasted, *Ancient Records of Egypt*, I.221, note d (No. 460).
8. William C. Hayes, "Chronology: Egypt to The End of the Twentieth Dynasty," *Cambridge Ancient History*, I.1.174 (note 2).
9. James Breasted (Trans.), "The Teaching of Ammenemhet," *Ancient Records of Egypt*, I.228 (616).
10. William C. Hayes, "The Middle Kingdom in Egypt," *Cambridge Ancient History*, I.2A.504.
11. Petrie, *History of Egypt*, I.151.
12. Baines, "Egypt," *New Encyclopaedia Britannica*, 18.113.
13. James Breasted, *Ancient Records of Egypt*, I.302-304.
14. Breasted, I.250,272,279-81.
15. William C. Hayes, "Chronology: Egypt to the Twentieth Dynasty," *Cambridge Ancient History*, Vol. I, Part 1, 174 (see also footnote no. 2 on this same page).
16. Hayes, *Ibid.*
17. Baines, "Egypt," *New Encyclopaedia Britannica*, 18.113.
18. W. M. Flinders Petrie, *A History of Egypt*, I.150.
19. Breasted, *Ancient Records of Egypt*, I.221, footnote h.
20. Josef Wegner, "The Nature & Chronology of the Senwosoret III-Amenemhet III Regnal Succession," *Journal of New Eastern Studies*, " 55. No. 4. (1996), 249-279.
21. Peter Huber, *Astronomical Dating of Babylon I & Ur III, Monographic Journals of the Near East, Occasional Papers*, 1/4 (June, 1982), 131-135.
22. Peter Huber, *Ibid.*, 131-135.
23. Breasted, "Chronological Table of Kings," *A History of Egypt*, 599.
24. W. M. Petrie, *History of Egypt*, Vol. I.150-151

BIBLIOGRAPHY

Aaboe, Asger. "Babylonian Mathematics, Astrology," *Cambridge Ancient History*. 2nd ed. New York: Cambridge University Press: 1991. III.2: 280.

Aardsma, Gerald. *A New Approach to the Chronology of Biblical History*. El Cajon, Ca: Institute for Creation Research, 1992.

Aardsma, Gerald. "Tree-Ring Dating and Multiple Ring Growth Per Year," *Creation Research Society Quarterly*. March, 1993. Vol. 29: 186.

Aharoni, Yohanan and Michael Avi-Yonah. *The Macmillan Bible Atlas*. New York, 1968.

Aling, Charles. *Egypt and Bible History*. Grand Rapids: Baker, 1981.

Albright, William. *Archaeology of Palestine*. Gloucester: Peter Smith, 1971.

Albright, William. *Cambridge Ancient History*. New York: Cambridge University Press, 1973. II: 1.33,39.

Albright, William. Translation of "The Moabite Stone," *Ancient Near Eastern Texts*. Ed. Pritchard. Princeton, New Jersey: Princeton University Press, 1969. 320.

Alden, R. L. "Sodom," *Zondervan Pictorial Bible Dictionary*. 1976. 5: 466-68.

"Aleppo." *New Encyclopaedia Britannica*. Chicago: 1991. I: 237.

Ali, A. Yusef. "Index," *The Holy Quran*. Brentwood, Md.: Amana Corp., 1983. 1838-1846.

Ashkenazi, Micah. Personal Interview, P.O. Box 2316, Jerusalem, 91022, Israel. Tel. 02-41-4697.

Astour, Michael C. "Arioch," *Anchor Bible Dictionary*. New York: Doubleday, 1992. I: 378.

Astour, Michael C. "Ellasar," *Anchor Bible Dictionary*. New York: Doubleday, 1992. II: 476-477.

Astour, Michael C. "Tidal," *Anchor Bible Dictionary*. New York: Doubleday, 1992.,VI: 551.

Baines, J. R. and Jaromir Malek. *Atlas of Ancient Egypt*. New York: Facts on File Pub.,1982.

Baines, J. R. and E. F. Wente. "Egypt," *New Encyclopaedia Britannica*. Chicago: 1991. 18: 109-121.

Beitzel, B. J. "Hebrew People," *International Standard Bible Encyclopedia*. Grand Rapids: Eerdmans, 1982. II: 657.

Beitzel, B. J. "Habiru," *International Standard Bible Encyclopedia*.. Grand Rapids: Eerdmans, 1982. II: 586-588.

Beitzel, B. J. "Zaphenath-Paneah," *International Standard Bible Encyclopedia*.. Grand Rapids: Eerdmans, 1982. IV: 1173.

Bowman, S. G. E., J. C. Ambers and M. N. Lee. "Reevaluation of British Museum Radiocarbon Dates Issued Between 1980 and 1984," *Radiocarbon*. 1990. Vol. 32: No. 1, 59-79.

Brenton, Sir Lancelot. *The Septuagint Version: Greek and English*. Grand Rapids: Zondervan, 1970.

Breasted, James. *Ancient Records of Egypt*. 5 Volumes. New York: Russell Inc., 1962.

Breasted, James. *A History of Egypt*. 2nd Ed. New York: Charles Scribner's Sons, 1937.

Bright, John. *A History of Israel*. 3rd Ed. Philadelphia: Westminister Press, 1981.

Brisco, T. V. "Pithom," *International Standard Bible Encyclopedia*. Grand Rapids: Eerdmans, 1986. 5: 376.

Brown, Francis, S.R. Driver and Charles Briggs. *New Brown Driver Briggs Gesenius Hebrew and English Lexicon*. Lafayette, Indiana: Associated Publishers and Authors, 1980.

Brugsch. *Egypt Under the Pharaohs*. Trans. P. Smith, 2nd Ed. (1881), cited by Donovan Courville, *The Exodus Problem and Its Ramification*. Loma Linda,Ca.: Challenge Books, 1971. I: 134.

Budge, E. A. Wallace. *Egyptian Hieroglyphic Dictionary*. 2 vol. New York: Dover Pub., 1978.

Burchell, S. C. *Building the Suez Canal*. New York: Harper & Row, 1966.

"Calendar, The." *New Encyclopaedia Britannica* . Chicago: 1991. 18: 109-121; 15: 436,1991.

"Carbon-14 Dating." *New Encyclopaedia Britannica*. Chicago: 1991. 2: 850.

"Catastrophism and Ancient History," 3431 Club Drive, Los Angeles, Ca. 90064, advertizement in *Biblical Archaeology Review*. Washington D.C.: May/June, 1991. XVII: 3, 9.

Chapront-Touze, Michelle and Chapront, Jean. *Lunar Tables and Programs From 4000 B.C. to A.D. 8000*. Richmond, Va.: Willmann-Bell, Inc., 1991.

"Chronological Tables." *Cambridge Ancient History*. New York: Cambridge University Press, 1971. I.2B: 994-1000.

"Chronological Tables." *Cambridge Ancient History*. New York: Cambridge University Press, 1973. II.1: 818; II.2: 1038.

Cook, E. M. "On." *The International Standard Bible Encyclopedia.* Grand Rapids: Eerdmans,1986. III: 604.

Courville, Donovan. *The Exodus Problem And Its Ramifications.* 2 vol. Loma Linda, Ca.: Challenge Books, 1971.

David, John J. *Moses and the Gods of Egypt.* 2nd Ed., Grand Rapids: Baker, 1986.

Derricourt, Robin M. "Radiocarbon Chronology for Egypt and N. Africa," *Journal of Near Eastern Studies.* Chicago: Oct., 1983. 42.4: 271.

Dever, William. "Bar Interviews With William Dever, Part I." *Biblical Archaeology Review.* Washington D.C.: July/August, 1996.

Dever, William. "The Middle Bronze Age," *Biblical Archaeologist.* September, 1987. 171.

Devries, C. E. "Zoan," *International Standard Bible Encyclopedia.* Grand Rapids: Eerdmans, 1988. IV:1201.

Drower, Margaret. "Syria *c.* 1550-1400 B.C.," *Cambridge Ancient History.* New York: Cambridge University Press, 1973. II:1:417-525.

Edwards, I. E. S. "The Early Dynastic Period in Egypt," *Cambridge Ancient History.* 3rd Ed. New York: Cambridge University Press, 1971. I.2A: 1-70.

Edwards, I. E. S. "The Old Kingdom in Egypt," *Cambridge Ancient History.* 3rd Ed. New York: Cambridge University Press, 1973. I.2A: 189.

Eissfeldt, O. "Palestine in the Time of the Nineteenth Dynasty." *Cambridge Ancient History.* 3rd Ed. New York: Cambridge University Press, 1975. II.2.307-308.

Emery, Prof., Excavator. Cited by T. Save-Soderbergh and I. U. Olson, "C14 and Egyptian Chronology, " p.44. *Radiocarbon Variations and Absolute Chronology,* New York: John Wiley and Sons, 1970.

Eusebius. *Preparation for the Gospel.* Box IX. Ch. XXVII, cited by Velikovsky, *Ages in Chaos,* New York: Doubleday. 1951, p. 31.

Finkelstein, Israel. "Searching for Israelite Origins," *Biblical Archaeological Review.* Washington D.C.: Sept/Oct, 1988.

Gadd, C. J. "Babylonia: *c.* 2120-1800 B.C.," *Cambridge Ancient History.* New York: Cambridge University Press. 1971. I.2B, 604, 624-5, and "Chronological Tables," I.2B.998.

Gardiner, Sir Alan. *Egypt of the Pharaohs.* London: Oxford University Press, 1961.

Gardiner, Sir Alan. *Egyptian Grammar.* 3rd Ed.. London: Oxford Univ. Press, 1957.

Gardiner, Sir Alan. "Admonitions of Ipuwer," quoted by J. Pritchard, introduction to "The Instruction of Amenemhet," translated by John A. Wilson, *Ancient Near Eastern Texts.* 3rd Ed. Princeton, New Jersey: Princeton University Press, 1969. 418.

Gardiner, Alan. *Admonitions of an Egyptian Sage.,* p. 111, cited by Miriam Lichtheim, *Ancient Egyptian Literature.* Berkeley: University of California Press, 1980. I:19,149.

Geisler, Norman and Ron Brooks. *When Skeptics Ask.* Wheaton, Il: Victory,1990. 191-198.

Gilula, M. "The Smiting of the First Born — An Egyptian Myth?" *Tel Aviv 4* (1977) cited by Ziony Zevit, "Three Ways to Look at the Ten Plagues," *Bible Review,* Ed. Hershell Shanks, VI.13, Washington D.C. : June, 1990. 21, 42.

Goedicke, Hanks. "Another Look At An Old Object," *Bulletin of the Egyptological Seminar.* 1982. 4, 71-77.

Goodrick & Kohlenberger. *NIV Exhaustive Concordance.* "Egypt" and "Moses," Grand Rapids: Zondervan, 1990. 336-339 and 764-766.

Grayson, A. K. "Assyria: Sennacherib and Esarhadddon," *Eastern Occasional Papers.* June, 1982. III: 2.103-141.

Grayson, A. K. "Assyria: 668-635 B.C.: The reign of Ashurbanipal." *Eastern Occasional Papers.* June, 1982. III:2.141-161

Green, Jay (Ed.). *Interlinear Hebrew-Aramaic Old Testament.* Peabody: Hendricksen Pub.,1985.

Hallo, William C. *Ancient Near East: A History.* New York: Harcourt/Jovanovich Pub.,1971.

Halpern, Dever and McCarter, "Rise of Ancient Israel," Audio Cassette Set," *Biblical Archaeological Review.* Washington D.C., Nov., 1991.

Harrison, R. K. "Asenath," *International Standard Bible Encyclopedia.* Grand Rapids: Eerdmans, 1979. I:314.

Harrison, R. K. "Chedorlaomer," *International Standard Bible Encyclopedia.*. Grand Rapids: Eerdmans, 1982. II:638-9.

Hartley, J. E. "Job," *International Standard Bible Encyclopedia*. Grand Rapids: Eerdmans, 1982. II:1066-67.

Hayden, R. E. "Hammurabi," *The International Standard Bible Encyclopedia*. Grand Rapids: Eerdmans, 1982. II:604.

Hayes, William C. "Chronology: Egypt to the End of the Twentieth Dynasty," *Cambridge Ancient History*. New York: Cambridge University Press, 1970-73. I:1.174, 183.

Hayes, William C. "Egypt: Internal Affairs From Tuthmosis I to Amenophis III," *Cambridge Ancient History*. New York: Cambridge University Press, 1970-73. II:1.313-416.

Hayes, William C. "Egypt: From the Death of Ammenemes III to Seqenenre II, *Cambridge Ancient History*. New York: Cambridge University Press, 1970-73. II:1.44-54.

Hayes, William, C. "Middle Kingdom of Egypt," *Cambridge Ancient History*. New York: Cambridge University Press, 1970-73. I: 2A.493-531.

Hayes, William C. "Reforms of Sesostris III," *Cambridge Ancient History*. New York: Cambridge University Press, 1970-73. I:2A.506-507.

Hayes, William C. *The Scepter of Egypt*. 2 Volumes. New York: Metropolitan Museum of Art, 1990.

Hendel, Ronald. "Finding Historical Memories in the Patriarchal Narratives," *Biblical Archaeological Review* Washington D.C.: July/August, 1995. p, 56.

Herodotus. *The Histories*. Translated by Aubrey de Selincourt. New York: Penguin Books, 1972.

Hinz, Walther. "Persia *c*.1800-1550 B.C," *Cambridge Ancient History*. New York: Cambridge University Press, 1973. II:1.256-261.

Hoehner, Harold. "The Duration of the Egyptian Bondage," *Bibliotheca Sacra*.1969.CXXV: 501,1 13.

Howard, D. M., Jr. "Sodom," *International Standard Bible Encyclopedia*. Grand Rapids: Eerdmans, 1988. IV.560.

Huber, Peter. "Astronomical Dating of Babylonia I and Ur III," *Monographic Journals of the Near East*. June, 1982.

Ingham, M. F. "The Length of the Sothic Cycle," *Journal of Egyptian Archaeology*.1969. 55:39-40.

James, Peter. *Centuries of Darkness*. New Brunswick: Rutgers Univ. Press, 1993,

James, T. G. H. *Ancient Egypt. The Land and Its Legacy*. London: British Museum Pub.,1988.

James, T. G. H. "Egypt From the Expulsion of the Hyksos to Amenophis I," *Cambridge Ancient History*. 3rd Ed. New York: Cambridge University Press, 1973. II:I.289-312.

Janzen, J. Gerald. "Job, Book of," *Harper's Bible Dictionary*. San Francisco: Harper & Row, 1985. 492.

Jaroff, Leon. "Lost and Found in Orbit," *Time*. New York: Sep't 14, 1998. I:152, No. 11, p. 66.

Josephus, Flavius. "Antiquities of the Jews" and "Against Apion.," *Complete Words of Josephus*. Grand Rapids: Kregel Pub., 1981.

Josephus, Flavius. "Wars of the Jews," *Complete Words of Josephus*. Grand Rapids: Kregel Pub., 1981. Book IV, Chapter 8.

Kaiser, Walter C. "Exodus 2:1-4," *Expositor's Bible Commentary*. Grand Rapids: Zondervan,1990.

Keil & Delitzsch. *Old Testament Commentaries: The Pentateuch*. Grand Rapids: Eerdmans, 1959.

Kenyon, Kathleen. *Archaeology in the Holy Lands*. 5th Ed. Nashville: Nelson Pub.,1985.

Kenyon, Kathleen. "Palestine in the Middle Bronze Age," *Cambridge Ancient History*. New York: Cambridge University Press, 1973. II:1.88.

King, L. W. (Translator). "Code of Hammurabi," Law No. 133, *Encyclopaedia Britannica*. copied from the Internet,1910.

Kitchen, K. A. "Exodus," *Anchor Bible Dictionary*. New York: Doubleday,1992.II:705

Kitchen, K. A. "Goshen," *Zondervan Pictorial Bible Encyclopedia*. Grand Rapids: Zondervan, 1976. II:779.

Kitchen, K. A. "Hyksos," *Zondervan Pictorial Encyclopedia of the Bible*. Grand Rapids: Zondervan, 1976. III:232-233.

Kitchen, K. A. "Joseph," *International Standard Bible Encyclopedia*. Grand Rapids: Eerdmans, 1982. II:1130.

Kitchen, K. A. "Patriarchal Age: Myth or History?" *Biblical Archaeological Review*. Washington D.C.: March/April,1995.

Kitchen, K. A. "Pithom," *Zondervan Pictorial Bible Encyclopedia*. Grand Rapids: Zondervan, 1976. IV:804.

Kitchen, K. A. "Potiphar," *Zondervan Pictorial Bible Encyclopedia*. Grand Rapids: Zondervan, 1976. IV:823.

Kitchen, K. A. "Raamses, Rameses (City)," *Zondervan Pictorial Bible Encyclopedia*. Grand Rapids: Zondervan, 1976. 5:14.

Kitchen, K. A. "Shishak," *International Standard Bible Encyclopedia*. Grand Rapids: Eerdmans, 1980. IV: 489.

Kitchen, K. A. "Zoan," *Zondervan Pictorial Encyclopedia*. Grand Rapids: Zondervan, 1976. 5.1068.

Krauss, Rolf. *Sothis-und Monddaten*, Germany: Hildeshimer Agyptologische Beitrage, 1995.

Kupper, J. R. "Northern Mesopotamia and Syria," *Cambridge Ancient History*. New York: Cambridge University Press, 1973. III:1.8; I:.1.7-10.

Kupper, J. R. "Chronological Tables," *Cambridge Ancient History*. New York: Cambridge University Press, 1973: II.1.820.

Lammerts, W. E. "Are Bristlecone Pine Trees Really So Old?" Cited by Gerald E. Aardsma, "Tree Ring Dating and Multiple Ring Growth Per Year," *Creation Research Society Quarterly*. March, 1993: 29:186.

Lewthwaite, G. R. "The Dead Sea," *Zondervan Pictorial Encyclopedia of the Bible*. Grand Rapids: Zondervan, 1976. II:50-52.

Lichtheim, Miriam. *Ancient Egyptian Literature*. 2 Vols. Berkeley: Univ. of Calif. Press, 1976.

Luckenbill, Daniel (Translator). *Ancient Records of Assyria and Babylonia*. New York: Greenwood Press Pub., 1927.

Luft, Ulrich. *Chronologische Fixierung*. 1991.

Mallowman, Max. "The Early Dynastic Period in Mesopotamia," *Cambridge Ancient History*. 3rd Ed. New York: Cambridge University Press, 1971. I:2A.242.

Mazar, Amihai. *Archaeology of the Land of the Bible*. New York: Doubleday, 1990.

McCarter, P. Kyle Jr. "Exodus," *Harper's Bible Commentary*. San Francisco: Harper & Row, 1988.

McFall, L. "Hebrew Language," *International Standard Bible Encyclopedia*. Grand Rapids: Eerdmans,. 1982. II:660.

Meek, Theophile J. (Translator). "The Code of Hammurabi," *Ancient Near Eastern Texts*. Princeton, New Jersey: Princeton University Press, 1979: 179.

Mellaart, J. "Anatolia, *c.* 4000-2300 B.C.," *Cambridge Ancient History*. New York: Cambridge University Press, 1971. I:2A.368-386.

Mellaart, J "Anatolia, *c.* 2300-1750 B.C.," *Cambridge Ancient History*. New York: Cambridge University Press, 1971. I:2B.688, 691.

Mitchell, T. C. "Israel & Judah until the Revolt of Jehu," *Cambridge Ancient History*. New York: Cambridge University Press, 1982. III:1.442-487.

Mitchell, T. C. "Israel and Judah (750 to 700 B.C.)," *Cambridge Ancient History*. New York: Cambridge University Press, 1991. III:2.322-370.

Mitchell, T. C. "Judah Until the Fall of Jerusalem," *Cambridge Ancient History*. New York: Cambridge University Press, 1991. III:2.372-409.

Moran, William (Editor and Translator). *The Amarna Letters*. Baltimore: John Hopkins University Press,1992.

Morgan, D. F. "Horse," *International Standard Bible Encyclopedia*. Grand Rapids: Eerdmans, 1982. II.759.

Mulder, Martin. "Sodom and Gomorrah," *Anchor Bible Dictionary*. New York: Doubleday, 1992. VI.99-103.

Negev, Avraham (Editor). *The Archaeological Encyclopedia of the Holy Land*. Nashville: Thomas Nelson, Inc., 1986.

NIV Study Bible. Comments on Job 2:11, Grand Rapids: Zondervan, 1985.

Oppenheim, A. Leo (Trans.). "The Story of Idrimi, King of Alalakh," *Ancient Near Eastern Texts*. 3rd Ed. Princeton, New Jersey: Princeton University Press, 1969. 557.

Opperwall-Galluch, Nola J. "Zaphenath-Paneah," *International Standard Bible Encyclopedia*. Grand Rapids: Eerdmans, 1988. IV:1173.

Parker, Richard. *Calendars of Ancient Egypt*. Chicago: Univ. of Chicago Press, 1950.

PC Globe (Computer software on Population Information and Growth Rates), 1990.

Petrie, W. M. F. *A History of Egypt*. 10th Ed., 3 volumes. London: Methuen & Co., 1923.

Pettinato, Giovanni. *The Archives of Ebla*. New York: Doubleday, 1981. 287.

Pierce, R. W. "Rameses," *International Standard Bible Encyclopedia*. Grand Rapids: Eerdmans, 1988. IV:39.

Pinches, T. G. H. "Amraphel," *International Standard Bible Encyclopedia*. Grand Rapids. Eerdmans, 1979. I:118-119.

Posener, G. "Syria and Palestine During the Twelfth Dynasty," *Cambridge Ancient History*. New York: Cambridge University Press, 1971. I:2A.535-558, and I:2B.954, no. 53.

Pratico, G. "Potiphera," *International Standard Bible Encyclopedia*. Grand Rapids: Eerdmans, 1986. III:913.

Pritchard, James, Ed. *Ancient Near Eastern Texts*. 3rd Ed. Princeton, New Jersey: Princeton University Press, 1969. 18, 22, 247, 418, 557,

Redford, Donald B. "Heliopolis," *Anchor Bible Dictionary*. New York: Doubleday, 1992. III:122.

Redford, Donald B. "Zoan," *Anchor Bible Dictionary*. New York. Doubleday, 1992. VI:1106.

Rohl, David. *Pharaohs & Kings*. New York: Crown Pub.,1995.

Rose, Lynn. "Astronomical Evidence for the Dating the End of the Middle Kingdom," *Journal of Near Eastern Studies*. Chicago: University of Chicago Press, 1994. 53.4.

Rowton, M. B. "Ancient Western Asia," *Cambridge Ancient History*. New York: Cambridge University Press, 1970. I:1.210.

Save-Soderbergh and I. U. Olsson. "C-14 Dating and Egyptian Chronology," *Radiocarbon Variations & Absolute Chronology*. New York: John Wiley and Sons, 1970.

"Septuagint." *New Encyclopaedia Britannica*, Chicago: 1991. 10.643.

Shanks, Harold, Editor. *Bible Review*, Washington D.C., various articles:
   "Shank and Dever, "Bar Interviews with William Dever, Part I," *Biblical Archaeology Review*. Washington, D.C., Nov., 1991.

Shanks, Harold, "The Biblical Minimalists," *Bible Review*, June, 1997.

Shaw, Ian M. F. "Egyptian Chronology & the Irish Oak Calibration," *Journal of Near Eastern Studies*. Oct., 1985. 44:4.311.

Shea, W. A. "Exodus, Date of," *International Standard Bible Encyclopedia*. Grand Rapids: Eerdmans Pub., 1982. II:231.

Silberman, Neil. "Lure of the Holy Land," *Archaeology*, (Nov./Dec., 1990).

Simpson, William Kelly. "Egypt," *The Ancient Near East: A History*. New York: Harcourt, Brace & Jovanovich, 1971.

Smick, E. "Job," *Zondervan Pictorial Bible Encyclopedia*. Grand Rapids: Zondervan, 1976. 3:602-3

Smick, E. "Job," *NIV Study Bible: Job 2:11*. Grand Rapids: Zondervan, 1985.

Smith, W. S. "The Old Kingdom in Egypt," *Cambridge Ancient History*: New York: Cambridge University Press, 1971. I:2A.145-207.

Spalinger, Anthony. "Some Remarks on The Epagomenal Days in Ancient Egypt," *Journal of New Eastern Studies*, 1995. 54: No. 1, p. 34.

Steindorff, G., Cited by C. E. DeVrie, "Zaphenath-Paneah," *Zondervan Pictorial Encyclopedia of the Bible*. Grand Rapids: Zondervan, 1976. V:1033-34.

Thiele, Edwin. *Mysterious Numbers of the Hebrew Kings*. Grand Rapids: Zondervan, 1983.

Time Magazine. "What Does God Really Think About Sex?" June 24, 1991. 48-50.

Thompson, Thomas L. "Can Your Understand This?" and William G. Dever, "Save Us from Postmodern Malarkey," pp. 28-35; *Biblical Archaeology Review*. March/April, 2000.

Ussishkin, David. "Scholars Speak Out," *Biblical Archaeology Review*. May/June, 1995.

Velikovsky, Immanuel. *Ages in Chaos*, New York: Doubleday, 1952.

Velikovsky's Followers: "Catastrophism and Ancient History," 3431 Club Drive, Los Angeles, Ca. 9-64, advertizement in *Biblical Archaeology Review*. XVII.3, p. 9, May/June, 1991.

Wegner, Josef. "The Nature & Chronology of the Senwosoret III-Amenemhet III Regnal
    Succession," *Journal of New Eastern Studies*. 55. No. 4. 249-279. 1996.
Wei, Tom. "Pithom," *Anchor Bible Dictionary*. New York: Doubleday. 1992. 5:377.
Welch, E. D. "Goshen," *International Standard Bible Encyclopedia*. Grand Rapids: Eerdmans. 1982.
    II:529.
Wente, Edward F. "Rameses," *Anchor Bible Dictionary*. New York: Doubleday. 1992. 5:617-618.
Winkler, Hugo (Translator). *Tell-El-Amarna Letters*. New York: Lemcke and Beuchner, 1986.
Wilson, John A. (Translator). *Ancient Near Eastern Texts*. Ed. James Pritchard. Princeton, New
    Jersey: Princeton Univ. Press, 1969.
Wilson, John A. (Translator). "The Admonitions of Ipuwer," *Ancient Near Eastern Texts*. Ed. James
    Pritchard. Princeton, New Jersey: Princeton Univ. Press, 1969. 441.
Wilson, John A. (Translator). "Asiatic Campaigning of Amenhotep II," *Ancient Near Eastern Texts*.
    Ed. James Pritchard. Princeton, New Jersey: Princeton Univ. Press, 1969. 245-248.
Wilson, John A. (Translator). "Egyptian Myths, Tales and Mortuary Texts: The Story of Sinuhe,"
    Ancient Near Eastern Texts. Ed. James Pritchard. Princeton, New Jersey: Princeton Univ.
    Press, 1969. 18-23.
Wilson, John A (Translator). "The Execration of Asiatic Princes," *Ancient Near Eastern Texts*. Ed.
    James Pritchard. Princeton, New Jersey: Princeton Univ. Press, 1969. 328-29.
Wilson, John A. (Translator). "Hymn of Victory of Merneptah," *Ancient Near Eastern Texts*. Ed.
    James Pritchard. Princeton, New Jersey: Princeton Univ. Press, 1969. 376-78.
Wilson, John A. (Translator). "In Praise of the City Ramses," *Ancient Near Eastern Texts*. Ed. James
    Pritchard. Princeton, New Jersey: Princeton Univ. Press, 1969. 470-471.
Wilson, John A. (Translator). "The Instruction of King Amen-emh-het," *Ancient Near Eastern Texts*.
    Ed. James Pritchard. Princeton, New Jersey: Princeton Univ. Press, 1969.418-419.
Wilson, John A. (Translator). "The Taking of Joppa," *Ancient Near Eastern Texts*. Ed. James Pritchard.
    Princeton, New Jersey: Princeton Univ. Press, 1969. 22
Wilson, John A. (Translator). "The Tradition of Seven Lean Years in Egypt," *Ancient Near Eastern
    Texts*. Ed. James Pritchard. Princeton, New Jersey: Princeton Univ. Press, 1969. 31-32.
Wood, Bryant. "Did the Israelites Conquer Jericho?" *Biblical Archaeology Review*. March/April,
    1990.
Wyatt, Ron. *Discovered Noah's Ark*. World Bible Society, 1989.
Zevit, Ziony. "Three Ways to Look at the Ten Plagues," *Bible Review*. June, 1990.

Printed in the United States
6124

9 780971 868007